4 DEC 23

THE FUNDAMENTAL TECHNIQUES OF
CLASSIC ITALIAN CUISINE

For my wonderful friend, DAVID:
Learn well
cook well
Eat well
Food is our Friend

Your friendship has certainly been a highlight
of these past few years —

Marco

THE FUNDAMENTAL TECHNIQUES OF
CLASSIC ITALIAN CUISINE

The International Culinary Center's
School of Italian Studies

with Cesare Casella

and Stephanie Lyness

Photographs by Matthew Septimus

Stewart, Tabori & Chang *New York*

Published in 2012 by Stewart, Tabori & Chang
An imprint of ABRAMS

Props for the photography were generously provided by Richard Ginori 1735
(www.richardginori1735.com), Sferra Fine Linens (www.sferra.com), Rosenthal Sambonet
(www.rosenthalusa.com), and Alessi (www.alessi.com).

Library of Congress Cataloging-in-Publication Data:

Casella, Cesare.
  The fundamental techniques of classic Italian cuisine / with Cesare Casella and Stephanie Lyness ;
the International Culinary Center's School of Italian Studies ; photographs by Matthew Septimus.
     p. cm.
  Includes bibliographical references and index.
  ISBN 978-1-58479-990-0 (alk. paper)
  1. Cooking, Italian. I. Casella, Cesare. II. Lyness, Stephanie. III.
International Culinary Center's School of Italian Studies. IV. Title.
  TX723.C29739 2012
  641.5945—dc23
                          2012004135

Editor: Natalie Kaire
Project Manager: Kate Norment
Designer: Liam Flanagan
Production Manager: Kathy Lovisolo

The text of this book was composed in Trade Gothic and Granjon.

Printed and bound in China
10 9 8 7 6 5 4 3 2 1

ABRAMS
THE ART OF BOOKS SINCE 1949
115 West 18th Street
New York, NY 10011
www.abramsbooks.com

Contents

Foreword **6**

Preface **7**

Acknowledgments **9**

The Flavors of Italy **10**

Foreword

Good food has no boundaries. France slips into Italy, China touches Thailand, and the Pacific waters bridge the California beaches to the Japanese shores.

So it was not surprising when two dapper men from Italy came to visit The International Culinary Center in New York in 2004. Albino Ganapini and Riccardo Carelli had a dream to create a culinary school outside Parma with one of the greatest chefs in Italian history, Gualtiero Marchesi (known as Il Divino!). Their vision was to bring young budding chefs from all over the world to study Italian cuisine in a gorgeously renovated palazzo in the picture-perfect town of Colorno.

After a very agreeable lunch, our French dean, Chef Alain Sailhac, and I decided to visit with Ganapini and Carelli in Italy. We discovered their passion as well as their commitment to quality and experienced some of the most delicious food we had ever tasted. It reminded me of when I had visited the Ferrandi school in Paris twenty years earlier as I considered starting The French Culinary Institute. When Chef Alain said, "This is great; we should do it," I knew an Italian school was in our future. What fun!

But challenging. The course in Colorno would be very different from the courses we had previously offered. First, our students would be going abroad. Second, the Colorno course was primarily based on the cuisine of the region, Emilia-Romagna and northern Italy. Our students would need a broader curriculum that encompassed all the regions of Italy, and they would need to be adequately prepared for international living and learning.

Who could help us form a comprehensive preparatory course so our students would be able and ready to attend the program in Italy? Who could help us negotiate with the Italians for a broader curriculum?

Everyone we asked, from Marcella Hazan to Arlene Feltman Sailhac (founder of De Gustibus at Macy's), responded emphatically, "Cesare!" Of course, they were referring to the great Tuscan chef Cesare Casella, who had taken New York by storm. The idolized chef from Lucca once prompted shopkeepers to yell, "Cesare! Cesare! Come back! Come back!" when we walked down the town's main street together.

Cesare agreed to be our dean and we were off to an exciting start. To house this dynamic program, we even created a new school, The School of Italian Studies at The International Culinary Center. In order for the students to fully extract the glories of the cuisine during their stay in Italy, they needed to be well armed. A new ten-week curriculum was created that included intense immersion in the Italian language, an overview of all the regions of Italy, and an introduction to the basic techniques common to all styles of Italian cooking.

In 2006, we accepted our first students and began to prepare them for a nine-week intensive program at the school in Colorno followed by a nine-week "stage" (internship) in an authentic regional Italian restaurant. Cesare not only displayed a voluminous knowledge of cooking from the Alps to Sicily, but he also seemed to know personally every major chef from both sides of the Apennines. His passion for teaching was immediately obvious. His love of sharing his expertise was infectious.

He labored for two years with one of our seasoned teachers, Chef Susan Lifrieri, and the terrific food writer Stephanie Lyness to present our students with a binder full of history, techniques, tips, and recipes that would serve as the curriculum for our new program. After hundreds of hours of refinement, it is ready to be put into a text.

This book will cut a swath through Italy and get to the core of the techniques and products that a good cook needs to know in order to be a good "Italian" chef. There truly is no course that has been so lovingly and painstakingly conceived and presented. We are happy now to share it with you.

Dorothy Cann Hamilton

Preface

Today is a fantastic moment for Italian cuisine.

Our cuisine is at once ancient and very young. Regional Italian cooking, *la cucina regionale*, has a rich and vibrant story that dates back hundreds of years. It is based on a love and knowledge of the earth and its harvest—what Italians call *territorio*. Regional cuisine is a celebration of local agriculture. It is a reflection of the skills and history of people who have lived and worked on the land.

By the time Italy was unified in 1861, there were so many different ways of cooking that it was not possible to talk about a national cuisine. Yet despite their differences, the foods of each region were unified by a universal philosophy. It was about simplicity, respect for ingredients, and a sense of place. That is still very true today. Italian food is based on the idea that culinary expression starts with the ingredients. To cook Italian is to highlight the flavors of the products—whether you talk about the food of Toscana, of Sicilia, or of Alto Adige, this principle is the same. Yes, the ingredients are different. The land and climate have produced different peoples, different lifestyles, and different foods. But the philosophy is a constant.

For me, the unification of Italian cuisine—and the beginning of something we can call *la cucina Italiana*—was set in motion in the 1960s. Fueled by curiosity and a fervent entrepreneurial spirit, Italian chefs and restaurateurs began to travel extensively and to pursue a wider culinary education. They experimented with new flavors, products, and cooking techniques. In French kitchens, they were exposed to a sophisticated restaurant culture. They returned home with a passion to advance and professionalize Italian cuisine.

We began to see the fruits of this work in the seventies and eighties. That was the era of Mirella and Peppino Cantarelli, Angelo Paracucchi, and, of course, Gualtiero Marchesi. A new *cucina Italiana* was taking root. It built on regional cooking by making use of new culinary technologies, retooled old ideas, and brimmed with curiosity. Today that *cucina Italiana* is in full bloom with chefs like Massimo Bottura and Massimiliamo Alajmo, who are admired around the world.

This cuisine is not divorced from traditional *cucina regionale*. It is based on it. Contemporary Italian cuisine *is* regional cuisine, executed with modern techniques and ideas. The current generation of Italian chefs understands the chemistry of cooking. Their choices are based on tradition, but the tradition has been elevated. *Zuppa di Pesce* (page 240), for example, has been made all over Italy, with variations, for centuries. Traditional recipes may call for the fish to be cooked all together, regardless of individual cooking times, and for a long time. Now, with greater technical knowledge, a chef can adhere to the soul of the dish and enhance it. A fish broth is used as a base of flavor, and the seafood is added sequentially, or even cooked separately. This technical "upgrade" demonstrates a respect for and understanding of each variety of seafood and its cooking time while remaining consistent with what has always made Italian food great.

Contemporary chefs may choose ingredients based on something other than proximity or custom. A chef may make *Spaghetti alla Carbonara* (page 104), from Lazio, with *speck* in lieu of the *guanciale* that is traditional to the region. Or the dish may be deconstructed and presented in an entirely contemporary way. Classic Italian cuisine? Yes! There is still a respect for the ingredients, which form the basis of culinary expression. This is simply a more contemporary expression.

I'm sometimes asked whether it's difficult to cook Italian food in America. Italian food can be cooked well wherever good-quality products are available, where there is the desire to learn, and where there is a passion for the food. This curriculum will give you the traditional foundations and the technical skills to cook great Italian food wherever you find yourself. *Fantastico.*

The curriculum teaches authentic Italian cuisine. What distinguishes the cuisine is its strong focus on *i prodotti*—raw materials and products such as olive oil, cheese, and *salumi*—and its reliance on traditional "forms" of foods, such as pasta, gnocchi, and risotto. These forms survive without formal codification throughout the twenty regions of Italy, varying with the products available. They exist as basic evolutionary structures—general themes—created over time, through opportunity and necessity, to reveal the intrinsic goodness of the ingredients. While cooking techniques certainly play a part, they are traditionally in the nature of approaches, rather than rules.

To reflect the spirit of the cuisine, this book is divided into two major parts. The first, "Recipes," is a collection of the traditional forms that compose the cuisine. Recipe introductions supply information on regional particularities. Since this is a teaching curriculum, recipes were chosen to demonstrate a full range of culinary skills, from butchering to baking.

The second part, "Lessons," is a detailed discussion of cooking techniques and processes taught at The School of Italian Studies at The International Culinary Center as well as information about restaurant organization and practices useful to readers in the industy. Many techniques are illustrated by step-by-step photography. The lessons may be used in conjunction with the recipes in this book (if, for example, the reader encounters an unfamiliar technique while cooking, he or she can turn to the relevant lesson for help), as an aid when cooking from other cookbooks, or on its own, as inspiration. The School of Italian Studies at The International Culinary Center was founded on the principle that excellent cooking begins with excellent technique. This training gives students the professional foundation that turns a good Italian cook into a great one. In addition, The International Culinary Center believes that to understand a cuisine, one must understand the culture. To give a taste of how the curriculum does this, we have included some of the Italian-cooking vocabulary that is used in our Italian-language classes, in our kitchen classrooms, and in Italian restaurant kitchens.

In using this book, you will notice that the introduction to each recipe chapter includes a short section entitled *Le Tecniche* (Cooking Skills). This section indicates the skills that are employed in the chapter. It also notes page references to those lessons that are relevant. In addition, recipe chapters include sidebars that deliver brief explications of cooking techniques as they arise throughout the course.

Throughout this book, we have used metric measurements (as students are taught at The International Culinary Center) followed by equivalents in American units, either in weight or cup measure, in parentheses. Our assumption is that professionals will adhere to the metric measure, while home cooks will find the parenthetical measure more helpful. In all cases, the metric measure is exact; the American may be rounded where practical. Very small amounts of ingredients—those too slight to be weighed on most scales—are expressed in teaspoon, half teaspoon, and quarter teaspoon, without a metric equivalent.

Because of its diverse and ancient history, Italy is a nation of regions and regional differences. Any attempt at making a generalization about Italy will inevitably run squarely into this historical truth. Consequently, information about specific regions is interspersed throughout the book. Quotes from Italian restaurant chefs who work with International Culinary Center students in Italy further highlight regional characteristics. (We can only begin to cover the cultural context of Italian cuisine, however. For those who are interested in more in-depth reading, see the bibliography on page 496.)

We believe that this is the most authentic and professional traditional Italian cooking curriculum in America. It differs even from classes taught in most schools in Italy precisely because it seeks to unite Italian home cooking with the level of professional technical training for which The International Culinary Center is known.

Cesare Casella

Acknowledgments

Let's start at the beginning. I want to thank Albino Ganapini and Riccardo Carelli for sparking the flame that grew into the Italian program at The International Culinary Center. With a curriculum that starts in the United States and continues in Parma, Italy, we realized that we needed a total immersion program to give our students a fundamental grounding in Italian foods and techniques before leaving for the motherland. To accomplish this goal, we found there was no one better suited to the role than Cesare Casella, who was appointed dean of Italian studies. For more than a year he worked with Stephanie Lyness, our gifted writer, and Chef Susan Lifrieri to design the basic curriculum.

When it was time to create this monumental book, we needed to perfect and adapt the curriculum for the publication. A huge thank you to Cesare, Stephanie, and Chef Jessica Botta for tirelessly working on this opus for two years.

Once again our immensely talented "court photographer," Matthew Septimus, photographed the most exquisite Italian dishes I have ever feasted my eyes upon. Thank you, Matthew! Our food stylist, A. J. Battifarano, made these dishes look both mouthwatering and classic, the essence of *cucina Italiana*. Thanks also to our prop stylist, Pam Morris, who provided the perfect settings to accompany the gorgeous food.

Making a book of this caliber takes the commitment and support of our team at Stewart, Tabori & Chang. My sincere thanks to Leslie Stoker, publisher; Kate Norment and Natalie Kaire, editors; and Liam Flanagan, designer. Their commitment to creating the highest-quality book possible is so appreciated by all of us at The International Culinary Center.

Last but not least, my heartfelt thanks go to Melanie Miller, our senior marketing director, for shepherding the book throughout the process. Like any true pro, Melanie never lost her focus, her enthusiasm, or her cool. Tara Hill and the marketing team also deserve accolades for bringing worthy attention to this project.

Finally, we are grateful to our literary agent, Kim Witherspoon, for all her support of this endeavor. As always, her help was invaluable. *Brava!*

Dorothy Cann Hamilton

The Flavors of Italy

Italian cuisine is defined by its native ingredients: its wealth of produce; its multiplicity of beans and grains; its abundance of oils, wines, and vinegars; and its livestock, from which a profusion of cheeses and cured meats have been made for centuries. These products intimately reflect the geographies, histories, and distinctive characteristics of the twenty regions in which they are produced.

While it is still true that eating in Italy operates as a kind of gustatory GPS—the regional differences are so evident in the cuisine that you can at the very least make an educated guess as to where you are by the food you're eating—the homogeneity resulting from modern communication and global influences has not gone unnoticed. Pizza, for example, once the defining food of Naples, is now ubiquitous in Italy (and in the world). Conversely, the Alpine regions of Valle d'Aosta and Trentino–Alto Adige, once isolated by their treacherous geographies, now have access to products that were never historically part of their cuisines. Italian chefs, intrigued by contact with cuisines and technologies so radically different from their own, have begun successfully and creatively to incorporate these influences into their cooking.

At the same time, a concerted effort exists in Italy to hold to tradition. This is reflected in the institution of two product designations approved by the European Union: *Denominazione di Origine Protetta* (DOP) and *Indicazione Geografica Protetta* (IGP). These trademarks have been put in place to preserve and protect the diversity and peculiarities of artisanally produced foods, and to act as a measure of quality control for the consumer. (These programs have been modeled after similar programs used for wines of controlled origin: *Denominazione di Origine Controllata* [DOC], *Denominazione di Origine Controllata e Garantita* [DOCG], and *Indicazione Geografica Tipica* [IGT].)

A designation of DOP links a food to the area in which it has traditionally been produced. All phases of its production—from the raw material through the processing—must be carried out in that area. A DOP-designated sheep's-milk cheese, for example, must be made with milk from sheep raised in the area and manufactured by local producers who are versed in the traditional manner of production. A designation of IGP (most common for fruits and vegetables) reflects less stringent regulations. Certain traditional conventions must be respected in the manufacture of the product, and the product must be historically linked to that area. But only one phase of the production is required to be carried out in the designated area. So, for example, certain breads may be designated IGP because they are manufactured in a specific region, but the flour may be from elsewhere.

DOP and IGP products include produce, grains, cheeses, meats, olive oils, and balsamic vinegars produced throughout the twenty regions of Italy. (It must also be noted that many fine products are made in Italy that do not carry an IGP or DOP certification.)

This cultural defense of traditional and local cuisines was also reflected in the birth, in 1986 in Piemonte, of what three years later was to become Slow Food, an international food movement with associations around the world. The movement's mission is to protect the heritage, tradition, and culture of food in the face of the homogeneity encouraged by the existence of industrial agriculture and a multinational food industry.

Given Italy's passionate attachment to its culture and customs, a study of its cuisine must open with a discussion of those products that are integral to it, beginning with the occasion that unites them: the Italian meal. Traditionally, an Italian meal should take at least an hour or two so that one has the leisure to enjoy the food and company. The pace of modern life has encroached to some extent on this practice, but Italians still hold to it when possible.

The main meal customarily consists of several different courses:

Antipasto: *Antipasto* translates to "before the meal" and refers to a food that is served before the meal begins. *Antipasti* include such preparations as salads, raw and marinated vegetable and seafood dishes, raw and cured meats, and toasts spread with savory toppings.

Primo (or primo piatto): The first course usually consists of a small serving of soup, a rice dish such as risotto, or pasta.

Secondo (or secondo piatto): The second course is the meat course. Portions are small and the preparations are simple—grilled or roasted chicken, beef, lamb, game, and fish, perhaps with a very light sauce, are popular. Italian cuisine also boasts many braises and stews.

Contorno: This is a vegetable side dish that accompanies the *secondo*. Loosely translated, *contorno* means "contours," because Italians believe that the role of vegetables is to define the shape of a meal by orienting it in terms of seasonality, color, and texture. A salad may be served as a *contorno*.

Dolce: From the Italian word for "sweet," the *dolce* is the final course of a meal. It may be a complex pastry preparation, but it is likely to be a simple *frutta* (fruit) served with biscotti, particularly during the summer.

Formaggio: A cheese course is served at the end of a meal, often before or in place of dessert.

Pane: Bread is a fundamental and ubiquitous part of Italian life and is served at almost every meal. Every region has its specialties (as do geographical areas within regions), and hundreds of breads of varied styles, shapes, textures, and flavors are baked throughout the country. *Pane Siciliano*, for example, is made with semolina and sprinkled with sesame seeds; *casareccio* is another Sicilian semolina bread. *Pane Toscano*, famously saltless, is made with white or whole-wheat flour. *Pane Pugliese* is characterized by its thick crust and chewy interior.

To some extent, these differences are related to the types of grains available in the areas in which the breads are traditionally made. So, for example, the further south one goes, the more one finds breads made with semolina flour. In northern Italy, darker breads are made with rye, buckwheat, corn, and whole-wheat flours. Most Italian breads are not made at home but rather purchased at bakeries (*panifici*).

Breads taught in this curriculum—*pizze*, calzone, *focacce*, and *grissini*—are covered in Chapter 9.

The following products (*prodotti*)—vegetables, oils and vinegars, grains, cheeses, and preserved meats—are integral to the making of Italian food, and appear regularly in this book and in Italian restaurant kitchens.

Verdure (Vegetables)

The Italian climate, protected from the cold of northern Europe by the Alps, is conducive to agriculture, and varied microclimates and soil types in Italy encourage cultivation of many types of produce. In addition to the vegetables that are indigenous to Italian soil, invasions, notably Greek and Muslim, and the conquest of the Americas during the fifteenth century brought new crops: tomatoes, sweet peppers, chili peppers, beans, squashes, potatoes, and corn. (Tomatoes were not commonly acccepted into Neapolitan cooking until the 1700s.)

Vegetables are crucial in forming the identity of regional cuisines. Each region in Italy has its specialties, depending on what vegetable flourishes in that geography and climate. The Veneto is famous for its radicchio, for example, and a special variety of white asparagus, *asparago bianco di Cimadolmo*. Toscana is known for its beans, Umbria for its lentils, and the southern regions for their tomatoes, peppers, and eggplants. Piemonte is famous for its cardoons; Calabrian cooking would be unrecognizable without its spicy *peperoncini*.

Traditionally, Italian chefs have cooked with seasonal local produce—asparagus in the spring, tomatoes in the late summer, and mushrooms in the fall. This tradition has a great deal to recommend it; fruits and vegetables typically taste better in season, and if they can be purchased locally, they are more likely to be fresh.

It is essential to be able to recognize high-quality produce and to clean, store, and handle it correctly so that it does not deteriorate too quickly.

As a general rule, fresh produce looks fresh—crisp, with vibrant colors and no obvious blemishes or soft spots. Yellowing or browning is a sign of age, as is limpness.

Perishable produce should be inspected and refrigerated as soon as possible after receiving. Do not allow it to sit out on a counter and wilt. Fruit that needs ripening, such as tropical fruit, pears, and stone fruit, should be left out to ripen at room temperature before refrigeration.

Purchasing and storage information for specific vegetables is given below; methods for cleaning are included in those cases in which instructions do not appear in individual recipes.

Carciofi (Artichokes)

Purchasing: Leaves should be tightly closed around the heads; stems should be firm, not rubbery; leaves should snap rather than bend. Color will vary depending on variety, but should not be brown.

Storage: Like flowers and asparagus, the best way to store artichokes is stems down, in shallow water. In a restaurant, they will be stored in plastic bus tubs or hotel pans. They will last at least 1 week.

Asparagi (Asparagus)

Purchasing: Heads should be tightly closed with compact buds; stalks should be dark, bright green, and firm. Stalks should snap when broken.

Storage: Refrigerate for up to several days. Store upright, if possible. The fresher the asparagus, the sweeter.

Fagiolini, Fagioli, e Piselli
(String Beans, Beans, and Peas)

String beans are a category of fresh bean encompassing a variety of shapes, colors, and sizes. String beans acquired their name from their long, narrow shape and because of the stringlike fibers that often cling to the tops of the beans. The entire bean is edible, pod and all. Shell beans—such as fava and cranberry beans—have a tough pod that is not usually eaten.

Purchasing: Green and yellow string beans and haricots verts should be firm, without wrinkled ends, and snap crisply when broken. Color is deep with no brown spots. Pods on shell beans and peas should be bright colored and plump, with no sign of dryness or browning.

Storage and Cleaning: As with all vegetables, sugars in beans and peas turn to starch with age, which negatively affects flavor; refrigerate beans and use as soon as possible. Shell beans are shucked before cooking. To clean string beans, snap off the stem end and pull down the length of the bean to remove the "string." The small, pointy end of the bean may also be snapped or cut off.

Broccoli, Cime di Rapa, e Cavolfiori (Broccoli, Broccoli Rabe, and Cauliflower)

Purchasing: Broccoli florets should be a deep green color and their buds compact, with no yellow flowers. Stems on broccoli rabe should be firm and slender, the buds dark green and tightly closed. On both, leaves should be dark green, not yellowed nor wilted. Cauliflower should be ivory colored, with no black or brown spots, and its leaves firm. Heads should be tightly packed.

Storage: Refrigerate for up to several days.

Preparation: In Italian cuisine, broccoli rabe is often, but not always, blanched and refreshed before sautéing in order to soften its bitterness and set its color.

Cavoli e Cavoletti (Cabbages and Brussels Sprouts)

Cabbages include a wide variety of vegetables eaten for their heads, flowers, or leaves, such as turnips, Brussels sprouts, and cauliflower. Cabbages typically have a short stem upon which rests a mass of leaves or a compact, round cluster.

Purchasing: Leaves on head cabbage and Brussels sprouts should be tightly closed; leaves on Brussels sprouts should be a deep green color. Check for browning or wilting at stem ends; leaves should show no signs of drying or wilting. Head cabbage should feel heavy. Buy Brussels sprouts on the stalk, if possible.

Storage: Refrigerate for up to several days.

Melanzane, Peperoni, Pomodori, e Zucchine (Eggplants, Peppers, Tomatoes, and Summer Squash)

The nightshade family includes vegetables such as potatoes, eggplants, and tomatoes. Members of this family contain capsaicin, a defensive chemical that has proven useful throughout history. After hundreds of years of farming, the processes of selection and breeding have reduced these defenses, although the leaves are often still toxic.

The tomato's unique chemical composition makes it a natural complement to the complex flavors of meats and sauces in classic Italian cuisine.

Purchasing: For eggplant, whatever the size or color, skin should be shiny and smooth, without blemishes or spots; it should feel firm and plump. Its cap should be bright green. Smaller, narrower eggplants contain fewer seeds. Ripe tomatoes should give when touched, without being soft. Regardless of color, skin on peppers should be smooth, shiny, and not wrinkled. Flesh will be firm. Zucchini and yellow squash (summer squash) should be firm; skin should be smooth and without obvious damage. Smaller squash contain fewer seeds.

Storage: Refrigerate eggplants, peppers, and squash for up to several days. Do not refrigerate tomatoes; store ripe tomatoes at room temperature and use them as soon as possible. Tomatoes may also be ripened at room temperature.

Finocchio (Fennel)

Fennel is used as a vegetable (the bulb), an herb (the leaves), and a spice (the seeds). The bulb has short, tight stalks with feathery leaves, and the flavor is similar to anise or licorice.

Purchasing: Buy bulbs with stems and fronds attached; fronds and stems should be fresh, not limp. Bulbs should be firm and whitish-green with little browning and should show no signs of drying out.

Storage: Cut off fronds and stems; refrigerate for up to several days.

Verdure a Foglia (Leafy Greens): Lettuces

Purchasing: Look for bright color with no browning or yellowing leaves. Texture will depend on the variety of green, but leaves should never be limp: Hardier lettuces such as romaine and varieties of chicory such as *puntarelle* should be crisp with fleshy, crunchy ribs; tender lettuces such as Boston, loose-leaf, and butter lettuce should be soft but not limp; arugula should be crisp with dark color—smaller, younger leaves are milder tasting. Belgian endive and radicchio should have tight heads; endive leaves should show no brown or green color.

Storage: Remove any damaged leaves and refrigerate. Softer lettuces and arugula should be used as soon as possible, as they wilt quickly.

Verdure a Foglia (Leafy Greens): Cooking Greens

Purchasing: For spinach, kale (including the Italian variety known as *cavolo nero*, or black kale), Swiss chard, and beet, turnip, mustard, collard, escarole, and dandelion greens, leaves should be bright colored, with no signs of drying or decay, and not limp. Stems should also be firm.

Storage: Remove any damaged leaves and refrigerate. Wrap ends in damp paper towels.

Funghi (Mushrooms)

White "button" mushrooms and cremini mushrooms—used often in this curriculum—are different strains of the *Agaricus bisporus* mushroom. (Portobello and cremini mushrooms are actually the same strain, harvested at different times of the growing process. Portobello mushrooms are allowed to mature to a much larger size.) Porcini mushrooms are common in Italian cuisine but difficult to find here in America; cremini are usually substituted at The International Culinary Center.

Purchasing: Regardless of variety, mushrooms should be firm and dry, not wilted, and with no evidence of damage. On white mushrooms, the cap should be closed, with no dark-colored gills visible.

Storage: Refrigerate out of plastic and keep very dry; dampness causes mushrooms to rot quickly. Do not remove the stem until ready to slice. (See sidebar on page 130 for general instructions on cleaning mushrooms.)

Preparation: For white and cremini mushrooms, trim the stems (discard if dark or soft) and cut the mushrooms as desired.

For portobello mushrooms, trim the stems flat to the cap; cut the mushrooms as desired.

For porcini mushrooms, remove the gills if they are dark or mushy (as the mushroom ages, the underside of the cap darkens; the gills should be tan in color). Trim the stem ends and peel the stems with a vegetable peeler if they are hard or dry. If the porcini are large, separate the cap from the stem, then cut as desired.

For chanterelle and black trumpet mushrooms, trim the stems; cut the mushrooms as desired.

For shiitake mushrooms, gently pull off the stems; cut the mushrooms as desired. The stems are not edible but add excellent flavor to stocks.

For oyster mushrooms, trim the bases; cut the mushrooms as desired.

For morel mushrooms, wash carefully and trim the stem ends.

Cipolle (Onion Family)

Purchasing: Red onion is used for cooking throughout Italy, with the exception of a pickling preparation known as *saor*, in which white onion is traditional. Typically, white onions are eaten raw. Fresh garlic is preferred; never use garlic that is sold peeled. Skins on garlic, onions, and shallots should be dry and papery without soft spots or mold. Spring garlic, also called green or immature garlic, has a milder flavor than mature garlic. The outer layer of the bulbs should be soft, like a scallion but thicker, and not dry; peel before using. (See "Preparing Spring Garlic" on page 354.) The bulbs should be firm, with no green sprouts emerging. Leeks should be firm, their leaves white and bright green, with no sign of drying.

Storage and Cleaning: Store garlic, onions, and shallots in a cool place, ideally outside of the refrigerator; the humidity in refrigerators will cause them to rot. Refrigerate leeks, however, for up to 1 week. Peel garlic, onions, and shallots and trim the stem ends. The root ends may be left attached for ease of dicing, or be trimmed and cut as desired. (See sidebar on page 278 for detailed instructions on cleaning leeks, and page 348 for tips on how to easily peel small onions such as cipollini.)

Tuberi (Root Vegetables)

Purchasing: Buy beets, carrots, and turnips with leaves if possible. Crisp, fresh-looking leaves indicate a fresh vegetable. Trim leaves before refrigerating. Potatoes should not have sprouted or have spots or bruises; a greenish color indicates bitterness. Jerusalem artichokes (sunchokes), in season from fall through early spring, are very firm when fresh and spongy when old.

Storage and Cleaning: Refrigerate beets, carrots, and turnips for up to 1 week. Store potatoes in a cool, dry place, preferably outside of the refrigerator; the humidity in refrigerators will cause them to sprout. For beets, wash and trim the stems, leaving 1 to 2 centimeters (about ½ inch).

Zucche (Winter Squash)

Purchasing: Regardless of variety, squash should be firm, without soft spots. In Italy, a delicious variety of pumpkin called *zucca* is available. The standard American sugar pumpkin is not comparable because it contains too much water, but butternut squash makes an excellent substitute.

Storage and Cleaning: Store in a cool, dry place or refrigerate. Squash may be peeled with a knife or vegetable peeler.

Erbe e Odori (Aromatic Herbs)

The flavor of basil leaves depends on the variety, the growing conditions, and even the stage at which they are harvested. Young basil leaves have a much larger proportion of aroma compounds than older leaves, by as much as five times. For the recipes in this book, basil leaves are torn into pieces (or in half for smaller leaves) rather than chopped. Chopping will bruise the herb and cause it to blacken, which is undesirable in uncooked or lightly cooked dishes.

Bay leaves, the leaves of the bay laurel tree, grow all over Italy. The trees are traditionally planted in lines between properties to make a natural divider. Fresh bay leaves are always used. Bay leaves are not edible.

Dried oregano is commonly used in Italian cuisine. It is one of only a few dried herbs used at The International Culinary Center because its flavor is not diminished by the drying process.

Purchasing: Fresh herbs (parsley, basil, chives, dill, chervil, tarragon) should be unblemished, with soft, bright leaves. They should not look wilted.

Woody herbs (thyme, rosemary, sage, oregano, marjoram) should not be brown or black.

Storage: Store fresh herbs wrapped in paper towels, then in plastic, in the refrigerator. Do not wash until ready to use. Basil and parsley may be stored standing in water, the leaves covered loosely with plastic. Store dried oregano in a tightly closed container.

Oils and Vinegars

In Italy, olive oil is used for both cooking and seasoning, as well as for salads and other raw *antipasti* such as *tartara,* carpaccio*,* and *crudo* (see sidebar on page 53). Neutral oils, such as peanut and grapeseed oils, may also be used for frying.

The smoke point of an oil, or the temperature at which the oil breaks down, depends on a variety of factors. The smoke point of unrefined oil, for example, is substantially lower than that of oil that has been refined. Therefore, smoke points are usually expressed as ranges of temperature.

Olio di Oliva (Olive Oil)

Humans have extracted oil from olives for over five thousand years. Olive oil was used by the ancient Greeks as a food, as fuel for lighting, and as a medicinal ointment to soothe wounds. The word *oil* is derived from the Latin *oleum,* which refers to the oil pressed from *olivae* (olives).

Olive trees are indigenous to the Mediterranean areas of Italy, France, Spain, and Greece, and the olive tree is a cultural symbol of those regions. Production of olive oil was the primary trade of the Mediterranean for thousands of years, where it has always been an essential element of the diet.

Italy produces nearly one-third of the world's olive oil. Extra-virgin oils are produced in all regions of southern and central Italy, and sparsely in the north. The taste and aroma of the oil depend on a number of factors: the terrain, the climate, the variety of olive used to make the oil, and the way the olives are harvested. Fine-quality olive oil will be anywhere from golden yellow

to almost bright green in color and will have a definite aroma. Flavor and aroma can range from slightly sweet, delicate, and nutty to almost grassy. (Oils from southern Italy, for example, tend toward a heavier flavor and a darker green color.) Oils made from hand-picked, under-ripe olives are a deep green color, with a fruity aroma and full-bodied flavor, while oil produced from mature olives is paler in color, with a subtler flavor.

Olive oils should be purchased a small amount at a time because they turn rancid very quickly, particularly the highest-quality oils. Store olive oils in a cool place, out of the sunlight.

Production

The production of olive oil begins with the harvest. In most instances, the olives are hand-picked or shaken from the trees in a time-consuming process. They are harvested at different stages of maturity to yield oil with specific characteristics. Each olive tree may be harvested several times during the picking season, to produce either a few oils with distinct characteristics or one oil with complexity.

To reduce their moisture content, olives are allowed to rest before production begins. After resting, they are crushed into a paste or formed into cakes that are then pressed to extract oil. The simplest method for crushing, still used in many areas of the Mediterranean, is a very ancient, primitive one employing a large granite stone in combination with a screw or hydraulic press, which does the actual crushing. The best producers accomplish this task without the aid of heat or water, which affect the purity of the finished oil. Smaller producers allow the fresh oil to settle, then filter it or leave it unfiltered, depending on the final product. The resulting oil is called "cold-pressed." These unrefined oils have distinctive rich, delicate flavors and aromas and retain essential nutrients. Cold-pressed olive oils are used raw. Their smoke point is low; high heat destroys their fine aroma and taste.

Most commercial olive oils go through additional processing, and some are made from second pressings. Larger producers use other methods of extraction that may involve the use of heat, solvents, and chemicals, which greatly affect the integrity of the oil. Several different oils from various countries may also be combined to arrive at a balanced oil. These oils constitute much of the inexpensive olive oil available in the commercial marketplace.

Traditionally, olive oils were made with a combination of olive varieties. Production methods for extra-virgin olive oil, however, are becoming more sophisticated, and oils may be made using a single variety to give a particular flavor.

Grading

Commercially, and by law, Italian olive oil is graded according to its acidity. The level of oleic acid contained in an olive oil indicates the degree to which the fat has broken down into fatty acids. The percentage of fatty acids determines the smoke point of the oil. The acidity rises with the decrease in quality.

Since heat destroys the flavor of olive oils, more expensive, high-quality extra-virgin oils are reserved in this book for uncooked preparations, and to drizzle over finished dishes as a seasoning oil. When recipes call for "olive oil," a less expensive extra-virgin olive oil is recommended.

Smoke points of olive oils range from 210°C (410°F) to 238°C (460°F), with extra-virgin oils registering at the lower end of the range and light olive oil at the higher end.

The grades are as follows:

Olio extra vergine di oliva (extra-virgin olive oil): Produced by the first cold press of high-quality olives, extra-virgin olive oil has an acidity level of less than

1 percent. Used in dressings, emulsions, sauces, and condiments, and as a finishing oil.

Olio vergine di oliva (virgin olive oil): The next highest quality oil, virgin olive oil is also the result of a first pressing, with an acidity level of no greater than 3 percent. It is used for frying, sautéing, and baking.

Olio di oliva (pure olive oil): This oil is the result of the second or third pressing of olive cakes, with up to 10 percent virgin olive oil added, and an acidity level of no more than 4 percent. The process used to produce pure olive oil, whether heat or chemicals, permits a longer shelf life than that of virgin or extra-virgin, but also yields an oil with little flavor or color. It is a good cooking oil when delicate flavor is unimportant or when the oil will be subjected to high heat.

Light olive oil: A recent introduction to the American market, light olive oil has the same properties and caloric count as pure olive oil, but through an exceptionally fine filtration process, it is lighter in color, with almost no flavor or aroma. It is used for cooking with high heat and for any dish calling for no additional flavor.

Other Oils

A number of other oils are used in Italian cuisine.

Nut oils, including hazelnut (*olio di nocciola*), walnut (*olio di noci*), pine nut (*olio di pinoli*), pistachio (*olio di pistacchi*), and almond (*olio di mandorle*): Most nut oils carry the flavor of the nut from which they have been made and impart a very defined character to foods. Since they are unstable oils that are very perishable, nut oils should be purchased in small amounts from reputable vendors and refrigerated once open. Italian chefs use these oils for sauces, for dressing salads, for seasoning vegetables, as a flavoring for *crudo*, and as a "finishing" flavored garnish on the plate. Some may also be used for light sautéing. In the past, hazelnut and walnut oils were sometimes used in *Bagna Cauda*

(page 38), because they were less expensive than olive oil, which is not widely produced in the Piemonte region, where those recipes are traditional.

Olio di semi di arachide (peanut oil): One of the heavier oils, peanut oil is used for frying, deep-frying, and emulsions. Its smoke point is 216°C (420°F) to 221°C (430°C). At The International Culinary Center, peanut oil is used for deep-frying.

Olio di vinaccioli (grapeseed oil): A by-product of wine-making, this light, neutral oil is extracted from grape seeds. With a very high smoke point of 216°C (420°F) to 248°C (480°F), it is useful for frying and sautéing.

Infused oils: These oils are made by infusing fine-quality oils, even highly fragrant extra-virgin olive oil, with herbs; spices; aromatics such as garlic, shallots, or ginger; fruits; or fruit peels. They can be used in vinaigrettes but are used mainly as a flavored garnish or plate accent. *Olio santo*, olive oil infused with chilis and garlic, is a local tradition in Puglia.

Aceti (Vinegars)

Vinegar has been used for centuries for the preservation of foods, as a component of light and often healing beverages, as a deodorizer and cleanser, and even as a health aid. Vinegar is the result of the natural acid fermentation that occurs in wine or other alcoholic liquids. The first fermentation converts sugars in liquids such as grape juice or malt wort into alcohol; the second, known as acetous fermentation, converts the resultant alcohol liquid into vinegar. This acetous fermentation results from the action of the bacterium *Acetobacter xylinum*. This bacterium occurs naturally in wine-growing areas, and the first vinegar was probably made accidentally when wine was left out in the hot sun.

Today, most vinegar is produced with the addition of a cultivated bacteria starter. The bacteria react with the alcohol in the wine and turn it into acetic acid. Vinegar

is produced all over the world, with wine vinegars generally made in wine-producing areas, and grain or other fruit vinegars made in regions producing grains or particular fruits.

The basic vinegar types are those made from wine or champagne, distilled alcohol, sherry, or cider. The quality of the vinegar depends on the quality of the wine or alcohol used to make it. It must contain between 4 percent and 7.5 percent acetic acid to be labeled vinegar. (Vinegar is occasionally marked in terms of "grains," with every 10 grains equaling 1 percent acidity. Therefore, a vinegar marked "50 grain" would contain 5 percent acidity.)

The commonly used vinegars in Italian cuisine are:

Aceto di vino rosso (red wine vinegar): Sharp, sweet, and full-bodied, red wine vinegar complements intensely flavored foods such as bitter greens.

Aceto balsamico tradizionale (traditional balsamic vinegar): A traditional vinegar produced from the white Trebbiano grape in Modena, through a years-long process of aging in barrels made of a variety of different woods—including chestnut, cherry, ash, mulberry, pear, and oak—and in graduating sizes. The vinegar is moved from one barrel to the next after a one-year aging, with the complete aging process taking at least five years. Natural evaporation takes place during the aging process, infusing the vinegar with the scent of the wood and dramatically decreasing the yield. Traditional balsamic vinegar, labeled *aceto balsamico tradizionale*, is extremely expensive and thicker than

ordinary vinegars. It should be almost molasseslike in consistency, with a mildly acidic aroma and a smooth, yin-yang taste of sweet-sour. Like fine-quality olive oils, it is often used as a condiment for a flavored garnish on the plate. Two balsamic vinegars have been classified DOP: *aceto balsamico tradizionale di Modena* and *aceto balsamico tradizionale di Reggio Emilia*, and they are distinguished by their specific bottle shapes (slender and bullet-shaped for Reggio Emilia, rounded for Modena).

Aceto balsamico di Modena (balsamic vinegar): Commonly available and more affordable than traditional balsamic vinegar, *aceto balsamico di Modena* (or *aceto balsamico industriale*) is a red wine vinegar fortified with caramelized sugar, herbs, and other flavorings. It is now widely used in the United States in vinaigrettes, dressings, and marinades.

Aceto di sidro di mele (cider vinegar): This vinegar is produced from naturally sweet apple juice with yeast added to convert the sugar to alcohol. The resulting hard cider is converted into vinegar following the usual process. Cider vinegar has a low percentage of alcohol and acidity and is used in dressings and in pickling solutions. Apple cider vinegar is produced in the regions of Friuli–Venezia Giulia, Trentino–Alto Adige, and Piemonte, where apples are grown.

Infused and flavored vinegars: Vinegar can be flavored with a wide variety of ingredients. The most common are infusions of herbs (particularly tarragon and basil), fruit (raspberry and pear), garlic, and shallots.

Formaggi d'Italia (Italian Cheeses)

Every region in Italy produces cheese. As a whole, the country produces nearly 450 different types. In the United States, we are exposed to only a small fraction of the cheeses available in Italy. Pictured at right is a sampling of cheeses available in the United States and used in the recipes in this curriculum.

Then there are vast numbers of subdivisions that classify a specific cheese by its texture, the place from which it originated, the mechanics of its manufacture, the ripening process, and many other delineations. A classification is also altered by the aging process. A young, unripened cheese is an entirely different entity from the same cheese when it has fully matured.

Cheeses may also be loosely categorized by cheese-making process and texture. While there is some variation and overlap among chefs and cheese-makers, a rough overview of categories is presented below.

The simplest cheeses, called **fresh cheeses**, are those in which the milk is simply pasteurized (as required by law in the United States), soured and/or coagulated with rennet, drained, molded, salted, and perhaps pressed. These soft cheeses have a high water content and are made to be consumed soon after production. Examples are fresh goat cheeses.

Classifying Cheese

There are various ways to classify the Italian cheeses available to the American consumer. One is by type of milk: *vaccino* (cow's milk); pecorino (sheep's milk), *caprino* (goat's milk), *bufalino* (buffalo milk), and *latte misto* (mixed milk). Northern Italy is particularly famous for several cow's-milk cheeses, specifically the nutty, granular Parmigiano-Reggiano and Grana Padano. Fontina, Gorgonzola, Taleggio, and Asiago are other well-known cow's-milk cheeses produced in northern and central Italy. Once more common in the mountainous regions of central and southern Italy, sheep's-milk cheeses (collectively called pecorino, from *pecora*, the Italian word for sheep) as well as goat's-milk cheeses are now produced in most regions. Buffalo-milk cheeses are traditionally connected to the area around Rome and southern Italy, particularly Campania.

Italian cheeses can be further divided into two broad categories: fresh (or unripened) and aged (ripened).

Ricotta is a special case. It is called a "secondary" fresh cheese because it is made by recuperating the residual whey drained from the "primary" cheese (usually a sheep's-milk cheese), cooking it, and scooping out the resulting solids into a draining mold. The residual whey has enough fat and protein to make this second cheese. One particular whey protein, lacto-globulin, coagulates to allow the creation of ricotta and other whey cheeses. In Italy, sheep's-milk ricotta is common; in the United States, one is more likely to see cow's-milk ricotta.

Soft-ripened (or bloomy-rind) cheeses are those that have been coagulated, drained, and molded, then ripened by dipping or spraying the rounds of fresh ("green") cheese with bacteria that encourage a rind to develop. (Some soft-ripened cheeses are inoculated with bacteria in the liquid stage.) The mold ripens the cheese from the outside in, developing the texture from chalky and dry to creamy and runny. A mature soft cheese will run when cut into. A cheese that is not yet mature has a softened outer rim, while the center remains chalky and firm. Maturing also develops flavor in the cheese. Examples of soft-ripened cheeses are Robiola and Robiola Bosina. The soft rind is edible.

Semifirm cheeses are those in which the curds have been coagulated, drained, and pressed in a perforated mold to allow the whey to continue to drain. In some cases, the curds have been cooked and cut in a variety of sizes. (Cooking is a technique for further expelling whey. The longer the curds are cooked and the higher the temperature, the drier the cheese; the smaller the curds are cut before cooking, the more whey is expelled, further drying the cheese.) As opposed to the softer cheeses described above, semifirm cheeses will hold their shape when sliced. Semifirm cheeses are aged for a short period of time and may be coated with wax to maintain moisture. Many goat cheeses are semifirm cheeses.

Washed-rind cheeses such as Taleggio are washed with brine, beer, wine, or another liquid during their aging process to ripen their surface. The liquid feeds the bacteria that break down the surface proteins and cause the rind to develop a brown color and a strong odor. These cheeses, which range from semisoft to creamy, are made from raw or pasteurized milk.

Firm cheeses are those in which the curds have been coagulated, drained, cooked (or not), pressed, and aged in a controlled environment that allows them to continue to dry and develop character. Asiago d'Allevo belongs in this category. Firm cheeses are aged for at least 45 days, and they can continue aging for several years, if properly stored.

Hard cheeses are crumbly cheeses that have been pressed and aged (some have been cooked), and are dry enough that they will no longer slice easily; they are often used grated or shaved. Parmigiano-Reggiano, Grana Padano, and aged pecorino are examples.

Blue cheeses such as Gorgonzola are made by exposing the cheese to specific molds, either by inoculating the milk or by sprinkling a powdered form of the mold on the curd. The cheese is pressed and aged; it is typically pierced at some time during the aging process to allow the necessary oxygen into the center of the cheese so that it develops veins of blue or green mold running throughout. Textures of blue cheeses vary from creamy to drier. For example, there are two types of Gorgonzola, one creamy and one "natural."

Pasta filata, which means "pulled curd," is a uniquely Italian process by which the drained curds are immersed in a bath of very hot water to soften them, then worked by hand or machine to stretch the cheese in thick strands until pliable. The cheese can then be shaped. *Pasta filata* cheeses are very common in the southern regions of Italy. Mozzarella, Caciocavallo, and provolone are examples of this technique.

Guidelines for Storing Cheeses

In general, keep cheese and everything it touches clean, cold, and covered. Cheese is a living organism; it contains enzymes and bacteria that need air and moisture to survive. After opening cheese, always cover it in a fresh wrapping (waxed or parchment paper is ideal, but semipermeable plastic wrap is acceptable) to prevent it from drying out or picking up neighboring flavors. If possible, store cheeses separately to prevent flavor transfer.

Double-wrap pungent cheeses, such as blue or washed-rind varieties, to prevent their aromas from permeating other foods. Store them in an airtight container to further ensure against aroma leakage. However, no matter how cheese is wrapped, be sure to use it within a few days after purchase to avoid loss of flavor.

Avoid exposing cheeses to strong fluctuations of temperature and light. According to the American Cheese Society, the recommended temperature range for storing cheese is from 1.7°C to 7.2°C (35°F to 45°F). Cheese that is stored at too low a temperature may become dry and lose flavor. Cheese that is too warm may weep or even collapse. Cheese should be stored at a high humidity level, preferably in the bottom vegetable/fruit bin of the refrigerator, and never near meat.

Note the expiration date on cheeses. If cheeses other than fresh cheeses and blues have passed their expiration dates, or if the cheese develops a blue-green mold on the exterior, cut it approximately 1 centimeter (about ½ inch) below the mold. Discard the moldy portion; the rest of the cheese will be fine.

In general, never freeze natural cheeses, as this may damage texture. In some cases, their flavors will also be seriously affected. If cheese must be frozen, allow it to defrost slowly in the refrigerator and use it only for cooking (defrosted cheese often has a crumbly, dry texture).

Check cheeses every day to make sure they remain healthy and to ensure that there is proper air exchange. Rewrap cheeses if necessary.

If stored cheeses become overly dry or develop a slimy texture or any "off" odors, it's best to discard them. If these characteristics appear too frequently in cheeses from one retailer, it may be advisable to find another source for your cheese.

Serving Cheese

When designing a menu, first consider when the cheese will be served. For instance, a cheese course after the main course and prior to or in place of dessert can add an elegant touch to casual dining. Present cheeses of diverse sizes, shapes, and flavor and texture profiles. Strong, pungent cheeses should not be placed next to delicate-flavored cheeses. Make sure each cheese has its own knife, to keep the flavors distinct.

Even modest cheese courses can be elegant when served attractively using a wooden board, marble slab, straw mat, flat wicker basket, or other innovative presentation. Be sure not to overcrowd the tray, as guests will need room to slice the cheeses. Serve bread and/or plain crackers on a separate plate. Fruit can add variety to a cheese board, especially if cheese is being served with cocktails. Additional accompaniments can include nuts such as walnuts or Marcona almonds, fig cakes, floral honeys, wine jellies, or Italian *mostarda*. It is best to cut cheese while it is still chilled, so the cut line remains clean. Cold cheese is also easier to handle. Some hard cheeses, such as Parmigiano-Reggiano, cut better when brought to room temperature.

Fresh cheeses may be served slightly chilled; however, most other varieties should be allowed to sit at room temperature for at least 30 minutes to release the best flavor and aroma prior to serving.

Salumi (Cured Meats)

Historically, every region in Italy developed methods to preserve fresh meat before access to refrigeration. Archeological evidence suggests that such preservation practices have been followed for thousands of years. Most often the meat was pork, but beef, goose, wild boar, and turkey were also used. Technology, refrigeration, and freezing, as well as other methods of preserving, have reduced the importance of curing, since these foods no longer need to serve the same function. However, Italians still make these cured products—though perhaps not in their original regions or with the same local ingredients—by incorporating new technologies into traditional recipes.

The general word for cured meats is *salumi*, which can be roughly divided into two categories. The first is whole cuts, such as hams (prosciutto and *speck*) and pork belly (pancetta), that are cured in salt and aged in a temperature- and humidity-controlled environment. The second category, *insaccati*, or *salami*, are meats that are ground and packed into casings. This category includes such products as *cotechino* and mortadella. *Insaccati* or *salami* may be fresh, cooked, or aged. Some aged *salami*, such as *cacciatorino*, are also fermented. Fresh *salami* are usually, but not always, cooked before eating (sausage is commonly consumed raw in Italy). Aged *salami* may be sliced and eaten, while fresh *salami* must be eaten within a specific amount of time or they will spoil. Traditionally the casings were natural (bladder, intestine, or pigskin); many producers now use artificial casings.

Salumi are not usually smoked. A famous exception is *speck*, a cured, lightly smoked, aged ham produced in the northern region of Trentino–Alto Adige.

Below are some common types of Italian *salumi* and fats (*grassi*), most of which are used in this curriculum (see photo on opposite page).

Prosciutto crudo: Salted, aged, cured ham. Many regions produce prosciutto. Two of the most famous types are Prosciutto di Parma, from Emilia-Romagna, and Prosciutto di San Daniele, made in the region of Friuli–Venezia Giulia. The latter is unique in that the pig's trotter is attached, and the shape of the leg is somewhat flattened, giving it its signature violin shape.

Prosciutto cotto: Cooked ham.

Pancetta: Salt-cured and aged pork belly. Pancetta is sold rolled up into a cylinder (*arrotolata*) or as a slab (*tesa*). *Pancetta arrotolata* is the more common of the two forms in the United States and the form used in this curriculum.

Speck: Boned hog's leg that is cured, cold-smoked, and aged. It is unusual in that the majority of Italian *salumi* are not smoked. Speck dell' Alto Adige IGP is a specialty of the province of Bolzano, in Trentino–Alto Adige.

Guanciale: From the Italian word *guancia*, or "cheek," *guanciale* is cured pork jowl. It features prominently in the cuisine of Umbria and Lazio, where it is a main ingredient in such classic dishes as *spaghetti alla carbonara* and *bucatini all'amatriciana*. In many recipes, *guanciale* can be substituted for pancetta. However, the pork flavor of *guanciale* is generally stronger than in pancetta and the texture is more delicate.

Mortadella: Cooked sausage made with finely ground, smooth pink meat, at least 15 percent of which must be mixed with pure white animal fat.

Bresaola: Air-dried, salted, and aged beef from the leg. Bresaola della Valtellina IGP has been made in Valtellina, an Alpine valley in the northern region of Lombardy, since 1400. *Bresaola* is eaten raw.

Strutto: Soft-textured pork fat found in various locations (notably around organs) on the inside of the carcass and rendered. Do not confuse *strutto* with *lardo* (see below), which is made from subcutaneous pork fat. *Strutto* is used in some traditional pastries (see *Pastiera* on page 295) and for cooking.

Lardo: Cured pork fatback. Uncured fatback, also called *lardo*, is used for larding meats and as an element in *salumi* such as mortadella and *cotechino* (see page 213). The most famous cured fatback is Lardo di Colonnata IGP, made in the town of Colonnata, in Toscana, near the town of Carrara. The region of Valle d'Aosta makes another form: Valle d'Aosta Lard d'Arnad DOP. *Lardo* is also served finely sliced as an antipasto or snack, or finely chopped as a condiment for bread.

Guidelines for Storing *Salumi*

Salumi—fresh, aged, and cooked—are ready to eat and at their best at the moment of purchase. Once sliced, they deteriorate quickly, so serve *salumi* as soon as possible.

Store *salumi* in the refrigerator.

The best way to hold *salumi* is in Cryovac, which maintains appropriate humidity and keeps the meat from drying out. Otherwise, once *salumi* have been cut into, wrap them in plastic to prevent the meat from drying out and picking up flavors. A good way to hold prosciutto is to cover it with the skin or thin-sliced fat, then in plastic wrap.

to play with *salumi* of different styles from different regions. An appealing variety might include slices of prosciutto from Parma or San Daniele, *finocchiona* from Toscana, Bresaola della Valtellina from Lombardy, *coppa* from Emilia-Romagna, slices or cubes of mortadella from Bologna, and sliced *cacciatorino*, which is made in several regions. *Lardo* is delicious served on warm, toasted crostini so that the warmth of the toast melts the *lardo* slightly.

Salumi should be brought to room temperature before serving.

If the exterior of any meats, such as prosciutto or pancetta, is dry and hard, shave it off with a sharp knife and save for stock or soups.

Serving *Salumi*

Salumi are among the most popular choices for antipasto. It's traditional to serve several varieties. Count on about 50 grams (about 2 ounces) per person. Choose *salumi* with different shapes, tastes, textures, and styles. Combine whole cuts (prosciutto) with dry-aged *salami* and cooked meats. This is an opportunity

Slice meats with a very sharp knife or on a slicer. When slicing, use a gentle sawing motion rather than pressure, so as not to mash the meat. *Lardo* in particular must be cut when very cold or it will be difficult to get a thin slice.

Serve the meats on a *tagliere* (wooden board) or platter with bread and/or breadsticks (*grissini*), and perhaps a bowl of olives.

Fagioli (Beans)

Italy grows a huge variety of beans of different sizes, shapes, and colors, each with a distinct flavor and texture. Recipes in this book use *cannellini* beans, chickpeas, and lentils exclusively, but other varieties may be substituted. See pages 364–65 for detailed instructions on washing, soaking, and cooking beans. (Note that beans and other dried legumes—peas and lentils—vary enormously in quality and price. Some excellent-quality legumes have superb flavor and tender skin that is barely distinguishable from the flesh of the legume when eaten.)

Below is a sampling of several different varieties of Italian beans:

Fagioli cannellini Toscani have a creamy vanilla color, a delicious nutty flavor, and a slightly mealy texture.

Fagioli cocco di mamma have thin skins and a nutty, slightly sweet, buttery flavor.

Fagioli del papa, or pope's beans, are large purple-and-beige beans with a wonderful chestnut flavor and a dense, meaty texture. These beans originated in the mountains of Peru and are closely related to the lima bean.

Fagioli rosso di Lucca are small, red beans with a rich, earthy, nutty flavor. Dense and meaty, they are specifically grown to be used in soups, where their thick skins add beautiful color to the broth.

Fagioli saluggia are tan with purple speckles. Intensely flavorful and slightly grainy in texture, they have durable skins that make them great for stews and braised dishes. It is common in Piemonte to serve them with sausages and rice.

Fagioli sorana have been grown for centuries in a small valley in the province of Pistoia. *Sorana* beans come in two varieties: milky white, with a squashed shape; and wine red, with a cylindrical shape. Both varieties have rich but delicate taste and tender skins.

Fagioli stregoni are small, kidney-shaped beans of the *borlotti* family. They are used mainly in soups, where they maintain their beautiful color throughout cooking. They have a meaty, slightly earthy flavor.

Fagioli toscanelli have an irregular, elongated shape, tender skins, and a white, milky color. Their flavor is intense, creamy, and sweet.

Fagioli zolfino pratomagno are also called *burrino* because they melt in the mouth like butter (*burro* in Italian). They are also known as *fagioli del cento* (the hundred bean), because they are traditionally sown on the hundredth day of the year. They are small, round, yellow, and subtly flavored.

Ceci Toscani, nutty Tuscan chickpeas, are cousins of the pea that have been a staple on the Italian peninsula since the days of the Roman Empire.

Cicerchie, members of the chickpea family, date back to ancient Rome and are cultivated primarily in Puglia and Umbria. Tiny and irregular in shape and ranging in color from gray to brown, they look like miniature fava beans. They have a delicate flavor and tender skins.

Fagioli burrini hold their shape well when cooked and have a mild, buttery flavor with a long mineral finish.

Fagioli corona are large, hearty, cream-colored beans whose skins stay whole when cooked.

Fagioli diavoli are dark brown beans speckled with purple. Sweet, with a hint of olive, they have a chewy skin and creamy texture.

Fagioli scritti are sought after for their tender skins and earthy, chestnutlike flavor. Members of the cranberry family, *scritti* beans are off-white with red striations and are produced exclusively on centuries-old family farms in the Piemonte region.

Fagioli pavoni are plump, kidney-shaped beans with a creamy, smooth texture. Light brown with deep brown striations, they are sometimes called "peacock beans." Earthy and meaty, with hints of sweet chestnut, they retain their color during soaking and cooking.

Fagioli piattella are flat, oblong white beans with a creamy texture and an earthy, salty flavor.

Cereali (Grains and Flours)

Italian cuisine makes use of a variety of grains and flours in soups, risotto, risottolike *farrotto*, polenta, pasta, breads, and pastries.

Riso (Rice)

Italian rice is divided into four grades according to the length, shape, and size of the grain and the creaminess or texture of the rice when cooked.

The least expensive, lowest-quality grade, called **commune**, or **originario**, is characterized by short, round grains that cook quickly and break down to a mushy texture when cooked. This grade is used mostly for soups and desserts where firmness is unimportant.

Rice grains that are graded **semifino** are of medium length and retain a moderate firmness when cooked. *Semifino*-grade rice is used in soups and may be used in risotto, although higher grades will give a better product.

Fino-grade rice grains are longer and slightly larger, with an oval shape that narrows at each end. Rice that

is graded *fino* remains firm when cooked and is therefore a fine grade for *risotto*.

Superfino is the top grade, denoting rice grains that are long and fat. *Superfino* varieties take the longest time to cook because the grains can absorb more liquid while still remaining firm. *Superfino* is an excellent grade for risotto.

Italian Rice Varieties

Worldwide, rice is divided into three major categories: short-, medium-, and long-grain, each characterized by a unique texture and cooking property. Most of the rice varieties grown in Italy are strains of a thick, short-grained variety called japonica (*Oryza sativa japonica*). Although several of those varieties may be used for risotto, the three best, and most commonly used, are Arborio, *Vialone Nano,* and *Carnaroli*. For the purposes of risotto-making, the important distinction between the three lies in their differing percentages of two starches: amylopectin, which binds very effectively and is responsible for the creamy texture of risotto; and amylose, a harder starch that dissolves more reluctantly and is responsible for retaining the firmness of the grain.

Arborio is a *superfino*-grade rice. The grains are large and thick, and they contain a high percentage of amylopectin, which helps to produce the thick, compact style of risotto prevalent in Piemonte, Lombardia, and Emilia-Romagna. Arborio absorbs liquid readily and can become mushy if not carefully monitored.

Vialone Nano is a *fino*-grade rice, popular in the Veneto and Lombardia. A smaller-grained variety, it contains a lower percentage of amylopectin than

Arborio but is higher in amylose. *Vialone Nano* retains its firmness well, but its lesser percentage of amylopectin means that it does not bind as well as Arborio, creating the looser (brothier), less creamy *risotti* typical of the Veneto.

Carnaroli is a *superfino*-grade rice considered to have the best characteristics for a firm, creamy risotto. *Carnaroli* contains enough amylopectin to create an appropriately creamy texture; it also has a high percentage of amylose, which helps the rice to retain its shape and firmness. At The International Culinary Center, we use *Carnaroli* and *Vialone Nano*.

Farro

Farro (*Triticum dicoccum*) is a variety of hard wheat, an unhybridized ancestor of modern wheat recognized as the first known cereal in Western history. High in vitamins, mineral, and fiber, it was an important food of the ancient Etruscans, Egyptians, and Romans. Roman soldiers were given rations of *farro*, with which they made thick soups flavored with dried pork and vegetables. Ground into a paste and cooked into porridge, *farro* was also the major ingredient in *puls*, the ancient forerunner of polenta. With the development of other grains after the fall of the Roman Empire, the cultivation of *farro* was restricted to regions in central Italy, but it has regained popularity in recent years.

Unlike in modern wheat, the husk of the *farro* is attached to the grain, much like that of barley or oats, giving cooked *farro* a chewy texture, somewhat like wheat berries. The key to cooking *farro* is to use enough liquid, since it absorbs a great deal of water as it cooks. *Farro* is not generally served on its own, as a rice pilaf might be. Rather, it is cooked into a dish such as a regional soup or rustic minestrone (see *Zuppa di Farro* on page 87), and it adds excellent texture to salads. It is also the main ingredient in a risottolike preparation called *Farrotto* (page 134). *Farro* is now cultivated in a number of regions in Italy, but the only IGP-designated variety is grown in Toscana and Umbria. The *farro* from the Garfagnana area of Toscana is famous for its pure, nutty taste.

Make sure to buy *farro* rather than spelt (*Triticum spelta*), which it resembles. Cooked *farro* has a firm, chewy texture; spelt softens and becomes mushy. To get the correct product, look for *Triticum dicoccum*, or buy the IGP-designated Farro della Garfagnana from Toscana. (Buying the IGP product also guarantees that the grain has been properly husked.)

Polenta (Cornmeal)

Cornmeal is available in coarse, medium, and fine grinds. The preferred grind depends on the region (sometimes white and yellow cornmeal are mixed as well, or buckwheat added, creating *polenta taragna*), but as a general rule, coarse-ground cornmeal produces a thicker polenta, while a fine grind produces a softer, thinner polenta.

Polenta integrale is stone-ground cornmeal made from the whole grain—germ and bran. Whole-grain cornmeal looks speckled with light and dark bits rather than having a uniform color, and it has a richer corn flavor.

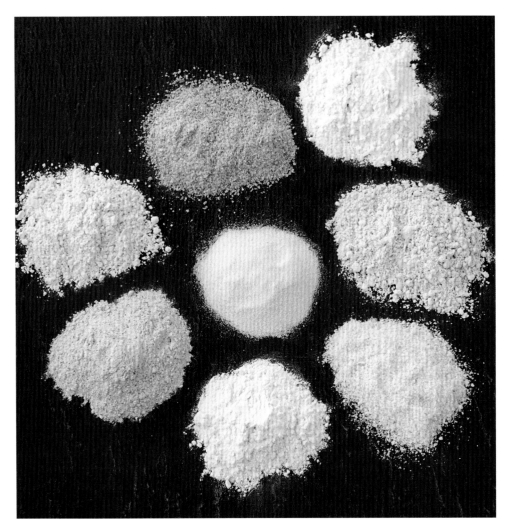

Farina (Flour)

Recipes in this book call for several different types of flour. Except when specialty flour is called for, such as semolina, *doppio zero*, or whole-wheat flours discussed below, recipes use **all-purpose flour**. Soft-textured **cake flour**, milled from soft wheat, is used in some pastry recipes, and **bread flour** is used in yeasted *bomboloni*.

Durum wheat (*grano duro*), which is milled into **semolina flour**, is used in the manufacture of dried pastas (*pasta secca*) and is also used to make some hearty fresh pasta shapes from central and southern Italy, such as *orecchiette*. **Whole-wheat flour** is used to make crisp *grissini*. *Tipo* (meaning "type") *00* (*doppio zero*, or **"double zero"**) **flour** is traditional for some fresh egg pastas, particularly in the cuisine of Emilia-Romagna; it creates very soft, tender noodles and filled pasta shapes. **Buckwheat flour** is used in combination with *tipo 00* flour to make some pastas, such as the *pizzocheri* of the Alpine area of Lombardy, in the north of Italy. The recipe for pasta dough in this curriculum uses a combination of *tipo 00* and semolina flours.

The recommended **flour for pizza** is a *tipo 00* flour formulated for pizza-making, which means it has a relatively high (11 to 12 percent) protein content. To approximate Italian pizza flour, mix equal parts (by weight) all-purpose and bread flours. However, the flour used will also depend on the type of crust desired as well as the type of oven the pizza will be cooked in.

Chestnut flour, made from ground dried chestnuts, was traditionally used in sweet and savory preparations by those regions that grew chestnuts. In this book, chestnut and **almond flour** are used in cakes. No recipes in the book call for **chickpea flour**, but it is a common product in Italian cuisine, particularly in certain traditional foods of Liguria, Campania, and other parts of southern Italy.

Sapori e Spezie (Flavors and Spices)

Some further pantry ingredients are essential to Italian cuisine.

Acciughe Sotto Sale (Salt-Packed Anchovies)

Anchovies are sold gutted, heads removed, skin and bones intact, and packed in salt; or filleted and packed in oil. At The International Culinary Center, we prefer the salted variety for its superior flavor. (Excellent salt-packed anchovies are produced in Sicilia.) To prepare them, see "Cleaning Salt-Packed Anchovies" on page 451.

Capperi (Capers)

Capers are the flowering bud of the caper bush, native to the Mediterranean. Most Italian capers come from the islands off Sicilia (famously, the island of Pantelleria) and from Sardinia. The best-quality capers are salt-packed rather than brined. To use, soak overnight in water to cover. Then drain and rinse well.

Sale (Salt)

Several regions in Italy are famous for their production of sea or mineral salt, notably Emilia-Romagna (in the province of Cervia on the Adriatic) and Sicilia (Trapani, Paceco, and Marsala). At The International Culinary Center, coarse (kosher) salt is always used.

Spezie Forti (Spices)

The first known reference to spices in a culinary context was in the first-century-BCE Roman cookbook, *De Re Coquinaria*, by Apicius. *Spezie forti* (which means "robust spices") is a mixture of spices used by Italian butchers to season cured meats and sausage mixtures. At The International Culinary Center we use it to flavor meat for roasts and braises, and for various fillings. A typical *spezie forti* will include many different spices, but common ones are cardamom, coriander, cinnamon, nutmeg, mace, star anise, fennel seeds, and ginger. Each butcher has his own custom recipe, usually a closely held secret; Dean Casella's contains seventeen different spices. Garam masala and freshly ground nutmeg are reasonable substitutes.

Recipes

Chapter 1

Antipasti

Bruschetta al Pomodoro
    (Grilled Bread with Tomatoes)
Bagna Cauda (Hot Dip with Garlic and Anchovies)
Fonduta (Valdostana Fondue)
Peperoni Arrostiti con Acciughe
    (Roasted Marinated Peppers)
Zucchine alla Scapece
    (Zucchini Marinated in Vinegar)
Verdure Sott'Olio
    (Vegetables Layered with Seasonings in Olive Oil)
Pomodori Arrostiti (Roasted Tomatoes)
Caponata (Sweet-and-Sour Eggplant)
Soppressata di Polpo (Octopus Terrine)
Crudo di Pesce (Crudo)
Tartara di Tonno (Tuna Tartare)
Insalata di Mare (Seafood Salad)
Capesante con Funghi Porcini
    (Scallops with Porcini Mushrooms)
Insalata di Pollo (Chicken Salad)
Fegatini (Chicken-Liver Crostini)
Involtini di Cavolo (Stuffed Cabbage)
Carpaccio di Manzo con Funghi
    (Carpaccio with Mushrooms)
Vitello Tonnato (Veal with Tuna Sauce)

Clockwise from bottom: *Bruschetta al
Pomodoro* (page 38), *Peperoni Arrostiti
con Acciughe* (page 42), and *Caponata*
(page 47)

The antipasto is the traditional prelude to the Italian meal. The literal translation of the word is "before the meal" and it refers to the array of savory nibbles and small bites that Italians traditionally lay out to accompany drinks, and conversation, before sitting down to the formal meal. The intention of *antipasti* is to whet the appetite, not sate it. So these dishes are traditionally light, with bright flavors—salty, acidic, and/or spicy. *Antipasti* may be hot or cold; they are often served at room temperature.

Historically, a formal restaurant meal in Italy would begin with an impressive collection of several different *antipasti*, presented buffet-style. In the home, the antipasto course is a much simpler affair—perhaps just a bowl of olives, or a few nice slices of cured meats (*affettati misti*).

As life becomes more pressured everywhere, dining is becoming more informal, and Italy is no exception. A current trend, particularly at a more casual restaurant such as an *osteria* (tavern, loosely translated), *trattoria* (bistro), or *enoteca* (wine bar), is for diners to make an entire meal of *antipasti* alone, much as Americans these days are eating meals composed of small plates, or tapas. And at home, Italians are just as likely to be buying their *antipasti*, ready-made, as to be making them in their own kitchens.

This chapter includes an assortment of traditional recipes that demonstrate several classic forms of, and approaches to, *antipasti*. Typical of *antipasti*, none are very fancy or difficult to make. Antipasto preparations vary a great deal from area to area, and there are a great many more options than are included in this chapter. Once you are familiar with some of these forms, they may be varied according to season, availability of ingredients, and personal preference.

Some traditional forms of *antipasti* are:

- Salads of all types

- Raw, cooked, and/or marinated vegetable dishes

- Raw, cooked, and/or marinated seafood dishes

- Raw, cooked, and cured meats

- Terrines

- Rolled meat and vegetable dishes (called *involtini*)

- "Toasts" spread with savory toppings (called bruschetta or crostini)

But the possibilities are practically endless, from *frittate* to mixtures of fried vegetables and seafood (called *fritto misto*), braised mussels, and stuffed clams, many of which are discussed in later chapters in this book. Slender breadsticks or *grissini* (page 152) often accompany *antipasti*.

Vegetable *Antipasti*

Vegetables are an ideal choice for *antipasti* because they are light and fresh, and offer the cook a myriad of choices, almost regardless of season. Some of the simplest vegetable *antipasti* combine raw, cut-up vegetables with some kind of flavorful dipping sauce; examples are *Pinzimonio* (see *Bagna Cauda*, page 38), a vinaigrette for cut-up vegetables, and the famous *Bagna Cauda* from Piemonte (page 38), in which vegetables are dipped into a pungent, warm, olive-oil sauce redolent of garlic and anchovies. Alternatively, raw vegetables may be served in a salad or dressed with olive oil, lemon, or vinegar, and perhaps herbs. (See Chapter 16 for more salads.)

Another common approach for enhancing the flavor of vegetables is to marinate or pickle them in flavorful liquids and seasonings. The vegetable soaks up the marinade, which transforms its taste—sometimes subtly, sometimes more aggressively. A simple example of marinating is demonstrated in the recipe for *Peperoni Arrostiti con Acciughe* on page 42, in which grilled or roasted bell peppers are marinated in olive oil with anchovies, capers, parsley, salt, and pepper. *Sott'olio* describes a technique in which cooked vegetables are marinated under a layer of oil and seasonings. Vegetables may also be pickled, a process called *sott'aceto* (see "Marinated, Pickled, and Oil-Cured Foods for *Antipasti*" on page 44).

More recipes for vegetable *antipasti* may be found in Chapter 16: *Insalata di Topinambur* (page 268), *Le Puntarelle* (page 265), *Panzanella* (page 265), *Insalata di Patate* (page 269), *Insalata di Barbabietole* (page 271), *Carciofi alla Giudea* (page 252), and *Carciofi alla Romana* (page 254). A recipe for *Frittata* is on page 143 in Chapter 8 and a recipe for *Mozzarella* is on page 68 in Chapter 2.

Seafood *Antipasti*

Italians make good use of the wealth of shellfish available on their coasts, including mussels, clams, and oysters, as well as shrimp, squid, and octopus, to make seafood *antipasti*, which is served both cooked and raw. Just as for vegetable *antipasti*, the seafood can find its way onto bruschetta or crostini, is served in salads, and is marinated. Clams and oysters are stuffed and broiled (page 242). *Soppressata di Polpo*, an octopus terrine, is thinly sliced and served with arugula and a spicy olive-caper dressing (page 48). Oysters and clams are often served raw on the half shell, but can be served in many kinds of *antipasti*. Clams are also used in a variety of antipasto preparations.

Raw fish makes a popular antipasto, presented in preparations called *crudo, tartara*, and carpaccio (see "*Crudo*, Carpaccio, and *Tartara*" on page 53). Small fish, whole or in fillets, may be steamed for a couple of minutes and then served with olive oil, salt, and lemon juice or vinegar.

More recipes for seafood *antipasti* may be found in Chapter 15: *Baccalà Mantecato* (page 226), *Vongole Ripiene* (page 242), *Anguilla in Carpione* (page 244), and *Fritto Misto di Pesce* (page 246).

Meat *Antipasti*

An important category of meat *antipasti* is *salumi*, which covers a huge variety of salt-cured, air-dried, and smoked meats. These include whole cuts of pork on the bone, such as prosciutto; the salted, dried beef, *bresaola*; ground meats packed into a casing, such as fresh sausage, salami, *coppa*, and mortadella. *Salumi* are cut into thin slices before serving, and any skin is removed. A variety of different types may be offered; they are traditionally served with marinated vegetables or cheese.

Beef and poultry are also served in salads, such as the *Insalata di Pollo* with julienned vegetables, raisins, and pine nuts on page 57. And chicken and duck livers make fine *antipasti*, served whole, or puréed and spread on crostini (see page 40).

Le Tecniche

These recipes were chosen to allow students to practice knife skills as well as techniques relating to vegetable and meat preparations as discussed in depth in the relevant lessons in Part II of this book. Some of the specific cooking techniques employed in this chapter and discussed in depth include *saltare* (sautéing), *deglassare* (deglazing), *affogare* (poaching), and *sbianchire* (blanching). The technique of *arrostire* (roasting) is also used in this chapter but the text for *arrostire* is found in Chapter 10, where it accompanies a recipe for *Pollo Arrosto* (page 161), one of the most basic and classic uses for this technique.

Variations

Rub the toasted bread with a clove of garlic, cut in half. Cut a ripe tomato in half and rub over the toast, until the toast is moistened and flavored with the juice. Season with salt and drizzle with olive oil.

Thinly slice a ripe tomato and place in a bowl. Season with salt, pepper, olive oil, and torn basil leaves, and toss. Spoon onto toasted bread.

Chef's Note

Both ground black pepper and red pepper flakes are used in this recipe because each contributes a unique flavor.

Bruschetta al Pomodoro

Grilled Bread with Tomatoes

Serves 4

Several variations of tomato bruschetta are possible using the same few ingredients, each with a slightly different flavor; some are given below. The uniqueness of each demonstrates the way in which Italian chefs personalize their cooking and express their individuality, even in such a simple dish and with few ingredients.

Bruschetta may be served just as it is or with an accompanying arugula and tomato salad (see page 156). In addition to its role as an antipasto, Italians also eat bruschetta as snack food.

At The International Culinary Center, we make bruschetta with breads delivered from that day's bread class: *pane Pugliese*, the Sicilian *casareccio*, and *pane comune*. These are appropriate choices because they have a crumb structure that is open and irregular but not so large that the topping is likely to fall. If none of these breads are available, any rustic bread with a medium crumb structure will work.

(For step-by-step instructions on peeling, seeding, and dicing tomatoes, see page 350.)

Ingredients

400 grams (14 ounces) ripe tomatoes, peeled, seeded, and diced (1½ cups)
3 fresh basil leaves, torn into small pieces
7½ milliliters (½ tablespoon) aceto balsamico di Modena
7½ milliliters (½ tablespoon) red wine vinegar
45 milliliters (3 tablespoons) olive oil
Pinch of red pepper flakes
Coarse salt and freshly ground black pepper

4 large slices bread (ideally this would be a large, oval- or tube-shaped, crusty loaf with fairly thick crust, such as pane Pugliese, casareccio, or pane comune)
1 clove garlic, cut in half

Combine the chopped tomatoes and basil in a bowl. Stir in the vinegars, oil, red pepper, and salt and black pepper to taste.

Grill or toast (*tostare*) the bread, and rub it with the garlic. Divide the tomato mixture between the bread slices.

Bagna Cauda

Hot Dip with Garlic and Anchovies

Serves 4 to 6

Bagna Cauda, which means "warm bath," is a classic winter recipe from Piemonte. Olive oil is simmered with anchovy, garlic, and wine, melding the ingredients into a pungent, light-brown dip. *Bagna Cauda* is eaten warm, with locally grown vegetables—traditionally cardoons, fennel, peppers, celery, and carrots, among other choices—which are served raw, grilled, or roasted. (*Pinzimonio*, called *bagné 'nt l'euli* in Piemonte and *cazzimperio* in the south of Italy, is an example of another traditional but simpler antipasto in which raw vegetables are served with a dip of extra-virgin olive oil seasoned with salt and cracked black pepper.)

(See "Cleaning Salt-Packed Anchovies" on page 451 for step-by-step instructions.)

Ingredients

225 grams (8 ounces or 1 cup) unsalted butter

180 milliliters (¾ cup) extra-virgin olive oil

6 cloves garlic, peeled but whole

4 anchovies, preferably salt-packed (see page 31), deboned and rinsed, 15 milliliters (1 tablespoon) of their residual water (colatura) reserved

1 teaspoon Dijon mustard

60 milliliters (¼ cup) chicken stock or water

Coarse salt, if necessary

Assorted raw vegetables, such as carrots, celery, cauliflower, fennel, a variety of bell peppers, beets, artichokes, cabbage, and sunchokes, cut into wedges, strips, or rounds, depending on the shape and size of the vegetables

Combine the butter and oil in saucepan (*casseruola*) over medium-low heat. Heat until the butter melts completely and just begins to foam (do not allow it to take on any color or get too hot).

Add the garlic and allow it to infuse the oil; do not let it take on any color.

Add the anchovies and cook at a simmer (*sobbollire*), mashing the anchovies with a wooden spoon or heat-proof spatula until they dissolve into a paste.

Reduce the heat to low, and cook 10 to 15 minutes to allow all the flavors to blend.

Add the mustard, chicken stock, and reserved anchovy water. Transfer to a blender and process until smooth and emulsified. Add the salt, if necessary.

Pour the *bagna cauda* into a heatproof serving dish and keep warm over a flame. Serve with the vegetables for dipping.

Chef's Note

The overnight soaking of the cheese in the milk softens the cheese so that it melts easily and uniformly.

Fonduta

Valdostana Fondue

Serves 4

This dish of Fontina cheese melted in warmed milk and thickened with egg yolks originates in the Alpine Valle d'Aosta region of northern Italy, where Fontina is produced. (The dish is also common in the adjoining region of Piemonte.) *Fonduta* is traditionally served over toast or meats, sometimes garnished with a shaving of white truffle. In the modern Italian kitchen, it may also be served as a sauce for meats, vegetables, or polenta, or as a filling for fresh pasta.

Ingredients

275 grams (9¾ ounces) Fontina Valle d'Aosta, diced
    (about 1¼ cups)
250 milliliters (1 cup) milk
4 large egg yolks
55 grams (2 tablespoons) unsalted butter, cut into pieces
110 milliliters (¼ cup plus 3 tablespoons) heavy cream
15 milliliters (1 tablespoon) brandy

Bruschetta, Crostini, and *Fettunta*

The tradition of serving bread with a topping appears to date to the Middle Ages, when bread was used in lieu of plates. These mouthfuls of toasted bread, spread with a raw (such as chopped fresh tomatoes) or cooked topping, and known variously as bruschetta, crostini, and *fettunta*, are quintessential *antipasti*—simple, seasonal, and endlessly variable.

There are subtle differences between the three, but the terms may be used interchangeably. The simplest version is composed of toasted or grilled bread rubbed with a clove of garlic and drizzled with olive oil. More elaborate toppings are made from vegetables, legumes, fish, and meat, but the hallmark of bruschetta is the unencumbered simplicity of the ingredients. The topping should never be so heavy as to obscure the taste of the bread.

The bread is best grilled, or it may be toasted in a hot (204°C / 400°F) oven, depending on the desired result. Grilled bread will have a crisp exterior but the interior will remain soft; bread toasted in the oven will be crisp throughout. Crostini are sometimes fried in a combination of butter and olive oil.

Bruschetta: Bruschetta are cut from large rounds of breads into pieces about 2 centimeters (¾ inch) thick and are therefore relatively large pieces of toast. Traditionally bruschetta were grilled over an open fire.

Crostini: These "little toasts" are typically cut from long, narrow loaves into slices about 1 centimeter (⅜ inch) thick and are usually no more than 5 centimeters (2 inches) in diameter.

Fettunta: Their name is derived from the Italian words *fetta*, meaning "slice," and *unta*, meaning "greasy." *Fettunta* are thick slices of Tuscan bread, similar to what you'd use for bruschetta, grilled and rubbed with a garlic clove cut in half, drizzled generously with olive oil, and seasoned with salt and pepper. *Fettunta* are most frequently associated with Tuscan cuisine.

Valle d'Aosta (Aosta Valley)

Tucked into the northwest corner of Italy bordering France and Switzerland, the Aosta Valley is the smallest of the country's twenty regions. Valle d'Aosta is situated in the Alps and surrounded by some of the highest mountains in Europe, including Cervino (the Matterhorn), Gran Paradiso, and Monte Bianco. The entire region is mountainous, dramatically punctuated by glaciated valleys and Alpine pastures. Because of its close proximity to France and Switzerland, both French and Italian are official languages of the region. The cuisine is also influenced by the cultures of its neighbors. The capital of the region is Aosta, which traces its Roman origins back to 25 BCE.

As a result of its mountainous geography, cattle- and sheep-raising have traditionally been the region's most important agricultural activities, leading to a meat- and cheese-based cuisine. Many cow's-milk cheeses are produced here: Fontina is celebrated, as well as *Toma*, and Valle d'Aosta Fromadzo, a distinctive variety of *Toma*. Fontina features prominently in the local cuisine, where it is used most famously in *fonduta*, a sauce of melted cheese served over meats, vegetables, bread, pasta, rice, and polenta. Fontina is also used in soups,

including a hearty bread soup layered with Fontina and cabbage; in *risotti*; to stuff veal chops for *Costolette alla Valdostana*; and as a filling for sandwiches.

Cured meats include the dried, cured haunch of chamois, goat, or ibex called *moccetta*. The region adheres to ancient (probably pre-Roman) traditions in the limited production of the raw ham called *jambon de Bosses*, manufactured from small, gray local pigs that develop a unique flavor from feeding on Alpine grasses and the by-products of milk-making. The artisanal cured lard, Valle d'Aosta Lard d'Arnad, is produced here; both may be accompanied by boiled chestnuts with butter.

Other agricultural products are rye, chestnuts, potatoes, berries, apples, and pears. Specialties of the region include rye bread, walnut oil, gnocchi baked with Fontina, *risotti*, and a variety of thick soups. The region is also known for an after-dinner tradition called *la grolla*, in which a wooden pot with several spouts containing a special coffee drink called *caffé valdostano*, spiked with locally made grappa (an alcohol made from the pomace of grapes used in wine-making), is passed among guests.

See our recipe for the regional specialty *Fonduta* on the facing page.

Combine the cheese and milk in a container and refrigerate overnight to allow the flavors to meld and to soften the cheese.

In a saucepan (*casseruola*), heat the cheese with the milk very gently over low heat, stirring constantly, to melt the cheese (do not boil).

Remove from the heat. In a bowl, stir some of the hot cheese mixture into the yolks to temper them.

Put the saucepan back over low heat and stir in the yolks.

Stir in the butter.

Stir in the cream and continue to stir constantly until the *fonduta* has thickened enough to coat the back of a spoon.

Stir in the brandy and remove from the heat. (See recipe introduction for serving suggestions.)

Peperoni Arrostiti con Acciughe

Roasted Marinated Peppers

Serves 4 to 6

Roasted, peeled bell peppers are traditionally marinated in olive oil with vinegar and seasonings. Roasting over a gas flame or grilling concentrates and intensifies the flavor and sugars in the vegetable and contributes a lovely charred taste. Soaking in garlic, oregano, anchovies, red wine vinegar, and olive oil infuses the peppers with their taste, creating a sublime marriage of flavors.

(See "Roasting and Cleaning Peppers" and "Cleaning Salt-Packed Anchovies" on pages 352 and 451, respectively, for step-by-step instructions.)

Ingredients

500 grams (18 ounces) red and/or yellow bell peppers
2 anchovy fillets, preferably salt-packed (see page 31), deboned, rinsed, and cut into thirds
2 cloves garlic, sliced
1 teaspoon capers, preferably salt-packed (see page 31), soaked, rinsed, and drained
1 teaspoon chopped fresh Italian parsley
20 milliliters (1½ tablespoons) red wine vinegar
70 milliliters (⅓ cup) extra-virgin olive oil
Coarse salt and freshly ground black pepper

Preheat a charcoal or gas grill, if using. Set the peppers over the heat, or directly over the gas burners, if using, and roast (arrostire) until the skins are blackened on one side, then turn with tongs and continue roasting until the skin is blackened all over. Remove the peppers to a bowl, cover tightly with plastic wrap, and let stand until cool enough to handle.

Wipe off the blackened skin with a towel or your hands. Cut the peppers in half through the stem ends and pull out the stems by hand. Pull out the seeds and remove the ribs. Cut the peppers lengthwise into thick strips (3 centimeters / 1 inch).

Put the the peppers in a bowl. Add the anchovies, garlic, capers, parsley, vinegar, olive oil, and salt and pepper to taste. Let marinate at least 2 hours and serve at room temperature.

Zucchine alla Scapece

Zucchini Marinated in Vinegar

Serves 4

This is an example of a traditional pickling method in which the zucchini is fried, then soaked in a vinegar–olive oil marinade. Zucchine alla Scapece is traditionally served as an antipasto, but may also accompany fish or meat, as a side dish.

The zucchini is dredged in flour and fried in oil to create a crust, which helps the vegetable to hold its shape during marinating. The zucchini is floured just before cooking to prevent the flour from absorbing moisture and becoming gummy. The marinade is added cold so that the delicate flesh of the vegetable doesn't continue to cook in the marinade.

(For a discussion of pickling, see sidebar "Marinated, Pickled, and Oil-Cured Foods for Antipasti" on page 44.)

Ingredients

For the zucchini:

Grapeseed or canola oil, for frying

300 grams (10½ ounces) zucchini, thinly sliced on an angle
   into rounds 1 centimeter (⅜ inch) thick

All-purpose flour seasoned with coarse salt and freshly
   ground black pepper

For the marinade:

45 milliliters (3 tablespoons) olive oil

50 grams (¼ cup) thinly sliced red onion

50 grams (¼ cup) thinly sliced celery

50 grams (¼ cup) thinly sliced carrot

Pinch of red pepper flakes

Coarse salt

90 milliliters (¼ cup plus 2 tablespoons) red wine vinegar

10 fresh mint leaves

Pinch of granulated sugar

Make the zucchini:

Add the oil to a skillet (*padella*) to come about 1
centimeter (⅜ inch) up the side of the pan. Set over
medium-high heat and heat until a small piece of zucchini tossed into the pan sizzles. Toss the zucchini in
the seasoned flour; pat off the excess flour.

Fry (*friggere*) the zucchini in the hot oil until golden
brown on both sides, about 1 minute each side.
Remove from the pan and drain on paper towels. Chill.
Discard the oil.

Make the marinade:

In the same skillet, heat the olive oil over medium
heat. Add the onion, celery, and carrot and sauté
(*saltare*), adding the red pepper flakes a few minutes
into the cooking to keep them from burning, until the
vegetables just begin to turn golden brown. Season to
taste with salt. Add the vinegar, 50 milliliters (3 tablespoons plus 1 teaspoon) water, the mint, and sugar
and bring to a boil. Remove from the heat and chill.

Arrange the zucchini slices in a container in a single
layer. Layer the cooled, marinated vegetables over the
zucchini. Pour the marinade liquid over and marinate
several hours.

Verdure Sott'Olio

Vegetables Layered with Seasonings in Olive Oil

Serves 4

This recipe demonstrates a traditional method of preserving vegetables under a layer of oil, called *sott'olio*,
found throughout Italy. The variety of vegetable varies
with the region; here, grilled eggplant and zucchini are
layered with seasonings and vinegar, then immersed
in olive oil to cover. Any vegetable prepared *sott'olio*
works nicely as part of a platter of mixed *antipasti*.

(See page 351 for step-by-step photos of disgorging.)

Ingredients

Grapeseed or canola oil, for oiling grill grates

450 grams (1 pound) eggplant, unpeeled, cut into rounds
   3 millimeters (⅛ inch) thick

Coarse salt

225 grams (8 ounces) zucchini, unpeeled, cut into rounds
   3 millimeters (⅛ inch) thick

4 fresh peperoncini or other spicy (warm to hot) fresh pepper

5 grams fresh Italian parsley, chopped (1 tablespoon)

2 cloves garlic, thinly sliced

70 milliliters (5 tablespoons) white wine vinegar

Olive oil, as needed to cover

Freshly ground black pepper

Marinated, Pickled, and Oil-Cured Foods for *Antipasti*

Italian cuisine offers various traditional methods for preserving foods. Once it was discovered that air and moisture were the primary culprits in food spoilage, summer vegetables were brined, pickled, or covered in oil to preserve them through the winter; fish and meats were salted, dried, and/or smoked; milk was preserved as cheese. Many of these methods make excellent *antipasti*. Although refrigeration has made these techniques far less important as means of preservation, they continue to be invaluable not only for the flavor they impart, but also as a bridge between the contemporary cook and the enduring traditions of Italian culinary culture.

Pickling is the process of steeping food in an acidic liquid, often vinegar. Pickling works to preserve food in two ways: Submersion in liquid protects the food from contact with air, while the acidity of the liquid itself makes the medium inhospitable to bacteria. For long-term preserving, the food is usually brined in order to pull out excess moisture, and then vinegar is added. Salt and sugar are usual ingredients in pickling mixtures, because both draw moisture out of the food.

Sott'olio is a method of submerging or coating food in oil. The food is sometimes cooked in an acidic medium, then covered entirely with oil; or it may be cooked, layered with seasonings and vinegar for additional flavor, then covered in oil (see *Verdure Sott'olio* on page 43).

Preparing foods *alla Scapece* (see recipe for *Zucchini alla Scapece* on page 42) is similar to the Spanish preparation *escabeche*: The food is fried, then soaked in an acidic marinade. Variations are found throughout Italy. Some recipes use vinegar, others use citrus. The flavor profile of this preparation is *agrodolce* (sweet and sour): The sour is represented by the acid, while the sweet is often represented by sugar, or sometimes by honey, reflecting traditions that persist from the cuisine of Imperial Rome. Italian cooks typically pair this method with both vegetables and seafood. Regional methods for this process differ slightly in technique and ingredients; the pickling mixture may be flavored with local herbs, and sometimes both egg and flour are used in the coating.

Scapece is the term used in the south; in Liguria, it's *scabecio*; in Piemonte, *in carpione*, where the method is typically associated with fish, in particular with the local freshwater carp. In Venetian cuisine, the marinade is flavored with raisins and pine nuts, and it is called *saor* (*Pesce in Saor* is a famous Venetian dish of sole fillets that are fried, then marinated in vinegar with onions, pine nuts, raisins, and a pinch of sugar). Italians love to prepare zucchini and eggplant in this manner, as well as small fish, such as sardines and anchovies, and eels.

Marinating is akin to pickling. It is the process of soaking a food in a seasoned liquid to preserve, flavor, or tenderize it; for *antipasti* such as roasted, marinated peppers (page 42), it is primarily a technique to develop flavor in a short period of time. Vegetables need only an hour or two to absorb flavor from marinades; cooked fish and meat need a longer soak—from several hours to overnight (see further discussion of marinades for meat on page 223). For sturdy foods, such as fish, a hot marinade is added to hot food to encourage the marinade to penetrate the flesh. For delicate foods such as zucchini, the marinade is added cold so that the vegetable doesn't overcook in the marinade.

Molise

Molise is a small, relatively unpopulated province to the south of Abruzzo. The Adriatic coast forms its eastern border; it is bounded to the west by the Apennines. The geography is mostly mountainous. Its capital is Campobasso.

Molise was part of Abruzzo until 1963 and the cuisines of the two regions are similar. The cooking of Molise is characterized by the use of tomato, garlic, beans, artichokes, the very spicy *diavolicchio* (or *diavolillo*—meaning "little devil") chile pepper, and a white celery from Campobasso. As in Abruzzo, some IGP cattle are raised in the region, and sheep and goats are farmed. The region produces a number of sheep's-milk cheeses—ricotta and pecorino—as well as cow's-milk Caciocavallo Silano and *scamorza* (a stringy cow's-milk cheese, often smoked).

Agriculture is important to this isolated region. Molise produces olive oil, durum wheat, corn, and other vegetables. The wheat is used in a host of fresh and dried pastas such as *sagne* (like lasagne), *laganelle* (like *tagliatelle*), and *crejoli*, which resemble Abruzzo's *maccheroni all chitarra*. Corn is used in polenta.

Specialties include pasta dishes sauced with a ragout of lamb and pork, polenta, an unusual smoked prosciutto called *prosciutto affumicato*, *baccalà alla cantalupese* (salted cod cooked with peppers, capers, black olives, grapes, and garlic), and a *calcioni di ricotta* (deep-fried pasta rounds filled with cheese and ham).

Its historical poverty is poignantly reflected in the story of the region's *Pesce Fuinte*, or "fake fish" soup: Three or four rocks from the sea are heated in olive oil with onion and tomato to infuse the oil with their saltiness. The rocks are removed, and small pasta shapes are added and cooked in the tomato mixture until tender.

Lamb is the most popular *secondo* in Molise, served grilled, roasted, or braised. Our recipe for roasted leg of lamb, *Agnello Arrosto*, appears on page 219.

Variations

The zucchini and eggplant may be broiled instead of grilled.

Roasted tomatoes (see *Pomodori Arrostiti*, page 46) may be interspersed between vegetable layers.

Artichoke hearts, braised in olive oil with lemon juice, sliced garlic, and herbs, are delicious prepared *sott'olio*.

Heat a gas or charcoal grill and brush the grill grate with grapeseed or canola oil.

Disgorge the eggplant with salt.

Lay the zucchini and eggplant on parchment paper. Season the zucchini with salt. (The eggplant will already be salted from the disgorging process.) Separately, grill (*grigliare*) the zucchini and eggplant (they will cook at different rates) until cooked through.

Line a nonreactive airtight container with a sheet of parchment paper. Arrange a layer of vegetables, slightly overlapping, over the bottom of the container. Break a *peperoncino* over the vegetables. Sprinkle with some of the parsley and sliced garlic. Drizzle with some of the vinegar. Make another layer of overlapping vegetables, and season with *peperoncino*, parsley, garlic, and vinegar. Continue in this way until you've used all of the vegetables and seasonings. Add olive oil to cover the vegetables entirely. Cover and refrigerate (chilling will harden the olive oil so that the vegetables absorb less oil.) Bring to room temperature before serving.

Pomodori Arrostiti

Roasted Tomatoes

Serves 2

Roasted tomatoes are used in a variety of different ways: as a topping for bruschetta, tossed with pasta or into *Insalata di Mare* (page 54), or as part of an antipasto platter.

Ingredients

Olive oil

Zest of ½ lemon, peeled off in strips with a vegetable peeler

Zest of ½ orange, peeled off in strips with a vegetable peeler

2 to 3 cloves garlic, unpeeled but smashed

300 grams (10½ ounces) plum tomatoes, peeled and seeded, cut lengthwise into halves or quarters (1¾ cups)

Coarse salt and freshly ground black pepper

2 to 3 sprigs fresh thyme, torn into pieces

Preheat the oven to 93°C (200°F). Drizzle olive oil over a parchment paper–lined sheet pan and scatter with the pieces of citrus peel and garlic. Arrange the tomato quarters or halves in a single layer in even rows across the tray. Season the tomatoes with salt and pepper to taste, and sprinkle with the thyme. Roast (*arrostire*) until the tomatoes are shrunken and caramelized. Cool completely on the sheet pan. Then layer in an airtight container, add more olive oil to completely cover, and refrigerate.

Caponata

Sweet-and-Sour Eggplant

Serves 3 to 4

Caponata is classically Sicilian, but many variations are found, even outside of Sicilia. The vegetables vary depending on the cook but the dish usually includes eggplant, celery, capers, green or black olives, and tomatoes. Unsweetened chocolate or cocoa powder is often used to deepen the flavor and cut the acidity of the vinegar.

In this version, the vegetables are seasoned with vinegar and a little sugar to create the subtle sweet-and-sour flavor palette called *agrodolce*. The eggplant, which is disgorged to remove bitterness and can be peeled or left unpeeled as desired, is fried in order to create a crust, adding flavor and texture to the dish. The remaining vegetables are sautéed separately to caramelize their natural sugars (see sidebar "Maillard Reaction" on page 158). Some of these sugars are inevitably left on the bottom of the pan; the addition of vinegar acts to deglaze the pan and recuperate these browned bits.

Caponata may be served warm but is traditionally served at room temperature. It tastes even better the day after it is made.

(See pages 351 and 350, respectively, for step-by-step photos of disgorging eggplant, and peeling, seeding, and dicing tomatoes.)

Ingredients

225 grams (2½ cups) diced eggplant

Coarse salt

100 milliliters (¼ cup plus 2½ tablespoons) vegetable or peanut oil, for frying

20 milliliters (1 tablespoon plus 1 teaspoon) olive oil

50 grams (¼ cup) diced red onion

25 grams (2 tablespoons) seeded and diced red bell pepper

25 grams (2 tablespoons) seeded and diced yellow bell pepper

25 grams (2 tablespoons) seeded and diced green bell pepper

50 grams (¼ cup) diced celery

Red pepper flakes

¼ teaspoon chopped fresh thyme leaves

10 grams (2 teaspoons) capers, preferably salt-packed (see page 31), rinsed, drained, and coarsely chopped

Freshly ground black pepper

20 milliliters (1 tablespoon) red wine vinegar, plus extra to soak raisins

10 grams (2 teaspoons) granulated sugar

100 grams (½ cup) peeled, seeded, and diced tomatoes

30 grams (1¼ tablespoons) raisins, soaked in red wine vinegar to plump

40 grams (1½ tablespoons) pitted black olives, roughly chopped

½ teaspoon chopped fresh basil

1 teaspoon chopped fresh Italian parsley

25 grams (¼ cup) pine nuts, toasted on a sheet pan at 149°C (300°F) until golden and fragrant, 5 to 7 minutes

1 teaspoon very finely chopped unsweetened chocolate

Disgorge the eggplant; squeeze out excess liquid and pat dry.

In a large, deep skillet (*padella*), heat the vegetable or peanut oil over medium-high heat until a pinch of flour sizzles. Working in batches, add the eggplant and cook (*saltare*) until well browned all over, 3 to 5 minutes; drain on paper towels.

Place the olive oil in a skillet along with the onion, bell peppers, and celery. Set over medium heat and sauté until the vegetables are wilted and beginning to color at the edges, about 10 minutes.

Add the red pepper flakes, thyme, and capers. Season lightly with salt (the eggplant will be salty already) and black pepper.

Add the vinegar and sugar and cook to reduce. (If needed, add a little water to melt the sugar.)

Add the tomatoes and cook 10 minutes.

Meanwhile, drain the raisins, reserving the vinegar.

Add the eggplant, raisins, olives, parsley, basil, and pine nuts. Taste and adjust seasoning with salt and black pepper to taste; cook 5 minutes to marry the flavors. The eggplant should be tender but still firm and the celery should still have tooth. Stir in the chocolate, adjust seasoning, and add a few drops of the reserved vinegar drained from the raisins, if necessary.

Le Tecniche: *Saltare* (Sautéing) and *Deglassare* (Deglazing)

The recipe for caponata introduces the techniques of *saltare* (sautéing) and *deglassare* (deglazing).

Saltare is a dry-cooking method that, more generally, means "cooking" in Italian. Cooking this way concentrates and intensifies the flavors of the food by evaporating the water and caramelizing natural sugars.

When vegetables are cooked using the *saltare* technique, they are placed in a *cold* pan and set over medium to high heat in a small amount of fat. In this way, the essence is coaxed out of the vegetables, gently and completely, while the oil is infused with their flavor. The vegetables may or may not take on color depending on the specific preparation.

Proteins, however, are started in a *hot* pan, in *hot* fat (see "Le Tecniche: *Saltare o Rosolare il Pollo*" on page 158 for a further discussion of the technique as it applies to proteins).

Whether vegetables or meats are being sautéed, some of the caramelized sugars are inevitably left on the bottom of the pan. It is important to recuperate these

browned bits by *deglassare* (deglazing) the pan, a process of stirring a liquid (usually wine or stock but in this case vinegar) around in a pan to dissolve any small pieces of food that may be stuck to the bottom.

Soppressata di Polpo

Octopus Terrine

Makes 1 small terrine (serves 6 to 8)

Soppressata di polpo is a simple way to prepare octopus, particularly for students who are new to it. The octopi are poached, then packed into a terrine mold with some of the poaching liquid. The gelatin in the octopus sets it into a silky-textured block; the terrine is cut into thin slices and served with a sauce of finely chopped black olives, tomatoes, capers, red onion, and parsley.

If necessary, the dressing may be made in the food processor, but students at The International Culinary Center chop the ingredients by hand instead. The processor will emulsify the sauce, creating a homogenous look; when chopped by hand, the sauce shows bits of pretty, contrasting color. Use the sauce sparingly so as not to drown the delicate flavor of the octopus. (This recipe makes more sauce than you will need for the *soppressata*; it refrigerates well for up to ten days, as long as the top is covered with oil. Leftover sauce is delicious with any cooked or raw seafood, or tossed with pasta.)

(See "Cleaning and Poaching Octopus" on page 466 for step-by-step instructions.)

30 grams (2 tablespoons) capers, preferably salt-packed (see
page 31), soaked, rinsed, and drained
60 grams (½ cup) finely chopped red onion
3 grams (1 tablespoon) chopped fresh Italian parsley
95 milliliters (⅓ cup plus 1 tablespoon) red wine vinegar
250 milliliters (1 cup) extra-virgin olive oil
1 teaspoon Worcestershire sauce
1 teaspoon hot pepper sauce
Pinch of red pepper flakes
Coarse salt and freshly ground black pepper

For the garnish:
Baby arugula, cleaned
Coarse salt and freshly ground black pepper
Olive oil

Ingredients

For the octopi:
2 to 3 octopi, 1 to 1¼ kilograms (2 to 3 pounds) each
(approximately 2½ kilograms / 5 pounds total)
Coarse salt
150 grams (5 ounces) red onion, cut into 5-centimeter (2-inch)
pieces (⅔ cup)
75 grams (3 ounces) carrot, cut into 5-centimeter (2-inch)
pieces (½ cup)
75 grams (3 ounces) celery, cut into 5-centimeter (2-inch)
pieces (½ cup)
3 cloves garlic
2 sprigs fresh sage
30 milliliters (2 tablespoons) red wine vinegar
¼ lemon

For the marinated onion:
50 grams (½ cup) thinly sliced red onion
125 milliliters (½ cup) red wine vinegar

For the dressing:
150 grams (5 ounces) drained, whole, canned Italian plum
tomatoes
125 grams (¾ cup) pitted black Italian olives, such as taggiasca
(a small Ligurian olive)

Clean the octopi:

Pull out the beaks from the undersides. Press and cut
out the eyes. Rub salt all over and massage it into the
flesh. Rinse well under cold running water.

Make the octopi:

Put the octopi in a large pot (*pentola*). Add cold water
to cover, and salt until the water tastes lightly salted.

Wrap and tie the onion, carrot, celery, garlic, and sage
in a square of cheesecloth and add it to the pot.

Bring to a boil, then reduce the heat to a gentle simmer and poach (*affogare*) 30 minutes. Add the vinegar
and lemon quarter.

Continue cooking until the octopi are tender (cut off a
little piece of tentacle to taste), 45 minutes to 1 hour
more.

Line a small terrine mold with two sheets of plastic wrap
so that the plastic overhangs on all sides by about 10
centimeters (4 inches). Remove the octopi immediately

Chef's Note

If no terrine mold is available, 1-liter (1-quart) loaf pans are a good substitute.

Variations

Lay several pieces of the *soppressata* on the plate, overlapping slightly, and drizzle with dressing; garnish with marinated onion.

Shingle 2 slices *soppressata* to make 1 wide slice. Lay a bouquet of dressed arugula in the center and roll like sushi.

Garnish with a small salad of julienned zucchini and carrot, tossed with the dressing.

to the prepared mold. Tuck in all of the tentacles and moisten with a small amount of the cooking liquid. Fold the plastic over to cover the octopi completely.

Place another terrine mold directly on top of the octopi and weight with cans. Wrap the stacked terrines in plastic wrap and chill in an ice bath for 1 hour, or until cooled. Refrigerate the wrapped, weighted terrine for at least 24 hours.

Make the marinated onion:

Marinate the onion in the vinegar for 2 to 3 hours.

Make the dressing:

Finely chop the tomatoes, olives, and capers, and place in a bowl with the chopped onion. Add the parsley.

Stir in the vinegar and then the olive oil. Stir in the Worcestershire and pepper sauces, the red pepper flakes, and 30 milliliters (2 tablespoons) of water. Season with black pepper to taste. Let stand before seasoning with salt to allow the salt from the olives to permeate the sauce.

To serve:

Remove the terrine from the mold, pulling it out with the help of the plastic wrap.

Slice the terrine very thinly on a slicer, or with a very sharp, thin knife (not a serrated knife).

Prepare the garnish:

Dress the arugula with salt, pepper, and olive oil.

Arrange the terrine slices on a plate and garnish with the arugula and red wine–marinated onion. Drizzle with the olive dressing.

Crudo di Pesce

Crudo

Serves 1

Crudo means "raw" in Italian. Raw fish, thinly sliced and variously dressed, is a popular and stylish dish in Italy, and in Italian restaurants in America.

Crudo should be served immediately once dressed; the acid in the dressing will quickly "cook" the fish, turning it opaque.

The fish may also be tossed in the dressing, then plated with the garnishes and served immeditately.

(See sidebar "*Crudo*, Carpaccio, and *Tartara*" on page 53 for further discussion.)

Ingredients

60 grams (2 ounces) firm-fleshed fish, skinned and filleted, such as branzino, fluke, rainbow trout, tuna, salmon, or hamachi
Extra-virgin olive oil
Coarse sea salt and freshly ground black pepper
Lemon juice
Assorted garnishes and seasonings, such as caperberries, thinly sliced cucumbers, lemon and orange segments, julienned radishes, green olives, fresh herbs, and fennel pollen

Cut the fish into very thin slices (6 millimeters / ¼ inch, or thinner) and arrange on serving plates.

Whisk the dressing ingredients in a bowl and pour over the *crudo*. Add garnishes as desired, and serve immediately.

Tartara di Tonno

Tuna Tartare

Serves 4

Tartara represents another presentation for raw fish. The fish is diced, combined with olive oil, herbs, seasoning, and sometimes a fresh vegetable or fruit (here, celery for texture, tomato for color). A fish fillet or steak, such as tuna, may be used but *tartara* is also a practical way for chefs to make use of small pieces of other fish and fish trimmings. As with *crudo*, the freshness of the fish is of the utmost importance.

(See sidebar "*Crudo*, Carpaccio, and *Tartara*" on facing page for further discussion.)

Chef's Note

If, as in this recipe, the dressing for the *tartara* contains lemon juice or another acid, the lemon juice should be added just before serving since the acid will cook and discolor the fish.

Ingredients

For the marinated onion:

15 grams (1 tablespoon) finely chopped red onion
60 milliliters (¼ cup) red wine vinegar

For the tuna:

225 grams (½ pound) tuna fillet
70 grams (⅓ cup) peeled, seeded, and diced tomato
10 grams (1 tablespoon) chopped celery
12 grams (1 tablespoon) chopped capers, preferably salt-packed (see page 31), rinsed and drained
1 teaspoon chopped fresh Italian parsley
30 milliliters (2 tablespoons) extra-virgin olive oil
8 milliliters (1½ teaspoons) lemon juice (from ¼ lemon)
Sea salt and freshly ground black pepper

Make the marinated onion:

In a bowl, marinate the onion in the vinegar for at least 1 hour.

Prepare the tuna:

Cut the tuna into 6-millimeter (¼-inch) dice.

In a bowl, gently mix the tuna with the tomato, celery, capers, parsley, and olive oil.

Just before serving, season to taste with the lemon juice, salt, and pepper.

Place an 8-centimeter (approximately 3-inch) ring mold on a serving plate. Spoon in about one-quarter of the tuna mixture, press, and even the top with the back of a spoon. Lift off the ring mold. Repeat with the remaining tuna mixture and three additional serving plates.

Drain the marinated onions and serve them as a garnish on top or on the side of the *tartara*.

Crudo, Carpaccio, and *Tartara*

There are a number of ways to prepare raw fish for antipasto in Italy, called variously carpaccio, *crudo*, and *tartara*. Broadly speaking, the different names represent various ways of cutting the fish: Carpaccio refers to very thin slices, *crudo* to thicker pieces, and *tartara* to small bits or dice. The decision about whether to serve carpaccio or *tartara* is also a practical one; after filleting and portioning a whole fish, for example, a chef may use leftover pieces (presuming excellent quality) for making a *tartara* because they are not large enough for a carpaccio. All three preparations are traditionally dressed with a few choice ingredients: extra-virgin olive oil, an acid (lemon juice or a vinegar), and salt (typically sea salt). The chef may embellish with whatever flavorings he or she likes, including but not limited to fresh herbs and spices (see below).

Each region of Italy with access to seafood has traditions for these dishes, and they will vary according to the seafood available locally and the specific oils and salt produced there. *Crudo* from each region will taste profoundly different, although the preparation is essentially the same.

In any of these preparations, the quality of ingredients is supremely important. A dish of *crudo* must be simple and perfect. The fish must be very fresh and the olive oil delicious, and whatever other seasonings are used must be of excellent quality.

For ease of slicing and precision, make sure that the fish is cold and that the knife is very sharp. (See "Preparing Fish for Carpaccio and *Tartara*" on page 452 for step-by-step instructions.)

Dressings and Garnishes for Raw Fish *Antipasti*

Dressings are whisked together in a bowl and poured over the fish just before serving. In consideration of the delicate taste of raw seafood, it is important to choose olive oils with a relatively light flavor. Also, it is important to dress the seafood in such a way that the dressing complements rather than overwhelms the taste. For more delicate-flavored seafood, such as fluke, choose a more subtle dressing. For oilier fish, or seafood with a more pronounced flavor (such as tuna), the dressing may be more robust. Dressings and garnishes should also complement the texture of the seafood.

Below are some traditional combinations of ingredients for dressing and garnishing raw seafood.

For seafood with delicate flavor:

- Olive oil, lemon juice, salt, and black pepper
- Olive oil, lemon juice, salt, and Tabasco sauce
- Olive oil, sea salt, black pepper, and *aceto balsamico di Modena* (season the fish with salt and pepper; pour oil over the fish, and dot the plate with vinegar)

For seafood with more robust flavor:

- Olive oil, lemon juice, red wine vinegar, and salt
- Olive oil, lemon juice, red wine vinegar, salt, and toasted walnuts
- Olive oil, lemon juice, red wine vinegar, salt, sliced arugula, and chopped onion marinated in red wine vinegar

Insalata di Mare

Seafood Salad

Serves 4

Every region with access to seafood boasts a version of this salad; this recipe demonstrates a basic method that may be adjusted according to market availability and the personal preferences of the chef. The key is to choose a balance of textures and flavors so that no one element overwhelms the others. The sweetness of the shellfish is balanced by the acidity of lemon juice, the shellfish broth, and olive oil.

All of the seafood, with the exception of the mollusks that are opened in a bit of water, is poached separately in a court bouillon, a vegetable stock acidulated with white wine, lemon juice, and/or vinegar, to respect individual cooking times.

(See "Le Tecniche: *Affogare*" on page 56 for a discussion of poaching seafood. Step-by-step photos for cleaning seafood can be found on pages 447–50 and 460–64; see "Working with Dried Legumes" on page 364 for step-by-step instructions on cleaning, soaking, and cooking beans).

Ingredients

For the court bouillon:

50 grams (2 ounces) red onion, cut into 2½-centimeter (1-inch) pieces (⅓ cup)

50 grams (2 ounces) celery, cut into 2½-centimeter (1-inch) pieces (⅓ cup)

20 grams (¾ ounce) carrot, cut into 2½-centimeter (1-inch) pieces (¼ cup)

Fresh thyme sprigs

Fresh Italian parsley sprigs

Fresh basil sprigs

1 teaspoon whole black peppercorns

30 milliliters (2 tablespoons) red wine vinegar

Coarse salt

½ lemon

For the salad:

20 grams (¼ cup) roasted and thinly julienned red bell pepper (4 centimeters / 1½ inches long)

20 grams (¼ cup) finely diced celery

30 grams (¼ cup) pitted black olives, preferably taggiasca, quartered lengthwise

30 grams (¼ cup) pitted green olives, such as Gaeta, quartered lengthwise

Pinch of red pepper flakes

Coarse salt

110 grams (¼ pound) small shrimp, peeled, deveined, and halved lengthwise

75 milliliters (5 tablespoons) olive oil, plus extra for serving

Two U10 sea scallops (55 grams / 2 ounces total), cleaned of crescent-shaped muscle (see "Shucking Scallops" on page 463) and halved or quartered, depending on size

1 whole small squid (110 grams / 4 ounces), cleaned, body cut into tubes 1 centimeter (⅜ inch) thick

9 mussels, scrubbed and debearded

9 Manila clams, scrubbed

15 grams (1 tablespoon) diced red onion, marinated in red wine vinegar to cover for at least 1 hour

100 grams (½ cup) peeled, seeded, and diced tomato

3 grams (1 tablespoon) chopped fresh Italian parsley

15 to 30 milliliters (1 to 2 tablespoons) lemon juice (from ½ to 1 lemon)

Freshly ground white pepper

240 grams (1½ cups) cooked white beans

Baby arugula, small basil leaves, or other greens, for garnish

Make the court bouillon:

Wrap the vegetables, herbs, and peppercorns in cheesecloth and tie with kitchen twine. In a large saucepan, add 3½ liters (3¾ quarts) water, the vinegar, and the cheesecloth bag; bring to a simmer (*sobbollire*) and cook 45 minutes. Discard the cheesecloth bag.

Chef's Note

Octopus and/or finfish may be used in addition to, or in place of, the shellfish listed in this recipe. Poach skinned fish fillets in the simmering court bouillon; break the fish into pieces and add to the bowl with the salad. To poach octopus, see page 466.

Season to taste with salt and squeeze in the lemon juice.

Make the salad:

Combine the roasted red pepper, celery, olives, and red pepper flakes in a large bowl.

Bring the court bouillon to a simmer. Add the shrimp and poach (*affogare*) until opaque, about 1 minute. Use a slotted spoon to transfer the shrimp to the bowl with the vegetables and olives. Add the olive oil and toss.

Poach the scallops in the simmering broth 2 to 3 minutes, or until just opaque; transfer to the bowl.

Poach the squid in the broth 1 to 2 minutes; transfer to the bowl.

Combine the mussels and clams in a saucepan (*casseruola*), add 25 milliliters (1 tablespoon plus 2 teaspoons) water, place over heat, cover, and steam until the mollusks open. Shell the mollusks and add to the bowl. Discard the shells.

Drain the onion from the vinegar (reserve the vinegar for another use) and add it to the bowl along with the tomato, parsley, and lemon juice to taste (remember that the marinated onion will add acidity).

Taste the salad. Add salt and pepper as needed, and a little bit of the court bouillon to balance the sweetness of the seafood.

Add the beans to the salad and let marinate.

To serve:

Spoon the salad onto plates, garnish with the greens, and drizzle with olive oil.

Le Tecniche: *Affogare* (Poaching)

The recipe for *Insalata di Mare* on page 54 introduces the technique of *affogare* (poaching), a common technique for cooking seafood.

Poaching means simmering in liquid at a constant low temperature (82°C / 180°F). Shellfish is often poached in a vegetable broth acidulated with white wine, lemon juice, and/or vinegar, called a court bouillon, that helps to impart flavor to the food being poached.

The length of time seafood cooks in a broth depends upon size. Seafood that is to be served cold should be allowed to cool in the broth. This must be taken into consideration when determining the total cooking time since the fish will continue to cook in the hot liquid after the liquid is removed from the heat. Because they are small and easily overcooked, shrimp are best poached by adding them to the simmering broth and then pulling the pan off the heat, thus allowing the shrimp to cook in the residual heat from the broth.

It is advisable to wrap aromatics in a cheesecloth bag so that they are easily removed once the broth has cooked, and the seafood poached therein needn't be cleaned of stray vegetables and herbs (see sidebar "Making a *Mazzetto Guarnito*" on page 359). A broth for poaching seafood should be well salted in order to season the seafood as it cooks.

When poached seafood is used in salads, the vinaigrette is often added to the still warm seafood because warm foods more readily absorb the flavors of the dressing.

Meats and poultry may be poached by the same system (see *Insalata di Pollo* on facing page, and *Vitello Tonnato* on page 64). Both are allowed to cool completely in the cooking liquid in order to prevent the meat from drying out.

Capesante con Funghi Porcini

Scallops with Porcini Mushrooms

Serves 4

Scallops, seasoned delicately with white wine, *aceto balsamico di Modena*, aromatics, and olive oil, and roasted with meaty porcini mushrooms, demonstrate the unabashed simplicity of the best of Italian *antipasti*. The wine and vinegar combine with the juices from the roasting scallops and porcini to create an intensely flavored sauce, earthy from the mushrooms and sweet from the scallops.

Cook the scallops in an oven-to-table baking dish so that the scallops come to the table warm. Serve with crusty bread to sop up all the delicious juices.

(See "Shucking Scallops" on page 463 for instructions on removing the crescent-shaped muscles.)

Chef's Note

Whole, unpeeled garlic cloves add a subtler flavor to this dish than would peeled, chopped garlic. Roasting in the skins also prevents the garlic from burning.

Ingredients

450 grams (1 pound) U12 sea scallops, crescent-shaped muscles removed
200 grams (7 ounces) porcini or cremini mushrooms, sliced 6 millimeters (¼ inch) thick (1½ cups)
4 cloves garlic, unpeeled, crushed with the heel of the hand or a knife
30 milliliters (2 tablespoons) dry white wine
15 milliliters (1 tablespoon) aceto balsamico di Modena
3 grams (1 tablespoon) chopped fresh Italian parsley
2 sprigs fresh thyme
Coarse salt and freshly ground black pepper
45 milliliters (3 tablespoons) olive oil

Preheat the oven to 232°C (450°F).

In a bowl, toss the scallops with the mushrooms, garlic, wine, vinegar, herbs, salt and pepper to taste, and 30 milliliters (2 tablespoons) of the oil.

Coat the bottom of a baking dish with the remaining 15 milliliters (1 tablespoon) oil. Lift out the scallops and set them in a single layer in the dish.

Scatter the mushrooms, garlic, and herbs over and in between the scallops.

Roast (*arrostire*) until the scallops are cooked through, 7 to 10 minutes. Serve with the mushrooms and sauce.

Insalata di Pollo

Chicken Salad

Serves 2

Chicken salads have been a feature of Italian cuisine since at least the first century BCE when Apicius, a Roman, wrote what is widely credited to be the world's first cookbook, *De Re Coquinaria*. This recipe, indigenous to Mantua, in Lombardia, dates to the Italian Renaissance, when it was traditionally made with capon.

The salad may be made with either chicken breast or dark meat. Dark meat has the advantage of richer flavor but requires careful cleaning of veins, fat, and connective tissue. This recipe is written for boneless, skinless chicken breast—the easiest solution to the question—but the choice is up to the cook. (At The International Culinary Center, students poach the whole chicken, slicing the breast meat and tossing the pulled dark meat in with the julienned vegetables; the broth is used elsewhere.)

Chef's Notes

Allowing the chicken to cool completely in the stock in which it was poached keeps the flesh moist.

Tossing the chicken with the marinade while the chicken is still hot encourages the chicken to absorb the marinade.

Ingredients

60 milliliters (¼ cup) dry white wine

20 grams (1½ tablespoons) dark raisins

250 to 300 milliliters (1 to 1¼ cups) chicken stock, or as needed

Coarse salt and freshly ground black pepper

250 grams (9 ounces) boneless, skinless chicken pieces, cleaned of all fat, veins, and connective tissue

15 grams (1 tablespoon) pine nuts

12 grams (¼ cup) julienned carrot

20 grams (¼ cup) julienned celery

45 grams (¼ cup) unpeeled and julienned Granny Smith apple

1 teaspoon chopped fresh chives

½ teaspoon chopped fresh tarragon

15 milliliters (1 tablespoon) lemon juice (from ½ lemon)

25 milliliters (1 tablespoon plus 2 teaspoons) red wine vinegar

Pinch of sugar

30 milliliters (2 tablespoons) extra-virgin olive oil

½ head Boston lettuce, cleaned and dried

Pour the wine over the raisins in a bowl and marinate.

In a saucepan (*casseruola*), season the chicken stock with salt to taste and bring it to a boil. Add the chicken (add more stock as needed to cover), reduce the heat to a bare simmer, and poach (*affogare*) gently until the chicken is cooked through, about 10 minutes. Remove the pan from the heat, cover, and let the chicken cool completely in the broth.

Preheat the oven to 177°C (350°F). Toast the pine nuts on a baking sheet in the oven 4 to 5 minutes, until they turn golden brown.

In a large bowl, combine the carrot, celery, apple, pine nuts, and herbs.

Drain the raisins, squeezing to extract the wine, and add to the bowl with the carrot mixture. (Save the wine for another use, or whisk into the dressing instead of some of the vinegar.)

In a small bowl, whisk together the lemon juice, vinegar, sugar, and salt and pepper to taste. Whisk in the oil. Taste and adjust the seasoning.

Thinly slice the chicken across the grain and add it to the bowl with the carrot mixture.

Pour half of the dressing over the chicken mixture and toss. Taste and season with salt and pepper as needed. Let marinate for at least 30 minutes, or until the chicken has cooled.

To serve, toss the lettuce leaves with the remaining vinaigrette and arrange on a serving plate; mound the chicken salad on top. Or tear lettuce leaves into wide strips and toss into the salad with the remaining vinaigrette.

Fegatini

Chicken-Liver Crostini

Serves 4

During the era of Catherine de' Medici (1519–1589), wife of Henry II of France, all innards, including chicken livers, were thought to be aphrodisiacs. This dish would have been embellished with cockscomb and wattle.

These days, sautéed chicken livers may be presented whole on bruschetta, or puréed or chopped (as in this recipe, with onions, anchovies, garlic, and sage) and spread on crostini. Dredging in flour before cooking ensures that the livers brown nicely, and a splash of Marsala wine picks up the caramelized flavors.

Since the livers spoil quickly at room temperature, they must be served either chilled or hot. Toasted or grilled crostini may be used in place of the fried.

(See "Le Tecniche: *Saltare o Rosolare il Pollo*" on

page 158 for a discussion of sautéing meats, and "Cleaning Salt-Packed Anchovy Fillets" on page 451.)

Ingredients

For the livers:
225 grams (½ pound) chicken livers
25 grams (2 tablespoons) all-purpose flour
Coarse salt and freshly ground black pepper
45 milliliters (3 tablespoons) grapeseed or canola oil
30 grams (2 tablespoons) chopped red onion
2 anchovy fillets, preferably salt-packed (see page 451), rinsed
    and chopped
1 small clove garlic, chopped
½ teaspoon chopped fresh sage
45 milliliters (3 tablespoons) Marsala wine
60 milliliters (¼ cup) chicken stock or water, or as needed
1 teaspoon chopped fresh Italian parsley

For the crostini:
30 grams (2 tablespoons) unsalted butter
15 milliliters (1 tablespoon) olive oil
8 slices narrow loaf bread, such as baguette (sfilatino)

Prepare the livers:

Trim the livers of fat and pat dry.

Season the flour with salt and pepper to taste. Dredge the livers in the flour.

Heat the oil in a medium skillet (*padella*) over medium-high heat. Add the livers and brown (*rosolare*) on both sides, 1 to 2 minutes. Remove the livers from the pan and coarsely chop (6-millimeter / ¼-inch pieces); set aside.

Add the onion, anchovy, garlic, and sage to the pan and sauté (*saltare*) over medium heat until the onion is translucent and the anchovy melts, 2 to 3 minutes.

Deglaze (*deglassare*) the pan with Marsala and simmer until reduced by half.

Add the stock and the parsley and simmer (*sobbollire*) until the stock is reduced almost to a glaze. Return the livers to the pan and toss to warm through. Add more stock if the mixture is dry.

Taste and adjust seasoning.

Make the crostini:

Heat the butter and the oil in a large sauté pan. Add the bread and cook until golden brown on both sides.

Drain on paper towels. Serve topped with the livers.

Involtini di Cavolo

Stuffed Cabbage

Makes 6 rolls (serves 3)

Involtini are foods in which a stuffing is rolled up in a wrapping of some sort, often thin-sliced meat, poultry, or fish. In this classic recipe, cabbage leaves make a delicate, edible wrapping for a ground-pork stuffing, fragrant with spices. Milk-soaked bread keeps the meat mixture moist, and an egg serves to bind it. Once assembled, the rolls are browned lightly in olive oil to add a bit of flavor, then braised in a tomato sauce seasoned with vinegar to enhance the flavors.

A mixture of aromatic vegetables, herbs, and spices cooked in oil, called a *soffritto* (see "*Soffritto*" on page 362), provides a base of flavor for the tomato sauce. As is usual for a *soffritto*, the vegetables are started in a cold pan, in cold oil, to gently coax the essense from the vegetables while infusing the oil with their savor.

Cabbage leaves are blanched prior to stuffing to make them flexible enough to roll. Refreshing them in ice water prevents them from overcooking.

Ingredients

For the stuffing:

40 grams (1½ ounces) day-old firm, country bread, crusts removed, cut into 1¼-centimeter (½-inch) cubes (1 loosely packed cup)

60 milliliters (¼ cup) milk

250 grams (½ pound) ground pork

50 grams (¼ cup) finely chopped red onion

1 teaspoon finely chopped garlic

5 grams (2 tablespoons) chopped fresh Italian parsley

1 large egg

15 grams (3 tablespoons) grated Parmigiano-Reggiano or Grana Padano

Pinch of spezie forti, garam masala, or freshly ground nutmeg

Coarse salt and freshly ground black pepper

For the cabbage:

8 medium leaves savoy cabbage, cores removed (see Chef's Note)

Red wine vinegar (see "Le Tecniche: *Sbianchire*" on page 62 for quantity)

For the sauce:

30 milliliters (2 tablespoons) olive oil

100 grams (½ cup) chopped red onion

100 grams (3½ ounces) carrot, halved lengthwise and thinly sliced into half-rounds (¾ cup)

50 grams (½ cup) thinly sliced celery

1 teaspoon chopped garlic

1 scant teaspoon fresh thyme leaves

Pinch of red pepper flakes

Coarse salt and freshly ground black pepper

125 milliliters (½ cup) dry white wine

45 milliliters (3 tablespoons) red wine vinegar

180 milliliters (¾ cup) tomato purée made from whole, canned Italian plum tomatoes with their juices, passed through a food mill

180 milliliters (¾ cup) chicken stock

For the rolls:

35 milliliters (2 tablespoons plus 1 teaspoon) olive oil, for browning the rolls

All-purpose flour seasoned with coarse salt and freshly ground black pepper, for dusting

1 lemon, cut in half

Grated Parmigiano-Reggiano or Grana Padano, for serving

Make the stuffing:

In a small bowl, soak the bread in the milk 15 to 20 minutes, until the bread is soft; squeeze out excess milk.

In another bowl, combine the soaked bread with the remaining stuffing ingredients and mix well. Sauté (*saltare*) a small piece of the stuffing in oil and taste for seasoning.

Prepare the cabbage:

Pull off and discard the outer leaves of the cabbage. Cut around the core and remove. Gently pull the whole leaves off the head, cutting more deeply around the core as necessary to remove the leaves.

Fill a pot (*pentola*) with salted water, add vinegar, and bring to a boil. Add the cabbage leaves and blanch (*sbianchire*) until flexible and tender but not mushy, 3 to 5 minutes. Refresh the leaves in an ice bath and pat dry.

Assemble the rolls:

Lay the cabbage leaves on a cutting board and cut out the thick, tough parts of the central ribs. (Torn leaves may be patched with pieces cut from other leaves and placed over the tear.)

Although this recipe only yields 6 cabbage rolls, it's practical to blanch 8 leaves in case leaves tear or need to be patched.

Divide the stuffing into six portions, and shape each portion into a cylinder on the top third of the cabbage leaves. Fold over the tops of the leaves to cover the stuffing, fold in the sides and roll to enclose the stuffing entirely. Set aside, seamed sides down.

Make the sauce:

Place the oil, onion, carrot, celery, garlic, and thyme in an ovenproof skillet (*padella*). Set over medium heat and sauté (*saltare*) until the vegetables begin to color, about 5 minutes. Add the red pepper flakes a few minutes into cooking to keep them from burning.

Season to taste with salt and add the wine. Stir to deglaze (*deglassare*). Cook about 2 minutes over medium heat to reduce the wine by about half.

Add the vinegar and reduce by half.

Add the tomato purée and bring to a simmer (*sobbollire*).

Add the chicken stock, season with salt and pepper, and bring to a simmer. Taste for seasoning.

Bake the rolls:

Preheat the oven to 260°C (500°F).

In an ovenproof skillet large enough to hold the rolls in a single layer, heat the oil over medium-high heat. Roll the cabbage rolls in the seasoned flour and gently tap off the excess flour. Add to the skillet, seamed side down first, and turn to brown (*rosolare*) on all sides. Drain on a sheet pan lined with paper towels. Remove the skillet from the heat.

Spread a little sauce over the bottom of the skillet. Arrange the rolls in the skillet in a single layer, seams down, and evenly spaced. Squeeze the lemon halves over the rolls and cover with the remaining sauce.

Cover with foil or a lid and bake (*cuocere in forno*) until the stuffing is cooked through, 15 to 20 minutes. Remove the rolls from the sauce and cut them in half on the bias. Degrease the sauce, if necessary.

Arrange two rolls on each of three serving plates. Spoon a little sauce over, and sprinkle with cheese.

Le Tecniche: *Sbianchire* (Blanching)

For the *Involtini di Cavolo*, the cabbage leaves are blanched (*sbianchire*) in heavily salted boiling water, chilled quickly by refreshing in a bowl of ice water, and drained. This is a common treatment for vegetables, particularly green vegetables, which will overcook and lose their bright green color if the cooking is not stopped immediately by refreshing (if color and texture are not a concern, refreshing is not necessary). This is a useful method for cooking vegetables prior to service: During service, they can be rewarmed in boiling salted water until just tender.

Italians add a little vinegar or lemon juice to the water when blanching cabbage, asparagus, and fennel. Acids such as vinegar bring out the flavor of the vegetable but often dull the color. As a general rule, add 60 milliliters (2 ounces) lemon juice or vinegar per 2 liters (8½ cups) water.

Carpaccio di Manzo con Funghi

Carpaccio with Mushrooms

Serves 4

Carpaccio is thinly sliced raw beef, traditionally served with a Worcestershire-and-mustard-flavored mayonnaise. It was invented in 1950 by Giuseppe Cipriani, who was at that time the owner of Harry's Bar in Venice. Mr. Cipriani is supposed to have created the dish for a Venetian countess, who was directed by her doctor to eat a diet of raw meat. The colors of paintings in a Carpaccio exhibit in Venice at the time inspired the name for the dish, which is meant to evoke the brilliant reds and yellows of the painter's work.

Carpaccio may also be drizzled with a simple dressing, as in this variation served at The International Culinary Center, and topped with a raw mushroom or artichoke salad, shaved cheese, arugula, or, more extravagantly, truffles.

Carpaccio is traditionally made with beef filet, a very tender, and expensive, lean cut. But it's quite acceptable to use a more modest cut, such as sirloin, or a top round, which has a large eye of lean meat perfect for thin slicing. Both of these tougher cuts will be tender in this preparation because they are sliced so thin.

(See page 418 for step-by-step instructions for "Trimming and Pounding Beef for Carpaccio.")

Ingredients

For the meat:
280 grams (10 ounces) filet mignon, beef top round, or sirloin

For the dressing:
125 milliliters (½ cup) extra-virgin olive oil
15 grams (1 tablespoon) trimmed and chopped scallion (white part plus about 2 centimers / 1 inch of the green part)
30 milliliters (2 tablespoons) lemon juice (from 1 medium lemon)
Hot pepper sauce, as needed
Coarse salt and freshly ground black pepper

25 grams (¼ cup) sliced porcini or cremini mushrooms
60 grams (2 ounces) Parmigiano-Reggiano or Grana Padano, shaved into thin slices
Arugula, as needed

Prepare the meat:

Tightly cover the meat in plastic wrap and tie with butcher's twine. Freeze the meat almost completely.

Using a meat slicer, slice the meat crosswise into very thin rounds. If slicing by hand, slice the meat against the grain as thinly as possible—(3 to 6 millimeters / ⅛ to ¼ inch thick)—with a very sharp, thin knife.

Place the slices between two lightly oiled sheets of plastic wrap. Using a flat meat mallet, gently pound the meat, dragging the pounder toward you at the same time to spread and enlarge the slice, until the meat is as thin as possible, but being careful not to make holes in the meat. Arrange the slices directly on a serving plate, slightly overlapping so that the plate is entirely covered.

Make the dressing:

In a bowl, whisk together the oil, scallion, lemon juice, hot pepper sauce, and salt and pepper to taste.

To serve:

Drizzle the dressing over the meat and top with the mushrooms, cheese, and arugula.

Vitello Tonnato

Veal with Tuna Sauce

Serves 4

This classic recipe is associated with the region of Piemonte. The *tonnato* sauce is versatile—it may be used to dress other foods such as fish and roasted or boiled meats. The classic *tonnato* sauce is made with canned tuna packed in oil. If possible, both meat and sauce should be prepared in advance and refrigerated to allow the flavors to develop overnight. The mayonnaise may be made with olive oil in place of a neutral oil.

Vitello tonnato may be garnished with fried capers and/or *insalata riccia* (frisée lettuce), as well as with the tender yellow leaves of celery. Thin slices of lemon add color and bright acidity to the dish.

Frying Capers

Fried capers are a contemporary adaptation of the traditional garnish for *Vitello Tonnato*.

To fry capers: Rinse the capers very well under cool tap water to remove excess salt, and dry thoroughly on paper towels. In a skillet, heat 2 to 3 centimeters (½ to 1 inch) canola oil to 177°C (350°F). Carefully add the capers and cook, stirring gently with a slotted spoon, until lightly browned, crisp, and dry, about 2 minutes. Drain on paper towels.

Ingredients

500 grams (18 ounces) veal top round or eye of round
Coarse salt and freshly ground black pepper
Celery leaves (for flavoring the veal and extra for serving
Fresh Italian parsley stems
2 liters (8½ cups) vegetable stock
2 to 3 fresh bay leaves
150 grams (5 ounces) canned tuna in olive oil, drained
12 capers, preferably salt-packed (see page 31), soaked, rinsed, drained, and fried (see "Frying Capers," left) (optional)
2 anchovy fillets, preferably salt-packed (see page 31), deboned and rinsed
80 milliliters (⅓ cup) Maionese (page 80)
Lemon juice
Lemon slices, for serving

Massage the top round with salt and pepper and stud it with celery leaves and parsley sprigs.

In a pot (*pentola*), bring the vegetable stock to a simmer with the bay leaves and salt to taste. Add the veal and simmer (*affogare*) until cooked but still slightly pink and moist, about 35 minutes. Let the veal cool in the stock completely. Remove the veal from the pot; reserve the stock.

In a food processor, process the tuna, capers, and anchovies to a paste. Pass the mixture through a fine-mesh sieve and return to the processor. Add the *maionese* and enough of the reserved stock to thin to a spreadable consistency, and process to blend. Add lemon juice to taste.

To serve, thinly slice the meat on a meat slicer or with a thin, sharp knife. Shingle the meat on four plates. Spread or drizzle the sauce over the meat. Decorate the plates with lemon slices, celery leaves, and fried capers, if desired.

Piemonte (Piedmont)

"Piedmont cuisine could not do without anchovies and garlic, the basic ingredients in bagna cauda."

—Chef Luigi Taglienti of Ristorante Delle Antiche Contrade, Cuneo

Situated in the northwest of Italy and sharing borders with France and Switzerland, Piemonte is a large region with a varied terrain. This landlocked territory is edged on three sides by the Alps. The lower elevations, fed by the Po River, are fertile agricultural areas. The home of FIAT, Piemonte is a highly industrialized region. Its capital is Turin.

Piemonte has a long historical connection with France. For several centuries, the region was ruled, along with parts of France, by the House of Savoy. Its cuisine is thus influenced by the cuisine of France, as well as that of neighboring Liguria.

The area of Piemonte around the Po River is Europe's major producer of rice, particularly *Carnaroli* rice, used for *risotti*. Wheat, corn, and grapes are also grown. In the fall, hilly areas produce game and mushrooms, and Piemonte is famous for its white truffles. Onions, grown here for centuries, are traditionally stuffed and baked; the fillings and preparations change from place to place throughout the region.

The region is rich with cattle and pigs. Several important cheeses, predominantly cow's-milk cheeses, including a special type of *Raschera* (Raschera d'Alpeggio), are produced high in the Alps. Pork is in a variety of cured meats, including cured fat called *lardo*.

Piemonte is particularly well known for its range of *antipasti*, beginning with the famous *bagna cauda*, a warm dip of olive oil, salted anchovies, and garlic, traditionally served with raw vegetables. Other *antipasti* include *fonduta* cheese sauce, *vitello tonnato*, pâtés and terrines, cured meats, and an array of salads.

Pastas, including the meat-stuffed, raviolilike *agnolotti*, are made with fresh egg dough. Slender *grissini* are reputed to have been invented in Piemonte.

Turin, famous for producing and selling chocolate since the seventeenth century, invented the hazelnut chocolate known as *gianduja*.

Piemonte boasts the greatest number of classified wines of all of the Italian regions, including the well-known reds Barolo, Barbaresco, Barbera, and Dolcetto.

What would become the Slow Food movement began in Piemonte in 1986.

See our recipes for the regional specialties *Vitello Tonnato* (facing page) and *Bagna Cauda* (page 38).

Chapter 2

Introduction to Cheese-Making:
Formaggi

Ricotta
Mozzarella

The term *cheese* describes a solid food derived from the curdled milk or cream of ruminating animals (animals that chew their cud). Cheese starts with milk, most commonly from cows, goats, and sheep, but other animals, notably the *bufala* (water buffalo) of southern Italy, are milked for cheese. Each type of milk has a unique flavor that is, in part, identified with its fat content.

Cheese-making is an ancient science of preserving that developed organically out of necessity, over a period of thousands of years. It is the result of the historical need to process milk in such a way that this nutritional but highly perishable food could be made to last. As with all processes of preserving food, the more moisture that is removed, the less chance there is of spoilage, and the longer the food will last. Most cheese-making techniques, therefore, are simply different ways of eliminating moisture, starting with the most obvious process of draining, and progressing to more specialized techniques of cooking, and eventually aging. If the cheese is made to be eaten fresh, it is quickly made with relatively few processes; if it is being made to last, the processes are more complicated and time-consuming. How the cheese is handled throughout develops its specific identity. This is the art of cheese-making.

Almost all cheeses are created by allowing the protein in milk to coagulate until it separates into whey (liquid) and curds (semisolids). The enzyme rennet (or another coagulating agent such as citric acid) is often added to speed the thickening process. Once separated, the whey is drained. The curds are either left as they are to be eaten as fresh cheese, or cured according to the type of cheese desired.

The recipes in this chapter are examples of cheeses that are made to be consumed fresh. The recipe for ricotta demonstrates the most basic steps in cheese-making: The milk and citric acid are reheated to encourage the separation of curds and whey, and the curds are drained in dampened cheesecloth (this tightens the fibers of the cloth). The recipe for mozzarella calls for a premade curd, sold in stiff-textured blocks in specialty stores and cheese shops. It is softened and stretched by hand under hot water, then shaped into balls. Once made, both cheeses should be eaten as soon as possible.

Cheese-making is far too complex a subject to treat completely in this curriculum; it has as many exceptions as it has rules. However, a few of the more common practices are covered on pages 355–57; cheese classifications are covered on pages 21–22.

Mozzarella (page 68)

Ricotta

Makes about 400 grams (14 ounces)

In Italy, most ricotta cheese is a by-product of the manufacture of other types of cheese, traditionally sheep's-milk cheese. The leftover whey drained during the production of the original cheese is cooked again to make ricotta (thus the name, which means "recooked"). But ricotta may also be made from cow's milk, as in this recipe.

(See "Making Ricotta Cheese" on page 356 for step-by-step photos.)

Ingredients

2 liters (8½ cups) whole milk
½ teaspoon citric acid
½ teaspoon coarse salt
Heavy cream (optional)

Draining Ricotta

For use in pasta fillings and some pastries, such as *Zuccotto* on page 303, ricotta cheese should be drained of as much excess water as possible for a tighter filling and a more concentrated taste. To drain the ricotta, scoop it into a fine-mesh strainer (*colino*) lined with a square of cheesecloth and set it over a container. Allow the cheese to drain in the refrigerator at least 2 hours or overnight.

Place the milk, acid, and salt in a small saucepan (*pentola*) and heat the mixture to 90°C (195°F), stirring often to avoid sticking and scorching. When the curds start to form and separate from the whey, turn off the heat and let the mixture rest undisturbed for about 10 minutes.

Carefully ladle the curds and whey into a fine-mesh or perforated strainer (*colino*) lined with dampened cheesecloth. Gather up the ends, tie into a knot, and let the cheese hang for about 1 hour.

Add a bit of cream, if desired, for a richer product.

Mozzarella

Makes about 500 grams (17 ounces)

Mozzarella is a member of the family of "pulled curd," or *pasta filata*, cheeses. It was traditionally made with milk of water buffalo (*bufala*), but cow's milk is also common. Mozzarella curd (made from milk that is treated with a coagulating agent to separate the curds, which are then drained) is sold in blocks. The cheese-maker washes and softens the curd in very hot water, then kneads it until the texture is smooth and elastic, and the curd is soft enough to shape into balls. A pair of insulated rubber gloves purchased from the hardware store may make this task easier at home; it's best, however, to go without so that you can feel the texture of the cheese.

At The International Culinary Center, the curd is shaped into small balls called *bocconcini*, which are sometimes marinated in olive oil with citrus rinds, herbs, spices, and *peperoncino* for flavor.

Fresh mozzarella is best eaten immediately. If it must be stored, refrigerate it in the liquid in which it was made, or in lightly salted water. If refrigerated, it should be brought to room temperature before serving.

(See "Making Mozzarella Cheese" on page 357 for step-by-step instructions.)

Ingredients

3 liters (12¾ cups) water
Coarse salt, as needed
500 grams (18 ounces) mozzarella curd (see Chef's Note)

Heat the water to 82° to 85°C (180° to 185°F), or as hot as you can stand it. Add enough salt so that the water tastes like seawater.

Cut the curd into small pieces and put the curds in a clean stainless-steel bowl. Add enough of the hot, salted water to cover.

Using both hands, stretch and pull the curds until the water is cloudy, 2 to 3 minutes.

Pour out the cloudy water and add fresh hot water. Work the curds until the texture is smooth and elastic, and soft enough to shape into balls.

Pull off a small portion of the softened curd. Working with the fingers below the surface of the hot water, form balls of the desired size, folding them underneath for a smooth appearance.

Set the shape of the mozzarella balls by dipping them in a salted ice bath for a few seconds.

Eat the cheese immediately, or refrigerate it in the liquid in which it was formed.

Chapter 3

Stocks and Some Basic Italian Sauces: *Fondi e Salse*

Brodo Vegetale (Vegetable Stock)
Fumetto di Pesce (Fish Stock)
Fondo Bianco di Pollo (Chicken Stock)
Fondo Bruno (Brown Veal Stock)
Salsa di Pomodoro (Tomato Sauce)
Ragù di Carne (Meat Sauce)
Pesto Genovese (Basil Sauce)
Besciamella (Bechamel Sauce)
Maionese (Mayonnaise)

A stock is an aromatic liquid made by simmering bones, trimmings, vegetables, and herbs gently in water until the solids give up their flavor to the liquid. An indispensable element of professional Italian cuisine, stocks are among the most basic and most important of kitchen preparations. Although it is not uncommon in Italian kitchens to find broths made from lamb, rabbit, game, beef, duck, and a variety of fish and shellfish, chicken and vegetable stocks are the most versatile and can be used in most of the recipes in this curriculum that call for stock. A few of the fish and shellfish recipes, such as *Pesce Spada all'Isolana* on page 230, and *Zuppa di Pesce* on page 240, require a fish stock. Veal stock is not common in traditional Italian cuisine, but it is important in professional training.

A stock is rarely used on its own. It is a building block, a neutral canvas on which to build dishes including soups, braises, stews, pasta sauces, and *risotti*. They are a key element in pan-reduction sauces that are served with sautéed or roasted meats and poultry (see *Pollo Arrosto* on page 161, and *Agnello Arrosto* on page 219). In some braised-meat dishes, such as *Ossobuco alla Milanese* on page 189, stock is used as the braising liquid that is later reduced to create a sauce. In *Pesce in Acqua Pazza* on page 234, stock becomes a brothy sauce for poached fish.

In addition to these stock-based sauces, a study of Italian cuisine requires knowledge of a few other important sauces, some of which will be covered in this chapter. *Salsa di Pomodoro* and *Ragù di Carne* rely on a *soffritto*, a mixture of aromatic vegetables, herbs, and spices cooked in oil or butter—possibly with pancetta or diced salt pork— that is the foundation for countless soups, sauces, and other dishes. These two sauces are commonly used to dress pasta, gnocchi, and polenta dishes.

Pesto Genovese, an ancient raw sauce from Genoa province, is a vibrant mix of pounded basil, garlic, pine nuts, olive oil, and grated cheese. *Pesto Genovese* typically dresses pasta (Ligurian *trenette* and *trofie* are traditional), but other regional kinds of pesto may be served with fish or spread on crostini.

Besciamella, a flour-bound white sauce, is one of the "mother sauces" (*salse madri*) of classic cuisine. It is used primarily as a base for other sauces. In the Italian repertoire it is an important component of baked pasta dishes such as *Lasagne di Carne* (page 116). It forms

Pesto Genovese (page 78)

the topping for gratinéed dishes such as *Uova alla Fiorentina* (page 140), and helps bind vegetables in molds or timbales, called *sformati* or *pasticci*.

Maionese is a cold, emulsified sauce used to dress meats, seafood, poultry, and salads.

Le Tecniche

In this chapter, students learn the fundamentals of stock- and sauce-making. Stocks, sauces, and *soffrittos* are covered more extensively on pages 358–63.

Brodo Vegetale

Vegetable Stock

Makes about 7½ liters (8 quarts)

A flavorful vegetable stock can stand in for more traditional meat stocks, particularly in vegetable risotto and soups. Vegetable stocks are also an important foundation of vegetarian cuisine.

Ingredients

250 grams (9 ounces) red onion, cut into eighths and stuck with 3 whole cloves (1½ cups)

200 grams (7 ounces) celery, cut into 5-centimeter (2-inch) pieces (1⅓ cups)

100 grams (3½ ounces) carrot, peeled and cut into 5-centimeter (2-inch) pieces (⅔ cup)

6 sprigs fresh Italian parsley

1 sprig fresh basil

3 cloves garlic, unpeeled, crushed

3 grams (1¾ teaspoons) whole black peppercorns

8 liters (2 gallons) cold water (or enough to cover the bones by 2½ centimeters / 1 inch)

Place the vegetables, herbs, and aromatics in a large stockpot (*pentola*), cover with the cold water, and bring to a simmer. Skim the foam that rises to the top.

Lower the heat and simmer (*sobbollire*) on the back of the stove 1½ hours. The solids should remain comfortably covered with water at all times; if too much evaporation occurs, add more water.

Ladle the stock carefully through a fine-mesh strainer (*colino*) lined with dampened cheesecloth. Chill completely in an ice bath. If not using immediately, refrigerate.

Fumetto di Pesce

Fish Stock

Makes about 5 liters (5⅓ quarts)

Fish stock is made with the bones and heads of white-fleshed fish, along with vegetables, aromatics, and herbs.

Ingredients

2 kilos (4½ pounds) bones from white-fleshed, non-oily fish, such as sole, turbot, flounder, or branzino
50 milliliters (3½ tablespoons) olive oil
250 grams (9 ounces) red onion, cut into eighths (1½ cups)
200 grams (7 ounces) celery, cut into 5-centimeter (2-inch) pieces (1⅓ cups)
100 grams (3½ ounces) carrot, peeled, cut into 5-centimeter (2-inch) pieces (⅔ cup)
100 grams (3½ ounces) fennel bulb, sliced ½ centimeter (¼ inch) thick (⅔ cup)
3 cloves garlic, unpeeled, crushed with the heel of the hand
6 sprigs fresh Italian parsley
1 sprig fresh basil
100 milliliters (⅓ cup) dry vermouth
6 liters (1½ gallons) cold water (or enough to cover the bones by 2½ centimeters / 1 inch)
3 grams (1¾ teaspoons) whole black peppercorns

Remove the gills from the fish. Cut and scrape out any pockets of blood in the vertebrae. Wash the bones by rinsing them several times in cold water to remove all traces of blood. Chop the spine in several places to aid in the release of gelatin and to eliminate blood.

Place the oil in a stockpot (*pentola*) along with the onion, celery, carrot, fennel, garlic, parsley, and basil, and cook (*saltare*) slowly over medium heat 5 to 10 minutes, until the vegetables soften but take on no color.

Add the bones and the vermouth and cook until the wine is reduced by about half.

Add the cold water and the peppercorns, bring to a simmer, skim well, and cook at a low simmer (*sobbollire*) 30 minutes. The solids should remain comfortably covered with water at all times; if too much evaporation occurs, add more water.

Turn off the heat and allow the stock to rest approximately 10 minutes.

Ladle the stock carefully through a fine-mesh strainer (*colino*) lined with dampened cheesecloth. Chill completely in an ice bath. If not using immediately, refrigerate.

Fondo Bianco di Pollo

Chicken Stock

Makes about 5 liters (5⅓ quarts)

This is a light-colored, delicately flavored stock made with chicken meat and bones (chicken backs and necks are a practical and flavorful choice), vegetables, aromatics, and herbs.

Ingredients

3 kilograms (6½ pounds) poultry bones, rinsed well under cold running water if bloody, and meat

8 liters (2 gallons) cold water (or enough to cover the bones by 2½ centimeters / 1 inch)

250 grams (9 ounces) onions, quartered and stuck with 3 cloves (1½ cups)

250 grams (9 ounces) carrots, peeled and cut in 5-centimeter (2-inch) pieces (2 cups)

100 grams (3½ ounces) celery, cut in 5-centimeter (2-inch) pieces (⅔ cup)

1 leek, green part only, rinsed well of grit

2 cloves garlic, crushed

1 fresh bay leaf

Fresh Italian parsley sprigs

Fresh thyme sprigs

3 grams (1¾ teaspoons) whole black peppercorns

Trim the bones and meat of fat and skin, and rinse them well under cold running water. Place the bones in a stockpot (*pentola*) and cover with the cold water. Bring the liquid to a simmer, skimming the foam and pockets of fat as they rise.

Lower the stock to a simmer (*sobbollire*) and continue to skim well. Add the onions, carrots, celery, leek, garlic, herbs, and peppercorns and simmer 2 hours; continue to skim as the stock cooks and more fat rises

to the surface. The solids should remain comfortably covered with water at all times.

Ladle the stock carefully through a fine-mesh strainer (*colino*) lined with dampened cheesecloth, and chill in an ice bath. If not using immediately, refrigerate.

Fondo Bruno

Brown Veal Stock

Makes about 5 liters (5⅓ quarts)

Brown veal stock is not a component in traditional Italian cuisine, but it is a necessity in the contemporary professional kitchen. Bones and vegetables are roasted, helping to create the deep, rich flavor and color associated with brown stocks.

Ingredients

5 kilograms (11 pounds) veal bones, rinsed well under cold running water if bloody

Olive or vegetable oil, for coating bones

500 grams (18 ounces) onions, quartered and stuck with 3 cloves (3¼ cups)

500 grams (18 ounces) carrots, peeled and cut in 5-centimeter (2-inch) pieces (4 cups)

30 grams (2 tablespoons) tomato paste

8 liters (2 gallons) cold water (or enough to cover the bones by 2½ centimeters / 1 inch), plus more for deglazing the pan

250 grams (9 ounces) tomatoes, chopped (1½ cups) (see Chef's Note)

1 leek, green part only, rinsed well of grit

2 cloves garlic, crushed

1 fresh bay leaf

Fresh Italian parsley sprigs

Fresh thyme sprigs

3 grams (1¾ teaspoons) whole black peppercorns

Preheat the oven to 204°C (400°F).

Coat the veal bones lightly with oil, transfer to a heavy roasting pan (*rostiera*), and place the pan in the oven. Stir the bones occasionally during roasting (*arrostire*). When the bones begin to caramelize, 20 to 25 minutes, add the onions and carrots and continue to cook until the vegetables begin to brown, another 10 to 15 minutes.

Spread the tomato paste over the bones and vegetables and stir. Return the roasting pan to the oven and continue roasting until the bones and vegetables are an even, rich brown color.

Place the bones and vegetables in a large stockpot (*pentola*), cover with the cold water, and bring to a simmer but do not allow to boil.

Pour the fat out of the roasting pan.

Deglaze (*deglassare*) the roasting pan with water. Using a wooden spatula (*spatola*), scrape all the browned bits off the bottom of the pan. Add the resulting liquid to the stockpot.

Skim the stock well. Add the tomatoes, leek, garlic, herbs, and peppercorns.

Simmer (*sobbollire*) on the back of the stove 8 to 12 hours. Continue to skim as the stock cooks and the fat rises to the surface. The solids should remain comfortably covered with water at all times; if too much evaporation occurs, add more water.

Ladle the stock carefully through a fine-mesh strainer (*colino*) lined with dampened cheesecloth, and chill completely in an ice bath. If not using immediately, refrigerate.

Chef's Note

Use tomato scraps in lieu of whole tomato, if available. At The International Culinary Center we save the scraps from dicing tomatoes (see "Peeling, Seeding, and Dicing Tomatoes" on page 350).

Salsa di Pomodoro

Tomato Sauce

Makes about 1 liter (1 quart)

This is an example of a long-cooked tomato sauce used in a variety of preparations, including pasta. (Other, shorter-cooked tomato sauces such as marinara are used in other recipes such as *Pizza Margherita*, page 147.) The recipe starts with a *soffritto*; the sweetness of the vegetables balances the acidity of the tomato. The sauce is passed through a food mill; alternatively, vegetables may be cut into small, uniform pieces—at The International Culinary Center, this is good knife-skills practice—and left in the sauce.

(For a further discussion of *soffritto*, see "*Soffritto*" on page 362.)

Ingredients

160 grams (5 ounces) red onion, cut into 3-centimeter
  (1¼-inch) cubes (1 cup)
80 grams celery, cut into 3-centimeter (1¼-inch) cubes (¾ cup)
40 grams (scant ¼ cup) diced carrot
3 cloves garlic, coarsely chopped
60 grams (¼ cup) torn basil leaves
3 grams (1 tablespoon) chopped fresh Italian parsley
45 milliliters (3 tablespoons) olive oil
Small pinch of red pepper flakes, or to taste
Coarse salt and freshly ground black pepper
950 grams (2 pounds) whole, canned Italian plum tomatoes
  with their juices, hand crushed

Combine the onion, celery, carrot, garlic, half of the herbs, and the oil in a cold saucepan (*casseruola*). Place the pan over medium heat and cook (*saltare*) until the vegetables are softened and begin to caramelize. Add the red pepper flakes a few minutes into cooking to prevent them from burning.

Season with salt and continue cooking until the vegetables are soft and golden brown, 15 to 20 minutes.

Add the tomatoes and bring to a simmer. Add 250 milliliters (1 cup) water and the remaining herbs. Season with salt and pepper to taste and simmer (*sobbollire*) very slowly for 30 minutes. Taste for salt and pepper. Purée in a food mill, return to the pan, and continue cooking 20 to 30 minutes more, until the sauce is no longer watery. Taste once more for salt and pepper and season as needed.

If possible, the prosciutto should be ground with the pork and beef to a very fine texture so that bits of the prosciutto are not apparent in the sauce. (For a different texture, the *Ragù di Carne* could be made with diced meat as well.)

(For further discussion of *soffritto*, see "*Soffritto*" on page 362.)

Ingredients

For the soffritto:

250 grams (9 ounces) red onion, cut into ½-centimeter (³⁄₁₆-inch) dice (1½ cups)

200 grams (7 ounces) celery, cut into ½-centimeter (³⁄₁₆-inch) dice (2 cups)

60 grams (2 ounces) carrot, cut into ½-centimeter (³⁄₁₆-inch) dice (¼ cup)

75 grams (3 ounces) pancetta, cut into ½-centimeter (³⁄₁₆-inch) dice (¼ cup)

60 milliliters (¼ cup) olive oil

Pinch of red pepper flakes

Pinch of spezie forti, garam masala, or freshly ground nutmeg

340 grams (¾ pound) ground pork

340 grams (¾ pound) ground beef

75 grams (3 ounces) prosciutto, ground or finely chopped (¼ cup)

Coarse salt and freshly ground black pepper

250 milliliters (1 cup) dry red wine

800 grams (28 ounces) whole, canned Italian plum tomatoes with their juices, puréed through a food mill

Ragù di Carne

Meat Sauce

Makes about 2 liters (8½ cups)

A mixture of ground meats—pork, beef, and prosciutto—flavored with a *soffritto*, red wine, and tomato, this sauce is traditionally served with pastas such as *Lasagne di Carne* (page 116) and *Gnocchi di Patate* (page 121).

Ragù di Carne is cooked very slowly to extract as much flavor from the ingredients as possible. To that end, the vegetables for the *soffritto* are cut into small dice, and, because this sauce will not be passed through a food mill, they are cut as precisely as possible for the best presentation.

Make the *soffritto*:

Place the onion, celery, carrot, and pancetta in a wide, unheated pan (*casseruola*) with the oil. Set over medium heat and cook (*saltare*), adding the pepper flakes and spices after a few minutes, until the water has evaporated and the flavor of the vegetables has deepened and the fat has rendered out of the pancetta, about 10 minutes.

Add the ground meats and ground or chopped prosciutto and cook, stirring almost constantly, until the meat has broken down entirely into bits and is cooked through, about 15 minutes. Season with salt and black pepper to taste about halfway through the cooking.

Pour off the fat from the pan. Add the wine and reduce until completely evaporated.

Add the tomato purée and simmer (*sobbollire*) very slowly until the liquid has almost evaporated and the mixture begins to stick to the bottom of the pan, about 20 minutes.

Add 250 milliliters (1 cup) water, season to taste with salt, partially cover, and simmer very gently until the ingredients are completely broken down and the flavor is rich and melded, 2½ to 3 hours. Add water periodically as the sauce reduces; the sauce should be thick but not dry. Taste and adjust seasoning.

Pesto Genovese

Basil Sauce

Makes about 375 milliliters (1½ cups)

Pesto Genovese is a very old sauce associated with the town of Genoa, on the Ligurian Sea, where it may have originated. The name comes from the Italian word *pestare*, which means "to crush" or "to beat," and refers to the traditional method of pounding the ingredients in a mortar and pestle. Pesto Genovese is a traditional condiment for the vegetable soup *Minestrone con Pasta* (page 88), and a sauce for pasta. There are other regional pestos: Pesto Trapanese, from Sicilia, for example, which includes tomatoes and almonds.

Pesto is rarely made in a mortar and pestle anymore, especially in professional kitchens. At The International Culinary Center, students are taught three methods in order to assess the different textures: chopping by hand, the food-processor method, and the mortar-and-pestle method. The hand-chopped sauce is rather rustic, with a coarse texture and distinctive flavor. The machine gives it a brilliant green color and a smooth texture, a particularly good choice if it is to be swirled into a soup or risotto. The mortar-and-pestle method produces a creamy, slightly grainy texture, somewhat like the food-processor style but less homogenized.

Pesto will hold very well for up to 2 days in the refrigerator. Add olive oil to cover, and press a layer of plastic wrap directly over the surface to inhibit oxidation.

In the mortar-and-pestle method, the salt is pounded with the pine nuts, garlic, and basil to act as an abrasive and help break down the other ingredients.

Ingredients

30 grams (¼ cup) pine nuts, lightly toasted on a sheet pan in the oven at 177°C (350°F) until golden

3 cloves garlic

120 grams (6 cups firmly packed) basil leaves

40 grams (¼ cup) grated Parmigiano-Reggiano or Grana Padano

15 grams (3 tablespoons) grated Pecorino Romano

125 milliliters (½ cup) extra-virgin olive oil

Coarse salt

Hand-chop method:

Finely chop the pine nuts and garlic together, and place the mixture in a small bowl.

Chop the basil finely by hand and add it to the garlic-nut mixture.

Stir in the cheeses and the oil and season to taste with salt.

Food-processor method:

Put the pine nuts and garlic in the food processor and process to chop fine.

Add the basil and process to chop fine.

Process in the cheeses.

With the food processor running, drizzle in the olive oil to emulsify. Season to taste with salt.

Mortar-and-pestle method:

Put the pine nuts, garlic, basil, and a pinch of coarse salt in a large mortar (marble is preferred). Pound to a paste with the pestle.

Continue pounding, gradually adding the grated cheeses. When the paste is smooth, stir in the olive oil. Season to taste.

Besciamella

Bechamel Sauce

Makes about 500 milliliters (2 cups)

Besciamella is a white sauce made of milk thickened with a cooked mixture of equal parts flour and butter, called a roux. *Besciamella* binds and enriches a variety of traditional baked pasta dishes such as *Lasagne di Carne* (page 116) and *pasticcio*, a dish traditionally encased in pastry.

(See "*Besciamella*" on page 363 for step-by-step instructions.)

Ingredients

30 grams (2 tablespoons) unsalted butter, plus about 5 grams (1 teaspoon) more for dotting the surface

30 grams (2 tablespoons) all-purpose flour

500 milliliters (2 cups) milk

Coarse salt and freshly ground black pepper

Freshly ground nutmeg (optional)

In a saucepan (*casseruola*), melt the 30 grams (2 tablespoons) butter over low heat. Slowly add the flour and stir to combine.

Cook 1 to 2 minutes, or until the mixture is bubbling and the ingredients are well blended and smooth. The roux should not color. Remove from the heat.

Add the milk gradually to the roux while whisking well. Return the saucepan to the heat and bring the mixture to a boil while whisking. (Any starch that is added to a sauce must come to the boil to achieve full thickening power.)

Lower the heat and simmer 10 to 15 minutes, stirring often. Season to taste with salt, pepper, and nutmeg, if using.

Strain the sauce through a fine-mesh strainer (*colino*). Dot the surface of the sauce with the remaining 5 grams (1 teaspoon) butter, and place plastic wrap or lightly buttered parchment directly on the surface of the sauce to prevent a skin from forming.

Maionese

Mayonnaise

Makes about 250 milliliters (1 cup)

All-purpose mayonnaise is made with a neutral oil such as canola or grapeseed, but for certain preparations, such as *Vitello Tonnato* (page 64), in which the flavor is desirable, olive oil may be used instead. *Maionese* should be used soon after preparing. Pasteurized egg yolks may also be used to avoid the risk of salmonella contamination.

Recouping a Broken *Maionese*

A *maionese* is said to "break" when the oil separates out of the mixture. To recoup a broken mayonnaise, whisk an egg yolk in a clean bowl. Whisk the broken *maionese* into the yolk.

Ingredients

1 large egg yolk (20 grams) or 15 milliliters (1 tablespoon) liquid pasteurized egg yolks
Coarse salt and freshly ground black pepper
1 teaspoon prepared mustard
150 milliliters (⅔ cup) grapeseed or canola oil
1 teaspoon lemon juice
½ teaspoon red wine vinegar

Make sure all ingredients are at room temperature.

Combine the yolk, a pinch of salt, and the mustard in a stainless-steel bowl and whisk 20 seconds.

Start incorporating the oil, drop by drop, whisking constantly until there is an emulsion. Add the rest of the oil slowly in a thin, steady stream until the desired consistency is reached.

Add the lemon juice, vinegar, and pepper to taste. Taste for salt. Thin with water, as needed.

Liguria

Liguria is a small, slender region in northern Italy that hugs the Italian Riviera. With the exception of the narrow coastline, the geography is hilly and mountainous. The capital is the port town of Genoa, one of Italy's most important ports and, at one point, one of the most powerful republics in the Mediterranean.

The cuisine reflects products harvested from both the sea and the land. From the sea, there are numerous preparations for anchovies and fish soups, called *burrida* and *ciuppin*. *Cappon magro* ("lean capon") is a famous salad of local seafood layered with vegetables and hard tack, traditionally served for meatless Christmas Eves.

From the land, garlic, basil, and olive oil are the most defining products of the region's cuisine. (Liguria's native-grown, intensely aromatic basil variety is DOP-classified.) The region's most famous specialty is undoubtedly the pounded basil-garlic sauce, pesto, served with *trenette* or the pasta spirals called *trofie* or *troffiette*; the recipe differs along the coast, and some-times pine nuts are replaced with walnuts. Another garlic-based sauce is the mayonnaiselike *aggiadda*.

Though Liguria was an important producer and exporter of pasta during the Middle Ages, the region is better known for its flatbreads: focaccia and the chickpea-flour *farinata*. Stuffed pasta is represented by *pansotti* (which means "pot-bellied" in Ligurian dialect) stuffed with ricotta, greens, and Ligurian herbs, and traditionally served with a walnut sauce.

Native vegetables and wild herbs are cooked into soups, and into pies such as the artichoke-filled *torta pasqualina* (Easter Pie), *torta verde*, and *torta marinara* with fish. Spanish and Portuguese invasions brought many dishes using dried cod (*baccalà* and *stoccafisso*); the Ligurian dialect, in fact, is a mix of Italian and Portuguese. Meat is used sparingly.

Cheese-making and pig-farming are industries of lesser importance.

Perhaps nothing evokes Liguria more than the aroma of freshly made pesto. See our recipe for *Pesto Genovese* on page 78, and use it as an addition to *Minestrone con Pasta*, page 88.

Chapter 4

Rustic Bean Soups:
Minestre e Fagioli

Fagioli (Beans)
Zuppa di Ceci (Chickpea Soup)
Zuppa di Farro (*Farro* Soup)
Minestrone con Pasta (Vegetable Soup with Pasta)
Zuppa di Lenticchie (Lentil Soup)

In a traditional Italian meal, soups are eaten as a *primo*. But soups are some of the most ancient and versatile of kitchen preparations and can stand alone as a meal. Thickened with beans, bread, rice, grains, and vegetables, or embellished with pasta, gnocchi, cheese, or meat, soups have offered Italians practical and inexpensive nourishment for centuries.

Soups may be categorized by main ingredient, by primary technique, and by region. In this chapter we address an important category of rustic soups based on legumes. Their natures change depending on region, to accommodate the native ingredients. Legumes have traditionally been particularly vital to the cuisines of central Italy, and in the area around Venice, where excellent varieties (some IGP designated) are grown. But bean soups are found all over Italy.

Legumes form a natural basis for soups. They contribute excellent flavor and sustenance, and their starch thickens the broth to such an extent that fine soups may be made with a simple *soffritto* and water instead of stock. Different varieties of beans may be used interchangeably, though some are more suited

to soup-making, such as *borlotti* and *fagioli stregoni*. Italian bean soups are typically flavored with a *soffritto*; the beans may be added to the *soffritto*, or the *soffritto* to the cooked beans. The chef will personalize the *soffritto* by using vegetables in proportions that he or she finds pleasing. For example, one might find the flavor of garlic to be particularly suited to chickpeas. Italian bean soups may be vegetarian, or the *soffritto* may be flavored with some form of meat, such as chopped pancetta or prosciutto, a prosciutto end, or a sausage.

Liquid saved from blanching vegetables and cooking beans will further boost a soup's flavor and body. The rind from a wedge of Parmigiano-Reggiano or Grana Padano will also enrich a bean soup. For a more robust product, soups may be thickened with potato. Hearty soups are also enriched and extended with grains (rice and *farro*, for example) or pasta.

Le Tecniche

In this chapter, students learn the fundamentals of cooking beans and *farro*, while they practice the skill of *saltare* (sautéing). For a more in-depth discussion of preparing and cooking beans and soups, see pages 358–61 and 364–65. For information about *farro*, see page 29. For step-by-step instructions for making a *mazzetto guarnito* (the Italian term for a collection of herbs for flavoring preparations such as stocks and beans) and a *soffritto*, see pages 359 and 362, respectively.

Minestrone con Pasta (page 88)

Fagioli

Beans

Makes about 770 milliliters (3¼ cups)

This basic recipe may be used to cook any dried legume. In addition to the aromatics listed below, ends of prosciutto or scraps of pancetta may be added for more robust flavor. Rinds of Parmigiano-Reggiano or Grana Padano may also be added, thus extracting maximum value from the cheese. (For this recipe, add a 5- to 8-centimeter / 2- to 3-inch piece of rind to the cheesecloth sachet.)

Dried beans and peas will increase in volume by about two and a half times when cooked.

Ingredients

For the mazzetto guarnito (sachet of aromatics):

50 grams (2 ounces) red onion, cut into 3-centimeter (1-inch) pieces, stuck with 3 cloves (⅓ cup)

50 grams (2 ounces) celery, cut into 3-centimeters (1-inch) pieces (½ cup)

25 grams (1 ounce) carrot, cut into 3-centimeter (1-inch) pieces (¼ cup)

1 small clove garlic, crushed

1 sprig fresh sage

1 sprig fresh Italian parsley

½ sprig fresh rosemary

½ fresh bay leaf

2 grams (1¼ teaspoons) whole black peppercorns

250 grams (1⅔ cups) dried beans, washed, soaked, and drained

1 heaping teaspoon coarse salt

Make the *mazzetto guarnito*: Wrap the aromatic vegetables, herbs, and peppercorns in a single layer of cheesecloth and tie with kitchen twine.

Put the beans in a medium pot (*pentola*) and cover with 10 centimeters (4 inches) cold water.

Place the pot over low heat and add the *mazzetto guarnito*. (Prosciutto skin, ends, bones, and rinds of cheese may be added for additional flavor.) Add the salt. Bring the beans slowly to a simmer over medium heat, skimming the gray foam that rises to the surface.

Simmer (*sobbollire*) gently, uncovered, until the beans are tender and the centers creamy, 30 to 60 minutes. Let cool in cooking liquid, and store covered in the broth.

Zuppa di Ceci

Chickpea Soup

Serves 6 to 8

This robust, puréed chickpea soup from Toscana is flavored with a *soffritto*, tomato, rosemary, and dried porcini mushrooms, which contribute an elegant, earthy taste. The *soffritto* is only roughly chopped because the soup will be puréed before serving.

Chef's Notes

Dried beans cook at different rates depending on their size and age. If you are cooking multiple bean varieties—for a colorful bean salad, for instance—each variety should be cooked separately.

When puréeing bean soups in a food mill, take care to scrape the bottom of the food mill and rinse it with water (start with about 500 milliliters / 2 cups) once the soup has been passed; in this way no soup is lost, and all of the flavor is recouped.

Ingredients

For the mazzetto guarnito (sachet of aromatics):

50 grams (2 ounces) red onion, cut into 3-centimeter (1-inch) pieces (⅓ cup)

50 grams (2 ounces) leek, white and green parts, rinsed well of grit and cut into 3-centimeter (1-inch) pieces (⅔ cup)

75 grams (3 ounces) celery, cut into 3-centimeter (1-inch) pieces (¾ cup)

20 grams (1 ounce) carrot, cut into 3-centimeter (1-inch) pieces (¼ cup)

1 fresh bay leaf

1 sprig fresh rosemary

3 grams (1 tablespoon) whole black peppercorns

450 grams (2¼ cups) dried chickpeas, washed, soaked, and drained

16 grams (2 teaspoons) coarse salt

30 grams (¼ cup) dried porcini mushrooms, soaked in 250 milliliters (1 cup) cold water 1 hour

For the soffritto:

75 milliliters (¼ cup plus 1 tablespoon) olive oil

60 grams (⅓ cup) chopped red onion

70 grams (¾ cup) cleaned and chopped leek, white and light green parts

150 grams (1¼ cups) chopped celery

30 grams (¼ cup) chopped carrot

25 grams (2 tablespoons) chopped pancetta

15 grams (1 tablespoon) chopped garlic (about 4 cloves)

5 grams (2 tablespoons) chopped fresh rosemary

Pinch of red pepper flakes

Coarse salt

350 grams (12 ounces) whole, canned Italian plum tomatoes with their juices, crushed

Coarse salt and freshly ground black pepper

Make the *mazzetto guarnito*: Wrap the aromatic vegetables, herbs, and peppercorns in a single layer of cheesecloth and tie with kitchen twine.

Put the chickpeas in a medium pot (*pentola*) and cover with 4 inches cold water. Cook over low heat 5 minutes, stirring frequently, to loosen any grit. Drain; rinse thoroughly with cold water.

Return the beans to the pot and refill with cold water to cover by 4 inches. Place over low heat. Add the 16 grams (2 teaspoons) salt and the *mazzetto guarnito*. Bring the beans slowly to a simmer over medium heat, skimming the gray foam that rises to the surface. Simmer (*sobbollire*) gently, uncovered, until the beans are tender and the centers creamy, 30 to 60 minutes.

Meanwhile, drain the porcini, reserving the soaking liquid; rinse and coarsely chop. Strain the soaking liquid through a fine-mesh sieve lined with cheesecloth or a coffee filter to remove grit.

Make the *soffritto*: Combine the oil, vegetables, pancetta, garlic, and rosemary in a medium, unheated stockpot (*pentola*). Set over medium heat and cook the *soffritto* until golden, 10 to 15 minutes, adding the red pepper flakes a few minutes into the cooking to keep them from burning. Season to taste with salt.

Add the porcini and cook 1 minute. Then add the mushroom soaking liquid and simmer until the pan is

dry. Deglaze (*deglassare*) the pan with a little water, scraping up all the caramelized bits; remove from the heat.

Add the *soffritto* and the tomatoes to the pot with the chickpeas, and cook 45 more minutes. Taste for seasoning.

Purée the soup in a food processor or blender or pass it through a food mill fitted with the fine blade, rinsing out the food mill once the soup has been passed with about 250 milliliters (1 cup) water to recover all of the flavor. Taste for seasoning, and continue cooking until the flavor is deep and rich and the soup is a thick but spoonable consistency.

Zuppa di Farro

Farro Soup

Serves 6 to 8

Zuppa di farro is a savory, rich-tasting soup featuring *farro*, an ancient grain with a satisfying chew (see page 29). The *farro* is cooked in a brothy mixture of puréed beans, tomato, *soffritto*, and diced pumpkin, so that the grain absorbs these flavors as it cooks.

This is a fine place to use meat scraps: Ends of pancetta, prosciutto, or sausage may be included. Or, for a vegetarian soup, the meat may be omitted (in the *soffritto* as well) and a piece of Grana Padano or Parmigiano-Reggiano rind added along with the aromatics.

Chef's Note

Instead of puréeing and passing the soup base, vegetables may be cut into an elegant brunoise (see *"Brunoise"* on page 348) and left in the soup as is.

Ingredients

For the mazzetto guarnito (sachet of aromatics):

40 grams (1½ ounces) red onion, cut into 3-centimeter (1-inch) pieces (¼ cup)

40 grams (1½ ounces) celery, cut into 3-centimeter (1-inch) pieces (⅓ cup)

20 grams (1 ounce) carrot, cut into 3-centimeter (1-inch) pieces (¼ cup)

1 small clove garlic, crushed

½ fresh bay leaf

1 sprig fresh sage

½ sprig fresh rosemary

1 sprig fresh Italian parsley

1 teaspoon whole black peppercorns

85 grams (⅓ cup) dried cannellini beans, soaked and drained

Scant ½ teaspoon coarse salt

100 grams (3½ ounces or ½ cup) sausage ends, pancetta ends, or prosciutto ends (optional)

175 grams (6 ounces) Idaho potatoes, peeled and cut into irregular (3- to 4-centimeter / 1³⁄₁₆- to 1½-inch) chunks (1¼ cups)

For the soffritto:

65 grams (⅓ cup) chopped pancetta

55 grams (⅔ cup) chopped red onion

25 grams (¼ cup) chopped celery

25 grams (¼ cup) chopped carrot

20 grams (¼ cup) cleaned and chopped leek

5 grams (2 tablespoons) chopped garlic

½ teaspoon chopped fresh rosemary

20 milliliters (1½ tablespoons) olive oil

Coarse salt

75 grams (½ cup) diced (6 millimeter / ¼ inch) butternut squash

30 grams (2 tablespoons) tomato paste

Coarse salt and freshly ground black pepper

70 grams (⅓ cup) farro, picked over and rinsed

Extra-virgin olive oil, for serving

Make the *mazzetto guarnito*: Wrap the aromatic vegetables, herbs, and peppercorns in a single layer of cheesecloth and tie with kitchen twine.

Put the beans in a large stockpot (*pentola*) with cold water to cover by 10 centimeters (4 inches). Cook over low heat 5 minutes, stirring frequently. Drain, rinse with cold water, and return to the pot. Add cold water to cover by 4 inches. Place over low heat. Add the salt, the *mazzetto guarnito*, the sausage, pancetta, or prosciutto ends, if using, and the potatoes. Bring to a simmer.

Meanwhile, make the *soffritto*: Combine the pancetta, onion, celery, carrot, leek, garlic, rosemary, and the oil in a cold skillet (*padella*). Set over medium heat and cook (*saltare*) until the *soffritto* turns golden, 5 to 7 minutes. Season to taste with salt.

Add the butternut squash to the skillet and cook 5 minutes. Stir in the tomato paste and cook 1 minute.

Add the *soffritto*-squash mixture to the pot with the beans, rinsing out the skillet with a little water to pick up all the caramelized bits. Continue simmering until the beans are tender (see Chef's Notes on page 85).

Remove the sausage, pancetta, or prosciutto, if using, and reserve. Measure 500 milliliters (2 cups) of the soup; reserve. Pass the remaining soup through a food mill fitted with a medium blade, rinsing out the food mill once the soup has been passed with about 250 milliliters (1 cup) water to recoup all of the flavor, then return the puréed soup to the pot. Slice the sausage, prosciutto, or pancetta, if using, and return it to the pot. Add the reserved (unpuréed) soup. Return to a simmer. Taste and adjust seasonings. Remove and reserve about 1 liter (1 quart) soup in a saucepan.

Add the *farro* to the pot, reduce the heat to very low, and cook until the *farro* is tender, about 45 minutes. As the *farro* absorbs the water and the soup gets very thick, heat the reserved soup and add it to the pot to thin. If soup is still too thick, add water or vegetable or chicken stock. Taste and adjust seasonings.

Serve the soup drizzled with extra-virgin olive oil and seasoned with black pepper, each bowl topped with a slice of meat, if using.

Minestrone con Pasta

Vegetable Soup with Pasta

Serves 6 to 8

All regions of Italy have their own versions of this classic mixed-vegetable soup, depending on what ingredients are available locally and seasonally. In Lombardia, it is typically made with pork, cabbage, vegetables, and perhaps rice. In the Italian Alps, it is sometimes made with chestnuts; in Toscana, it often contains locally grown *cavolo nero*, or black leaf kale.

This Ligurian version is finished with *Pesto Genovese* (page 78), the region's classic condiment. Alternatively, grated Grana Padano may be stirred into each bowl, to taste, and the bowls topped with slivers of basil.

(See "Working with Dried Legumes" on page 364 for instructions on washing, soaking, and cooking beans.)

Ingredients

250 grams (1 cup) cooked beans such as cannellini, borlotti, or chickpeas, with their liquid

25 milliliters (1 tablespoon plus 2 teaspoons) olive oil

250 grams (9 ounces) red onion, cut into ½-centimeter (³⁄₁₆-inch) dice (1½ cups)

100 grams (3½ ounces) carrot, cut into half-moons about 3 millimeters (⅛ inch) thick (⅔ cup)

40 grams (1½ ounces) celery, cut into ½-centimeter (³⁄₁₆-inch) dice (scant ¼ cup)

1 clove garlic, thinly sliced

Pinch of red pepper flakes (optional)

40 grams (1½ ounces) pancetta or prosciutto ends, cut into ½-centimeter (³⁄₁₆-inch) dice (¼ cup)

75 grams (2¾ ounces) black leaf kale (cavolo nero) or cabbage, thick ribs removed and leaves cut into 2½-centimeter (1-inch) squares (¾ cup)

150 grams (5½ ounces) Idaho potatoes, peeled and cut into ½-centimeter (³⁄₁₆-inch) dice (1 cup)

4 medium tomatoes, fresh or canned, peeled (if fresh), seeded, and diced

6 grams (2 tablespoons) chopped fresh Italian parsley

225 grams (8 ounces) zucchini, soft center section with seeds removed, and cut into ½-centimeter (³⁄₁₆-inch) dice (1 cup)

1 liter (4¼ cups) hot vegetable or chicken stock

Coarse salt and freshly ground black pepper

100 grams (¾ cup) dried, short pasta such as ditalini, maccheroni, or conchigliette

Pesto Genovese (page 78), for drizzling into soup

Extra-virgin olive oil, for serving

Freshly grated Grana Padano or Parmigiano-Reggiano, for serving

Strain the beans from their cooking liquid, reserving the liquid.

In a heavy-bottomed soup pot (*pentola*), heat the 25 milliliters (1 tablespoon plus 2 teaspoons) olive oil over medium heat until hot but not smoking. Add the onion, carrot, celery, and garlic and cook (*saltare*), stirring until the vegetables begin to turn golden, about 4 minutes.

Reduce the heat to low. Add the red pepper flakes, if using, and the pancetta or prosciutto and cook 5 more minutes.

Add the kale, potatoes, tomatoes, and parsley and cook 10 more minutes to meld the flavors.

Add the zucchini, the bean cooking liquid, and the hot vegetable or chicken stock and season to taste with salt and pepper. Simmer (*sobbollire*) 30 minutes.

Bring the soup to a simmer. Add the pasta and simmer gently until al dente. Adjust the seasoning. Add the beans.

Ladle the soup into bowls and drizzle with the pesto. Drizzle with more olive oil and serve. Garnish with the grated cheese.

Zuppa di Lenticchie

Lentil Soup

Serves 6 to 8

Lentils are probably the oldest cultivated legume. Umbria is known for its fine, IGP-designated lentils, *lenticchie di Castelluccio di Norcia*, which are grown in the high plains in the Monte Sibillini National Park. Castelluccio lentils are small, fragrant, and varied in color from speckled green to light yellow to brown. Because of their fine skins, they do not require soaking before cooking. This soup is seasoned with *spezie forti*, a "butcher's blend" of spices common to Umbrian and Tuscan cooking. (See page 31 for a discussion of *spezie forti*.)

Ingredients

For the soffritto:
60 milliliters (¼ cup) olive oil
100 grams (⅔ cup) finely chopped red onion
100 grams (⅔ cup) finely chopped celery
50 grams (⅓ cup) finely chopped carrot
10 grams (2 tablespoons) chopped garlic
4 teaspoons finely chopped sage
70 grams (½ cup) diced pancetta
Coarse salt and freshly ground black pepper

250 grams (9 ounces) Idaho potatoes, peeled and cut into ½-centimeter (³/₁₆-inch) dice (2¼ cups)
350 grams (¾ pound) fresh or canned tomatoes peeled, seeded, and diced (2 cups)
200 grams (7 ounces) lentils, picked over and washed (1¼ cups)
Pinch of spezie forti (see page 31), garam masala, or freshly ground nutmeg
Coarse salt and freshly ground black pepper
2 liters (8½ cups) vegetable stock or water
Extra-virgin olive oil, for serving

Chef's Note

This soup need not be puréed; the contrast of color between the whole lentils, diced potato, and tomato is beautiful. If the soup is not to be puréed, cut the vegetables into ½-centimeter (³/₁₆-inch) dice.

Make the *soffritto*: Combine the oil, vegetables, sage, and pancetta in a large, unheated saucepan (*casseruola*). Set over medium heat and cook (*saltare*) until the vegetables begin to turn golden, about 5 minutes. Season to taste with salt and pepper.

Add the potato and cook 10 more minutes.

Add the tomato, then the lentils, *spezie forti*, garam masala, or nutmeg, and salt and pepper to taste. Cook 5 minutes to allow the lentils to absorb the flavors from the *soffritto*.

Add the stock or water in two or three stages, cooking a few minutes in between additions. Bring the soup to a simmer and cook (*sobbollire*) until the lentils are tender, about 25 minutes. Season to taste with salt.

Coarsely purée the soup with a hand blender or food mill or in a food processor, just enough to break up the lentils and thicken the soup. Do not purée until smooth.

Return the soup to the heat and taste for seasoning, adding salt and pepper as necessary. Continue cooking gently, adding more vegetable stock or water as needed, to allow the flavors to meld and to correct the consistency. Taste again for salt and pepper.

Serve drizzled with olive oil.

Chapter 5

Pasta

Pasta all'Uovo (Fresh Egg Pasta)
Pasta Verde (Green Pasta)
Spaghetti con Vongole (Spaghetti with Clams)
Orecchiette con Cime di Rape
  (*Orecchiette* with Broccoli Rabe)
Pasta alla Norma (Pasta with Eggplant)
Spaghetti alla Carbonara
  (Spaghetti, Carbonara Style)
Pasta con le Sarde (Pasta with Sardines)
Tortellini alla Bolognese
  (Tortellini with Meat Stuffing)
Garganelli con Piselli (*Garganelli* with Peas)
Ravioli di Ricotta e Bietola
  (Ravioli with Swiss Chard and Ricotta)
Lasagne di Carne (Lasagne with Meat Ragù)

The origins of pasta in Italy have been hotly debated for years. Some sources still adhere to the popular story of Marco Polo returning from China in the thirteenth century with his discovery of noodles. Other historians have argued that pasta originated in Italy with the Etruscans, a race of people who predated the Romans and lived in central Italy. (This theory was supported by murals at Caere, an ancient Etruscan city about thirty miles north of Rome and dating back to about the fourth century, that show tools that look very like modern tools for making pasta.)

Fascinating new research compiled by authors Silvano Serventi and Françoise Sabban in their scholarly work,

Pasta: The Story of a Universal Food, compellingly suggests that while noodles did originate in China, pasta-making also evolved independently in the West. According to Serventi and Sabban, Western origins are complex, including contributions from ancient Greco-Roman and Arab cultures. As early as the ninth and tenth centuries, Arab texts and recipes reference dried pasta and products that are similar to *tagliatelle* and ravioli. And we know that the ancients had ready access to both soft and durum-wheat flours.

Nonetheless, the authors argue convincingly that while the Arabs helped to spread the use of pasta, especially beginning in the High Middle Ages, they were not the originators of pasta in Italy. And while Greco-Roman cultures grew, and consumed wheat in the form of bread and porridges, neither the Greeks nor the Romans made pasta as we know it today. Pasta as we know it probably didn't emerge in Italy until the Middle Ages, sometime during the thirteenth or fourteenth century.

Generally speaking, Italian pasta is made from wheat, although buckwheat is also used in some regions of northern Italy. Historically, each region had its own forms and ways of preparing pasta; now, modern transportation and distribution are such that regional specialties are no longer confined to their areas of origin. Nonetheless, it is still true that southern Italy, whose climate encouraged the industrial production of dried pasta hundreds of years ago, continues to favor dried pastas made from a variety of hard wheat (*grano*

Spaghetti alla Carbonara (page 104)

The "Bowl" Method

Home cooks who are making pasta for the first time may want to use the "bowl" method:

Sift the flour and semolina into a medium bowl.

In another large bowl, combine the eggs, salt, and olive oil.

With a fork, mix the flour into the wet ingredients a little at a time, until all of the liquid has been incorporated and a rough dough has formed. (Do not add all the flour at once.)

Gather the dough together with your hands and turn it out onto a lightly floured work surface.

Knead, roll, and cut the dough as in the recipe at right.

duro) native to that area of the peninsula. Fresh pasta is traditional to the northern regions south of the Po, where it is made with soft wheat (*grano tenero*) and usually with eggs. (Central Italy indulges in both traditions, as well as fresh pastas made with a combination of soft and durum-wheat flours.) Pasta made with durum-wheat (more commonly known as semolina) flour will be chewy and firm, while pasta made with finely milled, soft wheat flour will be tender, silky, and supple.

This chapter introduces preparations for fresh and dried pasta dishes. Recipes are chosen to demonstrate a range of shapes and regional preparations. Fresh pasta dough is rolled and cut into noodles or into sheets for lasagne; rolled into wide tubes for cannelloni or slender, ridged tubes from Emilia-Romagna called *garganelli*; stuffed and cut into squares for ravioli; folded around a filling for tortellini; or pressed into concave disks for *orecchiette*.

The basic egg-pasta recipe at right is Tuscan in origin. It is made with a combination of "00", or all-purpose, and semolina flours; the addition of the semolina yields a relatively firm noodle. This should not be understood as the only fresh pasta recipe available. In fact, Italian cuisine offers numerous fresh pasta recipes, some of which may be specific to certain shapes (such as the *orecchiette* on page 99, and *garganelli* on page 112), others of which may be used somewhat interchangeably. Delicate filled pastas, however, such as the tortellini on page 108, are best made with a lighter dough. There are also classic doughs characterized by their abundant use of egg yolks instead of whole eggs, such as Piemonte's *tajarin*.

The yields for these recipes assume that the dish is being served in small portions for a *primo*, as pasta is eaten in Italy.

Le Tecniche

In this chapter, students learn the fundamentals of shaping, cooking, and saucing pasta. Also covered is the importance of finishing the pasta—first cooked to nearly al dente—in a skillet with the sauce so that the pasta absorbs the flavor of the sauce while the starch from the pasta helps bind the sauce. Students continue to practice skills of *saltare* and *sbianchire* when saucing and stuffing pastas. For a discussion of methods for rolling, cutting, and cooking pasta, see pages 366–80.

Pasta all'Uovo

Fresh Egg Pasta

Makes about 450 grams (1 pound)

Recipes for fresh pasta differ by region. This dough of flour, egg, salt, water, and a little olive oil is typical of Toscana. The dough may be made by hand, in a food processor, or in a mixer. Additionally, ingredients such as spinach, for *Pasta Verde* (Green Pasta, page 96) and squid ink, for *pasta al nero di seppia* (see sidebar, page 367), are sometimes added to the dough for color and flavor.

This recipe demonstrates the traditional *fontana* (well) method in which the dry ingredients are formed into a well on a wooden board. The wet ingredients are combined in the center, and the flour is drawn into the wet ingredients with a fork until the dough comes together. The recipe for *Pasta Verde* demonstrates how to make the dough in a standing mixer or food processor.

The biggest problem new students have when learning to make pasta dough, however, is judging how much flour to add. Many students add too much flour and the dough is too dry. The "bowl" method (see variation on facing page) is a good way to practice because the flour can be added little by little to the wet ingredients. Students find it less cumbersome to add more flour to a wet dough than to attempt to work in moisture to an overly dry dough.

(See "Making Fresh Pasta Dough" on page 367 for step-by-step instructions.)

Ingredients

150 grams (1¼ cups) "oo" or all-purpose flour, plus more as needed for bench flour
150 grams (1¼ cups) semolina
4 large eggs
Pinch of coarse salt
10 milliliters (2 teaspoons) olive oil
Extra semolina and parchment paper for sheet pan

Set a bowl of flour to the side of a work surface as bench flour. Sift the flour and semolina onto a wooden board. Use a fork to make a well in the center. Add the eggs, salt, and olive oil to the well. Beat the wet ingredients with the fork to blend.

Use the fork to pull the flour gradually into the well, starting with the inner rim of the well, mixing to incorporate the flour with the wet ingredients. When all of the wet ingredients have been absorbed and the dough begins to come together, use clean hands to incorporate the rest of the flour into a rough dough.

Knead with the palm of one hand, pressing down and away from you, then fold the dough over with the other hand. Dust the dough with additional bench flour if the dough is sticky. Knead until the dough is smooth, silky, and elastic, 10 to 15 minutes.

Divide the dough into 2 balls. Sprinkle with flour. Cover with a clean cloth or wrap in plastic wrap; refrigerate at least 30 minutes or overnight. Bring to room temperature before rolling.

To roll the dough, dust a work surface with flour. Cut the dough balls in half and flatten each to a disk; keep the remaining dough covered while you work. Set the rollers on the pasta machine to the widest setting. Roughly flatten one piece of dough with your hand to an oblong thin enough to feed through the rollers. Dust with flour, then brush off excess flour with your hands or a pastry brush. Roll the dough through the machine. Fold the dough strip in half, and press down to seal. Feed one of the "open" ends of the dough into the rollers and roll through the machine again. Do this two or three more times, dusting the pasta with flour if it is sticky (and brushing off the excess), until the dough is smooth and satiny.

Adjust the machine to the next thinnest setting. Roll the dough strip through the machine, without folding.

Continue rolling the dough strip through the rollers, adjusting the machine to thin the dough, until the pasta strip is rolled to the desired thickness. If the strip is a little moist, let it stand at room temperature to dry for about 5 minutes. Roll the remaining dough through the rollers in the same way.

For **noodles**, the pasta is rolled to the next-to-thinnest setting and cut into wide or thin strands, as desired. Wrap the noodles loosely around your hand to make a "nest," and set the nest on a parchment-lined sheet pan sprinkled with semolina. For **lasagne**, the pasta is rolled to the next-to-thinnest setting, cut into rectangles, and arranged in a single layer on a parchment-lined sheet pan sprinkled with semolina. For **stuffed pastas**, the pasta is generally rolled to the thinnest setting. It is immediately cut into shapes and filled while the dough sheet is still slightly damp. It is stored on a parchment-lined sheet pan sprinkled with semolina.

Chef's Notes

Noodles can also be cut using the traditional pasta implement of Abruzzo, *la chitarra*. See page 372 for step-by-step instructions for rolling and cutting pasta with the *chitarra*.

Fresh pasta dough will turn an unappetizing gray color if left in the refrigerator for too long. Loosely cover noodles with plastic wrap and refrigerate if using within a few hours, or wrap well and freeze.

Pasta Verde

Green Pasta

Makes about 450 grams (1 pound)

The addition of blanched, puréed spinach (or other greens) to the dough is the traditional method for coloring fresh pasta dough green. Green pasta is used in some lasagne.

The spinach may be chopped by hand, to produce a green-speckled dough, or it may be processed to a purée, for a homogenous color. If hand-chopped, the spinach must be very finely chopped or the dough won't hold together. In both cases, it's important that the spinach be squeezed out after cooking so it is as dry as possible.

(See "Making Pasta Dough in a Food Processor or Standing Mixer" on page 369 for step-by-step instructions.)

Ingredients

2 large eggs

70 grams (⅓ cups un-packed) cooked spinach, squeezed dry very well, and chopped very, very fine or puréed

Pinch of coarse salt

10 milliliters (2 teaspoons) olive oil

225 grams (1¾ cups) "oo" or all-purpose flour, plus more for bench flour

Semolina and parchment paper for sheet pan

Set a small bowl of flour on a work surface as bench flour. Put the eggs, spinach, salt, oil, and flour into the bowl of a mixer fitted with the paddle attachment, or into a food processor.

Pulse to create a rough dough, scraping down the sides of the bowl as needed.

Using a plastic bowl scraper, scrape the dough out of the bowl onto a floured work surface. Knead with the palm of one hand, pressing down and away from you, then fold the dough over with the other hand. Dust the dough with additional bench flour if the dough is sticky. Knead until the dough is smooth, silky, and elastic, 10 to 15 minutes.

Divide the dough into 2 balls and sprinkle with flour. Cover with a clean towel or wrap in plastic wrap; refrigerate at least 30 minutes, or overnight. Bring to room temperature before rolling.

Roll and cut the dough as instructed in the recipe for *Pasta all'Uovo* on page 95.

Spaghetti con Vongole

Spaghetti with Clams

Serves 4

This is a classic dish of spaghetti dressed with clams steamed in white wine and seasoned with garlic and red pepper flakes.

Traditionally this dish is made with small clams (about the size of an adult fingernail), served in the shell. Any variety of small clam, such as New Zealand cockles or Manila clams, will work; the latter are particularly nice because they are plump.

The best method for cleaning clams is to soak them in cold salted (sealike) water for up to an hour so that they expel any grit.

Ingredients

30 Manila or other variety of small clams (1 to 1¼ kilograms /
2½ pounds), scrubbed
Coarse salt
40 milliliters (2½ tablespoons) olive oil
1 clove garlic, sliced crosswise into very thin rounds
Pinch of red pepper flakes
150 grams (5 ounces) spaghetti
70 milliliters (¼ cup plus 2 teaspoons) dry white wine
3 grams (1 tablespoon) chopped fresh Italian parsley

Place the clams in a bowl and add salted water to cover. Let stand 10 minutes, or up to 1 hour, to allow the clams to expel sand and grit contained in the shells. Lift the clams out of the water, leaving the sand in the bowl, and set aside.

Bring a large pot (*pentola*) of salted water to a boil for the spaghetti.

Combine the oil and garlic in a saucepan (*casseruola*). Set it over low heat and cook to warm the garlic and infuse the oil. Do not allow the garlic to take on color. After 1 to 2 minutes, add the red pepper flakes.

Add the spaghetti to the boiling water and cook 5 minutes. Drain, reserving about 500 milliliters (2 cups) of the cooking water.

Add the clams, wine, and a pinch of salt to the saucepan with the garlic. Cover the pan and cook, shaking gently every now and then, just until the clams open, 1 to 2 minutes. Remove the clams to a bowl; set aside.

Add the spaghetti to the saucepan, adding a little of the cooking water to emulsify. Continue cooking until the pasta is tender but al dente, approximately 3 minutes. Stir in the parsley and add the clams back to the pan to rewarm in the sauce.

The pasta should not be soupy, but some emulsified sauce will pool on the plate. Taste and adjust seasonings.

Orecchiette con Cime di Rape

Orecchiette with Broccoli Rabe

Serves 4

Orecchiette, which means "little ears" (a reference to their round, concave shape), are a regional symbol of Puglia. Traditionally, *orecchiette* are homemade. The combination of native, hard-wheat flour and water (instead of egg) yields a firm, textured pasta.

Wood is the ideal work surface for shaping *orecchiette*; a smooth surface will not create the rough texture that is characteristic of the pasta. (See "Making *Orecchiette*" on page 374 for step-by-step photos of shaping the pasta.)

The *orecchiette* are sauced with broccoli rabe that is cooked in olive oil seasoned with garlic, red pepper flakes, and chopped anchovy. (Anchovy is often used in combination with broccoli rabe and other bitter greens because the rich, salty flavor of the anchovy mellows the bitter taste of the vegetable.) The dish is finished with grated Pecorino Romano and, classically, with fried breadcrumbs. Crumbled sausage may be added; it also balances the bitterness of the broccoli.

The broccoli rabe is traditionally blanched in the water in which the pasta will be cooked, which serves to infuse the pasta with the flavor of the vegetable.

Ragù di Carne (page 77), *Salsa di Pomodoro* (page 76), and ricotta are also classic pairings with *orecchiette*.

(See "Cleaning Salt-Packed Anchovy Fillets" on page 451 for step-by-step instructions.)

Ingredients

40 milliliters (2½ tablespoons) olive oil, plus extra for the breadcrumbs

60 grams (½ cup) coarse breadcrumbs (made from day-old bread)

200 grams (about 10 stalks, or 7 ounces) broccoli rabe, thick stems trimmed

Coarse salt

150 grams (5 ounces) dried or fresh orecchiette (recipe follows)

2 cloves garlic, peeled and crushed with the heel of the hand

⅛ teaspoon red pepper flakes

2 anchovy fillets, preferably salt-packed (see page 31), deboned, rinsed, and chopped

150 grams (⅓ pound) pork sausage, casings removed (optional)

30 grams (6 tablespoons) grated Pecorino Romano

In a skillet, heat enough olive oil to generously cover the bottom over medium-high heat. Add the breadcrumbs and fry, stirring, until golden, about 30 seconds. Set aside to drain on absorbent paper.

Cut each stalk of broccoli rabe into 3-centimeter (1-inch) pieces. (You will have about 5 cups.)

In a large pot (*pentola*), bring salted water to a boil for the broccoli and the pasta. Add the broccoli and cook until it is tender and still juicy, and crushes when pressed between thumb and forefinger, 2 to 3 minutes. (Do not overcook; the broccoli will cook again in the olive oil.) Remove with a skimmer; set aside.

Add the *orecchiette* to the boiling water and cook until nearly al dente, about 2 minutes for fresh.

While the *orecchiette* cooks, combine the oil, garlic, red pepper flakes, and chopped anchovy in a large skillet (*padella*). Set it over low heat and cook until the garlic begins to turn golden, about 2 minutes. (Or, if using the sausage, cook the garlic only 1 minute until softened but not colored. Add the sausage and cook 1 minute.)

Drain the *orecchiette*, reserving about 500 milliliters (2 cups) of the cooking water.

Add the cooked broccoli rabe to the skillet, season with salt to taste, and toss. Cook 5 minutes.

Add the drained *orecchiette* to the skillet with enough reserved pasta water to bathe the pasta. Simmer until most of the water is evaporated and the pasta is cooked. You should see a little emulsified liquid surrounding the pasta. Adjust seasoning to taste. Toss with the cheese.

Sprinkle the breadcrumbs over the pasta and serve.

Orecchiette

Makes about 300 grams (11 ounces)

All-purpose flour, as needed for bench flour

200 grams (1⅓ cups) semolina, plus extra for dusting the sheet pan

2 grams (¼ teaspoon) coarse salt

95 milliliters (⅓ cup plus 1 tablespoon) warm water, or as needed

Olive oil

Set a bowl of bench flour to the side of a lightly floured work surface. Combine the semolina and salt in a bowl. Add the water a little at a time, and knead with your hand to combine. Add just enough water to form a stiff dough. (Avoid the temptation to add too much water or the dough will not be firm enough to hold it shape; it will hydrate as it rests.) Turn the dough out onto the work surface and knead with both hands until smooth and elastic, 10 to 15 minutes. The dough should be stiff and dry, and neither tacky nor sticky, and you should no longer feel the grain of the semolina.

Rub the dough with olive oil. Wrap in plastic and let rest at room temperature for at least 1 and up to 3 hours. (Or refrigerate overnight; bring to room temperature before shaping.)

To shape *orecchiette*, set a cup of water next to a work surface (preferably wooden); if the dough sticks or slides while you are working with it, dip your fingertips in water. Cut off a golf ball–size piece of dough; cover the rest of the dough with plastic wrap while you're working. Roll the dough into a rope about 1¼ centimeters (½ inch) in diameter. Using a small knife or a bench scraper, cut the dough rope into 6-millimeter (¼-inch) lengths. (Each of these will be an *orecchietta*.)

Set a piece of dough in front of you on the work surface. Using a butter knife with a rounded blade, or your thumb, press the blade or your thumb into the dough to flatten. Then drag blade or thumb across the dough, pressing down so that the dough thins and curls around the blade or thumb. Balance the *orecchietta*, rounded side down, on your thumb. Stretch it over the thumb, turning it inside out. The *orecchietta* should be deeply concave in shape, with a rough texture. Place the *orecchietta* on a sheet pan sprinkled with semolina. Continue to shape the rest of the *orecchiette*.

Cook immediately, or allow the *orecchiette* to dry completely and store in an airtight container at room temperature, or freeze.

Puglia (also called Apulia)

"[The most important geographical characteristics of the region are] the variety of landscapes and the possibility of fishing in two different seas with two different typologies of fish and shellfish. [It is a] chain of hills with two different sides. The presence of extra-virgin olive oil . . . is a prevailing element that links the various products together."

—Chef Antonella Ricci of Al Fornello da Ricci, Ceglie Messapica–Brindisi

Puglia is a narrow region on the southeast coast of Italy, forming the heel of the Italian "boot." The region is bordered by three bodies of water: the Adriatic on the east, the Ionian Sea on the southeast, and the Gulf of Taranto to the south. Inland one will find mountains, fertile plains, and uplands. The region's capital is Bari.

Agriculture has historically been very important in Puglia. It is an important producer of durum wheat, tomatoes, and olives, and the region produces a substantial percentage of Italy's total volume of olive oil. With meat in short supply, the cuisine has traditionally relied on vegetables: fava beans (traditionally cultivated in alternation with wheat) in particular, but also artichokes, chicory, turnip greens, rucola, eggplant, peppers, and the onionlike, slightly bitter *lampasciuoli*. Puglia produces more wine grapes than any other region in Italy.

Puglia is well known for its durum-wheat pastas, sometimes enriched with flour milled from *farro* (the ancient ancestor of modern wheat), and bread. Its most famous pasta is certainly the small, handmade, shell-shaped *orecchiette* (the name changes throughout the region), often served with *cime di rape* (broccoli rabe) and sheep's-milk cheese or tomato sauces. *Loane* is a traditional, fresh, *tagliatelle*-like pasta made with an eggless flour-and-water dough.

The area is also known for variations on pizza made with both wheat and potatoes (calzone, *calzuncieddi*, *panzerotti*, *sfogliate*) in which the filling is enclosed in the dough and then fried or baked.

Sheep- and goat-farming are important industries, and Puglia produces a number of sheep's-milk cheeses, including pecorino and the hard Canestrato Pugliese. *Pasta filata* cheeses (such as mozzarella), cow's-milk Caciocavallo Silano, and *burrata* (a creamy, fresh mozzarella cheese, traditionally made from water-buffalo milk) are produced here. Puglia also supports some pig-farming.

Seafood specialties include various versions of seafood soups, which change with the locale.

Orecchiette are often considered the culinary symbol of Puglia. Our recipe for *Orecchiette con Cime di Rape* appears on page 98.

Pasta alla Norma

Pasta with Eggplant

Serves 4

Pasta alla Norma is a traditional Sicilian dish of pasta dressed with fried eggplant, tomato sauce, basil, and *ricotta salata*. The dish, which was already a popular dish throughout Sicilia, got its name from the opera *Norma*, by Vincenzo Bellini, who was born in the city of Catania, in Sicilia. Rigatoni, derived from the word *rigato*, meaning "ridged," is a perennial favorite in parts of southern Italy, and particularly in Sicilia. The ridges on the rigatoni collect the sauce and cheese, but any ridged pasta—or even spaghetti—is appropriate. The shape of the pasta is not important: It is the sauce that makes the dish. The other key ingredients are the garnishes: *ricotta salata*, a hard cheese made by salting and pressing ricotta, and basil.

Flouring the eggplant before frying prevents the vegetable from absorbing too much oil during cooking. It also facilitates a crust on the eggplant and adds starch to the dish, which both thickens the sauce and helps it to adhere and meld to the pasta.

For a more delicate taste, the eggplant may be peeled and cooked without flouring. Fresh tomatoes will also result in a lighter sauce.

(See page 351 for step-by-step instructions for disgorging eggplant.)

Ingredients

---

250 milliliters (1 cup) canola or grapeseed oil
20 grams (3½ tablespoons) all-purpose flour
Coarse salt and freshly ground black pepper
170 grams (6 ounces) eggplant with skin, cut into
    1¼-centimeter (½-inch) dice (2 cups) and disgorged
30 milliliters (2 tablespoons) olive oil
60 grams (½ cup) sliced red onion, slices cut in half if onion is
    large
1 clove garlic, coarsely chopped
Pinch of red pepper flakes
Pinch of dried oregano
10 grams (⅓ cup) torn basil leaves
250 milliliters (1 cup) whole, canned Italian plum tomatoes
    with their juices, puréed in a food mill
60 milliliters (¼ cup) vegetable stock or water
170 grams (6 ounces) ridged pasta, such as rigatoni
70 grams (¼ cup) ricotta salata

Bring a large pot (*pentola*) of salted water to a boil for the pasta.

In a large, deep skillet (*padella*), heat about 6 millimeters (¼ inch) of canola or grapeseed oil until flour sizzles when a pinch is tossed into the pan.

Meanwhile, season the flour with salt and pepper to taste in a large bowl. Add the eggplant and toss to coat. Toss again in a fine-mesh or perforated strainer (*colino*) to remove excess flour.

When the oil is hot, fry (*friggere*) the eggplant in the oil until well browned all over, about 2 minutes. Do not crowd the pan; cook in batches, as needed. Drain them well on paper towels.

In a large skillet, combine the olive oil, onion, and garlic. Place over medium-low heat and cook (*saltare*) until the vegetables are softened and beginning to caramelize, 3 to 5 minutes. Add the red pepper flakes and dried oregano about 1 minute into the cooking.

Toss some of the torn basil leaves into the skillet, and add the fried eggplant. Cook 2 minutes.

Stir in the puréed tomatoes and cook 1 minute. Add the vegetable stock or water, season to taste with salt and pepper, and cook about 5 minutes to reduce.

Meanwhile, add the rigatoni to the boiling water and cook 6 to 8 minutes (the pasta will be undercooked).

Drain the pasta, reserving about 250 milliliters (1 cup) of the cooking water.

Add the rigatoni to the pan with the sauce. Add enough reserved pasta water to bathe the rigatoni and simmer until the rigatoni is al dente and the sauce is emulsified, adding the remainder of the water as needed. Season to taste with salt and pepper.

Stir in the rest of the basil leaves. Plate, and garnish with crumbled or grated *ricotta salata*. (The *ricotta salata* is not cooked; cooking will cause it to clump.)

Spaghetti alla Carbonara

Spaghetti, Carbonara Style

Serves 4

This pasta is from the region of Lazio, around Rome. Some sources believe the dish was developed at the end of World War II, when American soldiers stationed in Rome brought rations of eggs and bacon to Italian friends who turned them into this pasta sauce. Other sources suggest that it originated with coal miners (*carbonari*) in the region, because the specks of black pepper look like coal dust. It may be made with either pancetta or *guanciale*. Both are cured pork products: pancetta is made from pork belly, *guanciale* from pork jowl. Bacon (which unlike *guanciale* is smoked) is not commonly used in Italy, but it frequently appears in this dish in the United States.

The pancetta or *guanciale* should be cooked just to render the fat but not until crisp. The egg yolks, which serve to thicken the sauce, are whisked with cream, then cooked with the spaghetti—to ensure that the sauce is hot—but only briefly; exposure to heat will eventually scramble the eggs and ruin the smooth consistency of the sauce. (Cream is not traditional, but it is often used because it prevents the eggs from scrambling.)

Ingredients

100 grams (3½ ounces) pancetta, guanciale, or bacon, cut into ½-centimeter (³⁄₁₆-inch) dice (½ cup)

4 cloves garlic, peeled and crushed with the palm of the hand

45 milliliters (3 tablespoons) olive oil

Pinch of red pepper flakes

150 grams (5 ounces) spaghetti

2 large eggs

2 large egg yolks

30 milliliters (2 tablespoons) heavy cream (optional)

Coarse salt and freshly ground black pepper

20 grams (¼ cup) grated Parmigiano-Reggiano or Grana Padano

20 grams (¼ cup) grated Pecorino Romano

Bring a large pot (*pentola*) of salted water to a boil for the pasta.

Combine the diced meat, garlic, and oil in a skillet (*padella*). Place over medium heat and cook, adding the red pepper flakes about 1 minute into the cooking, until some of the fat is rendered but before the meat crisps, 3 to 5 minutes.

Cook the spaghetti in the boiling water until slightly undercooked, about 5 minutes.

While the spaghetti cooks, whisk together the eggs and egg yolks, the cream, if using, and black pepper to taste in a large bowl.

Drain the spaghetti, reserving approximately 500 milliliters (2 cups) of the pasta water, and add the spaghetti to the skillet.

Add enough pasta water to the pan to bathe the spaghetti, and simmer until the spaghetti is al dente and the water is reduced. Discard the garlic.

Transfer the spaghetti-meat mixture to the bowl with the egg mixture. Add the cheeses and toss well to combine.

Return the mixture to the skillet and toss over medium-low heat 30 to 60 seconds to warm and slightly thicken the sauce; do not overcook or the eggs will scramble. Taste and adjust seasonings. Serve hot.

Saffron

Saffron, the stigma of the saffron crocus flower, thrives in the Mediterranean climate, and saffron pasta is found throughout Italy. Saffron is expensive because it is so difficult and tedious to harvest the stigmas, of which there is only one per flower. The largest cultivation of saffron is found in three areas: San Gavino Monreale; Sardegna, near L'Aquila in Abruzzo; and San Gimignano, in Toscana.

Saffron is usually combined with a liquid (water, in this recipe, for both pasta and sauce) for even dispersal throughout the food it is flavoring.

It takes about 80,000 crocuses to yield 2¼ kilograms (5 pounds) of stigmas, which produce 450 grams (1 pound) of saffron. It takes about two hundred hours of labor to separate and harvest the stigmas by hand, making it the most expensive spice in the world.

The intense yellow color of saffron comes from a set of carotenoid pigments that account for 10 percent of the spice's weight.

Pasta con le Sarde

Pasta with Sardines

Serves 4

Pasta con le Sarde is a traditional Sicilian dish. It is at its best during spring and summer months, when fresh sardines are available. Ingredients vary depending on the area but the dish usually incorporates sardines, wild fennel, saffron, pine nuts, and raisins or currants. Wild fennel grows rampantly across Sicilia and the fronds add a beautiful potency to the dish.

The sauce features bright contrasting flavors—sweet, savory, bitter, acidic, and salty—and is reflective of the Arab influence in the region. Traditionally this would be made with a dried pasta, likely *percatelli,* spaghetti, *bucatini,* macaroni, or ziti. At The International Culinary Center, students are taught to make a fresh, saffron-flavored *taglierini* (a thin noodle), which while not traditional is nonetheless a logical choice for the dish, since southern Italy is an area where, in Roman times, saffron was cultivated.

(See pages 450 and 451, respectively, for step-by-step instructions for "Filleting Sardines"and "Cleaning Salt-Packed Anchovies.")

Ingredients

For the taglierini:

Large pinch of saffron, lightly toasted in a dry pan
50 milliliters (3½ tablespoons) warm water
100 grams (¾ cup) "oo" or all-purpose flour, plus more for bench flour as needed
150 grams (1¼ cups) semolina
Pinch of coarse salt
7 to 8 large egg yolks
Semolina or cormeal, for dusting the sheet pan

For the sardines:

4 fresh sardines
Coarse salt and freshly ground black pepper
Juice of 1 orange
Olive oil
50 grams (½ cup) panko or other coarse breadcrumbs
Grated zest of 1 orange
Pinch of fennel pollen or ground, toasted fennel seeds

For the sauce:

1 large bulb fennel (with fronds), trimmed and cut into ½-centimeter (³⁄₁₆-inch) dice (2½ cups) (reserve fronds)
Olive oil
110 grams (¾ cup) finely diced white onion
3 anchovy fillets, preferably salt-packed (see page 31), deboned, rinsed, and chopped
Generous pinch of saffron, soaked in a bit of water for even dispersal throughout the sauce
50 grams (¼ cup) pine nuts, lightly toasted
50 grams (¼ cup) dark raisins or currants, soaked in warm water and drained
Grated zest of 1 orange
A few sprigs of fennel fronds, chopped, and some small fronds reserved for garnish
Coarse salt and freshly ground black pepper

Make the *taglierini*:

In a small bowl, dissolve the saffron in the warm water.

Set a bowl of bench flour to the side of a lightly floured work surface. In a large bowl, sift the semolina with the flour and salt. Make a well in the center. Add the yolks and the saffron-water mixture. Beat the wet ingredients with a fork to blend.

Incorporate flour into the wet ingredients until the dough forms a ball and is no longer sticky when touched with clean fingers. Turn the dough out onto the work surface. Adding more bench flour if necessary, knead until the dough is smooth and silky, 10 to 15 minutes.

Divide the dough into 2 balls. Sprinkle with flour. Wrap in plastic and refrigerate at least 30 minutes, or overnight (bring the pasta to room temperature before rolling).

Follow the instructions in the recipe for *Pasta all'Uovo* on page 94 to roll the dough to sheets on the next-to-thinnest setting on the pasta machine. Cut the sheets into 28- to 30½-centimeter (11- to 12-inch) lengths, and lay on a parchment paper–lined sheet pan dusted with semolina flour. Cover with plastic wrap or a kitchen towel.

Move the machine crank to the noodle cutter and cut each sheet of pasta into *taglierini*. Lay flat or twist the cut *taglierini* onto a parchment paper–lined sheet pan dusted with semolina. Set the *taglierini* aside at room temperature until ready to cook.

Make the sardines:

Scale and fillet the sardines. Discard heads and backbones. Remove the pin bones from the fillets.

Lay the sardines skin side down in a half hotel pan, small tray, or baking dish. Season to taste with salt and pepper. Pour the orange juice over the fillets and allow to marinate until the fillets just begin to turn opaque, about 15 minutes.

Cover the bottom of a skillet (*padella*) generously with olive oil and heat over medium-high heat. Add the breadcrumbs and fry, stirring, until golden, about 30 seconds. Drain on paper towels. Transfer to a bowl and add the orange zest and fennel pollen or seeds. Season to taste with salt and pepper and set aside.

Preheat the oven to 177°C (350°F).

Sicilia (Sicily)

"As it is the largest island in the Mediterranean, it is a small continent. The coastal climate is different from the climate in the interior of the island, especially on Etna. It is rich in history and culture."

—Chef Giuseppe Cuttaia of Ristorante La Madia, Licata–Agrigento

Our recipe for the traditional Sicilian dish *Pasta con le Sarde* appears on page 105. Other dishes that reflect the international influences that continue to shape Sicilian cuisine are *Caponata* (page 47), *Pasta alla Norma* (page 102), and *Cannoli* (page 293).

This large island lies atop the "toe" of the Italian peninsula, separated from Calabria by the narrow Strait of Messina. The terrain of the island is largely hilly and mountainous, and includes the active volcano Mount Etna. The east coast is characterized by fertile plains. The region's capital is Palermo.

Sicilia's location has made it attractive to invaders—Greek, Roman, Byzantine, Arab, Aragon, Norman, and Hapsburg—all of whom left their mark on the cuisine. Agriculture has been an important industry here for millennia. The Greeks introduced grain, olives, and wine grapes to the island, and Sicilia was the principal source of wheat for the Roman Empire. Arab rule during the tenth and eleventh centuries introduced eggplant, cane sugar, citrus fruits, nuts, and spices to the cuisine. The Arabs may have introduced pasta to Sicilia; they certainly instituted its manufacture there in the twelfth century. The Arabic influence is also responsible for the sweet-and-sour flavor palate identified with Sicilian cuisine.

The Spanish brought New World vegetables—tomatoes, peppers, potatoes, and corn. Like all the cuisines of southern Italy, Sicilia uses these in abundance, along with eggplant. Sicilia produces a significant percentage of Italy's organic produce, second only to Sardinia.

Inland, sheep and goats are prevalent. A number of cheeses are produced here, especially the staple sheep's-milk ricotta, but also sheep's-milk *canestrato*, Pecorino Siciliano, and *ragusano* and Caciocavallo Siciliano, made from cow's milk. The region produces many wines; Marsala, Malvasia, and Moscato are the best known.

Sicilia is famous for its love of sweets, also a legacy of Arab culture. Nuts and fruit are used in extravagant desserts, often filled with a sweetened sheep's-milk ricotta mixture.

Trim off the sardine tails on an angle. Then cut each fillet, on the same angle, into 4-centimeter (1½-inch) diamond-shaped pieces. Place them skin side up on an oiled tray, sprinkle with the breadcrumbs and bake until the fish is just warmed through, 3 to 5 minutes. Set aside.

Make the sauce:

Bring a large pot (*pentola*) of well-salted water to a boil. Add the diced fennel and cook (*sbianchire*) until just tender, 3 to 5 minutes. Drain; set aside. Reserve the fennel cooking water for the pasta.

Coat the bottom of a wide skillet (*padella*) with olive oil and heat over medium-low heat. Add the onion and cook until softened and translucent, 7 to 10 minutes. Add the anchovies and cook until they have disintegrated into the onion, 1 to 2 minutes.

Add the blanched fennel, the saffron and its soaking liquid, the pine nuts, raisins, and orange zest and toss to combine.

Moisten with a little of the reserved fennel cooking liquid and cover to keep warm.

Cook and sauce the pasta:

Return the reserved fennel cooking liquid to a boil. Season with salt if necessary. Add the pasta and cook to al dente, about 2 minutes. Drain, reserving some of the pasta water. Transfer to the skillet with the sauce and place over medium heat. Add the chopped fennel fronds and toss to mix thoroughly. Season to taste with salt and pepper. Add more of the pasta water and/ or olive oil, and cook briefly to make a slightly thick, emulsified sauce.

Using tongs or a carving fork, twirl the pasta onto a plate or a wide bowl and garnish with the sardines and the reserved fennel fronds.

Tortellini alla Bolognese

Tortellini with Meat Stuffing

Serves 6 to 8

The classic *Tortellini alla Bolognese* from Emilia-Romagna are stuffed with a mixture of finely chopped mixed meats, as well as prosciutto di Parma, mortadella, Parmigiano-Reggiano, and freshly grated nutmeg. Traditionally, thumbnail-size tortellini are served in a meat broth (as pictured on page 110), often served at Christmas; larger versions of the pasta are served with a sauce, as in the recipe below.

A very tender dough, made with "00" flour, is traditional with tortellini. (This dough may be used with all filled pastas.) The suppleness of this lower-gluten dough makes it easy to encase the filling.

(See pages 376 and 378, respectively, for step-by-step photos of "Filling and Shaping Tortellini" and "Making Emulsified Sauces for Pasta.")

Ingredients

For the egg-pasta dough:
400 grams (3½ cups) "00" or all-purpose flour, plus more as
    needed for bench flour
4 large eggs
½ teaspoon olive oil
Pinch of coarse salt
Semolina, for the sheet pan

For the meat filling:

30 grams (2 tablespoons) unsalted butter

15 milliliters (1 tablespoon) olive oil

150 grams (⅓ pound) ground pork shoulder

150 grams (⅓ pound) ground turkey

150 grams (⅓ pound) ground veal

75 grams (3 ounces) prosciutto, diced (½ cup)

150 grams (⅓ pound) mortadella, diced (1 cup)

1 sprig fresh thyme

1 sprig fresh rosemary

40 milliliters (2½ tablespoons) dry white wine

1 large egg, beaten

1 large egg yolk

70 grams (¾ cup) grated Parmigiano-Reggiano or Grana
   Padano

Coarse salt and freshly ground pepper

⅛ teaspoon freshly grated nutmeg

1 teaspoon fresh thyme leaves, chopped

For serving:

Coarse salt and freshly ground black pepper

100 grams (⅓ cup) unsalted butter

5 sprigs fresh sage

40 grams (½ cup) grated Parmigiano-Reggiano or Grana
   Padano

Make the egg-pasta dough:

Set a bowl of bench flour to the side of a work surface. Mound 360 grams (3 cups) of the flour in the center of a large wooden cutting board or a large bowl. Make a well in the middle of the flour. Add the eggs, oil, and salt.

Using a fork, beat together the eggs and oil. Begin to incorporate the flour, starting with the inner rim of the well. As the flour is incorporated, keep pushing the flour up to retain the well shape. The dough will come together in a shaggy mass when about half of the flour is incorporated.

Start kneading the dough with both hands, primarily using the palms of your hands. Add more flour, in ¼-cup increments, if the dough is too sticky. Once the dough is a cohesive mass, remove it from the board and discard any leftover dry bits. Lightly flour the board and continue kneading 3 more minutes. The dough should be elastic and a little sticky. Continue to knead another 3 minutes, adding bench flour when necessary. Wrap the dough in plastic and set aside for 30 minutes at room temperature to relax the dough.

Make the meat filling:

In a Dutch oven or large, heavy-bottomed saucepan (*casseruola*), heat the butter and oil over medium-high heat until the butter foams and subsides.

Add the pork, turkey, and veal and cook (*saltare*), stirring occasionally, until the meat is well browned and begins to release some of its juices, 3 to 5 minutes. Add the prosciutto, mortadella, and herbs and cook 5 more minutes. Deglaze (*deglassare*) the pan with the white wine and cook to evaporate. Remove the pan from the heat and let cool.

Place the filling mixture in a food processor and process to a paste. Add the egg, egg yolk, and grated cheese and mix well. Season with salt and pepper to taste, add the nutmeg and chopped thyme, and mix again. Chill. Bring to room temperature before filling the tortellini.

Roll and fill the tortellini:

Line a sheet pan with parchment paper and sprinkle with semolina. Dust a work surface with flour.

Following the instructions in the recipe for *Pasta all'Uovo* on page 94, roll out the rested egg-pasta dough into a sheet using the thinnest setting on the pasta machine. Lay it on the work surface.

If serving *Tortellini in Brodo*, as pictured opposite, cook the tortellini in the simmering broth.

The dish can be finished with some freshly grated Parmigiano-Reggiano or lemon zest.

Frozen tortellini need not be thawed before cooking. Count on 3 to 4 minutes extra cooking time.

Cut the pasta into 4-centimeter (1½-inch) squares. Place ¾ teaspoon filling in the center of each square. Fold into triangles, press out any air around the filling, and press to seal the edges, using a little water if necessary. Bring the points of the long sides together to form a ring, and seal between your fingers.

Set the tortellini aside on the prepared sheet pan, and sprinkle with more semolina. Refrigerate until ready to cook.

To serve:

Bring a large pot (*pentola*) of salted water to a boil for the tortellini.

Working in batches, cook the tortellini in the simmering water until al dente, 2 to 4 minutes. Carefully remove with a skimmer or slotted spoon.

Meanwhile, melt the butter in a large skillet (*padella*) over medium-low heat. Add the sage and cook gently to flavor the butter, 3 to 5 minutes. (If the butter gets too warm and begins to brown, add a little pasta water to slow down the cooking.) Add the tortellini and enough of the pasta water to bathe them. Season to taste with salt and pepper and cook, swirling the pan, to reduce the water and emulsify the sauce.

Serve sprinkled with the cheese.

Garganelli con Piselli

Garganelli with Peas

Serves 4 to 6

A traditional pasta from Emilia-Romagna, *garganelli* are slender, ridged, quill-shaped tubes. The classic implement for creating the ridges is a small, grooved, comblike tool called a *pettine* used with a slender wooden dowel, but a grooved gnocchi board and dowel will also work. (The thickness of dowels varies by manufacturer.) *Garganelli* are named for *garganel*, or chicken's gullet (throat), which their shape resembles. The dough can be enriched with Parmigiano-Reggiano or nutmeg. *Garganelli* are traditionally served with meat *ragù* or capon broth. Their ridges are ideal for absorbing sauce.

(See page 373 for step-by-step instructions for "Shaping *Garganelli*.")

Ingredients

75 milliliters (5 tablespoons) olive oil
45 grams (3 tablespoons) finely diced shallot
150 grams (⅔ cup) speck, cut into julienne
150 grams (1 cup) peas, frozen or fresh, cleaned
½ recipe (225 grams / 8 ounces) fresh garganelli (recipe follows)
Coarse salt and freshly ground black pepper
40 grams (½ cup) grated Asiago Stagionato (see Chef's Note) or Parmigiano-Reggiano

Bring a large pot (*pentola*) of salted water to a boil for the pasta.

In a large skillet (*padella*), heat 45 milliliters (3 tablespoons) of the olive oil and the shallots over medium heat and cook until translucent, 2 to 3 minutes.

Chef's Note

Asiago Stagionato is a hard cow's-milk cheese made in the Veneto and in Trentino–Alto Adige. Parmigiano-Reggiano is a fine substitute.

Add the speck and cook until the fat is rendered but the speck is not crisp, about 3 minutes.

Add the peas and toss to combine.

Add the *garganelli* to the boiling water and cook 2 minutes. Drain, reserving 250 milliliters (1 cup) of the pasta cooking water. Add the *garganelli* to the skillet with 120 milliliters (½ cup) of the reserved water. Season to taste with salt and pepper. Add more of the cooking water, the remaining 30 milliliters (2 tablespoons) olive oil, and the grated Asiago. Stir or toss vigorously (*mantecare*) to emulsify the sauce. Taste and adjust seasoning.

Garganelli

This recipe yields twice as much *garganelli* as is needed for the *Garganelli con Piselli*. The remainder will keep in the refrigerator for up to 48 hours or in the freezer for up to 1 month.

Makes 450 grams (1 pound)

240 grams (1¾ cups) "oo" or all-purpose flour, plus extra for
    bench flour as needed
60 grams (⅓ cup) semolina
1 teaspoon coarse salt
30 milliliters (2 tablespoons) milk
3 large eggs
Semolina for the sheet pan

Set a bowl of bench flour to the side of a lightly floured work surface. In a large bowl, sift the flour with the semolina and salt. Make a well in the center. Add the milk and eggs and beat the wet ingredients with a fork to blend.

Use the fork to pull the flour gradually into the well, starting with the inner rim of the well, mixing to incorporate the flour with the wet ingredients. When all of the wet ingredients have been absorbed and the dough begins to come together, use clean hands to incorporate the rest of the flour into a rough dough. If the dough is sticky, add bench flour.

Turn the dough out onto the work surface. Knead with the palm of your hand, absorbing any leftover flour on the work surface. Dust the dough with additional flour if the dough is wet. Knead until the dough is smooth, silky, and elastic, 10 to 15 minutes.

Divide the dough into 2 balls. Sprinkle with flour, wrap in plastic, and let rest at room temperature at least 20 minutes.

To shape *garganelli*, cut off about one-quarter of the dough; cover the rest in plastic wrap. Follow the instructions in the recipe for *Pasta all'Uovo* on page 94 to roll the dough to the next-to-thinnest setting on the pasta machine. Cut the dough strip into 4-centimeter (1½-inch) squares.

Place a square of pasta on a *pettine* or grooved gnocchi board, rotating the square so that one corner points toward you (the square will look like a diamond). Tap the far corner of the diamond with a little water to help seal. Flour the dowel and lay it across the pasta square, perpendicular to the ridges of the *pettine* or gnocchi board. Pressing firmly on the sides of the dowel (not on the pasta), roll the dowel so that the top and bottom corners of the diamond overlap and seal, forming a hollow tube with a quill-like point at both ends and fine grooves all over. Slip the *garganelli* from the dowel and place in a single layer on a baking sheet sprinkled with semolina. Continue forming *garganelli* with the remainder of the dough.

Trentino–Alto Adige

"The Alto Adige is inextricably linked to the soil and nature, to its residents' meticulous character, the Mediterannean climate—mountainous; it is a region that, because of its climate and landscape, is said to have been 'kissed by God.'"

—Karl Baumgartner of Ristorante Schöneck 11, Molino di Falzes

Trentino–Alto Adige is in the far northeast of Italy, in the southern Alps. It borders Switzerland and Austria. The region is entirely mountainous, creased with Alpine valleys, rivers, and lakes. To the west and south, it is bordered by Lombardia and Veneto. Its capital city is Bolzano.

The region belonged to Austria-Hungary until it was annexed to Italy in 1919 at the close of World War I; as a result, it is split between two autonomous provinces, both of which maintain distinct cultures and languages. The area to the south (around the city of Trento) is Italian-speaking, while the northern Alto Adige area, or Südtirol, (around the city of Bolzano) is largely German-speaking.

Although modern communication has softened some of the differences, this sociopolitical division is still strongly reflected in the provinces' cuisines. The Alto Adige area is distinctly Austrian and German in nature. The region is celebrated for its smoked ham, called *speck*. Wurst is popular, as are German-style bread-dumpling soups called *knödeln*, *spätzli*, and *canederli* (bread gnocchi—sometimes flavored with bits of *speck*).

The southern province is strongly influenced by the cuisine of the Veneto. Polenta is a staple there, made with corn, buckwheat, or potatoes. *Smacafam* (a sausage-buckwheat casserole) is a specialty.

The region is an important producer of fruit. It is Italy's largest producer of apples, particularly from the Val di Non.

The Alto Adige's celebrated smoked ham called *speck* is used in our recipe for *Garganelli con Piselli* (page 111).

Ravioli di Ricotta e Bietola

Ravioli with Swiss Chard and Ricotta

Serves 3 to 4

These ravioli are stuffed with a Swiss chard filling flavored with ricotta and Grana Padano and bound with an egg. The Swiss chard leaves are blanched (see "Le Tecniche: *Sbianchire*" on page 62) in heavily salted boiling water, chilled rapidly in a bowl of ice water, then squeezed out well—first by hand and then in cheese-cloth—to prevent the filling mixture from being too wet. The ravioli are sauced with melted butter into which the flavors of marjoram and thyme have been infused, but tomato sauce makes an excellent alternative.

(See pages 367 and 375, respectively, for step-by-step instructions for making pasta and shaping and filling ravioli. See sidebar "Draining Ricotta" on page 68).

Ingredients

For the ricotta filling:
100 grams (3 cups) firmly packed, stemmed Swiss chard leaves
25 grams (1¾ tablespoons) unsalted butter or olive oil
Coarse salt and freshly ground black pepper
200 grams (¾ cup) ricotta, hung overnight in cheesecloth to drain
15 grams (3 tablespoons) grated Parmigiano-Reggiano or Grana Padano
1 large egg yolk
1 teaspoon chopped fresh marjoram
Freshly ground nutmeg

For the ravioli:
1 recipe Pasta all'Uovo (page 94), refrigerated 30 minutes and brought to room temperature
Semolina, for dusting the sheet pan
All-purpose flour, for dusting the work surface

For serving:
Coarse salt and freshly ground black pepper
100 grams (7 tablespoons) unsalted butter
3 sprigs fresh thyme
3 sprigs fresh oregano
40 grams (½ cup) grated Parmigiano-Reggiano or Grana Padano

Make the ricotta filling:

Blanch (*sbianchire*) the chard, drain, chill in a bowl of ice water, drain once more, and squeeze in your hands to force out the water. Wrap the chard in cheesecloth and twist to squeeze out as much water as possible.

Melt the butter in a skillet (*padella*) over medium heat. Add the blanched chard. Season to taste with salt and pepper and cook to dry out the chard and cook off as much water as possible.

Chop the chard and let cool. Transfer to a bowl. Add the drained ricotta, grated cheese, egg yolk, marjoram, and nutmeg. Mix with a fork to combine. Season to taste with salt and pepper.

Roll and fill the ravioli:

Scoop the filling into a pastry bag fitted with a large round tip; set aside.

Following the instructions in the recipe for *Pasta all'Uovo* on page 94, roll the pasta dough out into a thin sheet, using the thinnest setting on the pasta machine. (The pasta sheet should be about 10 centi-meters / 4 inches wide.) Dust a parchment paper–lined sheet pan with flour. Dust a work surface with flour, and lay the pasta sheet on the surface. Pipe rounds of filling about 4 centimeters (1½ inches) apart all along the bottom third of the dough strip. Brush the bottom half of the pasta strip with water.

Chef's Notes

The quality of the ricotta is essential in this recipe: The cheese should be sweet smelling, with a delicate flavor, and it should melt in the mouth.

The chard is chopped after sautéing to prevent little bits from sticking to the skillet.

Frozen ravioli need not be thawed before cooking. Count on 3 to 4 minutes extra cooking time.

Fold the top half of the sheet over the filling so that the top and bottom edges meet and gently press around the filling to press out any air pockets and seal the filling rounds. Starting at the folded edge and cutting down toward the bottom, cut between the rounds of filling to make the ravioli. Trim with a pasta cutter as necessary.

Set the ravioli on the prepared sheet pan. Sprinkle with semolina. Continue to roll, cut, and fill the remaining ravioli.

The ravioli may be refrigerated, in a single layer covered with plastic wrap, for up to several hours, or frozen.

To serve:

Bring a large pot (*pentola*) of salted water to a boil.

Working in batches, cook the ravioli in the boiling water until tender, 2 to 4 minutes (if it is freshly made, it will only take about 2 minutes). Remove with a wide skimmer, spider (*ragno*), or slotted spoon, reserving a little of the pasta cooking water.

Meanwhile, melt the butter in a large skillet over medium-low heat. Add the herbs and cook gently to flavor the butter, 3 to 5 minutes. (If the butter gets too warm and begins to brown, add a little pasta water.) Add the ravioli and enough of the pasta water to bathe the ravioli. Season to taste with salt and pepper and cook, swirling the pan, to reduce the water and emulsify the sauce.

Sprinkle with the cheese and serve.

Lasagne di Carne

Lasagne with Meat *Ragù*

Serves 8

This version of lasagne is layered with *Ragù di Carne*, *besciamella* (which serves to bind and moisten the layers), and grated Grana Padano. In southern Italy, lasagne is often made with mozzarella or ricotta, sometimes in place of the *besciamella*. This recipe uses green pasta (traditional in Emilia-Romagna), but plain egg pasta may be used, or a combination of the two.

(See pages 96 and 369, respectively, for step-by-step instructions for making green pasta and rolling pasta. See page 363 for a discussion of *besciamella*.)

Chef's Notes

Pasta dough may be rolled and cut into rectangles, then covered with plastic wrap and refrigerated overnight.

Lasagne may also be assembled and baked in individual ring molds, as might be done for restaurant service. Rewarm in the oven if necessary and turn out onto plates.

Ingredients

Semolina, for the sheet pan

1 recipe Pasta Verde (page 96), refrigerated 30 minutes, and brought to room temperature

1 double recipe Besciamella (page 79), made with 60 grams (4 tablespoons) unsalted butter, 60 grams (4 tablespoons) all-purpose flour, 1 liter (4¼ cups) milk, coarse salt and freshly ground black pepper, and freshly ground nutmeg; surface dotted with butter

1 recipe Ragù di Carne (page 77)

100 grams (1 cup) finely grated Parmigiano-Reggiano or Grana Padano

30 grams (2 tablespoons) unsalted butter

Roll the *pasta verde* dough:

Sprinkle a parchment paper–lined baking sheet with semolina.

Follow the instructions in the recipe for *Pasta all'Uovo* on page 94 to roll the dough to the next-to-thinnest setting on the pasta machine. Cut the dough strips into 8-by-13-centimeter (3-by-5-inch) rectangles. Place in a single layer on the prepared sheet pan, and dust with more semolina. Place a sheet of parchment on top, sprinkle with semolina, and continue rolling, cutting, and layering pasta strips in this way, placing a sheet of parchment between layers. Cover loosely with plastic wrap.

Assemble the lasagne:

Bring a large pot (*pentola*) of salted water to a boil. Prepare a container of ice water. Working in small batches, cook the pasta rectangles in the boiling water to al dente, 1 to 2 minutes. Use a pasta basket or spider (*ragno*) to transfer the cooked pasta to a sheet pan or other shallow dish to cool. (Add a little bit of the ice water and some oil to prevent the pasta from sticking together.) Drain and pat dry on paper towels. Repeat with all the pasta.

Preheat the oven to 191°C (375°F).

Butter a half hotel pan or a 21-by-21-centimeter (8-by-8-inch) baking dish. Spread the bottom with a thin layer of *besciamella*.

Cover with a single layer of pasta, cutting the rectangles to fit exactly with just a little overlap at the seams.

Spread with a thin layer of meat sauce, top with a thin layer of *besciamella*, and sprinkle with grated cheese.

Cover with a second layer of pasta. Continue this layering process, beginning with the pasta and ending with the cheese, to make 3 more layers. Dot with butter.

Bake until the top of the lasagne is golden, about 20 minutes. Let cool 10 to 15 minutes to firm up before cutting; lasagne cuts more easily when slightly cooled.

Chapter 6

Gnocchi

Gnocchi alla Romana (Semolina Gnocchi)
Gnocchi di Patate (Potato Gnocchi)
Strozzapreti (Swiss-Chard-and-Bread Gnocchi)
Gnocchi di Spinaci e Ricotta
   (Spinach-and-Ricotta Gnocchi)

Gnocchi are hand-formed dumplings. Their name stems from the Italian word for "lumps," which many styles of gnocchi do, in fact, resemble. (An exception is *gnocchi alla Romana*, a specialty of Rome made with semolina and cut into rounds or diamond shapes.) In *On Food and Cooking: The Science and Lore of the Kitchen*, Harold McGee writes that gnocchi "got their start in the 1300s as ordinary dumplings made from breadcrumbs or flour." Gnocchi derive from the culinary culture of *cucina povera*, an Italian phrase that means "cooking of the poor," referring to a style of peasant cooking necessitated by scarcity. Originally a hearty, filling, stick-to-the ribs food for those who had little else to fill their stomachs, potato and ricotta gnocchi are now valued for their delicacy and contemporary chefs strive to make them as light as possible.

The variety most familiar to American diners is made with potatoes, but potato gnocchi are far from the whole story. Other traditional styles are made with ricotta, various types of flour (including chestnut flour in Toscana, and buckwheat flour in Valle d'Aosta), pumpkin or squash, cheese, fish, bread, and semolina.

Methods of shaping and cooking gnocchi depend on the style and ingredients. The recipes in this chapter offer a sampling of basic methods for making, cooking, and saucing some standard forms of gnocchi: *gnocchi di patate* (with potato), *gnocchi alla Romana* (with semolina), *strozzapreti* (with bread and Swiss chard), and *gnocchi di spinaci e ricotta* (with spinach and ricotta). Although some forms of gnocchi are served in broth, generally speaking they are served with a sauce, like pasta.

Sauces vary by region and may be used interchangeably; some traditional sauces for gnocchi are tomato, mushroom, meat *ragù*, and herb-flavored butter—sage-flavored being the most classsic of the latter option. Gnocchi may be boiled or baked. Like pasta, they are often finished with a sprinkling of grated cheese.

The yields for these recipes assume that the gnocchi are served in small portions as a *primo*, as is customary in Italy.

Le Tecniche

In this chapter, students learn the fundamentals of making, shaping, cooking, and saucing gnocchi, while they continue to practice skills of *saltare* and *sbianchire*. See pages 381–84 for an in-depth discussion of gnocchi.

Gnocchi di Patate (page 121)

90 grams (6 tablespoons) unsalted butter, cut into pieces, plus
 30 grams (2 tablespoons) for finishing
110 grams (½ cup) cooked, chopped ham (prosciutto cotto)
 (optional)
35 grams (7 tablespoons) grated Parmigiano-Reggiano or
 Grana Padano, plus extra for finishing
2 large egg yolks
Pinch of freshly ground nutmeg

Bring the milk to a simmer in a heavy-bottomed sauce-pan (*casseruola*).

Reduce the heat to low. Add the semolina in a steady stream while whisking. Season to taste with salt and pepper and cook, stirring slowly and gently with a wooden spoon, until the semolina pulls away from the sides as a mass and a skin forms on the bottom of the pot, about 10 minutes.

Remove from the heat and stir in the 90 grams (6 tablespoons) butter, the ham, grated cheese, egg yolks, and nutmeg, stirring well between additions to incorporate. Season to taste with salt and pepper.

Pour the hot mixture onto a marble surface or a buttered, parchment paper–lined half sheet pan (about 31 by 45 centimeters / 12½ by 17¾ inches) or hotel pan. Spread with an offset spatula to a thickness of 1½ to 2½ centimeters (½ inch to 1 inch). Let cool.

Preheat the oven to 218°C (425°F). Butter a sheet pan.

Using a 7-centimeter (2¾-inch) round cutter, cut the semolina into rounds. (Or cut into 8-centimeter / 3⅛-inch squares.) Shingle the gnocchi, overlapping slightly, on the sheet pan. Dot with the remaining 30 grams (2 tablespoons) butter (see Chef's Note) and sprinkle with cheese. Bake until golden brown, about 10 minutes.

Gnocchi alla Romana

Semolina Gnocchi

Serves 4

These flat gnocchi, a specialty of Lazio, can trace their roots back to ancient Roman cooking. They are made from semolina, cooked with milk into a thick porridge, and enriched with butter, egg yolks, grated Parmigiano-Reggiano, and bits of cooked ham. The porridge is cooled in a thin layer, then cut into dumplings of various shapes. The gnocchi are finished in the oven with butter and more cheese, to brown.

Ingredients

1 liter (4¼ cups) milk
210 grams (1¾ cups) semolina
Coarse salt and freshly ground black pepper

Chef's Note

Traditionally, these gnocchi are served with no additional sauce, though herbs are common with the butter: Heat 30 grams (2 tablespoons) butter in a skillet over low heat until the butter is completely melted but still foaming. Add 1 teaspoon chopped fresh thyme or sage and warm 1 minute to release the aroma of the herb into the butter. Do not allow the butter to brown.

Gnocchi di Patate

Potato Gnocchi

Serves 4 to 6

Potato gnocchi are made from boiled or baked potatoes that have been passed through a ricer and bound with flour or a combination of flour and egg, to form a dough. The dough is rolled into ropes and cut into short sections; these pieces are pressed and curled on a gnocchi board, or over the tines of a fork or the holes of a grater to create indentations that catch and hold the sauce, and decrease the cooking time. Cooked spinach is sometimes added for color and flavor.

Chef's Notes

At The International Culinary Center, the potatoes are baked on a bed of salt to eliminate as much moisture as possible and encourage tender, light gnocchi (for further discussion, see "Potato Gnocchi" on page 381).

Gnocchi may also be served with *Salsa di Pomodoro* (page 76), *Ragù di Carne* (page 77), *Pesto Genovese* (page 78), and *Burro Nocciola* (see *Strozzapreti*, page 122).

Ingredients

For the gnocchi:
1 kilogram (2¼ pounds or about 4 large) Idaho potatoes
Coarse salt and freshly ground pepper
1 large egg yolk
1 large egg
25 grams (5 tablespoons) grated Parmigiano-Reggiano or Grana Padano
Freshly grated nutmeg
250 grams (1¾ cups) all-purpose flour, plus extra for rolling, shaping, and dusting the sheet pan

For serving:
100 grams (7 tablespoons) unsalted butter
2 sprigs fresh thyme
2 sprigs fresh oregano
Coarse salt and freshly ground black pepper
50 to 75 grams (½ to ¾ cup) grated Parmigiano-Reggiano or Grana Padano

Make the gnocchi:

Preheat the oven to 177°C (350°F). Place the potatoes on a bed of coarse salt on a sheet pan or a baking dish and bake until tender, about 1 hour. Peel as soon as the potatoes are cool enough to handle. Force the cooked potato through a ricer, food mill, or fine-mesh sieve into a large bowl or onto a sheet pan.

Add the egg yolk, whole egg, grated cheese, salt, pepper, and nutmeg to taste, and mix well to blend. Mix in 90 grams (½ cup) of the flour, gently kneading until combined. Add additional flour as necessary to form a soft dough that is not too sticky. Test the dough by shaping a few gnocchi and cooking in boiling water; if the gnocchi fall apart, incorporate more flour. Be careful not to add too much flour, and do not overwork. (Err on the side of too little flour—you can always add more.)

Transfer the dough to a floured work surface. Cut off strips of dough about 1 inch wide, and roll into long, thin ropes (about the diameter of a small coin). Dust the ropes with flour and cut into 2-centimeter (¾-inch) pieces.

Roll the pieces gently between your palms to give them a rounded shape. Roll each piece across the back of a fork or a gnocchi board, pressing down gently with your thumb as you roll to make an indentation. Place the gnocchi on a parchment paper–lined sheet pan dusted with flour, and cover with a clean towel.

To serve:

Bring a large pot (*pentola*) of salted water to a boil.

Meanwhile, melt the butter in a large skillet (*padella*) over low heat. Add the herbs and cook gently to flavor the butter, 1 to 2 minutes, or until you can smell the fragrance of the herbs.

Working in batches, add the gnocchi to the boiling water. Once they have risen to the surface, cook

10 more seconds. Transfer with a spider (*ragno*) or slotted spoon to the skillet. Add 30 to 60 milliliters (2 to 4 tablespoons) cooking water to the pan, season to taste with salt and pepper and cook 1 minute, swirling the pan, to reduce and emulsify the sauce. Divide among plates, sprinkle with cheese, and serve.

Strozzapreti

Swiss-Chard-and-Bread Gnocchi

Serves 4

The literal translation of *strozzapreti* is "priest chokers." One legend tells of priests dropping by the homes of unlucky parishioners just in time for Sunday dinner. According to the story, the greedy priests gorged themselves on their hosts' food. The dumplings are made with milk-soaked bread and Swiss chard, and bound with eggs and cheese. Additional breadcrumbs are added as needed to create a dry but malleable dough. The *strozzapreti* are served with a brown butter sauce called *burro nocciola*.

Traditionally, *strozzapreti* were made from leftover bread—typically from a rustic Italian loaf made without salt. It's important that the bread be rough-textured; fine-textured bread will make gummy *strozzapreti*.

(See pages 384 and 378, respectively, for step-by-step instructions for "Shaping Gnocchi into *Quenelles*" and "Making a *Burro Nocciola* Emulsion.")

Ingredients

For the strozzapreti:

250 grams (3 cups loosely packed) cubed (3 centimeter / 1¾₁₆ inch) day-old Tuscan bread, crusts removed

500 milliliters (2 cups) milk

300 grams (8 cups) stemmed Swiss chard leaves

1 large egg

40 grams (½ cup) grated Parmigiano-Reggiano or Grana Padano

2 teaspoon finely chopped fresh thyme

Pinch of freshly grated nutmeg

Coarse salt and freshly ground black pepper

55 grams (½ cup) dried breadcrumbs, plus more as needed

For serving:

Coarse salt and freshly ground black pepper

100 grams (7 tablespoons) unsalted butter

5 sprigs fresh sage

20 grams (¼ cup) grated Parmigiano-Reggiano or Grana Padano

Make the *strozzapreti*:

Soak the bread cubes in the milk for 30 minutes to soften. Squeeze out excess milk and transfer the bread to a bowl.

Blanch (*sbianchire*) the chard in boiling salted water until almost tender, about 3 minutes. Refresh in ice water; drain, and squeeze by hand to extract as much moisture as possible. Then, wrap the chard in cheesecloth and twist to squeeze out as much moisture as possible. Coarsely chop by hand or in a food processor.

Add the chard to the bowl with the bread. Add the egg, cheese, thyme, and nutmeg and season to taste with salt and pepper. Add half of the breadcrumbs and work the mixture with your hands until completely combined. Transfer to a food processor and process until smooth. Check the consistency—the dough should be dry to the touch but still hold its shape. If very wet, add more breadcrumbs.

Cook a small ball of the mixture in boiling water to test consistency and seasoning. A fork should cut through the gnocchi easily, and it should not feel gummy in the mouth.

To serve:

Bring a large pot (*pentola*) of salted water to a boil. Using two spoons, shape the gnocchi mixture into 4-centimeter-long (1½-inch-long) *quenelles* (or roll between the palms of your hands to balls about 2½ centimeters / 1 inch in diameter). Working in batches, add the gnocchi to the boiling water and cook until firm, about 4 minutes.

Meanwhile, melt the butter in a skillet (*padella*). Add the sage and cook over medium heat until the butter turns a golden brown color and smells nutty (*nocciola*). When the gnocchi are cooked, transfer to the skillet with a spider (*ragno*). Add a few tablespoons of the gnocchi cooking water; swirl the pan to reduce and emulsify the sauce. Season to taste with salt and pepper, and toss with the grated cheese. Serve sprinkled with more cheese.

Gnocchi di Spinaci e Ricotta

Spinach-and-Ricotta Gnocchi

Serves 4 to 6

These classic gnocchi are a variation on potato gnocchi flavored with spinach and ricotta. They are light-textured, pleasing to the eye, and simple to make.

(See sidebar "Draining Ricotta" on page 68 for step-by-step instructions.)

Ingredients

For the gnocchi:

700 grams (3½ cups) stemmed fresh spinach

250 grams (1 cup) ricotta, hung overnight in cheesecloth to drain

100 grams (1 cup) grated Grana Padano or other similar hard cheese

150 grams (1¼ cups) all-purpose flour, plus extra for rolling, shaping, and dusting the sheet pan

2 large eggs

Freshly grated nutmeg

Coarse salt and freshly ground black pepper

For the sauce:

115 grams (½ cup) unsalted butter

1 clove garlic, thinly sliced

1 sprig fresh thyme

1 fresh bay leaf

1 sprig fresh Italian parsley

Coarse salt and freshly ground black pepper

For serving:

Coarse salt and freshly ground black pepper

Grated Grana Padano or other similar hard cheese, for sprinkling

Make the gnocchi dough:

Blanch (*sbianchire*) the spinach in boiling salted water until wilted. Refresh in ice water; drain. Place the spinach in cheesecloth and squeeze out as much water as possible. (You should have about 200 grams / 7 ounces drained spinach.) Chop as finely as possible.

Place the ricotta in a large bowl and beat until smooth. Add the spinach, Grana Padano, flour, eggs, and a generous amount of nutmeg. Season well with salt and black pepper and mix, making sure all ingredients are evenly blended. Cover and refrigerate at least 1 hour.

Shape the gnocchi:

Dust a work surface well with flour. Roll small spoonfuls of the chilled gnocchi mixture on the floured surface into balls the size of a whole nutmeg. Follow the instructions in the potato gnocchi recipe on page 121 to shape each ball on the teeth of a fork or on a gnocchi board into ridged gnocchi. The gnocchi may also be shaped into *quenelles* like *strozzapreti* (see page 122). Place on a floured baking sheet. Continue to shape all of the dough into gnocchi.

Make the sauce:

Heat the butter with the garlic in a wide skillet (*padella*) over medium-low heat and cook until the garlic is tender, 2 to 3 minutes. Add the herbs. Season to taste with salt and pepper. Cook for a few minutes, adding water if the butter gets too hot. Remove the herbs and the garlic. Remove the skillet from the heat and set aside.

To serve:

Bring a large pot (*pentola*) of salted water to a boil. Reduce the heat so that the water simmers gently. Working in batches, add the gnocchi to the simmering water and cook, turning occasionally, until they are tender, about 3 minutes.

Friuli–Venezia Giulia

"This invisible mark [the difference in microclimates] left by nature has promoted the entrenchment of two different cultures. The first is in the city, on the plains, where the Mediterranean climate dominates with its olive oils, pastas, a culture of wine and foods that is tied to the soil and to the water, to Venice, to its Latin roots. As soon as you are in the mountains, [there is] meat and butter, melted pork fat, coarse grains, the great Austro-Hungarian pastries, Ottoman influences, the Slavic world."

—Chef Alessandro Gavagna of Trattoria al Cacciatore de la Subida, Cormons

Friuli–Venezia Giulia is a narrow region on the northeast edge of Italy. It is bordered by Austria and Slovenia to the northeast and the Adriatic to the south. The northern part of the region is mountainous; the southern part is characterized by river plains and the seacoast (lagoons).

Friuli–Venezia Giulia joins two regions—Fruili and Venezia Giulia. Venezia Giulia was part of the Austrian Empire for several hundred years. As a result, the region maintains Austrian and Slavic influences, and the cuisine offers well-defined Venetian and Hungarian traditions. The region's capital, Trieste, is an important Mediterranean port; it belonged to Austria-Hungary until the end of World War I.

The major agricultural products of the region are cattle, pigs, and corn. Fishing is important on the Adriatic, and the region shares a tradition of seafood cuisine with the neighboring Veneto, including numerous shellfish dishes, and seafood soups called *brodetto*, and *zuppa di pesce*. The fishing port of Grado produces a fish chowder, *boreto alla graisana*, seasoned with vinegar.

The most famous product of the region, produced in the Friuli area, is Prosciutto di San Daniele. Goose *speck* (cured and smoked breast) and other cured goose products are also prominent here. According to Chef Gavagna, "In Friuli, the goose was the poor man's pig." Every part of the goose was used: consumed fresh, cured, or smoked.

Central European influences show themselves in dishes such as *gulasch* (Trieste), sauerkraut, and *rambasici* (stuffed cabbage). Other specialties are *cjalçons* (stuffed pastas, often with sweet-and-sour fillings) and *sivilots* (pasta tubes). Polenta has also been important here for centuries.

The area produces fruity white wines, such as Tocai Friulano and the rare and prized sweet wine Picolit, as well as grappa.

In Friuli–Venezia Giulia, *Polenta* (page 136) is often sliced and toasted (see "Polentas," page 137), then served with sausages, beans, and cheese.

Rewarm the sauce over medium-low heat.

Transfer the gnocchi with a slotted spoon or spider (*ragno*) to the skillet with the sauce. Add a little of the cooking water and swirl the pan to form a smooth, emulsified sauce. Season to taste with salt and pepper and serve sprinkled with grated cheese.

Chapter 7

Risotto and Polenta

Risotto alla Parmigiana (Parmesan Risotto)
Risotto con Funghi (Mushroom Risotto)
Risotto alla Milanese (Risotto with Saffron)
Farrotto Primavera (*Farro* with Spring Vegetables)
Polenta (Cornmeal Porridge)

Rice and polenta, in various guises, have been important staples for Italians, particularly the peasantry, for centuries. According to historians Alberto Capatti and Massimo Montanari (*Italian Cuisine: A Cultural History*), "Almost unknown to Greek and Roman writers, rice was introduced into the West by the Arabs, who began cultivating it in Sicily and Spain." Its cultivation and consumption became important in Italy during the fifteenth century, in the north. Originally a food of the elite, it soon became a necessary staple for the poor, and does not appear to have returned to the tables of the upper classes until the eighteenth century, when genteel preparations such as risotto came into fashion.

Risotto is a dish of cooked rice that originated in Piemonte and Lombardia, though now it has variations in almost every region of Italy. It is usually but not always served as a *primo* (*ossobuco* is famously accompanied by *risotto alla Milanese*). The characteristic texture of risotto—firm grains of short, thick rice bathed in a small amount of creamy liquid—owes its consistency to the unique properties of special varieties of Italian rice grown throughout much of the Po valley—Lombardia, Veneto, and Piemonte—in northern Italy. These short-grain varieties have a high amount of a soluble starch called amylopectin—a higher amount than many long-grain varieties—that, under the correct cooking conditions, slowly dissolves, thickening the surrounding liquid and binding the grains to one another. (See page 28 for a discussion of rice for risotto.)

Styles of risotto differ by region. The *risotti* of the Veneto are looser and more liquid, and are traditionally flavored with vegetables and seafood. The *risotti* of Piemonte, Lombardia, and Emilia-Romagna are more compact and less runny, and are flavored more aggressively with cheese, meat, sausage, game, and wild mushrooms. The difference in texture and consistency is a function of the use of different varieties of rice and/or the amount by which the stock is reduced around the rice.

Other grains, including wheat berries, barley, and *farro*, an ancestor of modern wheat (see page 29), may be prepared in a manner similar to risotto. *Farrotto Primavera* (page 134) is such a preparation, in which *farro* is cooked in hot broth in stages until the grain softens to al dente. Despite the similar cooking processes, *farrotto* is chewier than risotto because, unlike with rice, the chewy husk has not been removed.

Polenta commonly refers to coarse cornmeal cooked into a porridge with water and salt. A version of the dish dates back at least to Roman times, when it was

Risotto con Funghi (page 130)

called *puls* or *pulmentum*. Polenta has been an enormously important food because the Italian peasantry historically relied on it to stave off starvation. Before maize was widely cultivated in Italy during the second half of the sixteenth century, the porridge was prepared with other grains, including *farro*, emmer, spelt, millet, sorghum, panic grass, and buckwheat, as well as with chestnut flour. (Ironically, the enthusiasm with which the Italian peasantry took to maize as a staple had the consequence of producing significant outbreaks of the skin disease pellagra among populations that depended on it.) Polenta as we know it today first took root in the Veneto, and is still traditionally more associated with northern Italy.

Polenta is wonderfully versatile. It can be sauced and served as a *primo*, much like pasta. It is also the traditional accompaniment to stews of meat or fish. If the porridge is allowed to firm up, it may be sliced and cooked again as is traditional in the Veneto, where slices are grilled and served as an accompaniment to meats and stews. This twice-cooked polenta may also be roasted or fried and used like bruschetta or crostini.

Polenta may also be employed as an element of a secondary dish. Twice-baked polenta may be sliced and baked between layers of *Ragù di Carne* (page 77) or *Salsa di Pomodoro* (page 76), liberally sprinkled with a grated hard cheese such as Parmigiano-Reggiano or Grana Padano (page 22), or fried and sauced with *Fonduta* (page 40). In the Veneto it is also served for breakfast, cut up into hot sweetened milk.

Styles of polenta vary by region. The corn may be coarsely ground, as in the polenta of the Alpine valleys, or finely ground, as it is in central Italy. In Friuli and Veneto, a fine, white polenta is ground from white corn. The water content of the finished polenta also varies depending on the desired consistency. In Veneto and Puglia, for example, a looser, delicate, and creamy polenta is made with white cornmeal; in Lombardia, a

mixture of cornmeal and buckwheat (*polenta taragna*) constitutes a more hearty meal.

The yields for these risotto recipes assume that the dish is being served in small portions, as a *primo*, or, in the case of *Risotto alla Milanese* (page 132) and polenta (page 136), as an accompaniment to another dish.

Le Tecniche

In this chapter, students learn the fundamentals of cooking risotto, polenta, and *farrotto*, and continue to practice the skill of *saltare*. See pages 385–87 for a more complete discussion of these dishes.

Risotto alla Parmigiana

Parmesan Risotto

Serves 4

This simple, delicate risotto *in bianco* (with butter and cheese) from Emilia-Romagna demonstrates the basic risotto technique.

Ingredients

1½ liters (6⅓ cups) chicken stock

120 grams (8 tablespoons) unsalted butter

70 grams (⅔ cup) finely diced white onion

250 grams (1¼ cups) Carnaroli rice

Coarse salt and freshly ground black pepper

175 milliliters (¾ cup) dry white wine

70 grams (¾ cup) grated Parmigiano-Reggiano or Grana Padano

Flavoring Risotto

As much as possible, ingredients to flavor risotto should be added before the rice is added, or during cooking. This allows the rice to absorb the flavors as it swells. There are exceptions: foods that will overcook, such as green vegetables, or shellfish.

Chef's Note

Carnaroli rice is almost always used for risotto at The International Culinary Center. Regardless of the variety, rice for risotto should be stored in a sealed container in the refrigerator, or at room temperature.

Bring the chicken stock to a simmer in a saucepan; adjust the heat so that the stock remains at a bare simmer.

Heat 60 grams (4 tablespoons) of the butter in a heavy-bottomed saucepan over medium heat. Add the onion and cook until softened but not colored, about 2 minutes.

Add the rice, season to taste with salt, and cook, stirring, until the rice smells toasted and is hot to the touch. (Neither rice nor onion should take on any color.)

Add the wine and cook until evaporated.

Ladle in enough hot stock just to cover the rice and simmer at a lively pace, stirring constantly, until the stock evaporates to the point that when you pull the spoon

through the rice, the stock no longer pools in the gap.

Add more stock just to cover the rice, ladling the stock around the sides of the pan to wash any starch back into the risotto. Continue cooking, stirring, until the stock has evaporated to the same degree.

Add more stock and continue this process until the rice is tender but still resistant at the core, 14 to 17 minutes. Add another ladleful of stock and remove from the heat. Add the remaining 60 grams (4 tablespoons) butter, cut into pieces, and the grated cheese, and stir vigorously (*mantecare*) to emulsify. The mixture should be creamy, but not soupy; the rice should be suspended in a broth that is thick enough to hold the risotto in a cohesive mass when it is flipped. Season to taste with salt and pepper.

Risotto con Funghi

Mushroom Risotto

Serves 4

This dish originates in the mountain communities of Italy where mushrooms grow. It is finished with grated Pecorino Romano, a mountain cheese. The tomato provides a subtle background, highlighting the taste of the mushrooms without overpowering their flavor. The mushroom sauce is made separately and added to the risotto in stages, in combination with the vegetable broth, so that the rice absorbs the flavors of the mushroom sauce as the kernels swell.

This dish is flavored with a typically Italian herb called *nepitella*. *Nepitella* is difficult to come by in the United States; it is replaced with a combination of fresh oregano, marjoram, and parsley—a fair approximation of the herb's taste.

(For step-by-step instructions for soaking dried porcini mushrooms, see "Working with Dried Porcini Mushrooms" on page 354.)

Cleaning Mushrooms

Most commercially produced mushrooms are relatively free of dirt, and are easily cleaned by brushing with a damp towel. If, however, the mushrooms need a more aggressive cleaning (wild mushrooms will be full of dirt and sand), wash them very fast with the stem on just before use (the stem protects the mushroom from exposure to oxygen that blackens the flesh), and dry them carefully. Morel mushrooms, in particular, must be washed several times; their corrugated flesh hides grit and dirt. (Wash morels repeatedly in bowlfuls of water until the water is clean.)

Ingredients

For the mushroom sauce:

17 grams (½ ounce) dried porcini mushrooms, preferably imported

225 grams (½ pound) cremini mushrooms, cleaned, stems removed

225 grams (½ pound) shiitake mushrooms, cleaned, stems removed

115 grams (¼ pound) oyster mushrooms, cleaned, stems removed

60 milliliters (¼ cup) olive oil

20 grams (2½ tablespoons) chopped garlic

2½ grams (1 tablespoon) chopped fresh oregano leaves

2½ grams (1 tablespoon) chopped fresh marjoram leaves

6 grams (2 tablespoons) chopped fresh Italian parsley

Coarse salt and freshly ground black pepper

1 liter (4¼ cups) whole, canned Italian plum tomatoes with their juices, puréed through a food mill

For the risotto:

1½ liters (6⅓ cups) vegetable stock

80 grams (6 tablespoons) unsalted butter

85 grams (½ cup) finely diced white onion

270 grams (1½ cups) Carnaroli rice

Coarse salt and freshly ground black pepper

120 milliliters (½ cup) dry white wine

75 grams (¾ cup) grated Pecorino Romano

Make the mushroom sauce:

Soak, drain, and coarsely chop the dried porcini, reserving the soaking liquid. Strain the soaking liquid through cheesecloth or a coffee filter to remove grit and set aside.

Cut the cremini mushrooms into 3-millimeter (⅛-inch) slices; cut the shiitake and oyster mushrooms into 6-millimeter (¼-inch) slices.

Chef's Notes

When cooking mushrooms, use a spoon rather than tongs, as tongs are likely to break the mushrooms. Stir only occasionally to allow the mushrooms to caramelize on the bottom of the pan.

Taste the mushroom soaking liquid after straining. If it is very strong, use less in the recipe, making up the remainder in stock or water.

When all of the mushroom sauce has been added to the risotto, the chef rinses out the pan with a little stock or water and adds it to the risotto in order not to lose any of the sauce; this determination not to waste, but to use everything, is consistent with the values of Italian cuisine.

Combine the olive oil and garlic in a large skillet (*padella*) and cook over medium heat until the garlic is softened but not browned.

Add the herbs and cook 1 to 2 minutes.

Add the fresh mushrooms and porcini. Season to taste with salt and pepper. Stir to distribute the garlic so that it doesn't burn on the bottom of the pan. (See Chef's Notes.)

Cook, covering the pan for a few minutes if the mushrooms are dry, until the mushrooms are wilted, about 5 minutes. Taste for seasoning.

In a separate skillet, season the tomato purée with salt and pepper to taste and heat until simmering at the edges. Pour the purée into the pan with the mushroom mixture and cook 2 minutes to reduce. Taste for seasoning.

Add the reserved porcini soaking liquid (see Chef's Notes) and continue cooking until the flavor of the tomato has melded with the mushrooms, and the sauce is reduced and thickened, about 15 minutes. Keep warm.

Make the risotto:

Bring the stock to a simmer in a saucepan; adjust the heat so that the stock remains at a bare simmer.

Heat 30 grams (2 tablespoons) of the butter in a heavy-bottomed saucepan over medium heat. Add the onion and cook (*saltare*) until softened but not colored, about 2 minutes.

Add the rice, season to taste with salt, and cook, stirring, until the rice smells toasted and is hot to the touch. (Neither rice nor onion should take on any color.)

Add the wine and cook, stirring, to evaporate.

Add enough of the simmering stock to barely cover the rice, and about half of the mushroom sauce. Season to taste with salt and pepper and bring to a simmer. Simmer at a lively pace, stirring constantly, until the liquid evaporates enough so that it no longer pools in the gap when you pull the spoon through the rice.

Add more stock just to cover the rice, along with some of the remaining mushroom sauce. Simmer, stirring, until the liquid has evaporated to the same degree.

Add more stock to barely cover, along with more of the mushroom sauce, and continue this process until the rice is tender but still resistant at the core, 14 to 17 minutes. Add a final ladleful of stock (use it to rinse out the skillet that held the mushroom sauce—see Chef's Notes) and remove the risotto from the heat.

Add the remaining 50 grams (4 tablespoons) butter, and the grated cheese, and stir vigorously (*mantecare*) to emulsify the butter and cheese into the liquid. Season to taste with salt and pepper. Serve immediately.

Risotto alla Milanese

Risotto with Saffron

Serves 4

The addition of saffron lends a lovely golden-yellow hue to this risotto. Saffron was historically used as a yellow-orange dye. During the years 1572 through 1576, the Flemish glass painter Valerio da Profondavalle was reported to have used saffron in his pigments to make the stained-glass windows of the Duomo in Milan more vibrant. When he wed, his apprentice allegedly added saffron to his master's risotto as a joke. *Risotto alla Milanese* is a classic accompaniment to *Ossobuco* (page 189)—one of the rare examples in the Italian repertoire of a *primo* being served with a main course.

(See "To Prepare Marrow" on page 423 for step-by-step instructions.)

Ingredients

1½ liters (6⅓ cups) chicken stock
60 grams (4 tablespoons) unsalted butter
15 milliliters (1 tablespoon) olive oil
75 grams (½ cup plus 1 tablespoon) finely diced white onion
50 grams (1¾ ounces) bone marrow or 30 grams (1 ounce) pancetta, chopped (optional)
250 grams (1¼ cups) Carnaroli rice
Coarse salt and freshly ground black pepper
125 milliliters (½ cup) dry white wine
Pinch of saffron threads
25 grams (5 tablespoons) grated Parmigiano-Reggiano or Grana Padano

Bring the stock to a simmer in a saucepan (*casseruola*); adjust the heat so that the stock remains at a bare simmer.

Heat 30 grams (2 tablespoons) of the butter with the oil in a heavy-bottomed saucepan (*casseruola*) over medium heat. Add the onion and pancetta, if using, and cook until the onion is softened but not colored, about 2 minutes.

Add the rice, season to taste with salt, and cook, stirring, until it smells toasted and is hot to the touch. If using the marrow, add it 1 minute into the cooking of the rice.

Add the wine and cook until evaporated.

Add simmering stock just to cover the rice. Crumble in the saffron threads and simmer at a lively pace, stirring constantly, until the stock evaporates enough so that it no longer pools in the gap when you pull the spoon through the rice.

Add more stock, just to cover the rice. Continue cooking, stirring, until the stock has evaporated to the same degree.

Add more stock and continue this process until the rice is tender but still resistant at the core, 14 to 17 minutes. Add another ladleful of stock and remove from the heat.

Add the remaining 30 grams (2 tablespoons) butter, cut into pieces, and the grated cheese, and stir vigorously (*mantecare*) to emulsify. The mixture should be creamy, but not soupy. Season to taste with salt and pepper and serve immediately.

Lombardia (Lombardy)

"Lombardy underwent various invasions prior to the formation of the Italian Republic. French and Austro-Hungarian cuisine left an important mark on local gastronomic culture."

—Chef Claudio Sadler of Ristorante Sadler and Chic'n Quick, Milan

Lombardia is a large, landlocked region of northern Italy. It shares a border with Switzerland. The geography is varied: From the Alps, Lombardia stretches south to the Po River and into the fertile Pianura Padana (the Po River plain). Shared between Lombardia, Piemonte, the Veneto, and Emilia-Romagna, the plain is the center of Italy's rice industry. Eastern Lombardia is distinguished by a series of lakes (Lago di Maggiore, Lago di Garda, Lago di Como). The Apennines are to the west. Milan is the capital of the region.

As in the neighboring regions of Piemonte and Emilia-Romagna, rice and corn are extremely important crops. (*Vialone nano* rice—for *risotti*—is grown in the province of Mantua, in Lombardia.) Risotto and polenta are staples. Rice is cooked in innumerable ways throughout the region, including in the famous saffron-infused *risotto alla Milanese*, in *risotti* garnished with seafood from Lake Como, and in soups.

Cattle-breeding is an equally important industry, and Lombardia is a major producer of cheeses. The region produces a relatively small amount of olive oil, and so the cuisine is historically marked by the use of butter, cream, and lard, and is heavily based on beef and veal dishes, such as *ossobuco alla Milanese* and breaded *cotoletta alla Milanese*.

Lombardia's pork industry is responsible for a selection of cured products, such as salami, pancetta, and *cotechino*, but curing is not limited to pork. A famous goose salami is produced in the town of Mortara, in the region of Pavia, for example, and the Alpine province of Valtellina, near Switzerland, produces an air-dried beef called *bresaola*.

The lake area boasts dishes of freshwater fish, including lake shad, perch, pike, eel, and frog.

Pasta dishes are traditionally homemade (*pasta fresca*). Mantua is celebrated for its pumpkin ravioli (*tortelli di zucca*) and meat-stuffed *agnolini*. Valtellina makes a predominantly buckwheat pasta called *pizzoccheri*, traditionally prepared with savoy cabbage, potatoes, sage, butter, and the local cow's-milk cheese, *bitto*.

See our recipes for the regional specialties *Risotto alla Milanese* (facing page) and *Ossobuco alla Milanese* (page 189).

133

Farrotto Primavera

Farro with Spring Vegetables

Serves 6

Farrotto is a dish made with *farro* (page 29), cooked in the style of a risotto. This recipe celebrates the vegetables that appear in Italian markets in the springtime—asparagus, artichokes, peas, and spring garlic—but the cook may substitute whatever is in season. Longer-cooking vegetables go into the pot first, followed by those that cook more quickly. (Alternatively, with the exception of the artichoke hearts, the vegetables may be blanched individually and added at the end, once the *farro* is fully cooked.) If you have access to spring garlic, use it in place of the onion and garlic in this recipe.

(For step-by-step instructions for preparing spring garlic, artichokes, and asparagus, see pages 353 and 354.)

Chef's Note

Marjoram is added twice in this recipe, once early on and a second time late in the cooking. This method helps chefs to layer the flavor of the long-cooked and briefly cooked herb. (See also "*Soffritto*" on page 362 for a discussion of building layers of flavor with herbs.)

Ingredients

2 artichokes
½ lemon
225 grams (about ½ pound) asparagus
2 liters (8½ cups) vegetable stock
Coarse salt and freshly ground black pepper
1 teaspoon olive oil
40 grams (¼ cup) chopped red onion
5 grams (½ tablespoon) coarsely chopped garlic
225 grams (1¼ cups) farro
10 grams (1 tablespon) chopped fresh marjoram leaves
140 grams (1 cup) fresh or frozen peas
40 grams (3 tablespoons) unsalted butter
40 grams (¼ cup) grated Parmigiano-Reggiano or Grana
　　Padano
6 grams (2 tablespoons) chopped fresh Italian parsley

Trim the artichokes and their stems, rubbing cut parts with the lemon to prevent blackening. Cut off the stems and slice on the bias, about 3 millimeters (⅛ inch) thick. Halve the hearts and thinly slice crosswise. Place in acidulated water until ready to cook.

Snap off the tips of the asparagus; reserve. Peel the stalks, if woody, and cut off the tips. Cut the stalks on an angle into 3-centimeter (1-inch) pieces; set the stalks and tips aside separately.

Wash the reserved asparagus ends well, then soak them in a bowl of water to rid them of any soil; drain. Place in a large saucepan (*casseruola*) along with the stock. Season to taste with salt and pepper. Bring to a simmer and cook 30 minutes. Strain, reserving the stock. Discard the asparagus ends. Return the stock to a low simmer.

Combine the oil, onion, and garlic in a heavy-bottomed saucepan. Place over medium heat and sauté 2 minutes, until the onion is softened but not colored.

Add the *farro*, season to taste with salt, and cook, stirring, until the grain is hot to the touch, about 2 minutes.

Add enough simmering stock just to cover the *farro* and simmer at a lively pace, 15 minutes, stirring occasionally.

Add the sliced artichokes and cook 5 minutes. Season to taste with salt and pepper. Add more simmering stock, just to cover the grains (about 250 milliliters / 1 cup), half of the marjoram, and the asparagus stalks. Cook, stirring occasionally, until the stock has reduced to the degree that it no longer pools in the gap when you pull the spoon through the grain.

Add more stock just to cover, and continue this process, reducing and adding more stock, until the *farro* is tender and retains a slight bite, 8 to 10 more minutes. Taste for seasoning halfway through the cooking.

Add the peas, asparagus tips, and the rest of the marjoram. Season to taste with salt and pepper. Add another ladleful of stock and remove from the heat. Taste again for seasoning.

Cut the butter into pieces and add to the *farro*, along with the grated cheese and parsley. Stir vigorously (*mantecare*) to emulsify the fat into the liquid. Serve hot.

Polenta

Cornmeal Porridge

Serves 8

Soft, or boiled, polenta is traditionally served as a *contorno* with stews and braises such as *cacciatore*, which agreeably soak into the grain. It may also be sauced and served as a *primo*, or twice-cooked—

sautéed, fried, grilled, roasted, or baked—and served in a variety of presentations. Grilled, it is a classic accompaniment to *Baccalà Mantecato* (page 226).

Ingredients

2½ liters (10½ cups) cold water
30 milliliters (2 tablespoons) olive oil
10 grams (1¾ teaspoons) coarse salt
300 grams (2½ cups) polenta

Polentas

Twice-Cooked Polenta

Once cooked, the soft polenta is scraped into an oiled container—a loaf pan for wider slices, a sheet pan for cutting other shapes—and the top is lightly oiled to prevent a crust from forming. The polenta is covered with plastic wrap and refrigerated. Once the polenta firms up, it may be sliced or cut into shapes (see "Shaping and Cutting Polenta" on page 387) and fried, roasted, or grilled, then sauced.

Fried Polenta

Cut polenta into thin (6-millimeter / ¼-inch) pieces, about 5 by 5 centimeters (2 by 2 inches) square. Sauté (*saltare*) in grapeseed oil until golden brown and crisp. Sprinkle with salt to taste and serve as crostini.

Roasted Polenta

Slice polenta 1 centimeter (⅜ inch) thick, turn onto an oiled sizzle platter or a small baking sheet or dish, oil both sides, and season to taste with salt and pepper. Roast (*arrostire*) at 232°C (450°F) until golden.

Polenta with Tomato and Cheese

Slice polenta into thin (1-centimeter / ½-inch) pieces, 5 by 12 centimeters (2 by 5 inches) large.

Spread *Salsa di Pomodoro* (page 76) on an oiled sizzle platter or small baking sheet or dish. Arrange 2 slices of polenta side by side on top; spread with tomato sauce and sprinkle with grated Parmigiano-Reggiano or Grana Padano. Set 2 more slices on top at a 90-degree angle; spread with tomato sauce and sprinkle with cheese. Bake (*cuocere in forno*) in a 191°C (375°F) oven until the polenta is warmed through and the cheese is melted. Cut into pieces and serve.

Variation: A similar dish is prepared using *Ragù di Carne* (page 77) in place of tomato sauce, and layered with *Besciamella* (page 79), as for a lasagne.

Grilled Polenta

A specialty of the Veneto, grilled polenta is traditionally served with meats and stews. Cut polenta into squares, rounds, or triangles, as desired, about 1 centimeter (⅜ inch) thick (see "Shaping and Cutting Polenta" on page 387), and cook (*grigliare*) on a hot grill until golden brown on both sides. Sprinkle with salt to taste and serve hot. (Or spread soft polenta in a buttered baking dish or sheet pan to a thickness of about 1¼ centimeter / ½ inch and let cool. Cut into whatever shape desired, and grill.)

Combine the water, olive oil, salt, and polenta in a saucepan (*casseruola*) and bring to a simmer over medium heat, whisking often. When the water comes to a simmer, the polenta will thicken.

Turn the heat down and cook slowly, stirring often with a wooden spoon, until the polenta pulls away from the sides of the pan and the texture is silky, about 45 minutes. (Be careful not to burn yourself; the polenta sputters in the pan and it is very hot.)

Serve hot.

Chapter 8

Eggs:
Uova

Uova alla Fiorentina (Eggs with Spinach)
Insalata di Uova e Carne Secca del Pontormo
　　(Scrambled Eggs with Mesclun and Pancetta)
Uova Fritte con Asparagi
　　(Asparagus with Parmesan and Fried Eggs)
Frittata di Cipolle (Onion Frittata)

Eggs have enjoyed a prominent place in Italian cuisine for centuries. Pellegrino Artusi, in his famous 1891 cookbook for middle-class cooks and housewives, *La Scienza in Cucina e L'Arte di Mangiar Bene*, extolled the value of their nutrition: "Eggs come immediately after meat at the top of the scale of nutritional value." Mr. Artusi goes on to recommend: "Spring is the season in which eggs taste best. Fresh eggs are given to birthing mothers to drink, and are also considered a good food for newlyweds."

Nor, seemingly, have modes of preparation changed dramatically. As noted in Capatti and Montanari's *Italian Cuisine: A Cultural History*, five hundred years before Artusi, the anonymous author of the fourteenth-century Tuscan cookbook *Libro della Cucina* writes, "There is so much known about fried, roasted, and scrambled eggs that it is not necessary to speak about them." In his multivolume *Opera*, published in 1570, the Renaissance chef Bartolomeo Scappi also includes recipes for eggs to be fried as well as baked; deviled, in which the eggs are hard-boiled and stuffed with the yolks mixed with sugar, raisins, herbs, and spices;

cooked into omelets; and poached in water, goat's or cow's milk, or melted sugar. (It is only the liberal use of sugar, cinnamon, and spices that places these recipes in Renaissance cuisine.)

Egg dishes were traditionally served as *antipasti* or *primi*, or as a light meal. In contemporary Italian culture, egg dishes such as those presented in this chapter—scrambled (*strapazzate*), baked (*al forno*) on a bed of spinach, fried (*fritte*) and paired with sautéed asparagus, or cooked in *frittate*—might also be served at lunch. *Frittate* are often eaten in the summertime at picnics or for snacks (which Italians call *merenda*). As in other parts of Europe, hard-cooked eggs (*uova sode*) usually constitute breakfast food. In Calabria, however, hard-boiled eggs are passed through a sieve, flavored with cinnamon and cocoa, dipped in whipped egg whites, fried, then served as a *dolce* called *uova alla monacella*.

Le Tecniche

In this chapter, students learn techniques for baking (*cuocere al forno*), scrambling (*strapazzate*) and frying (*fritte*) eggs, and preparing *frittate* while they continue to practice skills of *sbianchire* and *saltare*. For further discussion of eggs, see pages 388–89.

Frittata di Cipolle (page 143)

Uova alla Fiorentina

Eggs with Spinach

Serves 4

Spinach sautéed in garlic and olive oil serves as a bed for eggs baked under a blanket of *besciamella*, yolks exposed, with a crusting of Parmigiano-Reggiano. This dish may also be baked in individual gratin dishes.

Ingredients

15 grams (1 tablespoon) unsalted butter, plus extra for the gratin dish
40 milliliters (2½ tablespoons) olive oil
1 clove garlic, sliced
450 grams (1 pound) stemmed spinach
Coarse salt and freshly ground black pepper
4 large eggs
1 recipe Besciamella (page 79)
40 grams (¼ cup) grated Parmigiano-Reggiano or Grana Padano

Preheat the oven to 191°C (375°F). Butter a gratin dish large enough to hold the eggs in a single layer.

Cook the spinach: Place the oil and the garlic in a large, shallow pan, such as a rondeau (*casseruola*), and set over medium heat. Cook until the garlic begins to turn golden but not brown, 1 to 2 minutes.

Add the spinach (this may need to be done in batches) and cook, uncovered, until wilted but not colored, 3 to 5 minutes. Season to taste with salt and pepper.

Assemble and bake the dish: Spread the spinach over the bottom of the gratin dish. Break the eggs on top of the spinach in a single layer; season to taste with salt and pepper. Spoon *besciamella* on top, covering the spinach and egg whites but leaving the yolks uncovered. (You may not need all of the *besciamella*.)

Sprinkle all over (except the yolks) with the grated cheese and bake until the egg whites are set, the yolks are hot but still liquid, and the cheese is lightly browned, about 8 minutes.

technique for scrambling eggs.) These are cooked over relatively low heat in order not to toughen them.

Ingredients

60 milliliters (¼ cup) olive oil
100 grams (3½ ounces) diced pancetta
6 grams (1 tablespoon) chopped fresh Italian parsley
6 grams (1 tablespoon) chopped fresh marjoram
6 grams (1 tablespoon) chopped fresh thyme
15 milliliters (1 tablespoon) red wine vinegar
15 milliliters (1 tablespoon) aceto balsamico di Modena
Coarse salt and freshly ground black pepper
8 large eggs
120 grams (4 cups) mesclun or other soft lettuces, cleaned, and
   cut into 2-centimeter (¾-inch) strips

Insalata di Uova e Carne Secca del Pontormo

Scrambled Eggs with Mesclun and Pancetta

Serves 4

This warm salad of eggs scrambled with pancetta and tossed with soft lettuces, herbs, and vinegar was reputed to have been one of the favorite dishes of Pontormo, a sixteenth-century Florentine painter. Dean Cesare Casella was inspired to create this version after reading about the painter in a historical cookbook.

The salad requires no fat beyond that rendered by the pancetta and the oil used to cook the eggs; the red wine and balsamic vinegars, in combination with the rendered fat, create the dressing.

For this recipe, the eggs are not whisked before cooking. The goal is to retain the distinct colors and textures of the yolks and whites. (Note that this is not a traditional

Place the oil, pancetta, and herbs in a large skillet (*padella*) over medium-low heat. Cook until some of the fat is rendered from the pancetta but not browned, 5 to 7 minutes.

For the dressing, pour off most of the fat from the skillet into a bowl, leaving just enough to coat the bottom of the pan. Set the skillet aside. Drizzle the red wine and balsamic vinegars into the warm fat while whisking. Season to taste with salt and pepper; set aside.

Crack the eggs into a bowl; do not whisk. Pour the eggs into the skillet and cook over medium-low heat, stirring with a rubber spatula, until the eggs are lightly scrambled and still very soft, 1 to 2 minutes. Season to taste with salt and pepper. Remove the pan from the heat as necessary to keep the eggs from overcooking.

In a bowl, toss the lettuce with a drizzle of the warm dressing. Toss the eggs and the pancetta with a drizzle of the dressing, and taste for seasoning.

To serve, divide the dressed lettuce between four plates. Top with the hot scrambled eggs and serve immediately.

Chef's Note

The eggs may be served on a rustic style of toasted, crusty bread, such as *fettunta*, or with croutons, adding a pleasant crunch to the dish.

Ingredients

350 grams (¾ pound, or about 12 stalks) medium asparagus,
   tough ends snapped, and stalks peeled if woody
Coarse salt and freshly ground black pepper
8 milliliters (1½ teaspoons) red wine vinegar
60 grams (¼ cup) unsalted butter
4 large eggs
20 grams (¼ cup) grated Parmigiano-Reggiano or Grana
   Padano

Tie the asparagus into a bundle with kitchen twine.

Bring a pot of salted water to a boil, add the vinegar and asparagus and simmer (*sbianchire*) until the flesh of the asparagus gives when the stems are pressed between thumb and forefinger, 3 to 4 minutes.

Refresh the asparagus in ice water. Remove and discard the kitchen twine. Pat the asparagus dry.

Preheat the broiler.

Heat the butter in a skillet over low heat. Add the asparagus and season to taste with salt and pepper. Cook (*saltare*) without browning 2 minutes, to warm through.

Raise the heat to medium. Break the eggs into the pan, easing them between the asparagus stalks; sprinkle the eggs with salt and pepper to taste. Cook until the whites are set but the yolks are still runny, 2 to 3 minutes.

With a spatula, slide the eggs and asparagus out onto a heatproof plate or platter, sprinkle with the grated cheese, and heat under the broiler just until the cheese is melted.

Chef's Notes

The asparagus stalks are tied into bundles to protect the tips from breaking. They are blanched in acidulated water to enhance their flavor, and refreshed in cold water to hold their color.

This dish may also be baked: Cook the asparagus in butter as above, then transfer to a buttered baking dish. Break the eggs over the asparagus, sprinkle with salt and pepper to taste, and bake at 191°C (375°F) to set the whites, 5 to 7 minutes. Sprinkle with the cheese, return to the oven, and bake just until the cheese is melted.

Save the asparagus cooking water for use in soups or *risotti* that contain asparagus.

Uova Fritte con Asparagi

Asparagus with Parmesan and Fried Eggs

Serves 2

This delicate *primo piatto* combines sautéed asparagus and fried eggs. The dish is browned under the broiler with a dusting of grated Parmigiano-Reggiano or Grana Padano.

(See page 354 for step-by-step instructions for preparing asparagus for cooking.)

Making Clarified Butter

Clarified butter is butter that has been very slowly melted, allowing most of the water to evaporate and the milk solids to separate and settle in the bottom of the pan. The liquid is then carefully poured off the solids. The resultant clear, yellow liquid has a lighter flavor and much higher smoke point than pure butter, and can be used for frying and sautéing. To make clarified butter:

Place the butter in a small saucepan over low heat.

Bring the butter to a gentle simmer, skimming off the foam (milk solids) that rises to the surface. Simmer over low heat until the water evaporates, the milk solids settle to the bottom of the pan, and the butter is clear, 5 to 10 minutes. Be careful not to brown the solids at the bottom of the pan. (If the solids begin to brown, remove the pan immediately from the heat.)

Set the pan aside, off the heat, for 5 minutes, skimming any remaining foam off the top.

Strain the clear yellow butter through a chinois lined with cheesecloth, leaving the milk solids on the bottom of the pan.

Frittata di Cipolle

Onion Frittata

Serves 4

A frittata is something like an open-faced omelet; a thin round of egg is cooked in butter or oil until the egg is softly set but not runny, and the top of the frittata is nicely browned. *Frittate* are tremendously versatile: They are flavored with herbs and bolstered with cooked vegetables, cheese, meats, seafood, and pasta, any of which may be stirred into the beaten raw egg before the frittata is cooked. *Frittate* are cooked over medium-low heat to prevent the eggs from toughening.

Chefs differ as to the ultimate cooking technique, but all *frittate* are started, at least, in a skillet on top of the stove; once the egg is set, the frittata may be finished in an oven or under a broiler, or flipped and finished on top of the stove, as in this recipe. At The International Culinary Center, *frittate* are cooked entirely on top of the stove; Dean Casella finds that the stovetop encourages an even, golden color.

Frittate are served hot, warm, or at room temperature as an antipasto or a light meal.

(See "Making Clarified Butter" at left, and step-by-step photos for making *frittate* on page 389.)

Ingredients

350 grams (2 cups) thinly sliced red onion
15 grams (1¼ tablespoons) sliced garlic
80 milliliters (⅓ cup) olive oil
Coarse salt
Pinch of red pepper flakes
½ tablespoon chopped fresh thyme leaves
60 milliliters (¼ cup) white wine
6 large eggs
30 grams (6 tablespoons) grated Parmigiano-Reggiano or Grana Padano
2 teaspoons chopped fresh marjoram
30 milliliters (2 tablespoons) clarified butter

Combine the onion, garlic, olive oil, and salt to taste in a skillet (*padella*). Place over medium-low heat and cook until the onions start to wilt, about 2 minutes.

Add the red pepper flakes and the thyme. Cover and cook until the onions begin to brown, about 10 minutes.

Deglaze (*deglassare*) the pan with the wine. Uncover and continue to cook until the onions are softened but not mushy, about 20 minutes.

Drain the onions in a fine-mesh strainer (*colino*) and let cool.

Beat the eggs with a fork in a large bowl just until the yolks and whites are combined. Add the grated cheese, marjoram, and onion.

Heat the butter in a 20-centimeter (8-inch) nonstick skillet over medium-low heat. Add the egg mixture and cook, using a rubber spatula to push the sides of the firming egg in toward the center, until the bottom of the frittata begins to set, 1 to 2 minutes.

Let the frittata cook without moving until the bottom is golden brown and the center is set but just a little wobbly, 5 to 7 minutes.

Give the pan a sharp jerk away from you so that the frittata flips in the air. (Practice makes perfect with this.) Return to the heat and cook to brown the other side, about 2 minutes.

Turn the frittata out onto a plate. Cut into wedges and serve hot or at room temperature.

Chapter 9

Breads and Flatbreads:
Pizze, Calzone, Focacce, e Grissini

Pasta per la Pizza (Pizza Dough)
Pizza Margherita
    (Pizza with Tomato, Mozzarella, and Basil)
Pizza Bianca con Rucola
    (White Pizza with Arugula)
Calzone con Verdure Miste
    (Stuffed Pizza with Mixed Vegetables)
Focaccia (Focaccia)
Grissini (Breadsticks)

Wheat in the form of bread has been a staple of Italian culture for centuries. Existing artifacts suggest that some form of flatbread was made as early as the Neolithic period; primitive versions were made from ground wheat, kneaded into rough flatbreads or loaves and cooked on hot stones (Serventi and Sabban, *Pasta: The Story of a Universal Food*). Further historical evidence suggests that the origins of flatbreads in Italy may be credited to the Etruscans, ancient Greeks, or both. Some time later, the Romans appear to have cooked a flatbread called *panis focacius* in the ashes of their cooking fires, and the modern Italian word *focaccia* is derived from the Latin word for hearth (*focus*).

In this chapter, students are introduced to methods for making some of the more common descendants of these early flatbreads, all leavened with yeast.

Although some of these breads might be made by home cooks in Italian homes, most are purchased at *panifici*, *pizzerie*, or other food markets. Pizza and focaccia have traditionally been sold as street food and eaten out of hand. They are customarily cooked in wood-fired ovens.

Pizza, Focaccia, and Calzone

Pizza, focaccia, and calzone represent the triumph of imagination over scarcity: Inexpensive and practical, they require only wheat, water, and heat, and can be embellished with whatever ingredients may be available.

Pizza is a thin, flat round of yeast dough covered with a variety of toppings and baked. Pizzas are eaten in Italy as a snack or as a light meal. Tradition suggests that pizza as we know it originated on the streets of Naples sometime after the tomato was accepted into use in Italy. (Campania was the first region in Italy to use tomatoes and the region's volcanic soil proved to be an excellent medium for growing varieties such as the DOP-rated San Marzano tomato.) Before then, pizza would have been a simple flatbread seasoned with salt and oil. Pizza is now made throughout Italy—styles differing by region—and throughout the world.

Calzone are half-moons of doubled, thinly rolled yeast dough, stuffed with cheeses, meats, and/or vegetables. Tomatoes are a relatively recent addition; calzone were made without them up until the 1940s (Accademia Italiana della Cucina, *La Cucina: The Regional Cooking of Italy*).

Pizza Margherita (page 147)

Focaccia is somewhat thicker and chewier than pizza, rich with oil and usually baked into a rectangular shape. Depending on preference, it may be thicker or thinner, and the name changes with the region: In Florence, where flatbreads are very popular, the dough is seasoned with olive oil, rosemary, and sea salt, and the local name is *schiacciata*. Liguria is famous for its *focaccia Genovese*. Focaccia is eaten as an antipasto or out of hand as a snack.

Le Tecniche

In this chapter, students learn the fundamentals of making, shaping, and baking yeast doughs. The recipes are written to be prepared by hand as they are taught at the school, but all of the yeast doughs may also be made in a standing mixer fitted with a dough hook. Recipes for breads only include directions for baking in a static oven, but a convection oven may be used equally well. See "*Forno a convezione*" on page 346 for directions on how to calculate correct baking temperatures in a convection oven. For a more complete discussion of working with yeast doughs, see pages 390–95.

Pasta per la Pizza

Pizza Dough

Makes about 1 kilogram (2¼ pounds) dough (for 6 individual pizzas)

Every pizza chef has his or her own way of making pizza dough. Some methods are complex, using a variety of ingredients such as honey and wine, or a starter, to develop flavor and produce a particular texture (such as crisp, thick, or bready).

This is a relatively simple dough. A combination of flour, yeast, water, sugar, and oil, it produces a crisp crust of medium thickness. The use of pizza flour pro-

duces a delicate crust with a little chew and a crunchy texture, while the oil adds suppleness.

Ingredients

550 grams (4½ cups) Italian pizza flour, or equal parts all-purpose and bread flours, plus more as needed for bench flour

7 grams (2¼ teaspoons / 1 packet) active dry yeast

340 milliliters (1¼ cups plus 1½ tablespoons) warm water

¾ teaspoon sugar

25 milliliters (1 tablespoon plus 2 teaspoons) olive oil, plus extra for oiling the bowl and dough

¾ teaspoon coarse salt

Set a bowl of bench flour to the side of a work surface. Combine all of the ingredients in a large bowl and mix by hand until the dough comes together. Sprinkle with flour if the dough is sticky.

Knead until the dough is smooth, velvety, and elastic, about 5 minutes.

Transfer to a lightly oiled bowl, then oil the top of the dough to prevent a crust from forming. Cover with plastic wrap.

Let the dough rise until doubled in volume, a minimum of 3 hours at room temperature, or overnight in the refrigerator.

Divide the dough into six 150-gram (5-ounce) pieces. Form each piece into a ball and place on a parchment paper–lined sheet pan dusted with flour. Cover loosely with plastic wrap; let rest until almost doubled in volume, about 1 hour, depending on the temperature of the kitchen.

Chef's Notes

At The International Culinary Center, the dough is made the day before shaping and baking. Overnight refrigeration slows down fermentation and helps develop more flavor in the dough.

In a home setting, shape, top, and bake one ball of pizza dough at a time. Cover the remaining balls with a towel while you work.

Pizza Flour

The best flour for pizza has a relatively high protein content of 11 to 12 percent. Italian pizza makers use a *tipo "00"* (finely milled) flour with a suitable protein content. Sometimes they mix in a little higher-protein flour. This flour creates a dough that is soft and extensible and can easily be stretched very thin, in the style of Neapolitan pizza. The resulting crust is thin and delicate; the texture is a little chewy, but still crisp, and crunchy. Italian pizza flour is used at The International Culinary Center, but, to mimic this flour, bread flour may be blended with all-purpose flour in equal weights.

Variations

Marinara Sauce: To the cooked *salsa di pomodoro*, add chopped fresh rosemary and dried oregano.

In lieu of using the *salsa di pomodoro*, hand-crush drained, whole, canned Italian plum tomatoes onto the flattened dough, season to taste with salt and pepper, drizzle with olive oil, mozzarella, and basil, and continue with the procedure.

Pizza Margherita

Pizza with Tomato, Mozzarella, and Basil

Makes 6 individual pizzas

This classic pizza was named after Queen Margherita of Italy (1851–1926) in honor of her visit to Naples. The red, white, and green of the tomato, cheese, and basil symbolize the colors of the Italian flag. It is topped with a barely cooked tomato sauce, sliced mozzarella, and basil leaves.

Ingredients

For the salsa di pomodoro:
1 liter (4¼ cups) whole, canned Italian plum tomatoes with their juices, puréed through a food mill
10 grams (1 tablespoon plus ¼ teaspoon) finely chopped garlic
Coarse salt and freshly ground black pepper

Cornmeal or semolina, for dusting
1 recipe Pizza Dough (facing page), shaped into six 150-gram (about ¾-cup) balls and allowed to rise until almost doubled in bulk
150 grams (5 ounces) fresh mozzarella, thinly sliced
Fresh basil leaves
Coarse salt and freshly ground black pepper
Olive oil

Make the *salsa di pomodoro*:

Combine the tomato purée, garlic, and salt and pepper to taste in a saucepan (*casseruola*).

Bring to a simmer and cook (*sobbollire*) to reduce 5 minutes. Season to taste with salt and pepper.

Assemble and bake the pizza:

Preheat the oven to 260°C (500°F). Center a rack in the oven and preheat the pizza stone.

On a lightly floured work surface, using a rolling pin, roll a ball of dough into a thin round about 26 centimeters (10 inches) in diameter, or stretch the ball to a round over your knuckles. (Cover the remaining dough balls with a towel while you work.) The edges of the dough should be slightly thicker than the center, to better contain the toppings. Transfer the round to a wooden pizza paddle dusted with cornmeal or semolina.

Spread with a thin layer of *salsa di pomodoro* to within about 1 centimeter (½ inch) of the border.

Cover with the mozzarella and scatter basil leaves on top (the basil may also be placed under the cheese to prevent it from burning). Season to taste with salt and pepper and drizzle with olive oil.

Transfer to the hot pizza stone and bake (*cuocere in forno*) until the crust is crisp, about 5 minutes. Serve drizzled with olive oil.

Repeat with each of the remaining dough balls.

Pizza Bianca con Rucola

White Pizza with Arugula

Makes 6 individual pizzas

Pizza bianca signifies a pizza that is made with no tomato; in this case, the pizza is topped with ricotta and arugula.

(See sidebar "Draining Ricotta" on page 68 for step-by-step instructions.)

Ingredients

Cornmeal or semolina, for dusting

1 recipe Pizza Dough (page 146), shaped into six 150-gram (about ¾-cup) balls and allowed to rise until almost doubled in bulk

350 grams (1½ cups) ricotta, hung overnight in cheesecloth to drain

Coarse salt and freshly ground black pepper

Olive oil

Arugula

Preheat the oven to 260°C (500°F). Center a rack in the oven and preheat the pizza stone.

On a lightly floured work surface, using a rolling pin, roll a ball of dough into a thin round about 26 centimeters (10 inches) in diameter, or stretch the ball to a round over your knuckles. (Cover the remaining dough balls with a towel while you work.) The edges of the dough should be slightly thicker than the center, to better contain the toppings. Transfer the round to a wooden pizza paddle dusted with cornmeal or semolina.

Smear the dough round with 50 to 60 grams (about 3 tablespoons) ricotta, season to taste with salt and pepper, and drizzle with oil.

Transfer to the hot pizza stone and bake (*cuocere in forno*) until the crust is crisp, about 5 minutes. Brush the edge with olive oil. Scatter arugula on top and serve drizzled with olive oil.

Repeat with each of the remaining dough balls.

Calzone con Verdure Miste

Stuffed Pizza with Mixed Vegetables

Makes 4

Calzone are pizzas that have been folded into a half-moon shape to enclose the topping mixture. Here, the filling consists of roasted vegetables, sautéed pork sausage, mozzarella, and Parmigiano-Reggiano.

(To peel asparagus, see page 354.)

Ingredients

For the filling:

125 grams (5 ounces) unpeeled eggplant

55 grams (2 ounces) yellow bell pepper

65 grams (2½ ounces) red bell pepper

75 grams (3 ounces) zucchini

50 grams (2 ounces) asparagus, tough ends snapped, and stalks peeled, if woody

140 grams (¾ cup) red onion

1 large (65 grams / 2½ ounces) plum tomato

2½ grams (2½ teaspoons) chopped fresh thyme

70 milliliters (5 tablespoons) olive oil

Coarse salt and freshly ground black pepper

450 grams (1 pound) pork sausage meat, such as sweet Italian sausage

1 recipe Pizza Dough (page 146), shaped into four 180-gram (generous ¾-cup) balls and allowed to rise until almost doubled in bulk

without quartering. Slice the onion into rings. Cut the tomato into thin wedges.

In a large bowl, toss all of the vegetables with the thyme, 40 milliliters (3 tablespoons) of the oil, and salt and pepper to taste. Transfer to a sheet pan and roast until the vegetables are softened and caramelized, 15 to 20 minutes. Transfer the vegetables to a bowl. Leave the oven on.

In a skillet (*padella*), cook the sausage in the remaining 30 milliliters (2 tablespoons) oil over medium heat, breaking it up into very small pieces with a spoon, until the fat is rendered and the sausage is cooked through, 7 to 10 minutes. Drain the fat; discard. Add the sausage to the bowl with the vegetables and stir to combine.

Assemble and bake the calzone:

Place a pizza stone in the oven to preheat.

On a lightly floured work surface, stretch one of the dough balls over your knuckles to a thin round slightly larger than for an individual pizza, or roll with a rolling pin. Transfer to a wooden pizza paddle dusted with cornmeal or semolina.

Place about 50 grams (⅓ cup) of the vegetable mixture on the bottom half of the dough round, leaving a border around the edge. Sprinkle with 50 grams (⅓ cup) of the mozzarella and 10 grams (2 tablespoons) of the Parmigiano or Grana. Drizzle with olive oil.

Brush the bottom edge of the dough round with some of the egg wash. Fold the top half over the filling and crimp the edges to seal. Prick the top of the calzone to allow steam to escape. Brush the top of the calzone with some of the egg wash or olive oil, and sprinkle with salt. Transfer to the hot pizza stone and bake (*cuocere in forno*) until the crust is crisp and well browned, 10 to 11 minutes.

Cornmeal or semolina, for dusting
200 grams (1⅔ cups) shredded mozzarella
40 grams (¼ cup) grated Parmigiano-Reggiano or Grana
    Padano
Olive oil
1 large egg, beaten, for egg wash
Coarse salt

Make the filling:

Preheat the oven to 232°C (450°F). Center a rack in the oven.

Cut the eggplant, peppers, and zucchini into sticks about 1 by 8 centimeters (1 by 3 inches); set aside.

Cut the asparagus: If the stalks are thick, quarter them lengthwise and cut into lengths the same size as the other vegetables; if the stalks are thin, cut into lengths

Variation

Break an egg on top of the filling; fold and seal the calzone, and bake as in the instructions.

Focaccia

Focaccia

> Makes one bread, the size of a half sheet pan or a 43-by-30½-centimeter (17-by-12-inch) rimmed baking sheet

Focaccia is a soft flatbread, usually baked in a rectangular shape. At its simplest, focaccia is brushed with oil and sprinkled with coarse salt, although it is not unusual to find it topped with herbs, cheese, and/or vegetables. The topping is typically lighter than for pizza.

Although focaccia may be made with a pizza dough, focaccia dough usually contains a higher volume of olive oil, producing a crisp but moist textured bread with a rich olive-oil taste. Focaccia dough is dimpled with the fingertips before baking to create the signature crevices that collect oil or bits of topping.

Ingredients

550 grams (4½ cups) all-purpose flour

10 grams (1¾ teaspoons) coarse salt

7 grams (2¼ teaspoons / 1 packet) active dry yeast

300 milliliters (1¼ cups) warm water

3 grams (¾ teaspoon) sugar

150 milliliters (⅔ cup) olive oil, plus extra for drizzling

Very coarse sea salt, such as Maldon, as needed

Combine the flour, salt, yeast, water, sugar, and oil in a bowl and mix with clean hands until the dough comes together.

Knead on a lightly floured work surface until the dough becomes smooth, velvety, and elastic, about 5 minutes.

Place the dough in a lightly oiled bowl, then oil the top to prevent a crust from forming. Cover with plastic wrap.

Let the dough rise until doubled in volume, about 1 hour.

Press the dough into an oiled half sheet pan or 43-by-30½-centimeter (17-by-12-inch) rimmed baking sheet. Drizzle the surface with oil and sprinkle aggressively with the coarse sea salt (at least 20 grams / 1 tablespoon). Cover with plastic wrap and let rise again until almost doubled, about 1 hour.

Preheat the oven to 177°C (350°F). Center a rack in the oven.

Press indentations into the surface of the focaccia with oiled fingertips.

Bake (*cuocere in forno*) until the focaccia is golden brown on top, about 25 minutes.

Focaccia con Cipolle

Focaccia with Onion

Follow the first four steps in the recipe for Focaccia above. Press the dough into an oiled half sheet pan or 43-by-30½-centimeter (17-by-12-inch) rimmed baking sheet. Cover with plastic warp and let rise again until almost doubled in volume.

While the focaccia is rising and the oven preheating, cook 500 grams (4¼ cups) sliced red onion in 60 milliliters (¼ cup) olive oil until softened and beginning to caramelize, about 20 minutes. Season to taste with salt and pepper. Let cool.

Drizzle the surface of the focaccia with oil and sprinkle with about 1 teaspoon salt. Press indentations in the surface of the focaccia with oiled fingertips.

Spread with the onions, season lightly with salt and pepper, and bake (*cuocere in forno*) as in the recipe above.

Focaccia con Patate

Focaccia with Potato

Although some chefs prefer to slice potatoes by hand (they appreciate the multiple textures occasioned by the uneven thickness of the slices), the easiest way to cut regular, thin slices of potato is with a mandoline. For this recipe, adjust the straight blade to slice very thin. Then, using the guard to protect against injury, run the potato over the blade to cut thin rounds.

Follow the first four steps in the recipe for Focaccia on page 150.

While the dough is rising, soak needles from two 12½-centimeter (5-inch) sprigs fresh rosemary 1 hour in olive oil to cover (this keeps the rosemary from burning).

Press the dough into an oiled half sheet pan or 43-by-30½-centimeter (17-by-12-inch) rimmed baking sheet. Cover with plastic warp and let rise again until almost doubled in volume, about 1 hour.

Meanwhile, peel 450 grams (1 pound) Yukon Gold potatoes and slice paper-thin on a mandoline. Do not preslice; if you store the slices in water, they will lose the potato starch that is needed for the slices to adhere in a layer on top of the focaccia. Toss in a bowl with 60 milliliters (¼ cup) olive oil and the soaked rosemary leaves.

Drizzle the surface of the focaccia with oil and sprinkle with about 1 teaspoon salt. Press indentations in the surface of the focaccia with oiled fingertips.

Shingle the potato slices on top of the focaccia, interspersed with rosemary leaves. Season aggressively with the coarse salt (at least 20 grams / about 1 tablespoon). Drizzle with olive oil and bake (*cuocere in forno*) as in the recipe on page 150.

Grissini

Breadsticks

Makes about 80

Grissini are crisp, slender breadsticks that originated in Turin. Traditionally baked with a sprinkle of coarse sea salt and black pepper, *grissini* make an excellent antipasto, wrapped in thin slices of prosciutto.

Ingredients

460 grams (3¾ cups) all-purpose flour
110 grams (about 1 cup) whole-wheat flour
Pinch of sugar
10 grams (1¾ teaspoons) coarse sea salt, plus extra for sprinkling
7 grams (2¼ teaspoons / 1 packet) active dry yeast or 15 grams (1 tablespoon) fresh yeast
300 milliliters (1¼ cups) warm water
60 milliliters (¼ cup) olive oil
Freshly ground black pepper

In a bowl, mix the flours, sugar, salt, yeast, warm water, and olive oil until the dough comes together.

Knead on a lightly floured surface until smooth, velvety, and elastic, 8 to 10 minutes.

Place the dough in a lightly oiled bowl, then oil the top of the dough to prevent a crust from forming. Cover with plastic wrap and let rise until doubled in volume, about 1 hour. To make the dough a day ahead, let it rise 30 minutes, press it down with the heels of your hand to de-gas, cover with plastic wrap, and refrigerate. Return to room temperature before proceeding.

Line a baking sheet with parchment paper and lightly oil the paper. Preheat the oven to 177°C (350°F).

Turn the dough out onto a lightly floured work surface. Cut the dough in quarters. Work with one piece of dough at a time, and keep the remaining quarters covered with a clean kitchen towel or plastic wrap. Using a rolling pin, roll the dough into a thin sheet (about 6 millimeters / ¼ inch thick). Use a large knife to cut the sheet into strips 6 millimeters (¼ inch) wide.

Gently roll each strip of dough to round the cut edges.

Place the dough ropes 1½ centimeters (½ inch) apart on the prepared baking sheet. Sprinkle with sea salt and pepper, and roll the *grissini* in the oil to coat evenly with the seasoning.

Bake (*cuocere in forno*) until lightly browned and crisp, about 20 minutes. Cool on the baking sheet for about 5 minutes; transfer to a wire rack to cool completely.

Repeat with the remaining quarters of dough.

Chapter 10

Poultry and Game Birds:
Pollame e Selvaggina

*Petto di Pollo Impanato con Insalata di Pomodori
e Rucola* (Breaded Chicken Cutlets with
Tomato-and-Arugula Salad)
Piccata di Pollo con Fettuccine all'Uovo
(Chicken Scaloppine with Lemon, Butter, and
Fresh Egg Noodles)
Pollo Arrosto (Roasted Chicken)
Pollo alla Griglia (Grilled Chicken)
Pollo alla Cacciatora
(Braised Chicken with Tomatoes)
Pollo Fritto (Tuscan Fried Chicken)
Pollo alla Cacciatora in Bianco
(Braised Chicken with White Wine and Olives)
Anitra Arrosto (Roasted Duck)
Piccione in Casseruola (Braised Squab)
Quaglie alla Griglia (Grilled Quail with *Fregola*)

Chicken has been heralded as "the world's most
popular bird," and with good reason: According to the
USDA, it remains the most commonly available variety
of poultry in the world. In the United States, the
chicken industry is one of the largest sectors in agriculture. Chefs can choose from various chicken-farming
methods, ranging from "organic," "free-range," and
"natural" to "farm-raised." Poultry-farming practices
are similar in Italy.

Chicken consumption first surpassed that of beef in
the United States in 1992, and has continued to do so
each year since. Poultry and game birds have grown in

popularity here because of their versatility, low cost,
and lower fat and cholesterol relative to other meats.

While farmyard birds such as chicken and capon are
equally popular in Italy, Italian cuisine also has centuries-old traditions of preparing game such as duck,
guinea hen, capon, pheasant, squab, quail, goose,
thrush, and partridge. According to historians Capatti
and Montanari in their book *Italian Cuisine: A Cultural
History*, game came into fashion in courtly cuisine in
Europe during the thirteenth and fourteenth centuries,
when winged animals became symbols of elite culture,
"linking the 'higher' levels of the animal world and of
human society." At that point, fowl replaced large game
animals such as wild stag, boar, bear, and ox at table,
animals that had previously associated the elite classes
with their warrior identity.

Many of these game birds are available to the cook in
the United States, but wild meats, hunted for sport or
food, are banned from commercial use here because
they are not inspected or graded by USDA officials.
The "game" meats available in wholesale or retail out-
lets are actually raised on farms or ranches. So-called
game birds are also farmed in Italy.

This chapter demonstrates some classic methods for preparing poultry and game birds. Students are introduced
to a traditional mixture of chopped aromatics, called a
trito, used as seasoning for poutry as well as a variety of
meat preparations that appear in later chapters.

Pollo alla Cacciatora in Bianco (page 168)

Methods for cooking chicken and game on the bone include:

○ Trussing and roasting whole chicken and duck

○ Removing the backbone and butterflying whole chicken for grilling

○ Cutting chicken and squab into pieces for stews and deep-frying

Students also sauté thin scaloppine (cutlets) of chicken breast meat that are floured or coated in a more substantial breading.

Le Tecniche

In this chapter, students learn to fabricate chicken and poultry. These recipes were chosen to teach students to apply cooking techniques that have been introduced in previous chapters—*saltare* and *deglassare*—to poultry and game. New techniques of *brasare* (braising), *grigliare* (grilling), and *arrostire* (roasting) are demonstrated here. For a more complete discussion of poultry and game birds, see pages 396–411.

Petto di Pollo Impanato con Insalata di Pomodori e Rucola

Breaded Chicken Cutlets with Tomato-and-Arugula Salad

Serves 4

This classic technique for breading chicken cutlets is called *l'impanatura all'inglese*. Sliced into cutlets and pounded to an even thickness, the chicken breast meat is breaded with a coating of flour, egg, and breadcrumbs. The cutlets are sautéed in oil until the exterior is a crunchy, golden brown and the interior is cooked through but still moist.

This preparation is classically garnished with lemon wedges. It may also be served, as in this recipe, with a salad of tomato, baby arugula, and basil dressed with olive oil. (A pinch of sugar balances the acidity of the vinegar and tomatoes.) A simple arugula salad, dressed with lemon juice and olive oil, also makes an excellent accompaniment.

(See sidebar "Making Clarified Butter" on page 143 and step-by-step instructions for "Preparing Scaloppine" on page 403.)

Ingredients

For the chicken:

2 boneless, skinless chicken breast halves (from 1 chicken)

2 large eggs

Coarse salt and freshly ground black pepper

200 grams (1¾ cups) fine, dry breadcrumbs (see sidebar)

150 grams (1¼ cups) all-purpose flour

100 milliliters (about ½ cup) clarified butter

For the salad:

450 grams (1 pound) cherry tomatoes, cut in half or wedges

Coarse salt and freshly ground black pepper

15 milliliters (1 tablespoon) red wine vinegar

60 milliliters (¼ cup) olive oil

Pinch of sugar

12 fresh basil leaves, cut into chiffonade, or small sprigs of basil

100 grams (2 firmly packed cups) baby arugula, cleaned and dried

Cook the chicken:

Cut each chicken breast in half horizontally, to make four large, thin scallopine, or scallops. Place each scal-

lop between two sheets of plastic wrap and pound with a meat mallet to about 6 millimeters (¼ inch) thick.

Break the eggs into a bowl and beat lightly with a fork. Season to taste with salt and pepper.

Making Breadcrumbs

To make fine, dry breadcrumbs, arrange sliced sandwich bread or other leftover bread in a single layer on a sheet pan and bake in a very low oven (93°C / 200°F or lower) until the bread is dry but not browned, about 30 minutes. (It's important that the bread not take on any dark color.) Process the dried bread to crumbs in a food processor. For a very fine texture and regular size, pass crumbs through a china cap (*colino*) or a drum sieve or tamis (*setaccio*).

Place the breadcrumbs on a large plate, and the flour on another plate.

Sprinkle the scaloppine on both sides with salt and pepper. Dredge in the flour and pat off the excess. Dip the scaloppine into the egg, then into the breadcrumbs, pressing the crumbs into the flesh to evenly coat.

Heat the clarified butter in a large skillet (*padella*) over medium heat until flour sizzles when a pinch is tossed into the pan.

Slip as many of the scaloppine as will fit in one layer into the butter, being careful not to splatter. Sauté

(*saltare*) the scaloppine until browned on one side, 2 to 3 minutes. Turn and brown on the other side, 2 to 3 minutes. Transfer to a sheet pan lined with paper towels and drain, gently patting the top of the scaloppine to absorb the fat.

Make the salad:

In a bowl, season the tomatoes with salt and pepper to taste.

Add the vinegar, oil, sugar, and basil and stir well. Taste for seasoning.

Add the arugula and toss lightly to coat with the dressing.

To serve:

Divide the scaloppine between four serving plates, and top with the salad.

Maillard Reaction

The Maillard reaction is a complex series of chemical reactions between sugar and protein molecules, usually in the presence of high heat. The reaction is responsible for the characteristic brown color and "roasted" flavor many foods take on in the presence of high heat, including roasted meats, bones for stock, toasted bread crusts, chocolate, coffee beans, and even certain beers. The reaction is named for French physician and chemist Louis-Camille Maillard, who formally discovered the reaction in the early twentieth century, although it has been used in cooking for many centuries.

Maillard discovered that when a carbohydrate molecule (sugar) and an amino acid (protein) are heated to above 120°C (250°F), they bond, forming an unstable molecule. With continued, consistent heating, this unstable molecule undergoes additional changes, yielding hundreds of by-products, usually characterized by surface browning and increased flavor intensity. The results of the Maillard reaction are easily discerned by tasting the difference in flavor between a piece of meat that has been roasted and one that has been boiled or steamed.

Le Tecniche: *Saltare o Rosolare il Pollo* (Sautéing or Pan-Searing Chicken)

A fairly quick method of cooking, sautéing or pan-searing provides the best results with small items such as the scaloppine of chicken at right; pork, turkey, and veal scaloppine; and steaks, chops, and fish fillets. The high heat coagulates the protein on the surface of the food and produces the Maillard reaction (see sidebar at left), developing a flavorful brown crust on the surface (*rosolatura*). Caramelized juices, deglazed from the pan, may be thickened for sauces.

As in the recipe for the chicken scaloppine, meat, poultry, and fish are often dusted with flour before sautéing. The flour encourages browning, holds delicate fish fillets together during cooking, and helps to bind a pan sauce. If there is any question as to whether the flour will cook adequately (thin, quick-cooking cuts of meat and poultry, and fish fillets, may cook through before the flour has had a chance to lose its raw taste), it is best to use toasted flour (see sidebar on facing page).

Sautéing and pan-searing are also used in conjunction with other cooking techniques. Many braised dishes start by sautéing the food to develop flavor and color. (See page 165 for a discussion of braising.)

Guidelines for Sautéing Meats

It is important that the pan be hot. Foods will steam rather than brown if the pan is too cool. Or the food may stick to the pan, and any crust that has developed will pull off when the food is turned. (Vegetables are the exception to this rule; see "Le Tecniche: *Saltare*" on page 48.)

The pan is coated with a small amount of fat, enough so that the food to be sautéed doesn't stick to the pan. Aromatics may be used to flavor the oil, and subsequently the food as it cooks. If aromatics are used, they are started with the oil in a cold pan; the aromat-

ics will infuse the oil as the oil heats. (Garlic may be used whole and in the skin to prevent it from burning and to add a subtle taste of garlic to the dish.)

Ideally the food is at room temperature; it must be dry.

When the oil is hot, the food is added to the pan. The pan must be large enough so that the food is not crowded; in a crowded pan, the food will steam instead of sautéing. (With large amounts, cook in batches.)

The food is cooked, uncovered, and without shaking or stirring, until caramelization has occurred and a crust has formed. When cooking meats and poultry, lemon may be squeezed over the food as it cooks for flavor.

A quick pan sauce is made by deglazing the pan with a flavorful liquid and reducing. Alcohol is always added to the pan off the heat.

Piccata di Pollo con Fettuccine all'Uovo

Chicken Scaloppine with Lemon, Butter, and Fresh Egg Noodles

Serves 4

This is a basic method for sautéing poultry, pork, and veal cutlets, called scaloppine. Chefs vary ingredients to produce an array of pan sauces. *Piccata* refers to the piquant taste derived from lemon and capers.

The scaloppine are floured, then sautéed in oil that has been flavored with garlic. A quick pan sauce is made by deglazing the pan, first with white wine and then with stock, and finishing the sauce with capers, parsley, and lemon. Flour serves to encourage the chicken to brown, and eventually to thicken the pan sauce slightly.

Chef's Note

Unpeeled garlic cloves add a subtle flavor to sautéed food, without a strong garlic taste.

Toasting Flour

In Italian cooking, chefs may toast flour when it will be used to dredge foods, or to dust a sheet pan. Toasting ensures that the raw-flour taste is eliminated from the finished product, especially when the food will be cooked only for a short period of time.

To toast flour, spread a thin layer on a sheet pan and bake at 177°C (350°F) 5 minutes, or until golden brown.

This is a contemporary presentation with fettuccine; pasta would not traditionally be served with a *secondo*.

(For photos and step-by-step instructions for "Preparing Scaloppine," see page 403.)

Ingredients

For the chicken:

2 boneless, skinless chicken breast halves (from 1 chicken)

Coarse salt and freshly ground black pepper

150 grams (1¼ cups) toasted all-purpose flour (see sidebar, left)

125 milliliters (½ cup) olive oil, or as needed

2 cloves garlic, in the skin, crushed with the heel of the hand

Juice of 1 lemon

2 lemons, thinly sliced into rounds, seeds removed

30 grams (2 tablespoons) capers, preferably salt-packed (see page 31), rinsed and drained

150 milliliters (⅔ cup) dry white wine

150 milliliters (⅔ cup) chicken stock

3 grams (1 tablespoon) chopped fresh Italian parsley

½ recipe Pasta all'Uovo (page 94), cut into fettuccine

45 milligrams (3 tablespoons) unsalted butter

Prepare the chicken:

Cut the chicken breasts in half, horizontally, to make four large, thin scallopine, or scallops. Place each scallop between two sheets of plastic wrap and pound with a meat mallet to about 6 millimeters (¼ inch) thick.

Season the scallops on both sides with salt and pepper to taste. Place the toasted flour on a plate or in a shallow container. Dredge the scallopine in the flour and pat off the excess.

Bring a large pot (*pentola*) of salted water to a boil for the pasta.

Cook the chicken:

In a skillet (*padella*), add oil as needed to comfortably cover the bottom of the pan. Add the garlic cloves, place over medium heat, and heat until a pinch of flour sizzles when tossed into the pan. Working in batches as necessary, place the scaloppine in the pan, not touching, and sauté (*saltare*) on one side to brown, 2 to 3 minutes. Turn and cook about 1 minute on the other side to brown.

Remove the scaloppine, and pour off the fat from the pan.

Add the lemon juice, lemon slices, and capers. Add the wine to deglaze (*deglassare*), off the heat, and return to the heat. Cook to reduce until entirely evaporated.

Add the stock and reduce over medium-high heat until slightly thickened. Add the parsley and season to taste with salt and pepper. Remove the chicken from the skillet and set the chicken and the pan with the sauce aside.

Cook the fettuccine:

Place the fettuccine in the boiling water and cook to until about two-thirds done, about 2 minutes. Meanwhile, melt the butter in a separate skillet. Drain, and add the fettuccine to the skillet, along with enough of the cooking water to create an emulsion and finish cooking the pasta in the water, about 1 minute.

To serve:

Return the scaloppine to the pan with the lemon sauce. Return the pan to medium heat, and turn the chicken in the sauce to warm.

Twirl on a fork, and divide the pasta between four plates. Place the scaloppine on the plates. Spoon the sauce, lemon slices, and capers over the scaloppine.

Pollo Arrosto

Roasted Chicken

Serves 4

This is a basic method for roasting chicken. The chicken is stuffed with lemon, herbs, and garlic, and seasoned with salt, pepper, and a chopped herb-and-garlic mixture called a *trito*. Once seasoned, the chicken is trussed and roasted at 191°C (375°F).

The chicken is classically served with roasted potatoes (see *Patate Arrostite*, page 255). The oil drained from the chicken adds excellent flavor to the potatoes as they cook, or the potatoes may be roasted directly in the pan with the chicken (see "Le Tecniche: *Arrostire*" on page 162). The chicken may also be served with a pan sauce (as described in the same section on page 162).

If possible, the seasoned chicken should be refrigerated overnight to allow the flavors to permeate the flesh.

(See page 399 for step-by-step instructions for "Trussing Chicken and Poultry.")

Ingredients

For the trito:
Leaves from 2 sprigs fresh rosemary, finely chopped
Leaves from 2 sprigs fresh sage, finely chopped
2 cloves garlic, finely chopped
Coarse salt and freshly ground black pepper
Pinch of spezie forti, garam masala, or freshly ground nutmeg

For the chicken:
1 chicken, about 1⅔ kilos (3½ pounds)
Coarse salt and freshly ground black pepper
2 lemons, halved
2 sprigs fresh rosemary
3 cloves garlic, peeled and crushed with the heel of the hand

350 milliliters (1½ cups) olive oil, plus extra for the vegetables
100 grams (3½ ounces) red onion, cut into 5-centimeter (2-inch) pieces (¾ cup)
100 grams (3½ ounces) celery, cut into 5-centimeter (2-inch) pieces (1 cup)
80 grams (3 ounces) carrot, cut into 5-centimeter (2-inch) pieces (⅔ cup)
125 milliliters (½ cup) dry white wine

Make the *trito*:

Mix together the rosemary, sage, garlic, salt and pepper to taste, and the *spezie forti*. Set aside.

Prepare the chicken for roasting:

Pull out all excess fat from the neck and cavity areas. Remove the wishbone and thoroughly rinse the carcass.

With your hand, gently separate the skin from the breast meat without tearing the skin, and spread the *trito* over the breast meat. Make incisions through the skin into the joint between thigh and drumstick; stuff the *trito* into the joints and under the skin of the legs. (Reserve some *trito* for the outside of the bird.)

Season the inside of the cavity with salt and pepper and stuff with two of the lemon halves, the rosemary sprigs, and garlic cloves.

Truss the chicken, then rub a little of the *trito* over the outside of the bird.

Place the chicken in a container, and pour half of the oil (175 milliliters / ¾ cup) over it. Rub the oil all over the chicken; cover and let marinate at least 1 hour, or refrigerate up to 2 days. Bring to room temperature before roasting.

Roast the chicken:

Preheat the oven to 191°C (375°F).

Toss the onion, celery, and carrot in a bowl with a little olive oil and place in a roasting pan (*la rostiera*). Season the chicken with salt and pepper to taste and set it on top of the vegetables. Pour the remaining oil over the chicken.

Roast (*arrostire*) the chicken 25 minutes. Squeeze the remaining lemon halves over the chicken and toss the halves into the pan. Continue cooking 10 more minutes. Add the wine to the pan, and continue roasting, basting occasionally, until the internal temperature of the chicken registers 74°C (165°F) on an instant-read thermometer, approximately 30 more minutes. (If the pan becomes dry, add a little chicken stock or water to prevent it from burning.)

Remove the chicken from the roasting pan and set aside on a rack in a warm place to rest 10 to 15 minutes. Cut off the twine and carve, removing the legs and wings, then slicing the breast meat on the diagonal. Serve with *Patate Arrostite*, page 255.

Le Tecniche: *Arrostire* (Roasting)

As demonstrated in the recipe for *Pollo Arrosto* on page 161, roasting is a method of cooking by means of direct, radiant heat in the dry atmosphere of an oven. Roasting originally meant cooking on a spit above a fire in the open air. The spit was turned mechanically or by hand for even cooking. Through the Maillard reaction (see sidebar on page 158), roasting creates a savory, intensely flavored brown crust on the outside of the food. The coagulation of surface protein seals in the nutritive elements and juices.

The best candidates for roasting are foods that contain a certain amount of fat, or are basted during roasting to prevent the food from drying out. Roasting is a suit-

able method for young poultry (*Pollo Arrosto* on page 161) and game (*Anitra Arrosto* on page 169), as well as many cuts of beef, veal, pork (*Arista alla Toscana* on page 210), lamb (*Agnello Arrosto* on page 219 and *Costolette d'Agnello* on page 218), rabbit, seafood (*Pesce Intero Arrosto* on page 232), and vegetables (*Patate Arrostite* on page 255) throughout this book.

Guidelines for Roasting Chicken

The bird will benefit from being seasoned with a traditional mixture of chopped herbs and spices called a *trito*, coated with oil, and refrigerated for up to two days before cooking. Seasonings are massaged into the flesh, under the skin, before the oil is added; once the oil has been introduced, the seasonings will penetrate less well.

The bird may be stuffed with aromatic ingredients such as lemon, onion, and herbs for flavor, or an edible mixture such as a bread stuffing.

To improve the appearance of the roasted bird, many chefs prefer to truss poultry (see "Trussing Chicken and Poultry," page 399).

Bring the chicken to room temperature before roasting. It is seasoned and placed in a roasting pan in a preheated oven.

The bird is roasted with plenty of olive oil to add flavor and to keep the meat moist, and it is basted with the juices. Vegetables (traditionally carrot, onion, and celery, a classic combination known as mirepoix) are tossed with oil and added to the pan. Vegetables prevent the empty spaces in the pan from burning, and may eventually be used to make a pan sauce. Alternatively, potatoes may be roasted in the pan with the chicken and served alongside.

During roasting, lemon is squeezed over the bird for additional flavor. The pan may be deglazed with wine while the chicken roasts; pour the wine around, not over, the bird so as not to soften the crust that is developing.

The cooking time depends on the size and amount of chicken being cooked, as well as the oven temperature. Generally, smaller foods are cooked for a shorter time at higher heat, while larger pieces cook for a longer time at lower temperatures so that the heat can penetrate to the center before the exterior becomes overcooked.

Once roasted, the bird must be allowed to rest for 10 to 15 minutes on a wire rack in a warm place before carving. This allows the juices, forced to the center of the meat by heat during roasting, to re-disperse evenly in the meat.

Chefs may prepare a simple pan sauce. Once the chicken has been roasted, it is removed from the roasting pan. The fat is poured off, and the pan is deglazed with 250 milliliters (1 cup) chicken stock, scraping the bottom of the pan to pick up the browned bits. Pass the juices and the mirepoix through a food mill, with additional stock as needed to adjust the consistency. (Alternatively, the sauce can be strained through a fine-mesh strainer [*colino*]). Return the sauce to the heat, bring to a simmer, and cook to adjust consistency. Taste for seasoning.

Pollo alla Griglia

Grilled Chicken

Serves 4

In this classic preparation for grilling, also known as *al mattone*, the chicken is flattened to expose the maximum surface area to the grill. This technique allows the skin to crisp and brown evenly. A weight—traditionally a brick—is placed on top of the bird during cooking to hold it flat and prevent it from curling. Chefs may substitute a heavy pot wrapped in aluminum foil. Any bird may be prepared this way.

If time allows, it is best to season the chicken and let it marinate overnight in the refrigerator to allow the flavors to penetrate.

(See page 406 for step-by-step instructions for "Preparing Chicken for Grilling.")

Ingredients

---

1 chicken, about 1⅔ kilos (3½ pounds)
Coarse salt and freshly ground black pepper
Generous pinch of red pepper flakes
150 milliliters (⅔ cup) olive oil
7 cloves garlic, peeled and crushed with the heel of the hand
3 large sprigs fresh rosemary
Juice of 4 lemons
125 milliliters (½ cup) dry white wine

To prepare the chicken for grilling, first remove the wishbone. Cut down each side of the backbone with a heavy knife and remove. Make a small incision in the skin between legs and breast and insert the end of each drumstick into each incision. Remove the keel bone.

Place the chicken in a container. Massage salt, black pepper, and red pepper flakes into the meat. Pour the oil over the chicken, and massage into the meat. Add the garlic cloves and rosemary sprigs. Cover and marinate in the refrigerator at least 1 hour, or up to 2 days. Bring to room temperature before grilling.

When ready to cook the chicken, preheat a gas or charcoal grill to medium heat. Combine the lemon juice and wine in a bowl.

Lift the chicken out of the container, and wipe off the oil to limit flaming. Place the chicken on the grill, skin side down. Cover with a piece of foil and a weight to keep it flat. Grill (*grigliare*) until the skin is well browned, 5 to 10 minutes. Turn, replace the foil and the weight, and grill 5 more minutes. Continue this way until the chicken is well browned, about 20 minutes total.

Remove the weight and foil. Place the chicken, skin side up, on the grill. Baste thoroughly with the lemon-wine mixture and continue cooking, basting occasionally, until the internal temperature of the chicken registers 74°C (165°C) on an instant-read thermometer, another 15 to 20 minutes.

Le Tecniche: *Grigliare* (Grilling)

The recipe on page 163 for *Pollo alla Griglia* demonstrates the technique of grilling. Grilling is a method of cooking by radiant heat from below. The heat may be in the form of wood, charcoal, or a gas flame. Traditionally foods were grilled over a wood fire in the open air; charcoal and gas are common sources of heat now. Even when cooked over gas, foods that are grilled take on a smoky taste from the juices that drip onto the heat source.

Grilling is a suitable method for young poultry and game, as well as tender cuts of beef, veal, and pork, organ meats, and seafood. Longer-cooking foods may need to be moved to a cooler part of the grill to prevent the outside from burning before the interior is cooked through. Care must be taken not to grill poultry over too high a heat as the skin of poultry will burn.

Guidelines for Grilling

The grill must be absolutely clean and hot during cooking. It should be cleaned before use by brushing vigorously with a stiff wire brush to remove any charred pieces of food, then oiled with a cloth or folded paper towels dipped in oil (hold the cloth or paper towels with tongs).

The foods to be grilled are often but not always lightly oiled as well, depending on the food. Too much oil will cause the food to turn black as the oil burns.

Foods should not be transferred directly from the refrigerator to the grill, or the outside of the meat will be done before the inside reaches the desired internal temperature.

Foods may be marinated for several hours or overnight in oil and aromatics for better flavor. Foods also may be brushed with a marinade (*marinatura*)—oil, seasonings, lemon juice, and often wine—during grilling for additional flavor.

Grilled foods are usually marked with a crosshatch pattern (*quadrettatura*). Only the presentation side of the food need be marked. To mark foods with a crosshatch:

The grill is brushed with oil.

The food is placed on the grill at a 30-degree angle, toward the right.

The food is grilled, without moving, until marks form; then the food is turned at a 30-degree angle to the left.

Chef's Note

For practical purposes, in a professional setting (and at the school), the chicken may be grilled on the skin side to mark with a *quadrettatura* (see "Le Tecniche: Grigliare" at right), and finished in a 191°C (375°F) oven for 15 to 20 minutes, or until the internal temperature reaches 74°C (165°F).

*ADD -
green olives
black olives
red peppers
green peppers
mushrooms*

Pollo alla Cacciatora

Braised Chicken with Tomatoes

Serves 4

The chicken for this hearty rustic stew—called "hunter's style"—is braised (see "Le Tecniche: *Brasare il Pollo*" on page 166) in a mixture of puréed tomatoes, mushrooms, garlic, and rosemary. As with many braises, creamy polenta makes an excellent accompaniment.

When browning the chicken, make sure the oil in the pan is hot; if it is too cool, the skin of the chicken will stick to the bottom of the pan and will not brown well.

Braises may be cooked on top of the stove, as in this recipe, or in the oven, as in the "white" version of this stew, *Pollo alla Cacciatora in Bianco* on page 168.

(For step-by-step instructions, see "Quartering Chicken and Poultry," page 402.)

Ingredients

1 chicken, about 1⅔ kilos (3½ pounds), quartered
Coarse salt and freshly ground black pepper
125 milliliters (½ cup) olive oil, plus extra for serving
4 cloves garlic, peeled
3 sprigs fresh rosemary
450 grams (1 pound) porcini, shiitake, oyster, cremini and/or
    white mushrooms, stemmed and sliced 6 millimeters to
    1¼ centimeters (¼ to ½ inch) thick (5½ to 6 cups)
1 lemon, cut in half
Pinch of red pepper flakes
250 milliliters (1 cup) dry white wine
750 milliliters (3¼ cups) whole, canned Italian plum tomatoes,
    with their juices, puréed through a food mill
250 milliliters (1 cup) water or chicken stock
Extra-virgin olive oil, for serving

Cut the quartered chicken into 8 pieces: Cut through the joints to separate the thighs from the drumsticks. Cut the chicken breasts in half crosswise on the diagonal.

Toss the chicken pieces in a bowl with a generous sprinkling of salt and pepper, and massage the seasonings into the flesh.

Place the 125 milliliters (½ cup) oil, garlic, and rosemary in a deep vessel, such as a *sautoir* or a Dutch oven, large enough to hold the chicken pieces in a single layer. Heat over medium heat until the garlic and rosemary are aromatic. Increase the heat to medium-high, add the chicken pieces to the pan in a single layer, and sear (*rosolare*) to brown all over. Set the garlic cloves and rosemary on top of the chicken if they begin to burn.

Remove the chicken pieces from the pan.

Add the mushrooms to the pan and cook until nicely colored, about 5 minutes.

Add the lemon halves to the pan. Add the red pepper, then deglaze (*deglassare*) the pan with the wine. Cook until the wine evaporates entirely. Remove the lemons.

Add the tomato purée and the water or chicken stock. Season to taste with salt and pepper. Add the chicken back to the pan. Bring the tomato mixture to a bare simmer, cover, and cook until the juices run clear when the chicken is pierced with a small knife, and the internal temperature registers 74°C (165°F) on an instant-read thermometer, 15 to 20 minutes. Taste again for seasoning and serve the chicken with the sauce, drizzled with extra-virgin olive oil.

Le Tecniche: *Brasare il Pollo* (Braising Chicken)

In recipes for *Pollo alla Cacciatora* and *Piccione in Casseruola* on pages 165 and 172, respectively, chicken and squab are braised, a technique in which food is simmered, partially immersed in liquid. Braising is particularly well suited to less tender meats (highly active muscle) that are high in connective tissue, but all foods, including chicken and other poultry, may be successfully braised.

Braising begins by searing (*rosolare*) the chicken pieces in hot fat, then simmering them gently in liquid. (Searing and sautéing are related techniques: To sear means to brown the outside of the food, while sautéing implies that the food is cooked through.)

It is important that the oil be hot before the chicken is added to the pan. If it is not hot enough, the meat will stick to the pan.

Braising layers flavors into the dish. First, aromatics are used to flavor the oil. (In the case of *Pollo alla Cacciatora* and the "white" version of the same dish, *Pollo alla Cacciatora in Bianco*, garlic and rosemary are used.) The chicken is browned in the oil, creating a layer of caramelized juices that forms the foundation of the eventual sauce. The pan is deglazed with white wine, and the chicken absorbs the flavor of the wine. The fat is skimmed, tomato is added, and an exchange of flavors occurs as the chicken cooks in the tomato mixture.

Older, tougher poultry is best suited to braising, although the technique is commonly used with younger birds as well.

For a discussion of braising as applied to other meats, see "Le Tecniche: *Brasare*" on page 191.

Pollo Fritto

Tuscan Fried Chicken

Serves 4

The chicken is cooked in small pieces on the bone, coated in a light crust of seasoned flour and egg. Tarragon is commonly found in traditional Tuscan cuisine. At The International Culinary Center, this is served with Dean Cesare Casella's fresh slaw of savoy cabbage, radicchio, fennel, and carrots spiked with diced jalapeños and dressed with a tarragon vinaigrette. The recipe that follows is based on Chef Casella's recipe *Insalata di Lasagnino* (Tuscan Coleslaw) published in his book *True Tuscan*.

For step-by-step instructions on "Quartering Chicken and Poultry," see page 402. See "Le Tecniche: *Friggere*" on page 248 for a discussion of deep-frying.)

Ingredients

1 chicken, about 1⅔ kilos (3½ pounds), quartered

Coarse salt and freshly ground black pepper

45 milliliters (3 tablespoons) lemon juice (from 1 large lemon)

Grapeseed or canola oil, for deep-frying

150 grams (1¼ cups) all-purpose flour

2 large eggs

4 sprigs fresh thyme

4 sprigs fresh sage

4 sprigs fresh rosemary

4 cloves garlic in the skin, flattened with the heel of the hand

Cut the quartered chicken into 10 pieces: Cut through the joints to separate the thighs from the drumsticks. Cut the wing bones off the breast pieces, including as little of the breast meat as possible. Cut the remainder of the chicken breasts in half crosswise.

Season the chicken pieces in a container with salt and pepper to taste; massage the seasonings into the meat. Rub with 30 milliliters (2 tablespoons) of the lemon juice and marinate at least 1 hour.

Fill a deep pot or deep-fryer with a basket about half-way with oil. Heat the oil to 191°C (375°F).

Place the flour on a plate and season with salt and pepper to taste. Beat the eggs in a bowl.

When the oil is hot, dredge the chicken in the flour. Then, starting with the longer-cooking pieces (thighs and drumsticks), dip each piece in egg and let the excess drip back into the bowl; slide into the hot oil. Working in two batches if necessary, fry (*friggere*), regulating the heat to keep the oil at 191°C (375°F), until the internal temperature of the chicken registers 74°C (165°F) on an instant-read thermometer, 15 to 20 minutes. Add the herbs and garlic during the final 1 to 2 minutes of cooking (be careful not to burn them).

Drain the chicken, herbs, and garlic on a rack over a sheet pan or a sheet pan lined with paper towels. Drizzle the chicken with the remaining lemon juice and serve with the fried herbs and garlic.

Tuscan Slaw

450 grams (1 pound) savoy cabbage, julienned

75 grams (3 ounces) carrot, grated

170 grams (6 ounces) radicchio, julienned

75 grams (⅔ cup) thinly sliced fennel bulbs

2½ grams (1 tablespoon) chopped fresh tarragon

5 grams (1 tablespoon) finely chopped jalapeño pepper (seeds removed)

15 milliliters (1 tablespoon) red wine vinegar

45 milliliters (3 tablespoons) extra-virgin olive oil

Coarse salt and freshly ground black pepper

Combine the cabbage, carrots, radicchio, fennel, tarragon, and jalapeño pepper in a large bowl.

In a small bowl, whisk together the vinegar and olive oil to create an emulsification. Season to taste with salt and pepper. Just before serving, pour the vinaigrette over the slaw ingredients and toss to coat. Serve with the chicken.

Pollo alla Cacciatora in Bianco

Braised Chicken with White Wine and Olives

Serves 4

A "white" variation on the classic cacciatore preparation (see *Pollo alla Cacciatora*, page 165), this stew is made without tomato. Veal or chicken stock contributes the necessary liquid for braising. (Veal stock will create a thicker sauce and a more intense, meaty flavor; a combination can also be used.)

This preparation works very nicely with rabbit, as well as with chicken.

(For step-by-step instructions for "Quartering Chicken and Poultry," see page 402.)

Ingredients

1 chicken, about 1⅔ kilos (3½ pounds), quartered

Coarse salt and freshly ground black pepper

125 milliliters (½ cup) olive oil, plus extra for finishing

2 cloves garlic, in the skin, crushed with the heel of the hand

1 sprig fresh rosemary

1 lemon, cut in half

250 milliliters (1 cup) dry white wine

450 milliliters (2 scant cups) brown veal stock or chicken stock, or as needed

Pinch of red pepper flakes

110 grams (¾ cup) pitted black olives

Extra-virgin olive oil, for serving

Cut the quartered chicken into 8 pieces: Cut through the joints to separate the thighs from the drumsticks. Cut the chicken breasts in half crosswise on the diagonal.

Toss the chicken pieces in a bowl with a generous sprinkling of salt and pepper, and massage the seasonings into the flesh.

Preheat the oven to 191°C (375°F).

Place the 125 milliliters (½ cup) oil, garlic, and rosemary in a deep vessel, such as a *sautoir* or a Dutch oven, large enough to hold the chicken pieces in a single layer. Heat over medium heat until the garlic and rosemary are aromatic. Increase the heat to medium-high. Add the chicken pieces to the pan in a single layer, and sear (*rosolare*) to brown all over. Set the garlic cloves and rosemary on top of the chicken if they begin to burn.

Squeeze the lemon juice over the chicken. Pour off the fat from the pan. Deglaze (*deglassare*) the pan with the wine, pouring the wine around but not over the chicken, and cook until the wine evaporates entirely. Add enough stock to cover the chicken by about half. Add the red pepper flakes and olives, bring to a bare simmer, cover, and braise (*brasare*) in the oven until the juices run clear when the chicken is pierced with a small knife, and the internal temperature registers 74°C (165°F) on an instant-read thermometer, 10 to 15 minutes. Add more stock if the pan gets dry.

Remove the pan from the oven. Check the sauce for consistency; it should be thick enough to coat the back of a spoon. Reduce, if necessary. Taste for seasoning. Serve the chicken with the sauce, drizzled with extra-virgin olive oil.

Anitra Arrosto

Roasted Duck

Serves 4

This is a classic method for roasting duck. It is served with a simple pan sauce.

Ducks are trussed exactly like chickens. For step-by-step instructions, see "Trussing Chicken and Poultry," page 399. (For further information on roasting duck, see also "Methods of Cooking Duck," page 409.)

Ingredients

For the trito:

3 cloves garlic, chopped

Leaves from 2 small sprigs fresh rosemary, chopped

Leaves from 1 small sprig fresh sage, chopped

3 grams (1½ teaspoons) freshly ground black pepper

½ teaspoon spezie forti, garam masala, or freshly ground nutmeg

For the duck:

1 Long Island or Pekin duck (4 to 6 pounds), wishbone removed

Coarse salt and freshly ground black pepper

2 small sprigs fresh rosemary

2 sprigs fresh sage

1 lemon, cut in half

210 grams (7 ounces) red onion, cut into 5-centimeter (2-inch) pieces (1¾ cups)

115 grams (4 ounces) celery, cut into 5-centimeter (2-inch) pieces (1¼ cups)

50 grams (2 ounces) carrot, cut into 5-centimeter (2-inch) pieces (¾ cup)

Chicken stock or duck stock, as needed (see Chef's Note)

Season the cavity of the duck with salt and pepper to taste. Stuff the herbs into the cavity. Rub the outside of the duck all over with the lemon halves.

Truss the duck. Season with salt and pepper to taste. Refrigerate, uncovered, overnight.

Preheat the oven to 191°C (375°F). Season the outside of the duck with salt and pepper to taste, massaging the seasonings into the flesh. Place the duck, breast side up, on a sheet pan or in a roasting pan (*la rostiera*). Scatter the onion, celery, and carrot around the duck.

Roast (*arrostire*), pouring off the fat as it accumulates in the pan, until the juices run clear and an instant-read thermometer inserted in the thickest part of the thigh registers 82°F (180°F), about 2 hours.

Remove the duck from the pan and let rest 20 minutes.

Recuperate the pan juices; spoon off and reserve any remaining fat for another use. Pass the vegetables along with the juices through a food mill to purée. Add chicken or duck stock as necessary to thin the mixture to a saucelike consistency. Taste for seasoning and keep warm.

Carve the duck at the table, cutting the legs off the carcass and slicing the breasts. Serve with the sauce.

Make the *trito*:

Combine all of the ingredients in a small bowl; set aside.

Make the duck: Wash the duck, inside and out, and pat dry. Turn the duck over a gas flame or use a kitchen torch to singe off (*strinare*) any remaining pinfeathers, and rub a heated metal spoon around the cavity to melt internal fat. Cut off the glands on top of the tail.

Make small incisions in the skin of the duck between legs and body, and wings and body. Carefully loosen the skin on the breasts and stuff the *trito* between the skin and the breast meat. Use a finger to stuff *trito* into the joint and under the skin. Be careful not to rip or tear the skin; the meat should be evenly and fully covered by the skin.

Chef's Note

See "Making a Stock from Trimmings" on page 439 for step-by-step instructions for making duck stock.

Umbria

"You must establish a relationship with the past to be able to connect with the present; tie older traditions to more modern techniques. The exchange among regions brought elegance to traditional [Umbrian] cuisine. These changes wrought from interregional exchanges modify the format, yet change little of the substance."

—Chef Marco Bistarelli of Ristorante Il Postale, Perugia

Sometimes called "the green heart of Italy," Umbria is a landlocked region in the center of the peninsula, bounded on the north by Toscana, the east by Le Marche, and the south by Lazio. The terrain is hilly and mountainous, veined with rivers. The region is dotted with lakes and with citadel towns that perch atop steep hills. Its capital is Perugia.

Although Umbria makes use of the freshwater fish found in lakes and rivers (carp and tench are two common varieties), the cuisine has traditionally relied heavily on agriculture, meat, and game.

Hunting truffles (*tartufi*), both black and white, is an important industry. Norcia is Italy's major source of black truffles. Truffles find their way into a variety of dishes—on top of hand-rolled *strangozzi* (a spaghetti-like pasta made of flour, water, and salt), for example; pounded to a paste with anchovies; and in the locally produced Pecorino Tartufato.

Pork is also an important market, and fresh and cured pork are popular. With neighboring Toscana and Le Marche, Umbria shares a tradition of *porchetta* (spit-roasted suckling pig), and Umbrian butchers are famous for their cured pork products, including an IGP-rated Prosciutto di Norcia and *coppa*, a sausage that makes use of all parts of the pig that are not used elsewhere. Spit roasting is also popular for game, offal, and rabbit.

Umbria produces a DOP olive oil, and IGP-classified lentils (*Lenticchie di Castelluccio di Norcia*) from the medieval mountain town Castelluccio, in the Sibylline Mountains. Goat- and sheep-farming are common, and cheese is made from both milks, sometimes mixed.

Umbria is famous for its bread (often made without salt), grilled meats, porcini mushrooms, lentils, white wine from Orvieto, and fresh egg pasta (particularly *tagliatelle* with a meat sauce, and the hand-rolled spaghettilike shapes called *ciriole* and *stringozzi*).

The region hosts a large number of monasteries, which produce an array of cheeses, vinegars, and wines.

Umbria's IGP-designated *Lenticchie di Castelluccio di Norcia*, available in Italian specialty markets, are an excellent choice for *Zuppa di Lenticchie* (page 90) and *Lenticchie in Umido* (page 256).

Piccione in Casseruola

Braised Squab

Serves 2

For this dish, squab are stuffed with pancetta, garlic, and herbs, seared, then roasted with shallots and livers. The pan is deglazed with wine, chicken stock is added, and the squab braises in the oven or on the stovetop, in the simmering stock.

Some Italian chefs cook squab to medium or well done, but American chefs generally prefer to cook it to medium-rare. At the school, the squab is served as a garnish for squash risotto (see Chef's Note).

Ingredients

2 squabs, about 450 grams (1 pound) each
Coarse salt and freshly ground black pepper
30 grams (3 tablespoons) chopped pancetta
5 cloves garlic, in the skin, crushed with the heel of the hand
2 sprigs fresh sage
45 milliliters (3 tablespoons) olive oil
1 large sprig fresh thyme
250 grams (1½ cups) peeled and quartered shallots
250 milliliters (1 cup) dry white wine
20 milliliters (1¼ tablespoons) aceto balsamico di Modena
20 milliliters (1¼ tablespoons) red wine vinegar
250 milliliters (1 cup) chicken stock, or as needed

Chef's Note

At The International Culinary Center, the squab is often served on a bed of squash risotto (in which case two quarters are sufficient, and the recipe serves four). The risotto is made like the *Risotto alla Parmigiana* on page 128, but halfway through the cooking, 200 grams (½ cup) of roasted, puréed butternut or acorn squash is stirred into the simmering rice. (Alternatively, students cut the squash into dice, sauté it, and stir it into the risotto; for this preparation, butternut squash works better than stringier-textured acorn squash.) The risotto is finished as usual with the *mantecatura* (beating in) of butter and grated cheese.

Preheat the oven to 177°C (350°F).

Turn the squabs, one at a time, over a gas flame or use a kitchen torch to singe off (*strinare*) any remaining pinfeathers. Reserve the livers, gizzards, and neck.

Season the cavities with salt and pepper to taste; stuff each with half of the chopped pancetta, 1 garlic clove, and a sprig of sage. Season the squabs all over with salt and pepper to taste, and massage the seasonings into the birds.

Combine the oil, the remaining 3 cloves garlic, and the thyme in a saucepan (*casseruola*). Heat the oil over medium-high heat. Add the squabs and sear (*rosolare*) until well browned all over. Remove the squabs from the pan; set aside. Pour off some of the oil, leaving just enough to coat the bottom of the pan.

Add the quartered shallots to the pan and cook until they begin to color, 3 to 5 minutes.

Return the squabs to the pan and roast (*arrostire*) in the oven 10 minutes.

Add the reserved livers, gizzards, and necks to the pan and roast (*arrostire*) 5 more minutes.

Pour off any oil remaining in the pan. Add the wine, pouring it around, not over, the squabs. Return the pan to the oven and roast 15 more minutes, adding a little chicken stock or water if the pan gets dry.

Combine the *balsamico* and the red wine vinegars; drizzle over the breasts of both squabs and roast 5 more minutes.

Remove the squabs from the oven. Recuperate the shallots, gizzards, and livers; reserve. Discard the necks and the thyme. Place the pigeons in a saucepan (*casseruola*) and add the chicken stock. Cover with foil, return to the oven, and braise (*brasare*) 25 minutes.

Meanwhile, pass the reserved shallots, gizzards, and livers through a food mill along with any juices remaining in the saucepan.

Spoon the shallot mixture around the squabs, season with salt and pepper to taste, and continue to braise, covered, 15 more minutes. Add chicken stock as needed if the mixture gets dry.

Uncover and cook the squabs 5 more minutes, or until the breasts are medium-rare. Taste the sauce for consistency; it should be thick enough to coat the back of a spoon. Reduce as needed, and season to taste with salt and pepper.

Quarter the squabs and serve with the sauce.

Quaglie alla Griglia

Grilled Quail with *Fregola*

Serves 4

For this dish, semiboneless whole quail are stuffed with a mixture of diced pancetta, garlic, sage, parsley, fennel fronds, and fennel pollen, then grilled. The quail are served with *fregola*, a large form of couscous, and seasoned with herbs, onion, garlic, grilled corn, and red pepper.

Fregola (from the Italian verb *fregare*, meaning "to rub") is an ancient form of pasta originating in Sardinia (probably through contacts with Arab cultures of North Africa). It is made with coarsely ground semolina grains, sprinkled with warm water to form pellets that are dried and grated, then toasted. *Fregola* is produced in a variety of sizes.

Fregola is traditionally cooked like pasta but it may also be cooked in the manner of a risotto, as it is here: Onion is sautéed, *fregola* is added, then the *fregola* is moistened in stages with hot stock. The *fregola* needn't be stirred as constantly as a risotto—just enough to keep it from burning.

(See "Cooking Risotto" on page 385 and "Roasting and Cleaning Peppers" on page 352 for step-by-step instructions.)

Chef's Notes

A convenient form of quail for both cooking and eating is semiboneless, in which the breastbone, ribs, and wishbone of the quail have been removed, leaving the largest area of meat on the small bird free of bones.

Leftover game-bird meat can be picked from the bones and made into a *ragù* or filling for pasta.

Ingredients

For the quail:

4 semiboneless quail

Coarse salt and freshly ground black pepper

90 milliliters (6 tablespoons) olive oil, plus extra for rubbing the quail

120 grams (4 ounces) pancetta, diced

4 cloves garlic, finely chopped

15 grams (2 tablespoons) finely chopped fresh sage

3 grams (1 tablespoon) finely chopped fresh Italian parsley

5 grams (2 tablespoons) finely chopped fennel fronds

1 teaspoon fennel pollen, or ground toasted fennel seed

180 milliliters (¾ cup) dry white wine

15 milliliters (1 tablespoon) red wine vinegar

For the fregola:

1 liter (4¼ cups) chicken stock

45 milliliters (3 tablespoons) olive oil

175 grams red onion, cut into ½-centimeter (³⁄₁₆-inch) dice (1 cup)

220 grams (1⅓ cups) fregola

Coarse salt and freshly ground black pepper

2 ears fresh corn, husk and silk removed

150 grams (5 ounces) red bell pepper, roasted and cut into ½-centimeter (³⁄₁₆-inch) dice (¾ cup)

10 grams (3 tablespoons) chopped fresh Italian parsley

60 grams (4 tablespoons) unsalted butter

Prepare the quail:

Rinse the quail, inside and out, and pat dry. Turn the quail, one at a time, over a gas flame or use a kitchen torch to singe off (*strinare*) any remaining pinfeathers. Season the quail inside and out with salt and pepper to taste.

Place 45 milliliters (3 tablespoons) of the oil in a small, heavy-bottomed saucepan (*casseruola*) with the pancetta, garlic, and sage. Place over medium-low heat and cook (*saltare*) 5 minutes. Remove from the heat. Stir in the parsley, fennel fronds and pollen, and pepper to taste. Let cool, then stuff the cavities of the quail with the mixture. Secure the stuffing by tying the legs together and pushing them against the body, then secure the cavities with toothpicks.

Rub the quail with olive oil, cover, and set aside at least 1 hour, or refrigerate up to 2 days, to marinate.

Cook the *fregola*:

Bring the chicken stock to a bare simmer in a saucepan. Combine the 45 mililiters (3 tablespoons) oil and the onion in a skillet over medium-low heat and cook until the onion is softened and translucent, 5 to 7 minutes.

Add the *fregola* to the skillet and season to taste with salt. Add enough hot stock just to cover. Bring to a boil, reduce the heat, and simmer, stirring occasionally just as you would a risotto, until the stock has evaporated enough so that it doesn't pool in the gap when you pull a wooden spoon through the grain.

Add more stock just to cover, and continue cooking, adding more stock as it evaporates, until the *fregola* is al dente, 18 to 20 minutes. Taste for seasoning. Remove from the heat; set aside.

Preheat a gas or charcoal grill to medium heat. Grill (*grigliare*) the corn, turning, until the kernels are toasted and cooked through, about 20 minutes. (Keep the grill at medium heat for the quail.)

Cut the kernels off the cob.

Add the corn kernels to the pan with the *fregola*. Stir in the bell pepper and parsley. Taste for seasoning, and add salt and pepper as needed. (The butter will be added just before serving.)

Grill the quail:

Combine the wine, vinegar, and the remaining 45 mililiters (3 tablespoons) oil in a bowl; season with salt and pepper to taste.

Press down gently on the quail with the heel of the hand to flatten slightly. Grill, brushing with the wine mixture, until the quail are golden brown and the juices run clear when the quail are pierced with a small knife, about 5 to 8 minutes. (The breasts will cook quickly because they are boneless; the legs will take slightly longer.)

To serve:

Put the *fregola* over medium heat with a little stock to moisten, and heat through. Remove from the heat and beat in (*mantecare*) the butter, as for risotto. Taste for seasoning.

Split the quail in half lengthwise and serve with the *fregola*.

Sardegna (Sardinia)

"[Sardinia] is a region kissed by luck. Isolation was fundamental in preserving and caring for the culinary and gastronomic treasures."

—Chef Antonino Sanna of Hotel Excelsior Venice Lido Resort, Venice

Sardegna's toasted semolina pasta, *fregola*, is used in *Quaglie alla Griglia* (page 175).

Sardegna is the second-largest island in the Mediterranean, the largest being Sicilia. The coastline is predominantly rocky. The wild and mountainous topography of the interior is punctuated by valleys and plains. Prehistoric stone structures called *nuraghe* dot the landscape. The region's capital is Cagliari.

Historically, the population lived inland. Goat- and sheep-raising have been important industries for millennia: Prehistoric shepherds may have used the *nuraghe* to look after their flocks. Sheep-rearing has resulted in extensive production of cheeses, notably Fiore Sardo, an ancient brined sheep's-milk cheese, Pecorino Sardo and Pecorino Romano, and sheep's-milk ricotta. (Pecorino Romano was produced in the region of Latium, around Rome, until the end of the nineteenth century, at which time most of its manufacture was moved to Sardegna.)

The region is famous for its small, IGP-designated lambs; the lamb is often cooked with native wild fennel. Pork is also raised and used in sausage. Roasted and spit-roasted meats—*porchetta*, lamb, and kid—are popular. The island has a significant fishing industry as well.

Sardegna leads Italy in the cultivation of organic produce. Its cuisine is rich in tomatoes, artichokes, fava beans, eggplants, zucchini, and peas, and is characterized by the use of wild herbs. Like Sicilia, Sardegna was prey to waves of invasions; Spanish domination is reflected in meat-and-vegetable-filled pastries called *impanadas.*

Chapter 11

Beef and Veal:
Manzo e Vitello

Saltimbocca alla Romana (Veal *Saltimbocca*)
Polpettone (Meatloaf)
Bistecca alla Fiorentina (Florentine Beefsteak)
Braciole (Stuffed and Rolled Beef)
Coda alla Vaccinara (Braised Oxtail)
Stracotto (Braised Beef)
Ossobuco alla Milanese
    (Braised Cross-Cut Veal Shanks)

Up until the period after World War II, cattle were primarily used as work animals in Italy, and were too valuable for most families to eat. Nonetheless, by the middle of the nineteenth century, cattle had begun to be bred for their meat, particularly in northern and central regions of the country. Since then, three breeds have been designated IGP *Vitellone Bianco dell'Appennino Centrale* (which, loosely translated, means "white beef from the central Apennine Mountains"). These are the Chianina, Marchigiana, and Romagnola breeds, raised in the area around the central Apennines, in Emilia-Romagna, Toscana, Umbria, Le Marche, Lazio, Abruzzi, Molise, and Campania. To merit their IGP designation, cattle of either sex must belong to one of these three breeds and be between the ages of twelve and twenty-four months. The growth of the calves and structure of the carcasses must conform to certain specifications, as must the rearing methods and feeding techniques.

Ossobuco alla Milanese (page 189), served with *Risotto alla Milanese* (page 132)

The most famous Italian beef comes from the Chianina cattle, a breed that dates back to Roman times, raised near the Val di Chiana river in Toscana. The Chianina breed is celebrated for its combination of lean flesh and excellent flavor.

Veal has traditionally been more appreciated than beef in Italy. According to historians Capatti and Montanari, beef and veal had become popular in courtly and urban cuisines in Italy by the late Middle Ages. Veal was particularly admired for its delicacy and healthful properties, and Italy was precocious among European cultures in its regard for the meat, while fowl continued to be more popular elsewhere. Capatti and Montanari, in *Italian Cuisine: A Cultural History*, quote the physician Lorenzo Sassoli, who writes to advise a patient at the beginning of the fifteenth century. After recommending that his patient eat "as many turtle doves as you can . . . ," Sassoli continues, "my other recommendation is to put veal into your body in any way you can, since, with all its good properties, you will find no healthier form of food." The same authors quote the French philosopher Michel de Montaigne, who reported to his readers on the state of Italian cuisine in his *Travel Journal* that "a few cuts of veal or one or two brace of chicken" were standard fare at Italian banquets.

The recipes in this chapter demonstrate traditional methods for cooking beef and veal. Different parts of the animal lend themselves to different cooking methods—dry or wet heat—depending on the structure of the cut. Tender cuts such as rib-eye steak for

Bistecca all Fiorentina, or beef fillet, may be grilled or sautéed, while tougher cuts, such as beef or veal shin, top round, or chuck roast, benefit from braising in liquid. Veal scaloppine, traditionally sliced very thin from the leg of the veal and pounded thin, are excellent lightly floured and sautéed.

Le Tecniche

In this chapter students learn to fabricate beef and veal. The recipes were chosen to teach students to apply cooking techniques introduced in earlier chapters to a variety of beef and veal cuts. *Brasare* (braising) is discussed in detail in "Le Tecniche: *Brasare*" on page 191. For a more complete discussion of beef and veal, including information on nutrition, butchery, aging, grading, and cuts, see pages 412–21.

Saltimbocca alla Romana

Veal *Saltimbocca*

Serves 2

Saltimbocca means "jump in the mouth," and these small pieces of veal topped with prosciutto and sage are meant to be eaten in a single bite. Scaloppine for *saltimbocca*, which originated in Lazio, are traditionally cut from the leg of the calf but they may be made with whatever is available and inexpensive. The veal is sautéed in garlic-flavored oil and finished with lemon and white wine.

Chicken or pork scaloppine may be substituted for the veal cutlets.

(See page 420 for step-by-step photos of "Cutting Top Round of Veal for Scaloppine"; for instructions on how to toast flour, see sidebar "Toasting Flour" on page 159.)

Chef's Notes

Prosciutto should be cut into thin slices (*fette*) just barely large enough to cover the meat. Its purpose is to add flavor and it should not overpower the taste of the veal.

For variation, sprinkle the scaloppine with 5 to 10 grams (1 to 2 tablespoons) grated Pecorino Romano before saucing.

Use a skillet just large enough to hold the *saltimbocca* in a single layer. If the pan is too large, the caramelization will burn and the sauce will be ruined.

Ingredients

300 grams (10½ ounces) veal top round or eye of round, sliced thin, pounded thin, and cut into 6 pieces, about 8 centimeters (3 inches) square (50 grams / 2 ounces each)

Coarse salt and freshly ground black pepper

6 fresh sage leaves

30 grams (1 ounce) thinly sliced prosciutto, cut into 6 pieces

60 grams (½ cup) toasted all-purpose flour

60 milliliters (¼ cup) olive, grapeseed, or canola oil

1 clove garlic, in the skin, crushed with the heel of the hand

1 lemon, halved

60 milliliters (¼ cup) dry white wine

60 milliliters (¼ cup) chicken stock or water

Halved lemon slices, for garnish (optional)

Lay the veal pieces on a cutting board and season to taste with salt and pepper. Lay a sage leaf, then a slice of prosciutto on top of each. Thread a toothpick through each piece to hold the sage and prosciutto to the veal.

Sprinkle lightly with toasted flour on both sides, patting off the excess.

Combine the oil and the garlic clove in a small skillet (*padella*) and place over medium heat. When the oil is hot, increase the heat to medium-high, place the *saltimbocca* in the pan, prosciutto side down—working in batches if necessary so as not to crowd the pan—and sauté (*saltare*) to brown, about 2 minutes; turn and brown the other side, about 2 minutes.

Pour off the fat, but leave the meat in the pan. Remove the garlic clove. Return the pan to the heat and add the lemon juice, squeezing it over the meat. Drizzle the wine around (not over) the meat and deglaze (*deglassare*) the pan, turning the meat in the liquid, until the wine is reduced.

Remove the pan from the heat. Take the *saltimbocca* out of the pan, remove the toothpicks, and divide the meat between two plates.

Return the pan to the heat, add the broth or water, and reduce until it thickens slightly. Taste for seasoning, and pour the sauce over the *saltimbocca*. Garnish with halved lemon slices, if desired.

Variation

Divide the meat mixture into six or seven patties, about 65 grams (¼ cup–size) apiece. Brown on both sides in oil, spoon beans over as in the last step of the recipe, and bake 10 minutes.

Chef's Note

Be careful to press the meat mixture together lightly. If compacted, the *polpettone* will be tough. According to Harold McGee: "When you grind meat, you break the tissue up into tiny fragments, and that prebroken structure is what gives the cooked meat its light and tender texture, with little spaces that can hold some of the liquid that the meat tissue releases. The more you work the fragments, the more you squeeze them back together, and cooking glues them into a dense mass with no spaces for tenderness or moisture-holding."

Polpettone

Meatloaf

Serves 4

Ground beef, flavored with pancetta, grated cheese, and aromatics, and bound with breadcrumbs and egg, may be cooked in a loaf (*polpettone*) or in individual patties (see Variation). Either way, the mixture is seared in oil and braised in the oven with stewed beans, *cannellini all'uccelletto*.

Ingredients

40 milliliters (2½ tablespoons) olive, grapeseed, or canola oil, plus extra for browning the polpettone

80 grams red onion, cut into ½-centimeter (³⁄₁₆-inch) dice (½ cup)

1 clove garlic, finely chopped

30 grams (1 ounce) pancetta, cut into ½-centimeter (³⁄₁₆-inch) dice

1 fresh thyme sprig, torn into pieces

½ teaspoon red pepper flakes

70 milliliters (¼ cup plus 2 teaspoons) dry white wine

450 grams (1 pound) ground beef, chuck or round

1 large egg

10 grams (2 tablespoons) grated Parmigiano-Reggiano or Grana Padano

7½ grams (2 tablespoons) dried breadcrumbs

3 grams (1 tablespoon) chopped fresh Italian parsley

Coarse salt and freshly ground black pepper

1 clove garlic in the skin, crushed with the heel of the hand

1 recipe Cannellini all'Uccelletto (page 258)

For the *polpettone*, place the oil, onion, garlic, pancetta, and thyme in a skillet (*padella*). Set over medium heat and cook (*saltare*) 2 minutes. Add the red pepper flakes and cook 2 more minutes. Deglaze with 40 milliliters (2½ tablespoons) of the wine and cook until reduced and the onion is softened. Chill.

In a bowl, combine the ground beef, egg, grated cheese, breadcrumbs, parsley, and chilled onion mixture. Season to taste with salt and pepper. Work quickly and gently by hand to combine. Sauté a small piece to test seasonings. Shape into a loaf.

Preheat the oven to 177°C (350°F).

Coat the bottom of a cold skillet with oil, add the garlic clove, and set over medium heat. When the oil is hot, turn the heat to medium-high, add the meat, and brown (*rosolare*) on all sides. Discard the oil and garlic. Deglaze (*deglassare*) the pan with the remaining 30 milliliters (2 tablespoons) white wine.

Spoon the *cannellini all'uccelletto* over and around the meat. Cover with foil and bake (*cuocere al forno*) 20 minutes, or until the internal temperature of the meat reaches 68°C (155°F). Cut the meatloaf into slices and serve with the beans.

Bistecca alla Fiorentina

Florentine Beefsteak

Serves 2

Tuscan cuisine is famous for its grilled steaks cut from the local Chianina breed. The breed is prized for its musculature and the size of its haunch, which yields enormous steaks. These are traditionally cut thick and on the bone and weigh a minimum of 450 grams (1 pound). The exteriors are charred to a crust over coals and the steaks are served very rare, on the bone. In a restaurant setting, the steaks will be marked with a *quadrettatura*, or crosshatch pattern (see "Le Tecniche: Grigliare" on page 164).

At The International Culinary Center, this steak is served with *Cipolline in Agrodolce* (page 262).

Ingredients

2 bone-in porterhouse, T-bone, or strip steaks, at least 450
    grams (1 pound) each, 4½ centimeters (1¾ inches) thick
Sea salt and freshly ground black pepper
Olive, canola, or grapeseed oil, for the grill
Lemon wedges, for serving

Preheat a gas or charcoal grill to high heat. Sprinkle both sides of the steaks with salt and pepper to taste.

Brush the grill with oil. Place the steaks on the grill and grill (*grigliare*) until a dark brown crust forms, 4 to 5 minutes. Turn and grill until well browned on the other side, and very rare, 4 to 5 more minutes.

Let the steaks rest a few minutes before serving.

To serve, cut the meat off the bones. Thickly slice each piece and reassemble the slices with their bones.

4 pieces (225 grams / ½ pound each) beef top round, thinly sliced
(¼ to ½ centimeter / ⅛ to 3⁄16 inch thick) against the grain
Coarse salt and freshly ground black pepper
30 grams (5¼ tablespoons) chopped garlic
10 grams (3 tablespoons) chopped fresh rosemary
240 grams (8½ ounces) prosciutto, thinly sliced
24 very thin slices (280 grams, or about 10 ounces) fresh
mozzarella cheese
100 grams (¾ cup plus 1½ tablespoons) all-purpose flour
75 milliliters (5 tablespoons) olive, grapeseed, or canola oil
2 garlic cloves in the skin, crushed with the heel of the hand
3 sprigs fresh rosemary
150 grams (1 cup) finely chopped red onion
250 milliliters (1 cup) dry white wine
750 milliliters (3 cups) whole, canned Italian plum tomatoes,
puréed with their juices through a food mill
½ recipe Polenta (page 136), optional

Braciole

Stuffed and Rolled Beef

Serves 4

This dish originates in the region of Campania. The meat is pounded into a thin, even layer, seasoned with garlic, salt, and pepper, layered with prosciutto, cheese, and rosemary, then rolled. The rolls are seared and braised in a tomato mixture.

(See page 419 for step-by-step photos of "Trimming Top Round of Beef" and positioning the meat for rolling. See "Tying a Center-Cut Bone-in Loin of Pork for Arista" on page 430 for step-by-step instructions for tying.)

Place the meat on a cutting board; cover with a sheet of plastic wrap. Pound thin with a meat mallet, being careful not to create holes in the meat. Remove the plastic wrap.

Arrange the pieces of meat on a work surface so that the striations in the meat run parallel to the bottom edge of the table. Season the meat with salt and pepper to taste. Rub with the chopped garlic. Sprinkle with the chopped rosemary.

Cover the meat with the prosciutto slices, in a single layer. Place the mozzarella slices in a line across the center of the meat. Now, starting at the bottom edge, roll the meat up into a cylinder.

Tie each roll in three places with butcher's twine or tie the roll with hitch knots, as a roast. Season with salt and pepper. Dredge in flour; pat off excess flour.

Campania

"My evolution as a person and as a restaurateur was first tied to tradition and then little by little I applied personal techniques and know-how that I had obtained through experience. All this while staying true to the products and knowledge rooted in tradition. I can say that my personal cooking style is a modern Mediterranean cuisine closely tied to the area's products, with lots of room for research."

—Chef Gennaro Esposito of Ristorante Torre del Saracino, Vico Equense–Naples

Campania is a region on the coast of the Tyrrhenian Sea in southwest Italy. The inland geography is hilly and mountainous, grading to coastal plains. The region's capital is Naples.

Neapolitan cuisine is the defining style of the region. An ancient city, Naples was the capital of the Kingdom of Naples from the end of the thirteenth century until 1816, when the kingdom joined with Sicilia. Naples was a leading international power during the Italian Renaissance and again during the seventeenth through the nineteenth centuries.

Our recipes for *Braciole* (facing page), *Pizza Margherita* (page 147), and the traditional springtime pastry *Pastiera* (page 295) offer a taste of Campania.

Agriculture is an important industry. The region grows tomatoes (the San Marzano variety grows well in the volcanic soil of the region), olives, eggplants, artichokes, potatoes, lettuces, wheat, fruit (particularly lemons), and wine grapes. Cattle and water buffalo are raised on the lowlands, leading to the production of numerous dairy products, the most well known being the buffalo-milk *mozzarella di bufala* and ricotta from buffalo milk, as well as *fior di latte*, a cow's-milk mozzarella. Pig-breeding produces *soppressata* and sausages.

The cuisine is best known for its pastas and pizzas (nineteenth-century Neapolitans were famously dubbed *Mangiamaccheroni*, which means "macaroni eaters"). The pasta is *pasta secca*, made with the native durum-wheat flour. Native San Marzano tomatoes are used in a host of sauces, from the slow-cooking *ragù napoletano* to *pummarola*.

Seafood is common on the coast; specialties include an octopus stew, *polpi alla Luciana*, and the ever-present fried seafood dishes, *fritto misto alla napoletana*.

In a large skillet (*padella*) combine the oil and whole garlic cloves. Place over medium heat and cook (*saltare*) until the oil is hot and the garlic begins to color, but do not burn. Add the beef rolls and the rosemary sprigs, turn the heat to medium-high, and sear (*rosolare*) the beef very well all over, removing the garlic and rosemary as necessary to prevent them from burning. (Reserve the garlic and rosemary.)

Remove the meat from the pan and pour off most of the fat. Cut each roll between the strings into 3 even pieces. Set aside.

Add the onion to the pan, return to the heat, and cook over medium heat until the onion is softened, 3 to 5 minutes.

Add the wine and deglaze (*deglassare*), cooking to reduce. Add the tomato and 125 milliliters (¼ cup)

water, and return the rosemary sprigs and garlic cloves to the pan. Taste for seasoning. Bring the sauce to a simmer (*sobbollire*), return the meat to the pan, and simmer, covered, 15 minutes.

Remove the rolls from the sauce and place on a cutting board. Cut the twine. Arrange the rolls vertically on a plate (on top of the polenta, if desired), cut sides up, trimming the ends as needed so that the rolls stand upright. Taste the sauce for seasoning, spoon around the meat, and serve.

Coda alla Vaccinara

Braised Oxtail

Serves 4

Coda alla Vaccinara is a classic Roman dish. Its name derives from the slaughterhouse workers (*vaccinari*) who were paid by farmers with the entrails (*scarti*) of the slaughtered animals. The *vaccinari* transformed these less desirable cuts—oxtails in this case—into something good to eat.

Here, the oxtails are braised in a pot on top of the stove rather than in the oven, but the process is essentially the same as for *Stracotto* (page 188) and other braises. The finished braise is garnished with celery, raisins, and pine nuts. A small amount of extra-bitter chocolate adds depth of flavor to the sauce.

Ingredients

1¾ kilograms (4 pounds) oxtail, fat trimmed to a thin layer, cut in 8-centimeter (3-inch) pieces
Coarse salt and freshly ground black pepper
Olive, grapeseed, or canola oil
100 grams (3½ ounces) pancetta, cut into ½-centimeter (³⁄₁₆-inch) dice

125 grams (4½ ounces) red onion, cut into ½-centimeter (³⁄₁₆-inch) dice (¾ cup)
125 grams (4½ ounces) celery, cut into ½-centimeter (³⁄₁₆-inch) dice (1¼ cups)
125 grams (4½ ounces) carrot, cut into ½-centimeter (³⁄₁₆-inch) dice (1 cup)
75 grams (3 ounces) stemmed cremini mushrooms, cut into ½-centimeter- (³⁄₁₆-inch)-thick slices (1 cup)
3 cloves garlic, peeled and crushed
100 milliliters (6¾ tablespoons) white wine, plus extra to soak raisins
1 liter (4¼ cups) whole, canned Italian plum tomatoes, puréed with their juices through a food mill
Pinch of spezie forti, garam masala, or freshly ground nutmeg
4 large fresh bay leaves
1 liter (4¼ cups) brown veal stock, or as needed
25 grams (1 ounce / 2 tablespoons) finely chopped extra-bitter chocolate
30 milliliters (2 tablespoons) red wine vinegar, plus extra to soak raisins
30 grams (¼ cup) raisins, soaked in equal parts white wine and red wine vinegar to cover
150 grams celery, cut into 3-centimeter (1³⁄₁₆-inch) pieces (1½ cups), cooked in boiling, salted water for 10 minutes, drained, and shocked in ice water
30 grams (¼ cup) toasted pine nuts

Season the oxtail on both sides with salt and pepper.

Using a skillet (*padella*) large enough to hold all of the oxtails in a single layer, add oil to film the bottom and set over medium-high heat. When the oil is hot, add the oxtails and sear (*rosalare*) until the oxtails are well browned all over, 4 to 5 minutes each side.

Pour off most of the oil. Add the pancetta, vegetables, and garlic, tucking them into the space around the oxtails, and brown. Discard the remaining oil. Add the white wine and deglaze (*deglassare*).

Remove the oxtails to a large pot (*pentola*); set aside.

Chef's Notes

The celery is blanched separately so that it doesn't absorb too much of the flavor of the braise, and it brings a clean, bright flavor to the dish.

Raisins are soaked in wine and vinegar to cut their sweetness.

A trick for throwing off fat from a skillet holding meat is to set a lid over the skillet to hold the meat, then tip the skillet over a container so that the fat pours out.

For a more delicate flavor, use vegetable broth in place of veal stock, or cut the veal stock with water.

Add the tomato purée to the skillet along with 1 liter (4¼ cups) water. Season with salt and pepper to taste, the *spezie forti*, and the bay leaves. Bring to a simmer. Pour the sauce over the oxtails in the pot. Return to a simmer, cover, and simmer (*sobbollire*) until the oxtails are very tender, about 3½ hours. Stir occasionally to keep the oxtails from sticking, and check the level of the braising liquid to make sure that it doesn't evaporate too quickly; it should come about halfway up the sides of the oxtails.

After 2½ hours of cooking, add 500 milliliters (2 cups) of the stock and the chocolate. After 3 hours, add the remaining 500 milliliters (2 cups) stock, or as needed, along with the vinegar. Taste for seasoning a few times during the cooking and add salt and pepper as needed.

Ten minutes before the braise is finished, drain the raisins and add them to the pot with the oxtail along with the celery and pine nuts. Taste, and season with salt and pepper.

Stracotto

Braised Beef

Serves 4

Stracotto is a method as much as a recipe for braising meat, and the same dish is typically known as *brasato* in Piemonte and Lombardia. The meat is seasoned and marinated in a full-bodied red wine for one to two days, then braised in a combination of the red-wine marinade and puréed tomato. It is traditionally made with a lean cut of beef. Once braised, the meat is sliced thin, then baked and served with the reduced braising liquid; this offsets the dryness of the meat.

(See page 354 for instructions for "Working with Dried Porcini Mushrooms.")

Ingredients

For the trito:

3 cloves garlic, peeled

Leaves from 2 small sprigs fresh rosemary

Leaves from 1 small sprig fresh sage

2½ grams (1¼ teaspoons) freshly ground black pepper

1 teaspoon spezie forti, garam masala, or freshly ground nutmeg

For the braise:

450 grams (1 pound) beef top round or chuck roast

3 whole cloves

½ stick cinnamon

3 juniper berries

225 grams (8 ounces) red onion, cut into 3-centimeter (1³⁄₁₆-inch) pieces (1⅓ cups)

90 grams (3 ounces) celery, cut into 3-centimeter (1³⁄₁₆-inch) pieces (¾ cup)

55 grams (2 ounces) carrot, cut into 3-centimeter (1³⁄₁₆-inch) pieces (⅓ cup)

375 milliliters (1½ cups plus 2 tablespoons) full-bodied red wine

30 grams (¼ cup) dried porcini mushrooms, soaked in water to cover for 30 minutes

Coarse salt and freshly ground black pepper

45 milliliters (3 tablespoons) olive, grapeseed, or canola oil

30 grams (1 ounce) chopped pancetta

310 milliliters (1⅓ cups) whole, canned Italian plum tomatoes, puréed with their juices through a food mill

100 to 125 milliliters (7 to 8 tablespoons) veal or chicken stock, plus more as needed during braising

Prepare the *trito*:

Chop the garlic and herbs, and combine with the rest of the ingredients.

Marinate the meat:

Trim the beef of some of the fat and connective tissue, leaving the silverskin and a thin layer of fat. Make 6 or 7 slits (a little less than 3 centimeters / 1 inch deep) in the meat, starting at the top of the roast and cutting down. Stuff the slits with some of the *trito*. Rub the remaining *trito* all over the meat.

Place the beef, cloves, cinnamon, juniper berries, onion, celery, and carrot in a small, deep container. (The aromatics may also be tied up in cheesecloth for easier removal.) Pour the wine over the meat (the meat should be completely submerged). Cover and marinate overnight in the refrigerator.

Braise the meat:

Preheat the oven to 163°C (325°F).

Remove the meat from the marinade. Remove the vegetables and set them aside. Reserve the marinade and the spices.

Drain the mushrooms and strain the liquid through cheesecloth. Chop the mushrooms and add them to the vegetables. Taste the soaking liquid and reserve, diluting with water if it is very strong.

Rub the meat with salt and pepper. Rub with 15 milliliters (1 tablespoon) of the oil, and place in a small, high-sided cooking vessel. Pour the remaining 30 milliliters oil (2 tablespoons) around the beef. Add the pancetta and roast (*arrostire*) 15 minutes to brown the meat.

Arrange the reserved vegetables around the beef. Return it to the oven and roast 15 more minutes.

Pour about half of the reserved marinade around the meat. Return to the oven and cook 1 hour, stirring every 20 minutes. Add the porcini soaking liquid about halfway through the cooking.

Spoon off the fat. Add the tomato purée and the spices, tied up in cheesecloth, and stir; cook 15 more minutes to reduce.

Cover the dish with foil and braise (*brasare*), stirring and turning the meat in the braising liquid every 30 minutes, until the meat is very tender, about 2 more hours. There should always be enough liquid to cover the vegetables; if it reduces beyond that point, add stock or water.

When the beef is cooked, remove it from the pan. Remove the spices and pass the sauce (including the vegetables) through a food mill, rinsing out the food mill with water to catch all of the solids. Return the purée to the pan and add 100 to 125 milliliters (6 to 8 tablespoons) stock as needed for a saucelike consistency. Taste for seasoning and add salt and pepper as needed.

To serve:

Slice the meat as thinly as possible. Return the meat to the pan along with the sauce and bring to a simmer. Cover and bake 10 more minutes. Spoon the meat and sauce onto plates and serve.

Chef's Note

This dish improves if refrigerated for a few days after cooking.

Ossobuco alla Milanese

Braised Cross-Cut Veal Shanks

Serves 4

In the dialect of Milan, where this dish originates, *ossobuco* means "bone with a hole." The name refers to the fat bone in the center of the hind veal shank, filled with marrow that turns a rich, velvety consistency with cooking. The marrow itself is eaten as a delicacy, dug out with a narrow, long-handed spoon called an *esattore*, meaning "tax collector." A classic braise, *ossobuco* is made with veal shank cut into approximately 5-centimeter- (2-inch)-thick slices, which are tied around the circumference to better hold their shape. The meat is braised with *soffritto* in white wine and tomato until very tender.

Ossobuco is traditionally garnished with *gremolata*— a zesty mixture of lemon, garlic, and parsley—and served on a bed of *Risotto alla Milanese* (page 132).

(See page 420 for step-by-step instructions for "Braising Veal for *Ossobuco*.")

Ingredients

For the trito:
10 grams (5 tablespoons) rosemary leaves
10 grams (heaping ¼ cup) fresh sage leaves
2 large cloves garlic
5 grams (¾ tablespoon) freshly ground black pepper

For the braise:
4 slices (4 centimeters / 1½ inches thick) cross-cut veal shank, rinsed and patted dry
Coarse salt and freshly ground black pepper
Olive, grapeseed, or canola oil
3 cloves garlic in the skin, crushed with the heel of the hand
2 large sprigs fresh rosemary

375 grams (13 ounces) red onion, cut into ½-centimeter
  (³⁄₁₆-inch) dice (2¼ cups)

130 grams (4½ ounces) celery, cut into ½-centimeter (³⁄₁₆-inch)
  dice (1⅓ cups)

130 grams (4½ ounces) carrot, cut into ½-centimeter (³⁄₁₆-inch)
  dice (1 cup)

375 milliliters (1½ cup plus 2 tablespoons) dry white wine

500 milliliters (2 cups) whole, canned Italian plum tomatoes
  with their juices, chopped

500 milliliters (2 cups) brown veal stock, or as needed

For the gremolata:

1 clove garlic, finely chopped

Coarse salt

6 grams (2 tablespoons) chopped fresh Italian parsley

2 teaspoons grated lemon zest

Risotto alla Milanese (page 132)

Make the *trito*:

Chop the rosemary, sage, and garlic, and combine in a
small bowl along with the pepper.

Marinate the meat:

Make slits in the veal (look for the lines of white
cartilage, where the muscles meet, and make the slits
there rather than in the muscle itself) and stuff with
the *trito*. Stuff the *trito* around the bone as well. Tie the
slices around the circumference with butcher's twine.
Season to taste with salt and pepper, rub with oil, and
cover and refrigerate 1 hour, or up to 2 days.

Braise the meat:

Preheat the oven to 163°C (325°F).

In a skillet (*padella*) large enough to hold the veal
in one layer, combine 125 milliliters (½ cup) oil, the
whole garlic cloves, and rosemary sprigs. Place over

medium heat and heat until a leaf of sage or basil
sizzles when it hits the oil. Turn the heat to medium-
high, add the veal, and brown well (*rosolare*) on both
sides, 8 to 10 minutes total. Remove the garlic (or set
it on top of the meat) when it begins to brown.

Add the onion, celery, and carrot and cook (*saltare*)
over medium heat until the color of the *soffritto* darkens and the flavor concentrates.

Add the wine, off the heat. Reduce the wine over medium heat until the pan is almost dry.

Turn the meat in the pan. Add the chopped tomato and
enough stock to bring the liquid three-quarters of the
way up the meat. Cover and place in the oven to braise
(*brasare*) until tender, 3 to 3½ hours, basting every 25
to 30 minutes, and checking to ensure that the braising liquid covers the meat by about three-quarters; add
more stock or water as needed.

Remove the pan from the oven. Transfer the meat to a
plate. Degrease the sauce, and pass it through a food
mill with the stock, to purée. Return the sauce to the
pan. Remove the twine from the meat and return to the
pan with the sauce.

Make the *gremolata*:

Very finely chop the garlic with salt to taste. Combine
the garlic mixture with the parsley and lemon zest in a
small bowl.

To serve:

Heat the meat with the sauce 2 to 3 minutes. Season
to taste with salt and pepper. Serve the meat with the
sauce, sprinkled with the *gremolata*, on a bed of the
risotto.

Le Tecniche: *Brasare* (Braising)

In Italian cooking there has always been a heavy emphasis on wet-heat methods such as braising and stewing because these were suitable techniques for cooking less expensive, second- or third-category cuts of meat that would be tough if cooked by other methods. Braising is a method of cooking food partially immersed in a small amount of liquid, at a low temperature over a long period of time, until the food is very tender. As it cooks, the food renders its juices to the liquid, and the liquid tenderizes the meat. The slow interaction of the meat juices, herbs, wine, and aromatic vegetables creates a complex, multilayered flavor. Braises are traditionally served with polenta, gnocchi, or mashed potatoes. Braises also make excellent pasta sauces.

Braises may be cooked on top of the stove or in the oven. The oven method provides more even heat and is more consistent with the origins of the technique, in which the cooking vessel was placed in hot embers, and additional hot embers were placed on top of the lid so that the heat came from both top and bottom (technically, a braise differs from a stew in that a stew uses more liquid and, usually, smaller pieces of meat).

Braising does not make the meat juicy—in fact, meat loses weight in water during braising and also releases its flavor into the braising liquid. Braising is therefore best applied to cuts rich in collagen, which softens into gelatin during cooking, making the meat less likely to dry out. Braising may also be used for poultry and whole, firm-fleshed fish, as well as for vegetables such as cabbage, endive, artichokes, and lettuce.

Guidelines for Braising

Foods are frequently marinated prior to braising. They may also be seasoned with a *trito*, stuffed into shallow cuts in the meat.

It is important that the vessel used for braising be deep, and just large enough for the meat to fit into, so that the liquid evaporates very slowly. If liquid evaporates too quickly, the meat will not have enough time to cook properly, and the sauce will be over-reduced.

Many recipes call for searing the meat before braising. Color and flavor from the caramelization of the proteins will create a foundation for the sauce. When searing, it is important to keep in mind the following: If the pan is not hot enough, the meat will release its moisture and boil and steam rather than sauté; as a result, the meat will not caramelize, and the sauce will be robbed of its distinct flavor and color. If the pan is too hot, the meat will caramelize too much and the juices will burn; the resultant sauce will have a bitter flavor and the color will be too dark.

Once the meat is browned, a *soffritto* may be added to the pan; it is in turn lightly caramelized, to add its concentrated flavors to the dish. Lemon may be squeezed over the food for additional flavor.

Whatever the initial approach, the fat is thrown off, and the pan is deglazed.

The food is then moistened, usually with relatively little liquid, covered with a tight-fitting lid, and cooked in the oven or on the stovetop. The braising liquid should come about halfway to three-quarters up the sides of the meat and will need to be replenished during cooking. The amount of liquid is calculated to create an intensely flavored sauce.

The pot should be covered during cooking.

Once the food is cooked, it is removed from the pan, and the braising liquid is degreased. It may then be puréed with the *soffritto*, if there is one. Stock is added as needed to thin the sauce. The meat is returned to the sauce for a few minutes to rewarm before serving.

Chapter 12

Organ Meats:
Frattaglie

Animelle Saltate
(Sautéed Veal Sweetbreads with Moscato)
Fegato alla Veneziana
(Venetian-Style Liver and Onions)
Trippa alla Parmigiana (Tripe Stew)

Organ meats, or offal (*frattaglie*), such as trotters, tongue, tripe, and sweetbreads have held an important place in Italian cuisine throughout history, in part because the more desirable cuts were reserved for the elite, while those who raised the animals for slaughter made do with what was left over.

But offal was not disdained by the wealthy. In his *Opera* written in 1570, Bartolomeo Scappi includes numerous recipes for offal, including sweetbreads, kidneys, liver, brains, tongue, cow's udder, and calf's head. His recipes are not limited to beef and veal; one entry is entitled "To prepare every cut—that is, every part—of a goat and chamois"; he also recommends methods for cooking pig's head, as well as the head of a wild boar. In an earlier work, *Libro de Arte Coquinaria* (*The Art of Cooking*), the fifteenth-century Renaissance cookbook author Maestro Martino of Como also offers recipes for offal: Mutton's head is poached and boned; veal and kid sweetbreads are made into an egg-rich "pottage." And several centuries later, Pellegrino Artusi proposes recipes for beef tongue, goose liver, kidneys, tripe, sweetbreads, and "Lamb's Liver and Offal Bolognese Style," among other delicacies, in his cookbook *La Scienza in Cucina e L'Arte di Mangiar Bene* (*Science in the Kitchen and the Art of Eating Well*).

The recipes in this chapter demonstrate some classic preparations for calf's liver, sweetbreads, and tripe.

Le Tecniche

In this chapter, students learn the fundamentals of preparing offal and apply techniques of *sbianchire*, *saltare*, and *brasare* covered in previous chapters. For a more complete discussion of offal, see pages 422–25.

Trippa alla Parmigiana (page 198)

Animelle Saltate

Sautéed Veal Sweetbreads with Moscato

Serves 4

In Italy, sweetbreads are typically grilled or sautéed, after a preliminary soaking and blanching. (Sweetbreads may be soaked in water but, as with liver, they are often soaked in milk.) Once blanched, the sweetbreads are weighted to compress them to a firm, appetizing texture. For this recipe, the blanched sweetbreads are pulled apart where the lobe naturally breaks into rounded "nuggets." (Alternatively, the sweetbreads may be cut into 5- to 8-centimeter / 2- to 3-inch pieces.) The nuggets are floured and sautéed with some smoky bacon. A sauce is made by deglazing the pan with vinegar and Moscato, a sweet and slightly sparkling wine.

This dish is delicious garnished with mushrooms (as in the photo) sautéed separately and added to the pan after deglazing with the vinegar and wine.

(For instructions on toasting flour, see sidebar "Toasting Flour" on page 159.)

Ingredients

750 grams (1¾ pounds) veal sweetbreads

Milk for soaking (optional)

Coarse salt and freshly ground black pepper

Toasted all-purpose flour

Olive, grapeseed, or canola oil

2 garlic cloves in the skin, crushed with the heel of the hand

2 sprigs fresh sage

60 grams (2 ounces) bacon, cut into ½-centimeter (³⁄₁₆-inch) dice

60 milliliters (¼ cup) red wine vinegar

60 milliliters (¼ cup) Moscato wine

125 milliliters (½ cup) brown veal stock

Disgorge the sweetbreads under cold running water, then soak in milk or cold water overnight.

Place the sweetbreads in a pot (*pentola*) with cold, salted water to cover. Blanch (*sbianchire*) until firm, 10 to 15 minutes. Refresh in ice water; drain. Peel off the thin membrane that covers the sweetbreads and pull off any fatty parts, nerves, blood vessels, or cartilage. Place the sweetbreads on a sheet pan or baking dish or in a perforated hotel pan lined with cheesecloth. Cover with cheesecloth, place a second sheet pan, baking dish, or hotel pan on top, and weight at least 1 hour.

Separate the sweetbreads into rounded "nuggets" where they naturally break apart; pull off any remaining skin.

Season the sweetbreads with salt and pepper to taste and toss in the toasted flour; shake off the excess.

In a large skillet (*padella*), combine the oil, garlic, and sage and place over medium heat. When the oil is hot, increase the heat to medium-high, add the sweetbreads and the bacon, and sauté (*saltare*) until the sweetbreads are browned. Pour off the oil.

Add the vinegar and wine and toss with the sweetbreads over medium-high heat until the liquid evaporates. Divide the sweetbreads and bacon between four plates. Deglaze (*deglassare*) the pan with the stock, reduce to sauce consistency, and taste for seasoning. Spoon the sauce over the sweetbreads.

Fegato alla Veneziana

Venetian-Style Liver and Onions

Serves 2

An overnight soak in milk cleans the liver of blood while it softens the taste and smell. In this classic Venetian presentation, liver slices are cut into smallish strips, dredged in flour, sautéed in oil, and served *agro-dolce*, with caramelized onions and vinegar. The flour helps develop a crust and thickens the pan sauce.

Capers are an excellent addition to this dish. Add them when the cooked onions are returned to the pan.

Chef's Note

It is typical to serve this classic dish with polenta that's been cooled and cut into squares or rounds, then grilled or sautéed. White polenta would be traditional in the Veneto.

Ingredients

200 grams (7 ounces) calf's liver, cleaned, membrane peeled

Milk, for soaking, as needed

200 grams (7 ounces) red onion, cut in half through the equator and sliced thin (¾ cup)

45 milliliters (3 tablespoons) olive, grapeseed, or canola oil

5 fresh bay leaves

Coarse salt and freshly ground black pepper

35 grams (¼ cup plus 1 teaspoon) all-purpose flour

20 milliliters (1¾ tablespoons) white wine vinegar

1 tablespoon capers, preferably salt-packed (see page 31), rinsed and drained (optional)

Chicken or vegetable stock or water, as needed

3 grams (1 tablespoon) chopped fresh Italian parsley

Rinse the liver under cold running water. Place in a container and add milk to cover. Refrigerate overnight.

Cut the liver into slices, 6 millimeters (¼ inch) thick.

Combine the onions, 25 milliliters (1 tablespoon plus 2 teaspoons) of the oil, the bay leaves, and a sprinkling of salt and pepper in a cold skillet (*padella*). Set over medium-low heat and cook until the onions are softened but not mushy, and well browned but not burned, about 20 minutes. (The onions will first give up their liquid, and then caramelize.) Season to taste with salt and pepper. Set aside.

In a second large skillet, heat the remaining 20 milliliters (1 tablespoon plus 1 teaspoon) oil over medium-high heat until a leaf of sage or basil sizzles when tossed into the hot oil.

Season the liver well on both sides with salt and pepper. Dredge the liver in the flour, tap off the excess, and sear (*rosolare*) on both sides until a well-browned crust forms, 3 to 4 minutes on each side. Remove the liver from the pan. (Do not overcook: The liver should remain slightly pink in the center.)

Deglaze (*deglassare*) the pan with the vinegar and cook to reduce by half. Add the onions and the capers, if desired, to the pan with liver, and stir gently to warm them. Add stock or water if the pan gets dry; the onions should be surrounded by a lightly thickened liquid. Toss in the freshly chopped parsley. Serve the liver with the onions and sauce.

Trippa alla Parmigiana

Tripe Stew

Serves 4

Tripe is prepared all over Italy in a variety of ways; in this classic dish, it is braised in tomato and white wine. To finish, butter and grated cheese are vigorously stirred into the stew—just as for a risotto—to thicken and emulsify the braising liquid.

Tripe must be well cleaned before cooking by washing several times in cold water. Then it is blanched in two changes of salted water, with vegetables, for additional flavor.

Chef's Notes

The cooking time for the tripe is necessarily approximate; it varies with the quality of the tripe and the size of the pieces.

Very little oil is needed for cooking the *soffritto* because the tripe will give off enough fat and gelatin as it cooks to keep the mixture moist.

Ingredients

450 grams (1 pound) honeycomb tripe
50 grams (2 ounces) red onion, cut into 3-centimeter
    (1³⁄₁₆-inch) pieces (⅓ cup)
50 grams (2 ounces) celery, cut into 3-centimeter (1³⁄₁₆-inch)
    pieces (½ cup)
30 grams (1 ounce) carrot, cut into 3-centimeter (1³⁄₁₆-inch)
    pieces (¼ cup)
3 sprigs fresh Italian parsley
Coarse salt

For the soffritto:
30 milliliters (2 tablespoons) olive, grapeseed, or canola oil
50 grams (2 ounces) red onion, cut into ½-centimeter
    (³⁄₁₆-inch) dice (⅓ cup)
50 grams (2 ounces) celery, cut into ½-centimeter (³⁄₁₆-inch)
    dice (½ cup)
20 grams (¾ ounce) carrot, cut into ½-centimeter (³⁄₁₆-inch)
    dice (2 tablespoons)
1 clove garlic, chopped
3 grams (1 tablespoon) chopped fresh Italian parsley
1 gram (½ tablespoon) chopped fresh rosemary leaves

30 grams (1 ounce) pancetta, cut into ½-centimeter
    (³⁄₁₆-inch) dice
Pinch of red pepper flakes

Coarse salt and freshly ground black pepper
60 milliliters (¼ cup) dry white wine
Grated zest of ½ lemon
150 grams (5½ ounces) whole, canned Italian plum tomatoes
    with their juices, puréed through a food mill
4 fresh bay leaves
100 milliliters (scant ½ cup) brown veal stock
30 grams (2 tablespoons) unsalted butter
20 grams (¼ cup) grated Parmigiano-Reggiano or Grana
    Padano, plus extra for serving

Wash the tripe well in cold running water. Soak overnight in cold water to cover. Drain.

Place half of the onion, celery, carrot, and parsley in a large saucepan (*casseruola*). Add 3 liters (3 quarts) cold water, or enough to cover the tripe, and 2 tablespoons salt. Bring to a boil. Add the tripe, cover, and simmer 30 minutes. Remove the tripe, and discard the blanching water and vegetables. Repeat the process with clean water and the remaining vegetables. Cool the tripe in an ice bath. Drain; discard the vegetables.

Thinly slice the tripe into strips on a bias.

Make the *soffritto*: Combine the oil, vegetables, garlic, parsley, rosemary, and pancetta in a large, unheated saucepan (*casseruola*). Set over medium heat and cook (*saltare*) the *soffritto* until golden, 10 to 15 minutes, adding the red pepper flakes a few minutes into the cooking to keep them from burning. Season to taste with salt.

Add the tripe slices and stir. Season to taste with salt and pepper.

Deglaze (*deglassare*) the pan with the wine and cook until the wine has evaporated.

Veneto

"Given that Venice is a seaport, products from all over the world arrived here, and therefore there were many influences. In all the dishes in the Veneto there is a frequent use of spices, and products (particularly fish) that are preserved in salt, or dehydrated, or marinated with spices."

—Chef Nicola Portinari of La Peca Restaurant, Lonigo–Vicenza

Our recipes for the regional specialties *Fegato alla Veneziana, Baccalà Mantecato*, and *Radicchio Trevisano Brasato* appear on pages 197, 226, and 263, respectively.

The Veneto is a region of varied geography in northeastern Italy, bounded to the south by the Adriatic Sea. The northern part of the region is covered by the Alps. The southern part is a flat area of river plains through which the Po, Adige, and Piave rivers flow, while the coastline is characterized by a series of lagoons. The coastal city of Venice is the region's capital.

The Venetian Republic was a leading commercial and naval power during the Renaissance. As a result, the cuisine benefited from the importation of products from the New World and the Far East (such as corn and a variety of spices), as well as foreign culinary techniques. Techniques for preserving fish were responsible for the creation of innumerable seafood dishes, such as *sarde in saor* (marinated sardines), *aringhe in graticola* (grilled herring), and *baccalà* ("in a

thousand forms," according to Chef Portinari): *baccalà all Vicentina con l'uvetta* (Vicenza-style *baccalà* with currants), and *baccalà mantecato* (in which the cod is puréed with olive oil, parsley, and garlic).

Venetian cuisine is shaped by its access to saltwater creatures from the Adriatic such as cuttlefish, prawns, spider crabs, clams, mussels, scallops, tuna, eel, and sardines. But *Vialone Nano* rice and corn are grown on the plains of the Veneto, and the region is equally famous for its dishes of rice (*risi e bisi*) and polenta.

Fishing and cattle-breeding are important industries, as is the production of cheeses, Asiago and Grana Padano in particular, and cured pork products, such as *cotechino* and prosciutto.

Add the lemon zest and cook a few minutes.

Add the tomato purée, bay leaves, and 200 milliliters (¾ cup plus 2 tablespoons) water. Cover and cook 20 minutes.

Add the stock and continue cooking at a slow simmer (*sobbollire*) over very low heat until the tripe is very tender, 1 to 1½ hours more. (Check to make sure that

the liquid doesn't evaporate entirely; add more water as needed to prevent the pan from burning.)

Taste for seasoning, adding salt and pepper as needed. Remove from the heat. Add the butter and cheese and stir vigorously (*mantecare*) to emulsify. Return to the heat and warm, stirring constantly, to get the tripe very hot but not so hot that the butter separates out of the sauce. Serve with grated cheese.

Chapter 13

Pork:
Maiale

Hardy and high-yielding, pigs are bred almost exclusively for consumption. Nearly every part of the animal may be used for food, cooking, apparel, and more.

Pigs are raised all over Italy, and every region boasts characteristic pork products. Traditionally, pigs grew fat in the autumn, on harvest leftovers and from the nuts and acorns falling off trees. In the winter, when nutritious waste was not readily available, the farmer had to choose between feeding pigs valuable foods or slaughtering them and preserving their meat. Because pigs do not provide labor as cows do, the farmer often opted for slaughter. The techniques of curing pork and sausage-making were developed to use all parts of the pig efficiently. In areas where meat was too scarce to be consumed fresh, most of the animal was dedicated to cured products. As Capatti and Montanari explain in *Italian Cuisine: A Cultural History*, "No part of the pig should be thrown away" is an ageless saying in Italy that reflects the importance of the animal to the culture.

Pork fat has traditionally been as valuable as the meat itself. Some fat (such as the soft-textured fat surrounding the organs) is rendered and used as a cooking medium or ingredient (lard, or *strutto*); pork fat adds flavor and succulence to lean meats. Other types of fat are used for different purposes. *Rete,* or pork caulfat (see "*Rete*" on page 425), is a weblike membrane that is used as a wrapping to protect and moisten foods such as pork tenderloin during cooking (see *Filetto di Maiale*, page 204). Pancetta (see "Pancetta," page 25) is made, as is bacon, with the firm layer of thick, meat-striped fat located under the skin of the pork belly, while fatback (*lardo*), found under the skin of the back, is preferred for sausage-making or is cured in whole pieces (see "*Lardo*" on page 25).

Pigs are omnivores. They can survive on nearly anything and require little care, a fact that historically made their domestication much easier than that of other livestock animals, such as cattle and sheep. However, a pig's diet affects the flavor and texture of its meat. Pigs that eat a diet high in nuts, for instance, have a soft, oily fat that is well suited for making ham. Those that are allowed to range put on additional fat that may be used in cooking.

Arista alla Toscana con Patate alla Paesana
(page 210)

This chapter demonstrates classic cooking techniques for several cuts of pork:

Tender chops, scaloppine, and loin are cooked by dry-heat methods.

Chewier cuts—ribs and legs—are braised.

Pork chops are sautéed and served with a pan sauce made from the caramelized pork juices.

Thin scaloppine, cut from the tenderloin, are gently pounded to an even thickness and sautéed.

Pork loin and tenderloin are suitable cuts for sautéing and roasting.

Ribs are marinated, then braised in a spicy tomato sauce.

Cubes of leg (wild boar, in this chapter, but pork would work equally well) are braised in a stew.

Students also learn to make two varieties of pork sausage: a fresh sausage of seasoned ground pork; and a cured sausage, *cotechino*, made with cubed pork, pork fat, and pork rind.

Le Tecniche

In this chapter, students learn to fabricate pork and to apply techniques of *saltare*, *arrostire*, *brasare*, *affogare*, and *grigliare* covered in previous chapters. See pages 426–34 for an in-depth discussion of pork, with instructions for fabrication and sausage-making.

Costine

Tuscan-Style Pork Spareribs

Serves 4 to 6

Pork spareribs are marinated in an herb rub, browned in the oven, and then braised in a spicy tomato sauce in this luscious, mildly spicy preparation. Ribs give off a great deal of fat; therefore, as much oil as possible should be removed from the sauce once the ribs are cooked.

This recipe uses a cut called Saint Louis–style ribs, cut from a rack of spareribs.

(See "Cleaning Pork Spareribs" on page 428 for step-by-step instructions.)

Ingredients

For the spareribs:

30 grams (5¼ tablespoons) chopped garlic
15 grams (¼ cup) chopped fresh sage
15 grams (¼ cup) chopped fresh rosemary
30 grams (1¾ tablespoons) coarse salt
10 grams (1¾ tablespoons) freshly ground black pepper
5 grams (1 tablespoon) spezie forti, garam masala, or freshly ground nutmeg
5 grams (1 tablespoon) red pepper flakes
3 to 4 kilograms (7 to 8 pounds) pork spareribs (2 racks), membrane and skirt removed and rack trimmed of large areas of fat (see Chef's Note)
Olive, grapeseed, or canola oil
250 milliliters (1 cup) dry white wine

Preheat the oven to 177°C (350°F).

Place the ribs in a roasting pan (*la rostiera*) and roast (*arrostire*), turning twice during roasting, until well browned, about 50 minutes.

Deglaze (*deglassare*) the pan with the wine and return to the oven to evaporate the wine completely, 10 to 15 minutes. Remove from the oven and pour off the fat. Cut the ribs into individual bones. Return the ribs to the roasting pan; set aside.

Make the sauce:

In a large saucepan (*casseruola*), add enough oil to coat the bottom of the pan. Add the garlic, place over medium-low heat, and cook until the garlic is soft and just beginning to color. Stir in the red pepper flakes and cook 15 seconds. Add the crushed tomatoes, 750 milliliters (3 cups) water, the Worcestershire sauce, and hot pepper sauce. Bring to a simmer and season to taste with salt and pepper (be careful with the salt—the herb rub is salty).

Cook the ribs in the sauce:

Pour the sauce over the ribs and return them to the oven. Continue roasting, stirring occasionally, until the sauce reduces to the point where it comes about halfway up the sides of the ribs (this may take 5 to 10 minutes).

Cover and braise until the ribs are very tender and the sauce has thickened enough to coat the ribs, about 30 more minutes. (If the sauce is still too thin, braise the ribs uncovered to reduce.)

Spoon off as much fat as possible. Serve the ribs with the sauce.

Chef's Note

Use spareribs in preference to baby back ribs. Baby back ribs are cut from the rib side of the loin portion of the pork, and are relatively lean. Spareribs are cut from the front of the rib cage, on the belly portion; their natural fat contributes to the excellent flavor and melting texture of this dish.

For the sauce:

Olive, grapeseed, or canola oil, for sautéing

10 grams (1¾ tablespoons) sliced garlic

2 grams (2 teaspoons) red pepper flakes

1 kilogram (2¼ pounds) whole, canned Italian plum tomatoes with their juices, crushed

30 milliliters (2 tablespoons) Worcestershire sauce

25 milliliters (1 tablespoon plus 2 teaspoons) hot pepper sauce

Coarse salt and freshly ground black pepper

Marinate and roast the spareribs:

In a bowl, combine the garlic, sage, rosemary, salt, black pepper, *spezie forti*, and red pepper flakes. Rub the mixture all over the ribs. Drizzle the ribs with a little oil. Wrap in plastic and refrigerate overnight, or up to 48 hours.

Filetto di Maiale

Roasted Pork Tenderloin with Bay Leaves

Serves 4

Tenderloin is a tender, lean cut suitable for dry-heat methods of cooking such as sautéing, grilling, and roasting. Wrapping in caulfat (*rete*) helps the meat to hold its shape and protects the lean flesh from drying out during cooking. (The caulfat will melt away during roasting.) Vegetables roasted alongside the pork add moisture to the pan, preventing the pan juices from evaporating and burning; they are eventually deglazed to make a pan sauce.

The variation below demonstrates the technique of sautéing tenderloin.

(See "Wrapping Pork Tenderloin in Caulfat for Roasting" on page 431 for step-by-step instructions.)

Ingredients

450 grams (1 pound) pork caulfat
2 pork tenderloins, about 900 grams (about 2 pounds) total
Coarse salt and freshly ground black pepper
6 to 8 fresh bay leaves
100 grams (3½ ounces) red onion, cut into 5-centimeter
    (2-inch) pieces (¾ cup)
100 grams (3½ ounces) celery, cut into large 5-centimeter
    (2-inch) pieces (1 cup)
60 grams (2 ounces) carrot, cut into large 5-centimeter (2-inch)
    pieces (½ cup)
15 milliliters (1 tablespoon) olive, grapeseed, or canola oil
Pinch of red pepper flakes
125 milliliters (½ cup) dry white wine

Soak the caulfat in water to cover overnight in the refrigerator. Drain and squeeze to eliminate excess moisture. Pat dry.

Trim the tenderloins of fat. Season to taste with salt and pepper. Fold the skinny tail ends under the body of the tenderloin to equalize the diameter. Arrange a row of 3 to 4 bay leaves on top of each.

Lay a sheet of caulfat on a work surface. Place a tenderloin at one end and roll, giving it two turns to completely encase the pork in the membrane. Cut off the excess caulfat, including the ends. Wrap the second tenderloin in the same way. Season again with salt and pepper.

Preheat the oven to 191°C (375°F).

In a bowl, toss the vegetables with the oil and red pepper flakes. Place the pork and the vegetables in a roasting pan (*la rostiera*) just large enough to hold the tenderloins and arrange the vegetables around them.

Roast (*arrostire*) until the tenderloins are well browned.

Add the wine to the pan and continue roasting until the internal temperature of the pork reaches 63°C (145°F), about 20 minutes. Add water if the pan gets dry. Remove the bay leaves and slice the pork. Strain the pan juices through a fine-mesh strainer (*colino*) and serve with the sliced pork.

Sautéed Pork Tenderloin

2 pork tenderloins, about 900 grams (about 2 pounds) total
Coarse salt and freshly ground black pepper
8 fresh bay leaves
Pork caulfat, soaked in water overnight
2 cloves garlic in the skin, crushed with the heel of the hand
60 milliliters (¼ cup) olive, grapeseed, or canola oil
125 milliliters (½ cup) dry white wine

Follow steps 2 and 3 in the preceding recipe for *Filetto di Maiale* to season the tenderloins, and wrap in caulfat, placing 6 of the bay leaves on the tenderloins (3 on each). Cut both tenderloins in half.

Place the remaining 2 bay leaves, the garlic, and oil in a skillet large enough to hold the pork. Place over medium heat and cook until the garlic begins to color. Add the pork, increase the heat to medium-high, and sauté to brown all over. Pour off the fat.

Deglaze the pan with the wine and cook until reduced, turning the meat in the wine. Cover and cook until the internal temperature of the pork reaches 63°C (145°F), about 30 minutes. Uncover and cook to reduce the juices. Remove the bay leaves and cut the pork into slices. Serve with the pan juices.

Bistecchine di Maiale in Padella

Sautéed Pork Chops

Serves 4

For this recipe, pork chops are marinated in olive oil, garlic, and rosemary. Once the chops are sautéed, the pan is deglazed with wine and the chops finish cooking in the oven. A quick sauce is made with the pan drippings and stock. *Radicchio Trevisano Brasato* (braised radicchio) on page 263 makes a delicious *contorno*.

Cooking times for the chops are approximate because pork chops cook differently, depending on where they are cut from the animal: Cut from the shoulder end, they take longer to cook but the meat is often more tender. In Italy, pork chops are traditionally cooked to medium.

(See "Preparing Pork Chops for Sauté" on page 431 for step-by-step instructions.)

Chef's Notes

Olives are not pitted because pitting will break the flesh and release too strong an olive taste into the sauce.

The garlic and rosemary are added to the pan after the pork so that they won't burn.

Ingredients

4 pork chops (2 to 4 centimeters / ¾ to 1½ inches thick), trimmed, bones cleaned of meat (frenched), connective tissue slit at edges of chops
Coarse salt and freshly ground black pepper
8 cloves garlic, peeled and crushed with the heel of the hand
4 sprigs (15 centimeters / 6 inches long) fresh rosemary, cut in half
45 milliliters (3 tablespoons) olive, grapeseed, or canola oil, plus a little for marinating
125 milliliters (½ cup) dry white wine
60 grams (¾ cup) black olives, with the pits (see Chef's Notes)
100 milliliters (scant ½ cup) vegetable stock, plus 250 milliliters (1 cup) stock or water for deglazing
1 recipe Radicchio Trevisano Brasato (page 263) (optional)

Season the pork with salt and pepper to taste, place in a container with the garlic and rosemary, drizzle with a little oil, and massage the seasonings into the meat. Cover and refrigerate at least 1 hour, or overnight.

Preheat the oven to 232°C (450°F).

In a large, ovenproof skillet (*padella*), heat the oil over medium-high heat until hot but not smoking.

Remove the garlic and rosemary from the chops; reserve. Add the chops to the pan and brown (*rosolare*), 3 to 4 minutes on each side. A few minutes into the cooking, add the garlic and rosemary to the pan. When the garlic turns golden brown, place the garlic and rosemary on top of the chops to prevent burning.

When the chops are well browned, pour off the fat. Deglaze (*deglassare*) the pan with the wine, turning the pork in the wine. Add the olives and cook to reduce the wine by about half.

Add the 100 milliliters (scant ½ cup) vegetable stock.

Place the pan in the oven and roast (*arrostire*) the chops, turning once, until the pork is cooked to medium doneness, 5 to 10 minutes, depending on the cut.

Remove the chops from the pan and deglaze the pan with the 250 milliliters (1 cup) stock or water. Bring to a simmer over medium-high heat and reduce to the consistency of a sauce. Serve the pork with the sauce and the radicchio, if desired.

Cinghiale in Agrodolce

Sweet-and-Sour Wild Boar

Serves 6

The meat for this stew is cubed and marinated overnight with juniper berries and bay leaves. Then the recipe follows the traditional procedure for a braise (see "Le Tecniche: *Brasare*" on page 191): The meat is seared to brown it, then cooked with aromatic vegetables. The pan is deglazed, and the meat is moistened with tomato and simmered. The stew is finished with raisins and a little extra-bitter chocolate to deepen the flavor.

As with all braises, the stew may be cooked on the stovetop or in the oven. In class, it is served with couscous studded with herbs, pine nuts, and raisins. This recipe may also be made with cubed pork leg or shoulder meat.

Ingredients

550 grams (1¼ pounds) wild boar, cut from the leg or shoulder, trimmed and cut into 3- to 5-centimeter (1- to 2-inch) cubes

Coarse salt and freshly ground black pepper

1 fresh bay leaf

5 juniper berries

Olive, grapeseed, or canola oil, as needed

75 grams (3 ounces) red onion, cut into 1-centimeter (⅜-inch) pieces (½ cup)

40 grams (1½ ounces) celery, cut into 1-centimeter (⅜-inch) pieces (⅓ cup)

40 grams (1½ ounces) carrot, cut into 1-centimeter (⅜-inch) pieces (⅓ cup)

30 milliliters (2 tablespoons) red wine vinegar

12½ grams (1 tablespoon) sugar

Pinch of red pepper flakes

125 milliliters (½ cup) dry white wine

½ teaspoon spezie forti, garam masala, or freshly ground nutmeg

200 grams (7 ounces) whole, canned Italian plum tomatoes with their juices, crushed by hand

25 grams (3 tablespoons) golden raisins, soaked in white wine to cover

12½ grams (½ ounce) extra-bitter chocolate, finely chopped or grated (1½ tablespoons)

In a container, season the boar with salt and pepper to taste. Add the bay leaf and juniper berries, and rub with oil. Cover and refrigerate overnight.

Preheat the oven to 177°C (350°F).

Coat a large skillet (*padella*) with oil and heat over medium heat until a leaf of basil or sage sizzles when tossed into the pan. Add the boar along with the bay leaf and juniper berries, and sear to brown (*rosolare*).

Pour off most of the fat. Add the vegetables. Transfer to the oven and roast 5 minutes, or until the vegetables are browned.

Deglaze (*deglassare*) the pan with the vinegar. Stir in the sugar and the red pepper flakes.

Reduce the oven heat to 163°C (325°F). Deglaze the pan with the wine. Stir in the *spezie forti*. Return to the oven and cook 5 more minutes to reduce the wine.

Add the crushed tomato and 125 milliliters (½ cup) water and return to the oven for 15 minutes to reduce.

Stir, cover with foil, and braise (*brasare*) 1½ hours.

Add the raisins and the wine in which they soaked, and the chopped chocolate. Cover, return the pan to the oven, and continue cooking until the meat is very tender, about 30 more minutes. Taste for seasoning.

Salsiccia

Fresh Pork Sausage

> Makes about 2.3 kilograms (5 pounds) sausage or approximately 15 links, each 150 grams (5 ounces)

In this recipe fresh sausage is made with ground pork shoulder, seasoned and stuffed into casings. In Italy, fresh sausage is commonly eaten raw as a form of fresh *salame*, but it may also be grilled, sautéed, or roasted.

This is a basic recipe for pork sausage. Students are taught to personalize the recipe with various herbs and spices, including sage and red pepper flakes.

(For further information on pork sausage, including step-by-step instructions for stuffing sausage casings, see "Pork Sausage" on page 432.)

Chef's Note

The sausages may be poached before grilling or sautéing, to minimize the possibility of bursting.

Ingredients

2.3 kilos (5 pounds) pork shoulder, or "Boston Butt"

45 grams (2 tablespoons plus 1½ teaspoons) coarse salt

10 grams (1½ tablespoons) freshly ground black pepper

10 grams (1¼ tablespoons) spezie forti, garam masala, or freshly ground nutmeg

5 grams (2½ teaspoons) fennel pollen or ground toasted fennel seed

5 grams (¾ tablespoon) chopped garlic, mashed to a paste with the side of a large knife, and marinated 1 hour in red wine to cover

225 grams (8 ounces) natural hog casings, flushed well and soaked overnight in cold water to cover

Dice the meat. Chill. (The meat should be kept very cold to prevent the fat from smearing.)

Sanitize and chill the grinder head and all the grinder parts in ice water, the freezer, or the refrigerator. Grind the meat through the 10-millimeter (½-inch or ⅜-inch) plate. In a large bowl, mix the pork, salt, pepper, *spezie forti*, fennel pollen or ground fennel seed, and the garlic and the wine it was marinated in. Beat slightly or mix with gloved hands, adding ice water as needed to develop the primary bind; the meat should feel like a sticky homogenous paste.

Put the sausage mixture into the bowl of a sausage machine. Gather the entire casing onto the extruder, leaving about 5 centimeters (2 inches) hanging.

Feed the sausage mixture into the casing, pricking the casing as necessary to release the air. When all of the meat has been extruded, twist the casing to seal the sausage. Then twist off one sausage about the length of your palm; each link should weigh approximately 150 grams (5 ounces). Repeat the process to twist off a second sausage, twisting the casing in the opposite direction. Continue to twist off all of the sausages.

Let the sausages dry for several hours or overnight in the refrigerator.

Light a gas or charcoal grill.

Grill (*grigliare*) the sausages until well browned all over and cooked through, about 15 minutes.

Arista alla Toscana con Patate alla Paesana

Roasted Pork Loin with Potatoes

Serves 6

This is a classically Tuscan dish of pork loin, seasoned with a *trito* of chopped garlic, herbs, and spices. It is roasted with the traditional accompaniment of sliced potatoes tossed with onion, fennel, and herbs. The meat is cut from the bones in one piece and marinated; meat and bones are reassembled before roasting, and served together.

The potatoes may be roasted in the same pan as the pork (as is traditionally done), or cooked separately; either way, they are crisp and golden.

(See page 429 for step-by-step instructions for "Preparing Center-Cut Bone-in Loin of Pork for Arista.")

Chef's Note

Pellegrino Artusi, in *La Scienza in Cucina e L'Arte di Mangiar Bene*, ascribes the origin of the name of this dish to the Council of 1430, assembled in Florence to settle differences between the Roman and Greek churches. According to Artusi, when this roast was served, the cries of approbation, in Greek, from the council members were "*arista, arista*," which means "good, good!" And the name stuck with the dish.

Ingredients

For the trito:

6 cloves garlic, chopped

Leaves from 3 sprigs fresh rosemary, chopped

Leaves from 1 sprig fresh sage, chopped

5 grams (2 teaspoons) freshly ground black pepper

1 teaspoon spezie forti, garam masala, or freshly ground nutmeg

For the pork:

2 kilograms (4½ pounds) center-cut, bone-in pork loin

175 milliliters (¾ cup) olive oil

Coarse salt and freshly ground black pepper

250 milliliters (1 cup) dry white wine

1 recipe Patate alla Paesana (page 256), prepared from step 2 through step 4 (optional)

Make the *trito*: Combine the garlic, rosemary, sage, pepper, and *spezie forti* in a small bowl; set aside.

Cut the pork off the bones in one piece. Cut incisions in the meat 2½ to 5 centimeters (1 to 2 inches) deep, and stuff with most of the *trito*. Rub the meat and bones all over with the remaining *trito*. Tie the meat back onto the bones with butcher's twine. Set the roast in a container and pour the olive oil over. Cover and refrigerate 1 to 2 days.

Preheat the oven to 191°C (375°F).

Season the pork with salt to taste. Place the pork in a roasting pan (*la rostiera*) and roast (*arrostire*) 30 minutes.

Add the wine, pouring it around but not over the pork so as not to disturb the crust that is forming, and roast 10 minutes to reduce.

Arrange the potatoes, if using, around the pork and continue roasting, basting the pork every 10 minutes, until the internal temperature of the pork registers 63°C (145°F) on an instant-read thermometer, 35 to 40 more minutes. Ten minutes before the pork is cooked, pour off the fat from the pan.

Remove the pork from the roasting pan and let rest 15 minutes. Cut off the twine. Cut the pork into ½-centimeter- (³⁄₁₆-inch)-thick slices and cut the bones into individual ribs. Serve each slice of pork with a rib bone, and the potatoes, if using.

Toscana (Tuscany)

"We talk a lot about cuisine, but in reality, we are restricted to a few recipes. My cuisine is 'mine'; however, I have been influenced by the Tuscan stubbornness as regards their traditions and their beliefs."

—Chef Paolo Lo Priore of Il Canto Restaurant, Siena

Toscana is a region of hills, mountains, rivers, and plains in west-central Italy. Its western border is the Tyrrhenian Sea; to the east it is bordered by Emilia-Romagna, and to the south by Umbria and Lazio. The coastline is alternately rocky and sandy and includes the largely flat coastal area of Maremma.

Toscana is the home of the Italian Renaissance and Catherine de' Medici, whose marriage to Henri II of France was a testament to the power of the Medici family, and who is reputed to have introduced Italian Renaissance cooking to France. Florence, the capital of the region, was a leading center of politics, commerce, finance, and culture throughout the Italian Renaissance.

Toscana's most important agricultural products are olive oil (of which several are DOP and IGP rated), cattle (including the famous Chianina breed), and wine (best known are Chianti, Brunello di Montalcino, Vino Nobile di Montepulciano, the red Carmignano, the white Vernaccia di San Gimignano, and the dessert wine Vin Santo). Chianina cattle are traditionally used for the region's hefty steaks of *bistecca Fiorentina*, charred over wood.

Seafood from the Tyrrhenian is used in seafood soups called *cacciucco*, of which the region boasts innumerable variations, including the *cacciucco* from the coastal town of Livorno, which calls for five different fish in its preparation. Salted cod and eel are also popular.

Pig-farming is an important industry, with much of the meat going to cured meats such as prosciutto and *finocchiona* (fennel *salame*). Some of these products are made with the native *Cinta Senese* pig. Toscana also produces *lardo di Colonnata*, the famous cured fatback from the town of Colonnata, which is near the town of Carrara, renowned for its marble. *Porchetta* (spit-roasted suckling pig) is another Tuscan specialty, as is wild boar (*cinghiale*).

The Tuscan diet is also famous for its beans (particularly *toscanelli*, *cannellini*, and *zolfini*), vegetables, *farro*, and the unsalted bread *pane Toscano*. The bread is a crucial element in the bread-and-vegetable soup *ribollita* and in *panzanella* (bread salad), or rubbed with garlic, grilled, and seasoned with olive oil for *fettunta*. The French herb tarragon—particularly associated with Siena—is used in the cuisine. (Chef Lopriore says: "This herb, which is very green and typically French, has a delicate scent and flavor. In Siena it was called 'Dragoncello' and traditionally it became the best friend of *finocchiona* . . . and part of the base of the *salsa verde* that accompanies our boiled meat dishes.")

Other baked specialties are the focaccialike flatbread *schiacciata*, biscotti from Prato called *cantucci*, and *panforte* from Siena.

Toscana produces a variety of cheeses, predominantly made with sheep's milk, such as Pecorino Toscano.

See our recipes for the savory classics *Arista alla Toscana* (facing page) and *Bistecca alla Fiorentina* (page 182), as well as the charming *Zuccotto* (page 303), which evokes Florence's Duomo.

Cotechino con Lenticchie e Salsa Verde

Poached Pork Sausage with Lentils and *Salsa Verde*

> Serves 6 (Makes two 23- to 26-centimeter / 9- to 10-inch-long sausages)

Cotechino is a cooked *salame* or pork sausage that originated in Modena and more generally throughout Emilia-Romagna. The sausage is made from the pig shoulder and the skin (*cotenna*), which is ground, seasoned with spices such as cinnamon, cloves, and nutmeg, and stuffed into beef casings. The *cotechino* is poached in an aromatic broth or court bouillon, and traditionally served with lentils and a spicy condiment such as *mostarda*, *salsa verde* (see recipe below), or a red pepper sauce called *salsa rossa*. *Cotechino* with lentils is a popular dish for the New Year, when its consumption is thought to bring good fortune. *Cotechino* is also a traditional component of a *bollito misto* ("mixed boiled dinner"), a classic northern Italian dish of meats (typically more than one variety) simmered in water and aromatic vegetables. The *cotechino* is poached separately.

Beef bung and middles are common casings for *cotechino*. Bung casings are typically 10 centimeters (4 inches) in diameter; middles are smaller, measuring approximately 6 centimeters (2⅜ inches) in diameter.

Salsa verde ("green sauce") is an ancient sauce of pounded herbs and greens. The recipe below is made with parsley. Pellegrino Artusi recommends adding some basil to the parsley (*La Scienza in Cucina e L'Arte di Mangiar Bene*) while Bartolomeo Scappi's version combines parsley with spinach, sorrel, burnet, rocket, and mint (*The Opera of Bartolomeo Scappi*).

(See "Pork Sausage" on page 432 for further information on sausage-making, and page 434 for step-by-step instructions for "Preparing *Cotechino*.")

Ingredients

For the spice mix:
Pinch of freshly ground nutmeg
½ teaspoon ground Ceylon cinnamon
½ teaspoon ground clove
½ teaspoon dried thyme leaves
½ teaspoon ground fennel seeds
Pinch of ground caraway seeds
Pinch of ground mace

For the cotechino:
1 kilogram (2¼ pounds) boneless pork shoulder, cleaned of sinews
400 grams (14 ounces) fatback
600 grams (21 ounces) pork rind
250 milliliters (1 cup) red wine
50 grams (2 ounces / 3¼ tablespoons) Morton's Tender Quick
2 cloves garlic, peeled and crushed
10 grams (1½ tablespoons) coarsely ground black pepper
Beef middles or bung casings, for stuffing

For the poaching liquid:
100 grams (3½ ounces) onion, cut into 3-centimeter (1³⁄₁₆-inch) pieces (¾ cup)
35 grams (1½ ounces) carrot, cut into 3-centimeter (1³⁄₁₆-inch) pieces (¼ cup)
50 grams (2 ounces) celery, cut into 3-centimeter (1³⁄₁₆-inch) pieces (½ cup)
3 fresh bay leaves
2 sprigs fresh thyme
1 cinnamon stick
½ teaspoon crushed coriander seed
15 whole black peppercorns
Coarse salt

For the salsa verde:

120 grams (2 cups) fresh Italian parsley leaves, stemmed

3 anchovy fillets, preferably salt-packed (see page 31), rinsed, deboned, and finely chopped

15 grams (1 tablespoon) capers, preferably salt-packed (see page 31), soaked, rinsed, and drained

15 grams (1 tablespoon) finely chopped shallots

30 milliliters (2 tablespoons) dry white wine

15 milliliters (1 tablespoon) white wine vinegar

125 milliliters (½ cup) extra-virgin olive oil

Coarse salt and freshly ground black pepper

1 recipe Lenticchie in Umido (page 256)

Make the spice mix:

In a small bowl, combine all of the ingredients for the spice mix; set aside.

Make the *cotechino*:

Sanitize and chill the grinder head and all the grinder parts in ice water, the freezer, or the refrigerator.

Dice the pork shoulder.

Dice or cut the fatback into strips; chill in the freezer until firm.

Slice the pork rind into strips; chill in the freezer until firm.

Grind the pork and fatback separately through a 10-millimeter (½- or ⅜-inch) plate, keeping the meat and fat cold at all times; place in a large bowl.

Grind the pork rind through a 10-millimeter (½- or ⅜-inch) plate; then grind again through a 6-millimeter (¼-inch) plate. Add it to the bowl with the pork and fatback.

Mix in the wine, Morton's Tender Quick, garlic, pepper, and the spice mix, to taste (Note: Start with a teaspoon; not all of the spice may be needed). Sauté a small patty to taste the seasonings.

Beat slightly or mix with gloved hands, adding ice water as needed to develop the primary bind; the meat should feel like a sticky homogenous paste.

Put the sausage mixture into the bowl of a sausage machine. Gather the entire casing onto the extruder, leaving about 5 centimeters (2 inches) hanging.

Feed the sausage mixture into the casing, pricking the casing as necessary with a sausage pricker to release the air. When all of the meat has been extruded, twist the casing to seal the sausage. Then twist off one sausage about 26 centimeters (10 inches) long. Repeat the process to twist off a second sausage, twisting the casing in the opposite direction.

Hang or refrigerate the sausages at least overnight or up to a few days to improve and develop flavor.

Poach the *cotechino*:

Combine all of the ingredients for the poaching liquid in a pot (*casseruola*) large enough to hold both sausages. Mix well.

Add the sausages and water to cover and bring the poaching liquid to a bare simmer over very low heat. Poach (*affogare*) until the sausage reaches an internal temperature of 68°C (155°F), about 1 hour.

Make the *salsa verde*:

Combine the parsley, anchovies, capers, shallots, wine, and vinegar in the blender and process to a smooth paste.

Chef's Notes

Cotechino is poached over very low heat because the pork skin in the mixture will toughen and develop a grainy texture if exposed to high heat. Long simmering over low heat will also help convert the collagen in the skin to gelatin. Some recipes also suggest poaching the skin prior to grinding.

If not serving the *cotechino* immediately, let cool in the poaching liquid, then refrigerate in the poaching liquid (to prevent the sausage from drying out) for up to several days.

Emilia–Romagna

"As it is a region that is rich in water and 'herbs,' it has become the Italian food valley. From the milk (ricotta, milk, Parmigiano), from the flour (soft wheat) and from the herbs, the tortello di erbetta *(tortello with herbs) was born and it is representative of the evolution of the Emilian geographic reality."*

—Chef Massimo Spigaroli of Antica Corte Pallavicina Restaurant, Parma

The Po River forms the northern boundary of Emilia-Romagna and creates the fertile plains of this wealthy region. The eastern boundary is the Adriatic Sea; the Apennines are to the south. Bologna, at the center of the region, is its capital; the province of Emilia lies to the west, Romagna to the east.

Agriculture is the most important industry in the region, which grows corn, cereals, potatoes, and wine grapes (Lambrusco and Sangiovese). Pork and cattle are important industries, and the cuisine traditionally relies on butter and lard in preference to olive oil.

This region has some of the best-known Italian exports, including an important cheese industry that produces the famous Parmigiano-Reggiano, Grana Padano, and provolone cheeses. The pork industry of Emilia-

Romagna produces a quantity of cured meats such as Prosciutto di Modena, Prosciutto di Parma, Mortadella Bologna, *salame di Felino*, and pancetta. *Aceto balsamico* is made here as well.

Emilia-Romagna is famous for its fresh egg pasta; specialties include *tagliatelle con ragù* and lasagne. The region boasts many other pasta shapes, including tortellini, *cappellacci, cappelletti, garganelli* (ridged tubes), *passatelli* (dumplings), *tortelli* (ravioli shapes), and *anolini* (stuffed rounds). The names of the shapes and their fillings change with the towns.

Specialties from the Adriatic include *brodetti* (seafood soups) and eel. Polenta is common, although not as popular as pasta.

The cooked pork sausage called *cotechino*, which originated in Emilia-Romagna, is featured in our recipe for *Cotechino con Lenticchie e Salsa Verde* (page 213).

Add the olive oil in a steady stream while the blender is running.

Season with salt and pepper to taste.

Transfer to a bowl and chill on ice until ready to serve, to preserve the bright green color.

To serve:

Spoon the lentils into a serving bowl. Make a slit in the casing of the *cotechino* and pull off the casing; discard. Slice the *cotechino* 6 millimeters (¼ inch) thick, and shingle it on top of the lentils. Drizzle with some of the *salsa verde*, and serve the remaining *salsa verde* on the side.

Chapter 14

Lamb and Rabbit:
Agnello e Coniglio

Costolette d'Agnello (Roasted Rack of Lamb)
Agnello Arrosto (Roasted Leg of Lamb with
    Potatoes)
Coniglio all'Uva Passa e Pinoli
    (Braised Rabbit with Raisins and Pine Nuts)

Lambs are among the oldest known domesticated animals used for meat. According to the USDA, there is evidence that lambs were raised by humans as early as nine thousand years ago.

Although sheep have traditionally been raised throughout Italy, the island of Sardegna, in particular, is celebrated for its ancient tradition of sheep-rearing. Sardinian lambs are unusually small and lean, raised exclusively on sheep's milk to produce a very light-colored meat. Sardinian lamb (designated IGP) is sold in three categories: *da latte* (milk lamb), weighing a maximum of 1.4 kilograms (3 pounds); *leggero* (light lamb), weighing from 1.4 to 2 kilograms (3 to 4½ pounds); and *da taglio* (for slicing), weighing from 2 to 2.7 kilograms (4½ to 6 pounds).

Every region in Italy cooks with rabbit, introduced by the Romans into the Mediterranean through Spain and Italy by the middle of the third century. The Romans captured and domesticated wild rabbits, establishing protected habitats from which the rabbits could be harvested.

This chapter demonstrates classic methods for cooking rack and leg of lamb, and for braising rabbit. Leg of lamb may be cooked on the bone or boned entirely before roasting. The bone contributes juiciness and flavor to the roast, but a boned leg is easier to slice, and one can use bones and trimmings for stock. For both preparations, the leg is seasoned with fresh lemon juice to soften the gamey flavor of the meat.

Rabbit is marinated and braised.

Le Tecniche

In this chapter, students learn to fabricate lamb and rabbit. Recipes are chosen to allow students to apply skills of *brasare*, *arrostire*, and *saltare*. See pages 437–42 for step-by-step photos of preparing rack and leg of lamb for roasting and cutting rabbit into pieces.

Costolette d'Agnello (page 218)
with *Carciofi alla Romana* (page 254)

Costolette d'Agnello

Roasted Rack of Lamb

Serves 4

This is a basic method for roasting rack of lamb. The rack is trimmed of the chine bone, and the ribs are cleaned for presentation. All bones and trimmings are used for stock. Because it cooks too quickly to brown adequately in the oven, the rack is seared to brown on top of the stove in oil infused with garlic and thyme, then finished in the oven. *Carciofi alla Romana* (page 254) is an appropriate *contorno* for this dish.

(See "Making a Stock from Trimmings" on page 439, and "Trimming a Rack of Lamb for Roasting" on page 437 for step-by-step instructions.)

Chef's Note

New Zealand lamb is smaller than domestic lamb and will cook faster.

Ingredients

½ rack of lamb (8 rib bones)

50 grams (2 ounces) red onion, cut into 5-centimeter (2-inch) pieces (½ cup)

50 grams (2 ounces) carrot, cut into 5-centimeter (2-inch) pieces (⅓ cup)

1 clove garlic, peeled and crushed with the heel of the hand, plus 2 cloves garlic in the skin, crushed with the heel of the hand

Coarse salt and freshly ground black pepper

25 milliliters (1 tablespoon plus 2 teaspoons) olive, grapeseed, or canola oil

2 sprigs fresh thyme

½ lemon

125 milliliters (½ cup) dry white wine

250 milliliters (1 cup) strained lamb stock

Remove the chine bone and trim the rack of all but a thin layer of fat. Cut all fat and meat off the rib bones and scrape them clean. Chop the chine bone into 3 pieces and recuperate as much meat as possible from the trimmings. (The clean weight will be about 550 grams, or 1¼ pounds.)

Place the trimmings and the bone in a saucepan along with the onion, carrot, and peeled garlic clove. Sauté (*saltare*) over medium-high heat to brown well. Add water to cover and simmer (*sobbollire*) slowly 1 hour. Strain; reserve the stock. (You will need 250 milliliters / 1 cup for this recipe.)

Preheat the oven to 177°C (350°F).

Season the rack with salt and pepper to taste. Place the oil, 2 unpeeled garlic cloves, and the thyme in a cold, ovenproof skillet (*padella*) and cook over medium heat until the garlic just begins to color. Add the rack, increase the heat to medium-high, and sear (*rosolare*) all over.

Put the pan in the oven and roast (*arrostire*) until the internal temperature of the lamb registers 57°C (135°F) on an instant-read thermometer, 15 to 20 minutes depending on the origin of the lamb (see Chef's Note) and the length and strength of the heat during initial searing. Squeeze the lemon over the lamb halfway into the cooking.

Transfer the pan to the stovetop and set over medium heat. Deglaze (*deglassare*) with the wine and cook to reduce, turning the lamb in the wine.

Remove the lamb from the pan and let rest. Pour off the fat. Add the strained lamb stock to the pan and reduce to thicken. Taste, and season the sauce with salt and pepper as needed.

Slice the lamb into chops and serve with the sauce.

Agnello Arrosto

Roasted Leg of Lamb with Potatoes

Serves 8

This is a basic method for roasting leg of lamb. The leg is boned by a "tunneling" method, in which the bones are removed, leaving the shape of the leg intact. The interior is seasoned with a *trito* and chopped anchovy. Potatoes are traditionally roasted alongside the lamb. Lamb and potatoes are served with a pan sauce made by reducing lamb stock made from bones and trimmings from the leg.

(See "Preparing a Leg of Lamb for Roasting" on page 438, and "Making a Stock from Trimmings" on page 439 for step-by-step instructions.)

(See "Preparing a Leg of Lamb for Roasting" on page 438, and "Making a Stock from Trimmings" on page 439 for step-by-step instructions.)

Chef's Notes

If the leg browns too much during roasting, cover with aluminum foil. Remove the foil 5 minutes before removing the lamb from the oven.

Because leg of lamb is lean, it may alternatively be wrapped in caulfat before roasting.

Ingredients

For the trito:

10 grams fresh rosemary leaves, chopped (5 tablespoons)
10 grams fresh sage leaves, chopped (5 tablespoons)
35 grams (5½ tablespoons) chopped garlic
8 grams (1¼ tablespoons) freshly ground black pepper
5 grams (¾ tablespoon) spezie forti, garam masala, or freshly ground nutmeg

For the lamb:

1 leg of lamb (about 2.5 kilograms / 5½ pounds)
5 anchovy fillets, preferably salt-packed (see page 31), rinsed, deboned, and finely chopped
350 milliliters (1½ cups) olive oil
Coarse salt and freshly ground black pepper
1 lemon, halved
350 milliliters (1½ cups) white wine, or to taste

For the lamb stock:

25 milliliters (1 tablespoon plus 2 teaspoons) olive, grapeseed, or canola oil
Bones and trimmings from the leg
50 grams (2 ounces) red onion, cut into 5-centimeter (2-inch) pieces (½ cup)
50 grams (2 ounces) carrot, cut into 5-centimeter (2-inch) pieces (¼ cup)
1 clove garlic, peeled

For the potatoes:

800 grams (1¾ pounds) Idaho potatoes, peeled and cut into 3-centimeter (1 3/16-inch) pieces (5½ cups)
150 grams (5 ounces) red onion, peeled and cut into 3-centimeter (1 3/16-inch) pieces (1 cup)
4 sprigs fresh sage
Coarse salt and freshly ground black pepper
95 milliliters (⅓ cup plus 1 tablespoon) olive oil

Make the *trito*:

Combine all of the ingredients for the *trito* in a small bowl.

Bone the leg of lamb:

To prepare the leg, cut through the socket of the hip joint and remove the tailbone and hip bone in one piece. Trim most of the exterior fat from the leg, leaving a very thin layer. Remove the femur by cutting around the joint at the top of the femur to expose it. Scrape down the bone to free it entirely. Scrape around the joint and then cut through it; remove the bone. Scrape around the shank bone and remove it. Cut the trimmings in pieces and reserve them, with the bones, for the stock.

Marinate the lamb:

Rub the *trito* all over the interior of the leg where the bones were removed; then rub with the anchovy and a little oil. Tie the leg so that it lies fairly flat, folding the

meat over to close the open end. Sprinkle with pepper. Put the leg in a container, pour half of the olive oil over it, and massage the oil and seasonings into the meat. Refrigerate at least 1 hour, or up to 2 days, to marinate.

Make the stock:

Heat the oil in a saucepan (*casseruola*) over medium heat. Add the bones, trimmings, onion, carrot, and garlic. Sauté (*saltare*) to brown well. Add water to cover and simmer (*sobbollire*) slowly 1 hour. Strain; reserve.

Preheat the oven to 191°C (375°F). Bring the lamb to room temperature.

Meanwhile, prepare the potatoes: Toss the potatoes with the onion, sage, a sprinkling of salt and pepper, and the oil; set aside.

Season the lamb with salt to taste. Place the lamb in a roasting pan (*la rostiera*); pour the remaining olive oil over. Roast (*arrostire*) 25 minutes.

Squeeze the lemon over the lamb and add the lemon halves to the pan. Roast 10 more minutes.

Pour off some of the fat from the roasting pan. Deglaze (*deglassare*) the pan with the wine, pouring it around but not over the lamb. Arrange the potatoes and onion around the lamb and stir to coat with the oil remaining in the pan. Continue roasting until the leg is well browned, 15 to 20 more minutes.

Baste, and continue roasting 20 to 25 more minutes. Then pour off the oil remaining in the pan. Continue roasting until the internal temperature of the lamb registers 57°C (135°F) on an instant-read thermometer.

Remove the lamb from the pan and let rest at least 20 minutes. Remove the potatoes and keep them warm in the oven. Deglaze the roasting pan with the reserved stock and reduce until slightly thickened. Taste for seasoning and add salt and pepper as needed.

Cut the lamb into very thin slices and serve with the sauce and the potatoes.

Coniglio all'Uva Passa e Pinoli

Braised Rabbit with Raisins and Pine Nuts

Serves 4

This recipe is from Mantova, in Lombardia. Traditionally, it is made solely with butter, as olive oil was rarely used in that part of Italy. The rabbit is cut into pieces, marinated in white wine, seared in butter, and braised in the marinade. At The International Culinary Center, students make a rabbit stock from the trimmings and add it to the braising liquid for a more robust flavor.

A fryer is recommended for this dish, rather than a roaster; a roaster is likely to be older, and the meat tougher.

(See "Cutting a Rabbit into Pieces" on page 441, and "Making a Stock from Trimmings" on page 439.)

Ingredients

For the marinade:
115 grams (¼ pound) red onion, cut into ½-centimeter (³⁄₁₆-inch) dice (¾ cup)
2 sprigs fresh Italian parsley

5 fresh bay leaves
3 cloves
725 milliliters (3 cups) dry white wine
45 milliliters (3 tablespoons) red wine vinegar
Freshly ground black pepper

For the braise:
1 rabbit (1 to 2 kilograms / 2¼ to 4½ pounds), preferably a fryer
Coarse salt and freshly ground black pepper
60 grams (½ cup) all-purpose flour
130 grams (7 tablespoons) unsalted butter
115 grams (¼ pound) red onion, cut into ½-centimeter (³⁄₁₆-inch) dice (¾ cup)
40 grams (¼ cup) golden raisins soaked in dry white wine to cover
20 grams (¼ cup) pine nuts, toasted
Rabbit or chicken stock, or water, as needed to thin the sauce

Make the marinade:

Combine all of the ingredients in a saucepan (*casseruola*) and bring to a simmer. Let cool to room temperature.

For the braise:

Cut the rabbit into 10 pieces. Reserve the liver.

Wash and dry the rabbit pieces. Pour the marinade over the rabbit and marinate 4 hours. Remove the rabbit from the marinade and pat dry. Strain the marinade through a fine-mesh strainer (*colino*); set aside.

Season the rabbit with salt and pepper to taste. Toss the pieces in flour and pat off the excess.

Preheat the oven to 177°C (350°F).

Heat the butter and onion in a large ovenproof skillet (*padella*) over medium-high heat. When the butter

Chef's Notes

At The International Culinary Center the students often practice boning out the rabbit saddle (see "Deboning the Rabbit Saddle" on page 442 for step-by-step instructions). The boneless saddle is stuffed with chopped pine nuts, raisins, and seasoned breadcrumbs, rolled, tied, and braised with the legs. It cooks faster so it should be removed before the other pieces.

This dish is also very good prepared with red wine and olives (see *Pollo all Cacciatora in Bianco* on page 168); substitute red wine for the white in the recipe, and 1 cut-up rabbit for the chicken.

Working with Marinades

In the recipe for *Coniglio all'Uva Passa e Pinoli*, the rabbit is marinated in a white-wine marinade (*marinata*), an aromatic liquid in which meat, poultry, game, fish, and even vegetables may be soaked to add flavor and tenderness, and to help protect the food from drying out during cooking. (Here we focus on marinades for meat; see page 44 for a discussion of marinades for vegetables.)

The components of a marinade depend on the size of the meat and its toughness. The flavoring elements should be based on what the final dish will be, though often they are composed of an acidic liquid such as vinegar, buttermilk, wine, yogurt, or fruit juice. (Acid helps to denature protein, weakening muscle tissue and allowing the marinade to penetrate.) In addition to an acid, a marinade generally contains oil, and may also contain herbs and spices for flavoring. The meat should be submerged in the liquid, then the mixture should be refrigerated for a period of time—from thirty minutes to several days, depending on the size and thickness of the meat, and desired result. (See also *Stracotto* on page 188, *Cinghiale in Agrodolce* on page 208, and *Anguilla in Carpione* on page 244.)

Tips for Working with Marinades

Never put bare hands in the marinade, as it is a perfect habitat for bacteria growth. A marinade can be used as a sauce only after it is has been boiled—otherwise there is a risk of recontamination of the cooked meat with bacteria from the raw marinade.

When removing meat or fish from a marinade, be sure to wipe off excess liquid, to avoid flare-ups in the pan or on the grill.

Be sure to discard marinade after it has been in contact with raw meat, unless it is being boiled for a sauce.

When marinating fish, be sure to leave the fish in the marinade only for the recommended time, as the marinade can start to break down the delicate flesh of the fish.

stops foaming, add the rabbit pieces, including the liver, and sear (*rosolare*) to brown on both sides. Pour off the fat.

Drain the raisins. Add the raisin soaking liquid and the cooled marinade to the skillet; reserve the raisins. Simmer (*sobbollire*) until the marinade is reduced to almost a glaze.

Add the raisins to the rabbit along with the pine nuts. Taste the sauce, season with salt and pepper as needed, and add a little more wine if it lacks acidity.

Place the skillet in the oven and braise until the loin and saddle are cooked through, 15 to 20 minutes. Remove, and set aside in a warm place. Continue cooking the rabbit legs until they are tender, about 50 more minutes.

Replace the loin and saddle in the skillet and cook over low heat until warmed through. Thin the sauce with stock or water and bring to a simmer. Taste and adjust seasoning. Serve the rabbit with the sauce, the liver, and with *Polenta* (see page 136) or mashed potatoes, if desired.

Chapter 15

Fish and Shellfish:
Pesce e Frutti di Mare

About 70 percent of the Earth's surface is covered with water, so it is no wonder that fish has figured so prominently in the development of global cuisine. Italy is endowed with long coastlines that have historically provided an abundant variety of seafood, while rivers and lakes offer freshwater species.

Italian cuisine encompasses a variety of methods for cooking fish. Whole fish, stuffed with aromatics for flavor, may simply be roasted with a coating of olive oil, or encased in a salt crust. Fillets and steaks may be sautéed, grilled, poached, or braised. Cooking *al cartoccio*—baking small, whole fish or fillets in a parchment or aluminum-foil pouch—is also an excellent method of preserving the delicate flavor and aroma of fish.

The category of shellfish (*frutti di mare*, or "bounty of the sea," as Italians say—an apt name that captures the multiplicity of shapes, sizes, and colors of animals that are commonly lumped into this category) encompasses such a variety of structures and textures that it's fair to say that they may be cooked by all techniques. With the exception of cephalopods (squid, octopus, and cuttlefish), the connective tissue of shellfish is very delicate, and there is little fat. Many shellfish, including clams, oysters, mussels, scallops, shrimp, and sea urchins, are commonly eaten raw. They are also poached, stewed, braised, sautéed, and deep-fried.

Le Tecniche

In this chapter, students learn to fabricate round-fish and flatfish, and to prepare various shellfish for cooking or eating raw. Students apply skills of *saltare*, *grigilare*, *arrostire*, *affogare*, and *brasare*. *Friggere* (deep-frying) is introduced on page 248. See pages 443–66 for an in-depth discussion of fish and shellfish, and step-by-step instructions for fabrication.

Sogliola alla Mugnaia

Sole in the Style of the Miller's Wife

Serves 2

This preparation takes its name from the miller's wife because it was traditionally she who had access to the flour in which the fish is classically dredged. The flour ensures browning, and creates a savory crust when whole, small fish or fish fillets are sautéed in clarified butter or oil. The fish is sauced with a quick pan sauce made with browned butter, chopped parsley, lemon, and capers. Roundfish, including sea bass, sea bream, and trout, are also excellent prepared *alla mugnaia*. The brown butter sauce (*burro nocciola*) is also served with pasta and gnocchi (see *Strozzapreti* on page 122).

Thin flatfish fillets will cook through on top of the stove. Thicker fillets and whole, small fish are finished in a hot oven so that the outside of the fish does not burn and dry out before the interior is cooked through (see Chef's Notes).

(See "Making a *Burro Nocciola* Emulsion," page 378.)

Ingredients

30 milliliters (2 tablespoons) olive, grapeseed, or canola oil, or clarified butter

2 fillets of sole or other flatfish, such as flounder (150 to 200 grams / 5 to 7 ounces total), skinned

Coarse salt and freshly ground black pepper

30 grams (¼ cup) all-purpose flour

75 grams (3 tablespoons) unsalted butter

30 grams (2 tablespoons) capers, preferably salt-packed (see page 31), soaked, rinsed, and drained (optional)

5 grams (2 tablespoons) chopped fresh Italian parsley

1 lemon, halved

Lemon slices, for garnish

Place the oil or clarified butter in a skillet (*padella*) large enough to hold the fish. Heat over medium-high heat until the fat is hot enough that a piece of sage sizzles when tossed into it.

Season the fish on both sides with salt and pepper to taste. Dredge in the flour, patting off the excess.

Place the fish in the pan, skinned side up for presentation, and sauté (*saltare*) until golden brown, 3 to 5 minutes. Turn and cook until browned on the second side and cooked through, but still translucent at the center, 3 to 5 more minutes. Remove the fish to a serving plate and hold in a warm oven.

Throw off the fat from the pan. Return the pan to medium heat. Add the whole butter and cook until golden brown and nutty smelling (*nocciola*). Add the capers, if using, and the parsley, and squeeze in the lemon juice.

Pour the sauce over the fish. Garnish the plate with lemon slices.

Chef's Notes

For thicker fillets and whole, small fish: On the stovetop, brown the fish on one side and baste with the fat in the pan. Transfer to a 191°C (375°F) oven and bake for 5 minutes. Check for doneness, and baste again. Continue baking as necessary until the fish is cooked through. Turn off the oven. Transfer the fish to a plate and set in the still warm oven to stay warm. Make the sauce as in the recipe at right.

Check that the oil is hot before adding the fish; if the oil is too cool, the fish will stick to the pan and the crust will be lost.

Baccalà Mantecato

Whipped Salted Cod

Serves 4

The use of salted and dried fish such as cod dates back more than a thousand years and is found in the regional cuisines of South America and the Caribbean, western Africa, northern Europe, and particularly the Mediterranean. Food historians point to the use of salted fish as a pivotal development in human history, since its hardiness and versatility enabled long travel across lands, fostered trade, and powered global economics.

Baccalà Mantecato, or whipped salted cod, is a specialty of the Veneto but variations are also found in other

In a container, soak the cod in water to cover, refrigerated, until tender, about 48 hours. Change the water two to three times during soaking. Drain. Bring the milk to a simmer in a saucepan (*casseruola*). Add the soaked, drained cod, and cook (*affogare*) until tender, 20 to 30 minutes.

Remove the cod with a slotted spoon to a cutting board. Remove bones and skin, if there are any. Reserve the milk.

Pound the fish to a paste with a mortar, or purée in a food processor.

In a saucepan, heat 25 milliliters (1 tablespoon plus 2 teaspoons) of the oil over medium heat. Add the chopped onion and garlic, if using, and cook (*saltare*) until softened, 7 to 10 minutes. Add a few tablespoons water if necessary to prevent the onions from taking on color. Press the onions and garlic through a drum sieve or tamis (*setaccio*) and return to the pan.

Add the cod and cook over low heat, adding some of the reserved milk as necessary, until the mixture is soft and smooth, 5 to 7 minutes.

Add the bread and the remaining olive oil. Stir vigorously with a wooden spoon to blend (*mantecare*), until the mixture looks like a white paste. Season to taste with salt and pepper. Continue whipping with the wooden spoon until the mixture attains the consistency of a mousse.

Taste for seasoning, stir in the parsley, and more oil, as needed; the mixture should be shiny, creamy, and moist with oil. Serve drizzled with olive oil.

regions, including Emilia-Romagna and Friuli–Venezia Giulia. Traditionally, the fish was creamed with a little of the poaching liquid; in this recipe, milk is used instead for a creamier texture. The mixture is often served on top of grilled or toasted polenta, or on toasted bread as a snack or *stuzzichino*.

(See "Preparing *Baccalà* and *Stoccafisso*" on page 456 for a discussion of salted cod.)

Ingredients

250 grams (9 ounces) salted cod

1 liter (4¼ cups) milk

200 milliliters (¾ cup plus 2 tablespoons) extra-virgin olive oil, plus extra for serving

150 grams (1 cup) finely chopped onion

1 small clove garlic (optional)

75 grams (2½ ounces) bread, crusts removed, cut into 2½-centimeter / 1-inch cubes (1½ loosely packed cups)

Coarse salt and freshly ground pepper

3 grams (1 tablespoon) chopped fresh Italian parsley

Choosing Fresh Fish

Fish are available in a variety of sizes, shapes, and even colors, but there are some commonalities for chefs to keep in mind as they select fresh fish. Characteristics of freshness in fish include:

○ A shiny, brilliant appearance, and scales firmly in place

○ Bright, shiny, convex eyes that fill the eye socket; cloudy, sunken eyes are a sign of decay

○ Moist, brightly colored gills that are full of blood

○ A firm and intact stomach, a tightly closed anal cavity, and firm flesh that is resistant to the touch

○ A clean, fresh odor: Fish should smell of the ocean or the flora of the lake or river where they were farmed. A "fishy" smell indicates that the fish is not freshly caught.

Pesce al Cartoccio

Fish Cooked in Parchment

Serves 2

This recipe demonstrates a common method for baking whole, small flatfish or fish fillets in parchment bags on a bed of mixed vegetables. The vegetables are cut into 2-millimeter-by-6-centimeter (1/16-by-2½-inch) julienne so that they cook at the same rate, and relatively quickly. Softer, quicker-cooking vegetables such as zucchini and onion are cut thicker than dense, long-cooking carrots, to equalize cooking times.

At The International Culinary Center, sole or flounder fillets are used, but branzino, hake, or cod would be equally delicious. Thin fillets will take about 7 minutes; thicker fillets will need about 9 minutes.

(See pages 348 and 350, respectively, for instructions for cutting vegetables into julienne and peeling tomatoes. See "Cooking Fish *al Cartoccio*" on page 455 for instructions for wrapping fish in parchment.)

Ingredients

30 grams (1 ounce) carrot, cut into 2-millimeter-by-6-centimeter (1/16-by-2½-inch) julienne (⅓ cup)

30 grams (1 ounce) red bell pepper, seeded and cut into 2-millimeter-by-6-centimeter (1/16-by-2½-inch) julienne (⅓ cup)

30 grams (1 ounce) yellow bell pepper, seeded and cut into 2-millimeter-by-6-centimeter (1/16-by-2½-inch) julienne (⅓ cup)

50 grams (2 ounces) tomato, peeled and cut into thin wedges (¼ cup)

50 grams (2 ounces) red onion, cut into thin wedges (½ cup)

90 grams (3¼ ounces) zucchini, cut into 2-millimeter-by-6-centimeter (1/16-by-2½-inch) julienne (¾ cup)

2 sprigs fresh thyme

2 sprigs fresh Italian parsley

4 fresh basil leaves

Pinch of red pepper flakes

2 fillets of flounder or sole, about 150 grams (5 ounces) each, skinned

Coarse salt and freshly ground black pepper

30 milliliters (2 tablespoons) dry white wine

10 milliliters (2 teaspoons) olive oil, plus extra for brushing the pouch and serving

1 large egg white, beaten with a fork

Sea salt

Preheat the oven to 246°C (475°F).

Combine the carrot, red and yellow bell peppers, tomato, onion, zucchini, herbs, and red pepper flakes in a bowl. Season with salt and black pepper to taste and mix well.

Cut two pieces of parchment paper for the pouches.

Place one-quarter of the vegetable-herb mixture on half of each of the parchment pouches. Set a fillet on top of each. Season with salt and pepper to taste. Drizzle each with the wine, olive oil, and 5 milliliters (1 teaspoon) water. Brush the bottom edge of each pouch with the egg white. Then fold over the top and make a series of short folds along the edges. For an extra secure seal, brush again with egg white and repeat the short folds. Brush the entire pouch lightly with olive oil to get a nice golden color.

Place the pouches on a baking sheet and bake (*cuocere in forno*) 7 minutes. Remove from the oven, and immediately make a small slit at one end of each pouch; this will prevent the pouches from collapsing, and help maintain their shape.

Place each pouch on a serving plate. At the table, cut or tear open the top of each. Drizzle with olive oil and season to taste with sea salt.

Sgombro con Scarola
e Fagioli

Mackerel with Sautéed Escarole and Beans

Serves 2

Mackerel is popular in Italian cuisine. In this recipe, the fillets are served on a bed of sautéed escarole with *cannellini* beans. Liquid reserved from cooking the beans binds a simple sauce.

(See "Filleting a Roundfish" on page 448 for step-by-step instructions for removing pinbones; "Scoring and Sautéing Fish Fillets" on page 453; and "Working with Dried Legumes" on page 364 for instructions on soaking and cooking beans.)

Ingredients

For the escarole and beans:

30 milliliters (2 tablespoons) olive oil

1 small clove garlic, sliced

Pinch of red pepper flakes

70 grams (2½ ounces) escarole, cut into 5-centimeter (2-inch) pieces (2 cups)

Coarse salt and freshly ground black pepper

125 grams (¾ cup) cooked cannellini beans

150 milliliters (⅔ cup) bean cooking liquid, or as needed

For the mackerel:

1 mackerel (about 600 grams / 1⅓ pounds), filleted and pinbones removed (to yield 2 fillets, approximately 200 grams / 7 ounces each)

Coarse salt and freshly ground black pepper

All-purpose flour, for dredging

60 milliliters (¼ cup) olive, grapeseed, or canola oil

2 cloves garlic, unpeeled

1 large sprig fresh sage

60 milliliters (¼ cup) dry white wine

125 milliliters (½ cup) bean cooking liquid

Make the escarole and beans:

Combine the oil, garlic, and red pepper flakes in a skillet (*padella*). Place over medium heat and cook until the garlic begins to color, 2 to 3 minutes.

Add the escarole and sauté (*saltare*) 3 minutes, seasoning to taste with salt and black pepper.

Add the beans and their cooking liquid. Simmer gently about 10 minutes, adding more cooking liquid as needed. Set aside.

Cook the mackerel:

Cut each mackerel fillet in half on the bias to yield 4 pieces. Score the skin to keep it from curling.

Season the fish with salt and pepper to taste and dredge in flour; pat off excess flour.

Combine the oil, garlic, and sage in a cold skillet (*padella*). Place over medium heat and heat until a leaf of sage sizzles when tossed into the oil. Add the fish to the pan, increase the heat to medium-high, and sear (*saltare*) to brown, about 2 minutes on each side.

Pour off the oil. Return the pan to the heat, pour the white wine around (not over) the fish so as not to disturb the browned crust; cook to reduce. Add the bean cooking liquid and reduce to thicken. Discard the garlic and sage. Season to taste with salt and pepper.

To serve:

Warm the bean-and-escarole mixture and spoon into bowls. Place the fish on top and pour the pan juices from the mackerel over.

Pesce Spada all'Isolana

Swordfish Braised with Tomato and Oregano

Serves 2

This recipe demonstrates braising as a method for cooking fish. Swordfish steaks are browned (caramelization of the proteins provides a layer of flavor: see sidebar "Maillard Reaction" on page 158) and then simmered, partially immersed in liquid consisting of fish stock, chopped fresh tomato, and aromatic vegetables. The swordfish infuses the braising liquid with flavor; the tomato and aromatics, in turn, contribute flavor to the fish. The braising liquid serves as a sauce.

Branzino or sea bream also works well in this preparation.

(See page 350 for step-by-step instructions for peeling tomatoes.)

Ingredients

60 milliliters (¼ cup) olive, canola, or grapeseed oil, plus extra-virgin olive oil for serving

2 swordfish steaks, about 175 grams (6 ounces) each, skin on

Coarse salt and freshly ground black pepper

½ lemon

75 grams (3 ounces) red onion, sliced 3 millimeters (⅛ inch) thick (¾ cup)

15 grams (2 tablespoons) coarsely chopped garlic

4 leaves fresh basil

Pinch of red pepper flakes

600 grams (1⅓ pounds) fresh tomatoes, peeled and cut into 1-centimeter (⅜-inch) dice, or canned Italian plum tomatoes, strained of their juice and cut into 1-centimeter (⅜-inch) dice (3⅓ cups)

5 grams (2 tablespoons) chopped fresh basil

3 grams (1 tablespoon) chopped fresh Italian parsley

50 grams (¼ cup) pitted black Gaeta olives

2 teaspoons dried or 1 teaspoon fresh oregano, chopped

30 grams (2 tablespoons) capers, preferably salt-packed (see page 31), soaked, rinsed, and drained

125 milliliters (½ cup) fish stock

Heat the oil in a skillet (*padella*) over medium-high heat. Sprinkle the fish on both sides with salt and pepper to taste, add to the pan, and sauté (*rosolare*) on both sides to brown. Squeeze the lemon over the fish. Remove the pan from the heat and place the fish on a plate; set aside.

Add the onion and garlic to the pan. Place the pan over medium heat. Add the basil and red pepper and sauté (*saltare*) until the vegetables begin to caramelize, 5 to 7 minutes.

Add the tomato, chopped basil and parsley, and salt and pepper to taste. Cook 3 minutes. Taste and adjust seasoning.

Add the olives, oregano, and capers and cook 2 minutes.

Add the fish stock and taste for seasoning. Bring to a simmer and cook to reduce by about half. Return the swordfish to the pan and simmer (*brasare*) until the fish is cooked through but still translucent in the center, 3 to 4 minutes.

Place the fish on plates. Taste the sauce for seasoning and spoon over the fish. Serve drizzled with extra-virgin olive oil.

Pesce Intero Arrosto

Whole Roasted Fish

Serves 2

This is a basic method for roasting whole fish. Cooking times in this recipe are for branzino, but any appropriately sized roundfish may be substituted. Whole fish stays moist during cooking, and roasting on the bone maintains flavor.

The fish is seasoned and rubbed with olive oil. The cavity is stuffed with aromatics: whole garlic cloves, sprigs of thyme, and lemon slices. Partway through the roasting, the fish is basted with lemon juice and white wine. Once filleted, the herb-and-garlic-infused fish may be served simply with olive oil and lemon.

(See "Filleting a Cooked Roundfish for Service" on page 237 for step-by-step instructions.)

Ingredients

1 whole roundfish, such as branzino, bream, dorade, or wild striped bass (450 to 575 grams, or 1 to 1¼ pounds), gutted and scaled

Coarse salt and freshly ground black pepper

1 clove garlic, in the skin

2 sprigs fresh thyme

1 lemon, cut in half (cut 1 half into thin slices, reserve the other half for squeezing over the fish)

Olive oil, for rubbing the fish

30 milliliters (2 tablespoons) dry white wine

Lemon wedges, for serving

Extra-virgin olive oil, for serving

Preheat the oven to 191°C (375°F).

Season the fish on both sides and inside the cavity with salt and pepper to taste. Stuff the cavity with the garlic clove, thyme, and the slices cut from half of the lemon. Rub the fish all over with olive oil and place in a baking dish. Oil a piece of aluminum foil and wrap it around the tail to prevent it from burning.

Roast (*arrostire*) the fish 10 minutes. Remove from the oven and remove the foil from the tail. Squeeze the remaining lemon half over the fish and drizzle with the wine. Return to the oven and continue roasting until the fish is cooked through, 15 to 20 minutes longer.

Skin and fillet the fish. Place the fillets on plates, squeeze the lemon wedges over, and serve drizzled with extra-virgin olive oil.

Pesce alla Griglia

Grilled Fish

Serves 4

This recipe demonstrates a method for grilling boned, whole trout, but any thick fillet such as salmon or striped bass may be substituted. *Salmoriglio*, a classic sauce typical of the south of Italy, especially in Calabria and Sicilia, is a mixture of olive oil and lemon juice, seasoned with oregano, parsley, garlic, and salt and pepper. It is a traditional sauce for and delicious with most grilled or roasted fish.

(See "Butterflying a Trout for Grilling" on page 452 for step-by-step instructions and photos.)

Ingredients

For the salmoriglio:
1 clove garlic, peeled
Coarse salt and freshly ground black pepper
Leaves from 4 sprigs fresh oregano, chopped
Leaves from 4 sprigs fresh Italian parsley, chopped
50 milliliters (3 tablespoons plus 1 teaspoon) lemon juice
150 milliliters (⅔ cup) extra-virgin olive oil

4 trout, 450 grams (1 pound) each, gutted and scaled, head and fins removed, but tails left on
Coarse salt and freshly ground black pepper
Olive oil, for grilling

Make the *salmoriglio*:

Place the garlic with salt to taste on a cutting board and mash to a paste. Transfer the paste to a bowl; add the herbs, lemon juice, 30 milliliters (2 tablespoons) water, and the extra-virgin olive oil and stir to combine. Season to taste with salt and pepper and set aside.

Butterfly the trout:

Slide the knife along both sides of the rib cage to release it from the meat. Cut through the backbone. Slide the knife all the way down the backbone to release it from the meat. Pull off the backbone and ribs in one piece, leaving the tail.

Grill the trout:

Preheat a charcoal or gas grill to high heat.

Season the trout on both sides with salt and pepper to taste and coat lightly with olive oil. Grill (*grigliare*) until golden and cooked through, 2 to 3 minutes each side. Spoon the sauce over and serve.

Pesce in Acqua Pazza

Fish in a Vegetable Broth

Serves 2

The literal translation of *acqua pazza* is "crazy water," so named because this simple dish of fish poached in vegetable broth is made at the whim of the chef, with whatever ingredients and seasonings are available. Some sources suggest Neapolitan fishermen developed this method of cooking fish.

The broth is made with sliced vegetables, herbs, and water acidulated with white wine and wine vinegar. The fish fillets are dredged in flour and sautéed on both sides to brown before poaching. The flour thickens the broth very slightly; the finished broth is served with the fish and the vegetables.

This preparation was traditionally used for whole fish; in contemporary kitchens, however, it is often made with fillets, as it is here. Depending on the chef, the fish may be served swimming abundantly in broth, or with just enough broth to moisten. Some chefs prefer to cook this dish in the oven (uncovered, so that the top of the fish browns); others cook it covered.

Fish stock may be substituted for the vegetable broth.

(See pages 350 and 354, respectively, for step-by-step instructions for peeling tomatoes and preparing asparagus.)

Ingredients

125 grams (4½ ounces) tomato, peeled, cored, and cut into wedges (1 centimeter / ⅜ inch) (¾ cup)

50 grams (2 ounces) red onion, cut into wedges (1 centimeter / ⅜ inch) (⅓ cup)

30 grams (1 ounce) fennel, sliced (6 millimeters / ¼ inch) (¼ cup)

15 grams (2 tablespoons) sliced garlic

40 milliliters (2½ tablespoons) dry white wine

10 milliliters (2 teaspoons) white wine vinegar

2 sprigs fresh basil

2 sprigs fresh Italian parsley

30 grams (about 1 ounce) asparagus, trimmed and large or woody stems peeled

Coarse salt and freshly ground black pepper

Pinch of red pepper flakes

2 pieces fish fillet, such as red mullet, striped bass or cod (200 grams / 7 ounces total)

Extra-virgin olive oil, for serving

Calabria

"Some dishes in Calabrian cuisine are rooted in Arabic cuisine; they are similar, but they are prepared in a simpler fashion. Sweet and spicy approaches: 'bewitched meat with a honey and hot pepper sauce.'"

—Chef Gaetano Alia of La Locanda di Alia, Castrovillari–Cosenza

Calabria is at the southernmost tip of the Italian peninsula, covering the toe of the Italian "boot." The interior ranges from hills near the coast, to mountains inland, with the Apennines running down the center of the peninsula. To the north is Basilicata. Sicilia lies to the south, across the narrow Strait of Messina. The region's capital is Catanzaro.

Calabria is one of Italy's poorest regions. The cuisine relies on vegetables (tomatoes, eggplants, peppers, purple onions from Tropea, artichokes, asparagus, potatoes, peas, and beans), durum-wheat pastas, seafood, and pork. Hot chile peppers, *peperoncini* in particular, are an omnipresent seasoning.

Nonetheless, Calabria is an important producer of olive oil and citrus fruits, particularly the IGP-classified *Clementine di Calabria*. The lemonlike *citron* (used in candied fruits) is grown near the coast; the region is also known for its figs. Calabria produces both red and white wines.

Pork represents the region's major source of meat, and it is preserved in hams and *salami*. Calabria maintains traditions of curing meats dating back to the ancient Greeks. *Capocollo*, pancetta, *salsiccia*, and *soppressata* from Calabria have gained DOP status. Goat- and sheep-farming are important industries, and cheeses from the milk of both animals are produced here, as well as the DOP-classified cow's-milk cheese Caciocavallo Silano.

The cuisine is rich in vegetable pastas, seafood, and soups. Specialties include local pasta shapes such as *lagane* (like fettuccine), *ricci di donna*, and *capieddi'e prieviti*. Other specialties of the region are *melanzane alla Parmigiana* (eggplant Parmesan), stuffed eggplant, and dishes made with locally caught swordfish and tuna.

Swordfish recipes, especially prepared with capers, olives, and tomatoes, are popular all along the Tyrrhenian coast of Calabria. Our version, *Pesce Spada all'Isolana*, appears on page 230.

Combine the tomato, onion, fennel, garlic, white wine, vinegar, basil, and parsley in a saucepan (*casseruola*). Cut off the tips (about 8 centimeters / 3 inches) of the asparagus and reserve; cut the stems on an angle into 4-centimeter (1½-inch) lengths and add them to the pan. Add water to cover generously (about 1¼ liters / 5¼ cups), salt and black pepper to taste, and the red pepper flakes. Bring the water to a boil, cover and simmer (*affogare*) 15 minutes. Taste and season the broth with salt and black pepper.

Season the fish on both sides with salt. Add the fish and the reserved asparagus tips to the saucepan. Simmer gently (*sobbollire*) until the fish is cooked through, 4 to 5 minutes.

Spoon the fish into shallow bowls and spoon the vegetables and some of the broth over. Serve drizzled with extra-virgin olive oil.

Pesce in Crosta di Sale

Whole Fish Baked in a Salt Crust

Serves 2

Fish, lean meats (beef tenderloin, for example), and even potatoes can benefit from baking in a salt crust. The crust encourages the food to cook evenly, while keeping it moist. The salt in the crust also serves to season the food, while the egg whites seal the crust so that the steam doesn't escape.

Here we use branzino and serve it with a sauce of lemon juice whisked with olive oil, salt, and pepper. Alternatively, the fish may be served with *salmoriglio* (page 233). Orata, snapper, or black bass would also be good choices.

(See "Filleting a Cooked Roundfish for Service" on page 237 for step-by-step instructions for serving this dish.)

Chef's Notes

The smallest size of fish that can be cooked by this method is one weighing 450 grams (about 1 pound). Smaller fish will overcook before the crust bakes through entirely.

Aromatic elements such as herbs or citrus zest can be added to the salt crust to impart subtle flavors to the fish and provide a wonderful aroma.

Ingredients

For the salt crust:
675 grams (2¾ cups) coarse salt
6 to 8 large egg whites

For the fish:
1 whole fish, about 450 grams (1 pound), such as branzino, gutted and scaled
Coarse salt and freshly ground black pepper
1 sprig fresh rosemary
½ lemon, sliced
Extra-virgin olive oil
Lemon juice

Make the salt crust:

Mix the salt and egg whites until the mixture is the consistency of wet sand.

Roast the fish:

Preheat the oven to 191°C (375°F).

Pat the fish dry with paper towels. Season the cavity with salt and pepper to taste. Place the rosemary inside the cavity, and line with the lemon slices. Rub the outside of the fish all over with oil.

Place the fish on a baking sheet lined with parchment paper. Completely cover the fish in the salt crust.

Place the baking sheet in the center of the oven and roast (*arrostire*) until the crust turns a light, golden brown, about 25 minutes. Serve immediately, or allow the fish to rest in the crust on the baking sheet at room temperature up to 1 hour before serving; the fish will remain warm.

To serve:

Cut around the circumference of the salt crust close to the bottom. Lift up like a hinge to expose the fish.

Skin and remove the top fillet and place on a serving plate. Remove and discard the bone.

Skin and remove the bottom fillet and place on another serving plate.

Whisk together a mixture of olive oil, lemon juice, and salt and pepper, using 3 parts oil to 1 part lemon. Season to taste with salt and pepper. Serve the fish drizzled with the sauce.

Aragosta Fra Diavola

Lobster in Spicy Tomato Sauce

Serves 4 as an appetizer, 2 as an entrée

The culinary term *fra diavolo* means "Friar Devil," and indicates a spicy dish. The name appears to have originated with an Italian bandit known for his red cape who was hanged by the French in the early nineteenth century.

The lobster is poached in vegetable stock and shelled. The shells are simmered in vegetable stock to create a lobster stock. Once strained, the stock moistens a spicy tomato sauce, served with the lobster over spaghetti.

(For instructions on cooking and cleaning lobster, see "Preparing Lobsters" on pages 458.)

Ingredients

For the lobster and lobster stock:
2 liters (8½ cups) vegetable stock
1 lobster (680 grams / 1½ pounds)
Coarse salt and freshly ground black pepper

15 milliliters (1 tablespoon) olive oil, plus extra for drizzling
4 grams (1¼ teaspoons) chopped garlic
Pinch of red pepper flakes
3 grams (1 tablespoon) chopped fresh Italian parsley
15 milliliters (1 tablespoon) brandy
175 milliliters (¾ cup) whole, canned Italian plum tomatoes, with their juices, puréed through a food mill
110 grams (4 ounces) spaghetti

Prepare the lobster:

Bring the stock to a boil in a large pot (*pentola*). Add the lobster to the pot and return the stock to a boil.

Remove the pot from the heat and let the lobster cool completely in the stock.

When the lobster is cool, remove from the pot. Reserve the stock.

Working over a hotel pan, rimmed sheet pan, or baking dish to collect the juices and the empty shells, twist off the claws where they attach to the body. Then pull the claws off the "knuckles." Crack both sides of the claws with the back of a large knife. Move the claw's pincers side to side, then bend them away from the claw while pulling them out. The feather-shaped piece of cartilage embedded in the claw should come out with the pincers. Push the claw meat out in a single piece; set aside.

Twist off the tail; reserve the head. Working on the underside of the tail, snip between the shells to cut down the length of the tail, on both sides. Pry open the shell and pull the tail meat out. Reserve the juices, roe, and shells.

Cut the tail in half lengthwise and remove the intestinal vein, or cut crosswise into medallions, about 1½ centimeters (½ inch) wide.

Make the lobster stock:

With a large knife, split the lobster head in half lengthwise.

Place the head along with the shells in a pot.

Add enough of the reserved vegetable stock to cover the shells; discard the remaining stock. Bring to a simmer and cook (*sobbollire*) 20 minutes. Strain, taste, and season to taste with salt and pepper. Measure 110 milliliters (¼ cup plus 3 tablespoons) for the sauce; reserve the remainder for another use.

Cook the sauce and the spaghetti:

Bring a large pot of salted water to a boil for the spaghetti.

Meanwhile, combine the oil, garlic, red pepper flakes, and half of the parsley in a large saucepan (*casseruola*). Place over medium heat and cook until the garlic begins to color at the edges.

Carefully introduce the brandy to the pan, off the heat, and flambé (*flambare*) to evaporate the alcohol.

Add the tomatoes, bring to a boil, and simmer 5 minutes.

Add the reserved lobster stock. Bring to a boil and simmer 5 minutes to reduce.

Add the reserved lobster juices and roe. Stir, and cook 2 minutes. Season to taste with salt and pepper and remove the sauce from the heat.

When ready to serve, add the spaghetti to the boiling water and cook until about two-thirds done. Drain and add to the pan with the sauce; add pasta water or lobster stock as needed to thin the sauce, and cook 2 to 3 more minutes. Stir in the lobster pieces (reserving a tail piece and claw for garnish) and the remaining parsley. Season to taste with salt and pepper.

Reheat the reserved tail piece and claw in the oven with a little of the lobster stock and a drizzle of olive oil to keep them moist, and serve with the sauced pasta.

Zuppa di Pesce

Fish Soup

Serves 6

This recipe demonstrates a basic method for making a seafood soup. All regions of Italy that have access to seafood have their own styles of *zuppa di pesce*. The soups are called by specific names in each region, such as *brodetto*, *cacciucco*, and *ciuppin*, to name a few. In addition to the seafood, the essential ingredients are red and/or black pepper, garlic, salt, herbs, vegetables, and spices.

The soup begins with a *soffritto*, to which the different varieties of seafood are added in the order of their cooking time (longer-cooking varieties first). The soup is moistened with white wine, tomatoes, and fish stock.

Ingredients

For the soffritto:

170 grams (6 ounces) red onion, cut into ½-centimeter (³⁄₁₆-inch) dice (1 cup)

120 grams (4½ ounces) celery, cut into ½-centimeter (³⁄₁₆-inch) dice (1¼ cups)

40 grams (1½ ounces) carrot, cut into ½-centimeter (³⁄₁₆-inch) dice (⅓ cup)

1 clove garlic, thinly sliced

90 milliliters (⅓ cup) olive oil

1 teaspoon red pepper flakes

5 fresh sage leaves

Leaves from 2 sprigs fresh basil

For the soup:

300 grams (11 ounces) octopus, cut into 2-centimeter (¾-inch) pieces

225 grams (½ pound) squid bodies and tentacles, bodies cut into 2-centimeter (¾-inch) strips

Coarse salt and freshly ground black pepper

6 grams (2 tablespoons) chopped fresh Italian parsley

250 milliliters (1 cup) dry white wine

500 milliliters (2 cups) whole, canned Italian plum tomatoes with their juices, puréed through a food mill

250 milliliters (1 cup) fish stock or water

Pinch of spezie forti, garam masala, or freshly ground nutmeg

1½ liters (6⅓ cups) vegetable or fish stock

225 grams (½ pound) shrimp, peeled and deveined

550 grams (1¼ pounds) mussels, bearded and scrubbed

700 grams (1½ pounds) clams, scrubbed and soaked to remove grit

450 grams (1 pound) lean, firm fish fillet such as red mullet, scorpion fish, snapper, monkfish, or branzino, skinned, cut into 5-centimeter (2-inch) pieces

Toasted bread (fettunta) rubbed with split garlic cloves and drizzled with olive oil

Make the *soffritto*:

Combine the vegetables and garlic in a cold pot (*pentola*), add the oil, and place over medium heat. Cook (*saltare*) 3 to 4 minutes.

Add the red pepper flakes, sage, and basil and cook until the vegetables have deepened in color and their flavors concentrated, 5 to 10 minutes.

Make the soup:

Add the octopus to the pot with the *soffritto* and cook 20 minutes.

Add the squid, salt to taste, and half the parsley and cook 20 more minutes.

Add the wine and cook (*sobbollire*) until reduced by half.

Add the tomato purée, the fish stock or water, and a pinch of *spezie forti* and cook 10 more minutes.

Add the vegetable or fish stock, and bring to a boil. Add the shrimp, and simmer until almost cooked through, about 5 minutes. Add the mussels and clams, season with black pepper to taste, and simmer until they just open, about 5 minutes.

Add the fish fillet and simmer until just cooked through. The broth should be reduced and deep flavored.

Stir in the remaining parsley. Season to taste with salt and pepper.

To serve, set one or two pieces of toast (*fettunta*) in each serving bowl and ladle the soup over.

Vongole Ripiene

Stuffed Clams

Serves 4 to 6

Stuffed clams are traditionally broiled or baked and served as an antipasto. In this recipe, the clams are topped with breadcrumbs seasoned with garlic, herbs, and olive oil, then broiled in the shell to brown the coating and warm the clam through.

Littleneck or cherrystone clams may be replaced with oysters or mussels.

(See "Cleaning and Shucking Clams" on page 461 for step-by-step instructions.)

Ingredients

40 grams (⅓ cup) fine breadcrumbs (see page 157)

30 milliliters (2 tablespoons) olive oil

50 grams (1¾ ounces) pancetta, finely diced

2 to 3 cloves garlic, finely chopped

20 grams (¼ cup) grated Parmigiano-Reggiano or Grana Padano

10 grams (3 tablespoons) finely chopped fresh Italian parsley

1 teaspoon chopped fresh thyme

Coarse salt and freshly ground black pepper

24 littleneck or cherrystone clams, scrubbed and soaked in salted water

Lemon wedges, for serving

In a bowl, combine the breadcrumbs, oil, pancetta, garlic, grated cheese, parsley, and thyme; mix well. Season with pepper and taste for salt; you may not need additional salt because both the pancetta and cheese are salty.

Preheat the broiler to high.

Cover the bottom of a sheet pan with a thin layer of coarse salt to stabilize the clamshells. Open the clams. Leave the clams in the bottom shells, and discard the top shells. Spoon the breadcrumb mixture over the clams (do not pack tightly) and place on the prepared sheet pan. Broil (*gratinare*) until the topping is golden brown and crisp, about 1 minute. Serve with lemon wedges.

Le Marche (The Marches)

"It is necessary to repeat that eating is an agricultural act. We use, and we have always used, small producers who encourage local consumption. It is a closed region that can 'make do' with all of its internal products. It has always been a poor and 'recycled' cuisine (offal from the capon eaten by the masters, used for at-home cooking) that was optimized with creativity and good taste."

—Chef Lucio Pompili of Symposium 4 Stagioni, Carteceto–Serrungarina

Le Marche is a rugged, mountainous strip of land in central Italy, bounded on the west by the Apennines, and to the east by the Adriatic Sea. Its capital is the port city of Ancona. Its cuisine is rich in both seafood and meat.

The seacoast has given rise to a tradition of seafood soups, called *brodetto*, of which there are innumerable variations, depending on the town. Some variations use saffron, some tomato; some call for flouring and browning the fish before adding liquid; some require as many as thirteen different varieties of seafood, while others specify a single fish. Pig-farming is an important industry in the hilly interior, and *porchetta* (spit-roasted suckling pig) is a popular dish.

The cuisine is similar to that of the contiguous, central Italian regions of Umbria and Tuscany. The geography encourages the production of olives and olive oil, as well as the mountain cheese pecorino. The cuisine also reflects the influence of Emilia-Romagna to the north, with its tradition of fresh egg pasta in dishes such as *vincisgrassi* (a version of lasagne made with mushrooms, or with white truffles, in season), and *passatelli di carni*, a variation on the egg dumplings of Emilia-Romagna called *passatelli*, and its production of *salumi*, including a DOP-classified prosciutto and an IGP-classified Mortadella Bologna. According to Chef Pompili, Le Marche is the largest European producer of eggs.

Along with seafood and pork, the cuisine is characterized by meat—chicken, goose, duck, lamb, beef, and veal, and mountain game, such as thrush, partridge, quail, pigeon, and pheasant.

Le Marche produces the well-known white wine Verdicchio.

Our version of the regional specialty *brodetto*, or *Zuppa di Pesce*, appears on page 240.

Anguilla in Carpione

Pickled Eel

Serves 3 to 4

Pickling *in carpione* is a traditional method for preparing freshwater eel. Pickled eel is customarily eaten on Christmas Eve, especially in southern Italy. Any firm-fleshed fish may be substituted for the eel; red mullet, with its orangey-red skin, makes a particularly beautiful presentation.

(See sidebar "Marinated, Pickled, and Oil-Cured Foods for *Antipasti*" on page 44 for further discussion of *in carpione*. See also "Preparing Eel for Cooking" on page 453.)

Ingredients

For the eel:

1 eel, about 300 grams (11 ounces), gutted, disgorged, and cut
    into 4-centimeter (1½-inch) pieces, skin on
Coarse salt and freshly ground black pepper
Juice of ½ lemon
110 grams (scant 1 cup) all-purpose flour
Olive, canola, or grapeseed oil

For the marinade:

45 milliliters (3 tablespoons) olive oil
50 grams (⅓ cup) thinly sliced red onion rounds
50 grams (½ cup) thinly sliced celery
50 grams (⅓ cup) thinly sliced carrot rounds
3 garlic cloves, sliced
Pinch of red pepper flakes
10 fresh mint leaves
Pinch of sugar
Sea salt and freshly ground black pepper
200 milliliters (¾ cup plus 2 tablespoons) red wine vinegar

Cook the eel:

Season the eel pieces with salt and pepper to taste, and squeeze the lemon juice over. Place in a fine-mesh or perforated strainer (*colino*) and toss with the flour; shake off the excess.

Heat about 2 centimeters (¾ inch) oil in a large skillet (*padella*) over medium-high heat. Working in batches, sauté (*saltare*) the eel pieces in the oil until cooked through. Drain on a rack. Place in a single layer in a container.

Prepare the marinade:

In a separate skillet, combine the olive oil, onion, celery, carrot, and garlic. Place over medium-high heat and sauté until the vegetables begin to color. A few minutes into the cooking, add the red pepper flakes and mint leaves.

Add the sugar, and salt and pepper to taste.

Add the vinegar and 60 milliliters (¼ cup) water and simmer 2 minutes. Taste for acidity: The mixture should not be overly acidic. If necessary, dilute with an additional 40 milliliters (3 tablespoons) water. Cook 3 more minutes.

Pour the marinade over the eel and marinate at least 1 day. Bring to room temperature before serving. This will keep several days in the refrigerator.

Seppie in Zimino

Cuttlefish Stewed with Swiss Chard

Serves 6

Cooking *in zimino* refers to stews that include chard or spinach and *cumino*, or cumin. The preparation is especially popular in Toscana and Liguria, and may be made with cuttlefish, *baccalà* (salted cod), legumes such as chickpeas and beans, and often tripe. Here, cuttlefish is cut into pieces, dusted with flour, and sautéed in oil. Once cooked, it is layered with Swiss chard that has been stewed with a *soffritto*, cumin, white wine, and tomato. The dish is finished in the oven.

Most cuttlefish in the United States is sold precleaned and frozen. The same quantity of squid may be substituted.

Ingredients

For the soffritto:
175 grams (6 ounces) red onion, cut into ½-centimeter (³⁄₁₆-inch) dice (generous 1 cup)
150 grams (5 ounces) celery, cut into ½-centimeter (³⁄₁₆-inch) dice (1½ cups)
50 grams (2 ounces) carrot, cut into ½-centimeter (³⁄₁₆-inch) dice (⅓ cup)
3 cloves garlic, finely chopped
6 grams (2 tablespoons) chopped fresh Italian parsley
Red pepper flakes

60 milliliters (¼ cup) olive oil
250 milliliters (1 cup) dry white wine
Coarse salt and freshly ground black pepper
500 grams (6 cups packed) Swiss chard, leaves and stems separated, stems cut into 3-centimeter (1-inch) pieces, leaves chopped
5 grams (2 teaspoons) ground cumin

300 milliliters (1¼ cups) whole, canned Italian plum tomatoes with their juices, puréed through a food mill
250 milliliters (1 cup) vegetable stock

For the cuttlefish:
400 grams (14 ounces) cleaned, frozen cuttlefish, thawed in the refrigerator
Olive, grapeseed, or canola oil, as needed, for frying
Coarse salt and freshly ground black pepper
½ lemon
110 grams (1 scant cup) all-purpose flour

Prepare the chard:

Combine all of the ingredients for the *soffritto*, except for the red pepper flakes, with the olive oil in a cold pot (*pentola*). Set over medium heat and cook (*saltare*) until the onions start to color and the flavors concentrate, adding the red pepper flakes a few minutes into cooking.

Add the wine, season with salt and pepper to taste, and cook until the wine is reduced by one half.

Add the chard stems and cumin; cover, and cook 10 minutes to soften.

Add the tomato purée and vegetable stock, cover, and cook 15 minutes.

Add the chard leaves, cover, and cook 15 more minutes until tender. Season to taste with salt and pepper. Set aside.

Cook the cuttlefish:

Cut the cuttlefish into ½-centimeter (³⁄₁₆-inch) pieces. Refrigerate until ready to use.

Preheat the oven to 177°C (350°F).

Heat about ½ centimeter (¼ inch) oil in a large skillet (*padella*) until a leaf of basil or sage sizzles when added. Season the cuttlefish with salt and pepper to taste, and squeeze the lemon juice over. Place in a fine-mesh or perforated strainer (*colino*) and toss with the flour; shake off the excess. Working in batches, fry (*friggere*) the cuttlefish pieces in the oil, turning to brown all over, until cooked through completely. Drain on a rack or paper towels.

Spoon a layer of the chard mixture over the bottom of a baking dish. Arrange the cuttlefish on top, in a single layer. Cover with the remaining chard mixture and season with pepper to taste. Cover with foil and bake (*cuocere al forno*) 15 minutes. Remove the foil and bake 5 more minutes.

Fritto Misto di Pesce

Mixed Fried Fish

Serves 4

Fritto misto—a preparation of crisp, deep-fried seafood and vegetables—is found all over Italy. This grand "mixed fry," a well-documented menu item of the Italian bourgeois in the seventeenth century, often included—in addition to meat—fish and vegetables, pastries, cheeses, and sweets. The mixture of foods changes depending on region and availability of ingredients; in Roman, Piemontese, and Lombardian versions, for example, offal is a common element.

The key to this dish is threefold: the freshness of the ingredients, the quality of the frying oil, and the effectiveness of the batter or coating, called *pastella*, in creating a crisp crust.

In this case, the *pastella* is created by dipping the ingredients first in milk, then in seasoned flour and cornmeal. The milk helps the dry ingredients stick to the food and the caramelization of milk solids during frying enriches the flavor. Cornmeal adds texture. Alternatively, a breadcrumb coating might be substituted or a light, tempura-style batter.

Fritto misto is traditionally served as an antipasto. In Italy, the vegetables would be fried and served separately from the seafood so as not to pick up its stronger taste.

Ingredients

Peanut or grapeseed oil, for frying

1 liter (4¼ cups) milk

Coarse salt and freshly ground black pepper

140 grams (1 cup plus 2 tablespoons) all-purpose flour

15 grams (3 tablespoons) fine cornmeal

300 grams (11 ounces) zucchini, cut into 1-by-8-centimeter (⅜-by-3-inch) sticks (2 cups)

150 grams (5 ounces) eggplant, cut into 1-by-8-centimeter (⅜-by-3-inch) sticks (2 cups)

225 grams (8 ounces) cleaned squid, sliced into 1-centimeter (⅜-inch) rings

150 grams (5 ounces) white-fleshed fish, such as red snapper or grouper, cut into 3-centimeter (1-inch) cubes

150 grams (5 ounces) shrimp, peeled and deveined

1 sprig fresh basil

1 sprig fresh Italian parsley

1 sprig fresh sage

Lemon wedges, for serving

Fill a deep-fryer with a basket about halfway to the top with oil. Heat to 163°C (325°F).

Pour the milk into a large bowl and season with salt and pepper to taste. Combine the flour and cornmeal on a plate and season with salt and pepper to taste.

Place the vegetables and seafood in the milk. Then, working in batches, remove them from the milk, allow-

ing the excess to drain over the bowl. Place in a perforated or fine-mesh strainer (*colino*) and toss with the seasoned flour-cornmeal mixture; shake off the excess. Gently slide the vegetables and seafood into the hot oil and fry (*friggere*), stirring so they cook evenly, just until golden brown and crisp, about 1 minute. Transfer with a spider to a sheet pan covered with a wire rack or paper towels to drain. Drop the herbs into the oil and fry until crisp; transfer to the rack.

Place the vegetables, seafood, and herbs on a serving plate. Season with salt to taste and serve immediately, with lemon wedges.

Le Tecniche: *Friggere* (Deep-Frying)

The recipe for *Fritto Misto di Pesce* on page 246 demonstrates the technique of deep-frying, an important cooking method in Italy, where it is said that "even old shoes will taste good fried." All regions of Italy have fried-food specialties, called *frittura*.

To deep-fry is to submerge food entirely in hot oil or other fat until the food is cooked. The goal is to obtain a golden brown crust caused by the coagulation of the external protein, and for the inside to be cooked through. Caramelization of the food's natural juices and sugars transforms starch into dextrin. For this to occur, the food being fried must be dry on the surface. Foods should be cut into small, regular pieces of uniform size so that the interior of the item is cooked by the time the exterior is crisp and golden brown. Potatoes can be fried uncoated, but moister items should first be dredged in flour, breadcrumbs, or a batter. When fried properly, this outer crust forms immediately and prevents the food from absorbing oil. For this reason, deep-frying is considered a dry-heat method.

Guidelines for Deep-Frying

Food may be cooked in a deep-fryer, which allows for precise temperature control; in a large, heavy pot; or in the case of very small foods, such as sage leaves, in a deep skillet. Do not fill the vessel more than halfway with oil or it will overflow when the food is added. A frying basket is recommended so that finished foods can be easily lifted out of the oil.

Avoid combining different types of oils; they can foam up and cause fires. There are additional reasons for fires: The oil may catch fire if it gets very hot, and if oil splashes out of the pot and onto the stove, it may ignite. If the oil does catch fire, never pour water on the fire. Turn off the flame and cover the pot with a metal tray or lid to smother the flames. If it continues to burn, call the fire department and use a fire extinguisher intended for grease fires. Evacuate the area if necessary.

The fat used for deep-frying is typically a vegetable oil with a high smoke point and mild flavor, such as grapeseed or peanut. Oil can be reused once or twice, depending on what has been cooked in it, but it must be strained after each use and stored covered. (Various strongly flavored foods, such as fish, can impart an undesirable flavor to the oil that will be transferred to the next food cooked in that oil.) Do not mix used with fresh oil. Oil should be discarded when it foams up, smells unpleasant, or darkens in color. Note also that the quality of the oil degrades each time it is used, lowering its smoke point. Avoid overheating the oil or preheating it too far in advance, because both can cause it to decompose more quickly.

The oil in the cooking vessel should be a minimum of 6 to 8 centimeters (2⅜ to 3⅛ inches) deep. It must be completely hot before the items are added, or they will absorb too much fat before cooking through. The temperature desired depends on the item being cooked, but it should never exceed 218°C (425°F). Always test the oil with one piece of the item being fried before adding the entire batch. When the oil is ready, the item being fried must be added in small quantities to prevent the oil's temperature from dropping significantly and to allow it to circulate freely around each piece. The food is lowered into the oil a few pieces at a time, or placed in a basket that is carefully lowered into the hot oil. To prevent being splashed with fat, place the food into the pan so that the farthest edge falls away from you. Do not salt the item before cooking.

Pan-frying is similar to deep-frying in that the food is almost always coated, and the goal is to create a crisp crust. Pan-frying, however, uses only enough oil to come about halfway up the side of the food. As a result, once the food is browned on one side, it is turned so that the other side browns. Quick-cooking foods are suitable for pan-frying.

After cooking, fried foods should always be drained on a rack or paper towels to absorb excess grease, salted while hot, and served immediately. Draining on a wire rack over a sheet pan helps keeps fried food crisp because the space between rack and pan helps to dissipate the steam that eventually causes the food to become soggy.

One- and Two-Step Methods for Deep-Frying

There are two basic frying techniques: one-step and two-step methods. In the one-step method, the food is fried completely at one temperature, usually at 177°C to 191°C (350°F to 375°F). In the two-step method (used for deep-frying some vegetables such as potatoes and artichokes), the food is first partially cooked in fat (also called blanching) at a lower temperature 135°C (275°F) to cook the food through, without coloration. The food is then finished at 177°C to 191°C (350°F to 375°F) to brown the outside quickly.

Coatings for Deep-Fried Foods

There are many ways to coat food in order to create a crust while deep-frying. These include dredging in flour or a combination of flour and egg; dipping in a heavier breadcrumb mixture; and covering in a batter.

Quick-cooking raw vegetables and fish may very effectively be dredged in seasoned flour and fried; the flour helps the exterior brown and crisp, and adds a very light crust. The addition of a small quantity of cornmeal to the flour will add an appealing texture.

Dredging the food in flour and then beaten egg will produce a light, puffy, crisp crust slightly more substantial than if flour alone is used, and is suitable for all of the ingredients that work well with just flour.

A breading of fresh or dry breadcrumbs, in which the food is dipped after first being moistened with beaten egg to help the breadcrumbs adhere, will produce a thicker, more substantial crust. This treatment is suitable for seafood and many quick-cooking vegetables, including mushrooms. Longer-cooking vegetables such as fennel, broccoli, and cauliflower are excellent breaded and fried, but must first be blanched in boiling salted water.

Food may also be crusted with a coating, or *pastella*. Batters are particularly useful for small and crumbly foods that might otherwise fall apart in the cooking. Italian batters are made with egg, water, milk, flour, and/or egg whites, in various combinations.

Chapter 16

Vegetables and Salads:
Contorni e Insalate

Clockwise from top left:
Cavolini con Prosciutto (page 255),
Cipolline in Agrodolce (page 262),
Finocchi Gratinati (page 259),
Piselli al Prosciutto (page 262),
and *Peperonata* (page 259)

One cannot overestimate the importance of vegetables in Italian cuisine. In part, this is because meat was historically too expensive for regular consumption; vegetables and grains have always been a staple of *cucina povera*. However, in *Italian Cuisine: A Cultural History*, historians Alberto Capatti and Massimo Montanari argue that vegetables have always held a special place in Italian culture. They note that the oldest Italian cookbook, *Liber de Coquina*, written in Latin at the end of the thirteenth or the beginning of the fourteenth century, begins with a chapter on vegetables. Since this cookbook was written for the Angevin court of Naples, a population that was certainly not confined to a diet of vegetables, the authors infer that even then and among all classes, vegetables have been uniquely esteemed.

Contorni are the vegetable accompaniments that are served alongside the main course during the Italian meal. Traditionally, and still in most cases today, *contorni* are served on a separate plate or platter and ordered à la carte. (These days, in some more international, contemporary restaurants in Italy, vegetables may be served on the same plate as the protein.) Vegetables also feature strongly in *antipasti*. (This is particularly true for salads.)

In addition to being eaten raw, vegetables are cooked in numerous ways. Often times, vegetables are first boiled, and then finished by some other method. Potatoes, for example, may be boiled and mashed; boiled fennel may be sliced, sprinkled with cheese, and browned under the broiler; and boiled broccoli rabe is often sautéed in olive oil with garlic and red pepper.

Roasting is an excellent method for cooking vegetables, as it concentrates their flavors, by evaporating water and caramelizing their juices. Vegetables are almost always roasted with oil to encourage browning:

radicchio may be additionally seasoned with vinegar while it roasts; potatoes are cut up and tossed with oil, sliced fennel, red onion, garlic, and herbs.

Italians love deep-fried vegetables, usually cut into regular pieces and fried just as they are. Potatoes and artichokes, for example, are prepared this way (*Carciofi alla Giudea*, right). Alternatively, the vegetable may be treated in a coating of flour, egg, or a combination of the two, a breadcrumb mixture, or a batter.

Italians are also fond of braising and stewing vegetables. The vegetable may be sautéed first to create a layer of caramelization, and then braised in a liquid with seasoning (*Cipolline in Agrodolce* on page 262). Artichokes are braised whole in a seasoned mixture of olive oil and water; peas are braised in stock seasoned with prosciutto, shallot, and tomato. Sweet peppers need no additional liquid, as they produce their own juices.

Many vegetables are suitable for grilling: Eggplant, fennel, radicchio, zucchini, and peppers, to name a few, are first brushed with olive oil and then grilled. Quick-cooking vegetables such as spinach, Swiss chard leaves, and mushrooms are quickly dispatched by sautéing.

Le Tecniche

In this chapter, students learn to apply all cooking methods—*saltare, brasare, sbianchire, friggere, grigliare, arrostire*—to vegetables.

Carciofi alla Giudea

Deep-Fried Artichokes

Serves 2

This dish originated in the Jewish ghettos of Trastevere, an area of Rome on the west side of the Tiber. Baby artichokes are fried twice: first at a relatively low temperature to cook them through, then at a higher temperature to brown and crisp them. The leaves are pressed open after the first frying to give the artichokes their characteristic flowerlike presentation.

This recipe uses baby artichokes, but larger globe artichokes can also be prepared in exactly the same way and are more traditional. (See "Preparing Artichokes for Cooking Whole" on page 352.) Fry the artichokes about 4 minutes at the lower temperature, then 1 to 2 minutes at the higher temperature to crisp. Jumbo-size artichokes should be avoided as they will not be tender.) *Carciofi alla Giudea* may be served as either a *contorno* or an antipasto. They may also be served with a *fritto misto*.

The chokes on baby artichokes are not fully developed, so they do not require as much work to remove.

Ingredients

1 lemon, cut in half
8 baby artichokes
Peanut or grapeseed oil, for frying
Coarse salt

Cut off the top centimeter (½ inch) of the remaining leaves, angling the knife so that the inner leaves are taller than the outer leaves. Rub all over with the lemon half.

Pull open the remaining leaves and scrape out the short, prickly leaves at the center and the fuzzy choke they cover.

Trim any remaining tough green skin from the base of the artichokes; rub all exposed surfaces with the lemon half. Place in the bowl of acidulated water.

Fill a deep-fryer fitted with a basket about halfway to the top with oil. Heat to 149°C (300°F).

Dry the artichokes well, then slide them into the hot oil and fry (*friggere*) 2 minutes, until softened.

Transfer the artichokes to a rack. While they are still hot, use a spoon to open out the leaves. Holding the artichokes stem ends up, press the leaves down and open on the rack, so that they open like a rose. Let drain and cool on paper towels, stem ends up.

Heat the oil to 177°C (350°F). Season the artichokes with salt to taste, return to the oil, and cook until golden brown and crisp, 1 to 2 more minutes. Transfer to a bowl with a spider or skimmer. Season with salt to taste. Squeeze the reserved lemon half over, and toss. Serve hot.

Fill a bowl with water and squeeze in the juice from 1 lemon half; drop in the juiced half. Reserve the second half for rubbing over the artichokes to prevent blackening and for juicing just before serving.

To prepare the artichokes, use a knife or vegetable peeler to trim all of the dark-green outer skin from the stem until you reach the white interior. Rub all over with the reserved lemon half to prevent blackening.

Snap off the outer few rings of leaves near the stem, bending them back and pulling them down toward the stem. Continue in this way, snapping off the leaves a little higher on the leaf with each successive layer, until you reach the pale, yellowish inner cone of leaves, green only at the tips.

Carciofi alla Romana

Artichokes, Roman Style

Serves 4

This recipe is traditionally made with the large (about 13 centimeters / 5 inches) Roman variety of artichoke, *mammola*. The artichoke is trimmed of all tough, inedible parts, stuffed with a mixture of garlic and herbs, and braised in a combination of olive oil and water. (In Rome, a wild Italian mint called *mentuccia* is used.) The braising liquid is reduced to evaporate the water, and the artichokes are served with the flavored oil that remains.

Carciofi alla Romana are traditionally served as either a *contorno* or an antipasto.

(See "Preparing Artichoke Hearts and Stems for Slicing" on page 353 for step-by-step instructions.)

Chef's Note

Damp towels placed over the pot make an effective seal so that the tops of the artichokes will steam as the bases cook.

Ingredients

4 large globe artichokes
½ lemon
10 grams (3 tablespoons) chopped fresh Italian parsley
10 grams (2 tablespoons) finely chopped garlic
15 fresh mint leaves, chopped
Coarse salt and freshly ground black pepper
125 milliliters (½ cup) olive oil

Fill a bowl with water and squeeze in the lemon juice; add the juiced half to the water.

To prepare the artichokes, snap off leaves until you reach the inner cone. Cut off the top two-thirds of the artichoke. Rub with the lemon half while you work.

Using a spoon, scrape out the prickly leaves at the center and the choke.

Trim all of the tough green skin from the base and stems of the artichokes; rub all exposed surfaces with the lemon half. Hold the cleaned artichokes in the bowl of acidulated water as you work.

In a small bowl, mix together the chopped parsley, garlic, and mint, and season to taste with salt and pepper. Press some of the garlic-herb mixture into the center of each artichoke, rubbing all around the sides of the hollow; rub the rest over the outsides.

Place the artichokes, stem ends up, in a pot (*pentola*) tall enough to hold them. Add the olive oil and enough water to come halfway up the bases. Dampen two towels: Cover the pot with one towel, then place the second towel on top, at a right angle to the first (see Chef's Note). Place a plate on top, wrap the towels up over the top of the plate, and set the pot over medium heat.

Cook until the bases of the artichokes are tender when pierced with a small knife, 35 to 40 minutes. (When lifting the plate, angle it away from you so as not to get burned by the steam.)

Remove the artichokes from the pot with a spoon and set them, stem ends up, on a plate. Reduce the cooking liquid until almost all of the water has evaporated and the garlic and herbs begin to sizzle.

Pour the oil over the artichokes and serve them warm or at room temperature.

Cavolini con Prosciutto

Brussels Sprouts with Prosciutto

Serves 4

Brussels sprouts are blanched in acidulated water to enhance their flavor, then sautéed in olive oil with chopped shallot, pine nuts, and julienned prosciutto.

Ingredients

475 grams (1 pound plus 1 ounce) Brussels sprouts, stem ends trimmed, outer leaves discarded (5¼ cups)
Coarse salt and freshly ground black pepper
Red wine vinegar
20 milliliters (1½ tablespoons) olive oil
25 grams (3 tablespoons) diced shallot or small red onion
Pinch of red pepper flakes
30 grams (¼ cup) pine nuts
80 grams (3 ounces) prosciutto, julienned

Cut the Brussels sprouts into quarters. Bring a large saucepan (*casseruola*) of salted water to a boil. Add a splash of vinegar, enough to add a mildly acidulated taste to the water.

Add the Brussels sprouts and blanch (*sbianchire*) until a knife pierces the sprouts easily, 3 to 5 minutes. Refresh in ice water; drain.

Place the oil and shallot or onion in a skillet (*padella*). Place over medium-low heat and cook (*saltare*) until the shallot or onion softens, 3 to 5 minutes. Add the red pepper flakes. Add the Brussels sprouts, pine nuts, and salt and black pepper to taste. Turn the heat to medium and cook until the sprouts begin to color, about 5 minutes. Add a little water if the pan begins to burn.

Stir in the prosciutto and toss over medium heat to warm the meat and render the fat, 1 to 2 minutes. Season to taste with salt and pepper.

Patate Arrostite

Roasted Potatoes with Garlic and Herbs

Serves 4

These potatoes are excellent roasted with the fat of a roasting chicken or duck (see *Pollo Arrosto* on page 161, and *Anitra Arrosto* on page 169). Otherwise, use olive oil.

Ingredients

1 kilogram (2¼ pounds) Yukon Gold potatoes, peeled and cut into 3-centimeter (1³⁄₁₆-inch) pieces (about 6½ cups)
8 cloves garlic, skin on, crushed with the heel of the hand
4 sprigs fresh rosemary
4 sprigs fresh sage
260 milliliters (1 cup plus 1½ tablespoons) olive oil or, preferably, the fat from a roasting chicken or duck
Coarse salt and freshly ground black pepper

Preheat the oven to 191°C (375°F).

Toss the potatoes in a bowl with the garlic, herbs, and oil or fat.

Place the potatoes in a roasting pan (*la rostiera*) or on a sheet pan and roast 35 minutes, turning every 10 minutes.

Pour off excess oil and continue roasting (*arrostire*) until the potatoes are crisp and golden, about 10 more minutes. Season to taste with salt and pepper.

Patate alla Paesana

Roasted Sliced Potatoes with Fennel and Pancetta

Serves 4

This dish of sliced potatoes roasted with onion, fennel, sage, and rosemary is traditionally made with *Arista alla Toscana* on page 210.

Chef's Note

Potatoes may be sliced by hand or on a mandoline. Slicing by hand will produce a more uneven and rustic texture (some slices will be crisper, some softer), which may be desirable.

Ingredients

375 grams (¾ pound) potatoes, preferably Yukon Gold
50 grams (2 ounces) fennel, halved and cored
30 milliliters (2 tablespoons) olive oil, plus extra for the sheet pan
50 grams (2 ounces) red onion, cut into ½-centimeter (³⁄₁₆-inch) slices (¼ cup)
30 grams (about 1 ounce) pancetta, cut in ½-centimeter (³⁄₁₆-inch) dice
8 grams (1 tablespoon) sliced garlic
3 fresh sage sprigs
6 fresh rosemary sprigs
Pinch of red pepper flakes
60 milliliters (¼ cup) dry white wine
Coarse salt and freshly ground black pepper

Preheat the oven to 191°C (375°F).

Peel the potatoes and slice them thinly. Drop them into a bowl of cold water, working quickly to prevent blackening. Rub the slices together under the water to rinse off the starch, which would cause the slices to stick together during cooking. Drain.

Place the fennel halves, cut sides down, on a cutting board and slice thinly (you should have about ½ cup). (Without the core, the slices will separate into pieces.)

Place the potatoes, oil, fennel, onion, pancetta, garlic, sage, and rosemary in a large skillet (*padella*) and

toss. Set over medium-high heat and cook (*saltare*) 2 minutes. Add the red pepper flakes and wine, toss, and remove from the heat. Season to taste with salt and black pepper.

Spread the potato mixture out on an oiled sheet pan. (Or if roasting with *Arista alla Toscana*, add them to the roasting pan with the pork now.) Cover with foil and bake 25 minutes. Uncover, stir, and return the potatoes to the oven to roast (*arrostire*) uncovered 15 more minutes.

Drain the fat. Return the potatoes to the oven and roast until they are crisp and golden, about 10 more minutes. Taste for seasoning.

Lenticchie in Umido

Stewed Lentils

Serves 4

This dish is traditionally served with *cotechino* sausage (see page 213) for the New Year. For best results, use the firm, brownish-green *lenticchie del Castelluccio*, an IGP lentil grown in the high plains of Castelluccio di Norcia, located between Le Marche and Umbria in central Italy. This variety of lentil remains firm when cooked but has a tender skin and an exceptionally earthy, sweet flavor. In addition to the *cotechino*, the lentils make an excellent accompaniment to grilled sausages, meatloaf, lamb, and assertive seafood dishes.

Ingredients

For the soffritto:

60 grams (2 ounces) red onion or shallot, cut into ½-centimeter (³⁄₁₆-inch) pieces (⅓ cup)
35 grams (1 ounce) celery, cut into ½-centimeter (³⁄₁₆-inch) pieces (¼ cup)

Basilicata

Basilicata is at the southern end of Italy, west of Puglia and north of Calabria (between the heel and toe of the "boot"). It offers two short coastlines: one on the Tyrrhenian Sea to the west, the second on the Gulf of Taranto to the south. The remainder of the region is almost entirely mountainous and often very dry. The capital of the region is Potenza.

Its inhospitable terrain has contributed to Basilicata's reputation as one of the poorest regions in the country. Meat is scarce, and the cuisine is plain, characterized by the use of olive oil, the hot chile pepper *diavolicchio*, and *lampascioni*, a variety of wild onion. Dishes made with dry or fresh durum-wheat pastas are traditional, as well as vegetables, vegetable and bean soups, and lamb, mutton, and kid, when available. Pork is largely reserved for cured products.

The area produces several mountain cheeses, including pecorino and *casiddi* (made from goat's milk). Cow's-milk cheeses are represented by Caciocavallo Silano, *caciocavallo*, *manteca* (a *pasta filata* cheese), and *burino facito*, a provolone-type cheese stuffed with butter (and sometimes *salame*). Sweet and savory dishes made with *grano* (wheat grains) are also traditional.

Basilicata produces a small amount of red wine, as well as the sweet white Moscato and Malvasia wines.

Basilicata produces the sweet white and slightly effervescent Moscato, which is an ideal choice for *zabaione* (page 289).

---

30 grams (1 ounce) carrot, cut into ½-centimeter (³⁄₁₆-inch) pieces (¼ cup)

8 grams (1 tablespoon) chopped garlic

40 grams (1½ ounces) pancetta, cut into ½-centimeter (³⁄₁₆-inch) pieces

5 grams (1½ tablespoons) finely chopped fresh sage

25 milliliters (1 tablespoon plus 2 teaspoons) olive oil

30 grams (2 tablespoons) tomato paste

60 milliliters (¼ cup) dry white wine

1 to 1½ liters (4¼ to 6⅓ cups) simmering chicken or vegetable stock

210 grams (1 cup) lentils, picked over and rinsed

Pinch of ground cumin

Coarse salt and freshly ground black pepper

Combine the ingredients for the *soffritto* and the oil in a cold saucepan (*casseruola*). Place over medium heat and cook (*saltare*) until the vegetables soften and deepen in color and the flavor concentrates, 10 to 15 minutes.

Stir in the tomato paste and cook 2 minutes.

Add the wine and cook until dry.

Add about 125 milliliters (½ cup) of the stock and simmer (*sobollire*) to reduce by half.

Add the lentils and the cumin. Bring to a simmer and cook, adding about 250 milliliters (1 cup) of the stock at a time, and cooking to reduce it before the next addition. (The lentils should always be bathed but never drowned.) Season with salt and pepper to taste. Continue cooking, uncovered, tasting for seasoning occasionally, until the lentils are tender but not mushy, about 30 minutes, depending on the lentils. The lentils should be surrounded by a lightly thickened liquid, as if for a stew. Season to taste with salt and pepper.

Cannellini all'Uccelletto

Stewed Beans with Tomato

Serves 4

Cannellini all'uccelletto means "beans, bird-style," referring to beans that are cooked in the same manner that a variety of tiny birds are traditionally cooked in Tuscan cuisine. The beans are fully cooked, then stewed in puréed tomato and seasoned with garlic and sage. *Cannellini Toscani* are used in this recipe, but IGP varieties such as *Sorana* (another Tuscan variety) or *Sarconi* (from Basilicata) would also work well.

(See "Working with Dried Legumes" on page 364 for step-by-step instructions for washing, soaking, and cooking beans.)

Ingredients

For the aromatics:

40 grams (1½ ounces) red onion, cut in 3-centimeter (1³⁄₁₆-inch) chunks (¼ cup)

40 grams (1½ ounces) celery, cut in 3-centimeter (1³⁄₁₆-inch) chunks (⅓ cup)

20 grams (¾ ounce) carrot, cut in 3-centimeter (1³⁄₁₆-inch) chunks (¼ cup)

1 small clove garlic, crushed with the heel of the hand

1 sprig fresh sage

1 sprig fresh Italian parsley

1 fresh bay leaf

1½ grams (2 teaspoons) whole black peppercorns

For the beans:

225 grams (8 ounces) cannellini beans, washed, soaked, and drained (1⅔ cups)

1 teaspoon coarse salt

45 milliliters (3 tablespoons) olive oil

3 cloves garlic, in the skin, crushed with the heel of the hand

2 sprigs fresh sage

Pinch of red pepper flakes

575 milliliters (2¼ cups) whole, canned Italian plum tomatoes with their juices, puréed though a food mill

Coarse salt and freshly ground black pepper

Tie the aromatics in cheesecloth.

Put the soaked beans in a saucepan and cover with 10 centimeters (4 inches) cold water. Cook over low heat for 5 minutes; drain, and rinse. Return the beans to a clean saucepan. Cover with cold water by about 10 centimeters (4 inches). Add the salt and the aromatics. Simmer gently (*sobbollire*) until tender; allow the beans to cool in the cooking liquid. Remove the beans with a slotted spoon and set aside. Reserve the bean cooking liquid.

Combine the oil and garlic in a large skillet (*padella*). Place over medium heat and cook (*saltare*) until the garlic just begins to take on color. Add the sage sprigs and red pepper flakes.

Add the tomato purée and simmer 5 minutes.

Add the cooked beans, black pepper to taste, and enough of the bean cooking liquid to make the beans soupy (about 150 milliliters / ⅔ cup). Bring to a simmer and cook, adding more of the bean cooking liquid as needed to maintain a loose consistency, about 10 minutes. (You'll probably use about 250 milliliters / 1 cup of the cooking liquid, but this will depend on the cooking vessel and the heat.) Taste for seasoning.

Finocchi Gratinati

Fennel Gratin

Serves 4

For this dish, thick slices of blanched fennel are coated with grated Parmigiano-Reggiano and thin slices of butter, and finished under the broiler to create a delicate, golden brown crust. Butter aids in the browning, while it keeps the fennel from drying out. This gratin is excellent served with *Filetto di Maiale* (page 204), *Arista alla Toscana* (page 210), and *Agnello Arrosto* (page 219).

Ingredients

325 grams (12 ounces / about 1½ medium) fennel bulbs
Coarse salt and freshly ground black pepper
½ lemon
50 grams (½ cup) grated Parmigiano-Reggiano or Grana
    Padano
30 grams (2 tablespoons) unsalted butter, cut into thin slices

Trim the fennel stalks, and trim the root end. Remove the outer layers, or peel with a vegetable peeler to remove any browned parts.

Bring a saucepan (*casseruola*) of salted water to a boil. Squeeze in the lemon juice; add the lemon half. Add the fennel and simmer (*sobbollire*) until a small knife pierces the fennel without resistance, about 10 minutes. Drain and cut into slices about 1½ centimeters (½ inch) thick.

Preheat a broiler to high.

Arrange the fennel slices in a single layer on a buttered sizzle platter. Season with salt and pepper to taste and sprinkle with the cheese. Lay the butter slices over the top. Broil (*gratinare*) until golden.

Peperonata

Stewed Bell Peppers

Serves 4

When bell peppers are stewed with onion, garlic, tomatoes, and a little vinegar, their flavor softens and sweetens. This dish is common all over northern Italy, where it has different names depending on the region. *Peperonata* may be served as a *contorno* (it is particularly good with a rich fish, such as mackerel, or pork sausages). It may be served hot or at room temperature.

If serving with fish, season the peppers more aggressively with additional vinegar.

(See "Peeling, Seeding, and Dicing Tomatoes" on page 350 for step-by-step instructions.)

Ingredients

825 grams (1¾ to 2 pounds) red and yellow bell peppers, seeded
    and cut into 5-centimeter (2-inch) squares (about 6½ cups)
200 grams (7 ounces) red onion, cut into ½-centimeter (³⁄₁₆-
    inch) slices (1¾ cups)
75 milliliters (⅓ scant cup) olive oil
5 cloves garlic, sliced
10 grams (½ cup) torn fresh basil leaves
Coarse salt and freshly ground black pepper
30 milliliters (2 tablespoons) red wine vinegar
250 grams (9 ounces) tomatoes, peeled, seeded, and cut into
    ½-centimeter (³⁄₁₆-inch) dice (1⅓ cups)
Vegetable stock or water, if needed

Chef's Note

Peppers usually don't require the addition of any liquid other than that of the tomato during cooking, as they give off their own juices. If, however, the pan gets dry, add a little vegetable stock or water.

Place the peppers, onion, oil, and garlic in a large saucepan (*casseruola*). Place over medium-low heat. Cover and cook (*saltare*) 5 minutes.

Add half of the basil and season to taste with salt and pepper. Cover and cook 5 more minutes.

Deglaze (*deglassare*) the pan with the vinegar. Add the tomatoes and season to taste with salt and pepper. (If the pan is dry, add a little stock or water to moisten.) Cover and continue cooking (*brasare*) until the peppers are tender and the tomatoes have melted, 5 to 10 more minutes. Add the rest of the basil and taste for seasoning.

Misto di Verdure Stufate

Stewed Mixed Summer Vegetables

Serves 4

Something between a sauté and a stew, and much like the French ratatouille, this is a method for cooking an array of summer vegetables. Green beans, asparagus, zucchini, and Swiss chard are first sautéed with herbs, then stewed in tomato. The vegetables will not entirely brown but they will form a slight crust and their juices will concentrate. The vegetables must not be stirred too much during cooking; rather, they should be allowed to sit undisturbed in the pan. In Toscana and particularly around Lucca, this dish is commonly known as *frissoglia*, or braised mixed-vegetable stew.

At The International Culinary Center, this dish is often served over polenta.

(For step-by-step instructions for peeling asparagus and peeling, seeding, and dicing tomatoes, see pages 354 and 350, respectively.)

Chef's Notes

Unless working with young zucchini, use only the outer portion of the vegetable, discarding the softer, seeded center core.

Rainbow Swiss chard varieties, such as Bright Lights, if available, are an excellent choice for this colorful dish.

When available, the flowers of zucchini make a lovely addition to this dish. Remove the stem and pistil and toss into the stew with the Swiss chard leaves.

Ingredients

60 milliliters (¼ cup) olive oil

10 grams (1¾ tablespoons) sliced garlic

½ teaspoon red pepper flakes

75 grams (½ cup) sliced scallion, white and green parts

220 grams (½ scant pound) green beans, cut into 3-centimeter (1³⁄₁₆-inch) lengths (about 1¾ cups)

250 grams (9 ounces) asparagus, trimmed, peeled if woody, and cut into 3-centimeter (1³⁄₁₆-inch) lengths, tips reserved separately

450 grams (1 pound) Swiss chard, leaves chopped (about 6½ cups, packed), stems sliced into 3-centimeter (1-inch) lengths and reserved separately

Coarse salt and freshly ground black pepper

650 grams (1½ pounds) zucchini, quartered lengthwise, and cut into 3-centimeter (1³⁄₁₆-inch) lengths

10 grams (½ cup) torn fresh basil leaves

2 teaspoons chopped fresh marjoram

900 grams (2 pounds) fresh tomatoes, peeled, seeded, and diced, or 300 grams (11 ounces) whole, drained canned Italian plum tomatoes, crushed by hand

125 milliliters (½ cup) dry white wine

Place the oil and garlic in a large skillet (*padella*). Place over medium heat and cook until the garlic is softened and just begins to color.

Add the red pepper flakes. Add the scallions, beans, asparagus stems, and Swiss chard stems. Sauté (*saltare*) until all the liquid given off by the vegetables has evaporated, about 10 minutes. Regulate the heat so that the vegetables neither burn nor steam. Season with salt and black pepper to taste about midway through the cooking.

Add the asparagus tips, zucchini, basil, and marjoram and sauté until the zucchini browns on the edges, raising the heat as necessary, 3 to 5 minutes.

Warm the tomatoes in a separate pan and season to taste with salt and pepper.

Use the wine to deglaze (*deglassare*) the skillet with the vegetables. Reduce.

Add the warmed tomatoes and cook 2 minutes.

Add the Swiss chard leaves and cook until the chard is tender and the tomatoes have reduced, 7 to 10 minutes; the vegetables should be surrounded by lightly thickened tomatoes. Season to taste with salt and pepper.

Cipolline in Agrodolce

Sweet-and-Sour Onions

Serves 4

Cipolline are small, flat onions native to the Italian Mediterranean, where they are often glazed with sugar and vinegar in a sweet-and-sour braise.

This dish may be served as a *contorno* with roasted or grilled meats, or as part of an assortment of *antipasti*, particularly with other vegetables.

Ingredients

30 milliliters (2 tablespoons) olive oil

325 grams (11½ ounces) cipolline onions, peeled, and dried on paper towels

30 milliliters (2 tablespoons) dry white wine

6 grams (1½ teaspoons) sugar

8 milliliters (1½ teaspoons) red wine vinegar, or as needed

8 milliliters (1½ teaspoons) aceto balsamico di Modena

Coarse salt and freshly ground black pepper

Heat the oil in a skillet (*padella*) over medium-high heat. Add the onions and sauté (*saltare*) until they begin to brown, about 10 minutes. Pour off the oil.

Deglaze (*deglassare*) the pan with the wine and reduce.

Stir in the sugar and the vinegars. Cover and cook 2 minutes.

Add water to cover the onions by about half; season with salt and pepper to taste. Cover and braise (*brasare*) until the onions are tender, 8 to 10 minutes. Uncover, and simmer until the liquid reduces around the onions to a glaze (*glassare*). Taste for acidity, adding a few drops of red wine vinegar if needed.

Piselli al Prosciutto

English Peas with Prosciutto

Serves 4

In this version of the classic *contorno*, English peas are braised with shallots, prosciutto, tomatoes, and herbs.

Ingredients

60 milliliters (¼ cup) olive oil

60 grams (2 ounces) shallot or red onion, cut to 6-millimeter (¼-inch) dice (½ cup)

Pinch of red pepper flakes

55 grams (2 ounces) prosciutto, cut to 6-millimeter (¼-inch) dice (¼ cup)

300 grams (11 ounces) fresh or frozen shelled English peas, thawed if frozen (1¾ cups)

100 grams (3½ ounces) tomato, peeled, seeded, and diced (1 cup)

90 milliliters (6 tablespoons) vegetable stock or water

Coarse salt and freshly ground black pepper

5 grams (2 teaspoons) fresh marjoram

10 grams (½ cup) fresh basil

3 grams (1 tablespoon) fresh Italian parsley leaves

Combine the oil, shallot or onion, red pepper flakes, and prosciutto in a saucepan (*casseruola*). Place over medium-low heat and cook (*saltare*) until the shallot or onion softens and the prosciutto just begins to crisp, 3 to 5 minutes.

Add the peas, tomato, and stock or water. Cover and braise (*brasare*) until the peas are tender, 5 to 7 minutes for fresh, 2 to 3 minutes for frozen. Adjust salt and pepper to taste.

Chop together the marjoram, basil, and parsley and add to the pan. Toss to combine.

Radicchio Trevisano Brasato

Braised Radicchio

Serves 4

The Veneto region has a long tradition of cultivating radicchio, and the best-known varieties are named after places in the region. This dish is made with radicchio di Treviso, which is less bitter than radicchio di Verona and radicchio di Chioggia. Its elongated shape holds together well during braising, which makes for an elegant presentation.

Ingredients

450 grams (1 pound) radicchio di Treviso, cut in half lengthwise
30 milliliters (2 tablespoons) olive oil, plus extra for drizzling
15 milliliters (1 tablespoon) dry red wine
15 milliliters (1 tablespoon) aceto balsamico di Modena
Coarse salt and freshly ground black pepper
Extra-virgin olive oil, for drizzling

Preheat the oven to 177°C (350°F).

Trim the root ends of the radicchio and remove any discolored areas with a paring knife so that the ends come to a point, but do not cut so deeply that the leaves detach.

Place the radicchio in a roasting pan (*la rostiera*) and drizzle with the olive oil, wine, and vinegar. Season with salt and pepper to taste.

Cover and braise (*brasare*) in the oven 20 to 25 minutes. Uncover and cook 5 more minutes. Reduce the liquid as necessary on top of the stove to achieve the consistency of a sauce or glaze.

Serve drizzled with extra-virgin olive oil.

Variations

Radicchio is also delicious charred on a grill or seared in a skillet, then tossed in the oil, wine, and vinegar, and braised.

To grill the radicchio, toss it with a little oil and salt and pepper to taste, and grill over high heat, turning, until charred and cooked through. Then transfer to a roasting pan and continue with steps 3 and 4 to braise.

Or, coat a large ovenproof skillet with olive oil. Season the radicchio with salt and pepper to taste and cook over medium-high heat until lightly browned and cooked through. Add 30 milliliters (2 tablespoons) of the olive oil, the wine, and the vinegar to the skillet and season with salt and pepper to taste. Continue to braise.

Spinaci Saltati

Sautéed Spinach with Garlic

Serves 4

In this simple preparation, spinach is sautéed in olive oil seasoned with sliced garlic. The garlic dissolves into the spinach so that the flavors are indistinguishable. This dish is delicious with beef, such as *Bistecca alla Fiorentina* (page 182), or with fish, such as *Pesce Intero Arrosto* (page 232) and *Pesce in Crosta di Sale* (page 237).

Ingredients

80 milliliters (⅓ cup) olive oil
30 grams (¼ cup) sliced garlic
575 grams (20 ounces, or two 10-ounce packages) stemmed baby spinach, washed
Pinch of red pepper flakes
Coarse salt and freshly ground black pepper

Combine the oil and garlic in a large skillet (*padella*) or pot (*pentola*). Place over medium-low heat and cook until the garlic begins to soften, but do not allow the garlic to brown.

Add the spinach in batches, by the handful, allowing it to wilt before adding more if the pan is not large enough to contain all of it. Increase the heat to high. Add the red pepper flakes and cook (*saltare*), turning with tongs, so that all the spinach cooks evenly. Season to taste with salt and black pepper and continue cooking, uncovered, until all of the water has evaporated and all of the spinach has wilted.

Preparing a Vinaigrette

To make a vinaigrette, set a bowl in a "collar" made by rolling a damp towel and wrapping it around the bottom of the bowl. Place the vinegar in the bowl. If chopped herbs, garlic, or shallots are being incorporated into the vinaigrette, add them to the vinegar before adding the oil. Salt and pepper should also be added to the vinegar at the beginning.

When all the flavorings have been added to the vinegar, pour the oil into the vinegar in a slow, steady stream while gently whisking. It is important that the components of the vinaigrette be well distributed before pouring it on the salad (give it a stir just before dressing).

Chef's Notes

If using fresh bread, toast it in a 149°C (300°F) oven until dry but not brown.

Use the best-quality tuna available. *Ventresca* is the meat from the tuna belly, preserved in oil and recognized for its soft texture and delicate flavor.

Panzanella

Bread Salad

Serves 6

Traditionally associated with Toscana, bread salad was, historically, a practical way to make use of bread that had hardened with age. The bread was soaked in water and vinegar to soften, tossed with whatever vegetables were on hand, and a protein, if there was any available. Featuring tomatoes, cucumbers, bell peppers, and basil, this is a summer garden recipe, but bread salads needn't be confined to that season. A winter version might include pickled or oil-preserved vegetables and preserved fish. The salad is also a feature of Campanian cuisine, where olives, peppers, anchovies, and garlic are added.

(For step-by-step instructions for cutting leaves into chiffonade, see page 350. For a discussion of vinaigrettes, see "Preparing a Vinaigrette" at left.)

Ingredients

350 grams (12 ounces) day-old country bread (see Chef's Notes), cut into 2½-centimeter (1-inch) cubes (2 firmly packed cups)
125 milliliters (½ cup) red wine vinegar
4 scallions, sliced into thin rounds
300 grams (11 ounces) cucumber, peeled and thinly sliced (2¾ cups)
120 grams (4½ ounces) yellow or red bell pepper, seeded, and sliced into thin strips (1¼ cups)
150 grams (5 ounces) plum tomatoes, peeled, seeded, and sliced (1 cup)
20 fresh basil leaves, cut into chiffonade
8 to 10 anchovy fillets, preferably salt-packed (see page 31), deboned, rinsed and chopped (optional)
180 grams (6½ ounces) canned tuna, packed in oil (optional; see Chef's Notes)

90 milliliters (6 tablespoons) extra-virgin olive oil
Coarse salt and freshly ground black pepper
4 grams (2 teaspoons) chopped fresh marjoram, or whole small leaves

In a bowl, soak the bread in 60 milliliters (¼ cup) of the vinegar about 2 minutes.

Squeeze the bread dry, and place it in another bowl with the vegetables, basil, anchovies, and tuna, if using.

In a small bowl, whisk together the olive oil, the remaining 60 milliliters (¼ cup) vinegar, and salt and pepper to taste. Pour over the bread-and-vegetable mixture and toss. Let stand 30 minutes at room temperature.

Stir, and serve sprinkled with the marjoram.

Le Puntarelle

Puntarelle Chicory Salad

Serves 4

Puntarelle is a variety of chicory with long, slender, serrated green leaves that look something like dandelion greens. During the winter months, hollow, whitish-green shoots grow from the center of the head. For this traditional Roman salad, the shoots are sliced very thin, soaked in cold water to soften the bitterness (soaking also causes the shoots to curl), and seasoned with a pungent garlic-anchovy dressing that further mellows the bitterness of the green.

Puntarelle is only rarely available in the United States and its season is short, but Italian cuisine also commonly pairs this dressing with endive and radicchio. If you cannot find *puntarelle*, you may substitute

450 grams (1 pound) Belgian endive (see Chef's Notes), young dandelion greens, or radicchio di Treviso, as well as mustard greens.

(For a discussion of vinaigrettes, see "Preparing a Vinaigrette" on page 265.)

Chef's Notes

If using Belgian endive, trim the ends and cut in half lengthwise. Put the halves cut sides down and slice lengthwise again. Hold in cold water to prevent browning.

The dressing may be made in the food processor; the processor will make a strong emulsion.

Ingredients

1 head (700 to 900 grams / 1½ to 2 pounds) puntarelle chicory

15 grams (2 tablespoons) finely chopped garlic

4 anchovy fillets, preferably salt-packed (see page 31), deboned, rinsed, and finely chopped

45 milliliters (3 tablespoons) red wine vinegar

Coarse salt and freshly ground black pepper

60 milliliters (¼ cup) olive oil

Pull off the outer green leaves of the *puntarelle* and detach the white stalks from the base of the head. Cut the stalks in half lengthwise, then, using a vegetable peeler and working downward along the cut edge, peel off long, thin strips of *puntarelle*, about 1 centimeter (⅜ inch) wide. Soak in ice water at least 1 hour.

Drain the *puntarelle* and spin dry.

Combine the garlic, anchovies, vinegar, and salt and pepper to taste in a bowl. Vigorously whisk in the oil to form an emulsion. Pour over the *puntarelle* and toss well.

Lazio (also called Latium)

"Rome was at the center of historic and religious events during the centuries that influenced not only Roman cuisine but the life of an entire nation. If we wanted to look for the most recent event that left its mark in Roman cuisine, we would find, for example, guanciale and eggs, which became the main ingredients with which one of the most famous and well-known dishes in the world was 'invented': carbonara."

—Chef Andreo Fusco of Giuda Ballerino, Rome

For the traditional Roman salad made with *puntarelle*, see our recipe on page 265. Other specialties from Lazio include *Spaghetti alla Carbonara* (page 104) and *Carciofi alla Giudea* (page 252), as well as Roman dishes such as *Gnocchi alla Romana* (page 120), *Saltimbocca alla Romana* (page 180), *Coda alla Vaccinara* (page 186), and *Carciofi alla Romana* (page 254).

Lazio is a region in central Italy, bordered on the west by the Tyrrhenian Sea. To the east lie Umbria and Abruzzo; to the north is Toscana, and to the south is Campania. The geography is extremely varied, ranging from the Apennines in the west, to hills, flatlands, and seacoast. The region's capital is Rome.

The diverse terrain of this pastoral region has encouraged varied agricultural production. Sheep, cattle, pigs, and water buffalo are raised here. Although lamb and beef are more common than fresh pork, pork is used in a wealth of cured meat products, including *guanciale* (cured pork jowl). The cuisine traditionally used pork fat (*strutto*), but that is now largely replaced by olive oil. The cuisine is famed for its offal dishes.

Wine grapes (for the white wines Frascati and Marino) and olives are important products. Other specialties from the garden include artichokes, *puntarelle* (a type of chicory), and fava beans.

The region is known for its extensive *antipasti*, including *supplì* (rice croquettes), bruschetta with olive oil and garlic, *frutti di mare*, *carciofi alla Romana* (braised artichokes), and stuffed vegetables. Jewish cuisine is important in the region, and *carciofi alla Giudea* (deep-fried artichokes) are a traditional specialty, as is the kosher *prosciutto di manzo* (beef prosciutto).

Lazio historically produced pecorino cheese, although most of the production has been moved to Sardinia. Lazio also produces *mozzarella di bufala* (made with milk from the water buffalo), which features prominently in the region's cuisine.

Sunchokes may be sliced very thin and eaten raw, in which case they have a mild nutty flavor. Cooking—in gratins, purées, or pies—enhances their sweetness. The thin skin is always removed before cooking.

Here the raw, sliced (unpeeled) sunchokes are dressed with a vinaigrette spiked with finely chopped shallot and a little sugar; the salad is finished with baby spinach and curls of Castelmagno cheese.

(For a discussion of vinaigrettes, see "Preparing a Vinaigrette" on page 265.)

Ingredients

225 grams (½ pound, or 4 to 6) sunchokes, washed and
    scrubbed well but not peeled
15 milliliters (1 tablespoon) red wine vinegar
45 milliliters (3 tablespoons) olive oil
Coarse salt and freshly ground black pepper
40 grams (⅓ cup) thinly sliced shallot, soaked for 1 hour in red
    wine vinegar to cover
Pinch of sugar
150 grams (5 cups) baby spinach, rinsed and dried
Castelmagno or other hard, aged cow's-milk cheese, such as
    Parmigiano-Reggiano or Grana Padano, for serving

Insalata di Topinambur

Sunchoke Salad

Serves 4

Sunchokes, also called Jerusalem artichokes, are the edible root of a variety of sunflower. Their Italian name is *topinambur*, which may be derived from *topino*, the Italian word for "mouse" (which is what a sunchoke resembles, to some), or they are sometimes known as *patate selvatiche* ("wild potatoes"). Sunchokes are grown in Piemonte and are a classic element of that region's *Bagna Cauda* (page 38).

Thinly slice the sunchokes. Hold in a bowl of cold water while you work, to prevent browning.

For the vinaigrette, whisk together the vinegar, oil, and salt and pepper to taste.

Drain the shallot, squeezing out the excess vinegar, and place in a bowl. Add the sugar. Add the sunchokes and toss well to season. Add half of the vinaigrette and toss well. Add the spinach and the remaining vinaigrette and toss again. Taste for seasoning.

Arrange the salad on four plates. Garnish with shaved Castelmagno.

Abruzzo

Abruzzo, or Abruzzi (the plural is a throwback to the administration of the region by the Bourbons, under whom it was divided into two parts), lies to the south of Le Marche and Umbria, and north of Molise. The region is largely mountainous, with the Apennines tapering to fertile foothills and the Adriatic seacoast at the eastern border. About two-thirds of the region is composed of national parks. The capital is L'Aquila.

Abruzzo cuisine is characterized by its abundant use of a locally grown hot pepper, the *diavolicchio*, olive oil, and tomatoes. Like other regions that face the Adriatic, the cuisine features seafood dishes—most famously its *brodetto*, a classic seafood stew that changes character from town to town, but is usually spicy.

Important agricultural products include olives, saffron, and wine grapes (Montepulciano and Trebbiano d'Abruzzo). IGP cattle are raised here, but sheep- and goat-farming are more prevalent. Dishes made with lamb, mutton, and kid are traditional. Although Abruzzo is not known as a major producer of cheeses, pecorino (including *farindola pecorino*, made with pig rennet), and *canestrato*, from Castel del Monte, are made here, along with other local sheep's- and goat's-milk cheeses. A few cow's-milk cheeses are produced in the region.

Other specialties include the fresh semolina pasta called *maccheroni alla chitarra* (squared-off spaghetti shaped on a special tool), other dried pasta dishes, sugar-coated almonds called *confetti*, and *torrone* (nougat).

Instructions for using the Abruzzese *chitarra* to cut fresh pasta sheets appear on page 372.

Insalata di Patate

Potato Salad

Serves 6

Potatoes are cultivated primarily in three regions in Italy—Campania, Emilia-Romagna, and Abruzzo—but they are one of the most popular *contorni* throughout Italy and feature prominently in local recipes in every region. Here, potato salad is made with firm-textured new potatoes because they remain intact during boiling.

The vinaigrette is added while the potatoes are still warm so that the potatoes drink up the flavors as they cool. Wine adds a subtle acidity. The salad should be allowed to stand for at least one hour at room temperature before serving to allow the flavors to meld and marry.

Ingredients

80 grams (3 ounces) red onion
40 milliliters (2½ tablespoons) red wine vinegar
1⅓ kilograms (3 pounds) Red Bliss potatoes, peeled, and cut into 4-centimeter (1½-inch) pieces
Coarse salt and freshly ground black pepper
30 milliliters (2 tablespoons) dry white wine
150 milliliters (⅔ cup) extra-virgin olive oil, plus extra for serving
6 grams (2 tablespoons) chopped fresh Italian parsley
30 grams (¼ cup) pitted and coarsely chopped Gaeta or other black olives
45 grams (3 tablespoons) capers, preferably salt-packed (see page 31), soaked, rinsed, and drained
Pinch of red pepper flakes

Slice the onion on an angle to make slender wedges. Marinate in the red wine vinegar about 1 hour, or until the taste is softened.

Place the potatoes in a large saucepan (*casseruola*), cover with cold water, and add enough salt so that the water tastes salty. Bring to a simmer and cook (*sobbollire*) until the potatoes slide off a knife when the blade is inserted into the vegetable, 12 to 15 minutes; drain and transfer to a bowl.

Before the potatoes have a chance to cool, add the wine and toss to allow the potatoes to absorb it.

Add the oil, parsley, olives, capers, and red pepper and stir gently to combine. Season to taste with salt and black pepper. Let stand 1 hour at room temperature. Serve drizzled with extra-virgin olive oil.

Insalata di Barbabietole

Roasted Beet Salad

Serves 6

This salad combines red and golden beets in a vinaigrette spiked with fresh spring onion, chopped chives, and crumbled *ricotta salata*.

The red and yellow beets are roasted separately so that the red color doesn't bleed into the yellow. Baby red and yellow beets work excellently here, too, because they cook quickly—25 to 35 minutes.

(For a discussion of vinaigrettes, see "Preparing a Vinaigrette" on page 265.)

Chef's Notes

Beets are roasted in water to keep the vegetable moist.

There are currently many varieties and colors of beets available to chefs; what is most important is to use whichever is freshest.

This dish is delicious and colorful when served with the beet greens: Boil or steam the greens, dress with some of the vinaigrette, and arrange them around the sliced beets.

Ingredients

1 to 1¼ kilos (2½ pounds, about 5 medium) red beets
1 to 1¼ kilos (2½ pounds, about 5 medium) yellow beets
Coarse salt

For the vinaigrette:

10 grams (¼ cup) finely chopped spring onion or shallot
3 grams (1 tablespoon) chopped fresh Italian parsley
25 milliliters (1 tablespoon plus 2 teaspoons) red wine vinegar, or to taste
60 milliliters (¼ cup) extra-virgin olive oil
Coarse salt and freshly ground black pepper
1 teaspoon chopped chives, for serving
50 grams (¼ cup) ricotta salata, grated or crumbled, for serving

Preheat the oven to 191°C (375°F).

Wash and trim the beets, leaving the roots and about 3 centimeters (1¼ inches) of the stem end to minimize bleeding. Put the red beets in one baking dish, and the yellow beets in another. Add water to come about halfway up the beets, and cover with aluminum foil. Roast (*cuocere in forno*) until a fork slides easily in and out of the beets, 45 minutes to 1 hour. Remove from the oven and let cool.

Wearing gloves to prevent staining hands with the beet juice, peel the beets. Trim stems and roots. Slice, cutting large beets in half first.

In a bowl, whisk together the ingredients for the vinaigrette and taste for seasoning.

Toss the beets with the vinaigrette. Taste again for seasoning and vinegar.

Divide the beets (and beet greens, if using) between the plates and finish with the chopped chives and grated or crumbled *ricotta salata*.

Chapter 17

Tarts and Doughs:
Crostate e Paste per Dolci

Pasta Brisée (Pastry Dough)
Pasta Frolla (Sweet Pastry Dough)
Pasta Bignè (Choux Pastry)
Pasta Sfoglia (Puff Pastry)
Torta di Pinoli (Pine-Nut Tart)
Torta di Porri (Leek Tart)
Crostata di Fragole e Kiwi (Strawberry-and-Kiwifruit Tart)
Crema Inglese (Custard Sauce)
Crema Pasticcera (Pastry Cream)
Profiteroles (Cream Puffs with Gelato)
Millefoglie (Napoleon with Strawberries)

Italian cuisine boasts an abundance of tarts, both savory and sweet, variously called *torta, pizze, focacce*, and *crostate*. Italian tarts may be two-crusted, open-faced, or topped with a lattice design.

Savory tarts (*torte salate*) are filled with meat, cheese, or vegetables, but most often feature vegetables and egg; the Ligurian artichoke tart, *torta pasqualina*, and Toscana's savory pies—*ciancifricola, erbolata*, and the *Torta di Porri* on page 278—are examples. Savory tarts such as these are made with *Pasta Brisée* (page 274), an all-purpose dough that can be used for savory and sweet alike.

Dessert tarts are lined with a sweet dough called *Pasta Frolla* (page 274) and filled with custards, creams, chocolate, fruit, cheese and/or nut fillings.

Many Italian desserts also employ the rich, delicate, crisp, and flaky *Pasta Sfoglia*, or puff pastry. *Pasta Sfoglia* (page 276) may be fashioned to line tart pans, or baked in sheets, cut into pieces, and layered with cream and fruit for *Millefoglie* (page 284).

Pasta bignè (see page 275), or choux pastry contains the same ingredients as the other basic doughs—flour, fat, water, salt, and sometimes sugar—but its form is radically different. Soft like a batter, it is piped onto a baking sheet; in the oven, the dough puffs up to create a crisp, hollow shape that is filled with sweet or savory ingredients.

This chapter teaches basic methods for making these four doughs, as well as examples of how to use each dough in a finished pastry. All may be cooked in a conventional or a convection oven; see *"Forno a Convezione"* on page 346 for temperature conversions for convection ovens.

Le Tecniche

In this chapter, students learn the fundamentals of making, shaping, and baking pastry doughs. They also learn the basics of custards, and how to apply these skills to stirred, baked, and starch-bound varieties. For an in-depth discussion and step-by-step instructions for making, shaping, and baking doughs, see pages 467–79. For an in-depth discussion and step-by-step instructions for making custards, see pages 480–84.

Torta di Pinoli (page 277)

Pasta Brisée

Pastry Dough

Makes enough for two 23-centimeter (9-inch) tarts

This is a good all-purpose dough for both savory and sweet tarts. The dough is made by cutting chilled butter into a mixture of flour and salt, then adding yolks and just enough cold water to bring the dough together in a ball. For instructions on making the dough using a standing mixer, see Chef's Note.

Ingredients

500 grams (4¼ cups) all-purpose flour, plus extra for dusting the work surface
½ teaspoon coarse salt
250 grams (1 cup plus 1½ tablespoons) cold unsalted butter
2 large egg yolks
30 milliliters (2 tablespoons) ice water, or as needed

Sift the flour and salt directly onto a work surface, or into a bowl. Cut the cold butter into very small pieces. Cut the butter into the dry ingredients with a plastic bowl scraper or metal bench scraper, or rub it in with your fingertips. (Work quickly to avoid melting the butter.)

When the mixture has a sandy texture, and when there are no large particles of butter visible, form a well in the flour-butter mixture. Add the egg yolks and the 30 milliliters (2 tablespoons) ice water into the well.

Begin to combine the liquid into the flour-butter mixture; be careful not to overwork the dough. Add more ice water, if needed, until the dough just comes together. Do not add too much liquid, however, or the dough will be sticky and tough.

Chef's Note

The dough may also be made in a standing mixer:

Place the flour and salt in the bowl of a standing mixer fitted with the paddle attachment.

Cut the butter into 1-centimeter (⅜-inch) cubes and add to the bowl. Beat on low speed until the butter pieces are reduced to the size of lentils (about 3 millimeters / ⅛ inch).

Beat in the egg yolks.

With the mixer still running, drizzle in the ice water a little at a time until the dough holds its shape when pieces are pressed together. If the dough feels sandy and falls apart, continue drizzling in ice water with the mixer running until the dough is the correct consistency.

To ensure a homogenous consistency, remove walnut-size pieces from the dough and smear them against a lightly floured work surface with the heel of your hand. Gather all the pieces together, shape into two disks, cover with plastic wrap, and refrigerate at least 30 minutes before rolling. (The dough may be refrigerated up to 2 days, or wrapped well and frozen up to 1 month.)

Pasta Frolla

Sweet Pastry Dough

Makes enough for two 23-centimeter (9-inch) tarts

This tender, sweet dough is made by creaming room-temperature butter with sugar, adding egg, then adding flour. It is used for dessert tarts, pies, and cookies. This recipe will line two tart pans, with a little dough left over for cookies or possibly a lattice top.

Ingredients

300 grams (1⅓ cups) unsalted butter, at room temperature
150 grams (¾ cup) granulated sugar
1 large egg, at room temperature
1 teaspoon pure vanilla extract
450 grams (3¾ cups) all-purpose flour, plus extra for dusting the work surface
½ teaspoon coarse salt

In a large bowl with a wooden spoon, or in the bowl of a standing mixer fitted with the paddle attachment, cream the butter with the sugar.

Beat in the egg. Beat in the vanilla extract.

In a separate bowl, combine the flour and salt. Stir or beat into the butter mixture until the dough comes together, about 45 seconds; be careful not to overwork the dough.

To ensure a homogenous consistency, remove walnut-size pieces from the dough and smear them against a lightly floured work surface with the heel of your hand.

Gather all the pieces together, shape into two disks, cover with plastic wrap, and refrigerate at least 30 minutes before rolling. (The dough may be refrigerated up to 2 days, or wrapped well and frozen up to 1 month.)

Pasta Bignè

Choux Pastry

Makes enough for 24 *bignè*

Pasta bignè is the dough used to make *bignè*, or cream puffs, tender balls of pastry that may be filled with savory or sweet fillings, such as *Crema Pasticcera* (page 281) or, as in *Profiteroles* on page 282, gelato or ice cream.

Chef's Note

The eggs for the *bignè* dough are broken into a separate bowl before they are added to the dough; this ensures that any bits of broken shell may easily be recuperated, and it allows the chef to add only as much egg as necessary.

The recipe for this dough is made with a pinch of sugar because the *bignè* are to be used in a sweet preparation. For savory preparations, omit the sugar.

Ingredients

110 grams (7¼ tablespoons) unsalted butter, cut into small pieces
Pinch of coarse salt
Pinch of granulated sugar (use for sweet, not savory, preparations)
140 grams (1 cup plus 1 tablespoon) all-purpose flour
4 to 5 large eggs, at room temperature

Place 250 milliliters (1 cup) water, the butter, salt, and sugar, if using, in a stainless-steel saucepan (*casseruola*) and bring to a boil.

As soon as the mixture reaches a boil and the butter is completely melted, immediately remove the pan from the heat and add the flour, all at once. (If the water boils too long, the proportion of the liquid to the dry ingredients will change.)

Return the pan to medium heat and stir vigorously with a wooden spoon about 30 seconds, or until the mixture thickens and forms a mass that does not stick to the pan. Then dry out the mixture by stirring over the heat another 1 to 2 minutes.

Remove the pan from the heat and transfer the mixture to a clean bowl.

Crack the eggs into a separate small bowl, one at a time, then stir each into the dough. Make sure that each egg is fully incorporated before adding the next. The eggs may be added by hand, stirring with a wooden spoon, or in a standing mixer fitted with the paddle attachment. Whisk the final egg with a fork to blend, and add it little by little; you may not need all of it. Enough egg has been added to the batter when a ribbon forms connecting the spatula to the batter when the spatula is lifted out of the bowl; a spoon run through the batter leaves a channel that fills in slowly; or a dollop of batter lifted on a spatula curls over on itself and forms a hook.

For best results, the dough should be formed into *bigné* and baked while it is still slightly warm (see *Profiteroles* on page 282 for instructions). Alternatively, the raw batter may be refrigerated 2 to 3 days or piped into *bignè* shapes and frozen.

Pasta Sfoglia

Puff Pastry

Makes about 450 grams (1 pound)

Pasta Sfoglia is a flaky, butter-rich, light-textured, multilayered pastry used for a variety of Italian desserts, including *Millefoglie* (page 284), as well as savory *antipasti* such as *vol au vents*, *pizzette*, and *salatini*.

Ingredients

For the lean dough (il pastello):
250 grams (2 cups plus 1 tablespoon) all-purpose flour, plus extra for dusting the work surface
3 grams (½ teaspoon) coarse salt
50 grams (3½ tablespoons) unsalted butter, cut into cubes and softened
150 milliliters (⅔ cup) cool water

For the butter (il panetto):
175 grams (12½ tablespoons) cold unsalted butter

Make the lean dough (*il pastello*):

Combine the flour and salt on a work surface or in a bowl, and form the mixture into a well. Cut in the softened butter with a bench scraper or mix in with your fingertips. Add just enough cool water to make a rough dough. Avoid overworking the dough: If too much gluten is developed at this stage, it will make the dough difficult to turn later. Gather the dough into a ball and form into a rough square on the work surface. With a sharp knife, cut a small, shallow X in the top and about halfway through the block. Cover the dough in plastic wrap and refrigerate at least 30 minutes.

Work the butter (*il panetto*):

When the dough has rested, remove the cold butter from the refrigerator. Place between two sheets of plastic wrap and pound with a rolling pin until pliable but still cool, and smooth, with no lumps. Form the butter into a square block and set aside in a cool place (do not refrigerate—the butter must remain pliable).

Make the pastry:

On a lightly floured work surface, roll out the dough to create a thicker center square with a flap at each edge just large enough to enclose and seal the butter. (Be sure to use sufficient flour when rolling and turning the dough; it must not stick to the work surface.)

Place the butter block diagonally on top of the thicker center square so that it looks like a diamond inside a square. Fold one set of opposite flaps of the dough over the butter to enclose it, then fold the remaining two flaps up to completely enclose the butter block, brushing off excess flour as you go. Pinch it lightly along the seams to seal.

Press on the dough with the rolling pin four or five times along its length, or until the dough lengthens to approximately 23 centimeters (9 inches). Be very careful at this point, as the butter is very thick and can easily break through the dough, destroying layers. Dust the work surface with flour, and roll the dough until it is about 56 centimeters (22 inches) long; do not roll its width. Keep the sides even and square as you work.

Using a pastry brush, brush off any excess flour and fold the dough into thirds.

Repeat the preceding two steps. The *sfoglia* now has had two turns. Make two finger marks in the *sfoglia* to indicate two turns, cover in plastic wrap, and refrigerate 20 to 30 minutes.

Repeat the preceding steps to make two more turns. This makes four turns, total. Mark the dough accordingly and refrigerate to rest.

Repeat the preceding steps for two more turns (six turns in total), refrigerate to rest, or freeze for future use.

Torta di Pinoli

Pine-Nut Tart

Makes one 23-centimeter (9-inch) tart

This dessert tart, a *pasta frolla* shell filled with almond cream and topped with pine nuts, is a good example of the lavish use of nuts in Italian pastry. The shell need not be prebaked; it cooks along with the filling. The pine nuts are sprinkled over the tart once the filling has set so that they sink in just slightly to create an even nut "crust."

Ingredients

½ recipe Pasta Frolla (page 274), refrigerated at least 30 minutes
All-purpose flour, for dusting the work surface

For the filling:

45 grams (3 tablespoons) unsalted butter
150 grams (1¼ cups) pine nuts
110 grams (1 scant cup) almond flour
135 grams (⅔ cup) granulated sugar
3 large eggs, at room temperature
35 grams (2½ tablespoons) cornstarch
½ teaspoon baking powder
Pinch of coarse salt
1 teaspoon finely grated lemon zest
80 grams (5¾ tablesoons) unsalted butter, melted and cooled

1 recipe Crema Inglese (page 281), chilled, for serving

Butter, flour, and chill a 23-centimeter (9-inch) tart pan with a removable bottom.

On a well-floured work surface, roll the *pasta frolla* to a round about 2 millimeters (1⁄16 inch) thick. Line the tart pan with the dough round. Lightly dock the bottom of the dough and refrigerate.

Preheat the oven to 191°C (375°F).

Make the filling:

Heat the 45 grams (3 tablespoons) butter in a skillet (*padella*) until foamy. Add the pine nuts and toast until they turn a light golden color. (Do not let them darken too much or they will burn when the assembled tart is cooking.) Drain; set aside.

In a bowl, mix the almond flour with the sugar. Beat in the eggs, one at a time, until light. Sift the cornstarch, baking powder, salt, and lemon zest over the mixture and fold very gently to combine. Fold in the melted butter.

Assemble and bake the tart:

Pour the mixture into the tart shell so that it reaches about two-thirds to three-quarters of the way up the sides (the filling needs space to rise); you'll have a little filling left over. Bake (*cuocere in forno*) until the filling just begins to firm but has not yet started to color, 3 to 5 minutes.

Cover the top of the tart with an even layer of the pine nuts. Return the tart to the oven and bake until the filling is firm and golden brown, about 20 minutes.

Transfer to a wire rack to cool completely. Remove from the tart pan, and cut into slices. Serve at room temperature with *Crema Inglese* (page 281).

Chef's Note

Instead of one large tart, this recipe can be used for individual-size tarts, as in the photograph opposite. The dough and filling will yield 20 to 24 tarts in 10-centimeter (4-inch) pans. The small tarts should be baked in the same way as the 9-inch tart, but for considerably less time, approximately 20 minutes.

Cleaning Leeks

Leeks are always full of grit that hides between the layers of leaves. To clean, cut the leek in half lengthwise. Hold each half upside down under cold running water, separating the leaves with your hands, all the way down to the root end, to expose and rinse out the dirt. If the leeks are extremely dirty, it's best to let them soak for several minutes to soften the dirt, and then rinse again.

Torta di Porri

Leek Tart

Serves 6 to 8

This is an example of a savory tart. The *pasta brisée* shell is filled with a leek custard flavored with pancetta and grated cheeses. The shell is precooked (blind baked) to ensure that it cooks through, then filled with the custard and baked to set.

This tart would traditionally be served as an antipasto or luncheon dish.

Ingredients

½ recipe Pasta Brisée (page 274), refrigerated at least
    30 minutes
900 grams (2 pounds) leeks, trimmed, rinsed well of grit, and
    sliced into rounds (10 cups)
60 milliliters (¼ cup) olive oil
Coarse salt and freshly ground black pepper
3 large eggs
250 milliliters (1 cup) milk
10 grams (2 tablespoons) grated Pecorino Romano
10 grams (2 tablespoons) grated Parmigiano-Reggiano or
    Grana Padano
100 grams (3½ ounces) pancetta, cut into ½-centimeter
    (³⁄₁₆-inch) dice

Preheat the oven to 191°C (375°F).

Roll the *pasta brisée* to a thin round and fit it into a 23-centimeter (9-inch) pie pan with a removable bottom (5 centimeters / 2 inches deep). With a fork, dock the dough gently (so as not to actually puncture the crust). Cover the shell with parchment paper and fill with beans or pie weights.

Bake (*cuocere in forno*) the shell until set, about 8 minutes. Remove the beans or pie weights and parchment and bake 5 more minutes.

Meanwhile, combine the leeks and oil in a large skillet (*padella*). Place over medium heat, season to taste with salt and pepper, and cook until the leeks are softened, 5 to 7 minutes. Remove from the heat and let cool.

In a bowl, beat the eggs with the milk and cheeses. Add the leek mixture and stir well.

Reduce the oven heat to 177°C (350°F). Arrange the pancetta over the bottom of the shell and pour in the custard mixture. Set the tart on a half sheet pan and bake 40 to 50 minutes, or until the custard is just set and the top is lightly browned. The custard should not soufflé; if it does, the oven is too hot.

Let cool briefly on a wire rack; unmold, slice, and serve.

Pasticcera on the facing page; let it infuse 10 minutes, off the heat. The zest will be strained out of the cream with the vanilla bean.

The tart may be finished with a sprinkling of superfine sugar, or apricot glaze; the glaze will protect the fruit and give the tart a longer shelf life.

Ingredients

All-purpose flour, for dusting the work surface
½ recipe Pasta Frolla (page 274), refrigerated at least 30 minutes
1 pint (about 450 grams / 1 pound) fresh strawberries
2 to 3 kiwifruit, peeled
1 recipe Crema Pasticcera (facing page), chilled
Superfine sugar or apricot glaze (optional; see Chef's Note)

On a lightly floured work surface, roll the dough to a circle about 2 millimeters (¹⁄₁₆ inch) thick. Line a 23-centimeter (9-inch) tart pan with a removable bottom with the dough round. Dock the bottom of the shell and refrigerate.

Preheat the oven to 177°C (350°F).

Cover the shell with parchment paper and fill with beans or pie weights.

Bake (cuocere in forno) the shell until set, about 15 minutes. Remove the beans or pie weights and parchment and bake 5 more minutes until lightly browned. Let cool on a wire rack.

Rinse the strawberries quickly under running water and dry immediately. Use the tip of a small knife to cut out the hulls. Stand the strawberries on their hull ends and cut into thin slices less than 6 millimeters (¼ inch) thick.

Cut the peeled kiwifruit in half lengthwise, then into slices 6 millimeters (¼ inch) thick.

Crostata di Fragole e Kiwi

Strawberry-and-Kiwifruit Tart

Makes one 23-centimeter (9-inch) tart

This is a basic fruit-tart recipe. The crust is baked separately, lined with vanilla pastry cream, and topped with sliced strawberries and kiwifruit. Kiwifruit was brought to Italy from New Zealand and is now grown in many regions, particularly in northern and central Italy. Other fruits may be substituted, and the pastry cream may be flavored as desired. Orange- or lemon-flavored pastry cream is particularly refreshing with strawberries and kiwifrit: Heat the grated zest of 1 lemon or orange with the milk in step 1 of the recipe for Crema

Chef's Note

The tart can be sprinkled lightly with superfine sugar; or melt apricot glaze over low heat in a small saucepan (casseruola), adding water as needed to bring the mixture to a brushing consistency, and brush over the fruit.

Spread the chilled *crema pasticcera* in the cooled shell. Arrange the strawberry and kiwifruit slices in overlapping concentric circles on top of the *crema pasticcera*, as desired.

Sprinkle the tart with superfine sugar or brush with apricot glaze, if desired (see Chef's note on facing page).

Crema Inglese

Custard Sauce

Makes about ½ liter (2 cups)

This is a recipe for a basic, stirred vanilla custard made with egg yolks, sugar, and milk, stirred constantly over gentle heat until thickened. Care must be taken not to cook the custard too quickly or over too high a heat, or the eggs will curdle and the sauce will be grainy instead of smooth and creamy, as it should be.

Chef's Note

In a professional setting, *crema inglese* may be pasteurized to address the risk of foodborne illness associated with lightly cooked egg. To pasteurize the cream, bring it to 79°C (175°F) and hold for 1 minute. Do not exceed 82°C (180°F) or the sauce will curdle.

Ingredients

500 milliliters (2 cups) whole milk
½ vanilla bean, split lengthwise and scraped, or 1 teaspoon
    pure vanilla extract
5 large egg yolks
100 grams (½ cup) granulated sugar

Bring the milk to a simmer in a saucepan (*casseruola*) with the vanilla bean half and scraped seeds. Remove from the heat and let infuse 10 minutes, or continue to the next step if using vanilla extract.

In a bowl, whisk the egg yolks with the sugar until the mixture is pale yellow.

Whisking constantly, gradually add some of the hot milk to the yolk-sugar mixture to temper. Whisk thoroughly to blend. Add the yolk-sugar mixture to the saucepan with the hot milk and cook over medium heat, stirring constantly with a wooden spoon or plastic spatula in a figure-eight motion; be especially attentive to the bottom and edges of the pan, as egg will coagulate there first.

Heat the custard until the mixture reaches 74°C (165°F), at which point it will become quite thick. The custard is done when it coats the back of a spoon. Stir in the vanilla extract, if using.

Strain the custard through a fine-mesh strainer (*colino*) into a bowl set over ice. Stir with a spoon until steam is no longer emitted. When cool, cover with plastic wrap laid directly on the surface to prevent a skin from forming, and refrigerate until cold. The *crema* will hold 1 day in the refrigerator.

Crema Pasticcera

Pastry Cream

Makes about ½ liter (2 cups)

Crema pasticcera is a flour- and/or cornstarch-bound cream used in Italian pastry-making for a multitude of purposes: as a filling for *bignè* and cakes; as a bed for fruit tarts; and as a filling for *millefoglie*, to name just a few.

This basic recipe for *crema pasticcera* is flavored with vanilla but typical variations employ orange, lemon, coffee, chocolate, brown butter, and a variety of liqueurs. Whipped cream or mascarpone may be folded into the cream to lighten and enrich it (this is a *crema leggera*), or gelatin may be added to stabilize it.

The mixture must be brought to a boil to activate thickening; the cream is boiled for three more minutes to sterilize the eggs.

Ingredients

500 milliliters (2 cups) whole milk

½ vanilla bean, split lengthwise and scraped, or 1 teaspoon
   pure vanilla extract

4 large egg yolks

75 grams (⅓ cup) granulated sugar

15 grams (2 tablespoons) all-purpose flour

15 grams (1½ tablespoons) cornstarch

Melted butter, for drizzling over finished cream (optional)

Sugar, for sprinkling over finished cream (optional)

Bring the milk to a simmer in a saucepan (*casseruola*) with the vanilla bean half and scraped seeds. Remove from the heat and let infuse 10 minutes, or continue to the next step if using vanilla extract.

In a bowl, whisk the egg yolks with the sugar until the mixture is pale yellow.

Sift the flour and cornstarch together and add to the sugar-yolk mixture. Whisk until smooth.

Whisk a little of the hot milk into the sugar-yolk mixture to temper it, then add the mixture to the pan, whisking to blend.

Using a whisk or a flat-edged wooden spoon, bring the cream to a boil over medium heat, stirring constantly to prevent lumps. Be sure to scrape the bottom and lower inner edges of the pan to prevent lumps and to keep the mixture from scalding.

Once the cream has come to a boil, continue boiling 2 or 3 more minutes to sterilize the eggs.

Transfer the pastry cream to a stainless-steel bowl. To prevent a skin from forming, dot the surface of the cream with melted butter and sprinkle with sugar, or press plastic wrap directly onto the surface of the cream. Chill in an ice bath. Stir in the vanilla extract, if using.

When it cools, the *crema* will become jellylike. Before using, work the *crema* with a spatula or whisk until smooth. (At this point whipped cream or mascarpone may be folded into the cream to lighten it.) Pastry cream will hold up to 2 days in the refrigerator.

Profiteroles

Cream Puffs with Gelato

Serves 4

In this classic recipe using *bignè*, or cream puffs, warm chocolate sauce provides a delicious contrast to the cold gelato.

It's important that *bignè* be completely cooked through and no longer wet on the interior, or they will collapse after they are removed from the oven. The dough accomplishes its rising during the first 10 to 15 minutes of baking; at this point, the *bignè* will be puffed and well browned. The oven is turned down to prevent the *bignè* from darkening excessively, and the pastries are cooked 5 to 10 minutes longer to dry out completely.

The dough for this recipe is made with a pinch of sugar because the *bignè* are to be used in a sweet preparation.

The chocolate sauce can be made ahead and gently reheated in a water bath.

Ingredients

1 recipe Pasta Bignè (page 275), prepared with the pinch of
   granulated sugar

Beaten egg for egg wash

Melting Chocolate

Chocolate must be melted over low heat to avoid scorching it; it is usually melted in the top of a double boiler. The chocolate is chopped into pieces and, once it begins to melt, stirred frequently until smooth.

If chocolate is being melted on its own, it is important that it not come in contact with liquid or steam as it melts. When it comes in contact with a small amount of liquid, it "seizes" and goes from a smooth consistency to a grainy, hard mass. If melted in a substantial amount of liquid (such as cream), the chocolate will not seize. Once the chocolate seizes, there is no remedy; it can no longer be used in sauces or glazes where a sheen is desirable. Allow the chocolate to harden and use it in baked goods such as cakes and cookies.

For the chocolate sauce:

20 grams (¼ cup) unsweetened cocoa powder

75 grams (3 squares or 3 ounces) unsweetened chocolate, chopped

80 grams (¼ cup plus 2 tablespoons) granulated sugar

140 milliliters (⅔ cup) heavy cream

For the panna montata (whipped cream):

300 milliliters (1¼ cups) heavy cream

10 grams (2½ teaspoons) granulated sugar

1 teaspoon pure vanilla extract

1 recipe Gelato di Crema (page 319) or Gelato di Cioccolato (page 320)

10 grams (1¼ tablespoons) confectioners' sugar, for finishing

---

Preheat a convection oven to 177°C (350°F), or a standard oven to 204°C (400°F).

Using a pastry bag fitted with a round tip, pipe the *pasta bignè* onto buttered baking sheets in 4- to 5-centimeter (1½- to 2-inch) balls, leaving 5 to 8 centimeters (2 to 3⅛ inches) of space between them.

Brush the *bignè* gently with the egg wash.

Bake (*cuocere in forno*) until the *bignè* are completely browned, 10 to 15 minutes.

Lower the oven temperature to 149°C (300°F), and break open one *bignè* to test; if the interior is still wet (it's likely to be), bake the *bignè* another 5 to 10 minutes to dry out. Remove the *bignè* from the oven when they are dry and feel light and hollow. Let cool on a wire rack.

Make the chocolate sauce:

Dissolve the cocoa powder in 60 milliliters (¼ cup) water.

In the top of a double boiler, combine the chocolate, cocoa-powder mixture, and sugar. Place over simmering water and heat, stirring constantly, until the chocolate melts, the sugar dissolves, and the sauce is smooth. (See sidebar "Melting Chocolate" at left.)

Stir in the cream until smooth. Remove from the heat and let cool slightly before serving.

Make the *panna montata* (whipped cream):

In a bowl set over ice, whip the cream with the sugar and vanilla to soft peaks. (See sidebar "*Panna Montata*" on page 284).

Assemble the profiteroles:

Cut the top third off each *bignè* with a serrated knife. Fill each with a spoonful of *gelato di crema* or *gelato di cioccolato* and replace the tops.

Sift the confectioners' sugar over the tops, and serve with the chocolate sauce and whipped cream on the side.

Panna Montata (Whipped Cream)

Whipped cream is an emulsion of air, water, and fat solids. The key to a stable emulsion is twofold: The cream must contain at least 30 percent butterfat to whip properly (but with a butterfat content of 36 to 40 percent, heavy cream, also called heavy whipping cream, is preferred for its ability to whip faster to a higher, more stable volume), and it must be cold while it is whipped. At The International Culinary Center, the cream is whipped over ice. The cream is beaten just until stiff peaks form; overbeating will cause the whipped cream to lose volume and weep, and eventually to turn to butter. If the whipped cream will be used to lighten another preparation, such as a mousse, *panna cotta*, or *crema pasticcera*, beat just until soft peaks form to avoid overbeating; the whipped cream will be worked further during the process of folding.

Whipped cream will hold, covered, in the refrigerator for several hours.

Millefoglie

Napoleon with Strawberries

Makes 8 individual pastries

Millefoglie ("a thousand leaves," in Italian) is a pastry that combines thin, crisp layers of *pasta sfoglia* with a sweet filling. This version features layers of sliced strawberries and a *crema pasticcera* flavored with brown butter. But a multitude of fillings might be employed—*panna montata* (whipped cream), preserved fruits, other fresh fruits, and flavored creams.

The *crema pasticcera* in this recipe is stabilized with gelatin and lightened with whipped cream. The combination creates a consistency that is fluid enough to pipe yet firm enough to stay put between the layers of pastry.

It's best to bake the dough in a convection oven if one is available; the circulation of air encourages the dough to rise.

(For further discussion of making and baking *pasta sfoglia*, including step-by-step instructions, see "*Pasta Sfoglia*" on page 276. Also see sidebar "*Panna Montata*" at left for a discussion of whipped cream.)

Ingredients

450 grams (1 pound) Pasta Sfoglia (page 276)
All-purpose flour, for dusting the work surface

For the brown-butter crema pasticcera:

1 gelatin sheet or 3 grams (¾ teaspoon) unflavored powdered gelatin
10 milliliters (2½ teaspoons) orange liqueur, such as Gran Gala
225 milliliters (1 scant cup) whole milk
¼ vanilla bean, split lengthwise and scraped, or ½ teaspoon pure vanilla extract

2 large egg yolks
60 grams (⅓ cup) granulated sugar
10 grams (3¼ tablespoons) all-purpose flour
10 grams (2 teaspoons) cornstarch
20 grams (1½ tablesoons) unsalted butter
125 milliliters (½ cup) heavy cream

450 grams (1 pound) strawberries, washed and sliced
Confectioners' sugar, for finishing

Roll and bake the *pasta sfoglia*:

Preheat the oven to 204°C (400°F).

On a lightly floured work surface, roll the pastry into a rectangular sheet about ½ centimeter (⅜ inch) thick and the size of a half sheet pan (23 by 33 centimeters / 18 by 13 inches) or baking sheet. Roll the pastry up onto a rolling pin, then unroll it onto a parchment paper–lined sheet pan.

Dock the pastry, using a roller-docker or the tines of a fork.

Cover the pastry with parchment paper and another sheet pan to weigh it down during the initial baking.

Place the pastry sheet in the preheated oven. After about 5 minutes, turn the oven down to 163°C (325°F) for a convection oven, or 177°C (350°F) for a standard oven. Bake (*cuocere in forno*) the pastry until golden, about 20 more minutes. Remove the top sheet pan from the pastry and invert the pastry onto a rack to cool; immediately remove the other sheet pan.

Make the brown-butter *crema pasticcera*:

If using sheet gelatin, lace the gelatin in a bowl with the orange liqueur and set aside to bloom. If using powdered gelatin, sprinkle it over 2 tablespoons cold water in a small bowl and set aside 5 minutes.

cream to a boil, whisking or stirring constantly. Simmer (*sobbollire*) about 3 minutes. Be mindful to scrape the spatula against the bottom and edges of the saucepan so none of the cream scalds or sticks.

Gently heat the butter in a heavy-bottomed saucepan until the milk solids coagulate and turn pale brown. Pass the butter through a fine-mesh strainer (*passasalsa*) and stir it into the pastry cream. Add the bloomed gelatin leaves and their soaking liquid and stir well.

Transfer the *crema* to a bowl set over ice and chill, stirring occasionally, until cold. Stir in the vanilla extract, if using. Remove the bowl from the ice. To prevent a skin from forming, dot the surface of the cream with butter and sprinkle with sugar, or press plastic wrap directly onto the surface. Refrigerate until ready to assemble.

In a bowl set over ice, whip the heavy cream to soft peaks. Give the *crema* a good stir to loosen it up. Gently fold in the whipped cream.

Assemble the *millefoglie*:

Cut the baked *sfoglia* into 3 strips measuring 10 by 30 centimeters (4 by 11¾ inches) each. Cut each strip crosswise into eight 4-centimeter (1½-inch) pieces.

Bring the milk to a simmer with the vanilla bean quarter and scraped seeds. Remove from the heat and let infuse 10 minutes, or continue to the next step if using vanilla extract.

In a bowl, combine the egg yolks with the sugar and whisk until pale yellow. Add the flour and cornstarch and stir until smooth.

Slowy pour half of the hot milk into the yolk-sugar mixture to temper, whisking vigorously. Add the yolk-sugar mixture to the saucepan with the rest of the milk. Using a whisk or a flat-edged spoon, return the

Arrange an even layer of strawberry slices over one pastry rectangle. Cover with a thin layer of the brown-butter *crema pasticcera*. Cover with a second pastry rectangle and layer the pastry with a second layer of sliced strawberries and a second layer of *crema*.

Choose the smooth-bottomed side of a third pastry rectangle and dust it with the confectioners' sugar. Caramelize a crosshatch pattern on the top of it using a heated metal skewer. Assemble the stack and place it on a chilled plate.

Repeat to make 7 more pastries.

Chapter 18

Traditional Italian Desserts:
Biscotti, Cannoli, Bomboloni, e Pastiera

Pere in Vino Rosso (Poached Pears in Red Wine)
Biscotti di Prato (Almond Biscotti)
Biscotti alle Mandorle con Pinoli
    (Almond Cookies with Pine Nuts)
Tiramisù (Tiramisu)
Cannoli (Cannoli)
Bomboloni (Doughnuts)
Pastiera (Neapolitan Ricotta Tart)

Italian cuisine boasts a rich tradition of classic and regional pastries. Sicilia, Piemonte, and the Veneto, in particular, are well known for their extravagant dessert cultures. Most of these pastries are purchased in pastry shops (*tiramisù* and *bomboloni* are exceptions), and most are associated with a particular holiday. This chapter covers some of these traditional preparations.

Italians enjoy fruit for dessert, often simply served fresh. But fruit is also baked (peaches are baked with an Amaretto filling in Piemonte), roasted, poached in sweetened red wine (see *Pere in Vino Rosso* on page 288), and baked into tarts and cakes. Deep-fried pastries are popular, including a host of sugar-dusted fritters such as *cenci*, *zeppoli*, the Sicilian ricotta-filled *Cannoli* on page 293, and the custard-filled *Bomboloni* on page 294. Many of the pastries that feature sweetened ricotta are associated with southern Italy; *Pastiera* (page 295), a traditional Easter pie filled with sweetened ricotta and wheat berries, is a specialty of Naples.

Cookies are made all over Italy, in many forms. Some examples include the crisp, pine nut–topped almond macaroons, *Biscotti alle Mandorle con Pinoli* on page 291 and twice-baked biscotti. This chapter demonstrates a style of almond-studded biscotti named after the town of Prato, in Toscana (*Biscotti di Prato* on page 290), and light-textured *savoiardi* cookies—named after the House of Savoy, which ruled Italy for several centuries from its seat in Piemonte—are soaked in espresso and layered with a mascarpone cream in the "spoon" dessert, *tiramisù*, which is said to have originated in the Veneto.

Dessert categories covered elsewhere in this book are:

○   Tarts (see Chapter 17)

○   Single-layer cakes (often made with nuts, such as the chestnut and almond cakes on pages 301 and 302, respectively) and layered cakes made with *Pan di Spagna* (page 300)

○   Pastries fashioned from *Pasta Sfoglia* (page 276), such as the *Millefoglie* on page 284

○   Soft, so-called spoon desserts such as custards, mousses, and *panna cotta*, which are traditionally served in a mold and eaten with a spoon (see Chapter 20)

○   Candylike confections such as the *Torrone* on page 312

Cannoli (page 293)

Chef's Notes

To serve the pears whole, peel them and core them from their base with a melon baller. Leave the stem on for a pretty presentation. Poach as in the recipe above for 20 to 30 minutes, depending on the ripeness of the pear. The cored centers of the cooled pears may be stuffed with chopped nuts—almonds, walnuts, pistachios, hazelnuts—sweetened with sugar or honey, and the pear served standing up, in the sauce.

For restaurant service in Italy, *zabaione* is traditionally made tableside and served with fresh fruit. It may be served warm or cold, and is also served spooned over cake, or with ladyfingers.

Le Tecniche

For step-by-step instructions for shaping and cooking biscotti, cannoli, and *savoiardi*, see pages 478, 479, and 487, respectively. For step-by-step instructions for making and frying *bomboloni*, see page 395.

Pere in Vino Rosso

Poached Pears in Red Wine

Serves 4, if pears are sliced; 2, if pears are left whole

This is a basic recipe for poaching pears in sweetened red wine. The technique applies equally well to other fruits: peaches, apples, plums, and nectarines. Bosc and Anjou pears work well because they stay firm in the cooking, and their pretty, elongated shape presents well.

Zabaione (also spelled *zabaglione*, from the Neapolitan word *zappillare*, meaning "to foam") is a frothy, egg-rich custard flavored with a sweet or sparkling wine such as Moscato, or the fortified Sicilian wine Marsala. The eggs are whisked over a bowl of simmering water (called a water bath, or *bagno maria*) to prevent the eggs from curdling while they are heated and aerated. The mixture is cooked until it reaches a temperature of 71°C (160°F).

This recipe suggests a variety of possible presentations (see Chef's Notes). At The International Culinary Center, the pears are served with the reduced poaching liquid, a *zabaione*, and a sprinkle of something to add texture: chopped toasted nuts, for example, or a little crumbled cookie. The pears may be served sliced, as in this recipe, or whole (see Chef's Notes).

The poaching liquid is intended to be very sweet; if it is not, it will leach sugar out of the fruit.

Ingredients

For the pears:
500 milliliters (2 cups) dry red Italian wine
150 grams (¾ cup) granulated sugar, or as needed
½ vanilla bean, split lengthwise and scraped
1 bay leaf
Juice of 1 orange
Zest of ½ orange, the zest peeled off in strips
Juice and zest of ½ lemon, the zest peeled off in strips
2 ripe pears, preferably Bosc or Anjou
Additional lemon juice, as needed

For the zabaione:
6 large egg yolks
75 grams (⅓ cup) granulated sugar
250 milliliters (1 cup) sweet white wine, such as Moscato

Poach the pears:

In a saucepan (*casseruola*), combine the wine, sugar, vanilla bean half and scraped seeds, bay leaf, and the citrus juices and zests and bring to a boil. Turn off the heat.

Peel, core, and halve the pears and add to the pan.

Return the pan to the heat and gently poach the pears about 15 minutes, or until tender when pierced with the point of a paring knife. Remove from the heat and let the pears cool in the poaching liquid, overnight if possible. (If holding overnight, refrigerate.)

Remove the pears with a slotted spoon and set aside. Strain and reduce the poaching liquid until somewhat syrupy (but not too viscous). Adjust the sweetness or acidity, with more sugar or lemon juice to taste.

Make the *zabaione*:

In the top of a double boiler, off the heat, beat the egg yolks and the sugar with a balloon whisk until light and foamy. Beat in the wine.

Place over simmering water and beat until the mixture is foamy and thick, has increased several times in volume, and reaches a temperature of 71°C (160°F) on an instant-read thermometer, 3 to 5 minutes. The mixture should be thick enough that it will mound in a spoon, and when you pull the spoon through it, it should be homogenous, with no liquid leaking from it. Remove the custard every now and then from the heat if the mixture gets too hot—you want to warm the eggs, not cook them.

To serve:

When the pears are cool enough to handle, slice and serve them with the *zabaione*.

Ingredients

300 grams (2 cups) all-purpose flour, plus extra for rolling the dough
140 grams (¾ cup) granulated sugar
½ teaspoon baking powder
½ teaspoon baking soda
¼ teaspoon coarse salt
3 large eggs
1 teaspoon pure vanilla extract
½ teaspoon almond extract
100 grams (¾ cup) whole almonds with skins, toasted and cooled (see sidebar "Toasting Almonds" at left)

Preheat the oven to 177°C (350°F), or to 163°C (325°F) if using a convection oven. Line a full sheet pan with parchment paper.

In the bowl of a standing mixer fitted with the paddle attachment, combine the flour, sugar, baking powder, baking soda, and salt.

Lightly whisk the eggs with the vanilla and almond extracts and add to the dry ingredients. Beat until almost combined.

Add the almonds and continue to beat until all the dry ingredients are incorporated.

Scrape the dough out onto a liberally floured work surface. Roll the dough into a log shape; it should be just well enough coated with flour to keep it from sticking to the work surface.

Cut the log into 4 even pieces and move to the edge of the floured surface.

Bring the parchment paper–lined sheet pan close to the work area. Shape one piece of the dough into a cylinder, as long as the sheet pan is wide. Quickly transfer

Biscotti di Prato

Almond Biscotti

Makes about 4 dozen

The word *biscotti* derives from an ancient word meaning "twice-cooked." The dough is baked first in a log shape to cook the dough through and brown the exterior. The log is sliced, and the long, flat slices are cooked for a second time until the interior is dry and crisp.

These almond-studded cookies, also called *cantucci*, are associated with Toscana. They are reputed to have been invented in the nineteenth century by a pastry chef, Antonio Mattei, who lived in the town of Prato, northwest of Florence.

Toasting Almonds

To toast almonds, place them on a sheet pan and roast 5 minutes at 177°C (350°F), or until they are slightly browned and give off a nutty aroma.

the cylinder onto the sheet pan, being careful not to stretch it. Press gently to flatten.

Repeat with the other 3 pieces of dough, spacing them equally across the pan.

Bake (*cucocere in forno*) 15 to 20 minutes, until golden.

Remove from the oven and let the biscotti cool on the sheet pan set on a wire rack until cool enough to handle, about 10 minutes. Lower the oven to 163°C (325°F), or 149°C (300°F) for convection ovens.

When the biscotti are cool enough to handle, place 1 piece on a cutting board and slice on a diagonal, 2 centimeters (¾ inch) thick.

Lay the biscotti flat on the sheet pan and repeat with the remaining pieces. Bake again until lightly toasted.

Let cool completely and store in an airtight container.

Biscotti alle Mandorle con Pinoli

Almond Cookies with Pine Nuts

Makes about 2 dozen

These pine nut–topped cookies, crisp on the outside with soft interiors, are very common in bakeries throughout Italy.

Ingredients

170 grams (1¼ cups) pine nuts
230 grams (1 cup plus 3 tablespoons) granulated sugar
450 grams (1 pound) almond paste
4 large egg whites, at room temperature
230 grams (2 cups) confectioners' sugar
¼ teaspoon coarse salt
110 grams (1 scant cup) all-purpose flour

Preheat the oven to 191°C (375°F). Line a sheet pan with parchment paper, or lightly butter it. Put the pine nuts in a shallow bowl; set aside.

In a bowl, beat together the granulated sugar, almond paste, and egg whites until creamy.

Sift in the confectioners' sugar, salt, and flour, and beat until blended.

Roll the dough into balls of 15 to 20 grams (1 to 1½ tablespoons) each. Dip each dough ball in the pine nuts, and gently press the nuts over the top half of the ball. Then set the balls on the prepared baking sheet, nuts facing up.

Bake (*cuocere in forno*) until golden and crisp on the outside, with a soft, marshmallowlike texture inside, 10 to 15 minutes. Cool for a few minutes on the baking sheet, set on a wire rack. Then remove the cookies from the baking sheet and cool them completely on the rack.

Tiramisù

Tiramisu

Serves 8

This classic dessert layers coffee-soaked ladyfingers (*savoiardi*) with a mousselike, coffee-flavored mascarpone filling.

(See pages 489 and 477, respectively, for step-by-step instructions for making *savoiardi* and using a pastry bag.)

Chef's Note

As *tiramisù* is made with raw egg, the use of pasteurized eggs, if available, will eliminate the risk of foodborne illness. Pasteurized eggs are sold whole, in the shell, and as whites or yolks only. *Tiramisù* is best eaten within two days; if the eggs are pasteurized, eat within three days.

Ingredients

7 large eggs (pasteurized, if possible), at room temperature, separated
125 grams (½ cup plus 2 tablespoons) granulated sugar
75 milliliters (⅓ scant cup) coffee-flavored liqueur, such as Kahlúa
500 grams (2 cups) mascarpone cheese
30 savoiardi (recipe follows)
500 milliliters (2 cups) freshly brewed espresso, cooled
Cocoa powder, for dusting

Place the egg yolks and 75 grams (¼ cup plus 2 tablespoons) of the sugar in the bowl of a standing mixer fitted with the whisk attachment. Beat on low speed to blend. Increase the speed to medium and beat until pale-colored and thick—almost the consistency of marshmallows—5 to 6 minutes.

Add the coffee liqueur and mascarpone and beat until thick and smooth.

In another bowl, beat the egg whites until soft peaks form. With the mixer running, gradually beat in the remaining 50 grams (¼ cup) sugar, and beat until the meringue is smooth and shiny and stiff peaks form. Fold the meringue into the mascarpone mixture; set aside.

Working with one at a time, dip the *savoiardi* into the espresso until they are wet on both sides, but still hold their shape. Arrange over the bottom of a 21-by-21-by-5-centimeter (8-by-8-by-2-inch) dish to cover. Spread with half of the mascarpone mixture. Cover with a second layer of soaked *savoiardi* and spread with the remainder of the mascarpone mixture.

Smooth the top of the dessert with a spatula and sift cocoa powder over to cover. Cover and chill for several hours or overnight before serving.

Savoiardi

Makes about 30

5 large eggs, at room temperature, separated
125 grams (⅔ cup) confectioners' sugar, plus extra for dusting
½ teaspoon pure vanilla extract (optional)
125 grams (1¼ cups) cake flour, sifted

Unsalted butter, softened, for the sheet pan and parchment paper

Preheat the oven to 177°C (350°F) and center a rack in the oven. Prepare a sheet pan: Draw a large X on the pan with softened butter and line the pan with parchment paper. (The butter will prevent the parchment from moving when the batter is spread into the pan.) Brush the parchment paper with softened butter.

Place the egg whites in the bowl of a standing electric mixer fitted with the whip attachment. Beat on low speed to aerate. Add the confectioners' sugar, raise the speed to high, and beat for about 4 minutes, until the peaks are firm but not dry.

In a small mixing bowl, combine the yolks and vanilla, if using.

Using a rubber spatula, fold the egg yolks into the meringue. Then carefully fold the flour into the meringue so as not to deflate the batter. Immediately transfer the batter to a pastry bag fitted with a plain tip. Pipe 8-centimeter-long (3⅛-inch-long) strips on the parchment, allowing at least 2½ centimeters (1 inch) between strips.

Dust the *savoiardi* lightly with confectioners' sugar.

Bake until the *savoiardi* are golden and the centers spring back when lightly touched, about 5 minutes.

Cool the *savoiardi* on a wire rack. Store, tightly covered, up to 3 days, or freeze.

Cannoli

Cannoli

Makes 15 to 20

Cannoli are made with a stiff dough flavored with wine or vinegar. The dough is thinly rolled—a pasta machine works very well for this—and cut into rounds or squares, which are shaped around a dowel or metal cannoli form to make a hollow tube. The pastry shells are deep-fried and filled with a cream. Traditionally the filling is sweetened ricotta cheese, but it is often replaced by vanilla or chocolate pastry cream.

(See pages 371 and 479, respectively, for step-by-step instructions for rolling dough with a pasta machine and making cannoli using a cannoli form. Also see sidebar "Draining Ricotta" on page 68.)

Ingredients

For the cannoli dough:

200 grams (1⅔ cups) all-purpose flour, plus extra for dusting the work surface

¾ teaspoon coarse salt

12 grams (1 tablespoon) granulated sugar

14 grams (1 tablespoon) unsalted butter, softened, in small pieces

15 milliliters (1 tablespoon) dry white wine, sweet wine such as Moscato, or vinegar

1 large egg, beaten, for egg wash, or water, as needed

Vegetable or canola oil, for deep-frying

For the filling:

200 grams (1½ cups) ricotta, drained

16 grams (2 tablespoons) confectioners' sugar

For the garnish:

Pistachios, crushed

Shaved chocolate

Candied fruit, diced

Make the cannoli dough:

Combine the flour and salt in a mixing bowl. Make a well in the center and add the sugar, butter, and egg.

Add the wine and stir with a fork, pulling the dry ingredients into the well, until the liquid is absorbed and the mixture comes together into a rough dough.

Turn the dough out onto a floured work surface and knead until smooth, about 5 minutes. Shape into a disk, cover in plastic wrap, and refrigerate 30 minutes.

Roll, form, and fry the cannoli:

Set up a pasta machine on a work surface. Divide the dough into 4 equal parts. Cover 3 of the dough pieces with plastic wrap and set aside. Lightly flour the dough

The cannoli shells can be made in advance, but they should not be filled until just before serving; once filled, the shells will become soggy.

quarter, and roll it through the pasta machine on the thinnest setting.

Lay the dough sheet on a lightly floured work surface. Cut into 9-centimeter (3½-inch) squares or rounds. Roll the dough rounds around a cannoli form (roll squares diagonally). Seal the overlapping edges with a little egg wash or water, as needed.

In a deep-fryer or deep pot, add oil to come about half-way up the sides of the pot. Heat to 191°C (375°F). Place a rack over a sheet pan, or line a sheet pan with paper towels.

Add the cannoli (still wrapped around the molds) to the hot oil and fry (*friggere*) until golden brown and crisp, about 1 minute. Remove from the oil to the prepared sheet pan. Remove the molds as soon as you can handle them, and cool completely. Roll, shape, cook, and cool the remaining cannoli.

Make the filling and assemble the cannoli:

Whip the ricotta with the sugar until fluffy. Spoon the mixture into a piping bag and pipe into the cannoli tubes. Garnish the tips with crushed pistachios, shaved chocolate, or diced candied fruit.

Bomboloni

Doughnuts

Makes about 3 dozen

Bomboloni are deep-fried pastries made with a butter-and-egg-rich yeast dough (similar to brioche), shaped into balls. The cooked *bomboloni* are often, though not always, filled with pastry cream, jam, or chocolate and finished with a sugar coating. They are eaten hot from the fryer, generally for breakfast.

The dough may be made by hand, but a standing mixer works very well. The key in either case is to mix or beat the dough sufficiently before adding the butter, which inhibits the necessary development of gluten.

(See page 395 for step-by-step instructions and photos for making *bomboloni*; page 477 offers step-by-step instructions for using a pastry bag.)

Ingredients

For the bomboloni:

500 grams (3⅓ cups) bread flour

70 grams (⅓ cups) granulated sugar

2 teaspoons coarse salt

30 grams (2 tablespoons) fresh yeast or 15 grams (1½ tablespoons / 2 packets) active dry yeast

50 milliliters (3½ tablespoons) warm water (40° to 46°C /
105° to 115°F)

5 large eggs

250 grams (1 cup) cold unsalted butter, cut into cubes

All-purpose flour for dusting the work surface

500 milliliters (2 cups) vegetable or grapeseed oil, for
deep-frying

1 recipe Crema Pasticcera, chilled (page 281)

Granulated sugar, for dusting

Combine the flour, sugar, and salt in the bowl of a standing mixer fitted with the paddle attachment and mix on low speed until thoroughly blended.

Dissolve the yeast in the water and add to the dry ingredients. Beat until combined.

Add the eggs, one at a time, beating until each egg is incorporated before adding the next. When all the eggs have been incorporated, increase the speed to me-dium, scraping the dough off the paddle several times during mixing, until the dough is smooth and satiny, 5 to 8 minutes. The dough is done when it is elastic,

Place the chilled pastry cream in a piping bag fitted with a small, plain tip.

Fill a deep-fryer or a wide, deep pan about halfway to the top with the oil, and heat to 176°C (350°F). Working in batches, fry (*friggere*) the *bomboloni* until they are a deep golden brown color and the dough is cooked through, 4 to 5 minutes. Do not crowd the pan, and turn the pastries once or twice while they fry for even coloring.

Remove with a skimmer to a pan lined with paper towels or a rack to drain. Let stand just until cool enough to handle.

Roll the *bomboloni* in sugar while still warm. Pierce each, on one side, with a chopstick, turning it to make a pocket in the center of the pastry. Fill each with the pastry cream.

Pastiera

Neapolitan Ricotta Tart

> Makes one 23-centimeter (9-inch) cake
> (serves 8 to 10)

This famous Neapolitan pastry was traditionally an Easter specialty, the wheat berries hearkening back to ancient Mediterranean rituals predating Christianity. These days, it's made year-round all over Italy.

The pastry is a version of *pasta frolla*, made with pure pork lard (*strutto*) instead of butter. (If lard is not available, substitute unsalted butter.) If you have *farro* on hand, it makes an excellent (and convenient) substitute for the wheat berries.

If there is time, macerate the ricotta with the 20 grams (1½ tablespoons) sugar overnight in the refrigerator to make it smooth and creamy.

pulls away completely from the sides of the bowl, and doesn't break when pulled.

Return the mixer to low, and beat in the butter, a few chunks at a time, until completely incorporated. Scrape the dough out onto a lightly floured work surface. Shape it into a ball, cover in plastic wrap, and refrigerate at least 4 hours, or overnight. (Chilling firms the dough, making it easier to shape.)

When ready to use, divide the chilled dough into 30-gram (2-tablespoon) pieces. On a lightly floured work surface, roll into balls. (Note that the dough may become sticky when it warms slightly. Resist the temptation to work in additional flour. Use only a pinch to "lubricate" the dough in order to shape it.) Place on a lightly floured sheet pan, cover loosely with plastic wrap, and let rise in a warm place until almost doubled in volume, 45 minutes to 1 hour.

Chef's Note

The granulated sugar may be flavored with vanilla (*zucchero vanigliato*), grated lemon zest, cinnamon, and/or nutmeg.

This tart tastes much better the day after it's made. In any event, at least twelve hours in the refrigerator makes it easier to unmold, though traditionally it is sold and sliced right in the pan.

(See pages 467–79 for an in-depth discussion of making, shaping, and baking pastry doughs; sidebar "Draining Ricotta" on page 68 offers step-by-step instructions.)

Ingredients

For the pastry:

450 grams (3¾ cups) all-purpose flour, plus extra for dusting the work surface

225 grams (1 cup plus 2 tablespoons) granulated sugar

225 grams (1 cup) lard or unsalted butter, plus extra for the cake pan

4 large egg yolks

For the filling:

225 grams (1¼ cups) wheat berries, soaked overnight in the refrigerator in water to cover, or farro, unsoaked

350 milliliters (1½ cups) whole milk

Finely grated zest of ½ orange, plus the juice of ½ orange

Finely grated zest of 1 lemon, plus the juice of ½ lemon

1 cinnamon stick

Pinch of coarse salt

40 grams (3 tablespoons) granulated sugar

15 grams (1 tablespoon) unsalted butter, as needed

280 grams (1 cup plus 2 tablespoons) ricotta, drained overnight in the refrigerator

3 large eggs, separated

30 milliliters (2 tablespoons) orange blossom water (acqua di fiori d'arancio)

Pinch of ground cinnamon

1 large egg, beaten, for egg wash

Make the pastry:

On a work surface or in a bowl, combine the flour and sugar. Cut in the lard or butter with a plastic bowl scraper, or rub it in with your fingertips, until the mixture reaches the consistency of fine crumbs. Make a well in the center and add the egg yolks; beat with a fork. With your hands, gradually incorporate the dry ingredients into the well, eventually pressing the mixture together with your fingers to create a rough dough. (Avoiding kneading to dough too much, or it will toughen.) Cut the dough in half and shape into two disks. Cover the disks in plastic wrap and refrigerate at least 30 minutes, or until chilled.

Butter and flour a 23-centimeter (9-inch) cake pan. On a lightly floured work surface, roll one dough disk to a round about 6 millimeters (¼ inch) thick and 33 centimeters (13 inches) in diameter. Line the prepared cake pan with the dough and refrigerate until chilled, at least 15 minutes.

Roll out the second disk of dough between sheets of parchment paper to 6 millimeters (¼ inch) thick. Chill the dough (if it is made with lard, it will soften quickly at room temperature). Cut the dough into strips 1 centimeter (⅜ inch) wide. Working on a parchment paper–lined sheet pan, assemble the lattice: Arrange 5 strips of dough on the parchment, 2 to 4 centimeters (¾ to 1½ inches) apart. Place a second layer of strips over the first, 2 to 4 centimeters (¾ to 1½ inches) apart. Put the parchment sheet into the refrigerator or freezer to chill the lattice until firm.

Prepare the filling and assemble the tart:

Drain the wheat berries, or *farro*, if using. In a saucepan (*casseruola*), combine the wheat berries or *farro*, the milk, 125 milliliters (½ cup) water, the grated orange and lemon zests, cinnamon stick, salt, and 20 grams (1½ tablespoons) of the sugar. Bring to a simmer and cook until the grain is al dente, about 25

(1½ tablespoons) sugar until the sugar dissolves.

In another bowl, beat the egg whites to soft peaks.

Beat the yolks into the ricotta mixture until well blended and lightened. Beat in the orange and lemon juices, the orange blossom water, and the ground cinnamon.

Stir in the grain mixture. Gently fold in the beaten whites until incorporated.

Pour the filling into the pastry shell.

For the top crust, lift the entire lattice construction off the parchment paper in one piece, and place on top of the filled pastry shell. (This is a little tricky and must be done quickly. If the lattice breaks, simply rejoin the dough pieces on top of the pastry shell, pressing the dough gently to adhere.) Press the edges together and cut off the excess dough at the edges, holding a small knife angled in toward the tart. Brush the pastry with the egg wash. Place on a sheet pan and bake (*cuocere in forno*) about 1 hour, until the filling is firm in the center and golden, and a toothpick inserted into the center comes out almost clean, with just a few bits of cheese clinging. Let cool completely in the cake pan set on a wire rack. Chill at least 12 hours.

To unmold, run a small spatula around the edge of the pie to gently loosen the crust. Place a 23-centimeter (9-inch) cardboard cake round over the pie. With one hand on the cake round and one hand on the bottom of the pan, quickly flip the pie so that it unmolds onto the cake round. Remove the cake pan. Place a second round on top (this is the bottom of the pie), and flip it again so that the lattice top faces up. Cut into wedges and serve.

Chef's Notes

Pastiera will keep for several days in the refrigerator.

Sometimes lightly toasted pine nuts or chopped almonds are added to the ricotta filling.

minutes. Remove the pan from the heat and let stand until cooled to room temperature, or chill in an ice bath. Discard the cinnamon stick. If, once cooled, the mixture is very thick, stir in the butter.

Preheat the oven to 191°C (375°F) and place a rack in the center.

In a bowl, whisk the ricotta with the remaining 20 grams

Chapter 19

Cakes:
Pan di Spagna, Zuccotto, e Torte

Pan di Spagna (Sponge Cake)
Torta di Castagne (Chestnut Cake)
Torta alle Mandorle (Almond Cake)
Zuccotto (Florentine Dessert)

Pan di Spagna (page 300), alternatively known as *pasta Genovese*, is an airy sponge cake based on beaten whole eggs, very little, if any, fat, and no chemical leavening agent. The basis for many Italian dessert preparations, it may be decorated and finished in a variety of ways, but it is usually cut into layers, soaked with a sugar syrup, and filled. Typical fillings include *panna montata* (whipped cream), and *crema pasticcera* (pastry cream). Unlike other, more buttery cakes, *Pan di Spagna* is dry because it is designed to be moistened.

Torta di Castagne (page 301) and *Torta alle Mandorle* (page 302) are typical Italian cakes made with nut flours. Many regional variations exist, with different names and combinations of ingredients. *Torta di castagne* is a chestnut cake that, like *pan di Spagna*, is leavened by eggs alone. *Torta alle mandorle* is an example of an almond cake with the addition of a chemical leavening: baking powder. This variation, inspired by a typical tart of Pavia (in western Lombardia), is made with cornmeal, which gives it a wonderful, slightly gritty texture. Both cakes are less fragile than the delicate *pan di Spagna*.

This chapter demonstrates the basic method for preparing these three cakes, as well as the traditional Florentine sweet *Zuccotto* (page 303). *Zuccotto* is composed of a flavored ricotta cream encased in strips of *Pan di Spagna* that are soaked in flavored syrup. The strips are used to line a bowl, and the lined bowl is filled with cream and frozen. The bowl gives the cake its unique domelike shape.

Le Tecniche

In this chapter, students learn the fundamentals of working with egg foams. See pages 485–89 for an in-depth discussion of egg foams and *Pan di Spagna*.

Torta di Castagne (page 301)

Pan di Spagna

Sponge Cake

Makes one 15-centimeter (6-inch) or one 21-centimeter (8-inch) cake

Pan di Spagna, also known as *pasta Genovese*, is a neutral sponge cake made with whole eggs. It is never served on its own; rather, it serves as the foundation for many dessert preparations in Italian cuisine. Intentionally a bit dry, the cake is designed to be moistened with a flavored sugar syrup, filled with creams or mousses, or used in *Zuccotto* (page 303). *Pan di Spagna* may be enriched with melted butter, for a moister cake.

Ingredients

Unsalted butter and all-purpose flour, for dusting the pan

For one 15-centimeter (6-inch) cake:

3 large eggs, at room temperature

75 grams (⅓ cup) granulated sugar

75 grams (¾ cup) cake flour, sifted

15 grams (1 tablespoon) unsalted butter, melted and cooled (optional)

Chef's Note

A chilled cake is easier to slice into layers.

For one 21-centimeter (8-inch) cake:

5 large eggs, at room temperature

125 grams (½ cup plus 2 tablespoons) granulated sugar

125 grams (1⅓ cups) cake flour, sifted

25 grams (1¾ tablespoons) unsalted butter, melted and cooled (optional)

Preheat the oven to 177°C (350°F) and place a rack in the center. Butter and flour the cake pan; refrigerate.

Bring a few inches of water to a simmer in a pot. Select a stainless-steel work bowl that fits the top of the pot snugly. (It is important that the bottom of the bowl is not in direct contact with the hot water.)

Combine the eggs and sugar in the bowl. Place the bowl on top of the pot of simmering water and whisk the mixture until it has doubled in volume and forms ribbons, about 5 minutes. The ideal temperature for the foam is 43°C (110°F). Do not allow the mixture to exceed 49°C (120°F) or the cake will be dry and tough. Turn the heat off under the water bath as needed.

Remove the mixture from the heat and beat until the mixture is cool and tripled in volume, about 1 minute.

Add the flour in several portions by sifting it directly over the egg-sugar mixture and folding it in with a rubber spatula.

If using the melted butter, fold it in completely after all the flour has been incorporated.

Pour the batter slowly into the prepared pan. Spin the pan to even the surface. Place the cake pan on a sheet pan.

Bake until no indentation remains when the cake is touched lightly in the center, it is a light golden color, and it begins to shrink slightly away from the sides of the pan, about 20 minutes for the 15-centimeter (6-inch) cake, or 35 minutes for the 21-centimeter (8-inch).

When done, turn the cake out immediately onto a wire rack to cool completely. Then wrap and refrigerate before cutting into layers and filling (see Chef's Note), or wrap and freeze up to 1 month.

Folding

Folding, the process of incorporating two preparations, generally one lighter than the other, into a homogenous mixture is a critical technique when making *Pan di Spagna* and other foods lightened with egg foams or whipped cream. Mixtures are usually folded with a rubber spatula. The heavier preparation (the flour, in this case) is pulled up over the lighter one (the warmed egg mixture). This motion continues as the bowl is turned slightly, to ensure even incorporation of the different mixtures. Folding should be done quickly and carefully; the mixture must not be overworked so as not to lose the airiness of the lighter preparation.

Torta di Castagne

Chestnut Cake

> Makes one 21- or 23-centimeter (8- or 9-inch) cake

This light, coarse-textured yet moist *torta* is only one example of a panoply of sweet chestnut cakes found throughout Italy. The cake is traditionally made with fresh chestnuts, which are blanched, peeled, and puréed. Peeled, frozen chestnuts are more practical, however: They need only be blanched in lightly salted water.

This cake may also be made with almond flour in place of the chopped almonds for a less coarse texture.

Ingredients

Unsalted butter and all-purpose flour, for dusting the pan

500 grams (17 ounces, or 3½ cups) fresh or frozen, peeled whole chestnuts

3 large eggs, at room temperature, separated

170 grams (¾ cup) granulated sugar

75 grams (4¼ tablespoons) unsalted butter, at room temperature

Finely grated zest of 1 lemon

75 grams (½ cup) skinned almonds, pulsed in a food processor or hand-chopped until finely chopped but not ground

1 teaspoon coarse salt

Confectioners' sugar, for dusting

Castagne

Chestnuts, the fruit of the sweet chestnut tree (*Castanea sativa*), are native to the Mediterranean and are a staple of the mountainous regions of Italy, particularly the Apennines. Several varieties are grown in Italy, and the nut is harvested during late autumn. With a carbohydrate content comparable to that of wheat and flour, chestnuts have constituted an important source of nourishment for the Italian peasantry for centuries.

Chestnuts, roasted or boiled, are employed in a variety of sweet and savory preparations. For the latter, they are found in soups, stuffings, and side dishes, and ground into flour for pasta or bread. They are also used to supplement potatoes. For sweets, chestnuts are made into *budini* (puddings or mousses), creams, and cakes. They are candied whole, and sweetened chestnuts are pressed through a ricer for the famous dessert *Monte Bianco*.

Preheat the oven to 191°C (375°F) and place a rack in the center. Butter and flour a 21- or 23-centimeter (8- or 9-inch) cake pan.

If using fresh chestnuts, in a saucepan (*casseruola*), cover the chestnuts with salted water and bring to a simmer; drain the chestnuts, let cool, and peel. Purée in a food processor until very finely chopped. If using frozen chestnuts, bring to a simmer in salted water, drain, let cool, and purée in a food processor until very finely chopped.

In a bowl, whisk the egg yolks with 85 grams (⅓ cup plus 2 tablespoons) of the sugar until light and fluffy.

In a separate bowl, beat the egg whites to soft peaks. While beating, gradually add the remaining sugar. Beat to stiff peaks.

In a third bowl, cream together the butter, lemon zest, chopped almonds, chestnut purée, and salt. Fold the chestnut mixture into the egg-yolk mixture.

Gently fold in the egg whites.

Pour the mixture into the prepared cake pan. Drop the pan gently onto a work surface from a height of about 1 centimeter (⅜ inch) to even the batter. Bake (*cuocere in forno*) until the center is just set and a cake tester inserted into the center comes out clean, about 40 minutes.

Turn the cake out onto a cooling rack and let cool completely. Before serving, sift confectioners' sugar over the top.

Torta alle Mandorle

Almond Cake

Makes one 21- or 23-centimeter (8- or 9-inch) cake

This is one of the multitudes of light, dry, nut-based cakes in Italian cuisine. The addition of polenta makes it pleasantly gritty and crumbly, like cornbread. Mascarpone can be used in place of the sour cream, resulting in a slightly more dense cake because of the higher fat content.

Ingredients

Unsalted butter and all-purpose flour, for dusting the pan
115 grams (¾ cup) fine polenta
115 grams (1¼ cups) cake flour
1 teaspoon baking powder
113 grams (½ cup) unsalted butter, softened, plus extra to butter the cake pan
60 grams (3½ tablespoons) almond paste, broken into small pieces
285 grams (2¾ cups) confectioners' sugar, plus extra for dusting the finished cake
½ teaspoon pure vanilla extract
½ teaspoon almond extract
2 large eggs
4 large egg yolks
60 grams (5 tablespoons) sour cream or mascarpone

Preheat the oven to 177°C (350°F) and arrange a rack in the lower third of the oven. Butter and flour a 21- or 23-centimeter (8- or 9-inch) round cake pan. Line the pan with a round of parchment paper. Refrigerate the pan until ready to use.

In a medium bowl, whisk together the polenta, cake flour, and baking powder and set aside.

In a standing mixer fitted with the paddle attachment, cream together the butter and almond paste on high speed until smooth, about 5 minutes.

Reduce the speed to low. With the mixer running, gradually add the confectioners' sugar and mix until thoroughly combined, and light and fluffy.

Raise the speed to high and add the vanilla and almond extracts, whole eggs, and egg yolks, one at a time, mixing well after each addition.

Reduce the speed to medium and add the sour cream and dry ingredients and mix until just incorporated.

Pour the batter into the prepared cake pan. Drop it gently onto a work surface from a height of about 1 centimeter (⅜ inch) to even the batter. Bake (*cuocere in forno*) until the cake is golden and pulls away from the sides of the pan, and a cake tester inserted into the center comes out clean, about 50 minutes.

Transfer the cake to a wire rack and let cool completely in the pan. Unmold, and dust with confectioners' sugar before serving.

Zuccotto

Florentine Dessert

One story behind this dome-shaped Florentine specialty is that it was inspired by the shape of the Duomo, the famous cathedral in Florence. Other sources suggest that the origin of the name is *zucchetto*, which means "skullcap," or *zucca*, which means "pumpkin," a reference to the shape. In any event, the rounded shape is achieved by assembling the *zuccotto* in a bowl: The bowl is lined with slices of *Pan di Spagna* soaked in a liqueur-flavored sugar syrup. Once lined, the bowl is filled with two sweetened ricotta creams, one flavored with candied fruit, the other with chocolate. The structure is topped with more soaked cake slices to cover.

The assembled cake is frozen for several hours before it is cut into wedges for serving.

(See "Assembling *Zuccotto*" and "Draining Ricotta" on pages 488 and 68, respectively, for step-by-step instructions.)

Ingredients

For the candied fruit:

175 grams (1 cup) chopped candied fruit
15 milliliters (1 tablespoon) orange liqueur, such as Gran Gala
1 vanilla bean, split lengthwise and scraped
Grated zest of 1 lemon
Grated zest of 1 orange

For the sugar syrup:

70 grams (⅓ scant cup) granulated sugar
45 milliliters (3 tablespoons) orange liqueur, such as Gran Gala
45 milliliters (3 tablespoons) framboise liqueur
15 milliliters (1 tablespoon) kirsch liqueur
125 milliliters (½ cup) grenadine

One 21-centimeter (8-inch) Pan di Spagna (page 300), made without butter, covered in plastic wrap, and frozen at least several hours, or overnight

For the fruit-ricotta filling:

350 milliliters (1½ cups) heavy cream
300 grams (1¼ cups) ricotta, hung overnight in cheesecloth, to drain
100 grams (½ cup) granulated sugar
Macerated candied fruit (from above)

For the chocolate filling:

125 milliliters (½ cup) heavy cream

8 grams (1 tablespoon) confectioners' sugar

100 grams (½ cup) ricotta

30 grams (3 tablespoons) granulated sugar

90 grams (3¼ ounces) bittersweet chocolate, melted and cooled but still fluid

---

Macerate the candied fruit:

Place the fruit in a bowl with the orange liqueur, the split vanilla bean, and the lemon and orange zests. Let macerate overnight.

Make the sugar syrup:

Bring the sugar and 120 milliliters (½ cup) water to a boil in a small saucepan (*casseruola*); cool. Add the liqueurs and grenadine. Transfer to a wide bowl.

Assemble the soaked *pan di Spagna* foundation:

Line a deep bowl (26 centimeters / 10 inches in diameter) with a damp cheesecloth. Cut the frozen *pan di Spagna* in half vertically into 2 semicircles (rather than horizontally into 2 thin rounds). Starting with the center of the cake (where the slices will be the longest), cut 1-centimeter (⅜-inch) slices, leaving top and bottom crusts intact: This will produce several long, rectangular slices, edged on all sides by crust. Cut the slices in half on the diagonal to form long, slender triangles, one side edged with crust.

Working with one cake triangle at a time, dip one side of each triangle in the syrup. Arrange the triangles side by side in the bowl, soaked sides facing down, so that the pointed ends meet in the center of the bowl, and all of the crusted edges face in the same direction. Overlap the triangles slightly, using as many cake triangles as needed to completely line the bowl. The wide ends of the triangles will overhang the edge of

the bowl; trim them with a knife. Set the bowl aside; reserve the remainder of the cake and the syrup to finish the *zuccotto*.

Make the fruit-ricotta filling:

In a bowl set over ice, beat the cream to soft peaks.

In the bowl of a standing mixer fitted with the paddle attachment, beat the ricotta with the sugar on medium speed 3 minutes, until smooth. Stir in the candied fruit. Fold in the whipped cream, half at a time. Refrigerate until ready to use.

Make the chocolate filling (see Chef's Note):

Beat the cream with the confectioners' sugar to soft peaks; do not beat over ice.

In the bowl of a standing mixer fitted with the paddle attachment, beat the ricotta with the granulated sugar on medium speed 3 minutes, until smooth. Beat in the cooled but still fluid chocolate. Fold in the whipped cream, half at a time.

Assemble the *zuccotto*:

Scoop the fruit-ricotta filling into the cake-lined bowl, smoothing it all over the sides so that it completely covers the cake; make an indentation in the center.

Scoop the chocolate filling into the center of the cake and smooth the top.

Dip more cake slices in syrup and use them to completely cover the top. Fold the cheesecloth over. Freeze for several hours, until set.

Unwrap the cheesecloth and turn the *zuccotto* out onto a plate. Remove the cheesecloth and cut the *zuccotto* into wedges.

Chef's Notes

The *pan di Spagna* is frozen before slicing because the fresh cake can fall apart easily.

The cream for the chocolate filling is not beaten over ice, as is usual, because if the cream is too cold when the chocolate is folded into it, the chocolate will seize in the cold cream and make the filling grainy. Make sure all the ingredients are at room temperature when you prepare the chocolate filling.

Chapter 20

Meringues, Mousses, and Confections:
Meringhe, Budini, e Torrone

Meringhe (Meringues)
Panna Cotta al Limone (Lemon *Panna Cotta*)
Dolci al Cioccolato (Warm Chocolate Cakes)
Budino di Cioccolato (Dark-Chocolate Mousse)
Torrone (Nougat)
Torrone al Cioccolato (Hazelnut-Chocolate Confection)
Semifreddo con Cioccolato, Mandorle, e Nocciole
    (*Semifreddo* with Nuts and Chocolate)

This chapter addresses a category of Italian sweets based on *meringa* (meringue) and *budini* (mousses). A meringue can stand alone as a crisp, dry, biscuitlike dessert (see *Meringhe* on page 308). Or it may be incorporated into a variety of hot and cold desserts as a distinct element, as it is in the *Budino di Cioccolato* on page 310, the *Dolci al Cioccolato* on page 309, or the almond-and-hazlenut-flavored *Semifreddo* on page 314. Meringue is also responsible for the light, crisp texture of *Biscotti alle Mandorle con Pinoli* (page 291), and when sweetened and stabilized with a cooked sugar, it forms the base of the Italian confection *Torrone* (page 312).

Mousses are made from a flavored base (fruit purées, egg yolks that have been poached by beating in hot syrup, and dark or white chocolate, to name a few) that is lightened with beaten egg whites and/or whipped cream, then chilled or frozen. The light-textured *Budino di Cioccolato*, the *Semifreddo* on page 314, and the *Panna Cotta* on page 308 are all examples of mousses with quite different characters, based on different procedures.

Le Tecniche

In this chapter, students learn the fundamentals of meringues (including the distinction between French, Italian, and Swiss meringues), mousses, and cooked sugars. See pages 490–93 for an in-depth discussion of meringues and mousses.

Dolci al Cioccolato (page 309)

Meringhe

Meringues

Makes 24

Crisp, light meringue cookies (*spumini,* in Emilia-Romagna) are made with Swiss meringue, piped into the desired shape and baked slowly at a very low temperature until the meringue dries. These cookies would normally be made as a way to use up the egg whites left over when yolks are needed for some other preparation. They are especially popular in Piemonte, where they are used as "sandwiches" and filled with whipped or flavored creams.

Chef's Notes

The circulating air in a convection oven works particularly well for baking meringues.

This recipe may also be used to create a layered dessert called *meringata*, filled with a *semifreddo* mixture (page 314). The meringue is piped out into two rounds the size of the desired ring mold. The disks are baked and cooled. One meringue round is fitted into the ring mold on a baking sheet. The mold is filled with *semifreddo* mixture and topped with the second meringue disk. The pastry is frozen as usual.

Ingredients

4 large egg whites
200 grams (1 cup) granulated sugar

Preheat a convection oven to 79°C (175°F), or a standard oven to 93°C (200°F). Line a sheet pan with parchment paper.

In a clean, empty bowl, whisk the egg whites with the sugar to combine. Place the bowl over a pan of simmering water and continue to whisk until the sugar dissolves and the egg whites are hot (about 54°C / 130°F). Continue whisking until the meringue is smooth and shiny.

Spoon the meringue into a pastry bag fitted with the desired tip, and pipe the meringue in a side-to-side, figure-eight motion, or a spiral, to produce "fingers" that are 4 centimeters (1½ inches) wide and 9 centimeters (3½ inches) long.

Bake (*cuocere in forno*) the meringues (on low fan, for convection) until they are completely dry, about 1 hour in a convection oven, or 1½ hours in a standard oven. Check the meringues after 1 hour. The time required will vary depending on the oven. Cool on a wire rack.

Panna Cotta al Limone

Lemon *Panna Cotta*

Serves 4

This traditional Italian dessert translates literally as "cooked cream," although the mixture is not, in fact, cooked. Rather, warm sweetened milk is infused with lemon zest and set with gelatin; once the gelatin begins to set, whipped cream is folded into the mixture. The mixture is poured into molds and refrigerated. *Panna cotta* may be served in the mold, but it is stable enough to be unmolded.

At The International Culinary Center, 125-milliliter (4-ounce) aluminum molds are used for the *panna cotta* and the desserts are unmolded before service. The molds have the virtue of being disposable, so holes can be poked gently through the aluminum to help release the pressure—the *panna cotta* will slip right out. But any attractive serving piece may be used: a shallow bowl, for example, or individual glasses, a soufflé mold, or martini glasses.

Ingredients

200 milliliters (¾ cup plus 2 tablespoons) whole milk
Zest of ¾ lemon, peeled off in strips (leaving behind as much
   of the white pith as possible)
50 grams (¼ cup) granulated sugar
1½ gelatin sheets, soaked in cold water to cover until softened,
   or 4½ grams (1 teaspoon) unflavored powdered gelatin
225 milliliters (1 scant cup) heavy cream

Bring the milk, lemon zest, and sugar to a simmer in a saucepan (*casseruola*), whisking to dissolve the sugar. Turn off the heat, cover, and let infuse for 20 minutes.

If using gelatin sheets, squeeze the excess water from the sheets and add the gelatin to the pan. If using powdered gelatin, sprinkle it evenly into the pan so it does not clump. Whisk until smooth.

Pass the mixture through a fine-mesh strainer (*colino*) and let chill in an ice bath until the mixture has begun to set to the consistency of yogurt, solid but still loose, about 10 minutes. (Do not allow it to set so that it stiffens completely or it will be difficult to fold in the whipped cream.)

Meanwhile, in another bowl set over ice, beat the heavy cream to soft peaks.

Check the consistency of the lemon mixture by giving it a stir with a rubber spatula; it will be lumpy. When the texture is yogurtlike, whisk the lemon mixture, still over ice, until smooth. Fold in the whipped cream in two batches. Transfer to four 125-milliliter (4-ounce) molds and refrigerate until set.

If unmolding, dip the bottoms of the molds into hot water very briefly to loosen the *panna cotta*, then run a slender knife around the edges to loosen. Invert onto serving plates, or just serve in the molds.

Dolci al Cioccolato

Warm Chocolate Cakes

Serves 4

These individual flourless chocolate confections are as much soufflés as they are cakes, incorporating a French meringue in a chocolate–egg yolk base. During baking, the meringue expands and the water in the mixture turns to steam, causing the cake to rise. The cakes are served warm, their centers still slightly liquid, in a pool of chilled, coffee-flavored custard cream sauce.

The cakes can be baked in 125-milliliter (4-ounce) individual soufflé molds, in fluted molds, or, as we do at The International Culinary Center, in aluminum cups.

(For step-by-step instructions for making the cream sauce, see *"Crema Inglese"* on page 482.)

Ingredients

For the espresso custard cream sauce:
350 milliliters (1½ cups) whole milk
350 milliliters (1½ cups) heavy cream
75 grams (1 cup) espresso beans, crushed
6 large egg yolks
155 grams (¾ cup) granulated sugar

For the cakes:
125 grams (4½ ounces) bittersweet chocolate, finely chopped (about ⅔ cup)
100 grams (7 tablespoons) unsalted butter, plus extra for the molds
50 grams (¼ cup) granulated sugar, plus extra for the molds
4 large egg yolks
2 large egg whites
Confectioners' sugar, for dusting

Make the espresso custard cream sauce:

In a saucepan (*casseruola*), combine the milk, cream, and crushed espresso beans and bring to a boil. Remove the pan from the heat and let infuse 20 minutes.

Return the pan to the heat and bring to a simmer.

In a bowl, beat the yolks and sugar until pale and lightened.

Temper the egg mixture with one-third of the hot espresso cream. Add the rest of the espresso cream mixture and whisk to combine.

Return the mixture to the saucepan and cook until the custard cream coats the back of a spoon and leaves a track when the spoon is run through it.

Pass the custard cream through a fine-mesh strainer (*passasalsa*) and cool in an ice bath.

Make the cakes:

Butter four 10-centimeter (4-inch) molds and line the bottoms and sides with granulated sugar.

In the top of a double boiler or in a bowl set over simmering water, melt the chocolate with the butter.

In a bowl, beat 25 grams (2 tablespoons) of the sugar with the yolks, reserving half of the sugar for the whites.

Gradually beat the warm chocolate mixture into the egg-yolk mixture; set aside.

In a separate bowl, prepare the meringue: Whip the egg whites to a soft peak. Gradually add the reserved sugar. Beat until stiff, smooth, and shiny.

Fold the meringue into the chocolate mixture and refrigerate until very cold.

Fill the prepared molds halfway with the chilled mixture. Chill at least 30 minutes.

Preheat the oven to 191°C (375°F) and place a rack in the center. Bake (*cuocere in forno*) the cakes on a sheet pan until the tops of the cakes crack, 7 to 8 minutes; the cakes will still seem moist and runny inside.

Remove from the oven and let stand 30 seconds, until the cakes begin to pull away from the sides of the molds.

Run a knife around the edges and unmold; dust with confectioners' sugar and serve hot, topped with the chilled espresso cream.

Budino di Cioccolato

Dark-Chocolate Mousse

Serves 4

This simple chocolate dessert is lightened by means of whipped cream and a French meringue. The usual technique for whipping cream is to beat it over ice (see sidebar "*Panna Montata*" on page 284). In this case, however, it is important not to; if the cream is too cold when folded into the warm chocolate mixture, the chocolate will seize in bits and the smooth texture of the dessert will be compromised.

Ingredients

150 grams (5 ounces) bittersweet chocolate, finely chopped (1 cup)
400 milliliters (1¾ cups) heavy cream
3 large egg whites, preferably pasteurized, at room temperature
30 grams (3 tablespoons) granulated sugar

With concerns about raw eggs and salmonella, the dark-chocolate mousse may be prepared by incorporating some Italian meringue in place of the raw egg white and sugar mixture; keep in mind that this will result in a sweeter dessert. Otherwise, pasteurized eggs may be used.

Place the chocolate in a bowl. Set the bowl over a saucepan (*casseruola*) of simmering water. Stir the chocolate gently with a spatula or a wooden spoon until it is completely melted. Turn off the heat and leave the bowl over the hot water to keep the chocolate warm.

In a bowl (not over ice), beat the cream until it forms soft peaks. Set aside at room temperature.

In another bowl, whip the whites. When soft peaks form, add the sugar gradually until the whites form firm peaks. Be careful not to overbeat the whites; they should be smooth and shiny, not stiff or dry.

Remove the bowl of chocolate from the saucepan and, using a whisk, fold in the egg whites in two batches. Be certain to scrape the bottom of the bowl.

When the whites are almost completely incorporated, fold in the whipped cream.

Cover the mousse and refrigerate approximately 1 hour, or until set.

Torrone

Nougat

Makes 25 to 40 squares or bars,
depending on size

The Italian version of the heavenly, nut-studded candy *torrone* (or its diminutive, *torroncino*) is an ancient sweet that dates back to Imperial Rome. Though it is available year-round in Italy, it remains a classic delicacy for the winter holidays.

The basic recipe of cooked egg white, sugar and/or honey, and nuts may be cooked to a range of textures, from silky soft and chewy to more brittle. It is embellished with a variety of extracts, spices, and liqueurs, depending on region. In Abruzzo, for example, the nougat may be softened with the addition of chocolate; in Sicilia, *torrone* is adorned with candied fruit, pistachios, and sesame seeds; in Campania, with the liqueur *Strega*; in Piemonte, with hazelnuts.

This recipe is made with pistachios, almonds, walnuts, and hazelnuts. Once toasted, it is important to keep the nuts warm before they are added to the *torrone*; if they are too cool, the egg white mixture will harden too quickly.

Torrone is traditionally formed into a single large block, from which smaller chunks are cut. It may also be cut into single-serving squares or bars, as it is here.

(See sidebar "Skinning Hazelnuts" on page 315 for instructions on toasting and skinning hazelnuts.)

Ingredients

40 grams (⅓ cup) shelled pistachios
160 grams (1 cup) walnuts
280 grams (2 cups) whole almonds, blanched
160 grams (1¼ cups) hazelnuts, skinned
240 milliliters (1 scant cup) corn syrup
280 milliliters (1¼ cups) honey
600 grams (3 cups) granulated sugar
2 large egg whites, at room temperature
Cornstarch, for dusting (optional)

Preheat the oven to 177°C (350°F). Toast the pistachios, walnuts, almonds, and hazelnuts on a sheet pan until fragrant, 5 to 7 minutes. Set aside in a warm place.

Combine 40 milliliters (2½ tablespoons) of the corn syrup and the honey in a saucepan (*casseruola*). Place over medium-high heat.

At the same time, combine the remaining 200 milliliters (¾ cup plus 2 tablespoons) corn syrup and the sugar in another saucepan and place over medium-high heat.

Chef's Notes

The varieties and proportions of the nuts in the recipe may be changed, but the total amount should remain the same.

Candied or dried fruit may be substituted for some of the nuts. Exotic honeys may be used to add interesting flavors.

Try to roll out the *torrone* while it is still warm, or it will become too stiff to work with.

The texture of the *torrone* depends on the degree to which the sugar is cooked. If the *torrone* is too hard once cooled, the sugar mixture was cooked to too high a temperature; if it is too soft, the sugar mixture was not cooked to a high enough temperature.

Put the egg whites in a standing mixer fitted with the whisk attachment.

When the honey mixture comes to a boil, begin beating the egg whites.

When the honey mixture reaches 130°C (266°F) on a candy thermometer, and the egg whites have reached soft peaks, with the mixer running, gradually pour the honey mixture into the egg whites; continue beating.

When the sugar mixture reaches 139°C (282°F) on a candy thermometer, with the mixer running, gradually pour the sugar mixture into the egg whites; continue beating.

When the meringue begins to stiffen, switch to the paddle attachment, add the nuts, and beat at low speed to combine.

Place a silicone mat on the work surface, or line a sheet pan with parchment paper and sprinkle with cornstarch (cornstarch keeps the candy from sticking to the paper). Scrape the *torrone* mixture onto the prepared mat or sheet pan and press with wet hands, or hands dusted with cornstarch, to a thickness of about 1½ centimeters (a little more than ½ inch). Or, pour the warm mixture into a loaf pan coated with nonstick spray. Allow the *torrone* to cool completely, then cut into squares or bars.

Torrone al Cioccolato

Hazelnut-Chocolate Confection

Makes one 43-by-30½-centimeter
(17-by-12-inch) pan

This is an entirely different version of *torrone*, made with chocolate, hazelnuts (both finely ground and whole), and the hazelnut-chocolate spread Nutella.

Like the *torrone* on the facing page, this candy would be served as a *piccola pasticceria* (small sweet pastry), in combination with other candies and cookies.

(See sidebar "Skinning Hazelnuts" on page 315 for instructions on toasting and skinning hazelnuts.)

Ingredients

500 grams (6⅓ cups) hazelnuts, skinned and finely ground
50 grams (¼ cup plus 1 tablespoon) confectioners' sugar
150 grams (⅔ cup) dark cocoa powder
300 grams (11 ounces) bittersweet chocolate, chopped
   (2½ cups)
200 grams (¾ cup) Nutella
1 teaspoon pure vanilla extract
500 grams (4¼ cups) hazelnuts, skinned and crushed with a
   rolling pin

Line a 43-by-30½-centimeter (17-by-12-inch) sheet pan with parchment paper; set aside. In a bowl, combine the finely ground hazelnuts and the confectioners' sugar.

In a double boiler over simmering water, melt the cocoa powder with the chocolate and heat to 40° to 45°C (104° to 113°F). Stir into the hazelnut–confectioners' sugar mixture.

Stir in the Nutella and vanilla.

Mix in the crushed hazelnuts.

Pour the mixture onto the prepared sheet pan, about 2½ centimeters (1 inch) thick. Refrigerate overnight.

To serve, cut the *torrone* into rectangles, or break into chunks.

Semifreddo con Cioccolato, Mandorle, e Nocciole

Semifreddo with Nuts and Chocolate

Serves 4 to 6

A *semifreddo* is a dessert based on a mousselike mixture of beaten egg yolk and sugar, whipped cream, and beaten egg white, frozen in a mold. The texture is similar to gelato, but airier and less dense. The whipped cream prevents the dessert from freezing completely, which gives the preparation its name, which means "half-cold." This version is flavored with Amaretto, chopped chocolate, and *granella* (an almond-and-hazelnut brittle).

In this recipe the mixture is unmolded and sliced for service, but *semifreddo* may also be served from the mold.

(See sidebar "Skinning Hazelnuts" on facing page for instructions on toasting and skinning hazelnuts.)

Chef's Note

Granella may also be broken into pieces and served as a candy, or as a garnish for other desserts.

Skinning Hazelnuts

Most recipes that use hazelnuts call for skinning them because the skin is bitter. To skin hazelnuts, preheat the oven to 177°C (350°F). Spread the hazelnuts on a sheet pan and toast until the skins are lightly browned and blistered, 10 to 15 minutes. Wrap the nuts in a kitchen towel and rub to remove as much of the skins as possible (some bits of skin will remain). Let cool.

Cooked Sugar

Italian cuisine uses sugar syrups made by heating sugar with a liquid for a variety of preparations. Some are thin syrups, boiled briefly to dissolve the sugar. Others are "cooked sugars" that are cooked beyond the boiling point in order to evaporate the water. A sugar syrup cooked to the caramel stage forms the basis of the *granella* in this recipe.

The key to making a sugar syrup is to keep the sides of the saucepan clean while cooking the syrup so that crystals do not form on the side of the pan. If crystals come in contact with the syrup, they will make it grainy. To prevent the formation of crystals, use a clean pastry brush dipped in cold water to clean the sides of the pan throughout the cooking process. The water in the brush will dissolve any sugar crystals that have formed and push the liquid down into the pan.

Ingredients

For the granella:

150 grams (¾ cup) granulated sugar
70 grams (½ cup) skinned almonds
70 grams (½ cup) skinned hazelnuts

For the semifreddo:

6 large egg yolks
70 grams (⅓ cup) granulated sugar
500 milliliters (2 cups) heavy cream
75 grams (2¾ ounces) bittersweet or semisweet chocolate, chopped (½ cup)
15 milliliters (1 tablespoon) Amaretto liqueur
180 grams (¾ cup) granella, plus extra for lining the mold (from above)
4 large egg whites
Coarse salt

Make the *granella*:

Line a sheet pan with a silicone mat or parchment paper.

Place a clean, dry saucepan (*casseruola*) over medium heat until the pan is hot. Add the sugar and let it cook, without stirring, until melted. Swirl the pan if the sugar melts unevenly.

Continue cooking, swirling as needed to maintain an even color, until the sugar caramelizes to a mahogany color.

Add the nuts and stir. Immediately pour the mixture out onto the prepared sheet pan. Let cool. Chop the *granella* until it is fine but still has texture; it should not turn into a powder. (This can also be achieved by pulsing in a food processor.) Measure 180 grams (¾ cup) of the *granella* for the *semifreddo* mixture; reserve the remainder to line the mold.

Make the *semifreddo*:

Line a 1-liter (1-quart) loaf pan or terrine mold with plastic wrap, so that the plastic hangs over the sides of the mold. Sprinkle about 30 grams (2 tablespoons) of the reserved *granella* over the bottom of the mold; set aside.

In a bowl, whisk the egg yolks with the sugar until the mixture is pale-colored and thickened almost to the consistency of a marshmallow interior, and holds a ribbon when the whisk is lifted from the bowl.

In another bowl set over ice, beat the cream to stiff peaks.

Fold the whipped cream, chopped chocolate, Amaretto, and the 180 grams (¾ cup) of *granella* into the beaten yolks.

Beat the egg whites with a pinch of salt until stiff but not dry. Fold into the egg-yolk base.

Pour the *semifreddo* mixture into the prepared mold and cover with the overhanging plastic wrap so that the plastic is in direct contact with the surface. Wrap the entire mold tightly in plastic so it does not absorb other flavors in the freezer. Freeze overnight.

To serve:

Dip the bottom of the mold in hot water to loosen the *semifreddo* from the mold. Invert the *semifreddo* onto a platter to unmold; remove the plastic wrap. The *granella* will now be on the top. Cut into slices and serve.

Chapter 21

Frozen Desserts:
Gelati, Sorbetti, e Granite

Italians have long been recognized for their supremacy in the realm of frozen desserts. Arabs brought what came to be known as *sorbetto* to Sicilia (the word is derived from the Arabic word *shariba*, meaning "cool drink"), but gelato is said to have been created by the court architect and artist Bernardo Buontalenti for the court of Francesco de' Medici in 1565. One hundred years later, frozen desserts appear to have been commonplace, at least in certain areas of Italy. According to historians Capatti and Montanari in their book *Italian Cuisine: A Cultural History*, "When Antonio Latini, a native of the Marches, took up service at the court of Naples in 1659, he had the impression 'that everyone [in the city] was born with a special skill and instinct for making sorbets.'" The first book devoted entirely to frozen desserts, called *De' Sorbetti*, written by Filippo Baldini, was published in Naples in 1775. It discusses *sorbetti*, as well as "milky sorbets," meaning ice creams.

This chapter addresses three types of frozen desserts: gelato, *sorbetto*, and granita.

Gelato, the past participle of *gelare*, which means "to freeze," is a dense style of ice cream based on a stirred custard made with cream and/or eggs and milk.

Sorbetto, which contains no dairy, is produced solely with sugar, water, and a flavoring—often, but by no means exclusively, a fruit.

Granita is a slushy, grainy-textured ice with a low sugar content. (The word is derived from *grana*, which means "grainy.")

Gelati, sorbetti, and *granite* may be flavored with seasonal fresh fruits and nuts, essences including coffee and chocolate, or dessert or fortified wines such as Vin Santo or Marsala, the lemon liqueur limoncello, or even grappa. Like gelato, *sorbetto* is made in an ice cream machine. To create its characteristic grainy texture, granita is frozen in shallow pans without churning, stirred every now and then to break up the ice crystals as they form.

Gelato desserts in Italy are often served at *gelateria* bars where the gelato is combined with syrups, sauces, and whipped cream. Each region of Italy has its own interpretation and ingredients.

Gelato di Crema (page 319),
Gelato di Cioccolato (page 320),
and *Gelato al Caramello* (page 319)

Affogato is a scoop of gelato served in a tall glass and topped with brandy, grappa, or espresso.

Frappés are concoctions of gelato blended with milk, fruit, or espresso.

Gelato is also served garnished with *macedonia* (fresh fruit salad) and topped with more gelato and *panna montata* (whipped cream).

Or, like ice cream, gelato can also be ordered simply in a cup (*coppa*) or a cone (*cono*).

Sorbetti are extremely light and refreshing. Made with varying levels of sweetness, they are served as desserts, or as palate cleansers in Italian restaurants (usually halfway through the meal to separate the fish and meat courses). A *sorbetto* anesthetizes the mouth in time for the arrival of the red wine.

Today, Italy has approximately 20,000 *gelaterie*, an astonishing number given that the country is roughly the size of Arizona. Italy's best *gelati* are made in the artisanal manner, "*prodotti artigianali*"; their commercial counterparts, *gelati industriale*, are produced with more fat and stabilizers to maintain their molecular structure.

The best *gelaterie* often display a sign, *Produzione Propria*, *Nostra Produzione*, or *Produzione Artigianale*— all indicating that their gelato is homemade. But only a small percentage of *gelaterie* still make their gelato from scratch on their own premises. Although they maintain a commitment to churning their gelato on-site daily, most shops buy pastes and flavorings. Making gelato from scratch is a dying art in part because it is so laborious, but also because the industrial companies that make flavorings do a good job of it, ensuring a more than acceptable final product. This makes it an easy business decision *not* to produce from scratch.

Americans are becoming ever more interested in premium ice cream and *gelati*, and Italy now estimates that the size of the gelato market in the United States will one day surpass its own.

Le Tecniche

In this chapter, students learn the fundamentals of making gelato, *sorbetto*, and granita, in several different traditional flavors. See pages 494–95 for an in-depth discussion of each.

Flavoring Gelato

Gelati may be flavored with any number of different ingredients and flavorings. An infusion is made by heating the milk, adding the flavoring element, and letting the mixture steep off the heat for as long as possible—overnight in the refrigerator is best. The milk-cream mixture is strained, and the *crema inglese* is made as usual. Some common flavorings for *gelati* include:

Finely grated zest of oranges, lemons, or tangerines added to the infusion

Cinnamon sticks or ground cinnamon added to the infusion

Coffee or roasted espresso beans added to the infusion

Almonds, hazelnuts, or other nuts, toasted, ground, or grated, added to the infusion and strained out after steeping

Melted bittersweet chocolate added to the warm *crema inglese* mixture

Liqueurs, generally added when the custard is finished and cool

Toasted coconut added to the infusion

Poached and puréed dried fruits added to the warm finished custard

Praline paste added to the finished mixture

Gelato di Crema

Vanilla Ice Cream

Makes about 1½ liters (3 pints)

Ingredients

500 milliliters (2 cups) whole milk
500 milliliters (2 cups) heavy cream
225 grams (1 cup plus 2 tablespoons) granulated sugar
Pinch of coarse salt
1 vanilla bean, split and scraped
6 large egg yolks

In a saucepan (*casseruola*), bring the milk, cream, 125 grams (½ cup plus 2 tablespoons) of the sugar, and the salt to a simmer with the vanilla bean and scraped seeds. Remove the pan from the heat, cover, and let infuse 20 minutes.

Meanwhile, whisk the yolks with the remaining sugar until lightened and pale-colored.

Whisking constantly, gradually pour half of the hot milk-cream mixture into the yolk-sugar mixture to temper the eggs. Add the tempered yolk-sugar mixture to the saucepan and stir to blend.

Return the pan to the stove and cook over medium heat, stirring with a wooden spoon in a figure-eight motion; be especially attentive to the bottom and edges of the pan, as egg will coagulate there first. The cream is done when it naps the back of the spoon and reaches 74°C (165°F), at which point it will become quite thick. Sterilize the custard by holding it at 79°C (175°F) for 1 minute. Do not let it boil; if the mixture reaches 82°C (180°F), it will curdle.

Pass the custard through a fine-mesh strainer (*passasalsa*) into a bowl set in an ice bath.

Chill completely, and process in an ice cream maker.

Gelato al Caramello

Caramel Ice Cream

Makes about 1½ liters (3 pints)

The sugar must be cooked to a deep mahogany color to ensure a strong caramel flavor. (See sidebar "Cooked Sugar" on page 315 for further discussion of cooking sugar and making caramel.)

Ingredients

225 grams (1 cup plus 2 tablespoons) granulated sugar
40 grams (2¼ tablespoons) unsalted butter
500 milliliters (2 cups) heavy cream
500 milliliters (2 cups) whole milk
½ vanilla bean, split and scraped
Pinch of coarse salt
6 large egg yolks

In a large stainless steel pot (*casseruola*), cook 150 grams (¾ cup) of the sugar over medium heat, without stirring, until it caramelizes to a mahogany color and starts to bubble. Remove the pot from the heat. Add the butter and swirl to combine. Add the cream, milk, vanilla bean and scraped seeds, and salt. Return the pot to the heat and bring to a boil, stirring with a wooden spoon.

In a bowl, combine the egg yolks with the remaining sugar and whisk until pale and thick.

Chef's Note

For all recipes in this chapter, there may be a small variation in yield depending on the ice cream maker. Machines incorporate different amounts of air into the mixtures during freezing.

Whisking constantly, gradually pour about half of the hot caramel mixture into the yolk-sugar mixture to temper the eggs. Add the tempered yolk-sugar mixture to the pot and stir to blend.

Return the pot to the stove and cook over medium heat, stirring with a wooden spoon in a figure-eight motion; be especially attentive to the bottom and edges of the pan, as egg will coagulate there first. The cream is done when it naps the back of a spoon and reaches 74°C (165°F), at which point it will become quite thick. Sterilize the custard by holding it at 79°C (175°F) for 1 minute. Do not let it boil; if the mixture reaches 82°C (180°F), it will curdle.

Pass the custard through a fine-mesh strainer (*passa-salsa*) into a bowl set in an ice bath.

Chill completely, and process in an ice cream maker.

Gelato di Cioccolato

Chocolate Ice Cream

Makes about 1½ liters (3 pints)

The percentage that is associated with chocolate refers to its total cocoa content (which can be in the form of cocoa powder, cocoa liqueur, ground cocoa nibs, or cocoa butter/fat), and indicates the balance of sweetness to intensity of flavor. The higher the percentage, the more intensely chocolate-flavored, and less sweet, the chocolate is. At The International Culinary Center we like to use a 60-percent chocolate for this recipe.

Ingredients

225 grams (8 ounces) bittersweet chocolate, finely chopped (1¾ cups)
500 milliliters (2 cups) whole milk
500 milliliters (2 cups) heavy cream
225 grams (1 cup plus 2 tablespoons) granulated sugar
Pinch of coarse salt
6 large egg yolks

Place the chocolate in a heatproof bowl; set aside.

In a saucepan (*casseruola*), combine the milk, cream, 125 grams (1 cup plus 2 tablespoons) of the sugar, and the salt. Bring to a simmer.

Meanwhile, whisk the yolks with the remaining sugar until lightened and pale-colored.

Whisking constantly, gradually pour half of the hot milk-cream mixture into the yolk-sugar mixture to temper the eggs. Add the tempered yolk-sugar mixture to the saucepan and stir to blend.

Return the pan to the stove and cook over medium heat, stirring with a wooden spoon in a figure-eight motion; be especially attentive to the bottom and edges of the pan, as egg will coagulate there first. The cream is done when it naps the back of the spoon and reaches 74°C (165°F), at which point it will become quite thick. Sterilize the custard by holding it at 79°C (175°F) for 1 minute. Do not let it boil; if the mixture reaches 82°C (180°F), it will curdle.

Pass the custard through a fine-mesh strainer (*passasalsa*) over the chopped chocolate in the heatproof bowl, and stir to melt the chocolate. Set the bowl over an ice bath.

Chill completely, and process in an ice cream maker.

Sorbetto di Lime

Lime Sorbet

Makes about 1½ liters (3 pints)

(See "Sugar Density" on page 495 for a discussion of the use of refractometers for making *sorbetti*.)

Ingredients

Finely grated zest of 4 limes
275 grams (1¼ cups plus 2 tablespoons) granulated sugar
75 grams (3 tablespoons) glucose syrup, such as Trimoline
250 milliliters (1 cup) lime juice (from 10 limes), strained of pulp
Pinch of coarse salt
Juice of 1 to 2 lemons, strained of pulp, if needed

Combine the grated lime zest, 1 liter (4¼ cups) water, the sugar, and the glucose syrup or paste in a saucepan (*casseruola*) and bring to a simmer. Simmer 2 to 3 minutes to infuse the syrup with the flavor of the zest.

Strain the mixture into a bowl and cool in an ice bath.

Add the lime juice and salt. (If using a refractometer, check the density and taste the mixture—the density of the finished mixture should range from 24° to 28° Brix.)

Adjust the acidity of the *sorbetto* base by adding some lemon juice, if necessary.

Chill completely, then process in an ice cream maker.

Sorbetto di Limone

Lemon Sorbet

Makes about 1½ liters (3 pints)

(See "Sugar Density" on page 495 for a discussion of the use of refractometers for making *sorbetti*.)

Ingredients

Finely grated zest of 4 lemons
275 grams (1¼ cups plus 2 tablespoons) granulated sugar
75 grams (3 tablespoons) glucose syrup, such as Trimoline
Pinch of coarse salt
Juice of 10 to 12 lemons, strained of pulp

Combine the lemon zest, 1 liter (4¼ cups) water, the sugar, and the trimoline or glucose in a saucepan (*casseruola*) and bring to a simmer. Simmer 2 to 3 minutes to infuse the syrup with the flavor of the zest.

Strain the mixture into a bowl and chill in an ice bath.

Add the salt and lemon juice. (If using a refractometer, check the density and taste the mixture—the density of the finished mixture should range from 24° to 28° Brix and the *sorbetto* base should be sufficiently acidic.)

Chill completely, then process in an ice cream maker.

Chef's Notes

For *sorbetti*, the amount of sugar syrup required will vary depending on the sweetness of the fruit itself, if using fresh fruit purée, or, for commercial purées, the quantity of sugar added, if any. Remember that the flavor will be muted—thus less sweet and less acidic—once frozen; beginning cooks will probably need to add more sugar and acid than expected.

In a professional kitchen, a device called a refractometer is used to measure sugar density. (See "Sugar Density" on page 495.)

Sorbetto di Fragola

Strawberry Sorbet

Makes about 2 liters (8½ cups)

(See "Sugar Density" on page 495 for a discussion of the use of refractometers for making *sorbetti*.)

Ingredients

300 grams (1½ cups) granulated sugar
50 grams (2 tablespoons) glucose syrup, such as Trimoline
600 grams (21 ounces / 2¾ cups) strawberry purée
Pinch of coarse salt
Lemon juice, strained of pulp

Combine the sugar, 250 milliliters (1 cup) water, and the glucose syrup in a saucepan (*casseruola*) and bring to a simmer. Chill in an ice bath.

Add the strawberry purée, salt, and lemon juice to taste and stir to blend. (If using a refractometer, check the density and taste the *sorbetto* mixture—the density should range from 24° to 28° Brix.)

Chill completely, then process in an ice cream maker.

Sorbetto di Mango

Mango Sorbet

Makes about 2 liters (8½ cups)

(See "Sugar Density" on page 495 for a discussion of the use of refractometers for making *sorbetti*.)

Ingredients

300 grams (1½ cups) granulated sugar
50 grams (2 tablespoons) glucose syrup, such as Trimoline
600 grams (21 ounces / 2¾ cups) mango purée
Pinch of coarse salt
Lemon juice, strained of pulp

Combine the sugar, 250 milliliters (1 cup) water, and the glucose syrup in a saucepan (*casseruola*) and bring to a simmer. Chill in an ice bath.

Add the mango purée, salt, and lemon juice to taste and stir to blend. (If using a refractometer, check the density and taste the *sorbetto* mixture—the density should range from 24° to 28° Brix.)

Chill completely, then process in an ice cream maker.

Granita di Pompelmo e Campari

Grapefruit-Campari Granita

Makes about 1 liter (1 quart)

Ingredients

200 grams (1 cup) granulated sugar
Finely grated zest of 2 grapefruits (about 2 tablespoons)
240 milliliters (1 scant cup) grapefruit juice, strained of pulp
Campari, for serving

Combine the sugar, 750 milliliters (3 cups) water, and half of the grapefruit zest in a saucepan (*casseruola*). Bring to a boil; immediately remove the pan from the heat.

Chill in an ice bath; strain.

Add the grapefruit juice and the remaining zest. (If using a refractometer, check the density, which should range from 13° to 17° Brix.)

Pour the mixture into a hotel pan or other shallow pan. Place in the freezer for 30 minutes. Using a large metal spoon, stir the frozen crystals from around the edges of the pan back into the liquid. Return to the freezer for 30 minutes. Stir as before, but as the mixture continues to freeze, scrape the spoon against the sides and bottom of the pan as well to loosen and break up frozen crystals.

Repeat this process every 30 minutes until the mixture is frozen and a bit creamy, about 3 hours.

Scoop into bowls, drizzle with Campari, and serve.

Granita di Limone

Lemon Granita

Makes about 1 liter (1 quart)

Ingredients

200 grams (1 cup) granulated sugar
Finely grated zest of 4 lemons
240 milliliters (1 scant cup) lemon juice, strained of pulp

Combine the sugar, 750 milliliters (3 cups) water, and half of the lemon zest in a saucepan (*casseruola*). Bring to a boil; immediately remove the pan from the heat.

Chill in an ice bath; strain.

Add the lemon juice and the remaining zest. (If using a refractometer, check the density, which should range from 13° to 17° Brix.)

Pour the mixture into a hotel pan or other shallow pan. Place in the freezer for 30 minutes. Using a large metal spoon, stir the frozen crystals from around the edges of the pan back into the liquid. Return to the freezer for 30 minutes. Stir as before, but as the mixture continues to freeze, scrape the spoon against the sides and bottom of the pan as well to loosen and break up frozen crystals.

Repeat this process every 30 minutes until the mixture is frozen and a bit creamy, about 3 hours.

Scoop into bowls and serve.

Granita al Caffe

Espresso Granita

Makes about 1 liter (1 quart)

Ingredients

½ teaspoon cocoa powder
100 grams (½ cup) coarsely ground espresso beans
200 grams (1 cup) granulated sugar

In a saucepan (*casseruola*), mix 1 liter (4¼ cups) water with the cocoa powder, and bring to a boil. Whisk in the espresso beans, remove from the heat, and let steep at least 15 minutes.

Strain out the espresso grounds with a coffee filter or clean cloth napkin, and dissolve the sugar into the espresso.

Cool in an ice bath.

Pour the mixture into a hotel pan or other shallow pan. Place in the freezer for 30 minutes. Using a large metal spoon, stir the frozen crystals from around the edges of the pan back into the liquid. Return to the freezer for 30 minutes. Stir as before, but as the mixture continues to freeze, scrape the spoon against the sides and bottom of the pan as well to loosen and break up frozen crystals.

Repeat this process every 30 minutes until the mixture is frozen and a bit creamy, about 3 hours.

Scoop into bowls and serve.

Part II

Lessons

Lesson 1

Introduction to the Professional Italian Kitchen

Whether one is working in the United States, Italy, or elsewhere, professional kitchens worldwide share a common language. It is the language of dress, organization, rigorous work habits, and hygiene. Before students can be schooled in Italian cuisine, it is critical for them to learn basic culinary terms and standards of food preparation, and to develop excellent kitchen protocol. In the professional kitchen, these principles and rules guarantee safety, hygiene, efficiency, ease of preparation, and unwavering standards of quality. Such disciplines are also useful in the home kitchen, where they can affect safety, efficiency, quality, and enjoyment of the work.

La Divisa (Chef's Regulation Dress Uniform)

The chef's uniform is standard attire throughout the world, designed to protect both the wearer and the food from harm. The complete, traditional uniform comprises a double-breasted white cotton jacket (*la giacca*) with long sleeves to protect against hot splashes and spills; a rectangular white neckerchief (*il fazzoletto*, or *la sciarpa*) tied around the neck to absorb perspiration; and black-and-white houndstooth pants (*i pantaloni*) with straight legs that limit the possibility of the pant legs getting caught on equipment. A white apron (*il grembiule*) is tied to the front to protect the chef's clothing; a dry, absorbent side towel (*l'asciugamano*, or *il torcione*) is always worn tucked into the apron strings to allow the chef to grasp hot dishes safely. Chefs wear a tall, white, pleated hat (*cappello da chef*) made of paper or cloth, and plain, closed-toe, black leather shoes to protect the feet against spills and falling knives.

In the more relaxed climate of recent years, some chefs who work in their own restaurant kitchens may be found in brightly colored pants and extravagantly embroidered jackets, as well as clogs or other utilitarian shoes. Chefs' uniforms are also being worn by home cooks, probably as much for their convenience as for the feeling of professionalism they impart. No matter how styles have changed, the entire *brigata* (brigade) in a large hotel kitchen anywhere in the world still wears the standard-issue uniform.

Organizational Structure: *La Brigata* (The Brigade)

The professional kitchen is a highly organized and efficient operation, in which each staff member knows his or her job and how it relates to the greater mission of serving high-quality food. Known as a brigade (*brigata*), this system was instituted in the vast kitchens of London's famed Savoy Hotel in the late nineteenth century by the esteemed French chef Auguste Escoffier (1847–1935). Escoffier is thought to have invented the classic concept of the kitchen brigade in an effort to streamline what he saw as the "grand confusion" in the menus and private kitchens of the French aristocracy. Escoffier's ideas were so successful that a version of his brigade system, and the uniform associated with it, is still used in many large restaurant and hotel kitchens around the world.

The classic kitchen brigade—strictly hierarchical, and designed to ensure efficiency, quality, and consistency—consists of a team of cooks and their assistants, who are divided into stations. The entire brigade is directed by the *capocuoco*, or head chef, whose job is to orchestrate the overall production of the food and ensure the efficiency of the kitchen stations. The *capocuoco* is assisted by the *sotto-capocuoco*, or sous chef, who works with individual station leaders called *caposettore*, or station chefs. Each *caposettore* is aided by assistants or apprentices.

The scope of the *brigata* in an Italian restaurant kitchen varies with the size of the kitchen and the requirements of the restaurant. A hotel kitchen, for example, requires a complex hierarchy with many specific stations and specialized tasks, while a smaller kitchen may manage with just the *capocuoco*, who covers many stations, and a *lavapiatti* (dishwasher). Many of the original French titles are still in use in Italian kitchens, and may be used interchangeably with their Italian counterparts.

In the years since Escoffier, the brigade system has been simplified and refined to reflect the demands of today's restaurant industry. Many of the positions and tasks have remained the same, but the brigade is modified and/or condensed as needed to accommodate the complexity or simplicity of the menu and the size of the staff. (Employees may cover multiple positions, for example.) The Italian kitchen has specific requirements as well, usually including a pasta station, which is separate from the *entremetier*. The pasta station may also be responsible for risotto preparations.

In its most classic structure, *la brigata* would consist of:

Capocuoco or *chef* (chef): An administrator whose responsibilities include all aspects of food production, including menu planning, costing, and training and scheduling of staff. The *capocuoco* is also responsible for maintaining communication with the department heads throughout the establishment.

Sotto-capocuoco, or *sotto-chef* (sous chef): The assistant under the *capocuoco*, traditionally charged with directly supervising production and production staff. In classic French kitchens, the sous chef also serves as the expediter and, as such, is responsible for receiving orders from the dining room and relaying them to the various station cooks. The expediter is also charged with calling orders to make sure they are assembled and plated on time, and inspecting each plate before it is served.

Caposettore or *chef di partita* (station chef): In charge of a specific station, with one or more assistants or apprentices, during preparation and service.

Specific stations may be:

Cuoco del pesce or *poissonnier* (fish chef): Responsible for the cleaning and preparation of all fish, along with their sauces and garnishes.

Salsiere or *saucier* (sauce chef): Responsible for the preparation of all stocks, sauces, stews, and hot hors d'oeuvres. The *salsiere* is also responsible for preparing sautéed items to order. (In a small kitchen, the *salsiere* and *cuoco pesce* may be the same person.)

Rosticciere or *rôtisseur* (meat chef): Responsible for all roasted, broiled, grilled, and braised meat preparations, jus, and related sauces.

Garde-manger (pantry chef): Responsible for preparing cold dishes (including salads and dressings, cold hors d'oeuvres, terrines, pâtés, galantines, and cold sauces). This position is extremely important in a large hotel kitchen that is responsible for large catered events, cocktail parties, and room service. In such cases, this station may have up to twenty-five people working in it.

Entremetier (side-dish chef): Responsible for all soups, as well as vegetable, starch, and egg dishes. Larger kitchens may divide this function between a soup cook (*potager*) and a vegetable cook.

Pasticciere or *pâtissier* (pastry chef): Responsible for producing all desserts and pastries. The *pasticciere* also supervises the bread baker.

Setting Up the *Piano di Lavoro / Postazione* (Work Area)

The professional kitchen workstation is a universal setup that never changes. It can carry over nicely to the home kitchen, as working in this systematic fashion reinforces good organizational skills. The *piano di lavoro*, or *postazione* (work area), is a standard way to arrange one's tools, food, and cutting board in order to work most efficiently and cleanly.

The *piano di lavoro* consists of an immaculate cutting board placed on one of the following to prevent slippage: a damp cloth towel, a cutting-board liner, or a damp paper towel. The *piano di lavoro* is arranged for fluid, efficient movement. If the cook is right-handed, knives and other necessary equipment are arranged to the right of the board. For those who are left-handed, materials are placed to the left. Work bowls to hold ready-to-prepare fruits or vegetables, dry goods, or other products are placed above the board. Each workstation should also include a bowl for a sanitation solution.

The *piano di lavoro* is where the cook prepares his or her *mise en place* for each dish. This French term, also used in Italian kitchens, means "put in place," and is used to describe the preparation and assembly of ingredients for cooking.

Principles for a Healthy Environment

Before any work can begin in a professional or culinary-school kitchen, standards of cleanliness must be set. Excellent health and external cleanliness are prerequisites for the maintenance of a hygienic, disease-free environment. Not only is personal sanitation required, but all materials and equipment, as well as the work space itself, must also be antiseptic. To the novice, these rules may seem unnecessary or extreme; however, any variance from these principles can result in extremely serious, even disastrous, results to the health of others. Adherence to the following principles will help ensure that this does not occur:

○ General daily hygiene must be practiced; bathing, shaving, and tooth brushing are mandatory.

○ Hands must be washed upon entering the kitchen and after touching raw ingredients, telephones, money, soiled linens, meat, chicken, fish, eggs in or out of the shell, fresh produce, and soiled equipment or utensils, as well as after using chemicals or cleaners; after picking up anything from the floor; after performing personal actions such as using the lavatory, coughing, sneezing, smoking, eating, or drinking; or at any time necessary when working to ensure that the hands are always immaculate.

○ Hair must be clean, well groomed, and covered with an immaculate hat to keep it out of food and machinery. If long, it should be restrained. Male students must be clean shaven and well groomed, or wear a beard guard.

○ Nails should be trimmed, clean, short, and polish-free. False nails are not allowed.

○ All jewelry should be removed before entering the kitchen to avoid mishap through loss or entanglement with utensils or machinery.

○ Perfumes, colognes, and aftershave lotions are not permitted.

○ The health department mandates that proper hand-washing techniques include generously soaping; vigorously rubbing for at least 20 seconds to cover the backs of the hands, the wrists, between the fingers, and under the nails; and rinsing under warm (38°C / 100°F) running water. Dry with a paper towel and use the towel to turn off the water and open any doors necessary to exit the washroom. Hand sanitizer is not FDA-approved and should never be used in place of hand washing.

○ Do not enter the kitchen if you have a skin or respiratory infection, intestinal problem, or rash of unknown origin, as these may cause the spread of disease.

○ Avoid direct hand/skin contact with products that spoil easily, including sauces and stocks, meats, egg-based products, cream, and ice cream. Do not use fingers for tasting; use a clean, unused spoon for this purpose.

○ In a school or professional environment, clean uniforms should be regularly issued and impeccably maintained. In a home kitchen, clothes should be clean and covered with a clean apron or smock. Street clothes should never be worn during food preparation.

○ Wear inexpensive and easily disposable rubber gloves when working with potentially hazardous foods: products that spoil easily or are known to readily transmit bacteria. These might include chicken, shellfish, sauces, eggs, stocks, meats, cream, and ice cream. Gloves should be worn over clean hands.

- Never use a kitchen towel, wipe cloth, or side towel to wipe your face, dry your hands, or for any other non-food-related purpose.

- Never smoke, drink alcoholic beverages, or use controlled substances in any kitchen. In the classroom kitchen as well as in restaurants, drinks and personal foods are not allowed at your workstation.

- Cover your face with an easily disposable paper towel or tissue when you sneeze or cough and discard it immediately. Wash your hands immediately. If the cough or sneeze seems to be an indication of the onset of an upper-respiratory infection, ask to be excused from kitchen duties.

- Never sit on worktables or preparation areas.

- In the event of an accidental cut or burn, make immediate use of a first-aid kit or, if necessary, call for emergency assistance.

Principles of Sanitation

Preventing foodborne illness is the moral obligation of every food professional and is essential to the success of any food-related business. State and local boards of health set rigid standards for food-service establishments, offer mandatory safety courses for food professionals, and routinely inspect all types of food establishments to ensure that their standards are upheld; however, it ultimately remains the responsibility of the establishment to impose the most rigorous standards in the working environment. In the home kitchen, it remains the responsibility of the main cook to create impeccably clean conditions.

There are numerous principles that must be observed in the purchase, storage, preparation, and service of food to prevent contamination from the three most common sources: biological, chemical, and physical.

Biological Contamination

Bacteria, the primary biological contaminants, are the cause of most foodborne illnesses. However, it is interesting to note that some bacteria are beneficial (such as those needed to produce some cheeses and cultured milk products, beer, and wine), and it is currently thought that most bacteria are benign or neutral. But those that are harmful can be deadly.

Bacteria are microscopic one-celled organisms that are present everywhere and on everyone. They multiply by splitting in two, and under ideal circumstances, one single cell can multiply into 281 billion cells in three days.

Undesirable bacteria that can cause spoilage in food can usually be identified by the presence of odor(s), a sticky or slimy surface, discoloration, or mold. Those bacteria that are also disease agents are known as pathogens. Pathogens may not be detectable through odor, taste, or appearance, and this makes them particularly insidious. They are the greatest concern in all kitchens. To lessen the risk of contamination, all food must be purchased from reliable sources and then protected from bacterial infection by the practice of good hygiene along with sanitary handling and proper storage.

The main factors affecting bacterial growth are:

Food: Almost all foods can be used as a host for bacterial growth. High-protein foods such as eggs or dairy products are very active supporters of speedy bacterial expansion.

Acidity or alkalinity: Acidity and alkalinity are measured by a pH factor. The term pH stands for *pondus hydrogenii*, which means "potential hydrogen." It is a measure of the balance between acid and base. pH measures range from 1 (strongly acidic) to 14 (strongly alkaline), with pure water measuring 7 (neutral) on the pH scale. Almost all bacteria thrive in a neutral or mid-level pH environment; the ideal pH for bacterial growth is 4.6 to 7.5.

Time: All bacteria need time to adjust to their host environment before beginning to grow. For cooks, this allows a brief period to leave food safely at room temperature as preparation is commencing.

Temperature: Bacteria grow best in temperatures ranging from 5°C (41°F) to 57°C (135°F). This range is referred to as the food danger zone, as it is in this range of temperatures that bacteria find a favorable climate for growth.

Oxygen: Most bacteria are aerobic, which means that they need oxygen to grow. However, some of the deadliest bacteria, such as those that cause botulism, are anaerobic, or able to grow without access to air (for example, in canned foods or vacuum-packed foods).

Moisture: All bacteria require liquid to absorb nourishment; therefore, moist, damp foods such as cream-based salads make the perfect host.

PHF: This acronym stands for potentially hazardous foods. These are foods that particularly support the rapid growth of bacteria and include dairy products, animal products such as raw or undercooked meat, and raw seeds or sprouts. A partial list of PHF items includes undercooked bacon, cut cheeses, fresh shelled eggs, unrefrigerated fresh garlic in oil, meats, cheeses, sour cream, soy protein and soy products, as well as any sauces containing PHF ingredients.

There are two categories of disease caused by pathogens: intoxications and infections. Both are potentially life threatening.

Intoxications are the result of poisons or toxins that enter the system after they have been produced in food as a result of bacterial growth rather than from the bacteria themselves. Infections are caused by bacteria or other organisms that enter and attack the human body.

Bacteria have no means of locomotion; they must be carried from one place to another. Travel may be instigated through hands, coughs, sneezes, other foods, unsanitary equipment or utensils, or environmental factors such as air, water, insects, and rodents. Only sterilization will eliminate bacteria, so it is extremely important to understand the simple rules governing bacteria's growth and travel to help prevent bacterial contamination in the kitchen:

Rule 1: Keep bacteria from spreading. Do not touch anything that may contain disease-producing bacteria. Protect food from bacteria in the air by keeping it covered at all times.

Rule 2: Prevent bacterial growth. Keep all food at temperatures that are out of the food danger zone.

Rule 3: Kill bacteria. Heat food to a temperature of 75°C (165°F) or above for 30 seconds using any heat source. Equipment used for cooking should be washed with *hot* water and detergent, then rinsed and sanitized.

Chemical Contamination

Chemical poisoning is the result of defective or improperly maintained equipment that has been incorrectly used. Such poisons might include antimony from chipped gray enamelware, lead found in containers or soldering material, or cadmium found in plating elements. All of the toxins found in these materials can cause illness in humans. Other chemical contamination can result from commercial cleaning compounds, silver polish, and insecticides.

To prevent chemical contamination:

- All food must be stored separately from cleaning or other chemically based materials.

- All containers must be properly labeled and washed or otherwise cleaned.

- All equipment must be thoroughly rinsed in extremely hot water.

Physical Contamination

Physical contamination is the result of the adulteration of food by foreign objects such as broken glass, hair, metal shavings, paint chips, insects, stones, and so forth. If you stringently follow safety guidelines, physical contamination should not occur. However, if it does, all raw and prepared foods affected should be discarded immediately.

Safe Food Handling and Food Storage

Temperature

Temperature control is critical to safe food handling. Bacteria grow best in warm temperatures, that is, those between 5°C (41°F) and 57°C (135°F). In this temperature range, disease and germs flourish, and most bacteria, including those that cause milk to go sour, grow best. Pathogenic bacteria find their nourishment in the 21°C to 52°C (70°F to 125°F) range. Temperatures of 77 °C (170°F) or over will kill most non-spore-forming bacteria and all pathogenic organisms. Although low temperatures (0°C / 32°F) will not kill bacteria, they will hamper or slow down growth so food can be preserved through refrigeration or freezing.

When an exact temperature reading is required, a food thermometer should always be used. Never use the hands-on method to make this determination.

Storage

In a professional kitchen, all products should be dated and labeled before storage and stored in a manner that prevents contamination from exterior sources and from the growth of any bacteria already in the product. Once stored, all foodstuffs should be rotated according to FIFO—the first in, first out system. Following are the basic guidelines for safe storage:

Dry Storage

Dry food storage refers to those foods that support less bacterial growth because they are dried or canned. This includes flour, sugar, salt, leavening agents, cereals, grains, oil and shortening, and canned and bottled foods.

All dry containers should be closed tightly to protect from insect or rodent infestation, and to prevent contamination from dust or other airborne materials.

Dry food should be stored in a cool, dry place and raised off the floor, away from the wall and not under a sewage line.

Refrigerated Storage

○ Other than those foods listed for dry storage, all perishable foods should be refrigerated to protect them from contamination.

○ Refrigeration may be done with the use of a walk-in refrigerator, reach-in refrigerator, refrigerated show-case, refrigerated counter, or refrigerated table.

○ All refrigerators must be equipped with a calibrated thermometer.

○ The interior walls and shelves of the refrigerator should be kept immaculately clean.

○ All refrigerated foods should be properly labeled and wrapped or stored in suitable containers to avoid contamination.

○ Within the refrigerator, raw and cooked foods should be stored separately, and cooked foods should be stored above raw meat and fish.

○ Do not allow any unsanitary surface (such as the outside of a container) to touch any refrigerated food or food product.

○ Air must be able to circulate around all sides of refrigerated items; therefore, do not overcrowd a refrigerator. Keep all products off the refrigerator floor.

○ Ensure that refrigerator doors are tightly closed.

Freezer Storage

○ All food items to be frozen must be tightly wrapped in plastic film followed by aluminum foil, packaged freezer bags, or Cryovac packaging to prevent freezer burn.

○ All stored items should be labeled and dated.

○ Frozen products must be kept completely frozen at 0°F (32°F) or lower until ready to use.

○ All freezers must be equipped with an outside thermometer so that the freezer temperature can be read without opening the door or entering the holding box.

○ Frozen products must be stored to ensure cold-air circulation on all sides. This means that food should not be stored directly on the freezer floor.

○ Frozen products must be thawed under refrigeration or under cool, running water with a temperature not above 21°C (70°F). Never thaw foods at room temperature because, at some point, this method will place the thawing product in the danger zone.

Holding Food for Later Use

○ Bring food to holding temperatures as quickly as possible.

○ Food should be cooked and processed as close to the time of service as possible.

○ Prudent menu planning prevents excessive leftovers. Leftovers are not to be mixed with fresh food during storage.

○ Chilled food should be kept at 5°C (41°F) or below at all times.

○ When holding cold food, such as protein salads, over ice or in a refrigerated table for service, do not mound food above the level of the container, as this food would not be kept sufficiently chilled.

○ Food that is going to be served hot soon after cooking should not be allowed to drop below an internal temperature of 57°C (135°F).

○ Hot perishable foods should not be kept below 57°C (135°F). Rare roast beef is the only exception to this rule. It may be held at 49°C (120°F).

○ If food is not to be served immediately, it may be kept at a temperature in excess of 57°C (135°F) by the use of warming cabinets, steam tables, or other devices suitable for this purpose. However, this should not be done for more than a couple of hours.

L'Attrezzatura: Equipment and Utensils Required for a Functional Kitchen

A well-stocked professional kitchen is built around a formal arrangement of restaurant ranges, stockpots or kettles, refrigeration, ice makers, dishwashers, workstations, and cleanup areas. The attendant cookware, knives, and other preparation materials can be expected to see long and hard use and should be made of exceptionally strong elements that wear well. Any well-supplied home kitchen will have much of the same equipment, with less emphasis on quantity and size but the same insistence on quality. Top-quality equipment and utensils purchased for the kitchen will offer many years of valuable use.

Materials

The following materials are those that are typically used for professional cookware. These same elements are also found in most commercially available home cookware.

Rame (copper) is the most even conductor of heat. It is often used for saucepans, sauté pans, and casseroles. Copper pans should be lined with nickel, tin, or stainless steel and will be extremely heavy. Unlined copper pots should never be used to prepare acidic substances (those having a high content of vinegar, wine, citrus juice, tomato juice, or sour milk, among other acids). The meeting of chemical compounds causes a toxic reaction that can lead to serious illness. Never cool cooked foods in an unlined copper pot, as it will affect the color and taste of the foods and can cause them to become toxic.

Alluminio (aluminum) is also an excellent heat conductor used for saucepans, sauté pans, and casseroles. Aluminum cookware is often lined with a layer of stainless steel or nickel to prevent a negative reaction (a metallic taste and color change) when used with acidic substances. Never cool cooked foods in an unlined aluminum pot, as it will affect the color and taste of the foods and can cause them to become toxic.

Ghisa (cast iron) is an extremely strong, heavy metal usually used for Dutch ovens, griddles, baking pans, frying pans, and skillets. Relatively inexpensive, it is long lasting and conducts and retains heat extremely well. It is available either uncoated or enameled (coated with a thin layer of borosilicate glass powder fused to the cast iron to prevent corrosion). Before use, uncoated cast iron must be seasoned by generously coating the inner surface with an unflavored cooking oil (such as peanut or canola) and placing the pan in a preheated 121°C (250°F) oven for two hours. This preliminary heating prevents the metal from absorbing flavors and prevents food from sticking. Once seasoned, the pan should be gently cleaned and wiped dry before storing.

Acciaio (black steel) is inexpensive, conducts heat quickly, and does not warp under high temperatures; it is used to make frying pans, *crespelle* (crepe) pans, woks, and deep-fryers. Black-steel pans are often not washed, as this causes rust. Instead, the pan is wiped clean, rubbed with salt to remove any remaining particles, and seasoned with a light coating of oil after each use to retain its nonstick capabilities.

Acciaio inossidabile (stainless steel) is an excellent nonreactive metal but an extremely poor heat conductor. It will not rust and does not require seasoning. To be useful in a professional kitchen, stainless-steel pots and pans must be quite thick, with an outer or internal layer of copper or aluminum to help conduct heat.

Ghisa smaltata (enameled cast iron) is inexpensive, with a decorative layer of enamel over thin steel. It is a poor heat conductor and food tends to stick to the bottom, scorching and burning. It is impractical for the professional kitchen.

Antiaderente (nonstick) cookware is often referred to by its various trade names, such as Teflon or T-Fal. Nonstick pans are useful because they require minimal fat for baking or browning, baked goods do not stick to the bottom or edge, and they are easy to keep clean. However, with heavy use, the coating wears off quickly, rendering the pan useless. Never heat a nonstick pan to a high temperature without any added fat, as the coating will be damaged and become toxic. Always use a wooden spoon or utensils made for cooking with nonstick pans.

Pentolame (Pots and Pans)

As you work in the kitchen, always use the appropriate name for each pot and pan. It is extremely important that the correct names be learned, as the chef or another cook may often call out for a piece of equipment that must be delivered as quickly as possible. If the name is not at the tip of the tongue, time will be wasted while the desired piece of equipment is searched for. The assortment of pots and pans in a professional kitchen is referred to as the *batteria di cucina* and will contain some of the following items:

Pentola alta, or *marmitta*: A stockpot of which there are two types: a tall and a short. Both can range in capacity from 9 to 150 liters (2.5 to 40 gallons).

Casseruola: A large, round, shallow, straight-sided pan with one or two handles that is used for searing, braising, and stewing, usually no more than 12½ to 15 centimeters (5 to 6 inches) deep. These pans can range in capacity from 11 to 28 liters (12 to 30 quarts) and should be of heavy construction. A key characteristic is that they are wider than they are tall.

Padella: A shallow pan with sloping sides. An American equivalent would be a skillet. At The International Culinary Center, nonstick *padellas* are also used for *fritatte* or *crespelle*.

Rostiera, or *rosticciera*: A large, rectangular, heavy-bottomed pan with low to medium-high sides and two handles. It is used for oven-roasting meats as well as roasting bones for brown stocks.

Pentola: A pot with one or two handles that is used mainly for making sauces, simmering broth, and cooking pasta.

Placca: A rectangular aluminum or stainless-steel sheet pan with very shallow sides that comes in various sizes; most typically a full sheet pan (46 by 66 centimeters / 18 by 26 inches) and a half sheet pan (46 by 33 centimeters / 18 by 13 inches). It is used for baking, roasting, and holding foods.

Teglia ovale (sizzle platter): Oval stainless-steel or aluminum platters with raised edges used to cook or finish items in the oven or under a broiler or salamander. The raised edge keeps the juices from spilling out. Available in various sizes ranging from 23 to 34¼ centimeters (9 to 13½ inches). When preheated, the platter is hot enough to cause the food applied to sizzle. (For the purposes of the recipes in this book, a gratin dish or baking dish may be substituted in the home kitchen.)

Recipiente gastronorm: A modular system of kitchen pans and containers used in the European Union, known as hotel pans or steam table pans in the United States. The *gastronorm*, or hotel pan, is a rectangular stainless-steel pan with a lip, enabling it to rest in a steam table or rack. It comes in various standard sizes, most typically a full hotel pan, which measures 325 by 530 millimeters by 65, 100, or 150 millimeters (12¾ by 20¾ inches by 2, 4, or 6 inches) deep, and a half hotel pan. They are also available at one-quarter, one-third, one-sixth, and one-ninth of the basic size. Solid hotel pans are used to cook, ice, store, or serve foods, and perforated ones are used to drain foods. Also included are square boys, or steam table pans. These are almost square, usually 176 by 162 millimeters (6⅞ by 6¼ inches) by 65, 100, or 150 millimeters (2½, 4, or 6 inches) deep. They are most often used to store items in the refrigerator or on the cooking line. Other sizes are also available. (In the home kitchen, a baking dish may be substituted.)

Ciotola or *bacinella*: A bowl.

Bagno maria: A double boiler or water bath used to keep preparations such as soups, sauces, and creams warm without placing them directly on the heat. Also used to refer to cylindrical stainless-steel containers in various sizes used for storing or heating foods in a steam table or a water bath.

Coltelli (Knives)

Knives are the most commonly used tool in the professional kitchen. They are usually the personal property of each chef, and an individual's knife kit is guarded with great care. In the beginning of a professional culinary career, prudent investment in fine knives will prove a lifelong one. Many kitchens also have an array of knives on hand for general use, but they are often not of the highest quality. Most knives are made either of forged high-carbon stainless steel or forged stainless steel. This metal is generally resistant to rust and corrosion and does not stain easily. The knife handle can be made of wood, plastic, metal, or natural substances such as horn, shell, or plastic wood. In fine knives, the end of the blade (called the tang) runs the length of the handle and is held in place by a number of rivets, creating a strong, well-balanced utensil. There are now very good knives of a one-piece construction. Currently knives are being made from an extremely hard, durable material called ceramic zirconia that reputedly does not rust, corrode, interact with food, or lose its edge. There are numerous styles of knives needed to properly cut and shape food. Each has a specific use that is often defined by its name.

One of the most important factors to consider when purchasing knives is the material. Some of the desirable materials used to make knives are:

Acciaio (carbon steel): An alloy of carbon and iron, its advantages is that it will hold a fine edge. Its disadvantage is that it requires a high degree of maintenance, as it corrodes very quickly and cannot be used in humid, salt-air climates or with highly acidic food.

Acciaio inossidabile (stainless steel): A combination of iron and chromium or nickel that is a very popular medium for chef's knives. It is resistant to abrasion and corrosion but it is also difficult to sharpen and does not maintain a fine edge.

Coltello in acciaio con alta contenuto di carbonio (high-carbon stainless steel): This material combines the best qualities of carbon and stainless-steel knives. High-carbon "no-stain" steel contains many different materials, such as chromium, molybdenum, and vanadium. Most knives made for professional use are made of such

17¾-centimeter (6- to 7-inch) curved blade, which is usually firm, not flexible.

Sfilettopesce, or ***coltello per sfilettare*** (filleting knife for fish) **(c)**: The most important feature of a fillet knife is a very sharp, flexible blade that is essential to the exacting process of filleting. The blade ranges from 15 to 17¾ centimeters (6 to 7 inches) in length.

Coltello da cucina, or ***coltello da chef*** (chef's knife) **(d)**: The most versatile of all knives, it is used for chopping, slicing, dicing, and filleting. The blade ranges from 15 to 35½ centimeters (6 to 14 inches) in length.

Coltello a sega (serrated knife) **(e)**: A bevel-edged blade that is used for slicing breads, rolls, and other soft items. The blade usually ranges from 26 to 30½ centimeters (10 to 12 inches) in length.

Trinciante (slicing knife) **(f)**: Used for slicing large cuts of meat or fish such as roasts, ham, or smoked salmon, with blades ranging from 30½ to 40½ centimeters (12 to 16 inches). Some may be round-tipped, while others have pointed tips. Pointed-tipped knives may also be used to make precise and smooth cuts such as those required when cutting large cakes.

Mannaia (cleaver) **(g)**: A large rectangular-bladed knife used for cutting through bones and designed to be swung like a hammer.

Acciaino (steel) **(h)**: A rod used to hone knives between sharpenings (see page 342).

Pietre per affilare (sharpening stones) **(i)**: Used to sharpen knives (see facing page).

Proper Care of Knives

Cleaning: Proper cleaning and sanitation are essential to prevent cross-contamination of foods. Wash and dry knives by hand immediately after each use. (The high

compositions. Blades made from this material are less resistant to abrasion than pure stainless-steel knives and are much easier to sharpen. They are also resistant to corrosion and, unlike carbon knives, do not rust.

Cotello di ceramica (ceramic): Made from a hard ceramic such as circonium dioxide, ceramic knives maintain a sharp blade and need not be sharpened as often as other materials. The material is brittle, however, and the blades may break. They should not be used for tasks, such as chopping bones, that may cause them to chip.

Most professional knife kits contain the following knives, along with auxiliary cutting and shaping utensils:

Spelucchino, or ***coltello da verdura***, or ***coltello da pelare*** (paring knife) **(a)**: A small-bladed knife used for peeling and turning vegetables. A paring knife is usually under 10 centimeters (4 inches) long.

Coltello per disossare (boning knife) **(b)**: Used to bone various meats and poultry. This knife has a 15- to

Name		What It's Used For
Chef's knife *Trinciante* *Coltello da cucina* *Coltello da chef*		Most versatile, this knife is used for chopping, slicing, dicing, and filleting; blade is typically 15 to 35 centimeters (6 to 14 inches) long
Boning Knife *Coltello per disossare*		Used for boning meats, poultry, and fish; blade, which is typically 15 to 18 centimeters (6 to 7 inches) long, can be firm or flexible
Filleting knife *Sfilettapesce* *Coltello per sfilettare*		Flexible, sharp blade for filleting fish
Slicing knife *Trinciante*		Round-tipped slicing knives are used for boneless roasts or salmon; pointed slicing knives are for carving roasted items with bones; most have blades 30 to 40 centimeters (12 to 16 inches) long
Paring knife *Spelucchino* *Coltello da verdura* *Coltello da pelare*		Used for peeling and turning vegetables
Serrated Knife *Coltello a sega*		Used for slicing bread

heat and heavy detergents used in commercial dishwashers can damage knife blades and handles.)

Affilatura dei coltelli (sharpening knives): Maintaining one's knives makes them safer to work with, while saving chefs time and money. Sharp knives work more efficiently and do not have to be replaced as often as those that are allowed to dull completely. While there is an array of knife-sharpening devices available, many chefs prefer to use a sharpening stone, or whetstone, to maintain their tools.

A whetstone is used to restore an edge to a dull knife without grinding away too much of the blade. Sharpening stones (*pietre per affilare*) include natural stones, Carborundum stones, and diamond-studded blocks. When sharpening knives on a stone, two different grits should be used: one coarse and one fine. The grit abrades the blade to create a sharp cutting edge. There are many different grades or grits. On Western stones, 300 and lower is considered coarse; 400 to 500 is medium; 600 to 1200 is fine; and above 1200 is extra fine. Drizzle water or a food-grade mineral oil on the stone when sharpening knives to keep the grit free of particles while sharpening.

Japanese water stones have a different grading system than Western stones. Below 1000 is considered coarse. Between 1200 and 2000 is medium and makes for a good all-purpose stone. Three thousand to 8000 is fine to extra fine. In a normal kitchen environment, there is no need to use a stone finer than 5000. Water stones are soft, and must be reshaped after some time; special stones exist for that purpose. A water stone is soaked in water for 5 to 10 minutes before use. (Using the stone dry will damage it.) Do not use oil on a water stone.

When sharpening a knife with a sharpening stone, put the stone on a nonslip surface or a towel to keep it in place. For Western-style knives, an angle of 15 to 20 degrees is recommended for both sides. On Japanese knives, a different angle is often used for each side of the knife; this makes the knife suitable for cutting sashimi, for example.

The *acciaino* (also *acciarolo*), a steel, is a hardened, finely ridged rod with a handle and guard and a round or flat profile. A steel is used to hone knife blades in between sharpenings. To use a steel, first place the blade against the steel at an angle of approximately 20 degrees. Then draw the blade against the length of the steel.

Miscellaneous Tools of the Professional Kitchen (*Utensili*)

All kitchens, whether professional or home, are equipped with an assortment of tools that go beyond the essentials. As with pots and pans and knives, when used carefully, the highest-quality tools will last the longest.

Some of the small tools that may be found in a professional kitchen are:

Rigalimoni (channel knife): A small knife used to channel citrus fruit and various vegetables into decorative patterns for garnishes.

Forchettone (chef's fork): A longer-handled, longer-tined fork that keeps the chef's hand slightly away from the heat when turning items during cooking. Also used to aid in slicing cooked meats and roasts, and for twirling pasta for presentation.

Mandolina (mandoline): Traditionally a flat, metal frame supported by folding legs with a number of different blades that cut vegetables quickly into a variety of shapes, sizes, and thicknesses that would be very time consuming to create by hand. A towel is often placed under the legs of a mandoline to prevent slippage on the work surface. Even if you feel that you are expert at its use, it is good practice to always use the protective guard when slicing with a mandoline. The less expensive, Japanese-style mandoline has a simplified design but is used for the same purpose.

Colino (chinois): A conical strainer with a handle. There are two types: One is constructed of fine-mesh metal, used for fine-straining liquids and purées; the other is perforated and used when fine-straining is not required. Both types are often referred to as "china caps" because of their distinct conical-hat shape. However, to give clarity to this nomenclature in the kitchen, it is useful to refer to the fine-mesh strainer as a "chinois" and the perforated chinois as a "china cap."

Passaverdura (food mill): A metal basketlike utensil with interchangeable disks and a hand-turned crank used to separate solids from seeds, skin, and tough fibers. Often used for puréeing sauces (especially canned tomatoes for sauce) and soups.

Bilancia (scale): A variety of scales are available that can give accurate measurements of all ingredients. Scales are essential in pastry making. Many chefs now prefer digital models.

Pinzette per spinare (needle-nosed pliers or tweezers): Very useful for removing fine bones from fish.

Scavino (scoop): This scoop is used to cut fruit or vegetables into small ball shapes.

Forbici (kitchen scissors): Sturdy shears used to cut butcher's twine or kitchen papers or for trimming fish and poultry.

Raschia (scraper): There are several styles of scraping utensils. For example, a metal bench scraper (*raschia dritta*) is used to cut or portion doughs and clean off a work surface; a plastic bowl scraper (*raschia in plastica*) is used to thoroughly remove doughs from mixing bowls.

Spatola (spatula): Large, wide, metal spatulas are used to flip or turn vegetables, meat, and/or poultry during cooking. Some of these also have offset handles. A variety of spatulas made of softer rubber (*spatola di gomma*) or composite materials are used for scraping bowls, folding ingredients, and spreading. High-heat silicone spatulas are used for stirring hot foods and making *frittate*. A *spatola di legno* (wooden spatula) is gentle on vegetables and delicate preparations cooked in nonstick, coated pans. They are also useful for stirring *pasta bignè*, stirring roasting bones for stock, deglazing pans, making roux, and stirring *crema inglese*.

Spatola angolata, or **spatola a ginocchio** (offset pastry spatula): A long, thin spatula with an offset handle used to assist in cake decorating and for spreading batters or icings.

Ragno (spider): A long-handled device with a shallow, almost bowl-shaped disk at the end made of mesh or perforated wire, used for scooping foods out of boiling water, or hot oil when deep-frying.

Cucchiai (spoons): A wide variety of sizes and shapes of metal and wooden kitchen spoons are available with whole, slotted, or perforated bowls.

Termometri (thermometers): Thermometers help chefs measure and manage temperature for an array of foods. A stem thermometer is provided to all students upon entering The International Culinary Center. It measures degrees through a metal stem just past the dimple, which is located about 5 centimeters (2 inches) from the tip. The dimple must be placed in the middle of the food item to record an accurate temperature reading. To calibrate a stem thermometer, place it in heavily iced water for 3 minutes, stirring occasionally. At this point, the thermometer should read 0°C (32°F). Inserting the thermometer in the provided groove of its handle, carefully adjust the nut under the reading dial if necessary. (This type of thermometer should not be placed in the oven as it will melt.)

Setaccio a tamburo (drum sieve, or tamis): A fine-mesh metal strainer used to sift dry ingredients such as flour, to pass purées, and to rice potatoes for gnocchi.

Pinze (tongs): An essential and versatile tool in every kitchen, tongs do not puncture food as forks do. They are helpful in turning foods; in lifting foods that are not easily picked up with spoons or forks; in lifting pans and platters out of the oven; and in plating foods. They are particularly useful when moving food items to be eaten raw or without further cooking so that contamination from hands and other substances can be avoided. (Cross-contamination may be an issue, however, when the same pair of tongs is used for multiple tasks.)

Ago (trussing needle): A long, skewerlike needle used to truss poultry or sew stuffed cuts of meat.

Fruste (whisks): Thin, flexible wire whips used to incorporate air into mixtures that are not very dense. A balloon whisk (*frusta a palla)* has large, somewhat spherical centers and is used to incorporate air into foods such as egg whites.

Pelapatate (vegetable peeler): A small fixed or pivoting blade with a handle used to peel vegetables and fruit.

Special Equipment for Pasta, Gnocchi, and Pizza

Macchina sfogliatrice (pasta maker or pasta machine) **(a)**: A piece of equipment designed to simplify the process of rolling and cutting pasta dough into sheets for filled pastas, lasagne, and noodles. The machine rolls the dough into progressively thinner sheets with each pass through the machine. The noodle-cutting attachment cuts the sheets into noodles of different widths.

Pettine per garganelli (**b**): A wooden comb for making ridged, quill-shaped pasta.

Rigagnocchi (**c, g**): A ridged wooden board for shaping gnocchi.

Rotelle (**d**): Straight and fluted roller cutters for cutting pasta.

Stampi per ravioli (**e**): Round and square cutters for making ravioli.

Stampi per corzetti (**f**): Wooden embossing stamps for making *corzetti*.

Chitarra (**h**): A traditional wooden implement from Abruzzo strung with music wire to cut pasta.

Mattarello: A rolling pin.

Schiacciapatate (ricer): A basket- or cone-shaped utensil with small holes and a plunger that is used to force solid foods into small grains resembling rice; used to rice potatoes for gnocchi.

Pala, or **paletta**: A metal or wooden pizza peel.

Spazzola: A brush used to clean the pizza oven.

Large Equipment

Macchina per gelato (a): A batch freezer for making gelato and *sorbetto* in which the mixture is simultaneously frozen and churned.

Cuocipasta (pasta cooker) (b): A large cookpot with automatic temperature control and removable wire-mesh baskets for high-volume production of cooked pasta.

Cutter (electric food processor): A machine with a heavy motor encased in a plastic or metal housing with a detachable bowl and cover, and various blades with specific functions. The food processor can purée, blend, mix, crush, chop, knead, grate, slice, and julienne. The machine processes best when the bowl is filled to no more than half its capacity, and it will work only when all the pieces are properly aligned.

Frullatore (electric blender): A machine that purées, emulsifies, grinds, and crushes, consisting of a solid bottom that houses the motor and a blender jar (often two different sizes) that sits on top of it. The jar is fitted with a removable lid. Never fill a blender jar to capacity. The force of action will raise the lid with cold items, and a combination of force of action and steam will raise the lid when blending hot items. Even when filled to the recommended two-thirds full, the lid, covered with a clean kitchen towel, should be held in place with both hands to prevent splattering or burning.

Minipimer (Bermixer): An electric or battery-driven immersion blender, often handheld, that can be placed directly into a mixture for blending.

Affettatrice (electric meat slicer): A substantial piece of machinery with a large, stable, metal-encased motor as the foundation and a circular cutting blade attached. The movable part is a carrier with a handle and a guard that slides along the blade. The blade can be adjusted to the desired degree of thickness. Use only with the guard, as the blade is extremely sharp and dangerous.

Pentola elettrica, or ***pentola a gas*** (steam-jacketed kettle, electric or gas): Ranging in capacity from 2 to more than 375 liters (2 quarts to over 100 gallons), these kettles are made from stainless steel, and are usually freestanding; some may be tilted or fitted with spigots. The lid is usually attached. Used for making large quantities of stocks, soups, and stews. Foods are heated by steam that circulates through the kettle wall and provides even heat.

Brasiera (tilting shallow kettle, electric or gas): Sometimes called a Swiss kettle, a large stainless-steel unit fitted with a hinged lid, used for making large quantities of sautés, braises, and stocks.

Large Appliances

Both professional and home kitchens require equipment for heating, refrigerating, and freezing food. Some of these appliances are:

Stoves, Ranges, and Ovens

There are many different types of stoves, ranges, and ovens available. Some of these have multiple uses, while others have a defined purpose.

Burners may be placed in a range top with an oven (or ovens) below or above, or they may be placed alone into a stovetop that is fitted into a specific place. The burner types available are:

Piano di cottura (open burner, gas): Direct, adjustable heat, generally from *fornelli a gas* (gas burners).

Piastra (flat-top, electric or gas): A thick plate of steel over the heat source that offers even, indirect heat, good for cooking stocks and sauces. A flat-top burner requires flat-bottomed cookware and time to adjust to changes in temperature settings.

Fornelli (ring-top, gas): Similar to a flat-top, but with concentric rings and plates that can be removed to expose the burner so that indirect heat can be converted to direct heat. These burners usually offer a higher BTU than a regular open burner. Particularly well suited to stir-frying, and reducing a liquid quickly.

Forno statico (conventional oven, electric or gas): The most familiar kind of oven, conventional ovens feature adjustable shelves for cookware and an indirect heat source, located below the oven floor.

Forno per pizza (deck oven, electric or gas): A type of conventional oven with one or more levels or decks. Food is cooked directly on the deck of the oven, which is typically made of stone or metal. Usually used for baking breads and pizza. Allow a minimum of 30 minutes to preheat to temperature.

Forno a convezione (convection oven, electric or gas): In a convection oven, a fan blows hot air through the interior, causing foods to brown more efficiently than in a conventional oven. Often used for pastry and baked goods. When a recipe designates a temperature for a conventional oven, the temperature in a convection oven, especially when baking pastries, should be lowered by 10 percent. Allow a minimum of 15 minutes to preheat to temperature.

Forno combinato (combi-oven): Includes features from a conventional oven, a convection oven, and a steamer—hence "combi." It may be used for both cooking and holding food, as accurate temperature, moisture content, and airflow are easily controlled in this oven. It is ideal for catering and banquets.

Salamandra (salamander/broiler, electric or gas): An open boxlike apparatus that usually sits above a range top with the heat source located in its roof. Fitted with adjustable racks to control cooking speed, it is generally used for intense browning and glazes.

Griglia (grill; electric, gas, or charcoal): The heat source is either built in (gas or electric) or added (wood or charcoal) and is located below a heavy-duty cooking rack. In many models, the distance between the grill rack and the heat source can be adjusted for temperature control. Preheating usually takes about 30 minutes.

Friggitrice (fryer): A tabletop or freestanding unit, with adjustable thermostats and hanging baskets, for frying.

Refrigeration and Freezing Equipment

All kitchens require some type of refrigeration and freezing devices. Some of those available are:

Cella frigorifera (walk-in refrigerator): A large, box-shaped unit with a door large enough to allow a person to walk through without bending. Walk-in refrigeration may be used for cold storage or freezing. Generally it is outfitted with storage shelves. The unit is cooled by a compressor, often located outside the box.

Frigorifero (reach-in refrigerator): A single- or multiple-unit commercial refrigerator that is simply a larger version of a home refrigerator. Reach-ins come in various sizes and are equipped with adjustable shelving.

Cassette (under-counter refrigerator and refrigerated drawers): Also known as a "low-boy," this is a small appliance used primarily around the work areas of professional kitchens to keep food cold until ready for cooking or service. Some refrigerated drawers are designed to hold special products such as fish.

Abbattitore (blast chiller): A unit that rapidly chills food such as stock.

Lesson 2

Working with Vegetables

Washing, Peeling, and Cutting Vegetables

Lavaggio (The Washing Process)

The washing process, *lavaggio*, eliminates impurities from vegetables by submersion in cold water. Washing is important for sanitary as well as aesthetic reasons, especially when the vegetables are to be eaten raw—dirt and grit carry bacteria and can cause foodborne illness. Before washing, vegetables and herbs should be checked for freshness—any rotting leaves or vegetation will disintegrate in the washing process and contaminate the remaining product by clinging to it.

Fill a large *ciotola* (bowl), *bagno maria* (cylindrical stainless-steel container), or sink with enough cold water to completely submerge the vegetables to be washed.

Gently agitate the items being washed in the water to loosen impurities (e.g., dirt, sand, and insects). Be sure to avoid bruising. Using both hands, lift the vegetables out of the water so that the impurities stay in the basin.

Rinse the bowl and repeat the process until the water is clear and clean, and no dirt at all is left on the bottom of the basin.

Some vegetables, such as spinach or Swiss chard, tend to be very dirty and must be rinsed at least three times. If very gritty, soak in cold water for 30 minutes.

Sbucciatura (The Peeling Process)

The process of peeling, unwrapping, or dissection is called *sbucciatura*. The term describes all activities used during the process, including peeling the skin or outer layer of a vegetable or fruit; shelling or hulling; and pulling off stringy side filaments, as in string beans.

Most items can be peeled using a paring knife with an 8- to 10-centimeter (3- to 4-inch) blade or a vegetable peeler (*pelapatate*). When peeling, it is important that only the peel or skin is removed, leaving as much flesh as possible.

Wash vegetables (see above).

Set up the work area as described on page 331. Place unprepared items in containers at the left; transfer them, as finished, to a bowl at the right. Catch the peelings in a bowl placed in the center of the board for easy cleanup.

Peel in a regular, consistent motion, taking care to remove as little of the flesh as possible. Throw away peelings and trimmings as soon as the work is completed.

Before peeling small onions such as cipollini, dunk them in a bowl of warm water for 5 minutes to rehydrate the skin; it will pull off easily with a small knife.

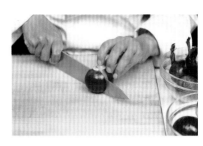

Knife Skills in the Traditional Italian Kitchen

Italians always use two words to describe the act of slicing, chopping, and dicing: one word that describes the shape of the cut (whether it be slicing or dicing), and one word that indicates the size. To describe a small cut, one can say: *fino*, *sottile*, or *piccolo* (small). For a larger cut, one would say *grosso* or *grande* (large). In Italy, a chef would say *affettare sottile* or *tagliare a fette grosse*, meaning "slice finely" or "slice thickly," respectively, rather than the word for slice—*affettare* or *tagliare*—alone.

Traditionally, Italian cuisine has been concerned with respecting the purity of foods. As a result, there has been less emphasis on manipulation and rigid guidelines for cutting, and more emphasis on preserving the natural shape of foods. The following Italian terms bear some relation to the rules of French *taillage* described below but are considerably less rigid.

Affettare or **tagliare a fette** (to slice): These terms describe cutting vegetables into slices. They do not imply a particular shape or size (e.g., carrot slices are round, onion slices are strips, celery slices are half-moons).

Tritare fino (small), **medio** (medium), or **grosso** (large) (to chop): These terms describe chopping vegetables into small, medium, or large pieces, depending on their ultimate use. ("*Tritare*" also describes the process of chopping fresh herbs; see "*Hacher* (tritare)" on page 350.) The pieces need not be of any particular shape, but they should all be of approximately the same size. When speed is important and it does not matter if juices are forced out of the vegetables, and when regular size is unimportant (e.g., the vegetables will be puréed or used as a foundation for a soup), a food processor, grinder, or food mill may be used for coarse or fine chopping.

Dadi (to dice): To cut vegetables into cubes of a specified size—for example, 6-millimeter (¼-inch) or 3-millimeter (⅛-inch) dice. In Italian, *dadi* denotes a relatively large dice, *dadini*, a smaller dice.

Taillage (Classic Methods of Cutting)

Taillage, the practice of cutting vegetables into uniform size and shape, is important for two reasons: Firstly, it ensures that food will cook evenly and at the same rate; secondly, it will enhance the visual appeal of a dish.

The practice of *taillage* in professional cooking is French in origin, dating back hundreds of years. However, these classic French cuts have, over time, become widely used by chefs around the world, and are used in traditional and modern Italian dishes.

Each *taillage* technique has a specific name, given below in French and parenthetically in Italian:

Tranches (*fette*): Standard slices into which items are cut during the initial stage of *taillage*, after the vegetables are first trimmed, or *parer* (*pareggiare*), to create flat surfaces.

Batonnet (*bastoncino*): Refers generally to sticks of vegetables of various thicknesses cut from *tranches*, or *fette*, and sometimes specifically to sticks cut 6 millimeters (¼ inch) thick. In French cuisine, certain sizes of *batonnets* have special names:

Jardinière (*giardiniera*): Thin sticks, ½ centimeter (³⁄₁₆ inch) wide, and 4 to 5 centimeters (1½ to 2 inches) long.

Julienne: Very thin sticks, 1 to 2 millimeters (¹⁄₃₂ to ¹⁄₁₆ inch) wide, and 6 to 7 centimeters (2⅜ to 2¾ inches) long.

Macédoine (*macedonia*): Small dice cut from *jardinière* vegetables, 5 millimeters (³⁄₁₆ inch) square.

Brunoise: Minute dice cut from julienned vegetables, 1 to 2 millimeters (¹⁄₃₂ to ¹⁄₁₆ inch) square. Throughout this book, this cut is referred to as "fine dice," or "finely diced."

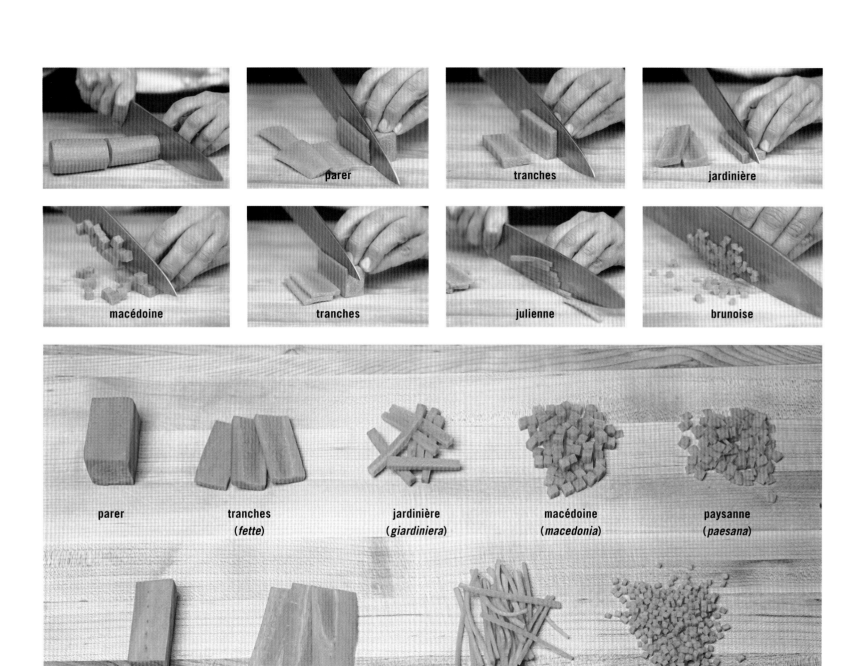

parer

tranches

jardinière

macédoine

tranches

julienne

brunoise

parer

tranches
(*fette*)

jardinière
(*giardiniera*)

macédoine
(*macedonia*)

paysanne
(*paesana*)

parer

tranches
(*fette*)

julienne

brunoise

Other Cuts

Mirepoix: Consistently sized, unshaped chunks, usually 1 to 2 centimeters (⅜ to ¾ inch). Used as aromatic elements to flavor the final product (such as stocks), they are usually strained out at the end of cooking; therefore, a perfectly regular appearance is not essential.

Paysanne (*paesana*): Tile-shaped or triangular pieces, usually cut from *jardinière* sliced to 1 to 2 millimeters (⅟₃₂ to ⅟₁₆ inch) thick.

Chiffonade: This method of cutting, shown above left, produces thin strips or ribbons of herbs or leafy vegetables. Clean the leaves. Make a small stack using three or more leaves. Roll the leaves into a tube. Finely julienne the tube crosswise to produce thin strips or ribbons.

Hacher (*tritare*): To finely mince herb sprigs in small bunches, which then are used to flavor dishes or to garnish finished dishes. For parsley, as shown left, pull all of the leaves off the stems (save the stems for stock). Bunch up the leaves in small batches, and finely julienne; then finely chop.

Cutting Zucchini into *Batonnets* (*Bastoncini*)

Often only the firm exterior portion of the zucchini is used for *bastoncini* (the interior is soft, and contains seeds). As shown above right, the skin is not peeled because it makes for an attractive presentation.

Trim the ends and cut the zucchini crosswise into 7-centimeter (2¾-inch) lengths.

Stand sections on end and slice off the sides in 4 pieces, leaving an interior square of flesh containing the seeds; the width depends on the size of *bastoncini* desired.

Discard the interior or reserve for another preparation.

Cut the slices lengthwise into the desired size. From here, the *bastoncini* may be cut crosswise, into dice.

Peeling, Seeding, and Dicing Tomatoes

When used in cooked dishes that will not be strained, tomatoes are usually peeled; unpeeled skin separates from the flesh and gets tough and unpleasant to eat. Some preparations may also require seeding.

Cut a cross on the top of the tomato with a paring knife.

Cut out the core in a triangular section.

Blanch the tomato in boiling water just until the peel starts to come off where the cross is cut (15 to 45 seconds). Immediately after removing the tomato from the hot water, set it in ice water to stop cooking.

Peel the tomato as soon as it is cool enough to handle.

To seed the tomato, cut it in half through the core end, and then in half again (through the core end) to make 4 "petals"; scrape out the seeds.

To dice the tomato, cut the "petals" into strips, lengthwise; cut the strips into dice.

Disgorging Vegetables

Disgorging draws out bitter juices from ingredients, usually watery vegetables such as eggplant or zucchini, and makes for a more delicate taste.

Cut the vegetable into slices or dice and put them in a colander or a sheet pan with a metal rack.

Sprinkle evenly with coarse salt and toss.

Let stand in a colander or perforated hotel pan, or on a cooling rack or on paper towels, for 15 to 30 minutes to drain.

The vegetable may be rinsed or not; rinsing will wash off the salt but also some of the flavor of the vegetable, making for a lighter taste. If rinsed, pat dry on paper towels.

Roasting and Cleaning Peppers

Peppers may be cooked on a charcoal grill or directly over gas burners. Peppers should be cooked as briefly as possible so that the skin is charred but the flesh is barely cooked. Peppers should never be rinsed to remove skin; rinsing will also remove the desirable charred taste and flavorful oils.

Set the peppers over the flame and roast until the skin is blackened on one side. Turn with tongs until the skin is blackened all over.

Remove the peppers to a bowl, cover tightly with plastic, and let stand until cool enough to handle; steam helps to loosen the skin.

Wipe off the blackened skin with a towel or your hands.

Cut the peppers in half through the stem ends and pull out the seeds by hand. Pull or cut out the ribs. Cut the peppers as desired.

Preparing Artichokes for Cooking Whole

Fill a nonreactive bowl with cold water and acidulate the water with the juice of half a lemon, and add the juiced lemon half to the water as well. (The other half of the lemon will be used for rubbing the artichoke, to keep it from turning brown.)

Starting with the leaves near the stem, bend back the outer leaves and pull them down toward the stem, snapping them off just before reaching the base. Continue in this way until reaching the pale, yellowish inner cone of leaves.

Shave off all the dark green from the base and stem of the artichoke with a paring knife or vegetable peeler to expose the light yellowish-green flesh. Remove as little flesh as possible, maintaining the natural shape of the vegetable.

Cut off the top two-thirds of the artichoke and discard.

Rub the bottom and stem with the lemon half to prevent discoloration.

Spread open the leaves. Pull out the purple-tipped interior leaves to reveal the fuzzy choke (*fieno* or *barba*). Remove the choke with a melon baller or spoon. Rub again with the lemon half.

Place the prepared artichoke in the acidulated water. (Artichokes will keep overnight in acidulated water; any longer, and the artichoke will take on the acidity and flavor of the lemon.)

Preparing Artichoke Hearts and Stems for Slicing

Sometimes just the hearts and stems of artichokes are used, as when preparing artichokes for *Farrotto Primavera* (page 134).

Prepare the artichoke as in the instructions above through rubbing the bottom and stem with the lemon half. Then cut the artichoke in half and scoop out the choke. Cut off and slice the stem.

Lay each half of the base on its flat side and thinly slice.

Peeling Asparagus

Green asparagus is grown in different sizes: pencil, standard, medium, medium-large, and jumbo. The rule of thumb is that if the skin is tender, as it is in younger and smaller asparagus, it needn't be peeled. Woody, jumbo, and white asparagus must be peeled.

Place a hotel pan or sheet pan on the work surface, and lay the asparagus flat on the pan.

Peel in one long, continuous movement from directly under the head of the asparagus down to the end of the stalk.

Rotate and continue peeling, maintaining even pressure with every stroke of the peeler so that the natural shape of the stalk is not distorted.

Preparing Spring Garlic

Spring garlic is the immature garlic bulb with the greens attached.

Trim off the hairy end of the garlic.

Wash in cold water, removing one or two layers of the outer leaves in order to clean the garlic of all soil.

Slice the bulb and greens.

Working with Dried Porcini Mushrooms

Dried porcini must be reconstituted in water before using (cold water is preferable but warm water may be used if time is short); the soaking liquid then becomes a vehicle for adding yet more flavor to the dish.

Soak the mushrooms in cold water to cover until soft, 30 minutes to 1 hour (or about 30 minutes in warm water).

Lift the mushrooms out of the soaking liquid and gently squeeze out as much of the water as possible; squeeze over the bowl so that the water returns to the soaking liquid. Rinse to remove any remaining grit.

Dry the mushrooms on paper towels and chop.

Pass the soaking liquid through a strainer lined with layered, dampened cheesecloth, or a coffee filter, to strain out any dirt. (Dampening the cheesecloth tightens the fibers of the cloth.)

Taste the soaking liquid to determine how strong it is. It should taste pleasant, not strong, particularly if it is to be reduced during cooking. Add water as needed if too strong, or use it sparingly.

Lesson 3

Cheese-Making

The History of Cheese

Cheese is a very old food. Historically, cheese-making was a means of preserving milk, an ancient science that developed organically out of necessity. While cheese-making is no longer a necessary method of storage and preservation, it retains an important role in Italian culture and cuisine.

Cheese-making probably happened by accident. Historians believe that it began as early as 7000 BCE in the region of the Tigris and Euphrates rivers. Nomadic sheepherders, who traveled with milk stored in stomach sacs from their herds, may have discovered that the milk, acted upon by the rennet remaining in the sacs, combined with the vigorous movement of traveling, had separated into curds and whey. From there came the practice of draining the curds and salting them for preservation.

It seems probable that many early civilizations produced some form of cheese, including the Tartars, Tibetans, Jews, Persians, Sumerians, Babylonians, and Egyptians. We know that sheep and goats were domesticated by the year 7000 BCE in the Middle East, and by 8000 BCE in Iran. There is also proof that the herding of cattle, buffalo, and sheep started in the year 600 BCE in Italy, France, and North Africa.

Cheese was an essential food of the ancient Greeks and Romans. Mixed with olive oil, fruit, and honey, it was reputed to be the athletes' main source of energy during the Olympic Games, and Virgil wrote about a daily ration of 27 grams of *pecorino* (sheep's-milk cheese) for Roman legionnaires. The Italian word *formaggio* (cheese) is derived from *formos*, the name given by the ancient Greeks to the vine baskets used to drain their curds. The Romans translated *formos* into *forma*, which eventually became *formaggio*.

Roman manufacturers made use of fig juice, twigs, cactus seeds, saffron, and vinegar to speed up the coagulation of the milk. In the first century BCE, Roman culture was responsible for the technological advancement of cheese-making by placing perforated weights on top of the curd during the aging process; this introduced the possibility of harder cheeses. In the third century CE, Emperor Diocletian dictated that soft chesses be sold wrapped in leaves and aged cheeses be coated with salt, probably in response to problems stemming from foodborne illness.

Cheese-making continued in the Middle Ages, when monastic orders developed new techniques for production, thereby creating new textures and flavors. During this period, cheese became an enormously important commodity in

Europe. During the Renaissance, in a fragmented Europe, cheeses from the original Roman formulas were adapted to the specific geographies and products of Italy's regions. From the fourteenth through the sixteenth century, Italian cheeses became identifiable as the products we know, and the basic principles of cheese-making have remained relatively unchanged since then, adjusting for the preferences of producers and consumers that occurred during various historical periods.

How Cheese Is Made

Cheese-making begins by separating the solid matter (curds) from the greenish-colored liquid (whey). There are three ways to accomplish this, depending on the desired result: The milk may be soured with an edible acidic substance such as lemon juice or vinegar (acid coagulation); it may be coagulated with rennet; or the two processes may be used in combination. Milk that has been left to sour (raw milk alone or pasteurized milk with added lactic-acid bacteria) will also naturally produce curds; sour-milk cheese is produced this way.

When the curds have coagulated, they may be cured by a variety of processes, all with the goal of eliminating more moisture. These include heating the curd, cutting the curd with an array of cutting and shaping tools, molding and pressing to expel even more moisture, salting the exterior, immersing the curd in brine, or a combination of methods. Once the cheese (now called a "green" cheese) is molded, it is ready to undergo further maturing processes to encourage it to dry and ripen. Naturally aged cheeses are ripened (usually uncovered) through a process of controlled storage that guarantees the appropriate humidity and temperature for the creation of the desired texture and flavor.

Making Ricotta Cheese

The technique illustrated at left is used when making *Ricotta* on page 68.

Heat the milk, acid, and salt to 90°C (195°F). When the curds start to form and separate from the whey, remove the curds from the whey with a skimmer or strainer.

Drain the curds in a sieve lined with dampened cheesecloth, over a bowl.

Flavors such as cinnamon or honey may be added to the finished ricottta, depending on the desired use. Additionally, for a creamier consistency, heavy cream may be added.

Making Mozzarella Cheese

The technique illustrated above is used when making *Mozzarella* on page 68.

Break or chop the curd into small pieces. Place the curds in a stainless-steel bowl and pour hot salted water at 82–85°C (180–185°F) over them.

Working with both hands under the water, stretch and pull the curd.

When the curds are softened, smooth, and elastic, shape and smooth them into balls.

Refrigerate the finished mozzarella in the liquid in which it was made, or marinate in olive oil, with added flavorings if desired.

Lesson 4

Working with Stocks and Sauces

Stocks (*Fondi e Brodi*)

The importance of quality in stock-making cannot be overstressed; the stock will have an impact on every preparation in which it is used. A well-made stock is clear in appearance, with a neutral, balanced taste and depth of flavor. Stocks are never salted. It is likely that the finished stock will be reduced during further cooking, making the taste of the salt more prominent.

Ingredients

Stocks, known as *fondi* or *brodi*, always begin with quality ingredients (fresh meat and bones, vegetables, herbs, and so forth). While it is useful and practical to use meat and vegetable scraps, both must be impeccably fresh and perfectly clean.

Solids

Vegetables stocks are made with vegetables and herbs; meat stocks are made with bones and lean meat trimmings, and a combination of vegetables and herbs. Meaty bones and carcasses add flavor, while the gelatin released from the bones gives the stock body. Bones may be roasted, blanched, or sautéed, depending on the desired stock. At The International Culinary Center, stock-making is often an adjunct to classes that teach butchering: When the students butcher chickens, for example, or break down a rack of lamb, the bones are chopped, roasted for brown stocks, and simmered with trimmings.

Aromatics for Stock

Stocks are typically cooked with "aromatics"—a collection of vegetables, herbs, and spices designed to contribute to a balanced, neutral flavor. (In the case of vegetable stocks, the aromatics are the total of the solids used to prepare the stock.) The choice of aromatics may vary depending on the end use of the stock. However, certain vegetables—onions, carrots, and celery—are classic. This combination is called *mirepoix* in French cuisine, a term also used by Italian chefs. The traditional proportion of onions, carrots, and celery in a mirepoix is 50:25:25. Garlic, fennel, leeks, and mushrooms may be included in the mix, too.

The amount of vegetables used in the mirepoix is usually 10 to 20 percent of the weight of the bones used. Aromatic vegetables for stock are roughly cut into a consistent size and, because they will be strained out of the liquid at the end of cooking, are added to the pot without further shaping. The size into which they are cut varies depending on how much time the stock needs to cook. Stocks that cook rapidly use smaller mirepoix than those that require a longer cooking time.

Making a *Mazzetto Guarnito*

Cut a single layer of cheesecloth in a square large enough to contain all the vegetables and herbs. Brush away any stray bits of fiber. Dampen the cheesecloth (this tightens the fibers of the cloth), place in a bowl, and add the herbs and vegetables. Pull together the edges of the cheesecloth and tie with butcher's twine.

The herbs are likely to be some combination of bay leaf, parsley, and thyme. (For all stocks made at The International Culinary Center, we save parsley, basil, and thyme stems for use in stocks; the leaves are reserved for other preparations.) Peppercorns and whole cloves are common spices, and some chefs add a piece of the rind from a wheel of Parmigiano-Reggiano or Grana Padano cheese. The herbs, called a *mazzetto guarnito*, may be added as is, or tied together into a cheesecloth bundle (see sidebar at left) for easy removal.

Liquid for Stock

Most stocks are made with water, but chefs may substitute other flavorful liquids. Stocks are begun with cold liquid to better facilitate the degreasing process (fats are not emulsified into the stock), to extract flavor, and to preserve clarity. Clouded stocks may contain impurities such as grease that can affect the flavor and texture of the stock. Enough liquid is added to comfortably cover the solids; more may be added during cooking, as necessary, to adjust for evaporation.

Making Stock

Stocks are cooked in a *pentola*, a tall pot with a narrow opening, to discourage evaporation. The stock is brought to a simmer (never allowed to boil) and skimmed well to remove fat and impurities. Only then are aromatics added to the pot: Foam, impurities, and grease are more difficult to remove from small pieces of vegetables and herbs.

The stock is simmered slowly, uncovered, allowing more fat and impurities to float to the surface of the stock to be removed. The stock should never be allowed to boil: The turbulence of the boiling liquid gives impurities a chance to be reincorporated into the stock. If this happens, the stock will become clouded.

The surface of the stock should be carefully skimmed and degreased as it cooks (be careful not to stir up the bottom during cooking, however, as this may also cloud the stock).

Cooking time is determined by the type of stock and the base ingredient. Generally speaking, *fondo bruno* (brown stock) requires a longer cooking time than *fondo bianco* (white stock). Veal and beef stocks require a longer cooking time than poultry or game stocks because the bones take longer to release their flavor into the surrounding liquid. *Fumetto di pesce* (fish stock) needs only 30 minutes of cooking time.

At the end of cooking, the stock should be ladled and passed through a fine-mesh strainer lined with dampened cheesecloth to leave settled sediment behind, and to ensure removal of small, fine bones and other impurities. (*Fumetto di pesce* [fish stock] should rest briefly after cooking and before straining so that fine sediment may settle to the bottom.) Stocks should be cooled quickly to preserve flavor and to prevent spoilage. By law, all restaurant kitchens in Italy must use blast chillers, devices that promote very fast, even cooling of foods. This not only preserves the taste of the stock, but also lengthens its shelf life. At The International Culinary Center, an ice bath is used.

Basic Stocks

Stocks generally break down into a few basic categories: *brodo vegetale* (vegetable stock), *fondo bianco* (white stock), *fumetto di pesce* (fish stock), and *fondo bruno* (brown stock). Each is named for its components or appearance.

Brodo Vegetale (Vegetable Stock)

The technique described below is used when making *Brodo Vegetale* on page 72.

Vegetable stocks are classically made with onion, carrot, celery, garlic, and herbs. Fennel may be added if the stock is destined for a particular dish in which that flavor is desirable, but typically a more neutral flavor profile is appropriate. Herbs should be as neutral as possible: Thyme, bay leaf, and parsley stems are classic.

The temptation to use leftover ingredients—which are not as fresh as they might be—should be resisted. Some chefs prefer to make fresh stock every day; it is better to use the freshest ingredients possible and freeze the stock than to use lesser-quality ingredients and make it less often.

Fondo Bianco (White Stock)

The technique illustrated above is used when making *Fondo Bianco di Pollo* on page 74.

White stocks are desirable for lighter-flavored and lighter-colored preparations. Like brown stocks, white stocks can be made using veal bones, chicken bones, or beef bones; chicken stock is the most common white stock used in restaurant kitchens.

In classic cuisine, the bones are blanched and immediately drained to remove surface impurities, excess blood, and coagulated proteins. In the contemporary kitchen, however, as at The International Culinary Center, chicken bones are usually not blanched due to the short cooking time of chicken stock, and to preserve flavor and gelatin content. (The technique of blanching is usually associated with vegetables that are cooked in boiling water; in the case of white stocks, the bones are placed in cold water that is brought quickly to a boil.)

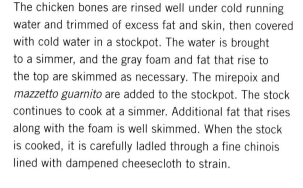

The chicken bones are rinsed well under cold running water and trimmed of excess fat and skin, then covered with cold water in a stockpot. The water is brought to a simmer, and the gray foam and fat that rise to the top are skimmed as necessary. The mirepoix and *mazzetto guarnito* are added to the stockpot. The stock continues to cook at a simmer. Additional fat that rises along with the foam is well skimmed. When the stock is cooked, it is carefully ladled through a fine chinois lined with dampened cheesecloth to strain.

The procedure for a white veal stock is largely the same as for a white chicken stock; however, the veal bones are rinsed under cold running water, if bloody, then blanched, and the cooking time is increased. White stocks may also be made using fish bones, but because their preparation is somewhat unusual, they deserve a separate discussion (see below).

Fumetto di Pesce (Fish Stock)

The technique illustrated opposite, top is used when making *Fumetto di Pesce* on page 73.

Lean, mild-flavored fish, such as sole, whiting, and flounder, are best suited to the task of stock-making. Fish with a high fat content, such as tuna and salmon, typically have strong, distinctive flavors that are less appropriate for a neutral-flavored liquid such as stock.

Fish bones are smaller and more delicate than those of beef or chicken, and release their flavor relatively quickly. It is important to clean the bones well as blood will make the stock bitter. Scrape out the bloodline (it looks like a vein that runs along the backbone, protected by a translucent membrane) under cold running water. Disgorge the bones of all remaining blood by rinsing very well under cold water. Cut the bones into pieces.

Because of the fragile nature and limited gelatin content of fish bones, the cooking procedure for fish stocks varies from other stocks in this curriculum in

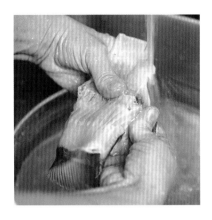

several ways: First the mirepoix and herbs are cooked, then the pot is deglazed with vermouth or white wine, then the bones are added directly to the pot, without prior blanching or roasting. Cold water is added, and the stock is simmered, skimmed, and strained. Fish stock cooks for no more than 30 minutes; any longer, and its taste becomes too strong.

Fondo Bruno (Brown Stock)

The technique illustrated below is used when making *Fondo Bruno* on page 74.

Brown stocks acquire their color and name from their principal element: roasted bones. When roasted, or "browned," in the oven, the bones develop a medium to dark brown color and enriched flavor. The color change and complex flavor are caused by the Maillard reaction, a series of chemical processes responsible for the characteristic brown color and "roasted" flavor of foods (see page 158).

A brown stock may be made with veal bones, beef bones, chicken bones, or other game bones. Mirepoix, usually carrots, onions, and celery, and *mazzetto guarnito* (see sidebar "Making a *Mazzetto Guarnito*" on page 359) are the standard aromatics; tomatoes, leeks, and garlic may be added. The mirepoix is added to the roasting pan about two-thirds of the way through the cooking—shortly before the bones are completely browned—to prevent the vegetables from burning. Tomato paste is spread over the bones and vegetables (the sugar in the tomato paste will increase caramelization), then the bones and vegetables are roasted to an even, rich brown color. The browned bones and vegetables are transferred to a large stockpot, covered with cold water, and brought to a simmer.

In order to recuperate as many of the caramelized juices as possible, the fat is poured from the roasting pan and discarded, and the pan is deglazed with water over heat, using a wooden spoon. The deglazed liquid is added to the stockpot and brought to a simmer. Then the herbs and optional tomatoes and garlic are added; the skimming continues as the fat and impurities rise to the surface. The finished stock is carefully ladled through a fine-mesh strainer (*colino*) lined with dampened cheesecloth.

Sauces (*Salse*)

Sauces (*salse*) may be defined as liquids that are used to complement—but never overwhelm—a dish by adding flavor, moisture, and visual appeal. Many sauces in Italian cuisine rely on a *soffritto*.

Soffritto

A *soffritto* is a mixture of aromatic vegetables and herbs—perhaps with the addition of pancetta or diced salt pork—that is cooked in oil. It serves as an omnipresent base of flavor for innumerable preparations including, but by no means limited to, *ragùs* and sauces. The *soffritto* mixture is traditionally very personal to the chef and is adjusted for each dish according to preference. (For example, a *soffritto* for tomato sauces typically uses more carrot than in other dishes because the sweetness from the carrot tempers the acidity of the tomato.) The *soffritto* is one of the ways the Italian chef customizes his or her cooking.

Vegetables for the *soffritto* are cut into larger or smaller pieces, depending on its intended use. Vegetables should be cut to approximately the same size so that they cook evenly. Optimally, carrots are cut slightly smaller than celery and onion because their hard texture takes longer to soften; garlic should be coarsely chopped (it should not be minced too finely) to prevent it from burning. If a sauce or soup is to be puréed after cooking, the size of the *soffritto* is unimportant; it may be cut fairly large so that the vegetables take relatively longer to cook, become well caramelized, and add rich flavor to the food. However, if a relatively smooth texture is required, vegetables may be finely chopped in a food processor.

The cooking of a *soffritto* must not be rushed. The *soffritto* is started in a cold pan with cold oil over moderate heat. (A more finely chopped *soffritto* will use less oil because the water given off by the vegetables will keep them from sticking and burning.) The heat gradually draws the taste of the vegetables into the oil, and the long, slow cooking process intensifies and develops the complexity of their flavor. As subsequent ingredients are added to the pan (in braises, for example), they are, in turn, infused with the flavors of the *soffritto*.

Correct cooking time is achieved by practice. The word *soffritto* roughly translates as "underfried," to suggest that the vegetables should not be cooked too quickly. They are cooked enough to concentrate their flavors and deepen their color (onions should be golden).

Once the *soffritto* is cooked, the pan is usually deglazed to pick up any caramelized food bits that adhere to the bottom of the pan.

Herbs vary in strength, and it's difficult to know how much to put in without tasting. Herbs may be added at various points in the cooking process to take advantage of the way their flavor changes during cooking. For example, in *Salsa di Pomodoro* on page 76, the chef builds layers of taste into the sauce by adding basil once with the *soffritto*, and again later, to simmer with the sauce. Herbs may also be tied up in cheesecloth for easy removal, when the appearance of bits of leaves in the finished dish is undesirable.

Battuto

A *battuto* (from the Italian word *battere*, "to strike") is a mixture of ingredients— typically onion, carrot, celery, and garlic—that have been chopped. (*Battere* describes the action of striking the vegetables on the cutting board as they are cut.) A *battuto* will usually become a *soffritto*.

Using a Food Mill to Purée Tomatoes, Sauces, and Soups

Either before or after cooking, tomatoes for sauce may be puréed in a food processor or food mill. An advantage to using a food mill is that it strains as it purées, depending on the size of the holes in the strainer plate. In addition, a food mill does not incorporate air into the purée as may a Bermixer or food processor.

If using a food mill, it is important to recoup as much as possible of the solid matter that invariably gets caught between the paddle and strainer plate; these solids contain a great deal of the flavor. Once most of the liquid is passed through and the solids are left, keep adding water, a little at a time, to continue to purée and force the solids through.

Salsa di Pomodoro (Tomato Sauce)

There are innumerable varieties of tomato sauces in Italian cuisine, and every Italian chef has his or her own. Tomato sauces may be roughly divided into two categories: long-cooked sauces for pasta, similar to *Salsa di Pomodoro* (page 76), and short-cooked sauces, such as those used for pizzas (page 147). Short-cooked sauces, such as *marinara*, may be seasoned quite simply with chopped garlic, salt, and pepper, and are cooked just long enough to reduce the tomato slightly, as they will cook again on top of the pizza. Long-cooked sauces are sweetened with a *soffritto* and simmered long enough to develop flavor and cook out the tomato's acidity.

Canned tomatoes work perfectly well for cooked tomato sauces and, in fact, are often preferable because good-quality canned tomatoes are dependably consistent and are processed at the peak of ripeness. A pinch of sugar may be added to compensate if tomatoes are very acidic. For best flavor, buy imported tomatoes packed without citric acid.

Besciamella (Bechamel Sauce)

The technique illustrated below is used when making *Besciamella* on page 79.

The first step in a *besciamella* is to make a roux. Measure out (by weight) a 50:50 ratio of sifted all-purpose flour to butter. The butter is melted in a saucepan. When the butter foams, the sifted flour is poured in all at once, while stirring, to disperse evenly. The roux is heated very slowly to ensure that the butter thoroughly lubricates and separates the particles of flour. (This will help the particles break up evenly when the milk is added and prevent lumps from forming.) If the roux is heated too quickly, the starch in the flour may shrink, inhibiting its ability to bind stocks and sauces. The roux is cooked very slowly until the mixture is bubbling and the ingredients are well blended and smooth. The roux should not color and it should be the consistency of sand at low tide. Allow the roux to cool slightly, but not so much that the fat solidifies.

Warm or room-temperature milk is added, while whisking vigorously, off the heat. The saucepan is returned to the heat and the sauce brought to a boil in order to achieve the full thickening power of the flour. (As the sauce heats, the starch granules in the flour absorb water and begin to swell, so the sauce begins to thicken. As the sauce reaches a boil, the starch granules continue to swell, the starch molecules migrate out of the granules and into the surrounding liquid, and the sauce achieves its maximum thickness.) *Besciamella* must be whisked constantly during this phase in order to prevent lumps from forming. The sauce is cooked slowly, over low heat, until thickened, stirring constantly. If necessary, the finished sauce can be strained to remove any lumps. If not using immediately, the sauce is dotted with butter or covered with plastic to prevent a skin from developing.

Lesson 5

Working with Dried Legumes

Beans were first imported to Italy from the Spanish colonies in the Americas during the 1500s. Today, a great many varieties are grown throughout the country and play a prominent role in Italian cuisine. Beans are served as *contorni* or as *antipasti* (puréed, for example, for crostini, or in salads), and are cooked into hearty soups (page 83).

Techniques illustrated below are used wherever cooked legumes are called for throughout the book.

Washing

It is important to wash all dried legumes carefully in order to remove any flavor or smell that will penetrate the legumes during eventual soaking and cooking.

First spread the legumes out in a single layer and check them carefully; discard any stones and shriveled, darkened, or broken legumes. Rinse well in a strainer under cold running water.

Soaking

Beans and peas should be soaked before cooking; lentils need not be.

Beans double in volume during soaking. Wash and drain the beans, put them in a stockpot or *bagno maria*, and cover them with cold water. Let soak overnight in the refrigerator. Smaller beans take less time to soak, as little as 4 hours. Very small beans, such as *zolfina* or *sorana*, need even less time. The soaking water should be discarded and fresh cold water should be added for cooking.

Note:

Dried legumes will increase in volume by about 2½ times when cooked.

Cooking

Dried legumes are always cooked before eating. It is best to use them within one year of their harvest. If they are of different ages, they should be cooked separately to prevent over- or undercooking, since older beans will take longer to cook.

Before cooking, pick out any beans or peas that have floated to the top during soaking; they are old and will not cook properly. Drain the beans or peas from their soaking liquid.

Prepare a *mazzetto guarnito* (see sidebar "Making a *Mazzetto Guarnito*" on page 359) with aromatic vegetables cut into 3- to 5-centimeter (1³⁄₁₆- to 2-inch) chunks and tied in cheesecloth for ease of removal. (The choice of aromatics is personal to the chef but carrot, celery, onion, fresh rosemary, sage, and black peppercorns are common.) Prosciutto skin, ends, or bones may be added for additional flavor, as well as the rinds from Grana Padano or Parmigiano-Reggiano cheese.

Return the legumes to the pot and refill with 10 centimeters (4 inches) of cold water or vegetable stock. Place the pot over low heat and add the *mazzetto guarnito*. The goal is to bring the legumes to a boil slowly so that they will absorb moisture gradually.

Add about 1 teaspoon coarse salt per 225 grams (8 ounces, or 1 cup) dried legumes.

As the legumes come to a simmer, skim the foam that forms on the surface. Cook the legumes, uncovered, at a very gentle simmer. Cooking time depends on the legumes' freshness, and the size of the legumes and the pot; it may take anywhere from 30 to 60 minutes. The legumes are perfectly cooked when their centers are very creamy, and the legume crushes easily between your tongue and the roof of your mouth. (Another good test is to pinch the legume between thumb and index finger; if it breaks open easily, it's cooked.)

Let the legumes cool completely in the cooking broth and then store covered in the broth to prevent them from drying out.

Save the cooking liquid for use in soups, or in dishes that use legumes, such as *Sgombro con Scarola e Fagioli* on page 229, or *Cannellini all'Uccelletto* on page 258.

Lesson 6

Working with Pasta

Fresh and Dried Pasta

The differences between *pasta secca* (dried pasta) and *pasta fresca* (fresh pasta) stem from differences in the character of the flours used and in the techniques by which the pasta is produced.

Pasta Secca

Pasta secca is a factory-made product fashioned from semolina flour, which is milled from the berry of a golden-colored variety of wheat called *grano duro* (durum wheat), a hard-wheat variety that originated in the Mediterranean. The dough is shaped by being pressed through perforated dies, then dried. The availability of the wheat, and a climate that was perfect for drying the dough, made southern Italy the natural home of *pasta secca*.

The quality of *pasta secca* is determined by the quality of the grain and the drying process. Artisanal *pasta secca* is made by essentially the same method as commercial dried pasta, with some important differences: The dies used to extrude modern, industrial dried pasta are made from Teflon, which produces a very slick, smooth surface on the pasta. Artisanal producers have returned to the use of traditional bronze dies that are more difficult to clean and maintain, but produce a pasta with a coarse and porous texture. The rougher surface of artisanal pasta captures sauce, giving it something to adhere to, while sauce tends to slide off the slick surface of standard-quality pasta. Additionally, artisanal pasta is dried at lower temperatures than industrial pasta; artisanal drying times are measured in days, rather than hours for standard-quality pastas. The longer drying time preserves the taste and aroma of the pasta. Artisanal *pasta secca* expands considerably during cooking, and maintains its firm, chewy "tooth" when cooked.

Dried pastas are available in a wide variety of shapes including spaghetti, rigatoni, fusilli, rotini, and penne, among others. The sturdiness of the semolina flour makes these shapes possible.

Pasta Fresca

Whereas the production of *pasta secca* was industrialized for export long ago (probably as early as the fifteenth century), *pasta fresca* was traditionally a handmade product, made in homes, restaurant kitchens, and local shops called *pastifici*. (Today, it is also produced in factories.) *Pasta fresca* is usually rolled, then cut or shaped by hand. It is usually softer, with a more delicate texture than dried, and it cooks faster. (There are some notable exceptions, including the robust, hand-shaped *Orecchiette* on page 98.)

Recipes for fresh pasta vary throughout the country, and the flour or combination of flours varies by region.

Fresh pasta is often, but not always, made with egg, but water or even wine may be used. In much of northern Italy, *pasta fresca* is traditionally made with flour milled from *grano tenero,* or soft wheat. In Emilia-Romagna, a region that is famous for its fresh pasta, the dough is made solely from flour (traditional Bolognese pasta is made from silky soft "00," or "*tipo 00*," flour, called *doppio zero,* or double zero) and egg. The province of Valtellina in Lombardia is known for short, wide noodles called *pizzoccheri,* made from buckwheat (*grano saraceno*). In Toscana, salt, water, and a little olive oil are used. In Apulia, fresh pasta is often made with water instead of egg, and the flour is semolina, which yields a chewier, coarser product. The Sardinian fresh pasta *malloreddus* is made with semolina flour, water, and saffron. The dough for some hand-shaped *cavatelli* is made with ricotta, flour, and salt.

Additional ingredients may be added to fresh pasta dough for color and flavor. Spinach and other greens produce the *Pasta Verde* on page 96; beets and tomato color the pasta pink; and squid or cuttlefish ink is used for the color of *pasta nera*, or black pasta (see sidebar "*Pasta al Nero di Seppia*" at left).

Pasta ripiena (filled pastas), such as ravioli, *agnolotti,* and tortellini, are made with fresh egg pasta dough. There is enormous variety in regional shapes, all with different names. Since these filled pastas are made throughout Italy, the name of a shape often changes with the region. Ravioli, for example, are also known as *tortelli*.

Filling mixtures are made from vegetables, meats, seafood, or cheese, often bound with egg and grated cheese.

Making Fresh Pasta Dough

The techniques illustrated below are used when making and rolling fresh pasta dough for *Pasta con le Sarde* on page 105, *Tortellini alla Bolognese* on page 108, *Garganelli con Piselli* on page 111, *Ravioli di Ricotta e Bietola* on page 114, and *Lasagne di Carne* on page 116.

Pasta al Nero di Seppia (Squid-Ink Pasta)

Ink sacs are found in the head cavity, as well as in two small depositories behind the eyes, of the cuttlefish. Freshly extracted ink must be used quickly or frozen to preserve its freshness. Extracting the ink is a delicate process and may not yield much, so oftentimes ink is bought in large quantities and stored frozen in jars. Cuttlefish and squid ink are used for color in pasta or risotto and have a fishy aroma that is desirable in these seafood dishes. *Pasta al nero di seppia* is found throughout coastal Italy.

The Traditional Method (*Fontana*)

Fresh pasta dough was traditionally made on a wooden board, but a variety of techniques are acceptable: A bowl may be used, as well as a food processor or a mixer. At The International Culinary Center, pasta is made by hand, either on the board or in a bowl, unless a large quantity is being made, in which case a large mixer is more practical.

Recipes for fresh pasta dough (*pasta fresca*) must be understood as a guide rather than an exact formula, because the exact proportion of flour to liquid depends on a number of factors, including how much flour the egg can absorb (for egg pasta), the age of the flour and how long ago it was milled, and even the humidity on the day the dough is made. When made properly, pasta dough is pliable and moist, neither too sticky nor too stiff. Pasta making is learned by experience. One good rule of thumb is 1 large egg per 100 grams (1 scant cup) flour.

The traditional method for making dough is the *fontana,* or "well," method: The flour is shaped into a well on a board (a large bowl may also be used); liquids, salt, and ingredients for colored pasta, if using, are added to the center of the well and mixed; then the flour is gradually incorporated into this liquid with a fork, until a workable dough is formed. A plastic bench scraper is helpful in gathering flour from the workbench to incorporate into the dough. *It is important to remember that all of the flour may not be necessary.*

Once the dough comes together, it must be kneaded until smooth and elastic. Kneading helps to develop the gluten in the flour. A container of extra flour (called "bench flour") is kept on the side of the workstation (the "bench"), so that dough may easily be sprinkled with flour if it feels wet. All-purpose or "00" flour may be used for bench flour; semolina should never be used for bench flour. The finished dough is divided into balls, sprinkled with flour, covered, and allowed to rest at least 30 minutes to allow the gluten to relax and the flour to hydrate.

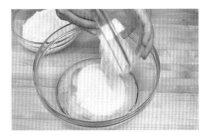

Making Pasta Dough in a Food Processor or Standing Mixer

Pasta may also be made in a food processor or mixer. Green dough is shown below.

Put the eggs, oil, salt, and spinach into the bowl of a food processor or a mixer fitted with the paddle attachment.

Add enough flour to create a rough dough, pulsing the machine and scraping down the sides of the bowl as needed until the dough comes together.

Scrape the dough out onto a work surface.

Knead the dough by hand or in a stand mixer with the dough hook, using bench flour as required.

The "Bowl" Method

The "bowl" method, shown above, is a good way for beginners to make pasta because the flour is added little by little to the wet ingredients in a bowl, preventing the common error of overly dry dough. The sifted flour is mixed with a fork or other utensil, a little at a time, into the wet ingredients until a rough dough is formed. Then the dough is scraped out onto a work surface and kneaded, as described above.

Rolling and Cutting Dough for Noodles (*Stendere e Tagliare la Pasta*)

Traditionally, fresh pasta was rolled by hand. The dough was progressively thinned and stretched to the desired thickness with a wooden dowel. Once thinned, the dough was cut into strips with a knife. Pasta machines (manual and electric) accomplish this task by rolling the dough through metal rollers to decreasing thicknesses, producing a long sheet of dough that is cut into strips on the machine, or by hand into whatever shape is desired.

In this curriculum, students roll the dough with a pasta machine. Unless making filled pasta, it is practical to roll all of the dough through each setting before moving to the next setting. While rolling, if the strips get too long to manage comfortably, they are cut in half, or into smaller segments, and worked one segment at a time. A bowl of bench flour is kept on the side of the workstation, so that dough may easily be sprinkled with flour if it feels sticky. In order to prevent clumps of flour being rolled into the dough, *excess flour is always brushed off the dough sheets after sprinkling*. To hold the finished rolled and cut pasta, sheet pans are lined with parchment paper, and sprinkled with semolina to prevent sticking.

Rolling and Cutting Dough
Using a Pasta Machine

Pasta machines (manual and electric) roll the dough through metal rollers (*rulli*) to decreasing thicknesses, producing a long sheet of dough that is then cut into strips on the machine, or by hand into whatever shape is desired.

Rolling the Dough

The most comfortable position for rolling the dough is to stand with your left hip perpendicular to the table, holding the handle with your right hand and guiding the pasta sheet with your left.

Flatten one piece of dough and dust it with flour.

Brush off excess flour with your hand or a pastry brush. Feed the flattened disk of dough into the machine. The dough will fold onto itself.

Flatten the strip, sprinkle with flour, and brush off the excess.

Fold the dough strip into thirds. Fold it so that the dough strip is the same width as the machine. Feed one of the open ends into the machine, so that the two folded edges are on the sides, to make nice, straight edges. Repeat five or six times until the dough is smooth and elastic.

Adjust the machine to narrow the opening by one notch. Dust the dough strip with flour, pat off the excess, and roll through the machine without folding; the strip will thin and lengthen. Do not pull the dough while guiding it out of the machine, or it will stretch and possibly tear.

Continue rolling the dough strips through the machine, dusting with flour and narrowing the opening by one notch each time, until all of the dough is rolled to the desired thickness. If your dough is a little wet, allow the strips to dry on a floured surface for a few minutes.

Cutting Noodles with the Pasta Attachment

The dough strips are cut into different lengths depending on the particular pasta; for our purposes, 26 to 30½ centimeters (10 to 12 inches) is usual. Run the dough strips through the cutters on the machine to cut noodles of the desired width.

Wrap the noodles loosely around your hand to make a "nest," and set the nest on a parchment-lined sheet pan. Sprinkle with more flour to prevent sticking.

Cutting Noodles by Hand

Before there were pasta machines, noodles were cut by hand with a knife. In the contemporary kitchen, wide noodles called *pappardelle*, cut from 21-centimeter (8-inch) lengths of dough, are still cut by hand with a knife or roller cutter because most pasta machines are not fitted with cutters for *pappardelle*. Noodles of all widths, however, can be cut by hand, following the steps below.

(At The International Culinary Center, *pappardelle* is sauced with *Ragù di Carne* [page 77] or *Coda alla Vaccinara* [page 186]; in the latter, the meat is picked

off the bones; gristle and fat are removed, cut into bite-size pieces, and mixed with the sauce from the braise.)

Sprinkle the sheets of dough aggressively with flour. Fold the dough strips in half and then in half again, sprinkling flour between folds.

On a work surface sprinkled with flour, using a knife or a roller/cutter, cut noodles 2 to 2½ centimeters (¾ to 1 inch) wide.

Cutting *Maccheroni alla Chitarra*

Maccheroni alla chitarra, a specialty of Abruzzo, is a square spaghetti cut from a durum-wheat flour dough. The dough is cut on a special instrument called a *chitarra* (as illustrated above), which means "guitar." The *chitarra* is a box with metal strings (thus the guitar reference). Sheets of pasta dough are laid over the

strings, one at a time, and rolled with a rolling pin to cut the dough. At The International Culinary Center, *maccheroni alla chitarra* is sauced with *Ragù di Carne* (page 77).

Roll the dough to sheets as if making noodles (see instructions in the recipe for *Pasta all'Uovo* on page 94). Cut the sheets to fit the length of the *chitarra*. Dust the pasta sheets aggressively with flour and lay the sheets, one at a time, on the *chitarra* strings.

Use a rolling pin to roll the dough through the strings.

Rolling will cut the dough, but it will not always release it: Strum your fingers over the metal strings to loosen the cut strands; the cut pasta will fall into the box below.

Lay the pasta strands on a sheet pan lined with parchment and dusted with flour.

Other Fresh Pasta Shapes

Shaping *Garganelli*

Follow the procedure in "Rolling the Dough" on page 371 to roll the dough until you can see color through the sheet (this will likely be the next-to-thinnest setting on the machine). Cut the dough strip into 4-centimeter (1½-inch) squares.

Place a square of pasta on a grooved *garganelli* comb (*pettine*), or gnocchi board (*rigagnocchi*), rotating the square so that one corner points toward you (the square will look like a diamond).

Tap the far corner of the diamond with a little water to help seal. Flour the dowel and lay it across the pasta square.

Pressing firmly on the sides of the dowel, not on the pasta, roll the dowel so that the top and bottom corners of the diamond overlap and seal, forming a hollow tube with a quill-like point at each end, and fine grooves all over.

Slip the *garganelli* from the dowel and place in a single layer on a baking sheet sprinkled with flour.

Making *Orecchiette*

Shaping *orecchiette* on a wooden board will create the rough-textured surface characteristic of this pasta.

Cut off a golf ball–size piece of dough and roll it into a rope about 1¼ centimeters (½ inch) in diameter. Using a small knife or a bench scraper, cut the dough rope into ½-centimeter (¼-inch) lengths.

Set a piece of dough in front of you on the work surface. Using the rounded blade of a butter knife or your thumb, press into the dough to flatten. Then drag blade or thumb across the dough, pressing down so that the dough thins and curls around blade or thumb. If the dough sticks or slides while you are working with it, dip your fingertips in water.

Balance the *orecchiette*, rounded side down, on your thumb. Stretch it over your thumb, turning it inside out. The *orecchiette* should be deeply concave in shape, and rough-textured on the exterior.

Rolling and Filling Shapes for Filled Pasta (*Pasta Ripiena: Stendere e Farcire*)

The dough for ravioli and other filled pastas is rolled just as for noodles, with one exception—the dough should be slightly softer and moister so that the layers stick together and the pasta does not crack when shaped and pressed around the filling. Therefore, one piece of dough is rolled through the entire thinning process and then cut and filled before moving onto the next one. To ensure that the two layers of dough adhere well, the dough is brushed with either water or beaten egg.

To maintain a delicate texture, the dough is rolled very thin because it will be overlapped to enclose the filling; if it is rolled too thick, the finished pasta will be dense and heavy around the edges. Once rolled, the dough sheet is placed on a work surface dusted with flour to prevent the dough from sticking.

Filled pastas may be refrigerated, covered with plastic, for up to several hours in a single layer so as not to crush them, and so they do not stick to one another. Turn them every now and then so that they dry evenly on both sides.

Filling and Shaping Ravioli

Pasta sheets are rolled to about 10 centimeters (4 inches) wide, and filled by spoon or using a pastry bag: Rounds of filling are piped about 4 centimeters (1½ inches) apart all along the bottom third of the dough strip, which is placed on a well-floured work surface so the pasta does not stick. It is important that the filling be moist but not so wet that it soaks the dough and causes it to tear. The dough strip is brushed with water to help the layers adhere. The top half is folded over to cover the filling and pressed to

seal. The air is pressed out from around the filling. Individual ravioli are cut with a knife, or a straight or fluted roller cutter (depending on the recipe), and trimmed as necessary.

Ravioli are placed on a parchment-lined baking sheet sprinkled with semolina or cornmeal, and more is sprinkled on top of the ravioli. Ravioli should be covered with plastic or a moist towel to keep the edges from drying and hardening, and should be turned every now and then so that they dry evenly on both sides.

Filling and Shaping Tortellini

Cut the pasta into 5-centimeter (2-inch) squares with a roller cutter or knife (use a ruler to notch the dough in order to make regular cuts).

Pipe ¾ teaspoon of filling in the center of each square. Moisten the edges of the pasta with water to help them seal.

Fold the squares into triangles, press out any air around the filling, and press to seal the edges.

Dab the points of the long sides with water, then bring them together to form a ring, and seal them between your fingers.

Set the tortellini aside on a sheet pan lined with parchment and sprinkled with semolina or cornmeal, cover well with plastic wrap, and refrigerate until ready to cook.

Cooking and Saucing Pasta

Al dente, which means "to the tooth," describes a point in the cooking process when the pasta gives slightly when one bites into it. It is used primarily in reference to dry pasta, or *pasta secca*. (Dry pasta will be chewier than fresh when fully cooked because hard-wheat flour does not absorb water as effectively as soft-wheat flour.) The exact point of al dente differs among regions in Italy; however, it is always recommended that the finished pasta should still have texture, without any raw taste. Many chefs believe that the only foolproof method of testing for doneness is to pull a strand out of the boiling water and bite into it.

The key to cooking and saucing pasta is to remember that the sauce is not separate from the pasta. To achieve this amalgamation, the pasta is cooked most of the way through in a pot of boiling water, then transferred to a skillet and cooked briefly with the sauce (*saltare in padella*). This way, the pasta absorbs the flavor of the sauce as it finishes cooking, and the starch from the pasta helps to bind the sauce. Pasta should never be oversauced. The pasta is the main attraction and the sauce should highlight and embellish it.

Pasta is cooked in a large, heavy-bottomed pot of boiling water. This requires at least 4 liters (1 gallon) of water per 450 grams (1 pound) of pasta. Cold tap water is always used for cooking pasta, as hot water picks up a metallic taste from the pipes.

Enough salt is added to the pasta water so that it tastes salty. Consideration should also be given, however, to the saltiness of the sauce that will accompany the pasta. If cooking long-dried pasta shapes such as spaghetti, gently bend the pasta with a long spoon as it begins to soften to submerge it in the hot water. Do not break the pasta.

Pasta secca is cooked until nearly al dente. (Once one is familiar with the pasta, it is possible to tell by sight when it is cooked. Until then, pull a piece out of the pot and taste it.) The pasta is drained, and about 500 milliliters (2 cups) of the cooking liquid is reserved for finishing. The drained pasta is added to the skillet in which the sauce has been cooking. Enough cooking liquid is added to bathe the pasta in the sauce. The pasta finishes cooking in the skillet, with more cooking liquid added as needed, until the pasta is al dente and the sauce has reduced and thickened slightly around the pasta. This step is particularly important in a restaurant setting because the additional liquid ensures that the pasta remains moist from the time it leaves the pan to the time it arrives at the client's table. The sauce should also remain emulsified for several minutes after plating.

Ravioli and other filled pastas are cooked in a large pot of simmering salted water. (The water should not be boiling rapidly as excessive agitation may harm the pasta.) The pieces of pasta are added all at once and stirred to prevent them from sticking to one another. Cooking time varies with the thickness of the dough. The pasta is carefully removed with a spider or slotted spoon (it is too delicate to pass through a strainer) and finished in a skillet with sauce and sufficient pasta cooking liquid, just as with other pasta shapes.

Making Emulsified Sauces for Pasta

A simple traditional sauce may be made by melting butter with whole herbs, such as sage, thyme, or marjoram. The drained pasta is added to the skillet with a few tablespoons of its cooking liquid. Cook, swirling the pan, until the pasta has absorbed the flavor of the sauce and the sauce has reduced and thickened slightly around the pasta. Once the emulsion has been achieved, the sauce must not be boiled or it will separate.

Making a *Burro Nocciola* Emulsion

An emulsion may also be made with butter that has been cooked to a golden brown color, called *burro nocciola*. Once the color is achieved, the sauce is emulsified with a little water, as above.

A *burro nocciola* is commonly served with gnocchi, such as *Strozzapreti* on page 122, and with fish (see *Sogliola alla Mugnaia* on page 226), flavored with lemon.

Pasta Shapes and Sauces

Italian culinary tradition ascribes specific sauces to specific pasta shapes, the result of centuries of regional traditions and local ingredients. In contemporary cooking, it is not always necessary to follow these traditions, but it is important to understand the spirit and thinking behind them so that intelligent substitutions can be made. The sauce is always meant to be eaten in the same mouthful as the pasta it accompanies. Therefore, it is important that the sauce adhere correctly to the pasta. Different types and shapes of pasta absorb and hold sauce in different ways. As a general rule of thumb:

○ Long, thin pastas are best with smooth or lighter-consistency sauces, and those with finely chopped ingredients—seafood or vegetables—that will easily coat the strands.

○ Long, wide noodles are particularly good with creamy sauces and will accommodate slightly larger chunks.

○ Thick, short pastas work well with heavier sauces.

○ Short, narrow tubes such as penne and ziti work well with sauces with small to medium-size chunks.

○ Large, tubular pastas will catch and hold large, chunky ingredients such as meat and beans.

○ Small, open shapes such as farfalle will tolerate sauces with medium-size chunks.

○ Very small pasta shapes are used only in soups.

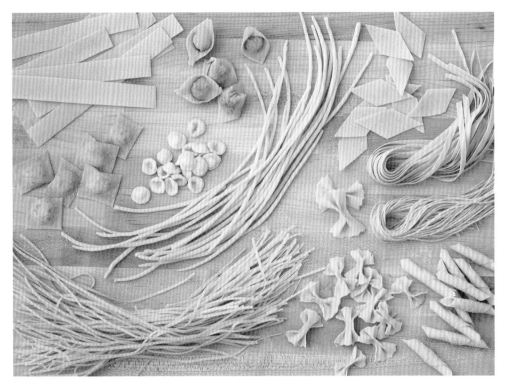

pinched in the center—the difference being that *strichetti* is slightly larger.

Garganelli: A handmade pasta shaped a little like penne; the dough is cut into squares, rolled over a tool called a *pettine*, or comb, to mark it, and rolled around a slender dowel to form a tube.

Maccheroni alla chitarra: A specialty of Abruzzo. Thick, squared strips (like squared spaghetti) are cut on a guitarlike device called a *chitarra*; the pasta is rolled slightly thicker than for noodles, laid over the wires of the *chitarra*, and cut using a rolling pin.

Orecchiette: Small, ear-shaped pasta rounds made by rolling and cutting small pieces of pasta, then pressing down and rolling on the cutting board with the thumb to make the indentation.

Pici: Long, handmade pasta made in Tuscany.

Bigoli: Long, round, thick strands from the Veneto (may also be dried).

Fresh Pasta Shapes

Flat Noodles

Tagliolini: 1½ millimeters (¹⁄₂₄ inch) wide and long

Trenette: 3 millimeters (⅛ inch) wide and long

Tagliatelle or fettuccine: 6 millimeters (¼ inch) wide and long

Pappardelle: 1½ to 2½ centimeters (½ to 1 inch) wide, 15 to 21 centimeters (6 to 8 inches) long

Lasagne: rectangles of varying widths

Other Shapes

Farfalle ("butterfly") or *strichetti* ("pinched"): Both refer to the same shape—a small rectangle of pasta,

Fresh Pasta Shapes for Soups

Maltagliati ("badly cut"): An irregular, lozenge-shaped cut classically used in bean soups and with *ragùs*

Quadrucci: Small squares

Filled Pasta Shapes

Ravioli (also *tortelloni*, *tortelli*): Square or round pastas

Cappelletti: Small, hat-shaped pastas

Pansotti: Triangular pastas

Anolini: Round pastas

Dried Pasta Shapes

Pasta Lunga (Long Pasta)

Capellini, *capelli d'angelo*: Very fine, threadlike, round pasta.

Spaghettini, spaghetti, vermicelli: Long, round strands.

Trenette, linguine: Long, flat strands. *Trenette* is traditional with pesto.

Lasagne, *lasagne festonate*, *tagliatelle*, *reginette*, *tripolini*: Long, flat, wide sheets (*tripolini* are narrower). *Lasagne festonate* have ruffled edges.

Bucatini, *perciatelli*, *maccheroncelli*: Long, tubular, hollow strands of varying thickness.

Pasta Corta (Short Pasta)

Rigatoni millerighe, penne, *sedani*, *maniche*: Tubular shapes of various sizes; they may be straight or curved, smooth or grooved.

Fusilli, *gemelli*, *conchiglie*, farfalle: Fusilli and *gemelli* are short spiral shapes; *conchiglie* are shells; farfalle are butterflies or bow ties.

Stelline, *anellini*, *alfabeto*, orzo: *Stelline* are small stars; *anellini* are rings; *alfabeto* are letters of the alphabet; orzo look like grains of rice.

Lesson 7

Working with Gnocchi

Italian cuisine boasts numerous different forms of gnocchi. Potato gnocchi are the most well known in the United States, and present a variety of issues to the cook that are addressed here.

Potato Gnocchi

Ingredients

Potato gnocchi require very few ingredients. At their most plain, they're made simply with potatoes, flour, and seasonings. Eggs are often added to bind the dough, along with grated cheese for flavor. Spinach is sometimes added for additional flavor and color, and some variations are made with ricotta cheese.

A well-made potato gnocchi is tender and ethereally light. This texture is achieved by using starchy potatoes such as Idaho (also called "mealy," "baking," and "all-purpose") potatoes, and as little flour as possible. Starchy potatoes concentrate dry starch in their cells, so they are denser than waxy potatoes. When cooked, the starch expands and separates, creating a dry, fluffy texture. (In contrast, waxy potatoes hold together when cooked, creating a dense, moist texture, making them more suitable for soups, stews, and salads.)

Recipes for making gnocchi, like those for making pasta dough, are more of a guide than an exact formula. The exact amount of flour will depend on the dryness of the potato, the dryness of the flour, and humidity. Gnocchi making is about developing intuition and understanding of the feel of the dough.

Flour, in combination with water, develops gluten; too much flour will result in gnocchi that are heavy and gummy. Since starchy potatoes contain less water than waxy potatoes, they require less flour to bind the dough.

Eggs create a dumpling with a firmer, spongier texture.

Making Potato Gnocchi

The technique illustrated below is used when making *Gnocchi di Patate* on page 121.

The Dough

Potatoes for gnocchi are traditionally boiled in their skins to absorb as little water as possible, but baking on a bed of salt as recommended at The International Culinary Center yields very good results; baking dries out the flesh of the potato, and the salt helps to draw out moisture from the vegetable. Once tender, the potatoes are peeled as soon as they are cool enough to handle. (If they are allowed to cool completely, they will

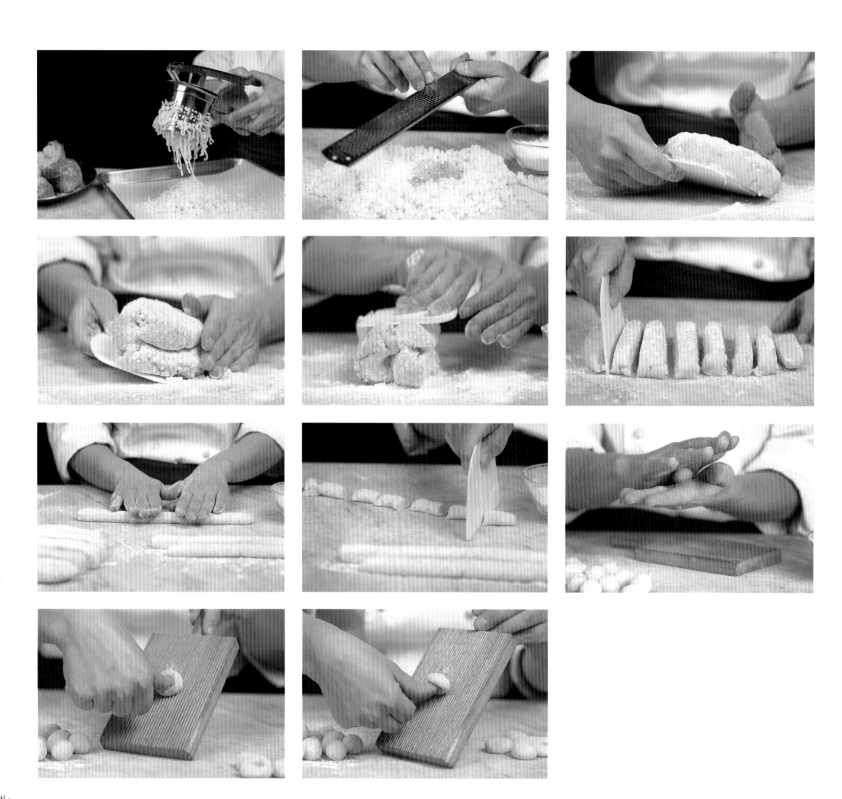

become gelatinous when passed.) While still warm, the potatoes are pressed through a ricer, food mill, or drum sieve onto a sheet pan or into a large bowl. The sheet pan allows the potatoes to be spread out sufficiently so that the residual moisture evaporates quickly.

The riced potatoes are mounded on a board or in a bowl. Eggs, if using, cheese, and seasonings are added and mixed until everything is well incorporated. The dough is turned out onto a clean board and sprinkled with the smaller amount of flour noted in the recipe. Slide the plastic bench scraper under the dough, fold the dough in half, and press. (This action involves folding and pressing, rather than the smearing action of kneading that is used to develop gluten for other doughs.) Turn the dough and fold and press it again. Continue folding and pressing in this way, five to eight times, until no more flour is visible. (Do not overwork; overworking will cause the gnocchi to become gummy.) The exact quantity of flour required is variable. It depends on the water content and age of the potato and the moisture content of the flour. The correct amount of flour will create a dough that is soft but not sticky. The finished dough should be light but not gummy.

A "test" *gnoccho* is pinched off the mound of dough and cooked in a pot of boiling water to determine whether the gnocchi will hold together. If the *gnoccho* falls apart, add a little more flour to the dough.

Shaping and Cooking Gnocchi

There are several methods for shaping potato gnocchi (by rolling them over the tines of a fork, across the large holes of a grater, or across a wooden gnocchi board), but the purpose is the same: to create indentations and crevasses to catch and hold the sauce.

On a lightly floured work surface, flatten the mound of dough to a rectangle with the bench scraper and square it up. Cut the rectangle into strips about 2½ centimeters (1 inch) wide. The strips are rolled underneath the fingers, starting from the center and working out to the ends, into ropes 26 to 30½ centimeters (10 to 12 inches) long, depending on the size of the rectangle. The ropes are dusted with flour and cut into 2½-centimeter (¾-inch) lengths. The lengths are then rolled gently in the palms to give them a rounded shape.

Place one dough piece across the ridges of the gnocchi board or a fork (tines curved down so that you are working on the back of the fork). Place your thumb on the dough. Press into the dough while you flick it down the board or off the fork, creating a concave shape that rolls over on itself. It should have a deep indentation on one side, and ridges on the other. Place on a parchment-lined sheet pan dusted with flour to keep the dumplings from sticking. Once formed, the gnocchi are cooked, or they may be wrapped and refrigerated for several hours or frozen.

Potato gnocchi are boiled, like pasta, in a large pot of salted water, in batches, to prevent them from sticking together. The gnocchi are cooked when they no longer taste floury—generally when they float to the surface. The cooked gnocchi are transferred with a spider or slotted spoon to the skillet with the sauce and cooked briefly in the sauce, like pasta, to absorb the flavors.

Other Forms of Gnocchi

Shaping Gnocchi into *Quenelles*

The dough for *Gnocchi di Spinaci e Ricotta* on page 124 can be shaped using two spoons into ovals called *quenelles*. *Strozzapreti* (page 122) and *Gnocchi alla Romana* (page 120) are also sometimes shaped into *quenelles*. *Gnocchi di Spinaci e Ricotta* are shown above.

Scoop a small amount of the gnocchi mixture onto one spoon. Use a second spoon to smooth over the mound. The *quenelle* should have a football shape, with three distinct rounded sides. Slide the second spoon under the gnocchi to gently roll it onto a parchment-lined sheet pan sprinkled with flour.

Making *Gnocchi alla Romana*

The technique illustrated below is used when making *Gnocchi alla Romana* on page 120.

Add the semolina in a steady stream to the heated milk, while whisking, and cook over low heat, stirring slowly until the semolina pulls away from the sides as a mass and a skin forms on the bottom of the pot. Remove from the heat and stir in the remaining ingredients.

Pour the hot mixture onto a marble surface or buttered, parchment-lined half sheet pan or hotel pan and spread with an offset spatula to 1½ to 2 centimeters (½ to 1 inch) thick. Flatten and level the mixture by pressing it with another pan. Let cool. Cut the cooled dough into rounds or squares. Shingle the gnocchi, overlapping slightly, on a buttered sheet pan, dot with butter, sprinkle with cheese, and bake until golden brown.

Lesson 8

Working with Risotto and Polenta

Risotto

Although risotto is sometimes made with water, it is normally cooked in stock. A light-flavored stock is preferable because the flavor will concentrate as the broth reduces during cooking. Vegetable, poultry, fish, and meat stocks are used, depending on the risotto. Veal stock is never used. While one can approximate the quantity of liquid necessary for a given weight of rice, the exact amount varies depending on a number of factors, including variety and age of rice, size and depth of cooking vessel, and rate of cooking. Liquid should be brought to a simmer separately so it is always added to the rice hot.

Cooking Risotto

The technique illustrated below is used to make several *risotti* in Chapter 7 as well as the *fregola* in the recipe for *Quaglie alla Griglia* on page 175.

The objective when cooking risotto is the even, gradual release of starch to create the distinctive creaminess of the dish. This is achieved in stages, and the rice is stirred constantly to help release the starch into the broth. For the even and gradual release of the starch, risotto should be cooked at a constant temperature; the flame should be high enough that the stock simmers aggressively.

The ideal pan for cooking risotto is heavy-bottomed, to prevent the rice and onion from burning, and shallow enough to facilitate the evaporation of the stock (preferably, the sides of the pan should be 6½ to 7½ centimeters / 2½ to 3 inches tall).

First, aromatics, if any (primarily onion), are cooked with butter and/or olive oil until softened and translucent. The onion is chopped very finely—as small as the grains of rice—so that it cooks completely and melts into the cooked dish. One doesn't want to encounter chunks of onion in the risotto. The onion should not take on color at this point because it will continue cooking with the rice. The onion and aromatics are started in cold oil (and/or butter that has been heated just enough to melt). Starting in a cold pan prevents the aromatics from burning; as the fat heats, the aromatics release flavor into it.

In the next stage, called *tostatura*, the raw rice is added to the pan and stirred with the butter and onion. This process not only develops flavor, but also coats the grains with fat, sealing in the starch and preventing too rapid an absorption of the cooking liquid.

Wine is added and cooked, stirring constantly, to evaporate. Then, in the *cottura* (cooking) phase, hot stock—enough to cover the rice (approximately 350 to 500 milliliters / 1½ to 2 cups)—is added. The stock is ladled along the side of the pan so as to wash any starch from the sides back into the risotto. The mixture

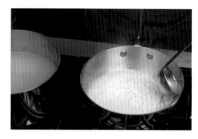

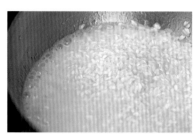

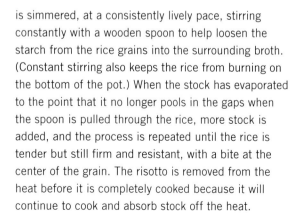

is simmered, at a consistently lively pace, stirring constantly with a wooden spoon to help loosen the starch from the rice grains into the surrounding broth. (Constant stirring also keeps the rice from burning on the bottom of the pot.) When the stock has evaporated to the point that it no longer pools in the gaps when the spoon is pulled through the rice, more stock is added, and the process is repeated until the rice is tender but still firm and resistant, with a bite at the center of the grain. The risotto is removed from the heat before it is completely cooked because it will continue to cook and absorb stock off the heat.

The final step is the *mantecatura* (from *mantecare*, which means "to make creamy"), the action of emulsi-

fying fat into liquid, in which butter and grated cheese are vigorously stirred into the risotto, off the heat, to create an emulsification that accentuates the creamy texture of the dish. The risotto must be somewhat liquid before the fat and cheese are added; to this end, a small ladleful of stock is added before the pan is removed from the heat. (Make sure the rice is hot—the cold butter will cool it down.)

The finished risotto should be suspended in a broth that is thick enough to hold the risotto in a cohesive mass when it is flipped. The risotto is flipped by jerking the pan toward you in a motion that causes the rice to flip back upon itself, like a wave breaking against the side of the pan—called *all'onda* in Italian.

The risotto is the correct texture when you hold the plate perpendicular to the table and the rice is loose enough to slide down the plate, but not soupy. If necessary, the finished risotto may be briefly returned to the heat and stirred constantly. *Do not boil*; the butter will separate out of suspension and the risotto will look oily.

Cooking Risotto in a Restaurant Setting

In a restaurant setting, it is usually impractical to cook risotto to order. The risotto is cooked through the *tostatura* phase, then quickly cooled, removed to a container, and later finished to order. Alternatively, the risotto may be cooked through one addition and reduction of stock, after which it is poured out and spread onto an unbuttered sheet pan. A spoon is gently dragged through the rice to expose as much surface area as possible, so that the rice cools as quickly as possible, after which the risotto is finished to order.

Cooking *Farro* in the Style of Risotto

Farro can be made just like risotto, with a different result. *Farro* is more forgiving than rice in that, although both grains continue to cook after removal from the heat, *farro* retains its firm texture far more effectively. Because *farro* does not have as much starch as short-grain rice, it need not be stirred constantly, and it will not create the creamy, surrounding liquid that characterizes risotto. (See *Farrotto Primavera* on page 134.)

Polenta

Polenta is traditionally made with water, but vegetable, poultry, fish, or beef stock may be used for additional flavor. Polenta is served soft and creamy, like a porridge, or it is allowed to firm up and cooked again ("twice-cooked").

Soft Polenta

The technique discussed below is used when making *Polenta* on page 136.

Polenta was traditionally made in an unlined copper pot called a *paiolo* that hung over the fireplace. A heavy-bottomed pot makes an excellent modern substitute.

In order to prevent lumps, polenta is started in cold water with a little olive oil, whisking often. As the water comes to a simmer, the polenta thickens. The mixture is cooked slowly, stirring often with a wooden spoon, until the polenta pulls away from the sides of the pan, is free of lumps, and has the consistency of soft mashed potatoes, with a silky texture resulting from the release of the cornstarch. Unlike risotto, polenta need not be stirred constantly—a stir every now and then with a wooden spoon is adequate.

To test the consistency of polenta, a small amount is spooned onto a plate and allowed to set for a minute; when the plate is tilted, the polenta should not run. Polenta may be held for several hours in a bain marie (*bagno maria)* or in a pan on the back of the stove.

The desired consistency of the polenta varies, depending on the ultimate dish. For a softer texture, a little stock may be added to thin. The finished polenta will look very much like *Gnocchi alla Romana* (see page 120).

Shaping and Cutting Polenta

Twice-cooked polenta may be firmed up in a loaf pan and sliced, or allowed to set on a sheet pan and cut into shapes.

Lesson 9

Working with Eggs

Eggs (*uova*) are among the most nutritious foods on earth. One large egg contributes approximately 6.5 grams of protein (about 13 percent of the average daily requirement), as well as substantial amounts of thiamin, iron, phosphorous, and vitamins A, D, and E. The yolk contains most of the fat, cholesterol, vitamins, and protein, while the egg white is composed mostly of water and albumen.

Chicken eggs may be the most commonly used in restaurant cooking, but the eggs of several game birds are popular, too. Duck eggs are slightly larger than chicken eggs and contain slightly more fat, which imparts a rich flavor. Goose eggs are significantly larger even than duck eggs, averaging 184 to 200 grams (6½ to 7 ounces). They have a more pronounced flavor than chicken eggs and a very hard, chalky-white shell. Speckled-shell turkey eggs are roughly the same size as duck eggs. Pigeon eggs are small, weighing about 14 grams (½ ounce) each. Tiny, speckled quail eggs are popular for their delicate, creamy texture. Ostrich eggs weigh slightly over 450 grams (1 pound) and have a distinctive flavor, but are often difficult to open.

Cooking Eggs

Methods of cooking eggs may be roughly divided into two categories: cooking in the shell and out of the shell.

Eggs Cooked in the Shell

This category includes soft-boiled (*uova bazzotte)* and hard-boiled (*uova sode)* eggs. Eggs cooked in the shell should be started in cold water to cover by 3 centimeters (about 1 inch), and timed from the point at which the water comes to a simmer. About 45 milliliters (3 tablespoons) of white vinegar per liter (quart) of water are added to the water to prevent albumen from leaking into the water if the egg shell cracks during cooking.

Soft-boiled eggs (yolks are warm but still liquid) are simmered for 3 minutes.

Medium-soft-boiled eggs (yolks have begun to firm) are simmered for 5 minutes.

Hard-boiled eggs (yolks and whites are firm but yolk is still moist and shiny) are cooked somewhat differently: Cold water is added to cover the eggs, and the water is brought to a simmer; the pan is removed from the heat, covered, and allowed stand for 11 minutes.

Eggs Cooked Out of the Shell

This category includes poached, fried, baked, and scrambled eggs.

Poached eggs (*uova in camicia*, also called *uova af-fogate*) are made in a shallow pan of simmering water acidulated with vinegar (30 milliliters / 2 tablespoons per liter / quart of water); vinegar helps to set the egg white. Do not add salt to the poaching water; it inhibits the coagulation of the whites. The eggs are poached for 3 minutes or until the whites are firm and the yolks are covered with a thin, almost transparent film and remain runny. Italians appreciate the taste of vinegar with poached eggs (it is said to soften the smell) so, unlike in French cuisine, the eggs are not rinsed before serving. If the eggs are to be reheated, rewarm in gently simmering (93°C / 200°F), salted water.

Fried eggs (*uova al piatto*, or *uova in padella*) are cooked in a skillet with lard, butter, or olive oil over medium-high heat until the white is set and the yolk is warm but still runny. The white alone is salted, as salt toughens the yolk. The yolk should remain intact during cooking. Fried eggs may be finished with a drop or two of vinegar.

Baked eggs (*uova al forno*) are traditionally served family-style. The eggs are cooked until the white is set and the yolk is warm but still runny.

Scrambled eggs (*uova strapazzate*) are cooked in a skillet or saucepan in olive oil or butter. The beaten eggs are stirred over a relatively low heat to encourage the formation of small, creamy curds. The finished eggs should be very soft and moist; the pan is moved on and off the heat as needed during cooking to prevent the egg from cooking too fast and hardening.

Frittate

The technique illustrated at left is used when making *Frittata di Cipolle* on page 143.

The pan is an integral element of the frittata-making process. Traditionally, *frittate* are prepared in a skillet reserved solely for this purpose. When necessary, the pan is cleaned with coarse salt. A nonstick pan, however, is an excellent substitute and can be cleaned after every use. The size of the pan is important—if it is too small, the frittata will take too long to cook and the texture will suffer. (A 21-centimeter / 8-inch skillet is the correct size for 6 eggs.)

The frittata is cooked in clarified butter (see "Making Clarified Butter" on page 143). Once the butter is heated in the skillet, the egg mixture is added. As the egg sets, a rubber spatula is used to push the sides of the firming frittata in toward the center to develop an even, firm, but creamy consistency. (The egg is going to cook first on the edges; the idea is to move the cooked egg from the edges into the center, and the egg from the center to the edges.) Shake the pan once in a while to prevent the frittata from sticking to the bottom of the pan. Once the egg is no longer runny, the frittata cooks without moving until it is golden brown on the bottom.

The frittata is flipped in the pan and cooked until both sides are golden brown and the frittata is cooked through but still moist. (This is accomplished by giving the pan a sharp jerk away from you so that the frittata leaps out of the pan and turns in the air. Students are taught to flip, but you may cheat, if you like: Cover the pan with a plate, overturn pan and plate, then slide the frittata back into the pan.)

Lesson 10

Working with Yeast Doughs (Sweet and Savory)

Working with Yeast (*Lievito*)

Doughs for breads such as pizza, calzone, focaccia and *grissini* are leavened by yeast, a living, single-cell organism that feeds on the starches in flour, converting them to alcohol and carbon dioxide. The action of the yeast creates pockets of carbon dioxide that, trapped in the dough, cause the dough to physically expand, or "rise." In addition to sugar (or sugar in the form of starch), yeast requires moisture and a controlled temperature in which to reproduce.

Unlike chemical leaveners such as baking soda and baking powder, yeast grows slowly. Therefore, while it is not necessary to add sugar to the dough (yeast will feed on the starch in the flour), it is practical to do so, because a small amount of sugar speeds the growth. The sugar also adds flavor, and when baked, in the case of breads, color.

Two types of yeast are available: compressed fresh yeast and active dry yeast. **Compressed fresh yeast (b)** is sold in a cake form. It is perishable and will hold in the refrigerator for only a very short time, 7 to 10 days. **Active dry yeast (a)** is sold in envelopes in the form of dehydrated granules. The yeast is dormant; it reactivates when dissolved in a warm liquid **(c)**. Active dry yeast may be refrigerated for up to 1 year.

Optimally, yeast should be dissolved in water at a temperature between 40° and 46°C (105° and 115°F). Yeast does not grow well in temperatures below about 21°C (70°F) and it dies at about 60°C (140°F); the heat of the oven during baking kills the yeast. The most common error students make with pizza dough is to use water that is too hot, so that the yeast is killed. The ideal temperature of 43°C (110°F) feels *warm* on the skin, not hot; until you are practiced, it is useful to test the water temperature with a thermometer.

Used properly, both compressed fresh and active dry yeasts are reliable enough products that they generally need not be proofed. But if there is any question as to the viability of the yeast, or if you are working in bulk, proofing is a good idea. To proof yeast, combine it in a bowl with warm water and a little bit of sugar and mix thoroughly. Cover and let stand. If the mixture becomes foamy, the yeast is alive.

If substituting active dry yeast for fresh, use approximately 50 percent of the weight of fresh yeast. The exact conversion will depend on the specific dry yeast being used. At The International Culinary Center, we also use instant yeast (different from "rapid" or "active dry"), which is a dry product that requires no predissolving or proofing.

Gluten and Kneading

Gluten is a protein found in wheat and some other cereals. It is a tough, stringy substance that gives dough the elasticity necessary to expand as the yeast grows. Gluten is formed when the protein molecules in the flour are moistened with liquid and the mixture is worked. Kneading, a process of working and stretching the dough, develops the strands of gluten so that the dough is strong enough to hold its structure as the yeast expands. (The action is slightly different from kneading pasta dough because the dough is stretched and pulled as it is kneaded in order to build structure.) The change in the dough is perceptible: Before kneading, the dough is soft and loose; after kneading, it is elastic and firm and springs back when pressed. Kneading may be accomplished by hand or with the dough hook of a standing mixer.

Making a Yeast Dough

While yeast doughs may be made by hand or by machine, students at The International Culinary Center are taught to do it by hand. The techniques illustrated below are used when making pizzas, calzone, focaccia, and *grissini* in Chapter 9.

The flour, oil, water, yeast, sugar, and salt are combined in a bowl. The ingredients are mixed with a wooden spatula until all of the liquid has been incorporated. Scrape any pieces of dough adhering to the spoon into the bowl. Then continue mixing with a bench scraper until the dough comes together in a shaggy mass.

The dough is turned out onto a work surface.

The dough is kneaded until smooth, satiny, and elastic. Additional water can be added, if necessary. This process will take 5 to 10 minutes: Push the dough away from you with the heel of the hand, stretching it as you push, then fold the dough back on itself. Give the dough a half turn, and repeat. (Kneading may also be done in a standing mixer with a dough hook.)

The dough is placed in a lightly oiled bowl, and the top of the dough is lightly oiled as well to prevent a crust from forming. The bowl is covered with plastic and the dough is allowed to rise until doubled in volume. The volume of the dough is tested by pressing a finger into it: If the indentation remains, the dough is sufficiently risen; if the dough is overproofed, the surface will have nooks and crannies like those on an English muffin.

The dough may be proofed in a warm place, in which case it will rise relatively quickly, or refrigerated to proof more slowly. Delayed fermentation at a lower temperature will develop more flavor in the dough and give a rich golden color to the crust. (To make the dough a day ahead, refrigerate after 30 minutes of rising, punch the dough down, cover with plastic wrap, and chill.)

Shaping and Cooking Yeast Doughs

Each dough is shaped by a specific technique.

Pizza

The risen dough is rolled or stretched over the knuckles to a thin round, then transferred to a pizza paddle. The dough is spread thinly with sauce, if using, and topped with additional ingredients. (Pizza sauce is a short-cooked tomato sauce because it will cook again and reduce in the oven. The sauce may be flavored as one likes, with or without garlic and herbs.) The pizza is drizzled with olive oil (a squeeze bottle is best for this) and baked on a heated pizza stone in a very hot oven until the edges are crisp.

The technique illustrated below is used when making *Pizza Margherita* on page 147 and *Pizza Bianca con Rucola* on page 148.

Use a bench scraper to divide the dough into pieces (150 grams / 5 ounces each). Roll each piece into a ball, then press each down with your palm to de-gas. Cup your palm and roll each piece on the board, using your palm and cupped hand to shape the dough into a ball. Place on a parchment-lined sheet pan dusted with flour. Cover loosely with plastic wrap and let rest until almost doubled in size.

The dough may be stretched over the knuckles or rolled with a rolling pin. To stretch the dough using your knuckles, lightly flour one dough ball and flatten gently with your fingertips. Working from the center of the dough, press down and out to thin it, while you rotate the dough in a clockwise motion. Gently stretch to a thin round over floured knuckles. The edges of the dough should be slightly thicker than the center, in order to better contain the toppings. To roll with a rolling pin, lightly flour the dough ball and roll it to a 26-centimeter (10-inch) round.

Calzone

The technique illustrated above is used when making *Calzone con Verdure Miste* on page 148.

Use a bench scraper to divide the dough into pieces (180 grams / 6½ ounces each). Cover loosely with plastic wrap and let rest until almost doubled in size.

The dough is rolled or stretched to a thin round, using the same technique as for a pizza. The round is slightly larger, however, to accommodate the filling and folding.

The edges are egg-washed to help seal.

The filling is spread over half of the dough, allowing a border around the edge to prevent the filling from leaking out; the dough is folded over the filling, and the edges are crimped.

The top of the calzone is pricked to allow steam to escape.

The calzone is brushed all over with egg wash or olive oil, sprinkled with coarse salt, and baked until the crust is well browned.

The calzone should rest a few minutes after baking to allow the filling to firm a bit, so that it does not run out.

Focaccia

The technique illustrated above is used when making *Focaccia* and *Focaccia con Cipolle* on page 150, and *Focaccia con Patate* on page 152.

Once risen, the dough is punched down and placed in an oiled pan. It is pressed out with fingertips to fill the pan, then allowed to rise again.

The risen focaccia is brushed with olive oil.

Fingertips dipped in oil are pressed into the dough to make dimpled indentations all over the top.

Any toppings are spread over the top and the focaccia is baked in a moderate oven until golden brown.

The easiest way to cut regular slices of potato for topping is with a mandoline.

Grissini

Once risen, the dough for *grissini* is cut into strips with a knife and rolled into slender ropes. Alternatively, it may be cut on a pasta machine at the next-to-widest setting, then cut as for fettuccine.

The technique illustrated below is used when making *Grissini* on page 152.

To shape *grissini*, turn the dough out onto a table and cut into quarters. Work with one piece of dough at a time, and keep the remaining quarters covered with a clean kitchen towel or plastic wrap.

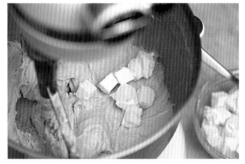

Bomboloni

Bomboloni are made from a yeast dough into which butter is beaten, like a brioche dough. The technique for making the dough is slightly different than for a basic yeast dough. The dough is rolled into balls just as for pizza dough (page 392) and deep-fried.

The technique illustrated at left is used for making *Bomboloni* on page 294.

Beat the flour, sugar, salt, and yeast in the bowl of a standing mixer fitted with the paddle attachment on low speed until thoroughly mixed.

The eggs are added, one at a time, each beaten well before the next is added. The dough is beaten on medium speed until smooth and satiny.

The dough is done when it is elastic, pulls away completely from the sides of the bowl, and doesn't break when pulled.

The butter is then beaten into the dough, a few chunks at a time, on low speed, until completely incorporated.

The key to this dough is to beat the dough sufficiently before adding the butter. Once added, the butter will inhibit the necessary development of gluten.

Roll the dough into a thin sheet (about 6 millimeters / ¼ inch thick) with a rolling pin, and use a large knife to cut 6-millimeter (¼-inch) strips.

Gently roll each strip of dough to round the cut edges.

Place the dough ropes 1½ centimeters (½ inch) apart on a baking sheet lined with lightly oiled parchment paper.

Sprinkle with coarse sea salt and pepper; gently roll seasoned *grissini* to coat evenly with the salt and pepper.

The dough is refrigerated and allowed to rise, then rolled into balls (see the technique for rolling pizza dough on page 392), and allowed to rise again.

Fry the balls without crowding the pan, until the *bomboloni* are a deep golden brown color and the dough is cooked through. Remove from the hot fat with a slotted spoon or skimmer.

The *bomboloni* are rolled in sugar while still warm and filled with pastry cream.

Lesson 11

Working with Poultry

According to the USDA, chickens are believed to be descended from red jungle fowl first domesticated in Southeast Asia before 7500 BCE. The birds were likely imported west through trade or military campaigns, and they can be seen in artifacts from parts of the Mediterranean dating to 500 BCE.

In the 1800s, importation of chickens from China led to the popularization of breeding in Europe and North America (McGee, *On Food and Cooking*). Mass production started in the twentieth century. Today, the vast majority of chickens for consumers are bred from the Cornish (developed in Britain) and the White Plymouth Rock (developed in New England) breeds to meet the needs of restaurants, food manufacturers, and supermarkets.

Anatomy and Structure of Poultry (*Pollame*)

Chickens should be plump, with full, round breasts. They should be odor-free, without red or dark spots, and not slimy. In younger birds, the breastbone is flexible, the spur is barely formed on the foot, and the neck is meaty.

In the United States, poultry is classified primarily by the size, weight, and age of the bird at the time it is processed. Classifications are similar in Italy. The age of the bird has a direct correlation with the appropriate cooking technique. A closer look at the anatomy and structure of chickens and other poultry clarifies this relationship.

Like all meat, poultry flesh consists of muscle fibers bundled together with connective tissue. The muscle is composed of about 75 percent water, 20 percent protein, and 5 percent fat, with trace amounts of other essential elements and carbohydrates (Wayne Gisslen, *Professional Cooking*). The tenderness of any cut of meat is dependent on the ratio of connective tissue to muscle fiber. Generally, the greater amount of connective tissue, the less tender the cut of meat. The amount of connective tissue increases with age and exercise. In other words, the leg meat of a young chicken will be more tender than that of a more mature bird. This fact, in part, explains why age is such an important factor as chefs select and develop chicken dishes. Moist-cooking methods, such as braising or stewing, are used often with more mature birds because their muscles are tougher. Dry-heat methods, such as frying and roasting, are often chosen for younger, more tender birds.

Meat Color and Taste

Chicken has muscle tissue of varying color; there is dark meat on the thighs and legs and white meat on the breasts and wings. To understand why this is and what it has to do with cooking, it is important to learn a little about muscles and how they work. Myoglobin is the protein responsible for these color differences in meat. Myoglobin helps store and carry oxygen to muscles for use during periods of high activity, such as running or flying. Like hemoglobin in the human body, myoglobin makes blood cells, and the muscles through which they circulate appear red or dark. Less active muscles receive less myoglobin and tend to be paler than more active ones.

Highly active muscles also possess a greater amount of fat and connective tissue than less active ones. During cooking, fat lubricates muscle cells and slows the escape of water, leading to the "juiciness" often associated with dark meat. White meat has little fat or connective tissue, which means there is little to slow the evaporation of water during cooking, making it much easier to cook a piece of white meat until it is overly dry.

Poultry Farming and Labeling

In the United States, poultry is labeled according to how it is raised. Practices of raising poultry in Italy are not substantially different. The following are some important terms used to identify chicken and poultry in the United States.

Fresh: Indicates that the chicken has never been cooled or held below -3°C (26°F).

Free-range: Indicates that the chicken has been given access to the outdoors, most typically a small, fenced area.

Organic: According to USDA rules, the label "organic" may be applied only if no pesticides or chemical fertilizers are used on the poultry feed, and no antibiotics are used at any stage of the production process, among other requirements. Chicken labeled "USDA Organic" must be raised free-range; however, not all free-range chickens are technically organic products.

Retained water: This term details the amount of water retained in the product as a result of mandated food-safety procedures.

Farm-raised: As used on most restaurant menus, this term indicates that the chicken has been raised on a local farm.

Natural: Indicates that the chicken contains no artificial ingredients, including coloring agents or preservatives, and has been minimally processed.

Produced without hormones: Indicates that no hormones were added during production. FDA regulations prohibit the use of artificial or added hormones in chicken production.

Antibiotic-free: Indicates that the chicken was raised without the use of antibiotics commonly used for health maintenance, disease prevention, or disease treatment.

Preparing Chicken for Cooking

Most restaurants in America purchase chickens and poultry already cleaned (RTC, or ready-to-cook). However, some free-range and hand-raised chickens are also sold in a less processed form. In this case, the cook must be prepared to fully clean the bird.

Preparing Whole, Undressed Chickens

If the chicken still has pinfeathers attached, hold it over a high flame or use a kitchen torch to singe them off. Follicles may also be plucked with fish tweezers.

Cut the skin on the back of the neck lengthwise and pull away. Remove the neck and head from the body. Trim the neck and save it for stock.

Cut off the feet and the wings at the second joint.

Insert one finger into the neck opening and detach the two red lungs from the thorax.

Cut off the circular anal opening and enlarge the opening.

Clean out the interior cavity, removing the liver, heart, windpipe, gizzards, and kidneys intact. Separate them on a cutting board. Trim the gizzards and separate the liver carefully from the gall bladder. The heart, gizzards, and feet may be used for stock. The liver, which is too strong-flavored for use in stock, is cooked separately. Discard the kidneys.

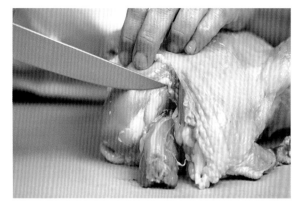 

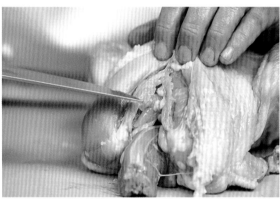 

Preparing Whole, Dressed Chickens

In the case of whole, RTC chickens, the prep work usually begins with trimming excess fat. Then the wishbone is removed, because this facilitates removal of the breast meat, both raw (for scaloppine) and cooked.

The wishbone is a type of fused clavicle, an adaptation made by dinosaurs and ancient birds to assist with flight. Removing the wishbone is often one of the first steps in preparing whole chickens for cooking.

Pull out excess fat near the tail.

To remove the wishbone, push the skin back on the breast. Make a small cut on either side of the bone and scrape. Reach into the incision with your fingers, forcing the meat away from the bone. Gently remove the bone, working carefully to prevent accidental breakage.

Trussing Chicken and Poultry

As the bird is roasted, muscle fibers begin to relax, even as surface proteins coagulate and brown. If cooked whole—that is, with meat attached to the carcass—the bird may droop somewhat. To improve appearance, many chefs prefer to truss, or secure, birds that will be cooked whole or carved tableside. Trussing also promotes even cooking and helps make it easier to hold stuffing inside the bird and to manipulate the bird when done.

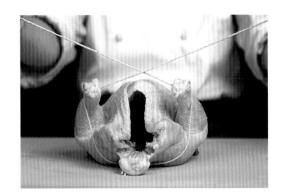  

There are several methods of trussing poultry; chefs have historically used twine (alone or in combination with a trussing needle), skewers, and even pins.

The trussing techniques illustrated above and opposite are used when making *Pollo Arrosto* on page 161 and *Anitra Arrosto* on page 169.

Trussing with Twine
(*Legare il Pollo con lo Spago*)

Prepare the chicken for cooking by trimming excess fat and removing the wishbone, as described in "Preparing Whole, Dressed Chickens" on the previous page. Cut a piece of twine about 75 centimeters (30 inches) long. Cut each of the wings at the second joint. Save trimmings for stock.

Season the cavity as desired. Push the legs of the bird toward its breast, and down, so that the breast pops up for a plump appearance and the skin is taut over the breast.

Slide the twine under the back of the bird next to the tail.

Lift the twine on both sides, bring it up over the drumsticks, and cross. Slide the twine under the tips of the drumsticks and pull tightly to secure.

Bring the twine along either side of the chicken, so that it crosses at the joint between thighs and drumsticks, compressing the bird into a neat package.

Turn the chicken on its breast, while holding the twine.

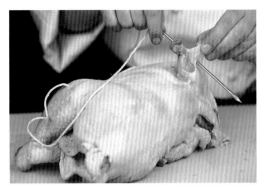

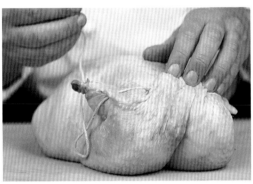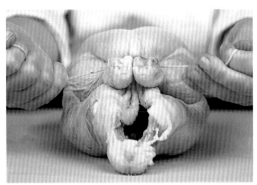

Bring one end of the twine over the wing and under the bone of the neck, securing the loose skin of the neck.

Secure both ends tightly with a single knot. Cut off and discard any excess twine.

Trussing with a Needle and Twine
(*Legare il Pollo con lo Spago e l'Ago*)

Follow the first two steps in the instructions for "Trussing with Twine" on the facing page, then thread the trussing needle with the string.

Turn the bird so the cavity is to the right. Lift up the drumstick nearest you and insert the needle in the skin under the knuckle.

Push the needle diagonally through the cavity, so the point comes through the articulation between the thigh and the drumstick.

Turn the chicken over on its breast, with the cavity facing away from you.

Thread the needle through the skin of the wing, then through the loose neck skin, the skin of the back, and the remaining wing.

Return the chicken to its back, with the cavity facing away.

Insert the needle through the articulation on the other side, coming out on the bias under the knuckle.

Pull tightly and tie down the drumsticks with a double, or butcher's, knot.

Cut off and discard excess twine.

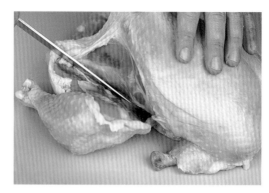 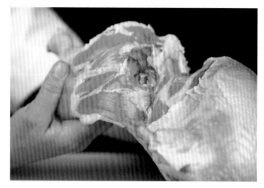 

 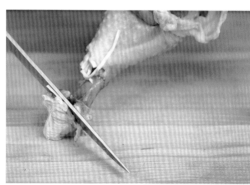 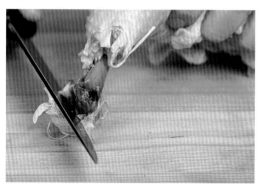

Quartering Chicken and Poultry

If not roasting or grilling a butterflied whole chicken, chefs must cut the chicken into parts. First, the chicken is quartered (*tagliare in quarti/squartare*). From this point, the chef can easily fabricate the chicken into smaller pieces, or use the quarters for roasting, braising, or grilling. In classic cuisine, the ends of the wings and the drumsticks are cleaned of cartilage to give the cooked bird a neat appearance.

There are several methods of quartering chicken and other poultry. The photos above and opposite may be used as a guide. They illustrate the technique used when making *Pollo alla Griglia* on page 163, *Pollo alla Cacciatora* on page 165, *Pollo Fritto* on page 166, and *Pollo alla Cacciatora in Bianco* on page 168.

Prepare the chicken for cooking by trimming excess fat and removing the wishbone as described on page 399. Cut off the wings at the second joint. Then place the chicken on its back.

Cut the skin between the leg and the breast, leaving a substantial amount of skin to cover the breast.

Pull the leg down to pop the thighbone out of the joint.

Cut around the thigh to completely separate it from the carcass. Be sure to include the oyster, the tender oval of meat that sits in a cavity along the backbone.

For an attractive presentation, cut through the skin and tendons above the knuckle of the drumstick. Chop away the cartilage, revealing the bone, and scrape down the skin. Do not cut through the bone; the bone will shatter. Repeat for the other leg.

With the chicken on its back, make an incision, inserting the knife through the neck end, on either side of the breast between the spine and the shoulder blades. Cut the whole breast section, including the bones, away from the backbone. (This may be done with poultry shears as well.)

Pull the freed side of the breast up, and cut down the other side of the backbone to remove.

Turn the breast skin side down and nick the top of the cartilage; pop out the keel bone (an oval bone that runs down the center of the breast, perpendicular to the ribs).

Cut the breast section in half lengthwise along the breastbone, separating the breast into two pieces.

Clean the wings bones just as with the drumsticks. Reserve bones, hearts, and gizzards for use in stock.

Preparing Scaloppine

Many chicken recipes use boneless chicken breasts cut into thin cutlets called scaloppine. The cutlets are pounded to an even thickness, for even cooking, and sautéed. The scaloppine may simply be floured, which aids in browning and helps to thicken the pan sauce (see *Piccata di Pollo con Fettuccine all'Uovo* on page 158). Or the cutlets may be breaded (*impanare*) with a coating of flour, egg, and breadcrumbs. Breading adds texture and flavor and helps seal in moisture; a very thin piece of meat can easily dry out during cooking (see *Petto di Pollo Impanato con Insalata di Pomodori e Rucola* on page 156). Toasted flour (see sidebar "Toasting Flour" on page 159) is sometimes used in the breading to ensure that the raw taste of the flour is cooked out.

Breaded meats are cooked in oil or clarified butter (see "Making Clarified Butter" on page 143). They are sautéed over medium heat in order to achieve the desired golden brown color while the meat cooks through. A balance must be achieved between the temperature of the meat and the color of the breading—it is difficult but important to finish both elements at the same time.

Scaloppine cut from veal and pork are cooked by this same method. Turkey cutlets (sliced from the breast) may also be used in place of veal, chicken, or pork, but turkey is always considered a less desirable choice.

Deboning Chicken Breasts for Scaloppine

Trim the fat and remove the wishbone as described on page 399. Cut the skin between the breast and thighs and peel the skin off of the breast meat.

Slide the knife along one side of the breastbone, holding the knife against the bone and pulling the meat away from the bone using the free hand. Continue in this way to remove the breast meat entirely from the bone, making sure to include the chicken tender, a

slender strip of boneless meat attached to the breast. Pull off the chicken tender and set it aside.

Repeat on the other side of the breastbone to remove the second breast.

Cut the breasts in half lengthwise to make two large, thin scaloppine.

Remove the tendon from the tenders; the tenders can be sautéed and sauced like scaloppine.

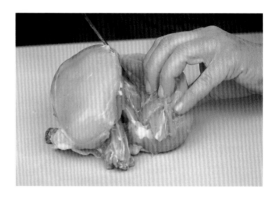
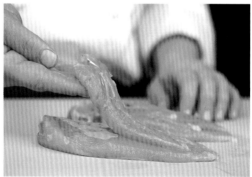

Breading (*Impanare*) for Chicken Scaloppine

When breading scaloppine, it's most efficient to use one hand to dip the meat in the egg, flour, and bread-crumbs, leaving the other hand clean.

Trim the breast meat of excess fat, if necessary. Using a meat mallet or the flat side of a cleaver, tap the meat flat between two pieces of plastic wrap or parchment paper.

Arrange three containers and fill each with one of the following ingredients: sifted flour, eggs beaten with salt and pepper, and dried breadcrumbs.

Season the meat on both sides with salt and pepper.

Lightly flour it on both sides, and pat off the excess.

With one hand, dip both sides of the scallopine in the egg wash. Make sure that the entire surface is coated.

Place in the breadcrumbs, and turn to coat. Pat the crumbs gently into the meat to adhere.

Cook the scaloppine in clarified butter over medium heat to crisp and brown the coating on both sides and to thoroughly cook the inside.

Remove the scaloppine to drain on absorbent paper.

Sautéing and Preparing a Pan Sauce for Scaloppine

The technique illustrated below is used when making *Piccata di Pollo con Fettuccine all'Uovo* on page 158, and is equally applicable to veal and pork scaloppine (see *Saltimbocca alla Romana* on page 180) and thin fish fillets.

Season the scallopine on both sides with salt and pepper. Flour the chicken and pat off the excess.

In a skillet, add oil as needed to comfortably coat the bottom of the pan. Add the garlic cloves and heat.

Place the scaloppine in the pan—do not crowd—and sauté on one side to brown. Turn and cook about 1 minute on the other side.

Remove the chicken. Pour off the fat from the pan.

Add the lemon juice, lemon slices, and capers. Add the wine, off the heat. Reduce. Add the stock and reduce until lightly thickened. Return the chicken to the pan, and turn in the sauce. Transfer the chicken to plates.

Preparing Chicken for Grilling

The breastbone of the chicken is removed, and the chicken is flattened before cooking to expose maximum surface area to the grill.

Trim the fat and remove the wishbone as described on page 399. Do not remove the wings. Remove the backbone by cutting down each side of the backbone with a heavy knife, through each side of the cavity of the chicken.

Make a small incision in the skin between each leg and breast tip and insert the end of each drumstick into each incision.

Remove the keel bone.

Place the chicken in a container and marinate in oil and seasonings.

Lift the chicken out of the container and wipe off the oil to limit flaming. Place the chicken on the grill, skin side down. Cover with a piece of foil and a weight to keep it flat. Grill until the skin is well browned. Turn, replace the foil and the weight, and grill 5 more minutes. Continue this way until the chicken is well browned.

Remove the weight and the foil. Baste thoroughly with the lemon-wine mixture. Return the chicken to the grill and continue cooking, basting every 5 to 10 minutes, until cooked through.

Roasting Chicken

Chicken will benefit from being seasoned with a *trito*, a traditional mix of chopped herbs and spices. This technique is used when making *Pollo Arrosto* on page 161 and is valid for all roasted meats and poultry (see also *Anitra Arrosto* on page 169, *Arista all Toscana* on page 209, *Costolette d'Agnello* on page 218, and *Agnello Arrosto* on page 219).

For the *trito*, mix together the chopped rosemary, sage, and garlic and the salt, pepper, and *spezie forti*.

Trim the fat and remove the wishbone as described on page 399. Cut off the wing tips.

With your hand, gently separate the skin from the breast meat without tearing the skin, and spread the *trito* over the breast meat. Make incisions through the skin into the joint between thigh and drumstick; stuff the *trito* into the joints and under the skin of the legs.

Season the inside of the cavity with salt and pepper and stuff with two of the lemon halves, the rosemary sprigs, and the garlic cloves.

Truss the chicken, then rub a little of the *trito* over the outside of the bird.

Toss the mirepoix in a bowl with a little olive oil and place in a roasting pan. Set the chicken on top. Pour oil over the chicken and roast, squeezing the lemon halves over the chicken.

Pour off the fat from the pan, and deglaze with wine, pouring it around—not over—the chicken, and continue roasting, basting every 10 minutes.

Set aside on a rack to rest 10 to 15 minutes.

Ladle any fat from the roasting pan. Deglaze with 250 milliliters (1 cup) chicken stock. Pass the juices and vegetables through a food mill. Pour the sauce into a saucepan; heat, and season to taste.

Carving a Whole Roasted Chicken

The technique illustrated below is used when serving *Pollo Arrosto* on page 161.

Make an incision between the breast and legs, and remove the legs in one piece, as well as the oyster (the tender oval of meat that sits along the backbone).

Cut down the breastbone and remove both sides of the breast.

Cut the breast pieces in half on the diagonal.

Cut between the thighs and drumsticks.

Manchonner the drumsticks (see "Quartering Chicken and Poultry" on page 402), if desired.

Working with Duck

The earliest ducks (*anatra*) were mallards, domesticated over 2,300 years ago in China, and as early as 1000 BCE in Greece (Christian Teubner, Sybil Gräfin Schönfeldt, and Siegfried Scholtyssek, *The Chicken and Poultry Bible: The Definitive Sourcebook*. The ducks found on contemporary restaurant menus are up to three times the size of their ancestors, and include the Rouen, the Aylesbury, the Nantais, and the Pekin.

Relative to chickens, ducks have a large skeleton, high fat content, and lower meat yield. Duck meat contains about 20 percent protein and 6 percent fat. A Pekin duck yields about 27 percent breast meat and 23 percent leg meat. A Muscovy duck yields about 25 percent breast meat and 28 percent leg meat.

Pekin/Peking

Most ducks commercially available in the United States are descended from the white Pekin, which was originally imported into the United States during the late 1800s and incorporated into traditional dishes cooked by immigrant groups, including the Chinese, the Germans, and the French. In the way of much immigrant cuisine, the Pekin duck eventually found its way onto American restaurant menus. Today, it is most frequently used in roasted dishes.

Just over 100 years ago, the business of duck-raising took root among American farmers in California and parts of Long Island, New York. At one time, Long Island produced 60 percent of the Pekins sold in the United States and the term *Long Island duck* generally referred to the Pekin breed. Today, Long Island produces less than 10 percent of the nation's Pekins and only birds raised in Long Island may be called Long Island ducks. Ducklings other than the Pekin are also produced in the United States, but in limited numbers from the domesticated Muscovy, mallard, and other imported breeds.

Mullard/Moulard

The Mullard is a large (approximately 1 kilogram / 2¼ pounds) crossbreed between a male Muscovy and a female Pekin duck. Widely used in the production of foie gras, Mullard meat has a different texture and a stronger flavor than the Pekin or Muscovy duck. After slaughter the carcass is often hung for a week to improve its tenderness. A *magret* is the breast of a Mullard duck.

Muscovy

Muscovy ducks are native to Central and South America. They are significantly leaner than Pekin ducks, and Muscovy meat is redder and has a gamier taste than that of Pekins.

Muscovy ducks have a large amount of breast meat. Male duck breasts are often used in sautéed preparations. (The tougher legs work well in braises and confits.) Small female birds are frequently served roasted. Muscovy ducks are also used to produce foie gras.

Mallards

Mallards can be wild or farm-raised. The breeding of these birds is not as widespread as that of Pekins. Mallards are seasonal, and their availability is limited. When available, they are usually obtained through the producer or specialty sources. Their flavor is close to that of wild duck, and the meat is known for its mouthfeel, which can be similar to beef. Meaty mallard breasts may also be sautéed and served along with the braised leg.

Methods of Cooking Duck

Duck lends itself to a wide array of preparations. Italians typically roast young ducks whole, while older ducks are cut into pieces and braised. Boneless duck breasts are sautéed or grilled. Traditional garnitures include olives or fruits such as oranges, figs, and cherries.

Duck livers may also be used in the preparation of pâtés and terrines. The gizzards may be cooked as confit and thinly sliced for salad. The skins can be used as cracklings. Duck fat may be saved and used for the preparation of many dishes, such as duck *prosciutto*. The carcasses may also be used for stocks and consommés.

Roasting poses certain problems because ducks tend to have a thick layer of fat just below the skin. If they are roasted to the point at which the breast meat remains pink, the fat under the skin will remain intact and the legs may be underdone. As a solution to this problem, in contemporary restaurant kitchens, whole ducks are often quartered and cooked by a combination of sautéing and braising.

Preparing Duck for Cooking

The technique illustrated below is used when making *Anitra Arrosto* on page 169.

Wash the duck, inside and out. Hold over a gas flame, turning, or use a kitchen torch to singe off (*strinare*)

any remaining pinfeathers. Heat a large metal spoon in the flame and rub it around the cavity of the duck to melt internal fat. Wash again. Place the duck on its breast with the feet toward you. Cut off the two olive-shaped glands on top of the tail in a V-cut (oil glands are eliminated to avoid imparting an unpleasant taste to the duck and the jus).

If roasting whole: Rinse the duck well, singe off any pinfeathers, and rub a heated kitchen spoon around the cavity to melt the fat as described above. Rinse well and pat dry. Season the duck with *trito* (see "Le Tecniche: *Arrostire*" on page 162), and truss exactly as for a chicken (see "Trussing Chicken and Poultry" on page 399). Remove excess fat from the pan as it accumulates during roasting. Carve the duck as for chicken (see "Carving a Whole Roasted Chicken" on page 161), but cut the breast off the carcass without the wing attached, and cut the breast into slices.

Sautéing the breast offers the advantage of allowing the chef to render the fat, leaving the outer layer crisp and the meat on the inside juicy and pink. **Grilling** the breasts is more problematic because ducks contain such a high fat/flesh ratio. When grilling, this fat must be first removed so that it doesn't melt or ignite over open flames.

Working with Game

Below is a discussion of some of the principal game birds used in Italian cooking. Duck is addressed separately, beginning on page 409.

Tacchino (Turkey)

Though not as usual in Italian cooking, turkeys are the largest and most widely used species of domesticated birds in the United States. Relatives of the grouse, most turkeys raised for food are descended from the Wild Turkey, which is native to many parts of North

America. A second species, the Ocellated Turkey, has been domesticated in the past and is native to the forest regions of Mexico's Yucatan peninsula; they were introduced to Europe through Spanish conquistadors, and to North America by early English colonists. Crossbreeding between Ocellated and native Wild Turkeys resulted in "the foundation stock of modern

American breeds" (Christian Teubner, Sybil Gräfin Schönfeldt, and Siegfried Scholtyssek, *The Chicken and Poultry Bible: The Definitive Sourcebook*.

High in essential amino acids, turkey breast and thigh meat contain in excess of 20 percent protein, and are low in saturated fat. Turkeys are also high-yield birds; the wings, breasts, and legs make up nearly 50 percent of the total carcass weight. According to the USDA, RTC (ready-to-cook), oven-ready turkeys are categorized by weight:

Light: 3½ to 5 kilograms (7½ to 11 pounds)

Medium: 5½ to 9½ kilograms (12 to 21 pounds)

Heavy: 10 to 12½ kilograms (22 to 27 pounds)

Very heavy: up to 18 kilograms (40 pounds)

Oca (Goose)

Geese have never been reared on the same scale as chicken, duck, and turkey. In the United States, geese are raised under cover for the first six weeks, then they are allowed to range from fourteen to twenty weeks, during which time their diet consists of local grass and grain. According to the USDA, California and South Dakota are the major geese-raising states.

According to the Food and Agriculture Organization of the United Nations (FAO), geese were likely among the first animals to be domesticated in Egypt about 3,000 years ago, although some research indicates that domestication may have occurred at an even earlier date. Several varieties arrived in the Americas with European settlers, and over the years, crossbreeding between the European varieties and local wild geese has resulted in the development of a number of breeds, including the Embden and Toulouse breeds, which are the most common in commercial use.

A dressed, oven-ready goose weighs between 72 and 75 percent of its live weight, and has the highest proportion of fat to meat of any poultry. Geese are traditionally roasted, though they may also be braised, boiled, or steamed.

Quaglia/Faraona (Quail/Guinea Hen)

Quail are naturally plump, high-yield, low-fat birds. Forty percent of quail meat resides in the breasts, and nearly 25 percent in the legs. Quail meat contains about 25 percent protein and 2½ percent fat (Teubner, Schönfeldt, and Scholtyssek, *The Chicken and Poultry Bible*).

The guinea hen, also known as the African chicken, is a member of the pheasant family. Domestication of guinea fowl dates back to ancient Greece.

Young guinea hens are often roasted to highlight the flavor and texture of the meat. Guinea fowl have the lowest fat content of any poultry, ranging from 1 to 3 percent in the breasts and legs, according to the USDA. They also yield the most meat after quail and turkey, and contain from 21 to 24 percent protein.

Piccione (Pigeon)

Squabs—highly prized for their tender, rich meat—are actually young pigeons. The meaty breasts of the White King, Texan Pioneer, Carneau, Mondain, Strasser, and Coburg Lark make them the most popular breeds for commercial use in the United States. Breast meat constitutes 26 percent of a squab, while leg meat makes up about 10 percent. Oven-ready birds weigh 225 to 400 grams (8 to 14 ounces). Common preparations for squab include roasting and braising.

Lesson 12

Working with Beef and Veal

Manzo (Beef)

"Beef," as defined by the USDA, is the meat of full-grown cattle (domesticated bovines, or cows), between eighteen months and two years old. A live steer weighs an average of 454 kilograms (1000 pounds). "Baby beef" and "calf" are terms used to refer to young cattle weighing approximately 318 kilograms (700 pounds).

It is unclear when humans first domesticated beef cattle. Some historians believe that domestication took place around 8000 BCE; there are records of its existence as early as 6500 BCE in the Middle East. The cattle breeds most often used today originated in Europe, Africa, and Asia. Although there are nearly fifty breeds of beef cattle, fewer than ten make up the core of today's cattle industry in the United States, including the Black Angus, the Hereford, the Texas Longhorn, and the Wagyu breeds of Japan. (The word *Wagyu* refers to all Japanese beef cattle; *wa* means "Japanese" or "Japanese-style," and *gyu* means "cattle." The meat from Wagyu cattle is known worldwide for its marbling, tenderness, and juiciness. Kobe beef, which has the highest market value of any breed, is the name given to beef from Wagyu cattle raised in the Kobe region of Japan.

Though beef cattle were first introduced to the Americas by European settlers around the fifteenth century (the Americas were home to bison, another member of the bovine family), beef was not widely consumed until around 1870, after the development of railroads and the refrigerated railway car. Today, the beef industry is one of the most successful in U.S. agriculture. According to the USDA, all cattle grown in the United States start out eating grass, and three-fourths of them are "finished" (grown to maturity) in feedlots where they are fed specially formulated feed based on corn or other grains.

Vitello (Veal)

Veal is the meat from calves, or young cows, ideally from animals that have not yet been weaned, weighing up to about 68 kilograms (150 pounds). Traditionally, calves two to three months of age are thought to provide the best veal, especially if they are exclusively milk-fed. Male calves are used for veal production, as females serve as dairy replacement stock. In Italy, a young calf is called a *vitello*; a slightly older calf that is still milk-fed is a *vitello da latte*; *vitellone* refers to nearly mature veal.

Beef (*Manzo*)

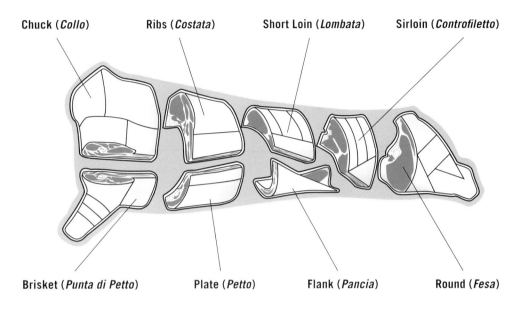

Chuck (*Collo*) Ribs (*Costata*) Short Loin (*Lombata*) Sirloin (*Controfiletto*)

Brisket (*Punta di Petto*) Plate (*Petto*) Flank (*Pancia*) Round (*Fesa*)

Veal (*Vitello*)

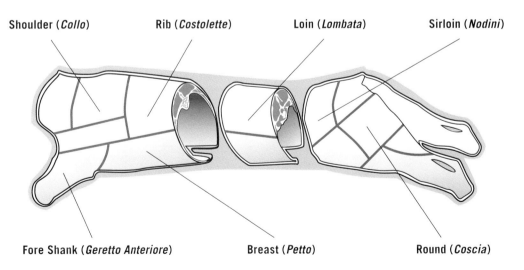

Shoulder (*Collo*) Rib (*Costolette*) Loin (*Lombata*) Sirloin (*Nodini*)

Fore Shank (*Geretto Anteriore*) Breast (*Petto*) Round (*Coscia*)

Veal is valued for its pale color, delicate flavor, and soft fat. Calves' feet are a practical addition to broths because the collagen in the feet readily dissolves into gelatin when cooked, adding body to the finished broth.

Though calves are separated from their mothers almost immediately, they receive her colostrum, or first milk, within twenty-four hours of birth. For the remainder of their lives, most calves are fed milk, along with a nutrient-rich milk-replacement formula with a limited iron content. The amount of iron they receive is carefully controlled so that the myoglobin in the muscle is maintained at a level that keeps the meat slightly rose in color, with an iridescent sheen. Some producers also raise calves on grass or grain in addition to the milk-replacement formula, and allow the animals to exercise. Both the feed (grass and grain) and exercise contribute to a darker meat that is more like beef in color, texture, and flavor.

The flesh of fine-quality veal should be slightly elastic but still firm to the touch, and the fat around the kidneys should be almost white. Inferior veal comes from calves that were weaned too early and/or that grazed in a pasture. Flesh from these calves is rose to red in color, stringy, and dry, and the fat is grayish. Meat from an animal that was harvested too young is soft, flaccid, and bland, and there is little fat.

Beef, Veal, and Nutrition

Beef and veal are good sources of essential B-vitamins and minerals such as zinc and iron. Iron and zinc are important for the production of hemoglobin and myoglobin (proteins that carry oxygen to red blood cells and muscle cells), cellular regeneration processes, and bone growth. Beef is high in vitamin B_6, which is used to make red and white blood cells and regulate blood sugar. Beef is also high in vitamin B_{12}, which is necessary for nervous-system function and healthy bones. There are approximately 100 milligrams of cholesterol in every 115 grams (4 ounces) of beef. About half of the fatty acids contained in beef are monounsaturated, and one-third of the remaining saturated fat is stearic acid, which has not been found to increase serum cholesterol levels.

To some extent, the nutritional value of beef is dependent on the animal's diet. For instance, in the 1950s, when corn and soybeans began to be grown inexpensively, farmers noticed that cattle grew faster on these grains, which, unlike grass, were available year-round. Feedlot cattle are about 30 percent fat by weight, while grass-fed beef is much leaner. However, among the consequences of the grain diet in cattle are stomach problems in many calves after they are first weaned from grass. Additionally, grain-fed beef has been found to contain fewer omega-3 fats, vitamin E, and beta-carotine than grass-fed beef (Nina Planck, *Real Food: What to Eat and Why*).

The appearance of brown meat might be a turn-off to some chefs and consumers. However, meat that isn't bright red is not necessarily a bad thing.

According to the USDA, brown meat does not necessarily mean that the protein has spoiled. It is an indication that the meat has not been exposed to oxygen (for example, meat in vacuum packaging). After exposure to the air for fifteen minutes or so, the residual myoglobin in muscle cells receives oxygen and the meat turns bright cherry red.

Some meat packers and wholesalers have been known to artificially dose meat with carbon monoxide, giving it a bright red color, to confuse buyers.

Harvesting and Processing

Primal and Subprimal Cuts, and Cooking Technique

During the butchering process in the United States, beef and other livestock meats are separated into primal and subprimal cuts (*tagli*). Primal cuts are those initially made as the meat is separated from the carcass. (See page 413 for diagrams of beef and veal.) Primal cuts may be sold or cooked complete, or further broken down into subprimal cuts.

Each cut corresponds to a different region or muscle group on the animal's body. Each region is composed of meat of variable tenderness, depending on how much work the muscles in that part of the body do. For example, leg and neck muscles do the most work in an animal's everyday life from walking, eating, and so forth; therefore, these muscles are likely to be fibrous and less tender than those along the animal's breastplate. As a general rule of thumb, meat becomes more tender as distance from "hoof and horn" increases.

In Italy, the cuts bear some relationship to American cuts, though the names change with the geographic area, and the cuts change subtly as well.

Italian cuisine designates four categories of meat, used to distinguish the different cuts and preparations suitable for cooking:

First-category cuts (*primo taglio*) are those that are tender enough for quick cooking by dry-heat methods such as sautéing, grilling, and roasting.

Second-category (*secondo taglio*) and **third-category cuts** (*terzo taglio*) are tougher meats requiring cooking methods that tenderize them, such as wet-heat methods of braising, boiling, and stewing.

The fourth category, **organ meats** (*frattaglie*), are cooked in a variety of ways, including sautéing, roasting, braising, and grilling.

La Frollatura (Aging)

After harvest, beef (and other livestock meat) is often aged, a process also known as conditioning or ripening. During the aging process, the natural action of enzymes and benign bacteria improve the taste and texture of the meat. After the initial period of rigor mortis has passed (usually within four to twenty-four hours), naturally occurring enzymes found in the muscles begin to break down protein components in the muscle fibers into smaller ones. The breakup of these protein strands is called fragmentation and accounts for the increase in tenderness.

Along with producing more tender meat, the loss of water associated with the aging process concentrates the flavor of the meat. The qualities of aged meat are improved by subjecting primal or subprimal cuts of meat (such as the rib and loin) to specific storage conditions of time, temperature, and, in the case of dry-aging, humidity and air circulation.

Dry-Aging

In a traditional dry-aging process for beef, whole carcasses or primal cuts are refrigerated for 21 to 28 days at 0°C to 1°C (32°F to 34°F), with 80 to 85 percent humidity and an air circulation velocity of 15 to 20 feet per minute.

The humidity levels are intended to limit microbial growth as well as excessive dehydration and shrinkage. Sufficient air circulation ensures that the environment is not so moist that water condenses on the meat's surface.

As the meat ages, it may lose up to 20 percent of its weight as water in the meat evaporates. Along with the chemical breakdown of muscle and fat, aging contributes to additional texture and aroma.

Aging can also cause the meat to develop a slightly moldy exterior crust similar to beef jerky that must be trimmed away (along with some fat) before portioning, which may account for another 25-percent loss in weight. Pieces of meat prepared for dry-aging should have a full "finish," or a thick and even external layer of creamy, waxy fat to prevent excessive loss of moisture during the process.

"Accelerated aging" is a process during which the meat is held at a higher temperature and lower humidity in conjunction with ultraviolet lighting to slow microbial growth. (Accelerated aging decreases the shelf life of beef, especially ground beef, due to elevated risk of microbial contamination.)

Wet-Aging

Although dry-aging can contribute to the quality of beef, it is often avoided in the modern meat industry, due to the large percentage of weight that is lost to evaporation and trimming. Producers may also choose to wet-age beef, a process during which it is held in vacuum bags or plastic wrap for up to several weeks. During wet-aging, the meat is shielded from oxygen and retains moisture while its enzymes work, thus preventing the expensive loss of weight associated with dry-aging. Although wet-aged meat may develop some of the tenderness of dry-aged meat, many chefs find that it does not have the same concentration of flavor.

USDA Grading

While federal inspection of meat is mandatory for safety reasons, grading for quality is not. In the United States, companies can choose to have their beef graded by the USDA. These grades range from U.S. Prime, which is the best quality and constitutes less than 5 percent of beef produced in the United States, to U.S. Utility, which is used mostly for pet foods; Cutter and Canner grades are used by processors and canners. Grades are assigned according to the amount of marbling and the age of the beef. For purchasers, the choice between grades of beef is often a monetary one. Here are the USDA grades in descending order of quality:

1. U.S. Prime	3. U.S. Select	5. U.S. Commercial	7. U.S. Cutter
2. U.S. Choice	4. U.S. Standard	6. U.S. Utility	8. U.S. Canner

Marbling and USDA Grades

There are many factors that contribute to the overall flavor, tenderness, and juiciness of beef, including genetics, exercise, feed, age, conditions during slaughter, and aging and storing conditions. Fat marbling, the white specks of fat within the muscle, contributes about a third of the juiciness, tenderness, and flavor to cooked beef. Today, beef is graded by its fat content. The difference in marbling is easily visible in a comparison between Prime, Choice, and Select cuts.

USDA GRADE	FAT CONTENT
Prime	10 to 13 percent
Choice	4 to 10 percent
Select	2 to 4 percent

Red-Meat Colors and Temperatures

Rare (*al sangue*) meat is red, and the center is cool or room temperature.

Medium-rare (*media al sangue*) meat is still red, but the center is slightly warm.

Medium (*media*) meat has a pink and warm center.

Medium-well (*media ben cotta*) meat has a center with a little color, perhaps a bit of pink.

Well-done (*ben cotta*) meat has no color. The steak may also be butterflied.

 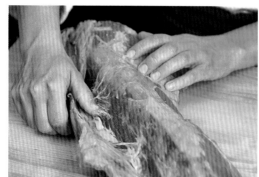

Trimming Beef

Trimming and Pounding Beef for Carpaccio

At The International Culinary Center, a "PSMO" (an industry acronym for "peeled, silverskin, side muscle on") cut of untrimmed beef tenderloin is used for *Carpaccio di Manzo con Funghi* on page 63.

To clean the tenderloin, pull off the long side muscle called the "chain."

Remove the silverskin, the tough, white sheath of connective tissue that covers some cuts of meat: Working from the tail end toward the wide end (the "head" of the tenderloin), cut into the edge of the meat just below the surface of the silverskin until you have freed a 2½-centimeter-wide (1-inch-wide) piece of silverskin. Grasping the silverskin with the hand that is not

holding the knife, run the knife between the silverskin and the meat to slice off a strip of silverskin. Hold the blade at a shallow angle, toward the silverskin, so as to cut as little of the meat as possible. Move to a new section of silverskin, and continue in this way to remove all of the silverskin in strips.

Trim the fat and connective tissue from the underside of the fillet.

Wrap the meat in plastic and tie with butcher's twine.

If you do not have access to a slicer, slice the meat as thinly as possible with a sharp knife, and gently tap it between two pieces of plastic wrap or parchment paper to flatten.

Trimming Top Round of Beef

The top round is a lean, tough piece of meat cut from the hind leg. For maximum tenderness, it is often braised: in chunks for stew, or tied in a single piece as for *Stracotto* on page 188. Or it may be sliced so that the muscle fibers are cut against the grain, as for *Braciole* on page 184.

To clean a top round of beef:

Trim the fat cap. If using the meat for a braise, leave a thin 3-millimeter (⅛-inch) layer of fat on the meat. For *braciole*, trim the fat completely.

Turn the top round over, trim off the soft side muscle, and remove any connective tissue and membranes.

Divide the meat along the natural seams to separate it into three pieces.

Braciole may be cut from any of those muscles. Each muscle has a unique texture when cooked.

To slice braciole, hold your hand flat against the meat and cut the meat into slices, on an angle, against the grain, about 6 millimeters (¼ inch) thick.

Pound the slices, and arrange so that the striations in the meat run parallel to the edge of the work surface.

Cover the meat with the filling and roll the meat up into a cylinder. Tie with butcher's twine.

Cutting Top Round of Veal for Scaloppine

Scaloppine is typically cut from the veal round or eye of round. As for braciole, the key is to cut against the grain for maximum tenderness. The veal sirloin or the loin (far more tender cuts) may also be used; they are sliced the same way.

The technique illustrated above is used when making *Saltimbocca alla Romana* on page 180.

Cut the veal into slices, against the grain, at a 45-degree angle, to cut the largest possible pieces of meat. Pound the meat as for chicken scaloppine on page 405.

Trimming Veal Shank for *Ossobuco*

Veal shank for *Ossobuco alla Milanese* on page 189 is cut into 4-centimeter-thick (1½-inch-thick) slices by the butcher. Trim the slices of excess fat, but leave the band of silverskin on the meat to hold the meat on the bones (the silverskin never completely breaks down in the cooking).

Braising Veal for *Ossobuco*

The illustrations opposite show veal shin being prepared and cooked for *Ossobuco alla Milanese* on page 189, but this basic method for braising may be used for any long-cooking meats, including poultry, pork, lamb, and beef.

Make slits in the veal along the lines where the muscles meet and stuff with *trito*. Secure the slices with butcher's twine.

Heat the oil with the aromatics to infuse the oil with their flavor. Add the meat and sear on both sides until browned.

Add the *soffritto* and cook until the color deepens and the flavors concentrate.

Deglaze (*deglassare*) the pan with wine to pick up the caramelized juices on the bottom of the pan. Pour the liquid around the meat (not on top of it), so as not to disturb the crust.

Add the tomato and enough stock to bring the liquid three-quarters of the way up the meat. Cover and braise in the oven or on top of the stove 1 hour, basting every 20 minutes.

Remove the meat from the pan. Degrease the sauce. Some fat is desirable for flavor but the sauce should not have fat pooling on top of it.

Purée the braising liquid with the *soffritto*, adding stock to thin the sauce. Return the meat to the pan with the sauce and continue cooking until the meat is done.

Lesson 13

Working with Organ Meats

Composition of Organ Meats (*Frattaglie*)

Bone and skeletal meat—meaning the shoulder, shank, loin, and so on—make up about half of an animal's body weight. Collectively, their purpose is to help the animal move around as needed during its life. The remaining weight is composed of nonskeletal meats—the heart, stomach, intestines, liver, brains, and so on—that are collectively referred to as organ meats (*frattaglie*) or offal.

Organ meats are secured inside the body and have specialized tasks (for example, storing nutrients for the body or filtering the blood of impurities) that require different cell structures. Due to their respective jobs, organ meats go through more physical stress than muscles, developing different flavors and textures as a result, and dictating certain cooking techniques.

According to Harold McGee, in *On Food and Cooking: The Science and Lore of the Kitchen*, "organ meats are generally similar to skeletal muscle in their chemical composition, but often contain substantially more iron and vitamins thanks to their special tasks." The cellular structure that enables organs to carry out these tasks may also be the reason organ meats contain higher amounts of cholesterol than muscle tissue.

McGee also states that certain organ meats—stomach, intestines, heart, and tongue—contain up to three times as much connective tissue as skeletal meat (partly due to the constant mechanical stress), and benefit from slow, moist-cooking methods to break down collagen. (Liver has a different structure, which will be discussed later.)

Commonly Used Organ Meats

The list below details some of the organ meats most commonly used by Italian chefs.

Midollo (Bone Marrow)

Rich in protein as well as flavor, bone marrow is a highlight of *ossobuco*. Bone marrow is a flexible tissue that fills the hollow interior of bones. It is found at the "spongy" end of long bones in such regions as the thigh, leg, and arm of many animals. Marrow performs a critical function in all animals by supporting the development of new blood cells.

To prepare marrow:

Pop the marrow out of the bone by pushing it through with your thumb. If the marrow will not disengage, blanch briefly to soften; then push it out.

Place in a bowl of cold acidulated water with salt, and soak to remove all of the blood until the marrow is completely white. The marrow may be poached briefly in stock, then drained if using as a garnish or to finish a sauce.

Rognone (Kidneys)

Kidneys are among the few organs that always appear in pairs. (Brains are almost always found in two bilateral parts, but are considered a single organ.) Like intestines, kidneys are charged with the task of helping the body to filter waste (kidneys accomplish this by generating urine). This specialized task contributes to the rich nutrient content and strong flavor of kidneys.

Lamb, beef, and pork kidneys are usually served sautéed, grilled, or braised. Kidneys from younger animals are invariably more tender than kidneys of mature animals.

To prepare kidneys for cooking:

Remove the fat and the thin membrane that surround the kidneys. (The fat that surrounds the kidneys is prized; for some dishes, this fat is melted and used to sauté the kidneys.) Remove only the fat and membrane from that portion of the kidneys that will be used; if the organ is left exposed to air for too long, it will oxidize, resulting in color, texture, and flavor changes.

Remove most of the white or light-colored center core tissue.

Lamb kidneys are usually just slit on one side to allow cleaning.

Fegato (Liver)

Its versatility and distinct flavor make the liver one of the most widely used of all organ meats. In Italian cuisine, it is thinly sliced and grilled or sautéed, or cut into pieces and cooked as a stew.

The liver is one of the most important organs in the body. It may be understood as the body's filtration system. It performs nearly five hundred different chemical functions, most of which aid in extracting impurities from the blood. Impurities are returned to the intestines for excretion through bile, which is also produced by the liver. The liver also manufactures proteins that are vital to blood clotting as well as the transport and metabolization of nutrients.

Although the liver undergoes much less physical strain than the heart, for example, it still requires a great deal of energy and oxygen to function. As a result, the liver has a deep red color, similar to that of the heart, kidneys, and tongue.

Liver has a characteristic flavor that is still in early phases of scientific investigation. Some researchers believe the flavor relies heavily on the naturally occurring sulfur compounds thiazole and thiazoline. As the animal ages, the liver's natural flavor grows stronger and more pronounced. Many scientists and agriculture experts also agree that the texture of liver grows firmer

with age. This is one reason that chefs prefer to work with liver from young animals—veal and lamb—rather than beef or mutton. Soaking liver overnight in milk will soften its taste.

The liver contains less collagen than the heart, and its connective tissue is far more delicate than that of other organs. With minimal cooking, this delicate tissue is tender and moist, but it grows crumbly and dry if overcooked.

The technique illustrated at left is used when making *Fegato alla Veneziana* on page 197.

To prepare veal or lamb liver:

Peel off the outside membrane with your fingers. (This thin, transparent film that covers the liver acts as a seal and prevents the liver from damage due to oxidation.) Peel only from the portion to be used; the remainder of the liver will oxidize quickly if exposed to air.

Cut out the ducts. Rinse, and soak the liver overnight in milk to cover.

Cut the liver in half lengthwise. Slice pieces 6 millimeters (¼ inch) thick on a shallow angle.

Stomaco/Trippa (Stomach/Tripe)

Tripe is the term used to refer to the stomach lining of ruminant animals. In the case of beef, tripe can come from the lining of any one of the animal's four stomachs. Tripe from oxen and sheep comes from their first and second stomachs.

Honeycomb tripe (from beef or veal), usually sold blanched and frozen, is the type most often consumed in the United States. Regional specialties in Italy use other types of tripe: lamb tripe, in Abruzzo; pig and beef tripe, in Lombardia; and beef tripe, in Lazio.

Tripe has a unique texture and a distinctive aroma. Around the world, tripe is served braised, poached, grilled, sautéed, or fried. Most tripe commonly sold in butchers' markets is blanched and/or bleached before sale to smooth out its natural taste.

The technique illustrated below is used when making *Trippa alla Parmigiana* on page 198.

To prepare stomach/tripe:

Wash the tripe well in cold running water. Soak overnight in cold water to cover. Cover the tripe with cold water, add vegetables for flavor, bring to a boil, and simmer 30 minutes.

Remove the tripe, and discard the blanching water and vegetables. Repeat the process, using more water and the remaining vegetables. Cool the tripe in the blanching liquid in an ice bath. Drain; discard the vegetables.

Thinly slice the tripe into strips, on an angle.

Rete (Caul, or Caulfat)

Caulfat is a thin, weblike, fatty membrane of connective tissue dotted with small fat deposits that covers organs in the abdominal cavities of pigs, cows, and sheep. Caulfat is often used to wrap forcemeats and lean skeletal cuts that are to be roasted or braised; it serves as a natural form of packaging to hold food together and to protect and maintain moisture. During cooking, much of the fat is rendered from the membrane and incorporated into the food.

The following technique is used when making *Filetto di Maiale* on page 204.

To prepare caulfat:

Soak the caulfat overnight in cold water to cover to remove any blood or impurities.

Drain; squeeze out excess moisture, and pat dry.

Animelle (Sweetbreads)

Sweetbreads are highly prized due to their mild, creamy, slightly sweet flavor and tender mouthfeel. In Italy, sweetbreads are typically grilled or sautéed, after a preliminary blanching.

The term *sweetbreads* refers to the pancreas or thymus glands of beef, veal, lamb, or pork. The exact origin of the term is unknown. Although "heart sweetbreads" (pancreas glands) and "throat sweetbreads" (thymus glands) come from two different regions of the animal, there is generally no distinction made between the two for purposes of purchasing and cooking.

The technique illustrated below is used when making *Animelle Saltate* on page 194.

Sweetbreads require some time to prepare.

Disgorge sweetbreads under cold running water to remove impurities. Cover with cold water or milk and soak overnight. Drain.

Blanch the sweetbreads: Cover with cold salted water, bring to a boil, and simmer until firm, 10 to 15 minutes. Refresh in cold water and drain.

When cool enough to handle, peel off the thin membrane that covers the sweetbreads and pull off any fatty parts, nerves, blood vessels, or cartilage.

Place the sweetbreads in a perforated hotel pan lined with cheesecloth. Cover with cheesecloth, place a second hotel pan on top, and weight at least 1 hour. This will give the sweetbreads a firmer texture.

Separate the sweetbreads into rounded "nuggets" where they naturally break apart.

Sweetbreads may also be sliced.

Lesson 14

Working with Pork

As with many cultivated animals, the domestication of wild pigs is believed to have occurred independently in different regions of the world. Anthropological evidence indicates that pigs were being domesticated up to 9,000 years ago in parts of southwestern Asia and China. From this region, it is believed that domesticated pigs—and the use of pork in local cuisine—spread throughout Asia, parts of Polynesia, Indonesia, and Europe. As the major world religions Judaism and Islam grew, their followers in the eastern hemisphere ceased to consume pork products, even as the number of consumers grew in the western hemisphere.

Domestic pigs were first brought to the continental Americas in the fifteenth century by conquistadors and settlers from parts of Europe, including Spain and England. The animals grew and bred quickly, and by the nineteenth century there was a flourishing pork industry in the United States. Today, pork (*maiale*) is one of the world's most widely consumed meats.

The Pork Industry in the United States

Commercially bred pigs are prolific; they mature quickly and are capable of having numerous young. After a gestation period of four months, a sow gives birth to an average of ten piglets, though the litter can be as large as thirty. These piglets can increase in weight by 5,000 percent in a six-month period.

In the United States, pigs are classified as lard, meat, or bacon hogs. Lard is the rendered fat tissue of pork. While crossbred pigs or hybrid pigs make up 80 percent of the commercial pork market, out of about three hundred different breeds, the eight most commonly used by pork producers in the United States are Berkshire, a black-haired pig renowned for its flavor and meatiness; Chester White, a white pig that originated in Pennsylvania; the fast-growing, mahogany-colored Duroc; the lean, muscular Yorkshire; Hampshire, a black pig with erect ears and a thick white band around its middle and its front legs; Landrace, a white pig descended from Danish stock; Poland China, a black-bodied pig, its nose and all four legs dipped in white; and Spotted Swine, a breed characterized by black and white spots.

Inspection and Grading

According to the USDA, all retail pork products are inspected by state authorities or the federal government for signs of disease. The "Passed and Inspected by USDA" seal ensures that the pork is wholesome and free of disease.

Grading for quality is voluntary, and pork producers pay to have their meat graded. USDA grades for pork reflect only two levels: "Acceptable" grade (fresh pork sold in supermarkets) and "Utility" grade (processed pork products, not available for consumer purchase).

The USDA grades pork carcasses based on the proportion of lean to fat. In descending order of quality, the grades are USDA 1, which has the highest proportion of lean meat to fat and is the most common grade, USDA 2, USDA 3, and USDA 4. Quality pork has a slightly pinkish color with firm, white fat.

Primal and Subprimal Cuts and Cooking Technique

As discussed on page 415, in the United States, all livestock meats, including pork, are divided into primal and subprimal cuts. Each cut corresponds to a different region on the pig's body. In Italy, the names of the cuts change depending on geographic region, and the cuts are subtly different as well.

In the United States, pigs are brought to the abattoir at approximately six months of age, at which point connective tissue is still relatively soluble and the meat is quite tender. Wild boar, or *cinghiale*, the ancestor of most domestic pig breeds, is farm-raised in the United States and in Italy, but it is also still found wild in Italy. It is particularly prolific in Tuscany, where it continues to be hunted in the wooded areas of the region. Its flavor is stronger than pork and its texture is tough and lean, so it benefits from wet-heat methods of cooking.

The variable muscle structure and the amount of fat and connective tissue contained in each cut help chefs determine the appropriate cooking technique. Shoulder cuts, for example, contain a high percentage of fat, which makes them an ideal choice for sausage. Relatively high in connective tissue, these cuts are also cooked by wet-heat cooking methods such as braises and stews (see *Cinghiale in Agrodolce* on page 208). The head, neck, and jowl contain medium fat content and a good amount of connective tissue; they are also best served by wet-heat methods such as braising or poaching. These cuts are also used in *salumi*, as are the feet, which are fatty and contain an abundance of connective tissue.

Cuts from the leg (medium fat content and some connective tissue) are cooked by wet-heat methods such as braising, stewing, and poaching. When thinly cut, as for scaloppine, the leg is also sautéed. The rack, loin, and tenderloin are very lean, tender cuts that contain little connective tissue; they are traditionally cooked by roasting, sauté, or grilling. Spareribs (see *Costine* on page 202) contain a great deal of fat and some connective tissue and are best cooked by a wet-heat method such as braising. (Because of their high fat content, spareribs may preliminarily be roasted for color and to render some of the fat before braising.) The pork belly is cured or braised.

Pork (*Maiale*)

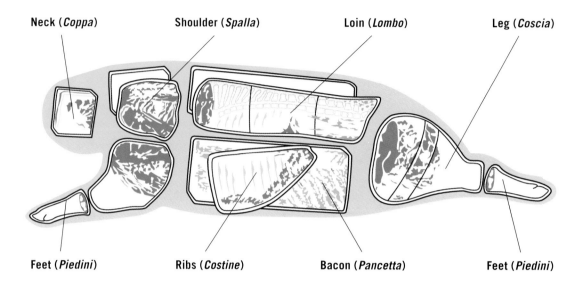

Neck (*Coppa*)   Shoulder (*Spalla*)   Loin (*Lombo*)   Leg (*Coscia*)

Feet (*Piedini*)   Ribs (*Costine*)   Bacon (*Pancetta*)   Feet (*Piedini*)

Trichinosis and Pork

There are several foodborne pathogens commonly associated with pork, including E. coli, salmonella, *Staphylococcus aureus*, *Listeria monocytogenes*, and *Trichinella spiralis*. Trichinosis is a parasitic infection caused by *Trichinella spiralis*, which is a roundworm whose larvae may migrate from the intestine and form cysts in various muscles of the body. According to the USDA, infections occur worldwide but are most prevalent in regions where pork or wild game is consumed raw or undercooked. While the parasite responsible for trichinosis has not been entirely eliminated, trichinosis-related illnesses are extremely rare. Since 1950, the incidence of trichinosis in the United States has declined sharply due to changes in hog-feeding practices. Years ago, some pigs were fed table scraps or garbage contaminated by the parasite. Today, this practice is prohibited, though it is still possible to contract trichinosis through the consumption of raw or undercooked meat. To prevent trichinosis, the USDA recommends that pork be cooked until it reaches an internal temperature of 63°C (145°F).

Cleaning Pork Spareribs

Pork spareribs contain eleven to thirteen ribs from the belly region. The breastbone may also be included and should be removed or notched.

The technique illustrated opposite, top is used when making *Costine* on page 202.

Place the slab of ribs on a board with the bone side up.

Place your boning knife flat against the rib bones. Remove the diaphragm, or skirt, by gripping the skirt meat and, as you lift up on it, cutting it as close as possible to the slab without cutting into or exposing the bones. (Removing the skirt ensures even thickness and therefore even cooking.)

Flip the ribs meat side up, and cut away the rib tips, or brisket bones, at the base of the ribs using a heavy chef knife or cleaver. (Squaring off the ribs in this manner makes for a cleaner presentation.)

Flip the ribs back to the bone side. Starting at the large bone end, insert the tip of your knife between the two membranes and peel up the top membrane. Insert your fingers or a butter knife to separate it further from the bottom membrane. (Do not attempt to remove the bottom membrane or the ribs will fall apart). Grip the loosened bit of the top membrane with your fingers or a paper towel and, holding the other end of the slab, pull the membrane away.

You will be left with three pieces: the skirt, the rib tips, or brisket bones, and the Saint Louis–style trimmed ribs. The brisket bones may be slow-cooked or used as a flavoring agent for soups. The skirt and the brisket bones may also be prepared just as the ribs. (In a restaurant setting, these cuts might also be braised for a family meal.) The skirt may be sautéed or grilled and thinly sliced like a beef-skirt steak.

Preparing Center-Cut Bone-in Loin of Pork for *Arista*

The technique illustrated below is used when making *Arista alla Toscana* on page 210.

Trim the finger bones off the underside of the loin.

Remove the piece of cartilage at the shoulder end of the loin.

Cut the pork loin in half to create roasts of 2 kilograms (4½ pounds) each.

Cut the rib bones off the loin roast in one piece.

Cut incisions in the meat 2 to 5 centimeters (1 to 2 inches) deep, and stuff with the *trito*. Rub the meat and bones all over with the remaining *trito*.

Place the meat against the bones, turning the bones inward so that they cradle the meat.

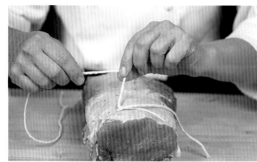

Tying a Center-Cut Bone-in Loin of Pork for *Arista*

The procedure for tying a pork roast is essentially the same as for tying any roast of meat. Tying creates a regular shape that facilitates even cooking and makes for an attractive presentation. Each chef has his or her own technique for tying; this is just one taught at The International Culinary Center. It is used when making *Braciole* on page 184, *Arista alla Toscana* on page 210, and *Agnello Arrosto* on page 219.

Cut a length of butcher's twine at least six times the length of the meat to be tied.

Slide one end of the twine under the bones, so that about 15 centimeters (6 inches) of twine extends out the other side.

Pull the two ends of the twine up and over the meat, and tie a butcher's knot by wrapping the short end of the string around the other end, twice.

To make a chain hitch knot, use your right hand to bring the long end of the string down toward you 2 to 3 centimeters (about 1 inch). Hold the string in place with the index finger of your left hand and, making an L with your right hand, pull the string across and under the meat again and back over to where the string is being held in place by your finger. Slip the string over and under the part held taut by your finger. Remove your finger, and gently pull the string and the hitch taut.

Repeat the steps, spacing the ties 2 to 3 centimeters (about 1 inch) apart, until the piece of meat is completely tied.

Turn the piece of meat over. Pull the remaining string around the bottom, and weave it over and under the links in the chain.

Flip the meat back over to the first side, and tie a knot using the short end of the string from the initial knot.

Preparing Pork Chops for Sauté

The bones of the chops are cleaned (frenched) for an attractive presentation.

The technique illustrated above is used when making *Bistecchine di Maiale in Padella* on page 207.

Starting 2 to 3 centimeters (about 1 inch) above the eye of the meat, cut around the bone to sever the membrane that covers the bone.

Holding the chop with one hand, scrape the bone to completely remove the membrane and scrape the bone clean.

Make a small slit in the sides of the chops to relax the connective tissue so that the chops will not curl.

Cut a piece of twine about arm's length from shoulder to wrist. Make a knot at the base of the bone, and wrap

the remaining string around the eye of the chop and tie to secure. This is for aesthetic purposes; it keeps the chops nice and round during cooking. This is particularly useful when working with chops that don't have a regular shape or won't easily hold one.

Wrapping Pork Tenderloin in Caulfat for Roasting

The technique illustrated below is used when making *Filetto di Maiale* on page 204.

Clean the tenderloin of silverskin.

Lay a sheet of caulfat on the work surface. Season the meat and place any aromatics on the meat (in this case, bay leaves). Place a tenderloin at one end (folding under the thin end to equalize diameter) and roll, giving it two turns to completely encase the pork in the membrane. Cut off excess caulfat.

Pork Sausage

Scrap meat has been preserved with salt, flavored with spices and herbs, and used for sausage since ancient Roman times. Each region in Italy has its own distinctive mix of flavors and meats in sausage.

Pork sausage is made of ground pork mixed with seasonings and fat. The ratio of fat to lean meat should range from 30 to 40 percent fat, to 60 to 70 percent lean meat so that the sausage will be moist. The pork shoulder contains about 30 percent mostly internal fat (within the marbling), making it an ideal cut for sausage-making. It may be practical to make sausage from trimmings from other pork cuts, in which case additional pork fat is added to achieve the proper ratio.

Salt is an important component in sausage-making, both for flavor and as a preservative. As a guideline, count 20 grams (¾ ounce) of salt per kilogram (2¼ pounds) of meat. Once seasoned, the meat is cured overnight in the refrigerator before it is stuffed into casings. The sausages are then hung overnight in the refrigerator.

Sausage Casings

Natural sausage casings come from pork, sheep, and beef. Pork casings are 4 to 5 centimeters (1½ to 2 inches) in diameter. Those from sheep are the smallest, at about 3 centimeters (1³⁄₁₆ inches) in diameter. There are two sizes of beef casings: Beef-bung casings are 10 to 11½ centimeters (4 to 4½ inches) in diameter; beef middles measure about 5 to 6 centimeters (2 to 2⅜ inches) in diameter. Wash well to remove the smell, and soak for 24 hours in cold water to cover.

Making Pork Sausage

The technique illustrated opposite is used when making *Salsiccia* on page 209.

Grind the chilled, diced meat through the 1½- or 1-centimeter (½- or ⅜-inch) plate of a chilled grinder.

Mix the ground pork with the seasonings. Cover and refrigerate 24 hours to cure the meat.

Put the sausage mixture into the bowl of a sausage machine. Attach one end of the casing to the open end of the extruder on the machine and gather the entire casing onto the extruder, leaving about 5 centimeters (2 inches) hanging.

Begin feeding the sausage mixture into the casing. Hold the casing onto the extruder as the sausage mixture feeds out, letting it go little by little and allowing the casing to fill to the correct diameter before releasing it. Prick the casing where air pockets develop. The sausage should be plump and tightly packed.

When all of the meat has been extruded, place your hand on top of one end of the sausage; using the width of your palm as a measurement, twist off one sausage the length of your palm. Repeat the process to twist off another sausage, but this time, twist the casing in the opposite direction to seal.

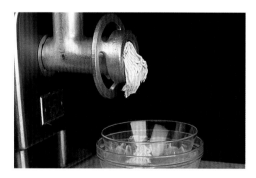

Preparing *Cotechino*

The only difference between stuffing *cotechino* and the *salsiccia* on page 432 is that the *cotechino* uses the shorter beef middles or bung as casing. Therefore, each piece of middle or bung will make one to two sausages; the *cotechino* is tied with twine.

The technique illustrated at left is used when making *Cotechino con Lenticchie e Salsa Verde* on page 213.

Clean the pork shoulder of sinews and cut it into small pieces.

Cut the fatback into strips or small pieces.

Cut the pork rind into strips.

Grind the pork and the fatback through a 1½- or 1-centimeter (½- or ⅜-inch) plate, keeping the meat and fat cold at all times.

Grind the pork rind: first through a 1½- or 1-centimeter (½- or ⅜-inch) plate, then through a 6-millimeter (¼-inch) plate.

Combine the pork, fatback, and pork rind. Mix in the garlic, black pepper, and spice mix. Add the wine: Beat slightly or mix with gloved hands, adding ice water as needed to develop the primary bind; the meat should feel like a sticky homogenous paste.

Stuff the mixture into beef-middle or beef-bung casings and poke holes intermittently using a sausage pricker.

Tie the stuffed *cotechino* with twine.

Lesson 15

Working with Lamb and Rabbit

Lamb

As with other livestock, lamb (*agnello*) is divided into primal and subprimal cuts (see diagram of lamb on following page). In Italy, the names of the cuts vary by geographic area, and the cuts themselves may vary subtly as well. As with other proteins, the structure of the muscles and the percentage of fat and connective tissue contained therein (see "Harvesting and Processing" on page 415) determine which cooking techniques are best suited to each cut. Cuts with more connective tissue, such as shoulder and neck, benefit from wet-heat techniques such as braising and stewing, while leaner cuts with less connective tissue, such as rack and leg, work well with dry-heat techniques such as roasting, sautéing, and grilling.

Lamb chops are cut from several different primals. Loin and rib chops from these respective regions tend to be the most tender. Blade and arm chops are cut from the shoulder region; sirloin chops are cut from the leg. These chops tend to be far less expensive than loin and rib chops because they contain greater bands of connective tissue.

Leg of lamb is suitable to wet- and dry-heat methods. It may be roasted on the bone, or deboned for ease of slicing. The outer fat of the leg is encased in a thin, paperlike covering called the fell. The fell helps the leg and other roasts retain shape and moisture. (According to the USDA, the fell is usually removed from smaller cuts, such as chops, prior to packaging for retail or wholesale.) The leg is also grilled, stewed, and braised.

Lamb breast is often stuffed, rolled, and braised.

The Sheep Industry in the United States

Lamb, defined as the meat of sheep less than one year old, is produced year-round in the United States. The USDA reports that most lamb is brought to market between six and eight months old, when the meat is still quite tender. Lambs are sold in a range of ages and weights of up to one year old and 45 kilograms (100 pounds). Younger lambs may be sold under the names "suckling," "hothouse," or "milk-fed." Lambs sold as "spring" or "Easter lamb" may be between three and nine months of age. (The name refers to traditional availability of lamb at this age, which was usually between March and October. However, advances in farming and animal husbandry have extended the availability of the meat.) New Zealand lambs are brought to market somewhat younger, at around four months old.

Lamb (*Agnello*)

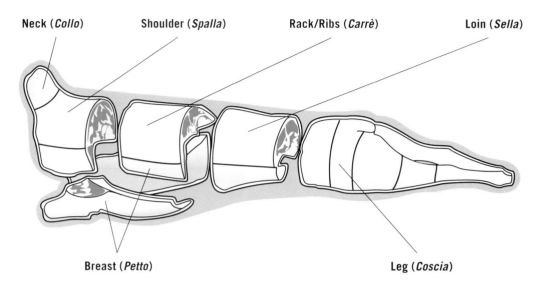

Neck (*Collo*) Shoulder (*Spalla*) Rack/Ribs (*Carrè*) Loin (*Sella*)

Breast (*Petto*) Leg (*Coscia*)

Mutton is the meat from sheep older than one year. Generally, mutton is less tender than lamb and has a much stronger flavor.

In the U.S. industry, lambs begin feeding on grass or coarse grain during weaning, according to the USDA's Food Safety and Inspection Service. As adolescents, they are fed hay and a feed mixture of corn, barley, milo, and/or vitamin-enriched wheat until maturity.

Inspection and Grading

As with beef, the maturity, color, firmness, and texture of lamb are all evaluated by the USDA in relation to its resultant flavor and tenderness. USDA grades for lamb in descending order of quality are: U.S. Prime, U.S. Choice, and U.S. Good. (Almost all lamb is graded as Prime or Choice.) Lower grades—U.S. Utility and

Cull—are usually used in processed products. Quality grades are not indications of high or low nutritional value (in other words, U.S. Prime lamb has a similar protein and nutrient content to U.S. Choice lamb).

Mutton, which has a proportionally higher amount of marbling, ranges from Choice to Cull.

Yield grades (assigned at meat-packing plants) designate the proportional amount of trimmed meat to bone and are listed as 1 (the leanest), 2, 3, 4, or 5 (the fattest).

Aging

Lamb may be wet- or dry-aged to develop additional tenderness and/or flavor. According to the USDA, the rib and loin sections (see diagram above) are most likely to be aged.

Trimming a Rack of Lamb for Roasting or Cutting into Chops

To prepare a rack, the chine bone is removed, and the ribs are meticulously cleaned above the eye, because any meat or membrane left on the bone will shrivel and burn in the oven, creating an unappetizing presentation.

The technique illustrated at left is used when making *Costolette d'Agnello* on page 218.

Remove the chine bone with a cleaver; reserve it for stock.

Set the rack on a cutting board. Score a line across the bones approximately 4 centimeters (1½ inches) from the eye.

Put the tip of the knife through each rib to make a slit on the rib side. Turn the rack over and connect the slits by cutting through to the bones across the fat layer.

Turn the rack back over so the bone side is up.

Score down the middle of each rib bone to loosen the membrane that surrounds each.

Pop the bones from between the score marks, and peel the meat and membranes back and away. The cleaned bones may require additional scraping.

Trim off the fat that covers the eye, leaving a 3-millimeter (⅛-inch) layer of fat to keep the meat moist during cooking. Recuperate as much meat as possible from the fat and reserve the meat for stock.

Preparing a Leg of Lamb for Roasting (Tunneling)

The following procedure is useful for deboning a leg to be roasted whole (see *Agnello Arrosto* on page 219). The femur is removed by "tunneling" into the leg rather than cutting through the outside, so that the leg holds its shape for roasting and cuts easily into neat slices.

Remove the flank—a piece of meat attached to the underside of the leg. Cut along the inside of the pelvic bone, pushing the meat away from the bone, until reaching the ball and socket that connect the pelvic bone to the top of the femur.

Cut through the joint and twist the hip bone to free it; pull it and the tail (if there is one) off in one piece.

Trim the thick pieces of fat along both sides of the leg. Trim most of the fat and membrane from the top of the leg, leaving a very thin layer of fat to keep the meat moist.

Remove the femur: Cut around the joint at the top of the femur to expose it. Scrape down the bone, cutting and scraping the meat away from it, until the joint that connects the femur to the shank bone is visible. Scrape around the joint to expose it and then cut through the joint. Twist the femur to free it entirely and then pull it out.

Remove interior clods of fat.

Scrape or cut around the shank bone and remove it.

Tie using butcher's twine, as for roast pork (see "Tying a Center-Cut Bone-in Loin of Pork for *Arista*" on page 430).

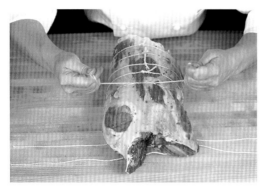

Butterflying a Leg of Lamb

If the leg is to be butterflied, it is not necessary to use the tunneling technique described above. However, the butterflied leg must still be tied before roasting.

Remove the pelvic bone as in the first step of "Preparing a Leg of Lamb for Roasting (Tunneling)" above.

Locate the femur bone by looking for a line of fat that runs parallel to the femur. Make a cut all the way down to the femur, following the line of fat, to expose the bone. Cut the meat away from the femur. Remove the femur. The shank bone will be exposed; cut the meat away from the shank and remove. Make sure to remove the kneecap and any interior clods of fat.

Smear the inside of the leg with *trito*.

Tie, as for roast pork (see "Tying a Center-Cut Bone-in Loin of Pork for *Arista*" on page 430), or with individual strings spaced 2 to 3 centimeters (about 1 inch) apart.

Making a Stock from Trimmings

When boning a leg of lamb, all bones and trimmings are reserved for stock. This technique applies equally to other meat, poultry, and rabbit:

Remove the fat from all meaty trimmings. Chop bones into 5- to 8-centimeter (2- to 3-inch) sections.

Combine the bones and trimmings in a stockpot; add aromatic vegetables and herbs, if desired.

Sauté to brown well.

Add cold water to cover and cook, skimming the foam that rises to the top. Cook about 1½ hours for lamb and other meats, about 1 hour for poultry and rabbit. Strain.

Rabbit (*Coniglio*)

Rabbits and hares belong to the same family but have different physical characteristics. Hares have longer rear legs and ears than rabbits, which are ideal for life in open country, where hares must be on constant alert and able to outrun predators. In contrast, rabbits tend to live in close quarters in wooded areas. Both are very lean and have a mild flavor.

Rabbits are farm-raised in the United States. The most widely available varieties are California and New Zealand white rabbits. They are raised on an all-natural diet, according to the USDA, and have been specially bred to have a higher meat-to-bone ratio than hares or wild rabbits. (See diagram below.)

Rabbits are labeled by the USDA as "fryers" and "roasters." The term **fryers** (also called "young rabbits") refers to rabbits of less than twelve weeks of age, weighing not less than 700 grams (1½ pounds) and rarely more than 1½ kilograms (3¼ to 3½ pounds). The flesh is fine-grained and pink in color. These animals are suitable for roasting, frying, and braising; all of the recipes in this book call for fryers.

Roasters (also called "mature rabbits") are rabbits of over eight months of age. The term does not imply a specific weight range but roasters are usually over 1¾ kilograms (4 pounds). The flesh is coarser-grained than a fryer. The muscle fiber is darker in color and the texture is tougher. Roasters are suitable for braising.

Rabbit (*Coniglio*)

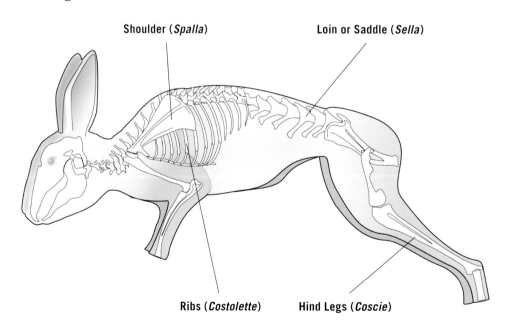

Shoulder (*Spalla*)   Loin or Saddle (*Sella*)

Ribs (*Costolette*)   Hind Legs (*Coscie*)

Cutting a Rabbit into Pieces

Cut into ten pieces this way, one rabbit can be stretched to serve at least three people (and more, if used in a sauce for pasta or a stew with other ingredients).

The technique illustrated at left is used when making *Coniglio all'Uva Passa e Pinoli* on page 221.

Place the rabbit on its back on a cutting board. Pull out internal organs and any clumps of fat from the interior.

Using a boning knife, cut underneath the shoulder blades at the natural seams to remove the forelegs.

Remove the hind legs by cutting along the pelvic bones to separate the legs from the carcass.

Cut each leg in two at the joint. Using a heavy chef's knife, cut through the vertebrae to remove the pelvic bone.

Cut away the neck bones.

Cut the rack from the saddle (loin). Trim the bones on the ends of the ribs.

Trim the thin flaps of meat on either side of the saddle (unless deboning the saddle; see following page), and cut the saddle into four pieces. Reserve the flaps for stock.

Reserve the liver.

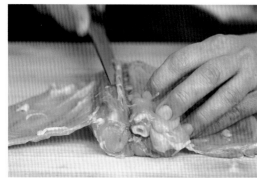

Deboning the Rabbit Saddle

For more refined presentations, the rabbit saddle, or loin, can be completely deboned, stuffed, and tied.

Place the saddle (do not remove the flaps) on its back. Using a boning knife, scrape way the tenderloins (the two thin muscles that run along the length of the saddle) from the underlying bone.

Slide the knife under the toothlike range of bones that were under the tenderloins and cut along the bones' contours, until you nearly detach the thicker loin. Continue, scraping now, until you reach the small cartilaginous bones at the underside of the backbone.

Scrape along those bones to release the flesh, but do not cut through the skin.

Repeat on the other side of the saddle, so that the flesh is hanging from the backbone only along the thin ridge of bones that almost protrudes through the back.

Keeping the skin intact, detach the backbone from the saddle by scraping the small bones with the boning knife as you pull up on the backbone. Continue until you have released each bone and the backbone comes away in one piece.

Season, stuff, roll, and tie the saddle as desired.

Lesson 16

Working with Fish

The term "fish" (*pesce*) is applied broadly to a class of aquatic, cold-blooded animals. The term is also frequently—if inaccurately—used to refer to shellfish, such as shrimp or clams. For the purposes of this curriculum, "fish" will refer to cold-blooded vertebrates that consist of four main parts: the head, the trunk or body, the tail, and the fins.

Most fish are 70 percent water and 10 to 20 percent protein, with traces of minerals, vitamins A, B, and D, carbohydrates, and lipids. Fish oil, or fat, has been hailed for its health benefits for centuries. The fattiest fish contain the most beneficial oils; all fish, however, provide high amounts of lean protein and nutrients. Fatty fish such as salmon and herring contain approximately 160 calories per 100 grams (3½ ounces). Lean fish such as bass and barramundi contain 70 calories per 100 grams (3½ ounces).

A fish is made up of muscles that are arranged in layers of short fibers, separated by delicate connective tissue, with a backbone and a tail that propels it. This connective tissue is weak because the collagen in the tissue has fewer amino acids than do other proteins. As a result, fish collagen requires significantly less cooking time than meat collagen. Fish scales are inedible rigid plates that grow from the animal's skin and assist in protection against the environment, including predators. Scales vary in size depending on the type of fish, but are generally arranged in overlapping rows.

Storage and Handling of Fish

Fish spoil very quickly due to the structure of their muscle fibers, connective tissue, and amino and fatty acids. With every degree over 0°C (32°F) that a fresh fish is allowed to go, its wholesomeness decreases rapidly. For instance, a fish held at 10°C (50°F) will deteriorate four times faster than one held at 0°C (32°F). Therefore, it is generally recommended that the time between fish capture and cooking be as brief as possible, and that careful attention be paid to storage and handling.

As soon as fish reach the kitchen, they should be gutted and refrigerated in crushed ice. In the **short term**, most whole fish with skin can be packed directly in the ice, in a fish storage unit with drainage holes to prevent the fish from soaking in water as the ice melts. For fillets and steaks, wrapping material such as parchment paper and/or plastic must be placed between the fish and the ice, since direct contact with the ice will damage the texture and flavor of the flesh. The ice should be changed as it melts.

Long-term storage can involve freezing, super-freezing, salting, smoking, pickling in brine, or canning. If freezing, the process must be completed as quickly as possible after capture to prevent damage to the natural texture of the fish and to ensure a fresh-from-the-sea taste. Before freezing, fish should be thoroughly wrapped and glazed with water to prevent freezer burn (first freeze the fish, then dip in water, then refreeze, and repeat, to build a protective ice layer). Never refreeze a product that has been thawed.

Classifying Fish

Fish are categorized in a number of ways: by habitat (freshwater, saltwater, brackish water); by harvesting technique (wild or farm-raised); by fat content; and by skeletal structure (roundfish or flatfish). It is particularly important that chefs be able to distinguish fish by fat content and structure, as these classifications affect methods of cleaning and cooking fish.

Classification by Fat Content

Fatty, or pelagic, fish (from the Greek *pelagos*, meaning "ocean") such as salmon, tuna, and eel swim over large distances, up and down currents. Constantly on the move, they require a consistent supply of fuel, which is provided by the oil stored in their muscle and tissue.

Lean fish, also called **whitefish** or **demersal** (from the Latin *mergere*, meaning "plunge" or "dive"), live just above the seabed, where they are less affected by ocean currents. These fish swim over much shorter distances, or in short bursts as needed to find food or escape predators. Demersal fish such as cod store most of their natural oils in the liver.

The difference in the fat content of fish is also determined by the quality and quantity of food consumed prior to harvest (Hugh Fearnley-Whittingstall and Nick Fisher, *The River Cottage Fish Book*. Fish harvested after harsh winters, or when less or poorer-quality food has been consumed, tend to be leaner than fish that have had bountiful, high-quality food.

On average, fish with less than 3 percent fat are considered "lean." Fish that contain 3 to 10 percent fat are considered "medium." "Fatty" fish are those that contain more than 10 percent fat.

Classification by Shape and Skeletal Structure

Roundfish (*pesce tondo*) have bodies that appear rounded, with eyes on either side of their heads; they swim vertically. Flatfish have asymmetrical bodies and swim in a horizontal position. Unlike on roundfish, the eyes of flatfish are located at the top of the head. (See diagrams on opposite page.)

Flatfish (*pesce piatto*) largely live at the bottom of the ocean. This category includes flounder, sole (e.g., English, Petrale, Dover, lemon), halibut, fluke, and turbot. Flatfish bodies are narrower than roundfish; they are compressed from the sides into a bottom-hugging shape. The skin on the top of a flatfish is dark, to act as camouflage from predators, and many have camouflaging abilities. Their dorsal and anal fins run the full length of their bodies.

Roundfish (*Pesce Tondo*)

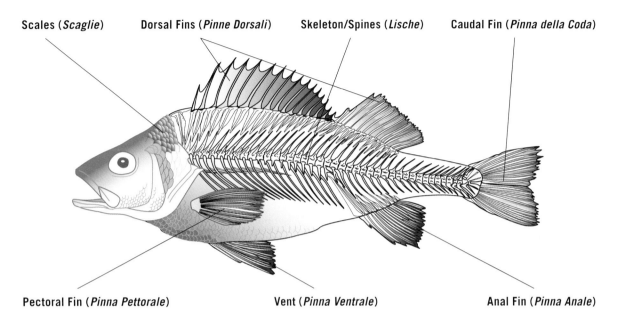

Scales (*Scaglie*) Dorsal Fins (*Pinne Dorsali*) Skeleton/Spines (*Lische*) Caudal Fin (*Pinna della Coda*)

Pectoral Fin (*Pinna Pettorale*) Vent (*Pinna Ventrale*) Anal Fin (*Pinna Anale*)

Flatfish (*Pesce Piatto*)

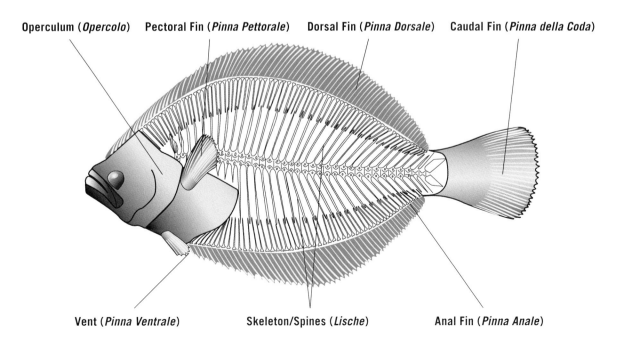

Operculum (*Opercolo*) Pectoral Fin (*Pinna Pettorale*) Dorsal Fin (*Pinna Dorsale*) Caudal Fin (*Pinna della Coda*)

Vent (*Pinna Ventrale*) Skeleton/Spines (*Lische*) Anal Fin (*Pinna Anale*)

Commonly Used Saltwater Fish

Market Name	Weight/Pounds	Category
Sea Bass	3 to 50	Round
Striped Bass	3 to 50	Round
Blackfish	2 to 5	Round
Bluefish	1 to 20	Round
Atlantic Cod	3 to 25	Round
Flounder (lemon, gray sole, Dover or English blackback	1 to 7	Flat
Fluke	1 to 5	Flat
Grouper	5 to 10, up to 1000	Round
Haddock	1.5 to 7	Round
Hake/Merluza	1 to 2, up to 30	Round
Halibut	5 to 75	Flat
Herring	0.12 to 0.25	Round
John Dory	2 to 5	Round
Boston Mackerel	1 to 2	Round
King Mackerel	5 to 15	Round
Spanish Mackerel	2 to 3	Round
Mahi-Mahi	5 to 10, up to 50	Round
Monkfish	1 to 50	Round
Mullet (American)	0.5 to 4	Round
Ocean Perch	0.5 to 2	Round
Pollock	1.5 to 8	Round

Commonly Used Freshwater Fish

Market Name	Weight/Pounds	Category
Arctic Char	4 to 25	Round
Bass	1 to 15	Round
Carp	2 to 10	Round
Catfish	1 to 5	Round
Eel	1 to 5	Round
Lake Herring	0.33 to 1	Round
Yellow Perch	0.5 to 1	Round
Pike	1.5 to 20	Round
Shad	3 to 8	Round
Smelt	1.5 to 5	Round
Sturgeon	10 to 30	Round
Tilapia	1.5 to 3	Round
Brook Trout	1 to 2, up to 6	Round
Lake Trout	10 to 100	Round
Rainbow Trout	0.12 to 6	Round
Steelhead Trout	8 to 12, up to 50	Round
Walleye Pike	1 to 2	Round
Whitefish	3 to 6, up to 20	Round

Preparing Fish for Cooking

Generally, the process of scaling, plucking, or otherwise cleaning fish, poultry, or game is known as dressing. There is considerable loss when cleaning and portioning fish. On average, gutting a fish removes 20 to 30 percent of its overall weight, depending on the species. Removing the head, skin, and bones can account for another 20- to 30-percent loss. The edible portion of a fish may only be 40 percent of its original weight. Generally, the portion of fish required for a main course is 100 to 150 grams (3½ to 5 ounces) per serving.

There are five basic steps to dressing a fish. Roundfish and flatfish require different methods.

Dressing a Roundfish

Cut off the fins using a pair of kitchen shears.

Scale the fish, as necessary: Hold the fish by the tail as tightly as you can, and use a fish scaler, the blade of a butter knife, or the back of the blade of a chef's knife to scrape down from the tail to the head with short, firm strokes. If the fish is very slippery, wrap a clean kitchen towel around your hand to help with the grip. This process can be done in a sink for ease of cleanup.

Snip out the gills.

Cut open the belly from the anal cavity to the gills and pull out the innards. Rinse the belly cavity carefully under cold running water.

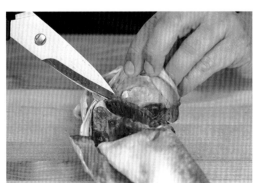

Dressing a Flatfish

Scale the fish with a fish scaler.

Cut off the fins with kitchen shears.

Cut out the gills with shears.

With a chef's knife, make a cut on the diagonal above the eyes and another under the jawbone, cutting all the way down to the work surface.

Pull the head up gently at an angle; the head and innards will come off in one piece. Thoroughly rinse the belly cavity under cold running water.

Filleting and Portioning Fish

Traditionally, roundfish are primarily cut into fillets (boneless sides) or steaks, or served whole. (Steaks, which are not shown here, are made by cutting across the fish with a large, sharp knife, through the backbone, into slices of the desired thickness. Very large fish, such as swordfish and tuna, are filleted: The large, wedge-shaped fillets are then cut crosswise into slices.) Flatfish are classically portioned into fillets or sections, as the structure of the fish does not allow for vertical slices.

Some fish, such as sardines, require different methods for cleaning and filleting (see "Dressing and Filleting Sardines" on page 450).

Filleting a Roundfish

The technique illustrated opposite is used when making several of the recipes in Chapter 15.

Score the tail end of the fish on both sides.

Place the knife behind the jawbone at an angle, and cut through to the backbone on both sides of the fish, angling the knife toward the tip of the head to maximize the yield on the fillet.

Using a fillet knife, make a 6-millimeter- (¼-inch)-

deep cut, from head to tail, alongside the backbone under the dorsal fin.

Insert the tip of the knife, at a shallow angle, at the head end of the incision.

Using smooth strokes and keeping the blade side of the knife as close to the skeletal structure as possible, separate the fillet, lifting the flesh away while working along the entire length of the fish.

Turn the fish around, and release the fillet from the belly side, from the tail to the belly cavity.

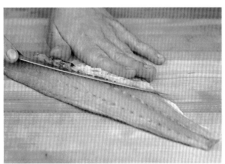

Using scissors, cut the ribs from the backbone, starting at the head. Lift the fillet completely off the bones.

Holding your knife almost parallel to the fillet, slide the knife under the rib bones and cut them off the fillet. Trim off the thin, fatty belly portion of the fillet; discard.

Place the fillet, skin side down, on the cutting board with the tail end at the bottom of the board. The pinbones run at an angle to the flesh; run your fingers gently down the fillet, from the head to the tail (this is against the grain of the flesh) to lift the ends of the bones so that they protrude slightly. Use fish tweezers or needle-nose pliers to grasp each pinbone and pull it out. Pull the bones away from you, in the direction in which they lie. Rinse the bones off the tweezers or pliers in a small bowl of cold water while you work.

Repeat to remove the rest of the pinbones, running your fingers against the grain of the fish to feel for any that remain.

Turn the fish over and repeat the process to remove the second fillet. Remove the pinbones in the same way.

Filleting a Flatfish

The technique illustrated at left is used when making *Sogliola alla Mugnaia* on page 226.

Score the tail of the fish. With a filleting knife, make a cut along the central backbone from the head to the tail.

Insert the blade of the knife at a shallow angle at either end of the backbone. Using smooth strokes and keeping the blade side of the knife as close to the rib bones as possible, begin to cut away the fillet. Keeping the knife angled toward the bones, continue working along the entire length of the fish. Repeat to remove the other fillet. Turn the fish over and remove the remaining two fillets.

Both the black and white skins are removed. To remove the skin: Lay the fillet, skin side down, on the board. Starting at the tail end, cut about 2½ centimeters (1 inch) of flesh away from the skin. Grasp the skin and pull it toward you, applying pressure with the knife, and making short, back-and-forth strokes with the knife to separate the fillet from the skin.

Dressing and Filleting Sardines

Sardines are easier to fillet than other roundfish. The bones are so soft that you can cut right through them.

The technique illustrated opposite is used when making *Pasta con le Sarde* on page 105.

Scale the fish. Cut off the head and remove the innards. Rinse.

Lay the fish on its side with the head to the right and the belly facing up. Place the tip of your knife on top of the backbone at the head end, steady the fillet with your other hand, and slide the knife through the bones and down to the tail end.

Now place the tip of your knife under the backbone and run the knife all the way down the length of the bone to remove the bottom fillet.

Trim the belly. Use tweezers to remove pinbones from the center of the fillet as described in the ninth step of "Filleting a Roundfish" on page 448. Rinse the tweezers in a small bowl of cold water between motions. Then pick up the fillet and pull out the pinbones from the side.

Cleaning Salt-Packed Anchovies

Salted anchovies are packed whole, with bones, but without heads.

As shown below, starting at the head end, use your fingers to pull off one fillet. Pull the second fillet off the bones; discard the bones. Rinse the anchovies under cold running water. Pat dry. Use within a few days or cover with oil and refrigerate.

The intensely flavored liquid called *collatura* is a by-product of the manufacture of salt-packed anchovies, created during the salting and weighting of the fish. *Collatura* is prized in Italy, where it is used in dressings, in *Bagna Cauda* (page 38), and for drizzling over roasted meats. While not precisely the same, the liquid from a can of salted anchovies is also very flavorful and can be reserved and used for the same purposes.

Preparing Fish for Carpaccio and *Tartara*

The technique illustrated at left is used when making *Crudo di Pesce* on page 50 and *Tartara di Tonno* on page 52.

For carpaccio, slice the fish thinly on an angle.

For *tartara*, cut a tuna loin into slabs. Slice each slab of tuna into 6-millimeter- (¼-inch)-thick slices. Cut the slices into 6-millimeter (¼-inch) dice. Areas of the tuna in which there is connective tissue are slightly tough; gently scrape the flesh from the connective tissue with a spoon. The connective tissue is not served.

Butterflying a Trout for Grilling

Prepare the trout as for a branzino (see "Dressing a Roundfish" on page 447) by scaling and gutting. Remove the head. Cut off the fins but leave the tail. Rinse well under cold running water.

The technique illustrated below left is used when making *Pesce alla Griglia* on page 233.

To butterfly, set the fish on its backbone and slide the knife along one side of the rib cage, then along the other side, to release the rib cage from the meat. Grasp the fish at the tail end, and cut through the backbone without cutting through the skin and meat of the bottom fillet.

Insert your knife at the head end so that it lies flat against the meat, and slide the knife all the way down the backbone to the tail. Do not cut through the fillet or cut off the tail. Pull the backbone and ribs off the flesh in one piece.

Scoring and Sautéing Fish Fillets

The skin of fish fillets is scored before sautéing to prevent the fish from curling in the pan during cooking. This ensures that the fillet lies flat in the pan, to encourage even browning and color.

The technique illustrated above is used when making *Sgombro con Scarola e Fagioli* on page 229.

Score the skin of the fish.

Season the fish with salt and pepper; sprinkle with flour and pat off excess.

Heat the oil with the aromatics over medium heat. When the oil is hot, add the fish, skin side down, and cook until well browned on both sides. Season with the juice of ½ lemon halfway through cooking.

Preparing Eel for Cooking

When working with eel, gloves should be worn to protect the hands from the secretions from the eel's skin, which can be irritating. Here, the eel is left on the bone, but the fillets may be removed from the bone just as for a roundfish. Eel skin is left on in many classic Italian recipes, but can also be removed.

The technique illustrated below is used when making *Anguilla in Carpione* on page 244.

Rinse the eel well under cold running water.

Score the skin below the head, all around the circumference of the eel.

Place the eel on a cutting board. With a filleting knife or kitchen scissors, cut along the underside of the eel from the head down the length of the belly.

Cut off the head and discard.

Disgorge the eel in cold water with vinegar added.

Cut the eel into pieces, discarding the tail end where there is very little meat.

To skin the eel, if desired, grasp the eel tightly at the head and pull the skin away from the flesh, revealing a dark gray, shiny membrane underneath. Pull the skin down and off in one piece.

Filleting a Cooked Roundfish for Service

The technique illustrated at left is used when serving *Pesce Intero Arrosto* on page 232 and *Pesce in Crosta di Sale* on page 237.

Cut behind the gills with a serving spoon. With a fork, lift the head from underneath and jimmy the head gently to detach. Place on a plate.

With the spoon, make a cut above the tail to loosen the fillet.

With a fork, gently scrape the fins off the fish.

Peel the skin off the top fillet with the fork and the spoon.

Use the spoon to cut down the dark line that runs the length of the top fillet and splits the fillet in two halves. Use the fork and spoon to push the fillets off the bone, on either side of that center line.

Lift each fillet half off the bone in one piece and place on a clean plate.

Use the fork to lift up the backbone and remove.

Repeat for the bottom fillet, to lift both halves of the fillet onto the plate.

Cooking Fish *al Cartoccio*

Steaming small, whole fish or fillets with a little liquid (usually wine) in a parchment or aluminum-foil pouch in the oven—*al cartoccio*—is a method designed to trap the flavor and aroma of the cooked fish. The liquid turns to steam in the package so that the fish cooks in its own juices; the juices are trapped to serve as a sauce. If assembly is properly done, the vapor created during baking puffs up the package dramatically.

Cooking time depends on the thickness of the fish. In general, expect 7 to 9 minutes for thinner (flatfish) fillets, 12 to 15 minutes for thicker fillets, and 15 to 20 minutes for whole fish, depending on the size (a whole trout will take less time than a larger fish such as a whole flounder).

This dish is served in its puffed parchment bag, which is cut open in front of the guest so that the diner can inhale the delicious aromas that would be lost if the packet had been opened in the kitchen.

The technique illustrated above is used when making *Pesce al Cartoccio* on page 228.

For each piece of fish, fold a piece of parchment paper in half and cut a rectangle 30 to 35 centimeters (11¾ to 13¾ inches) long and 23 to 26 centimeters (9 to 10 inches) wide. Open the paper out on a work surface.

Place the vegetable garnish, if using, in the center of the bottom half of the rectangle, and set the fish on top. Season with salt and pepper. Drizzle with a little wine, olive oil, and water.

Brush the bottom edge of the pouch with lightly beaten egg white. Fold over the top and crimp the edges to seal. Brush the seal again with egg white.

Place the parchment pouch on a baking sheet and bake.

Preparing *Baccalà* and *Stoccafisso*

Baccalà and *stoccafisso* represent ancient methods of preserving cod. *Baccalà* is salted, dried cod. *Stoccafisso* is air-dried but not salted. Both are prepared for cooking by soaking in water to cover until rehydrated, changing the water two to three times during soaking.

Preparing *Baccalà Mantecato*

Baccalà Mantecato (page 226) is a whipped mousse of puréed salted cod, enriched with olive oil.

Cook the soaked, drained cod in simmering milk until tender and whip to a paste in a stand mixer or food processor.

Return the mixture to the pot, and add the cooked onion and garlic, and milk as necessary, stirring with a wooden spoon until the mixture is soft and smooth.

Add the bread and the rest of the olive oil. Continue to whip with a wooden spoon until the mixture is soft and creamy, drizzling in some olive oil or a bit of extra milk if necessary.

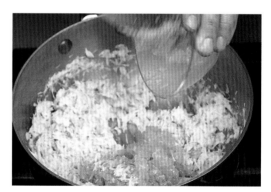

Lesson 17

Working with Shellfish

The word "shellfish" (*frutti di mare*) is misleading: Unlike roundfish and flatfish, shellfish are invertebrate animals. They do not have backbones or internal skeletons, and their physiology differs somewhat from their finned brethren. Shellfish are high in protein, iron, and vitamin B, and they are lower in calories and unhealthy fat than land-dwelling proteins such as beef, lamb, pork, and poultry. Shellfish may be divided into three distinct categories:

Crustaceans: A class of arthropod, a group of animals that have external skeletons or shells, segmented bodies, and jointed appendages. Lobsters, crabs, prawns, langoustines, crayfish, and shrimp are examples of commonly used crustaceans. All crustaceans share the same basic anatomy, made up of roughly two parts: the cephalothorax and the abdomen. The cephalothorax is the equivalent of the human head and trunk, composed of major organs and appendages, while the rear portion, or abdomen, is considered the tail, and is mostly composed of muscles for swimming.

Mollusks: A very diverse group of invertebrates. For the cook, the three important categories are bivalves, univalves, and cephalopods. **Bivalves** are saltwater creatures with two shells, such as oysters, scallops, and clams. **Univalves**, such as snails and winkles, have only one shell and can be either saltwater or land inhabitants. **Cephalopods**, including squid, cuttlefish, and octopus, have bilateral symmetry and are somewhat inverted—they have a muscular mantle on the exterior of their shell. They move by expelling water from a siphon under the head. Cephalopods generally have well-developed eyes, arms, or tentacles, and they can eject ink from an ink sac as a means of defending or hiding themselves from predators.

Echinoderms: A group of sea invertebrates that are found at every measurable ocean depth. Echinoderms may account for 90 percent of the biomass on deep-sea floors (Harold McGee, *On Food and Cooking*). Sea urchins are the most widely known edible echinoderms, used by chefs mainly for their creamy, flavorful reproductive organs and eggs. These organs can account for up to 60 percent of the animal's internal region.

Crostacei (Crustaceans)

Most edible crustaceans, including lobsters and crabs, are decapods, meaning they have five pairs of legs (the term *decapod* means "ten feet"), one of which is sometimes enlarged into a claw. Generally, the front two pairs of legs are pincers, and the back three are for crawling and swimming.

Crustaceans should be purchased as soon as possible after harvest. The longer they are in captivity, even alive, the more muscle mass they lose. (This is why the meat may seem to have shrunk when a lobster claw is cracked open.) The flesh of crustaceans breaks down very rapidly after death; over time, the flesh actually liquefies so that when the shell is opened it runs out as a transparent mucus.

Aragoste (Lobsters)

Claws in the American lobster can account for up to half of its total body weight. Its distant relatives, the spiny and rock lobsters, are considered "clawless"; their tails provide the meat.

Buying and Storing Lobsters

Lobsters are generally sold live or precooked. Lobsters should feel heavy and full, with all of their claws and feet intact. The tail of a live lobster will curl under strongly when the lobster is lifted.

Lobsters may be kept alive in a moist wrapping (wet newspapers are often used, or seaweed) in the refrigerator for up to 2 days; they must not be wrapped in plastic. Lobster tails freeze fairly well, and can be kept refrigerated for up to 48 hours.

Preparing Lobsters

Lobsters are cooked by a variety of methods: They are steamed, sautéed, grilled, poached, braised, and roasted. A popular method for cooking lobsters in Italy is to split them lengthwise down the middle, then grill them or roast them. Lobster tomalley, or liver, the pale mass that turns green when cooked, and coral, the ovary found in females that turns reddish-pink when cooked, can be removed before cooking, along with the stomach. The tomalley and coral are used in sauces and compound butters.

For humanitarian purposes, live lobsters may be anaesthetized in iced salt water for 30 minutes before being cut up or boiled, or they may be placed in the freezer (not to freeze them solid), and then dropped into boil-

ing water. The northern town of Reggio Emilia, in the province of Emilia-Romagna, has made boiling lobsters alive illegal.

Lobsters are sold with their claws bound in rubber bands; leave the rubber bands on the claws when cooking the lobsters.

Splitting a Live Lobster for Cooking

Lay the lobster on a board, belly side down. Straighten out the tail so that it lies flat. Insert the point of a large knife into the head just behind the frontal protrusion (the rostrum) and cut down the length of the lobster. Remove the coral (if it has any) and the tomalley for other use.

Break off the claws and cut off the legs as for cooked lobster (see next page).

Shelling a Cooked Lobster

The technique illustrated opposite is used when making *Aragosta Fra Diavola* on page 238.

Working over a bowl or other container to collect the juices and the shells, twist off the claws where they attach to the body. Then pull the claws off the "knuckles" that connect the claw to the body. Set the claws

on a cutting board, cover with a towel to prevent spraying, and crack both sides of the claws with the back of a large knife. Move the claw's pincers side to side, then bend them away from the claw while pulling them out. The feather-shaped piece of cartilage embedded in the

claw should come out with the pincers. Push the claw meat out in a single piece.

Twist off the tail. Put the point of your scissors on the underside of the tail, at one side, where the belly con-

nects to the hard, top shell. Snip between the shells to cut down the length of the tail. Repeat on the other side. Pry open the shell, jiggle, and pull the tail meat out. Remove and reserve the roe.

Cut through the shell of the knuckles and pull the meat out.

Remove the meat in the swimmers by rolling over them with a rolling pin.

Gamberi (Shrimp)

Along with prawns, shrimp are the most abundant shellfish in the world. There are about 300 species of shrimp, with the most common belonging to one semi-tropical and tropical genus. About a third of world's production is cultivated in Asia.

Buying and Storing Shrimp

Most shrimp are sold fresh, frozen, or cooked. The meat should look firm, springy, and moist. "Fresh" raw shrimp have usually been previously frozen, then thawed; they should be cooked the same day.

Shrimp are sold by number of shrimp to the pound. The number is usually expressed as a range: 16/20, for example, means 16 to 20 shrimp per pound. Very large shrimp may be sold as "U15" or "U10"; the "U" stands for "under," meaning that there are fewer than 15 or 10 shrimp per pound.

Preparing Shrimp

Shrimp are cooked by a variety of methods: They are poached, sautéed, grilled, and deep-fried.

Shrimp are commonly available "head-on" in Italy, and may be cooked in their shells or peeled with the fingers before cooking. The shells can be used for making stock. The dark vein along the outside curve of a shrimp is the end of the digestive tract, and can be gritty with sand. Make a shallow cut along the back of the shrimp. The vein is easily pulled out from the surrounding muscle.

Molluschi (Mollusks): Bivalves and Univalves

Bivalves such as clams and mussels spread their two-part shells open to allow water and food particles in, and pull the shells together with their adductor muscles to protect their innards from predators. Univalves are mollusks such as snails and periwinkles that have only one shell.

Buying and Storing Bivalves and Univalves

Bivalves and univalves should be purchased live in the shell when possible, and in a tightly closed shell; avoid any with cracked shells. Occasionally, live clams, oysters, and mussels are slightly open, but they should close quickly when tapped. Soft-shell clams always gape because of their protruding siphons, but they should retract the siphons when they are touched. Clams and oysters should sound full when tapped and feel solid; shellfish with slime or mud trapped inside will feel unusually heavy and must be discarded.

It's best to use clams, oysters, and mussels as soon as possible. If it's necessary to keep them for any period of time, store them in the refrigerator, loosely covered with a damp towel. Never store them in airtight con-tainers, wrapped in plastic, or submerged in water, as this will kill them.

Vongole (Clams)

Clams are burrowing bivalves: They dig themselves into ocean or river sediments. A pair of muscular tubes, or siphons, are used for inhaling and exhaling, as the clam needs to be able to reach water from its burrow in order to breathe and feed. Littleneck, or quahog, clams are considered "hard shell" and close completely, while steamers and longnecks are considered "soft shell" and their siphons are much longer than the actual shell.

The burrowing and siphoning musculature makes clams chewy. The tender part of a large clam may be cut out and prepared separately.

Preparing Clams

Clams may be immersed in salted water for about 20 minutes to eliminate any sand or grit. Scrub the shells to clean. Do not open clams until they are needed.

Clams may be served raw on the half shell. Cooked clams are typically served whole and gently poached in bouillon or sauce, or broiled (see *Vongole Ripiene* on page 242).

Cleaning and Shucking Clams

Clams should be opened just before serving, using a shucking knife. Be very careful since the knife can easily slip, and avoid losing the natural juices (liquor).

Scrub as needed, and soak the clams in water with enough salt added so that the water tastes salty.

Hold a clam in one hand protected with a folded towel, and place the sharp edge of the clam knife into the crack between the shells. Squeeze with the fingers of the hand that is holding the clam and force the knife between the shells.

Slide the knife against the top shell to cut the adductor muscles. Be careful not to damage the soft clam.

Open the clam and finish detaching the meat from the upper shell.

Cut the muscles against the lower shell to loosen the clam completely.

Ostriche (Oysters)

Oysters are the most tender bivalves. The shell-closing adductor constitutes just one-tenth of its body weight; the thin, delicate sheets of mantle and gills account for more than half; and the visceral mass accounts for a third. Oysters are largely farmed; their flavor is dependent on their home waters. The temperature of the water determines how rapidly an oyster grows, as well as its sex. An oyster with plentiful food will grow rapidly and develop into a plump female with millions of eggs. Cold water means slower growth, an indefinitely postponed sexual maturity, and a leaner, crisper texture. Oysters are most often served raw on the half shell, but may also be roasted, grilled, stuffed and baked, and served in soups and stews.

Storing and Preparing Oysters

Oysters can stay alive for a week or even longer if they are carefully stored, rounded side down, in the refrigerator, but they should not be frozen.

Oysters may be served raw on crushed ice, garnished with lemon. Cooked oysters are typically served whole and gently poached in bouillon or sauce, or broiled in the shell. (See *Vongole Ripiene* on page 242.)

Cleaning and Shucking Oysters

Oysters should be opened just before serving, using an oyster knife. Be very careful when opening oysters since the knife can easily slip, and avoid losing the natural juices (liquor).

Scrub the oysters clean. Hold an oyster in one hand protected with a folded towel, or set the oyster on a solid surface and hold it down with a towel.

Holding the knife in the opposite hand, insert the blade between the shell halves near the hinge. Do not push forward, but twist the knife to break the hinge.

Slide the knife under the flat top shell. Cut through the adductor muscle near the top shell; try not to damage the flesh of the oyster or lose its juices.

Remove the top shell. Carefully cut the lower end of the muscle from the bottom shell to loosen the oyster. Eliminate any small pieces of shell.

Cozze (Mussels)

Mussels anchor themselves with tough proteinaceous fibers called the byssus, or beard. A mussel has one large adductor at its wide end and one at its small end, which closes the shell and holds it tightly shut. The rest of its body comprises the respiratory and digestive systems, and the mantle. Coloration of the mussel depends on sex, diet, and species.

Preparing Mussels

Mussels are the easiest mollusk to prepare, as they readily come off their shells. The technique illustrated below is used when making *Zuppa di Pesce* on page 240 or *Insalata di Mare* on page 54.

Carefully scrape the shells with a paring knife to remove any small crustaceans (barnacles) and grit. If sandy, mussels may be soaked in salted cold water for about 20 minutes. (If mussels are cultivated, this step will probably not be necessary.) If any mussels are slightly open, push the shells sideways using the thumb and forefinger. The mussels should close; if not, discard. Debeard the mussel by pulling off any protruding filaments (the beard). Since the beard is attached to the body, tugging on it can injure the animal; mussels should be debearded just before cooking, so as not to damage or kill them.

If serving mussels raw, discard the top shell and eliminate any loose particles of shell in the remaining half. Cooked mussels are typically served whole and gently poached in bouillon or sauce.

Capesante (Scallops)

The meaty adductor muscle is generally the only part of the scallop that is eaten. Because they spoil quickly, scallops usually arrive at market shucked; most consumers never see a scallop in its shell.

American sea scallops are by far the most common in the marketplace. Local populations of bay scallops have decreased sharply in recent years due to a range of factors, including increased coastal development, habitat loss, and overfishing of sharks that feed on rays, a main predator of bay scallops.

As the only bivalves that can swim, many varieties of scallop are also notable for their hermaphroditism. Scallops may be both male and female at harvest,

or begin life as male and become female over time. In Europe, scallops are sold with the male or female reproductive organs attached. The bright-red roe is also widely appreciated. U.S. fishing boats discard everything but the adductor muscle before bringing scallops to market, and the roe has more of an orange color.

Buying and Preparing Scallops

Scallops should be creamy or slightly pink in color, and slightly sticky to the touch. Do not buy scallops that look dull or have a brownish tinge, as these may be signs of damage or decay. Also be on the lookout for scallops that are pure white, shiny, and wet looking: Because scallops are so perishable, they are often soaked in a chemical preservative to prevent spoilage and loss of moisture. Soaking compromises their flavor and causes them to absorb the soaking liquid, which will be expelled when the scallops cook, preventing them from searing correctly.

Shucked scallops are sold by the piece, or, like shrimp, by the number to the pound. "U10" scallops are "under 10 to the pound," "U12" are "under 12 to the pound," and so forth. U10 and U12 are standard sizes for sautéing.

If purchased in the shell, scallops should be tightly closed. Scallops are common in the Adriatic Sea, but are smaller than Atlantic sea scallops. In the United States, substitute bay scallops (pictured above).

Shucking Scallops

Use a thick towel to protect the hand. Hold the shell (a bay scallop is shown above) in your palm, with the muscle facing away, then carefully insert a rigid blade between the shells.

Cut or scrape away the white muscle from the top sides of the shell. (When this muscle is cut, the shell will open.)

Remove the band of nerves surrounding the muscle, as they will retract when cooked. Pull off the tough, crescent-shaped muscle on the side of the scallop (below). Rinse or briefly soak the shucked scallop in cold water to expel any excess sand.

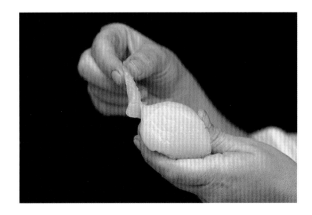

Cefalopodi (Cephalopods)

Cephalopods have more connective tissue and a greater amount of collagen in their bodies than other types of fish or shellfish. Squid and cuttlefish are either seared or grilled very briefly over high heat, or they are simmered at a low temperature for a long time to soften the collagen. (Otherwise their texture is tough and rubbery.) Octopus must always be cooked for a long period of time to tenderize the flesh.

Calamari (Squid)

Several species in a dozen families of squid are used in cooking. The most common edible squid of the Northeast Atlantic is *Loligo vulgaris*, and it is found in the Mediterranean and in the East Atlantic as far north as the English Channel.

The body of a squid has swimming fins projecting from its rear. At the front is the head, with two long tentacles and eight "arms" projecting from it. Squid are nearly transparent, making it a simple task to camouflage themselves from predators that might attack from below. (Their ink constitutes another form of protection.) Large, bulbous eyes give squid an advantage over their prey of small fish, prawns, and crabs.

Squid muscle fibers are extremely thin, producing a dense and fine-textured flesh. The fibers are arranged in multiple layers and attached with connective-tissue collagen, which behaves more like the collagen of meat animals than that of fish.

Buying and Preparing Squid

Squid is harvested with squid jigs, lures that resemble prawns. A squid wraps its tentacles around the jig, becomes entangled, and can then be scooped up with a landing net once it reaches the surface of the water.

Imported squid is sold deep-frozen, or previously frozen and defrosted. Squid cannot be stored alive but will keep fresh, refrigerated, for up to 3 days. Squid that is not fresh will have a gray, milky, wet appearance and a slimy residue.

Cleaning Squid

Very small squid may be cooked whole; larger squid are usually cut into pieces, or left whole and stuffed. Italians use the ink from cuttlefish, relatives of squid, in preference to squid ink, which is stronger and harsher tasting, to flavor pasta and risotto.

It is simple to pull out the innards of a squid, including the quill, which is actually a vestigial shell, leaving the body empty. The head and tentacles can be removed as well. If the body is sliced across, this will produce rings.

Rinse the squid well under cold running water. Holding the body in one hand and the tentacles in the other, pull the tentacles gently away from the body, removing the innards at the same time.

The ink sac is suspended in a silver pouch. Feel for the plasticlike, feather-shaped quill in the body, pull it out, and discard it.

Cut off the tentacles above the eyes; reserve the tentacles and discard the innards.

Feel for the bony squid beak at the base of the tentacles, press it out, and discard it.

Pull off as much of the gray skin from the body as possible.

Rinse the tentacles and body, inside and out, under cold running water, and dry well. Pull off the triangular "flippers" attached to the body and reserve. Cut the body, tentacles, and flippers as desired.

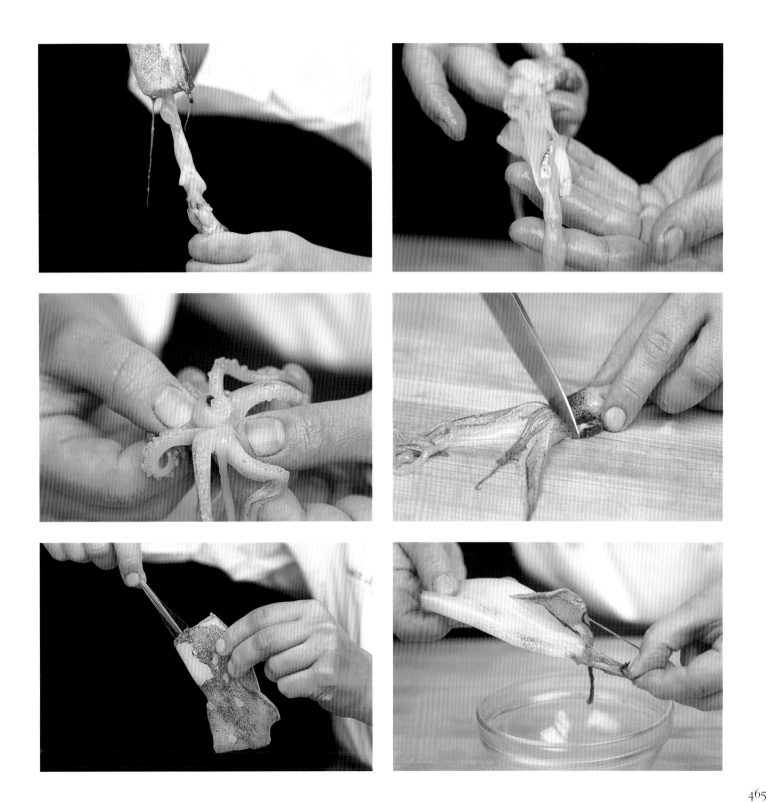

Seppia (Cuttlefish)

Cuttlefish do not inhabit U.S. coastal waters. They are usually imported from Europe and have a similar physiology and taste to cooked squid. In the United States, most cuttlefish are sold cleaned and frozen.

Cuttlefish contain far more ink than squid, and the flavor of the ink is preferable. The bountiful ink is often used to flavor and add color to sauces and stews. Cuttlefish are traditionally cut into strips and stewed (see Seppie in Zimino on page 245).

Polpo (Octopus)

Several varieties of octopus are commonly available, but they tend to be so similar that chefs do not usually worry about mixing types in dishes. The usual market length of an octopus is 51 to 102 centimeters (20 to 40 inches), but its maximum length is three times greater. It has eight arms clustered around its mouth. Each tentacle has a double row of suckers.

Buying and Preparing Octopus

Most octopi are sold dressed and ready to use, but whole octopi are also available. Octopus is poached in a flavored cooking liquid until tender. Once poached, the skin of the octopus and the suckers may be removed or not, as desired. When using octopus in a terrine, as on page 48, it is useful to retain the skin;

it contains gelatin that helps hold the terrine together. For a seafood salad, however, where the gelatin is unnecessary, skinning may be desirable. Note that the skin contributes a lovely purple color to the dish.

Baby octopus is tender enough that it may be briefly poached or fried, but mature octopus must be tenderized in some way. A variety of techniques are used for tenderizing, such as poaching for several hours.

Cleaning and Poaching Octopus

To prepare an octopus, as illustrated above, for cooking, the head must be removed just above the eyes, then turned inside out in order to remove the internal organs.

Rinse the octopus under cold running water. Press and pull out the beak from the underside.

Press and cut out the eyes.

Put the octopus in a bowl. Sprinkle with coarse salt and rub all over, massaging the salt into the skin. Rinse well under cold running water.

Place the octopus in a large pot with cold, salted water to cover and a mazzetto guarnito. Bring to a boil, reduce the heat, and poach for 1 hour. Add the vinegar and lemon quarter and continue cooking until the octopus is tender (cut off a little piece of a tentacle to taste), 1½ to 2 hours.

Lesson 18

Working with Pastry Doughs

Basic Tart Doughs: *Pasta Brisée* and *Pasta Frolla*

A dough is a flour-based preparation that, once formed and molded, acts as a container for a filling. Pastry dough that has been fitted into a mold and baked is called a tart or pie shell. All pastry doughs have four basic ingredients: **flour**, **fat**, **salt**, and a **liquid**. Different pastry types are achieved by varying the proportions of the basic ingredients and the methods of combining them.

In Italian pastry, two types of doughs are most frequently used for tarts: *pasta brisée* and *pasta frolla*. *Pasta brisée*, made without sugar, is the most basic tart dough and is suitable for both sweet and savory tarts. With the addition of **sugar**, the character of the dough changes, and it becomes *pasta frolla*.

Basic Italian tart doughs (as well as American pie doughs) can be classified by their texture—flaky or crumbly. Listed below are the main ingredients used, and a discussion of how each affects the dough. The choice of one dough over another depends on the requirements of the recipe. The doughs are almost interchangeable except in the case of savory tarts, when little or no sugar is desired.

Ingredients

Flour

A low-protein flour such as cake or pastry flour is best for producing the tender texture suitable for tart doughs, but all-purpose flour is very often used as well. Gluten is formed when the protein molecules in the flour are moistened with liquid and the mixture is worked. The less protein in the dough, the less gluten will develop during mixing, and the more tender and crumbly the dough will be.

The natural development of a small amount of gluten is necessary for the dough to hold together. If the dough is overworked, however, and the gluten overdeveloped, the pastry will become elastic, it will shrink in the oven, and it will be hard and tough when baked.

Fat

Although butter is almost always used in classic doughs, regional tart recipes often replace part of the butter with pork lard (*strutto*), which, like butter from a technical standpoint, has the advantage of solidity and malleability at room temperature. Oil can be used to make an extremely tender crust because it surrounds the flour proteins, making them resistant to water absorption and thus preventing gluten development.

Fats play two important roles in tart doughs: They tenderize and provide flakiness. Fats tenderize because they prevent the buildup of gluten by separating and lubricating the proteins in the flour. Fats produce flakiness by keeping the components of the dough separate until the dough starts to set its structure during the baking process. The ratio of flour to fat in a tart dough should be 2:1.

For *pasta brisée*, the fat must be very cold when added to the flour or it will soften and melt. Of the fats that can be used, butter is the most difficult to work with because it has a low melting point, so it must be well chilled at every stage: before it is added to the flour; in the completed dough; and in the completed tart shell, before baking. Butter also contains up to 20 percent water, which can activate the gluten in the flour.

Salt

Salt strengthens and tightens the gluten network, allowing the proteins to come closer together and bond extensively. Salt makes the structure of the dough more elastic and also adds flavor.

Liquid

Traditionally, the liquid used for tart dough is water. The amount of water determines the concentration of gluten. A small amount of water develops the gluten, though incompletely, and gives the pastry a crumbly texture; a greater amount of water dilutes the gluten and creates a softer, moisture texture. Milk, eggs, and juice may also be used instead of or in addition to water, and each will affect the dough in a different way. Milk will add some flavor due to its lactose (milk sugars); the lactose will also encourage color in the baked dough. Juices, especially acidic juices, will break down gluten but reduce browning.

When adding liquid ingredients to a dough, remember that the correct amount of liquid will vary according to the humidity in the air. It is important to add the liquid little by little and to learn to judge when the dough is moist enough. A dry dough will be very hard to roll out and may crack and fall apart. A dough that is too moist will stick to the work surface, will be difficult to mold, and will shrink when baked.

The liquid should be well chilled. The cold temperature hinders the development of gluten and prevents the fat from melting. The addition of acid, such as in lemon juice, also helps to make pastry flaky. Acid weakens the gluten network by increasing the number of positively charged amino acids (which make up proteins), thereby increasing the repellant forces between protein chains.

Eggs count as part of the liquid portion of the basic ingredients. Because of their viscosity, eggs should be well mixed (by themselves and/or with the other liquid ingredients) before addition to the flour-fat mixture. If incompletely mixed, the eggs will not combine easily with the flour, and the dough risks being overworked. Eggs, which contain fat and protein, prevent gluten development and contribute to the color of the pastry.

Sugar

Sugar affects taste, color, and texture in a tart dough. The large proportion of sugar in *pasta frolla* imparts sweetness and gives it a distinctly grainy texture. Sugar increases color by caramelization during baking. It prevents gluten development by cutting through gluten strands and diluting the flour proteins. It also preserves moistness and makes a crust tender.

Making *Pasta Brisée* and *Pasta Frolla*

When making *pasta brisée* and *pasta frolla*, the main objective is to work the dough as little as possible in order to minimize the development of gluten.

The techniques illustrated on the following pages are used when making sweet and savory tarts in Chapter 17.

Making *Pasta Brisée* by the Cut-In Method

Pasta brisée is a flaky dough that typically has little flavoring other than salt. It is made with a low-protein (pastry or cake) flour or all-purpose flour, fat (butter, lard, or shortening), salt, and water (other liquids, such as egg yolks, may be substituted, for flavor and appearance). The flakiness is a result of small pieces of cold fat in the dough, which, when they eventually melt in the oven, create voids or pockets that separate the dough into layers.

Mix the flour with the salt, then "cut" in the cold fat until the mixture has a sandy texture and there are no large particles of butter visible. The cutting can be done on a work surface with a plastic bowl scraper, with the paddle of a mixer, or with fingers. (If using fingers, however, one must work quickly so as not to warm the butter.) Ideally, the finished butter pieces are the size of dried lentils. If they are too small, the dough will be crumbly instead of

flaky; if too big, they can create holes that completely penetrate the dough when the fat melts.

Form a well in the flour-butter mixture. Add the water and any other liquid ingredients to the well. Begin to combine the liquid into the flour-butter mixture. Add just enough water to bring the dough together—too much water and the dough will be sticky and tough. Pull the dough into a rough mass. Work the dough as little as possible; overworking will develop the gluten and toughen the dough.

Crush walnut-size pieces of dough and smear them against the work surface with the heel of your hand to fully incorporate the ingredients. Press the pieces back into the dough.

If possible, press the dough into a shape that is roughly the form of the pan to be lined. Cover with plastic and chill.

Making *Pasta Frolla* by the Creaming Method

Pasta frolla means "tender dough." It is made with a high proportion of sugar and eggs, which gives it a crumbly, almost cookielike texture (it is often called shortbread dough). This delicate dough is used for tarts as well as for some biscotti. *Pasta frolla* can be made with either the cut-in method (see above) or the creaming method (*montare a crema*). In the creaming method, the room-temperature fat and the sugar are worked together until light and airy. The liquid (usually eggs) is added, and finally the flour. The high sugar and fat contents shorten and reduce the gluten structure, and the sugar and the eggs give the crust color. The high fat content necessitates chilling the dough for several hours to firm it up before rolling, or it can be difficult to work with.

In the bowl of a standing mixer, cream the butter with the sugar until light and airy. Beat in the eggs and the vanilla extract.

Beat in the flour and salt until the dough is combined. Gather all the pieces together and shape into disks. Cover with plastic and chill for at least 30 minutes.

Working with *Pasta Brisée* and *Pasta Frolla*

Despite the differences between *pasta brisée* and *pasta frolla*, the basic steps of rolling out the doughs are the same. Both doughs are high in fat and require a deft hand in preparation.

Chilling: This is an important part of the pastry-making process. Pastry dough should rest in the refrigerator for at least 30 minutes; it is even better if the dough is made the day before it is to be rolled out. Chilling firms up the fat and allows the moisture to distribute evenly throughout the dough; it also allows the gluten to relax and results in a tender, flaky pastry that does not shrink. In most cases, the dough is chilled again once it has been rolled, and once again after it is molded.

Rolling: The dough should be rolled on a clean, cool surface; marble is the best choice, but wooden, granite, or stainless steel will also work. Lightly flour the bench, the rolling pin, and the surface of the dough. If the dough is too firm, strike it a few times with the rolling pin to make it pliable enough to roll. Press the rolling pin into the dough in intervals to begin "walking the dough" out into a wider circle.

Begin rolling from the center of the dough away from you. Be careful not to roll off the edge of the dough, which will thin it out. The idea is to push *out* as well as down, in order to spread the dough while it flattens. Return to the center of the dough and repeat the process, this time rolling toward you. Roll forward and backward only—not side to side. After rolling just once in each direction, turn the dough 90 degrees. As the dough is turned, check that it is not sticking to the bench or the rolling pin. If more flour is needed, drag the dough through the flour on the bench. A little flour may be dusted on top as well.

Again, roll away from and toward you once in each direction and turn the dough 90 degrees. Continue rolling and turning the dough until the piece is several inches larger than the pan it will line. For a classic tart, the dough should be rolled into a circle approximately 3 millimeters (⅛ inch) thick and 5 centimeters (2 inches) larger than the diameter of the pan. 280 grams (10 ounces) of dough will roll to a 23-centimeter (9-inch) diameter.

Brushing: It is important to remove any excess flour from the dough before it is placed in the pan. Use a pastry brush to gently brush off the top of the dough. To brush the other side, roll the dough around the rolling pin, unroll it in the opposite direction, and brush off the excess flour.

Molding and Trimming: There are two basic methods of transferring the rolled dough to the pan or tart ring:

Roll the dough onto the rolling pin. Place the rolling pin at the bottom of the dough round. Lift up the bottom edge of the dough and place it on the rolling pin; roll the pin away from you to roll up the dough round. Place the flap of dough that is hanging off the rolling pin at the top of the pan, and unroll the dough over the pan.

Fold the dough in half and then in quarters; place the point where the two folds meet in the center of the pan and unfold the dough.

Once the dough is in the pan, it must be worked into the "corners." For this process, use a little of the excess dough, pressed into a ball and very lightly floured. Turning the pan as you work, lift up the dough as you gently tamp it into the corners of the mold. Be careful not to stretch the dough during this process; it will shrink when baked.

After the dough is properly pressed into the pan, the excess dough must be trimmed. Trim by rolling over the pan with the rolling pin.

If at any point, while rolling and lining the pan, the dough becomes too soft and warm to work with, place it in the refrigerator to chill.

Docking: Certain recipes call for the tart shell to be docked before it goes into the oven, to prevent the crust from rising as it bakes. Docking is the process of poking small holes in a raw dough to allow for the release of steam and trapped air during baking.

These holes can be poked into the dough using the tines of a fork or a roller docker. The dough can be docked either before it is placed in the pan or immediately after molding. A tart dough is docked when the filling to be used is not heavy enough to weigh it down, and for blind-baked tarts for which small holes in the finished shell will not cause problems. Do not dock the dough of a tart with a liquid filling that might seep through the holes in the bottom of the tart shell during baking and cause it to stick to the pan.

Baking: Tarts are filled and baked using different methods. The first, a one-step method, is the easiest. The raw shell is simply filled, and the tart shell and filling are baked together. This type of tart requires a long baking time to ensure that the dough is cooked through. (An example is the *Torta di Pinoli* on page 277.)

The second, a two-step method, requires that the tart shell be partially or completely baked, then cooled, before any filling is added. This method is referred to as blind baking. Blind baking is required for tarts in which the filling is not to be baked (fresh-fruit and cream tarts such as the *Crostata di Fragole e Kiwi* on page 280), or for tarts with fillings that bake quickly or require a low temperature such as the *Torta di Porri* on page 278.

To blind bake a tart shell, line the chilled, raw tart shell with a piece of parchment paper and fill the center with weights. Weights help the tart maintain its shape in the initial phase of baking and prevent the dough from forming air pockets. These weights can be dried beans, rice, or individual ceramic or metal pie weights. (Alternatively, a commercially made necklace of metal pie weights can be used.) Bake the shell at a relatively high heat until it looks white and chalky (the bottom of the shell is usually still raw at this point). Remove the weights and parchment paper, and return the pastry shell to the oven until it is baked through. Blind-baked tart shells can be prepared in advance, but there is a risk of the fragile crust being damaged if not stored properly.

Pasta Sfoglia

Sfoglia means "leaved." It refers to the layers (or leaves) that are formed by rolling and folding dough over and over until multiple layers are created. The individual layers of fat and dough created in the process are thinner than a sheet of paper, but when the dough is prepared properly, they will remain intact during the rolling, turning, and baking. The finished dough is light and flaky.

Leavening by Aeration

The leavening action that occurs in *pasta sfoglia* when it bakes is aeration by lamination—a method of mechanical leavening. The lamination leavens the dough and creates height by stacking the layers and entrapping pockets of air in between. Correctly made, *pasta sfoglia* can rise eight to ten times its original height when baked and can contain more than a thousand layers. This leavening occurs in two ways:

Enclosed/trapped air: During the preparation of the dough, a certain amount of air is trapped between layers each time the dough is folded. These air cells expand during baking and push the layers up and apart.

Steam: In the oven, steam is released from the water contained in the dough layers as well as from the butter; as the butter melts, it leaves air pockets that fill with steam. This steam pushes on the leaves of dough, forcing them to rise one by one. At the same time, the starch in the flour coagulates, strengthening the leaves and helping them stay apart.

Ingredients

Pasta sfoglia begins with the same four basic ingredients as the two previously discussed tart doughs: flour, fat, salt, and a liquid. The fat in *pasta sfoglia* has a significant influence on the quality of the final product. Historically many kinds of fat have been used in its preparation, including lard, goose fat, vegetable shortening, margarine, and pastry margarine, but the classic fat, and the best for flavor, is butter. The fat must be chilled and kept at roughly the same consistency as the dough.

Flour is also an important ingredient. The flour should have a high enough protein content to create a dough that can stretch without breaking during baking. However, if the flour is too "strong" (that is, too high in protein, such as 100-percent bread flour or high-gluten flour), the dough will develop too much gluten and, as a result, will be tough and overly elastic, will crack during use, and will be difficult to work. Conversely, if the flour is too low in protein (e.g., 100-percent cake flour), the requisite amount of gluten will not be created. The resulting dough will not have the necessary elasticity or stretching power to withstand the folding and rolling required to achieve the many layers; as a result, the layers will be fewer and lower.

Therefore, the best choice of flour is either all-purpose or equal parts bread and cake flours. While not necessary, the addition of an acid such as cream of tartar, lemon juice, or vinegar helps the protein (gluten) in the flour become more elastic and allows the dough to stretch rather than break. Keep in mind, however, that if the dough is to be held in the refrigerator for a substantial amount of time prior to baking, the addition of acid will have the opposite effect and will inhibit the dough from reaching its full rise.

Making *Pasta Sfoglia*

It is important that *pasta sfoglia* be made under proper conditions. If working in a very hot kitchen and/or if there is no marble surface, the dough will be difficult to handle. It will need to be chilled again as soon as it starts to get soft and before the butter starts to melt and ooze out; otherwise the dough will be impossible to manipulate.

The techniques illustrated above are used when making *Millefoglie* on page 284.

Pasta sfoglia consists of alternating layers of a lean-dough mixture, or *pastello* (composed of flour, water, salt, and a small amount of butter), and a butter block (*panetto*).

To make the *pastello*, combine the flour and salt and form the mixture into a well. Cut in the softened butter with a bench scraper or mix with your fingertips. Add just enough cold water to make a rough dough. Avoid overworking the dough: If too much gluten is developed at this stage, it will make the dough difficult to turn later. Shape the dough into a square. With a sharp knife, cut an X in the top and about halfway through the block. (This helps to cut the gluten strands so that they relax more quickly.) Wrap in plastic, and

refrigerate to allow the gluten to relax and the dough to become fully hydrated.

For the *panetto*, place the cold butter between two sheets of plastic wrap and pound with a rolling pin until pliable but still cool. The butter should be smooth, with no lumps, and the consistency should be as similar as possible to that of the lean dough. It must be cold so that it doesn't melt into the dough, but it must be pliable so that it does not break the layers when rolled. Fold and pound the butter into a square block the size of the lean dough.

Now the lean dough is rolled to encase the butter block. During this process, the temperature and consistency of the dough and the butter block should be carefully controlled; maintaining a similar consistency will allow the two to roll together easily. On a lightly floured surface, roll out the dough to create a thicker center square with a flap at each edge just large enough to enclose the butter. Place the butter block diagonally on top of the thicker center square so that it looks like a diamond inside a square. Fold one flap of the dough over the butter and brush off excess flour. Continue folding the remaining flaps over the butter, brushing excess flour from each as you go. Refrigerate if the dough gets sticky or begins to soften.

Now the package is repeatedly folded and rolled (a process called "turns"), to create many thin layers of dough and fat. These turns are done in sets, resting the dough in between. Long rest periods between turns will help to relax the dough and limit gluten development. When turning the dough, dust with as little flour as possible.

Press on the dough with the rolling pin four or five times along its length, or until the dough lengthens to approximately 23 centimeters (9 inches). Be very careful at this point, as the butter is very thick and can easily break through the dough and destroy layers. Dust the work surface with flour and roll the dough until it is about 56 centimeters (22 inches) long, about the length of the rolling pin; do not roll the width.

Using a pastry brush, brush off any excess flour and fold the dough into thirds. Make two finger marks in the *sfoglia* to indicate two turns, wrap in plastic, and refrigerate 20 to 30 minutes. Repeat this process to make six turns in total.

When incorporating the butter block and rolling out and turning the dough package, keep the dough in as even a rectangle and as even a thickness as possible. Keep squaring the sides of the dough package with the rolling pin as you work, and do not roll over the sides of the dough, which will compress the edges and interfere with the rising. The more evenly the layers are made when preparing the dough, the more evenly the pastry will rise when baked.

To shape the dough, roll it to the desired thickness and chill. This allows the dough to rest and prevents shrinkage when baking. When firm, cut the dough into the desired shape and chill again. The dough is usually docked before baking (see discussion of chilling, rolling, brushing, and docking doughs on pages 270–74).

Storing *Pasta Sfoglia*

Pasta sfoglia freezes well both as a dough and in pastry products assembled for later baking. It may also be refrigerated, but if held longer than a few days, it will begin to ferment, affecting both the taste and the color of the final product. *Pasta sfoglia* must be extremely well wrapped before storing to prevent the dough from drying out.

Tips for Rolling, Cutting, and Baking *Pasta Sfoglia*

When shaping the dough, roll it out to the desired thickness and chill it. This allows the dough to rest and prevents shrinkage when baking. When it is firm, it can be removed from the refrigerator or freezer, cut into the desired shape, and chilled again before baking.

When cutting *pasta sfoglia*, do not use a sawing motion—cut straight down. This will keep the edges of the dough straight and help it rise evenly during baking.

If applying egg wash to a puff-pastry product before baking, do not allow the wash to drip down on the cut sides of the pastry, which would seal the edges and inhibit the rise.

Make sure the pastry is completely baked before removing it from the oven. Puff pastry must be baked all the way through to be palatable; underbaked layers of dough inside the pastry are heavy and unpleasant to eat. The pastry should be baked until it is brown on the outside and, unless the pastry has been rolled very thinly, the temperature of the oven should be lowered and the baking continued to ensure that the pastry is baked through. The finished pastry should be an even, golden brown on the bottom, with no white spots. It should feel light, and if you cut into it with the tip of a sharp knife, you should see completely cooked, dry layers.

Pasta sfoglia scraps should never be wasted; it is a time-consuming dough to produce. When combined and rolled together, scraps are suitable for making many types of small pastries such as farfalle (puff-pastry butterflies), or anything that does not need a high rise. Combine the scraps by layering them as evenly as possible, chilling them, then rolling them out as desired.

Pasta Bignè

Pasta bignè falls somewhere in between the categories of batter and dough and behaves differently from either because of its higher water and egg contents. It is the only Italian dough that is cooked twice, first on top of the stove, and a second time in the oven. The correct amount of each of the basic ingredients is crucial in the formation of a successful dough.

Bread flour or another high-protein flour may be used to create an adequate gluten structure to contain the air, fat, and steam during baking, but all-purpose is more often used. (Bread flour contains approximately 13 percent protein, as compared to pastry or cake flour with protein content that falls between 6 and 9 percent.) If a pastry or cake flour is used, the dough will tear during baking.

The technique illustrated below is used when making *bignè*, or cream puffs, as in the recipe for *Profiteroles* on page 282.

Using a Pastry Bag

Fit the bag with a rounded tip. Twist and press the bag into the tip to lock.

Fold over the top of the bag.

Fill the bag halfway with batter, press the batter down toward the tip, and twist the top of the bag to close.

Nest the piping bag between the thumb and forefinger of your right hand. Wrap the top of the bag around the index finger of your left hand to stabilize.

Pipe the batter, squeezing from the top of the bag, onto baking sheets.

To form the initial dough, bring a mixture of water, butter, salt, and sugar to a boil. Add the flour immediately. The water must not be left to boil unattended, or it will evaporate and alter the proportions of the recipe. The fat should be cut up into small pieces so that it melts at the same time that the water comes to a boil. If the water boils before all of the fat melts, it will evaporate and throw off the proportions of the recipe. The flour is added all at once so that the starch can swell instantly and evenly in the hot water.

Cook the paste on top of the stove to dry out the mixture. The purpose of stovetop cooking is to extract enough moisture to enable the dough to absorb the eggs. When a paste forms a mass that pulls away from the side of the pot and the mixture begins to form a skin on the bottom, remove the mixture from the heat and beat vigorously with a wooden spoon (or in a mixer) to cool it and to develop its gluten structure. It will be thick at first, then start to thin and become glossy. (Avoid overcooking the dough, or the cream puffs will have an unpleasant reddish tinge.)

Beat in the eggs, one at a time. The number of eggs used is important to the success of the pastry, or choux. This amount will vary according to the size of the eggs, the amount of moisture in the air, and the amount of moisture extracted from the paste during the stovetop cooking. If too little egg is added, the dough will rise poorly; too much, and the dough will fail to shape well. If a lighter, crisper pastry is desired, one or two of the eggs may be replaced with egg whites.

Enough egg has been added when:

The batter falls in a ribbon from a spoon or paddle lifted out of it.

A trench made with the spoon in the batter closes slowly.

The batter forms a small hook or curl that flops over when pulled up.

Shaping *Bignè*

In order to produce the best rise, *bignè* should ideally be formed and baked while the initial dough is still fresh and slightly warm. The batter is piped onto buttered or parchment-lined baking sheets with a pastry bag (see sidebar "Using a Pastry Bag" at left). Pipe the *bignè* in alternating rows to allow the heat to circulate freely between them. Leave plenty of room (5 to 7½ centimeters / 2 to 3 inches) between them to allow for expansion during baking. Score the *bignè* to help them rise evenly, and brush with an egg wash. Egg wash should be applied just before baking, and not too heavily, or it may run onto the baking sheet, inhibiting rise and deforming the piped shapes.

Baking *Bignè*

Bignè are leavened by steam, a mechanical form of leavening. During baking, the moisture and the eggs in the dough expand and turn to steam, forming a cavity inside the pastry. The pastry puffs up and multiplies in size, but remains hollow inside. The exterior shell around the hollow partially dries out and becomes firm. This structure helps the shell to hold its shape when the pastries are removed from the oven and the steam pressure subsides. The *bignè* need to bake until they are completely dried out, or they will collapse as they cool. Therefore, they are baked at a relatively high temperature for 10 to 15 minutes as they puff and expand, then for several minutes more at a reduced temperature to dry out the interior without overly browning the outside. When properly baked and dried, the pastries will feel hollow and lighter than their size.

Storing *Pasta Bignè* and *Bignè*

Pasta bignè may be made in large batches and stored for future use. The only inhibitor is storage space. Raw batter may be refrigerated for 2 to 3 days, or the batter can be piped out into *bigné* shapes and frozen. Place the shapes, uncovered, in the freezer, and when the shapes are rigid, cover them well with plastic wrap. Defrost the *bignè* uncovered, in the refrigerator, then apply egg wash and bake as needed. This method will provide a crisp, fresh-tasting product.

Bignè may also be baked, cooled, and stored airtight for up to 3 days, or frozen, well wrapped, for 1 month. When baked *bignè* are removed from the refrigerator or freezer, they may be slightly soft due to condensation. Refresh them in a 350°F (177°C) oven for several minutes to dry out.

Other Pastry Doughs

Doughs for cookies and other pastries, such as biscotti and cannoli, are made following guidelines similar to those for tart doughs. They are then shaped and rolled in different ways.

Shaping and Cooking Biscotti

The technique illustrated above is used when making *Biscotti di Prato* on page 290.

Scrape the dough out onto a floured work surface. Roll the dough into a log; it should be just well enough coated with flour to keep it from sticking to the work surface.

Quickly transfer the log onto the sheet pan, being care-ful not to stretch it. The log can also be divided into smaller logs; space them evenly across the pan. Press gently to flatten and bake until golden. Let cool.

When the biscotti are cool enough to handle, place one piece on a cutting board and slice on a diagonal, 2 centimeters (¾ inch) thick.

Lay the biscotti flat on the sheet pan and repeat with remaining pieces. Bake again until lightly toasted.

Making Cannoli Shells

The technique illustrated here is used when making *Cannoli* on page 293.

Roll the dough through the pasta machine to the thinnest setting.

Lay the dough sheet on a lightly floured work surface, and cut into 9-centimeter (3½-inch) squares or rounds.

Roll the dough squares or rounds around a cannoli form (roll squares diagonally). Seal with a little egg wash or water, as needed.

Fry the cannoli (still wrapped around the molds) in hot oil until golden brown and crisp. Remove the molds as soon as you can handle them, and cool the cannoli completely on absorbent towels.

Lesson 19

Working with Creams and Custards

Custards (derived from *croustade*, a flaky pastry case) date back to the Middle Ages, when they were used as fillings for flans or tarts. A custard is a mixture of liquid and egg that, when gently heated, thickens or sets by the coagulation of egg proteins. Custards may be sweet or savory; they may use whole eggs, whole eggs plus yolks, or yolks alone. They usually contain cream, milk, or both, but they may also be made with liquids other than milk, as in fruit curds and *zabaione*. The consistency of a finished custard is determined by the ratio of eggs to liquid. (One whole egg or 2 egg yolks will set 1 cup of milk into a loose custard. A firmer gel requires more protein, usually 3 whole eggs per 2 cups of milk.)

Custards fall into three major categories: stirred, starch-bound, and baked. These basic mixtures may appear on their own or as components of other dishes. Stirred, starch-bound, and baked custards mostly start with the same ingredients, but their methods of preparation are quite different.

Eggs and the Science of Custards: Coagulation and Overcoagulation

The key to a successful custard is getting the eggs to thicken and set properly. In pursuit of that goal, it's useful to understand a little of the science behind eggs and custards.

Custards are made possible by the coagulation of egg proteins. Egg proteins begin as folded chains of amino acids. As the proteins are heated, their increased motion breaks some bonds, and the chains unfold. The newly unfolded proteins bond with one another, resulting in a continuous meshwork of long molecules. This creates a moist but solid egg mass.

Simple egg proteins, cooked on their own, coagulate over a relatively wide temperature range from 62°C (143°F) to 70°C (158°F).

Coagulation in the preparation of custards is a delicate process. Custards are sensitive to time and temperature as well as to other ingredients. Too much heat applied too quickly, or low heat applied for too long, will cause protein molecules to overcoagulate. When this happens, the molecules become too firm and rupture, squeezing out the liquid held within their molecular structure. (The scientific name for this is syneresis.) Tiny, liquid-filled holes in a baked custard, a grainy texture, and a separated or curdled sauce are all evidence of overcoagulation.

Coagulation occurs gradually in a custard cooked at a low temperature. At a high temperature, coagulation is almost instant. The line between the thickening point and the formation of curds is small. To lessen the risk of curdling, stovetop custards are cooked over low heat and stirred constantly; the stirring promotes even heating and ensures that parts of the mixture don't overcoagulate while the remainder continues to cook.

Insulation from direct heat also ensures gentle cooking. Stirred custards can be protected by using a heavy-bottomed pan, but a double boiler (*bagno maria*) is ideal because the water serves as an insulator. Unlike with stovetop heat, the temperature of water cannot exceed 100°C (212°F), ensuring that the heat is gentle and easy to control.

For the same reason, baked custards are usually cooked at a low temperature in a water bath, unless insulated by a pastry crust (see *Torta di Porri* on page 278). Water baths are also important in food safety, ensuring the even heat penetration necessary for destroying harmful bacteria.

Other Ingredients and How They Affect Custards

Liquids

The addition of milk, water, or another liquid to beaten eggs dilutes and separates the protein molecules, making it more difficult for the molecules to combine. This in turn raises the coagulation temperature and slows down thickening. The addition of milk, for example, allows a stirred custard to be heated to 71°C (160°F) before curdling, because the sugar in the milk dilutes the egg proteins.

The rate at which a liquid conducts heat also affects cooking time: Homogenized whole milk, for instance, conducts heat more slowly than skim milk.

Starches

Most starches—flour, cornstarch, potato starch, arrowroot, and tapioca—prevent egg and other proteins from curdling even when a mixture is brought to a boil. The theory is that before the egg protein coagulates, the starch swells and blocks the protein molecules from bonding. As a result, starch-based custards can be exposed to higher heat. In fact, it is essential to reheat a starch-based custard mixture after adding the egg yolks to deactivate an enzyme in the yolks (alpha-amylase) that destroys starch gels. Moreover, the more sugar the mixture contains, the higher the temperature needed to deactivate the enzyme. If the enzyme is not deactivated, it can turn a thick custard or cream pie to soup overnight in the refrigerator.

Sugars

Sugars also separate egg-protein molecules from one another, raising the temperature required for coagulation and slowing down the rate of coagulation in a mixture. Consequently, a sweet custard will require a longer cooking time than a savory one.

Salts

Salts, including the salts naturally found in milk, change the electrical makeup of egg protein and speed up coagulation. According to Harold McGee (*On Food and Cooking*), with the addition of salt and other minerals, positively charged ions cluster around the negatively charged egg proteins, creating a neutralizing shield. This shield makes it possible for the proteins to unfold near each other and bond extensively.

Acids

Acids, when added to eggs, also change the electrical environment, lower the coagulation temperature, and speed up coagulation. When an acid such as lemon juice or cream of tartar is added, the pH of the egg is lowered, thus diminishing the proteins' mutually repelling negative charge. Citrus curds and custards that contain fruits or vegetables (and therefore acids) will set faster than custards without such ingredients.

Stirred Custards

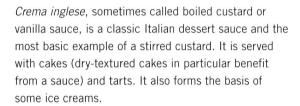

Crema Inglese

Crema inglese, sometimes called boiled custard or vanilla sauce, is a classic Italian dessert sauce and the most basic example of a stirred custard. It is served with cakes (dry-textured cakes in particular benefit from a sauce) and tarts. It also forms the basis of some ice creams.

Crema inglese is a combination of milk and/or cream, egg yolks, sugar, and flavoring that is cooked until thickened. The mixture must be stirred constantly during this thickening process. The stirring motion breaks the bonds of the proteins as they begin to set, creating a saucelike consistency. Thickening occurs when the temperature reaches approximately 160°F (71°C). Curds (scrambled eggs) will form at 180°F (82°C).

The technique illustrated at left is used when making custard sauce for the *gelati* in Chapter 21, and to serve with *Torta di Pinoli* on page 277 and *Dolci di Cioccolato* on page 309.

Bring the milk or cream to a boil in a saucepan. If the mixture is to be infused (see "Flavoring *Crema Inglese*" below), add the ingredient(s) as the mixture heats and allow the mixture to steep off the heat, if necessary.

Prepare an ice bath by setting a bowl over another bowl containing ice and water. (This is necessary to immediately halt the cooking when the stirred custard has reached consistency.)

Whisk together the egg yolks and sugar until the mixture is very pale-colored. This step is called *blanchir*: when sugar has been dissolved into the yolks sufficiently to lighten the color. Although this does not necessarily indicate any chemical change, it does mean that most of the sugar has dissolved and the mixture is thick.

It is important that sugar and yolks be whisked immediately once they are added to the bowl. If they are allowed to sit together unmixed, a chemical reaction will "scorch" or "burn" the eggs, causing hard bits to form. Some chefs add part of the sugar to the liquid and the balance to the egg yolks. This helps prevent scorching of the milk, and creates less foam, especially important in a baked custard.

Return the milk to the boiling point, if necessary, and add it slowly to the yolk-sugar mixture, whisking constantly, to temper the eggs. (Tempering is the process of stabilizing two different elements to a consistent temperature for incorporation—in this case, to avoid scrambling the eggs, which would occur if the hot milk were added all at once or the eggs were added directly to the milk.)

Pour the entire mixture back into the saucepan. Place it over low heat and cook it slowly, stirring constantly with a wooden spoon in a figure-eight motion, until the custard reaches the desired temperature, between 71°C (160°F) and 82°C (179°F), and is thick enough to coat the back of the spoon. If the mixture is heated above 82°C (180°F), it will curdle, and the mixture will be grainy instead of smooth and creamy. (Should the *crema inglese* exceed optimum temperature, immediately remove the pan from the heat and add cold cream to halt the cooking.)

When the custard has reached the desired thickness and temperature, it is passed through a fine-mesh strainer. Since the internal heat of the custard and the residual heat of the pan will continue to cook the custard, it must be chilled as soon as it is removed from the heat: Pour the mixture into the bowl in the ice bath, and stir it occasionally as it cools to release steam and ensure that it cools evenly. (Cooling quickly is also imperative for sanitary reasons.) The custard will continue to thicken as it cools.

Flavoring *Crema Inglese*

The *crema* may be flavored at several different stages, with any number of ingredients. Most often (but not always), the milk is infused with the flavoring: The milk is heated with the flavoring element, and the mixture is allowed to steep off the heat for as long as necessary to infuse it with the appropriate flavor. This can take as little as 1 to 2 minutes for a scraped vanilla bean, or up to 20 to 30 minutes for other ingredients. The milk is strained and reheated, and the recipe continues as usual. Some common flavorings include:

Citrus, such as finely grated zest of oranges, lemons, or tangerines

Cinnamon sticks or ground cinnamon

Coffee or roasted espresso beans

Almonds, hazelnuts, or other nuts, toasted, ground, or chopped

Praline paste (the milk is not strained)

Toasted coconut

Melted bittersweet chocolate (added to the warm finished *crema* mixture)

Liqueurs (added to the finished *crema* mixture)

Poached and puréed dried fruits (added to the finished *crema* mixture)

Zabaione

Zabaione is an aerated, stirred custard cooked on the stovetop, usually over a water bath (*bagno maria*). The bottom of the bowl must not touch the simmering water.

Zabaione should be made as close to serving time as possible. It tends to lose some of its aeration and will separate if allowed to stand too long. (Should this happen, return it to the stove and repeat the thickening process.)

To make *zabaione:*

Beat the egg yolks and sugar with a balloon whisk as for *crema inglese.*

Add the liquid flavoring.

Place the bowl over a simmering water bath. Heat the mixture, whisking constantly and vigorously to prevent curdling and to incorporate air. The mixture thickens as a result of heat coagulation: As the egg proteins bond, they form a strong yet flexible network that traps water and other liquid. Beat until the mixture is thick yet very light and foamy, and when a spoon is pulled through it, the mixture is homogenous with no liquid leaking from it. Remove every now and then from the heat if the temperature of the mixture risks exceeding 71°C (160°F). (If the mixture gets too hot, the proteins will become too firm and tight, and they begin to squeeze out the liquid. The eggs will curdle and the resulting sauce will become thick and pasty.)

Flavoring *Zabaione*

When selecting the flavoring for *zabaione*, remember:

Some juices or alcohols may not be strong tasting enough to adequately flavor the *zabaione*. Reducing the liquid before adding it to the egg foam will increase the flavor.

The reduced liquid must be cooled before adding it to the eggs, or the eggs may curdle.

An alcohol, when added as the flavoring, can help prevent curdling, as it will lower the boiling point of the custard.

Starch-bound Custards

Starch-bound custards are simply stirred custards that are thickened and made more stable with a starch. These custards represent an exception to the rule that custards should never be heated above 180°F (82°C): They must boil for at least 2 minutes to eliminate the raw-starch taste, destroy the starch-digesting alpha-amylase enzyme in the eggs (which will counteract the thickening power of the starch and thin out the custard), and thicken to the proper consistency. In a restaurant setting, the custard is usually boiled for 3 minutes to sterilize the eggs.

The starch (frequently cornstarch and/or flour, but other starches may be used) adds stability and protects the eggs from breaking or curdling during cooking. Starch-bound custards are more substantial and denser than other custards, and they can be prepared directly on the stovetop or baked in a moderate oven without a *bagno maria*.

The classic example of a starch-bound custard in Italian cuisine is *crema pasticcera* (pastry cream). *Crema pasticcera* is not served on its own; rather, it is used as a filling for cakes, fruit tarts (see *Crostata di Fragole e Kiwi* on page 280), and other pastries. It is also used as the basis for other dessert preparations, such as *crema leggera* (pastry cream lightened with whipped cream) used when making *Millefoglie* on page 284.

To make *crema pasticcera*:

Bring the milk to a simmer.

Whisk together the eggs and sugar in a bowl until the mixture is pale-colored, and add the starch to combine.

Temper the mixture with heated milk, whisking constantly, as for *crema inglese*.

Return the mixture to the heat and cook, whisking vigorously, until the custard is smooth and has boiled for at least 2 minutes to destroy the alpha-amylase enzyme and eliminate the taste of raw starch.

Immediately tranfer the custard from the hot pan to a bowl and cool in an ice bath. *Crema pasticcera* is always refrigerated until needed.

Dot the *crema* with melted butter, sprinkle with sugar, or press a piece of plastic wrap directly onto the surface. This step will prevent a skin from forming. The skin that forms on stirred custards, including *crema inglese* and *crema pasticcera*, is casein, a protein found in milk. It occurs as a result of evaporation on the surface of a hot milk or cream liquid, which causes the casein to dry out. If it is removed while the mixture is still hot, it will form again.

Lesson 20

Working with Egg Foams

When egg albumen is beaten vigorously, it foams and increases in volume six to eight times. Egg foams are essential to meringues as well as to certain types of cakes, such as *pan di Spagna* and *savoiardi*. Both preparations are leavened by egg foams alone; no chemical leavening agents, such as baking powder or soda, are used. The two preparations differ in that *pan di Spagna* is made with whole eggs, *savoiardi* with separated eggs. Products made with separated eggs are more malleable.

Working with *Pan di Spagna*, or *Pasta Genovese*

Pan di Spagna, also known as *pasta Genovese*, relies on whipped eggs for its light, spongy texture. The cake rises by mechanical rather than chemical means: The heat of the oven causes the air bubbles in the batter—trapped in the whipped eggs—to expand. The heat cooks and sets the proteins around the bubbles. It is therefore crucial that the eggs be correctly beaten.

The technique illustrated below is used when making *Pan di Spagna* on page 300 and *Zuccotto* on page 303.

To make *pan di Spagna*:

Combine the whole eggs and sugar in a heatproof bowl. Quickly move the bowl to a *bagno maria*, and stir the mixture. (Eggs and sugar left together unmixed will "burn" the eggs—cause hard bits to form—because of a chemical reaction.)

Warm the mixture *over* the water (the bottom of the bowl must not touch the water) until it reaches a temperature of approximately 43°C (110°F), stirring constantly to prevent the eggs from cooking. The heat helps to dissolve the sugar and to make some of the proteins in the eggs more elastic, allowing the eggs to trap more air and achieve greater volume. This results in a higher, lighter cake. Do not, however, heat the eggs above (49°C) 120°F—eggs will scramble at a higher temperature and lose their capacity to hold air bubbles.

Remove the bowl from the heat and whisk until tripled in volume. The completed egg foam should be pale yellow, and it should fall in a wide ribbon from the whisk; it should not disappear or be reincorporated into the remaining foam. (When whisking the warmed egg-sugar mixture in a mixer, watch the sides of the bowl to see when the batter ceases to rise. Once it has stopped rising, it is ready.)

Add the sifted cake or all-purpose flour slowly, in several additions, gently folding with a rubber spatula. Do not overwork the batter: Fold in each addition just until combined; streaks of flour should still be visible.

Gently fold in the flavorings and melted butter (if using). If using butter, it should be liquid but not hot. To incorporate the butter easily, add a small amount of the batter to the butter to bring it to a consistency closer to that of the batter. Then, fold the butter mixture into the batter.

Once mixed, the batter is extremely fragile. It must be handled gently, with great care taken to retain the air in the batter. It will deflate if allowed to sit before baking. Immediately pour the batter into the prepared pan (see "Preparing Cake Pans" on facing page). Gently spin the cake pan to even the surface of the batter, which will in turn help the cake rise evenly. Bake on the center rack of a preheated oven. The cakes should have ample space around them.

Until the last 5 minutes of baking, avoid banging into the oven, and opening and closing the oven door, which can cause the cake to collapse. The cake is finished when the top is golden brown, the cake pulls away from the sides of the pan, the center of the cake springs back with no indentation remaining when the surface is gently touched with a fingertip, and a skewer inserted into the center of the cake comes out clean with no crumbs sticking to it. Great care must be taken when testing a cake for doneness; testing too early can cause the cake to deflate.

After baking, immediately unmold the cake onto a cooling rack to allow air to circulate freely around it. (If the cake is left in the pan, the steam from the batter will be trapped, causing the cake to become soggy and the sides to cave in.) Once cooled, wrap the cakes tightly in plastic to prevent staling. If the cake is made in advance, it may be frozen for up to 2 weeks.

Preparing Cake Pans

A properly prepared pan ensures that the cake will not stick and that it will rise without obstruction.

Place a sheet of parchment paper on your work surface.

Fold the left half over the right, then the bottom half up over the top. Stabilizing the bottom left corner with your left index finger, fold the paper in half to make a triangle and continue folding a few more times until you have a tight, slim triangle.

Place the point of the cone in the center of the overturned cake pan and cut with a pair of scissors to fit just inside the pan.

Unfold into a round. Brush the pan with melted butter, brushing up the sides.

Insert the paper round, then brush the paper round with butter.

Flour the pan, tilting it to coat; tap out excess flour.

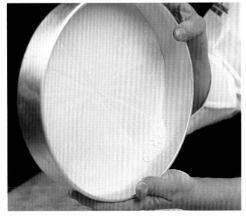

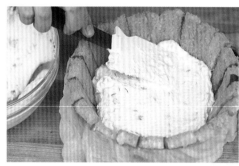

Assembling *Zuccotto*

The technique illustrated at left is used when making *Zucotto* on page 303.

Cut a frozen *pan di Spagna* into slices 1 centimeter (⅜ inch) thick, leaving top and bottom crusts intact, to produce several long, rectangular slices, edged on all sides by crust.

Cut the slices in half on the diagonal to form long, slender triangles, one side edged with crust.

Dip one side of each triangle in sugar syrup. Arrange the triangles side by side in a bowl, the soaked sides facing down, so that the pointed ends meet in the center of the bowl and all of the crusted edges face in the same direction, overlapping slightly as necessary. Trim the tops of the cake triangles that are hanging over the bowl.

Scoop the fruit-ricotta filling into the cake-lined bowl, smoothing it all over the sides so that it completely covers the cake; make an indentation in the center.

Scoop the chocolate cream into the center of the cake and smooth the top. Fold the overhanging cake over the filling. Dip more cake slices in syrup and use them to completely cover the top. Fold the cheesecloth over to secure. Freeze.

Working with *Savoiardi*

Care should be taken not to overbeat the egg whites; overbeaten whites lose their capacity to leaven the cake. The peaks should be firm but not dry.

The technique illustrated above is used when making *Savoiardi* on page 292.

To make *savoiardi*:

Beat the egg whites in the bowl of a standing electric mixer fitted with the whip attachment on low speed, to aerate. Add the confectioners' sugar, raise the speed to high, and beat until firm peaks form.

Whisk the yolks and vanilla to blend well.

Using a rubber spatula, fold the meringue into the egg yolks. Then carefully fold the flour into the meringue so as not to deflate the batter.

Immediately transfer the batter to a pastry bag fitted with a plain tip. Pipe 8-centimeter (3⅛-inch) strips on the parchment, allowing at least 2 to 3 centimeters (1 inch) between them. Dust the *savoiardi* lightly with confectioners' sugar and bake for 5 to 7 minutes, or until the *savoiardi* are golden and the centers spring back when lightly touched.

Lesson 21

Working with Meringues and Mousses

Meringhe (Meringues)

A meringue is an egg-white foam that has been reinforced and stabilized by the addition of sugar and/or heat. There are three types of meringues: French, Italian, and Swiss. For all three, it is crucial that neither the egg whites themselves nor the bowl in which they are whipped be contaminated with egg yolk or any other fat. Even the smallest amount of yolk will prevent the foam from forming correctly. It is equally important that the whites not be overbeaten. When overbeaten, the proteins in egg whites become dry, and the foam develops a grainy texture and loses volume. Meringues with low sugar content are very easy to overbeat. An acidic element such as cream of tartar or vinegar will increase the stability of the foam and helps to prevent overbeating.

French Meringue

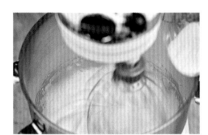

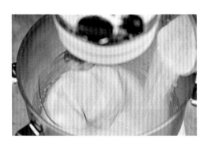

A French meringue is made from raw egg whites beaten with sugar. The sugar content of a French meringue helps determine how long the mixture should be beaten to achieve the correct consistency; the greater the sugar content, the more beating is required because sugar will inhibit the expansion of the egg protein.

Because it is uncooked, French meringue is usually used in products that will be baked. Piped into shapes and baked at a very low heat, a French meringue achieves a distinctive, crunchy texture that melts in the mouth. (If the mouthfeel is grainy or cottonlike, the egg white may have been beaten too much.) French meringue is also used for shells or rings in a variety of cakes.

To make French meringue:

Place the egg whites in the bowl.

Start the mixer on low speed to break up the whites and incorporate air. If using an acid, add it to the whites when they are just frothy.

Increase the speed to medium and beat the meringue to the soft-peak stage, meaning that the mixture will hold soft peaks when the beater is lifted from the bowl.

With the mixer running, add the sugar steadily, but not too rapidly (the sugar is referred to as "running sugar" in this process), and beat to soft or stiff peaks, as indicated in the recipe. (The more the added sugar, the longer it will take to beat to the desired consistency.)

At the end of the mixing time, "sear" the meringue by beating at high speed for a few seconds. This stabilizes the meringue by preventing it from expanding and then deflating. The finished meringue should be stiff and shiny.

Italian Meringue

An Italian meringue is made with a sugar syrup cooked to 112°C to 116°C (234°F to 240°F)—also called the "soft-ball" stage—and carefully drizzled into firmly whipped egg whites. During this process, the egg whites are cooked in the hot syrup, resulting in a stable meringue that is safe to eat.

Making an Italian meringue can be difficult: The beaten egg whites must be ready when the syrup reaches the correct temperature, or the finished meringue may turn out dull or heavy. Italian meringue is used in mousses, in *torrone* (the sugar is cooked to a higher temperature in order to create a stiff texture), and in some *semifreddi*, products that require volume but no additional cooking after the meringue is added.

To make Italian meringue:

Bring the water and sugar to a boil without stirring, washing sugar crystals down the inside of the pot with a clean pastry brush to prevent the syrup from crystallizing. (The amount of water used is variable; use just enough to moisten the sugar.)

When the syrup has come to a full boil, start beating the egg whites in the mixer. Begin on low speed, and increase to medium as the cooking of the sugar progresses. When the sugar reaches 112°C to 116°C (234°F to 240°F), the whites should be at the soft-peak stage. (This procedure may need to be regulated: If the whites are coming up faster than the sugar is cooking, slow down the speed of the mixer. If the sugar is nearing soft-ball stage and the whites are not ready, reduce the heat to low.)

Pour the syrup, slowly and carefully, down the side of the bowl into the whipping whites, with the mixer running. Avoid pouring it onto the whip; it will splatter onto the sides of the bowl instead of going into the foam.

Whip the meringue to the desired consistency, and "sear" by beating at high speed for a few seconds. The finished meringue should be light and shiny, with a soft, full, dense, creamy texture.

Swiss Meringue

Swiss meringue is made by heating egg whites and sugar over a *bagno maria* until the mixture reaches about 54°C (130°F) and the sugar granules are dissolved. At this point, the mixture is removed from the heat and beaten until cool. Its preliminary cooking makes it the most stable of the three meringues. Since, as in an Italian meringue, the eggs have been cooked to a safe temperature, the meringue requires no further cooking. Less airy and less fluffy than either French or Italian meringue, Swiss meringue is often used for decoration.

To make Swiss meringue:

In the bowl of a standing mixer fitted with the whisk attachment, beat the egg whites and sugar to combine.

Place the bowl over a *bagno maria* and heat, whisking slowly, until the whites come to a temperature of approximately 54°C (130°F).

Remove the bowl from the heat and place it on the mixer stand. Beat the meringue, slowly at first, then on medium speed, to the desired consistency. A Swiss meringue should be light, smooth, and very firm. Since Swiss meringue usually contains a high ratio of sugar, the meringue will probably be cool by the time it comes to firm peaks, which are needed for piping decorations, such as meringue mushrooms, for which a Swiss meringue would be used.

Tips for Working with Meringues

Be gentle when folding meringues; they deflate easily.

Meringues are extremely fragile and should be made right before they are to be used. Although some meringues are more stable than others, they will start to break down if they sit for any length of time.

When making a French meringue, the whites are beaten to soft peak before adding the sugar; more volume is achieved this way, and the whites will foam much faster.

When making an Italian meringue, sugar should always be added after soft-firm peaks have been formed.

Fresher egg whites are more viscous and therefore will produce a more stable meringue.

Older egg whites are less viscous and therefore will give greater volume to a meringue.

Adding a pinch of salt to egg whites reduces viscosity and thus will give greater volume to a meringue.

It is easier to whip air into room-temperature egg whites, thereby giving a meringue greater volume. However, cold egg whites will make a more stable meringue.

Fat interferes with the development of egg-white foam, and egg yolk contains fat. When breaking eggs open, make sure that no egg yolk mixes into the whites. The bowl and the whip should be clean. Egg whites beaten by hand with a balloon whisk will usually result in a more even-textured meringue than those beaten in an electric mixer.

If available, a copper bowl is a good container in which to beat egg whites. The copper reacts with the proteins in the egg whites, yielding more volume than with a stainless-steel bowl. A better consistency will be achieved and it will be more difficult to overwhip. Cream of tartar has the same effect as copper (don't use both). Before using copper bowls, clean them with salt and vinegar and dry with paper towels. Make sure there are no traces of fat in the bowl, on the whisk, or in the egg whites; otherwise the egg whites will not stiffen or achieve maximum volume. Never add acid to a mixture in a copper bowl—a toxic reaction occurs that turns the egg whites green.

Mousses

Mousses may be sweet or savory. Savory mousses are made from purées of meat, fish, or vegetables. Dessert mousses are made from several different bases, including fruit purées, egg yolks that have been poached by beating in hot syrup, and dark or white chocolate. The characteristic mousse texture is obtained by folding beaten egg whites and/or whipped cream into the base. The air bubbles from the beaten whites/cream are trapped inside the dessert, which provides the frothy, almost spongy texture. When making mousses, it is important that neither the egg whites nor the cream be overbeaten. Overbeaten whites will produce a deflated mousse; overbeaten cream will produce a heavy, buttery-textured mousse.

When folding, first fold in a quarter of the total volume to lighten the base, then fold in the remaining three-quarters all at once.

Gelatin is sometimes added to mousses for stability. A mousse made with a thin fruit purée, for example, may need gelatin to bind it. A mousse that is being served to a large number of people and must be held unrefrigerated for a period of time will also benefit from gelatin for stability. Gelatin does not enhance the texture or flavor of a mousse; it should be added sparingly.

Making *Panna Cotta*

Panna cotta is an eggless variation on mousse, thickened with gelatin, lightened with whipped cream, and molded. The technique illustrated below is used when making *Panna Cotta al Limone* on page 308.

The milk is heated and infused with flavorings, such as lemon, coffee, or spices.

The gelatin is soaked in cold water, squeezed out, and stirred into the warm milk. The mixture is removed from the heat, strained, and allowed to begin setting. This can be done over an ice bath or in the refrigerator to speed up the process.

While the base is chilling and beginning to set, the cream is whipped to soft peak. Once the base mixture has set to the consistency of yogurt, it is folded into the cream with a rubber spatula. Once the cream is completely incorporated, the *panna cotta* is molded and refrigerated for several hours to set completely.

To remove a *panna cotta* from the mold, warm the mold by either dipping it in warm water or using a propane torch. Once the mold has been slightly warmed, invert the dessert onto a serving plate or cake cardboard and remove the mold. Do not warm the mold too much, or the *panna cotta* will melt. The shelf life of any *panna cotta* is 2 to 3 days, refrigerated. Never freeze *panna cotta*.

Lesson 22

Working with Frozen Desserts

Gelato

Gelato is made from a stirred custard with a high proportion of natural flavorings such as fruit purées or chocolate. It is frozen using a machine that incorporates very little air, unlike American ice creams, which have air whipped into them to create volume (this added volume is called "overrun"). Less air makes for a denser and more intensely flavored product. Despite its lighter texture, American ice cream is actually much higher in fat: 10 to 30 percent for ice cream versus 2 to 8 percent for most *gelati*.

Gelato is an emulsified foam that has been stabilized by the freezing of much of its liquid. According to food scientist Harold McGee in his book *On Food and Cooking*, ice cream is a collection of four essential components: **Liquid** containing dissolved salt, sugar, and milk protein keeps the ice cream from freezing into a solid mass. **Ice crystals** act as stabilizing agents. Clumps of **milk fat** give ice cream its body and rich texture. And tiny **air cells** float in between the other elements and keep ice cream from becoming too dense. Occasionally, there are undesirable crystals of lactose that give ice cream a gritty texture; these usually occur in whole-cream custards.

Sorbetti and *Granite*

The basic ingredients for *granite* and *sorbetti* are the same: sugar, water, optional lemon juice for acidity, plus flavorings (fruit purées, fruit juices, liqueurs, wines, spirits, brewed teas, coffees, and herbal infusions). The difference between the two lies in the procedures for making them: *granite* are stirred very little while *sorbetti* are churned, like *gelati*.

Sorbetti are based on a mixture of sugar with a variety of fruit juices or purées, wines (Moscato, sherry, port, champagne), spirits (fruit brandies), or liqueurs, such as grappa. These frozen concoctions may also be based on infusions from aromatic plants (mint, tea, lemon verbena, lavender, thyme, or other herbs).

The texture of a *sorbetto* should be perfectly smooth rather than granular. In order to obtain this texture, the *sorbetto* is churned very rapidly so that ice crystals don't have time to form. When *sorbetti* sit overnight in a freezer, they have a tendency to crystallize. Those that have crystallized can be melted and put back into the ice cream machine to restore their texture (do not use this method with ice cream, which is far more perishable).

Sugar Density

The texture of *sorbetto* is controlled by the sugar content of its sugar syrup. If the sugar content is too low, the *sorbetto* will be grainy. If the sugar content is too high, the mixture will not freeze properly. Because different types of fruit and other ingredients have different sugar contents, there is no standard amount of sugar that should be added to a *sorbetto* mixture. The sweetness of a *sorbetto* base is adjusted by the addition of either water or sugar syrup. In a professional kitchen, testing the sweetness of a *sorbetto* base mixture is most easily done by using a refractometer, which registers the sugar density of the mixture. Refractometers measure in degrees Brix, which represents the sugar content as a percentage. A mixture registering 26° Brix contains 26 percent sugar. *Sorbetti* should range from 24° to 28° Brix. If no refractometer is available, follow the recipe and, if necessary, thaw the finished *sorbetto* mixture and adjust the sugar level—up by adding sugar syrup, or down by adding water.

Glucose, a liquid invert sugar, is sometimes added to *sorbetto* not only to contribute sweetness, but also to act as a stabilizer, to give the *sorbetto* a creamier texture, and to prevent the sugar from crystallizing. Glucose may be replaced by corn syrup.

When a *sorbetto* mixture has been adjusted to the correct sugar density, it may often be too sweet to the taste, in which case some lemon juice can be added for acidity. However, if the sugar density is lowered significantly, the *sorbetto* will not have a perfectly smooth texture.

To adjust the density of a *sorbetto* mixture:

If the *sorbetto* is not dense enough or sweet enough, add more sugar syrup.

If it already seems too sweet or the density is already high, stop adding sugar syrup.

If at this point the mixture seems thick, add water, or a mix of half water, half sugar syrup to thin it.

The ultimate flavor of the *sorbetto* will be affected not only by the sugar content but also by the natural acidity of fruit. Remember too that the unfrozen *sorbetto* mixture will taste sweeter and stronger than the finished product.

Granite

Granite can refer to any of a variety of frozen preparations in Italian cuisine, but generally speaking and for the purposes of this curriculum, it is a slushy, grainy-textured ice, based on a flavored sugar syrup with a relatively low sugar content. *Granite* are commonly served in well-chilled glasses and garnished, but they may be served plain or as a palate cleanser. They are most often found in bars and are more common in southern Italy.

A granita usually has a lower sugar content than a *sorbetto* and is prepared with little stirring during the freezing process, resulting in coarse ice crystals. *Granite* should register between 13° and 17° Brix on a refractometer. *Granite* are usually mixed and placed in a stainless-steel pan, placed in the freezer, and stirred occasionally at regular intervals as ice begins to form around the edges; this ensures the distribution of flavor and encourages the formation of ice crystals, while preventing the granita from freezing solid. In this method, *granite* are prepared for serving by scraping an ice cream scoop or a large spoon across the frozen surface, shaving off bits of the flavored ice.

Granite are also prepared by freezing completely without any stirring; the frozen mixture is then crushed in an ice crusher for a coarse texture or processed in a food processor for a finer texture.

Bibliography

Accademia Italiana della Cucina. *La Cucina: The Regional Cooking of Italy*. Translated by Jay Hyams. New York: Rizzoli, 2009.

Aidells, Bruce. *Bruce Aidells's Complete Book of Pork: A Guide to Buying, Storing, and Cooking the World's Favorite Meat*. New York: HarperCollins, 2004.

Apicius (Translated by Christopher Grocock and Sally Grainger). *Apicius*. Totnes, Devon [U.K.]: Prospect Books, 2006.

Artusi, Pellegrino. *Science in the Kitchen and the Art of Eating Well* [1891]. Translated by Murtha Baca and Stephen Sartarelli. Toronto: University of Toronto Press, 2003.

Bastianich, Lidia. *Lidia Cooks from the Heart of Italy*. New York: Alfred A. Knopf, 2009.

Bloom, Leslie Beal, and Marcie Ver Ploeg. *Seafood Cooking for Dummies*. Foster City, CA: IDG Books Worldwide, 1999.

Bugialli, Giuliano. *The Fine Art of Italian Cooking: The Classic Cookbook, Updated and Expanded*. New York: Gramercy Books, 2005.

Capatti, Alberto, and Massimo Montanari. *Italian Cuisine: A Cultural History*. Translated by Aine O'Healy. New York: Columbia University Press, 2003.

Casella, Cesare, and Eileen Daspin. *Diary of a Tuscan Chef: Recipes and Memories of Good Times and Great Food*. New York: Doubleday, 1998.

Casella, Cesare. *True Tuscan: Flavors and Memories from the Countryside of Toscana*. New York: HarperCollins, 2005.

Culinary Institute of America. *The Professional Chef*. 7th ed. New York: John Wiley, 2002.

Davidson, Alan. *The Oxford Companion to Food*. Oxford: Oxford University Press, 1999.

————. *Seafood: A Connoisseur's Guide and Cookbook*. New York: Simon and Schuster, 1989.

Della Croce, Julia. *Umbria: Regional Recipes from the Heartland of Italy*. San Francisco: Chronicle Books, 2002.

Editors of *Cook's Illustrated*. *The Cook's Illustrated Complete Book of Poultry*. New York: Clarkson Potter, 1999.

Fearnley-Whittingstall, Hugh. *The River Cottage Meat Book*. London: Hodder and Stoughton, 2004.

Fearnley-Whittingstall, Hugh, and Nick Fisher. *The River Cottage Fish Book*. London: Bloomsbury, 2007.

Field, Carol. *The Italian Baker*. New York: Harper & Row Publishers, 1985.

Gho, Paola, ed. *The Slow Food Dictionary to Italian Regional Cooking*. Bra, Piemonte [Italy]: Slow Food Editore, 2010.

Gisslen, Wayne. *Professional Cooking*. 6th ed. Hoboken, NJ: John Wiley, 2007.

Gordon, Peter. *Salads: The New Main Course*. New York: Clarkson Potter, 2005.

Green, Aliza. *Field Guide to Produce: How to Identify, Select, and Prepare Virtually Every Fruit and Vegetable at the Market*. Philadelphia: Quirk Books, 2004.

Hazan, Marcella. *Essentials of Classic Italian Cooking*. New York: Alfred A. Knopf, 1992.

Kiple, Kenneth F., and Kriemhild Coneè Ornelas. *The Cambridge World History of Food*. Vol. 1. Cambridge: Cambridge University Press, 2000.

Labensky, Sarah R., and Alan M. Hause. *On Cooking: A Textbook of Culinary Fundamentals*. Upper Saddle River, NJ: Prentice Hall, 2007.

Labensky, Steven, Gaye G. Ingram, and Sarah H. Labensky. *The Prentice Hall Essentials Dictionary of Culinary Arts*. Upper Saddle River, NJ: Prentice Hall, 2007.

Lang, Jenifer Harvey, ed. *Larousse Gastronomique*. New York: Crown, 1988.

MacNeil, Karen. *The Wine Bible*. New York: Workman Publishing, 2001.

Maestro Martino of Como. *The Art of Cooking: The First Modern Cookery Book*. Edited by Luigi Ballerini. Translated by Jeremy Parzen. (With fifty modernized recipes by Stefania Barzini.) Berkeley: University of California Press, 2005.

Malgieri, Nick. *Great Italian Desserts*. Boston: Little, Brown, 1990.

Marchesi, Gualtiero. *The Marchesi Code*. Translated by Kathleen Page. Milan: La Marchesiana, 2006.

May, Tony. *Italian Cuisine: Basic Cooking Techniques*. New York: Italian Wine and Food Institute, 1990.

McGee, Harold. *On Food and Cooking: The Science and Lore of the Kitchen*. New York: Scribner, 2004.

National Association of Meat Purveyors. *The Meat Buyer's Guide*. Reston, VA: The Association, 1992.

Norman, Jill. *Herbs and Spices: The Cook's Reference*. London: Dorling Kindersley, 2002.

Planck, Nina. *Real Food: What to Eat and Why*. New York: Bloomsbury/USA, 2006.

Roux, Michel. *Eggs*. Hoboken, NJ: John Wiley and Sons, 2005.

Sahni, Julie. *Savoring Spices and Herbs: Recipe Secrets of Flavor, Aroma, and Color*. New York: William Morrow, 1996.

Scappi, Bartolomeo. *The Opera of Bartolomeo Scappi* [1570]. Translated by Terence Scully. Toronto: University of Toronto Press, 2008.

Schlesinger, Chris, and John Willoughby. *Lettuce in Your Kitchen: Flavorful and Unexpected Main-Dish Salads and Dressings*. New York: William Morrow, 1996.

Schneider, Elizabeth. *Vegetables from Amaranth to Zucchini*. New York: William Morrow, 2001.

Schwartz, Leonard, and Sheila Linderman. *Salads: 150 Classic and Innovative Recipes for Every Course and Every Meal*. New York: HarperCollins, 1992.

Serventi, Silvano, and Françoise Sabban. *Pasta: The Story of a Universal Food*. Translated by Antony Shugaar. New York: Columbia University Press, 2002.

Sortun, Ana. *Spice: Flavors of the Eastern Mediterranean*. New York: ReganBooks, 2006.

Stewart, Martha, and Sarah Carey. *Martha Stewart's Cooking School: Lessons and Recipes for the Home Cook*. New York: Clarkson Potter, 2008.

Teubner, Christian, Sybil Gräfin Schönfeldt, and Siegfried Scholtyssek. *The Chicken and Poultry Bible: The Definitive Sourcebook*. New York: Penguin Studio, 1997.

Waters, Alice. *Chez Panisse Vegetables*. New York: HarperCollins, 1996.

Wolke, R. L. *What Einstein Told His Cook*. New York: W. W. Norton, 2002.

Conversion Charts

American and Metric Measurements and Conversions

American Volume Measurements

1 gallon	= 4 quarts	= 8 pints	= 16 cups	= 128 fluid ounces	
1 quart		= 2 pints	= 4 cups	= 32 fluid ounces	
1 pint			= 2 cups	= 16 fluid ounces	
1 cup				= 8 fluid ounces	
1 tablespoon				= ½ fluid ounce	= 3 teaspoons

Metric Volume Measurements

1 liter   = 10 deciliters   = 100 centiliters   = 1 mililiters

American Volume to Metric Volume

1 gallon	= 3.78 liters	
1 quart	= 0.946 liter	= 946 milliliters
1 pint	= 0.473 liter	= 473 milliliters
1 cup	= 236.6 milliliters	
1 fluid ounce	= 29.57 milliliters	

fluid ounces x 29.57 = # milliliters per # fluid ounces

Example: to determine the metric equivalent to 12 fluid ounces

12 x 29.57 = 354.8 milliliters in 12 fluid ounces

American Weight Measurements

1 pound = 16 ounces

Metric Weight Measurements

1 kilogram = 1000 grams

Metric Weight to American Weight

1 kilogram	= 2.2 pounds	= 35.2 ounces
1 ounce	= 28.37 grams	

\# grams / 28.37 = # ounces per # grams

Example: to determine the number of ounces equivalent to 750 grams

750 / 28.37 = 26.44 ounces = 1 pound 10.44 ounces

Temperature Conversions

0° Celsius	= 32° Fahrenheit
37° Celsius	= 98.6° Fahrenheit
100° Celsius	= 212° Fahrenheit

Degrees Fahrenheit to degrees Celsius [(F°-32) x 5] / 9 = C°

Example: 212°F converted to °Celsius

[(212°F −32) x 5] / 9 = [180 x 5] / 9 = 900 / 9 = 100° C

Degrees Celsius to degrees Fahrenheit [(C° x9) / 5] + 32 = F°

Example: 37°C converted to °Fahrenheit

[(37°C x 9) / 5] +32 = [333 / 5] +32 = 66.6 +32 = 98.6° F

Index